THE ORIGINS OF JAPANESE TRADE SUPREMACY

CHRISTOPHER HOWE

The Origins of Japanese Trade Supremacy

Development and Technology in Asia
from 1540 to the Pacific War

The University of Chicago Press

CHRISTOPHER HOWE is Professor of Economics with reference to Asia in the University of London. Trained in history, politics, and economics at Cambridge University, he later studied Chinese and Japanese at the School of Oriental and African Studies, London.

The University of Chicago Press, Chicago, Illinois 60637

C. Hurst & Co. (Publishers) Ltd., London WC2E 8JZ

© 1996 by Christopher Howe

All rights reserved. Published 1996

Printed in Hong Kong

04 03 02 01 00 99 98 97 96   1 2 3 4 5 6

ISBN: (cloth) 0–226–35485–7

Library of Congress Cataloging-in-Publication Data

Howe, Christopher.
  The origins of Japanese trade supremacy : development and technology in Asia from 1540 to the Pacific War / Christopher Howe.
    p.   cm.
  Includes bibliographical references.
    1. Japan—Commerce—History. 2. Industrial promotion—Japan—
  —History. 3. Technology—Japan—History. 4. Japan—Foreign economic relations. 5. Foreign trade promotion—Japan—History.
  I. Title.
  HF3824.H68   1996
  382'.0952—dc20   95–3400
                                                                            CIP

This book is printed on acid-free paper.

Fallen leaves pile high
  upon the path.
Sweep them away, and you shall
  see the footprints of the sun goddess.
      — Old Shinto poem

'The economist needs the three great intellectual faculties, perception, imagination and reason: and most of all he needs imagination, to put him on the track of those *causes of visible events* which are remote or lie below the surface, and of those *effects of visible causes* which are remote or lie below the surface.'
      — Alfred Marshall, *Principles of Economics*.

CONTENTS

Part III. THE ROLE OF TECHNOLOGY

FIGURES

TABLES

PLATES

MAP

PREFACE AND ACKNOWLEDGEMENTS

The emergence of the Japanese trade surplus is one of the key economic events of the twentieth century. Indeed, only the rise and fall of the Warsaw Pact economies rivals it in drama and global significance. The surplus first appeared in the mid-1960s and was initially modest in scale. In the economic turmoil of the 1970s the significance of Japan's achievement in reversing a century of almost continuous recorded deficits went largely unnoticed. However, during the early 1980s the surplus grew almost exponentially, reaching the extraordinary peak of over $100 billion in 1986. By 1994 95 it was $130 billion and had become a source of intense, intractable international friction, threatening to fracture the world economic community. Finally, in April 1995 the rise of the yen against major currencies was such that by nominal measures Japan had the highest *per capita* income in the world.

Yet surplus has proved to be a complex affair with many positive and unforeseen consequences. Its counterpart has been an outflow of capital that financed the American budget deficit, transformed the international aid programme, recovered for Britain its position as a net exporter of colour televisions and cars, and has purchased for Japanese interests (often controversially) some of the finest companies, properties, golf courses, vineyards and works of art in the western world.

It is the thesis of this book that the trade surplus and Japan's successive rise to competitiveness in one industry after another, which is an integral part of the story, are not purely post-war phenomena. Rather, their foundations lie buried in Japanese history, and in the accumulation and orchestration of many different skills which is the thread that binds the story together. The contemporary Japanese trade problem may correctly be thought of as macro-economic, caused by the strong propensity of Japan to consume less than it produces, but the macro-economic issue would not be an international one affecting entire regions and sectors of the world economy, if the Japanese economy were not itself now so large, so technically accomplished, and so competitively strong.

Although much that is said in this book is positive about Japan, readers should observe that this part of the research ends with the Pacific war — a catastrophic event in the sense that Japan's defeat was a political and moral disaster, as well as a physical one. The Pacific war led literally to the destruction of much of Japan's economy and its Asian empire, but this outcome resulted partly from the way Japan's outward economic expansion had turned eventually towards violence and oppression. I have tried to face the complexities and economic dimensions of all this as objectively as possible; for although the insights of economics are our primary concern, I believe that economists who abstract too far from the real world are ultimately unlikely to make much contribution to their science, and that the relationship between economics and wider issues must be considered. Thus, just as it is easy to overlook the point that the history of Stalin's Gulag reflected the economic as well as moral bankruptcy of the system, so we need to be reminded that some of the fundamental problems of Asian economic integration and leadership today are inextricably related to Japan's pre-war efforts to relate to the world and Asian economic systems, as well as to the long-drawn-out political retreat of the West. The feelings still generated by these events are not simply part of the problem; they also obscure analysis.

I came to the study of this enormous subject by a roundabout route, which I shall briefly describe not because the story is of any intrinsic importance, but because otherwise it may be difficult, especially for professional Japanologists, to grasp the book's particular viewpoint. I studied history and economics at Cambridge: benefiting from a golden age of Victorian historical studies and graduating in the twilight of an era dominated by Marshall and Keynes, and immediately before the University's economists largely split into the mathematical and Marxist factions. While a student, I had the good fortune to be supervised by Solomon Adler, a Rooseveltian New Dealer from Yorkshire who later worked as a financial adviser to both the Nationalist and Communist governments in China. As a result of interests aroused by Adler, I joined the School of Oriental and African Studies in 1963 as part of a programme to develop the study of the Chinese economy. But as opportunities to study contemporary China dwindled in the Cultural Revolution, I became increasingly interested in China's pre-war development, a subject requiring study of the Japanese language and economy.

These interests were pursued in Japan in the spring and summer of 1972 — an interesting time to be there, since the economy was just leaving the period of High Speed Growth and of relatively easy labour supplies and moving, unknowingly, towards the precipice of the oil shocks in the autumn of 1973. One indicator of this transformation was that although the economy was in a relatively slow phase of the economic cycle, the Spring Labour Offensive (*Shunto*) was unexpectedly tense. In place of old-style nominal stoppages, the unions organised strikes that actually caused inconvenience to the public. Among the disputes affecting Japan that summer was a seamen's strike which, according to the press, immobilised 8% of the world's active shipping in Japanese ports or their vicinity. I was forcibly struck by this statistic of Japan's place in the international economy and immediately began collecting materials for an eventual study of the matter.

These plans were held up for nearly a decade by other work, but I returned to the subject in the early 1980s when as a teacher of Japanese economic development I discovered that the only serviceable textbook was a study which, though carefully up-dated with supplementary chapters, was still largely the work that its author, Professor G. C. Allen, first drafted in 1939. I therefore decided to develop my interest into something that would provide both students and other readers with an introduction to the Japanese trade sector. In attempting to do this I have relied extensively on many remarkable pieces of research, in particular books by Yamazawa Ippei, Sugiyama Shinya and the recent volume edited by Hamashita Takeshi and Kawakatsu Heita. But for the purposes of explaining this subject to audiences with little background in either Japanese or world history, these works are not only rather sophisticated but also narrow in their interests and time-horizons.

Let me take the latter point first. Economists understandably choose subjects for which quantitative data are available. For Japan comprehensive data begin in the 1890s, and this is where most studies of the subject begin. Some authors do not even go back so far — claiming in effect that Japan's situation today requires study only of the years after the Second World War, in spite of the fact that reputable analysts had already proclaimed Japanese industrialisation a 'modern miracle' in the 1930s.[1] The problem, however, is that for almost the whole of the quantifiable period Japan's economic performance, whether measured in terms of domestic or of foreign trade

---

1. Eugene Staley, *The World Economy in Transition. Technology vs. Politics. Laissez Faire vs. Planning. Power vs. Welfare*, New York: Council on Foreign Relations, 1939, p. 142.

indicators, has been exceptional; and it seems improbable that the explanation of this can be found entirely in data and events contemporary with this modern trajectory. For while it is true that the 'convergence' theorists are just able to get Japan onto their charts — explaining Japan's exceptional performance by its exceptionally low starting point — this approach does not tell us why and how Japan managed this extraordinary feat, while many other economies not on the charts remained in states of chronic poverty and under-development.[2] There has to be more to it; and to some extent this must lie in the earlier, largely unquantifiable period. This was my view from quite early in the research, and happily I have been able in the course of it to benefit from very recent Japanese studies that enable us to reconstruct at least a rudimentary statistical outline of the pre-modern Japanese economy ('modern' is used here to refer to the economy before it came to be based on power-driven machinery).

It was originally my intention to cover the entire history of Japanese foreign trade in one book. This proved too ambitious and I therefore conclude this part of the story in the late 1930s — using the end-date flexibly. I believe that the work stands on its own, since it shows how in nearly all important ways Japan had demonstrated its economic capabilities before the Second World War. The post-war story is essentially the working-out of these capabilities in what was for nearly thirty years a different and altogether more favourable domestic and international climate.

Turning to the question of breadth, clearly the core of any analysis of Japan's foreign trade must be an examination of the basic information on trade and the issues to which it gives rise. However, indispensible as this may be, there are many reasons, some already mentioned, why studies of trade need to be set in a broad context. The story of Japan's trade sector is not a story merely of Japan's comparative advantage mechanistically evolving from exports based on natural resources to those based on rising competitiveness in labour, capital and knowledge-intensive industries. One reason for this was pointed out to me by Ohkawa Kazushi many years ago, namely that one cannot meaningfully separate the economy into distinct sectors serving domestic and foreign markets. Thus trade and Japan's more

2. William J. Baumol, 'Productivity growth, convergence, and welfare: what the long-run data show', The *American Economic Review*, vol. 76, no. 5, December 1986, pp. 1072–85.

general economic development have to be considered together in the context of economic policy and the wider context of international relations and politics. Further, below the macro-economic history of Japan lies the micro-history of individuals, households, firms and organisations of all kinds. For all these, contact and expansion into the outside world was a cultural, social and intellectual as much as an economic experience. The study of all this, especially the dimension of company activity, is beginning to be well developed, although the riches of the Japanese company histories and other sources remain largely unexplored by western scholars.

Finally, there is the geographical dimension. Most studies of Japan's trade focus on Japan and the West. But coming to the study of Japan from that of China, I started out conscious of Japan's economic role in Asia and of the importance of thinking in terms of the whole East Asian region and its relation to the rest of the world. That is why this study starts in the Tang Dynasty and ends in Shanghai. That interest in the Pacific economy is now so fashionable only shows how history is in some sense repeating itself. From the sixteenth century to the 1930s western activity in Asia was essentially that of interaction with a region rather than with its individual components, and if any one power above all others commanded the interest of outsiders, it was not Japan but China. The editor of a classic seventeenth-century work noted:

China is a Country so Vast, so Rich, so Fertile, and so Temperate; the Multitude of People so infinite, their Industry in Manufacture, and their Policy in Government so extraordinary, that ever since the undertaking of Long Voyages, there was never any Discovery made, that might stand in Competition with this Kingdom.[3]

That we have lost this perspective during the last fifty years reflects not only the events of post-war history but also, equally important, the post-war development of academic Asian studies. In the two countries that really count — Japan and the United States — these studies have been decisively shaped by China's Communism, which set China

---

3. *A New History of China, containing a Description of the Most Considerable Particulars of that Vast Empire, written by Gabriel Magaillans of the Society of Jesus, Missionary Apostolic*, London: Thomas Newborough, 1688, p. 2. Magaillans was a descendant of the circumnavigator who, as a young Jesuit, obtained permission to go to Japan. He arrived in Macau in 1636 but was too late to join the Japanese mission, eventually spending most of his life in the far western Chinese province of Szechwan.

apart politically and economically and destroyed many of its traditional Asian partnerships. The structure and financing of western academic study followed suit. This fact shaped the research agenda for our understanding of the long-term development of China and Japan, but when both countries — for very different reasons — began to accelerate their regional economic integration in the 1980s, the academic world, with its tendency to create islands of China and Japan specialists, was ill-equipped to understand the new phenomena.

In trying to draw these various strands together I have incurred many debts. Studying the economy of a society that is culturally so different from one's own and situated on the opposite side of the globe is intrinsically a strange and difficult experience, and the task would have been impossible without the firm foundation provided by a vast secondary literature and the guidance and help of friends in Japan in building upon it. The scale of Japanese publishing and reading is not yet remotely appreciated in the West. To take academic periodicals alone, a standard list contains 48,000 Japanese items, and in embarking on any major economic topic, one usually finds a three-figure list of journals to pursue.[4]

A second aspect of Japanese economic literature, which differentiates it from its western equivalents, is that it makes no sharp distinction between economics and economic history. In the premier Japanese economic journal, *Keizai kenkyu* (Economic research), an article on pure theory will sit side-by-side with a study of the role of traditional craftsmen in Meiji technology transfer. And most of the leading Japanese economists known for works in English on contemporary Japan have either done research on Japanese economic development since the nineteenth century, or are familiar with it.

There are two Japanese authors, neither of whom I ever met, to whom I feel particularly indebted, namely Takahashi Kamekichi and Miyamoto Mataji. Both were economic historians, both wrote more than 100 works, and I came across the writing of both by chance. I first located Takahashi while sheltering from a monsoonal rainstorm in a secondhand bookshop in Kyoto. He started writing in the 1920s and was an active participant in debates about Japan's return to the

---

4. *Tokyo daigaku gakujutsu zasshi sogo mokuroku* (University of Tokyo Catalogue of Scientific Periodicals in the Japanese Language), Tokyo, 1986. In more popular vein, there are over 200 series of Japanese paperback books covering every kind of reading material, of which one alone, *Iwanami Bunko*, had published 3,460 titles by 1991.

gold standard, and he later wrote on a wide variety of subjects, including contemporary studies of pre-war Taiwan, Manchuria and China. I have never located the Chinese study, but have made profitable use of the other two in this work. However, Takahashi's *magnum opus* was his six-volume history of the Japanese economy, covering the 1850s to the 1920s, a remarkable and exciting series which was an indispensable source until it was supplemented by the eight-volume history edited by Umemura Mataji and others.[5]

Miyamoto's writing was, qualitatively, as valuable as Takahashi's. His lifelong interest was the history of Osaka and its trade, and it was his writings on these topics that first opened my eyes to the subtlety and significance of Japanese economic development between the seventeenth and nineteenth centuries. In recent years this tradition has been carried on by his son, Miyamoto Matao, whose study of the Osaka rice market is one of the major works of post-war Japanese economic history.

The fundamental theme of this book is that the accumulation of a wide range of skills and technological capability lies at the heart of Japan's economic success, and that the study of this subject is necessarily a broad process. In developing these ideas, I was first inspired by the British economists Adam Smith and Alfred Marshall, both men of encylopaedic, worldwide interests in history and the economic problems of their day and both concerned to understand what determines economic development in the long run and hence the changing world economic order. Smith, in particular, was profoundly inductive in method and drew for arguments on the economic experience of Europe, the whole of Asia, and the Americas. He could explain with equal skill topics as diverse as the demography of southern France and the cultivation systems of Indo-China. Concerning Asia, Smith argued that the discovery of the Cape route to the East Indies was one of the two 'greatest and most important events recorded in the history of mankind', the other being the discovery of the Americas. He analysed the eighteenth-century French view that China had the world's highest standard of living, which he explained by its enormous internal market, minute division of labour, and exceptional transportation system. Moreover, on a practical level, his dissection of the inefficiencies of the East India Company monopoly paved the way for

5. Takahashi wrote an autobiography, *Watashi no jissen keizaigaku* (My practical economics), Tokyo: Toyo Keizai Shimposha, 1976.

its abolition, thereby triggering the dash for China in the late 1830s and indirectly that for Japan a few years later.[6]

Marshall was also an economist totally at ease with contemporary developments and issues. He was aware of Japan as a dynamic, private sector exporter (and of the contrast here with India), and above all he insisted that economics should not rest on an abstract concept of 'economic man' nor be based exclusively on the methodologies of logic and mathematics. On the contrary, he praised Ruskin and Carlyle for disputing (if misinterpreting) the narrow intellectualism of some Victorian economists while approving of the empirical approach of the earlier British economists and arguing that the great challenge to the economists of his day was to have the imagination to see the viewpoint of people in *other classes* of society. The only possible modification to that claim after a century is that today's great challenge to economists is to understand the people of modern and modernising economies embedded in foreign cultures and societies.[7]

Of particular help on industrial and technology issues was Marshall's second large work, *Industry and Trade*, which he wrote as an empirical exploration of many topics he had dealt with theoretically in his more famous *Principles of Economics*.[8] When I first read the Japanese literature of the 1920s on trade and industrial policy I found it an unfamiliar world, but it proved to be far more comprehensible after reading Marshall, who dealt with similar themes in an almost contemporary study of Europe and America. I was also impressed by Marshall's decision to visit the factories of almost every industry that he planned to write about, which he did in the belief that the exact details of technology were often crucial to a proper understanding of

6. An illuminating account of Adam Smith is found in the introduction to the Victorian edition of his work by J. E. Thorold Rogers, whose edition has the great merit that it provides the references that Smith had not troubled to include himself. The breadth of Smith's interests may also be judged from the contents of his library, which includes a vast sweep of works from the sixteenth to the eighteenth centuries and which is now housed, appropriately, in the Economics Department of the University of Tokyo. Adam Smith, *Wealth of Nations*, Oxford University Press, 1869.

7. Alfred Marshall, *Principles of Economics*, vol. 1, 2nd edn, London: Macmillan, 1891, 8th edn, 1936. This discussion is based on these two editions. The comparison of India and Japan occurs in Alfred Marshall, *Money Credit and Commerce*, London: Macmillan, 1923, p. 173.

8. Alfred Marshall, *Industry and Trade: A Study of Industrial Technique and Business Organization: and of their influences on the conditions of various classes and nations*, London: Macmillan, 1919.

the economics of an industry's operation. A later influence favouring the technology theme in development was Professor Bill Philipps, an engineer by training, who enthused me with the importance of the subject, although sadly he did not live to pursue his planned investigations of it in the context of Chinese economic development. More recently, Professor Isaac Ehrlich has drawn my attention to new and stimulating literature on technology and economic growth.

Western influences have been paralleled by important Japanese ones, among which I acknowledge particularly the help and detailed advice of Professor Ishikawa Shigeru and Professor Kiyokawa Yukihiko, both of the Hitotsubashi school; and of Professor Nakaoka Tetsuro of Osaka who, like Philipps, was an engineer before becoming an economist. I have read as many of their articles on technology and development as I could find and am grateful to each of them for discussing these with me and for sending me research materials. I am more generally indebted to Professors Ishii Kanji, Komiya Ryutaro, Odaka Konosuke and Nagura Bunji for help during my stay in Tokyo in 1988. My visits to Japan over the years have also benefited greatly from the library of the International House of Japan and from the support and hospitality of the University of Tokyo's Department of Economics, Professor and Mrs Paul Chen, Dr and Mrs T. Kambara, Mr Nagatomi Yuichiro and his colleagues at the Foundation for Advanced Information and Research, and the Nikon Corporation.

For travel to Japan I have had the privilege of many years' work on the Hong Kong University and Polytechnics Grants Committee and, more recently, the Hong Kong Research Grants Council. I am grateful to the staff of those bodies for the trouble they have so often taken to route me to meetings through Japan, at no expense to the public purse. A fellow-member of the Committee for many years, Dr David Bethel, kindly supplied me with information about his ancestor E. T. Bethell, who played an important role in reporting the Japanese colonisation of Korea in the early twentieth century.

In London I owe a great debt to many colleagues for discussions and help. I thank especially my teachers at the School of Oriental and African Studies, Professors Pat O'Neill and Charles Dunn; and Professor W. G. Beasley for endless encouragement and advice on Japanese history and for reading the manuscript. I am also indebted to Dr K. Sugihara for reading suggestions; to the late Caroline Dinwiddy for advice on statistics; to John Wright for help with computing; to Dr Richard Sims for loan of his important study of France and the opening of Meiji Japan; to Dr John Breen for translation of a Meiji text; to Dr Tim Fox for advice on difficult sentences; to Paul Fox for his excellent photography; and to Professor Terry Byres for providing a framework of calm departmental administration.

Without the benefit of daily conversations over several years with Professor K. N. Chaudhuri, now Vasco de Gama Professor at the European Institute in Florence, I could never have ventured into the early period covered by this book.

Professor Edith Penrose encouraged me to take an interest in Japanese affairs as long ago as 1969, and I am especially grateful to her for several items from the library of her late husband, Professor E. F. Penrose, who lived in Japan in the inter-war years, mastered the language and conducted research on Japanese agriculture, industry and demography that stands the test of time.

Finding the materials for research of this kind is very difficult. The late Brian Hickman, formerly the curator of the Japanese collection at the Library of the School of Oriental and African Studies, never failed either to help me locate sources already in his collection or to respond to often outrageously expensive requests to buy materials that I came across in Japan. As this work has never had the benefit of significant research grants, I am grateful to the School of Oriental and African Studies for several small travel grants, and in particular to Professor Sir Cyril Philips and Professor C. D. Cowan, both former Directors of the School, for giving me a start in this field and for subsequent support at critical junctures.

Quite early in the work I decided to acquire copies of the major early books on western interaction with the Far East and I later extended this collecting to prints, maps and other objects helpful to understanding the issues of this study. I am especially grateful to my old friend the bookseller Ronald Gooch of Ad Orientem Ltd., St Leonards-on-Sea, to Christer von der Burg, and to Pierre Joppen. I should also like to salute the many Japanese and French booksellers whose shops I have combed down the years.

I thank my wife Dr Patricia Howe for many insights into language and inter-cultural understanding, for encouragement, and for tolerating absences and much else besides; and, lastly, my cousin Mrs Rosamund Jonkers, for locating the photograph of our great-uncle Bunny Wesson, who was a first-hand participant in the transfer of western photographic technology to Japan before the First World War.

London
1995

CHRISTOPHER HOWE

NOTE ON ROMANISATION, NAMES
AND FOOTNOTES

Japanese romanisation follows the system of Kenyusha's *New Japanese–English Dictionary* (1954) with macrons omitted. Japanese family names are placed first throughout the text.

Chinese place names in the text and tables follow conventional or Wade-Giles spellings. This is because these forms are common in the secondary literature referred to. In other contexts, including bibliographical description, Pinyin is used.

The footnote system has been designed to be as comprehensive as possible for specialists, while also giving readers unfamiliar with Asian languages some indication of the character of the sources used. When a publication is referred to for the first time a full bibliographical description is given. Thereafter, references are to author and title or, more frequently, an abbreviated title.

For Asian-language material, second and subsequent references *use the translated title*, which can normally be identified by use of lower case letters. For the small number of Asian sources with no author, the Asian title is retained.

Six sources are indicated by acronyms in second and subsequent references. These are:

BPPJ British Parliamentary Papers, Japan
  EB *Encyclopaedia Britannica*
EHOJ Umemura *et al.* (eds), *Nihon keizaishi* (Economic history of Japan)
  FER *Far Eastern Review*
LTES Ohkawa *et al.* (eds), *Choki keizai tokei* (Long-term economic statistics)
MITI Ministry of International Trade and Industry
 NCH *North China Herald*

Part I
TRADE AND THE TRADITIONAL ECONOMY

1

THE JAPANESE TRADING WORLD BEFORE 1853 AND THE FIRST CYCLE OF CONTACT WITH EUROPEANS

'If only there had been more of the world they would have discovered it.'
— Camoens, on the greatness of the Portuguese navigators[1]

Japan has traded with its Asian neighbours for at least 1,400 years. Among early links, those with China and Korea were particularly important and for hundreds of years after the close of the Tang dynasty (618–907) in China, foreign boats were known in Japan as *tosen* ('Tang boats'), thus reflecting the dominance of China in the Japanese consciousness of the outside world.

These early economic exchanges were important not only for the commodities exchanged but also for the transfer of knowledge, writing systems and the traditional production techniques that accompanied them. On a small but important scale there was also a movement of people who either had special skills or were otherwise engaged in seeking new knowledge to take back to Japan.

Since the sixteenth century, this Asian world has twice been disturbed by a major European economic incursion. The first irruption reached its peak in the late sixteenth century, and both Japan and the West are still living with the consequences of the second, which started in the Far East in the 1830s. This chapter is concerned mainly with the impact of the first of these expansions, and with the development of Japanese foreign trade during the long period of seclusion from western contact, beginning in 1640, and extending to the second opening of Japan to western traders in the 1850s.

The beginnings of European trade in the Far East

Trade between Asia and Europe in the Middle Ages was based mainly on the long-distance land routes that connected the two continents. These routes were a result of the extension of Mongol power from the

1. 'E se mais mundo houvera, la chegara', quoted in Edgar Prestage, *The Portuguese Pioneers*, London: A. & C. Black, 1966, p. 310.

Chinese seaboard in the east to the Danube and Adriatic in the west. The Mongol political framework lasted from the mid-thirteenth to the mid-fourteenth century, and it protected two major highways from Europe to Asia: a northerly route via the Sea of Azov and Turkestan and a southerly one through Trebizond, Tabriz, Samarkhand and Kashgar.[2] These highways facilitated a variety of economic exchanges between the eastern Mediterranean and the greater part of Asia. Interest in these regions was sharpened by the Crusades, which increased contacts between Europeans and the Middle East and gave them valuable trading and fiscal privileges in the Holy Land.[3]

Trade and western knowledge of Asia interacted in strange ways so that medieval and renaissance conceptions of the world beyond Alexandria were based on a mixture of fable and carefully described realities. Thus while Marco Polo gave Europe a detailed and accurate account of his journeys and years in China, which had enormous subsequent influence, and the Florentine merchant Pegolotti included in his fourteenth-century compilation of merchant practice minute details of both the journey to Peking and the intricacies of trade with the Chinese,[4] Europeans of that time were equally enchanted and influenced by descriptions of imaginary, wonderful worlds. Especially influential was the image of the kingdom described in the forged letter from the fictitious Christian king, Prester John, which most authorities assigned to Abyssinia while others placed it to the

2. Boise Penrose, *Travel and Discovery in the Renaissance, 1420–1620*, Cambridge, MA: Harvard University Press, 1952, ch. 1; Sir Henry Yule and Henri Cordier (eds), *Cathay and the Way Thither: Being a collection of Medieval Notices of China* (2nd edn, 2 vols), London: The Hakluyt Society, 1913–16, esp. the Preliminary Essay, vol. 1, pp. 146–73; Jacques Bernard, 'Trade and finance in the middle ages, 900–1500' in Carlo M. Cipolla (ed.), *The Fontana Economic History of Europe*, vol. 1, *The Middle Ages*, London: Collins, 1972, pp. 274–80.

3. J. H. Parry, *The Discovery of the Sea*, Berkeley: University of California Press, 1981, pp. 47–8; E. LeRoy Ladurie, *Histoire du Languedoc*, Paris: Presses Universitaires de France, 1974, pp. 26–7; William W. Tarn, *The Greeks in Bactria and India*, 2nd edn, Cambridge University Press, 1951.

4. Yule and Cordier, *Cathay*, vol. III, pp. 137–83; Penrose, *Travel and Discovery*, p. 15; Francesco Balducci Pegolotti (ed. Allan Evans), *La Practica della Mercatura*, Cambridge, MA: Mediaeval Academy of America, esp. pp. 21–3. Pegolotti did not himself travel in Asia and it is significant that a great deal of his information on China is concerned with silk.

east of Marco Polo's Cathay.[5] Wherever its precise location, interest in Prester John persisted for centuries and his kingdom was believed to be immensely desirable and rich in both material and spiritual treasures. One authority wrote: 'Within the realm were the lands of the Amazons and Brahmins, the Shrine of St Thomas the Apostle, the Fountain of Youth, and rivers that ran gold and silver and jewels.'[6]

The articles of Asian commerce confirmed the fabulous character of the East. In the twelfth and thirteenth centuries, Genoese merchants were distributing superfine Chinese silks as far afield as France and London; and in the markets of Languedoc, in southern France, one could find pepper, spices, ginger, musk, cloves, rare medicinal herbs and other exotic products. These products were exchanged for textiles and metalwork and had found their way to France through Middle Eastern land routes and trading intermediaries from as far afield as Syria, Arabia, Persia, Ceylon, Tibet and the Moluccas. Moreover, eastern goods from the bazaars of Montpellier and St Gilles were redistributed up the great trading corridor of France to the Champagne region, Flanders and as far as London, ultimately constituting what Ladurie has described as 'an uninterrupted chain of commerce from Sumatra, Ceylon and Baghdad to the seaports of Northern Europe and the Baltic'.[7]

These patterns of exchange came to an end in the fourteenth century. In Europe the Black Death depopulated major centres of commerce, bringing depression and reduced demand, while in Asia Mongol power disintegrated and led to the closure of the overland routes taken by Marco Polo and others. Nonetheless, trade flows within Asia continued and indirect links with the eastern Mediterranean were maintained by Venetian and Genoese merchants, who purchased goods brought up through the Red Sea and taken overland for collection

---

5. With the true prudence of a Dutch Catholic who worked for the King of Spain, the definitive sixteenth-century cartographer, Abraham Ortelius, published maps placing the kingdom in both Abyssinia and Tartary.

6. Penrose, *Travel and Discovery*, p. 12. The early sixteenth-century Portuguese view of Prester John is reflected throughout in Mansel Longworth Dames (ed.), *The Book of Duarte Barbosa*, vol. 1, London: Hakluyt Society, 1918. Duarte Barbosa wrote it *ca.* 1518.

7. Donald Lach, *Asia in the Making of Europe* (3 vols in 9 books), University of Chicago Press, 1965–93, vol. 1, book 1, pp. 45–6; Ladurie, *Histoire du Languedoc*, p. 27; see also Fernand Braudel, *L'identité de la France. Les hommes et les choses*, Paris: Arthaud-Flammarion, 1986, pp. 132–8.

at Alexandria. In spite of this basic rupture, interest and a residual geographical knowledge of Asia remained alive in parts of Europe for which, by the fifteenth century, direct communication was only a memory.

The renewal of direct contacts between Asia and Europe, this time by sea rather than land, was the achievement of Portugal[8] — an unlikely base for such major exploration. The country was poor, had a small population, a precarious food supply and no traditions of long-distance seafaring. Less skilled than the Venetians or Genoese, the Portuguese limited their seamanship at first to coastal trading and the 'island hopping' that was to remain typical of Mediterranean Europe for centuries.[9]

However, Portugal's geographical situation and history were unusual. Situated in the far south-west of Europe, close to Africa, it combined elements of a hot, Mediterranean climate and culture with a coastline swept by strong winds and cold, open seas. The unknown limits of these seas were a constant challenge and at certain times of the year, the offshore winds were favourable to voyages out into the Atlantic and down the West African coast. The benefits of this location were reinforced by toleration of the Jews and former Cathar heretics and by proximity to Arab scientific discoveries, all of which combined to give the Portuguese élite early access to new cosmographical knowledge, a sense of being a chosen people and a deep tradition of secrecy.[10]

A major factor in Portuguese exploration and expansion was leadership, particulary that provided in its early stages by Prince Henry the Navigator. Born in 1394, Henry acquired a military reputation in North Africa as a young man that won him invitations to command the armies of the Holy Roman Empire, Castile, England and the Pope.[11] He declined all these offers, being more interested in what he

8. Henri Cordier, *Histoire Générale de la Chine, et de ses Relations avec les Pays Étrangères*, Paris: Paul Geuthner, 1920, vol. 3, ch. 9, *passim*; Parry, *The Discovery of the Sea*, pp. 81–7.

9. Fernand Braudel, *The Mediterranean and the Mediterranean World in the Age of Philip II*, (2 vols), London: Collins, 1972, vol. 1, pp. 103–8.

10. Mascarenhas Barreto, *The Portuguese Columbus. Secret Agent of John II*, London: Macmillan, 1992, *passim*. The key figures in the Portuguese expansion were members of the Order of Christ, successors to the Order of Templars.

11. C. R. Beazley, *Prince Henry the Navigator*, New York: G. P. Putnam, 1903; Cordier, *Histoire Générale*, vol. 3, p. 97.

had discovered during his campaigns of internal African trade routes. These routes, he learned, stretched from Tunisia and the Barbary coast down to the goldfields of Gambia and Timbuktu. Armed with this knowledge, Henry sought direct access by sea to West Africa and its wealth. The voyages he inspired and supported established a tradition which, within a century, had led the Portuguese down the West African coast, round the Cape of Good Hope, across the Indian Ocean, and on to South-East Asia and, finally, to China and Japan.

Japan was an early and persistent factor in Portuguese thinking. Henry himself knew of the country from a manuscript copy of Marco Polo's travels that had been given to his brother. In this Polo, without first-hand knowledge, had included long passages on the wealth and precious metals to be found there.[12] Later, when Christopher Columbus discussed his Atlantic voyages with John of Portugal and offered his services to the Spanish, the specific, alluring objective of reaching 'China, Japan and other unknown lands' via a westward route was high on the agenda.[13]

The motivation behind the Portuguese voyages was complex. Economic aspirations were central, since the early African voyages were a search for gold, spices and slaves,[14] and with these external

---

12. The references to Japan and its gold may be found in Sir Henry Yule and Henri Cordier, *The Book of Ser Marco Polo* (3rd edn), London: John Murray, 1903, 1920, vol. 2, p. 253.

13. The plan to reach Japan by sailing west was given credibility by the erroneous Ptolemaic view that Asia extended much further to the east (see Ortelius's map, pp. 104–5). The quotation is from João de Barros and Diego de Couto, *Da Asia, Dos Feitos, que os Portuguezes fizeram no descubrimento, e conquista dos mares, e terras do Oriente*, Lisbon: Na Regia Officina Typografia, 1778–88, dec.I, liv.III, cap.X1. '. . . e lia per Mario Polo que falava moderamente das cousas Orientas de Reyno Cathayo, e assi da grande Ilha Cypangao, veio a fantaziar que per este mar Oceano Occidental se podia navegar tanto tie que fossem dar nesta Ilha Cypango e em outras terras incognitas.' A controversial recent study has suggested that Columbus, as a Portuguese agent, deliberately misled the Spanish about the possibility of a westward route to Japan, thus giving the Portuguese more time to consolidate their voyages via the Cape, which were in any case based on far superior cosmographical knowledge and cartographic resources. Barreto, *The Portuguese Columbus*, passim.

14. C. R. Boxer, *The Portuguese Seaborne Empire, 1415–1825*, London: Hutchinson, 1969, ch. 1; R. P. Giovan Pietro Maffei, *Le Historie delle Indie Orientali tradotte di Latino in Lingua Toscana da M. Francesco Serdonati Fiorentino, con una scelte di lettere scritte delle Indie*, Venice: Damian Zenaro, 1589. This book has many interesting comments on Portuguese ambitions and strategy, esp. in ch. 3. The letters from 'the Indies' are from Japan, in line with normal sixteenth-century usage.

resources the Portuguese may well have hoped to improve and stabilise their domestic economic base.[15] They also believed that economic success would undermine Muslim and Venetian power, and apart from trade, constant themes of Portuguese expansion were a chivalric quest for 'praise and honour', the discovery of Prester John and other lost kingdoms and, later, the zealous Catholic evangelism of the Counter-Reformation.[16] As achievements multiplied, the Portuguese sense of the uniqueness of their destiny appears to have grown. By the early sixteenth century they had accomplished the discovery of an entire new world, an achievement unparalleled in either the classical or modern eras.[17] It is thus hardly surprising that the sixteenth-century Portuguese historian de Barros believed that Henry had gone straight to live with the elect in Paradise or that his compatriot Camoëns could sum up the lives of the Portuguese explorers with the immortal lines quoted at the beginning of this chapter.[18]

In practice the originality of the Portuguese lay in their finding solutions to the problems of navigating the open, pathless Atlantic. Thus, while superficially unremarkable, the rounding of Cape Bojador on the tip of West Africa in 1434 was a critical achievement precisely because it involved going out of sight of land.[19] Subsequent land-mark voyages were the rounding of the Cape of Good Hope by Dias in 1486 and the return voyage of da Gama from Lisbon to Calicut in the Red Sea in 1497–98.

15. According to Jones, one in three Portuguese harvests was inadequate to feed the population, hence basic needs had an important influence in the Portuguese expansion. See E. L. Jones, *The European Miracle. Environments, economies and geopolitics in the history of Europe and Asia* (2nd edn), Cambridge University Press, 1990. The key references are in ch. 4, 'The Discoveries and ghost acreage'.

16. Maffei described the Portuguese as 'molto desiderosi d'acquisitar lode e honore', *Le Historie*, p. 133. See also R. H. Major, *The Life of Prince Henry of Portugal. Surnamed the Navigator; and its results*, London: A. Asher, 1868. For an early account of the importance of the Prester John motif, see de Barros, *Da Asia*. dec. I, liv. III, cap. V. The persistence of Prester John is illustrated by a full discussion of the kingdom in Philip Avril, *Voyages en divers États d'Europe et d'Asie, Entreprise pour découvrir un nouveau chemin à la Chine*, Paris: Claude Barbin, 1692, pp. 184–90.

17. de Barros, *Da Asia*, dec. I, liv. V, cap. I; de Couto, *Da Asia*, dec. V, liv. I, cap. II. The latter includes a remarkable letter outlining the significance of the Portuguese achievement in world history, addressed to Pope Paul III (Farnese), who established the Jesuits in 1540.

18. de Barros, *Da Asia*, dec. I, liv. I, cap. XVI and note 1.

19. Major, *The Life of Prince Henry*, p. 1. de Barros likened the rounding of the Cape to a labour of Hercules, *Da Asia* (dec. I, liv. I, cap. IV).

Recent European scientific and technological discoveries made important contributions to these voyages and to the ability of the Portuguese to establish themselves militarily and politically across Asia. More advanced mapping and navigation, especially the use of the quadrant and astrolabe, made navigation possible in the open seas and in the Southern Hemisphere.[20] Improvements in shipbuilding played a role too. The first Portuguese success in this field was the development of the caravel, a small craft, only 20–30 metres long but rigged with a lateen sail that enabled it to manoeuvre close to the wind and hence made possible the return voyages up the African coast against the prevailing trade winds.[21] Dias actually rounded the Cape with three small caravels, and the Venetian traveller Cadamosto described them as the 'best ships that travel on the seas of the winds'.[22] Later, as the needs of trade and empire took over from simple exploration, the Portuguese began the construction of enormous ships for the journey to India. These were of up to 1,600 tons displacement, carried as many as 1,000 people and at full sail were described as being 'as big as castles'.[23]

Portuguese military capacity was also strengthened by sixteenth-century innovations. Metallurgical techniques improved the firepower of both small and large arms. Thus the guns, instead of being mounted on the upper deck and the poops, were increasingly placed between decks to fire through ports.[24] The Portuguese took advantage of all these changes, allying them with brilliant psychological tactics

20. Parry, *The Discovery of the Sea*, ch. 8; Edgar Prestage, *The Portuguese Pioneers*, ch. 14. A near-contemporary account of the significance of the astrolabe is in Maffei, *Le Historie*, p. 6.

21. J. H. Parry, *The Age of Reconnaissance, Discovery, Exploration and Settlement 1450–1650*, Berkeley: University of California Press, 1981, p. 53.

22. 'Sendo le caravelle di Portugallo i migliori navigli che vadono sopra il mare di vella,' quoted in Major, *The Life of Prince Henry*, p. 309.

23. 'Si mandano quasi ogn'anno quattro o cinque navi di carico nell' India, di grandezza tanto meravigliosa, che quando vanno a piene vele paiono quasi tante castella,' Maffei, *Le Historie*, p. 205. A modern source with details of Portuguese shipbuilding achievements (and of every other practical aspect of Portuguese activity in sixteenth-century Asia) is Georg Schurhammer, *Francis Xavier: His Life, His Times* (4 vols), Rome: Jesuit Historical Institute, 1977, esp. vol. 2, ch. 1.

24. J. H. Parry, *Europe and a Wider World, 1415–1715*, London: Hutchinson, 1969, pp. 24–5.

that exploited their terrifying potential on land and at sea.[25] Although the Japanese and others eventually learned many of the secrets of foreign gun manufacture, the Portuguese foundry in Macau remained an important source of large armaments for Asian rulers until the end of the eighteenth century.[26]

During the sixteenth century, the economic aspects of this expansion became increasingly visible as the Portuguese laid the foundations of an empire in Asia, the skeletal remains of which are at the time of writing still visible: indeed, only the reversion of Macau to China in 1999 will bring the formal Portuguese presence finally to an end. The Portuguese imperial strategy was to establish a series of land bases from which to conduct their operations. The four key points established by Alfonso Albuquerque were Aden, Ormuz, Goa and Malacca.[27] All four cities were to varying degrees already important centres of intra-Asian trade, and two of them — Ormuz and Malacca — remain as strategically critical today as they were in the sixteenth century because of their control of narrow straits. Another feature of these cities was that Chinese traders were present in at least three of them. In Ormuz they jostled with Persians, Armenians and others.[28] In Goa they were noted for their strange crafts,[29] and in Malacca most of all they were a substantial social and economic presence,[30] arriving in huge, painted Canton junks loaded with vegetables and coops of live ducks.

The importance of Malacca as a centre of Asian trade reflected its geographical position at the intersection of two zones of circulation: the South-East Asian trade winds and the monsoon system of the

25. Carlo M. Cipolla, *Before the Industrial Revolution: European Society and Economy, 1000–1700* (2nd edn), London: Methuen, 1980, pp. 177–8. de Barros and other sources are replete with examples of Portuguese tactical skills.

26. Anders Ljungstedt, *An Historical Sketch of the Portuguese Settlements in China and of the Roman Catholic Church and Mission*, Boston, MA: Munroe, 1836, repr. Hong Kong, 1992, pp. 23–4.

27. C. R. Boxer, *The Portuguese Seaborne Empire*, pp. 46–8.

28. de Barros, *Da Asia*, dec. II, liv. II, cap. I.

29. Penrose, *Travel and Discovery*, p. 65.

30. de Barros, *Da Asia*, dec. II, liv. VI, cap. I; K. G. Jayne, *Vasco De Gama and his Successors*, repr. London: Methuen, 1970, p. 227; a slightly later account concerning Malacca of great interest is in John Huighen Van Linschoten, *His Discours of Voyages into ye East and West Indies*, London: John Wolfe, 1598, p. 31.

Indian Ocean. As a result, the city is a natural meeting-point, available all year round to seaborne traders originating anywhere between Arabia and the Chinese seaboard.[31] The Portuguese rightly saw it as the key to future trade with Sumatra, Siam and the Far East, and after a preliminary reconnaissance took control of it.

The final steps that brought the Portuguese to China and Japan were not taken for some decades after their establishment in Malacca. The Portuguese entered the Pearl River Delta as early as 1513, and in 1517 Rafael Perestrello became the first European to reach the Chinese mainland by sea.[32] Despite the profitability of Perestrello's trade, the Chinese regarded the Portuguese as pirates and refused official contact. During the 1550s the Portuguese went to annual markets on Chinese islands in the Pearl River Delta and in the late 1550s were finally allowed to settle in Macau.[33] Meanwhile, the first Portuguese arrival in Japan had occurred in 1542, as the accidental result of a junk *en route* from Malacca to China being blown off course. And in 1549 the Jesuit Francis Xavier, who had heard of the Japanese in Malacca, landed at Kagoshima to found a mission which was to become an integral part of the Portuguese economic and political presence in Japan.

The problem of Asian trade. As the Portuguese moved across Asia, many of their high but often fanciful expectations were fulfilled. In Ormuz and Calicut they found cities with magnificent

---

31. Fernand Braudel, *Civilisation and Capitalism 15th–18th Century*, vol. 3: *The Perspective of the World*, London: Collins, 1984, p. 524. See Cordier, *Histoire Générale*, for an account of Sequeira's instructions to enquire into Chinese shipping and trade. Maffei described Malacca as 'mercato nobilissimo' and the key to the Far East, *Le Historie* (ch. 3), and Pyrard de Laval, a French observer, reported that the city was a market for goods from Europe and the Cape of Good Hope in the West to China and Japan in the East. See also Albert Gray (ed.), *The Voyage of François Pyrard of Laval to the East Indies; the Maldives, the Moluccas and Brazil*, London: Hakluyt Society (2 vols), 1887–88, vol. 2, part 1, pp. 168–72.

32. Cordier, *Histoire Générale*, vol. 3, p. 118; de Barros, *Da Asia*, dec. IV, liv. II, cap. VI. The Perestrello family uniquely united the eastward and westward Portuguese discoveries in one family. Bartholomeu Perestrello explored the Atlantic and his papers and charts went with his daughter as a dowry for his son-in-law, Christopher Columbus. See other dimensions of this relationship in Barreto, *The Portuguese Columbus*, *passim*.

33. C. R. Boxer, *Fidalgos of the Far East, 1550–1770* (2nd edn), Oxford University Press, 1968, pp. 2–5.

buildings.[34] In India, they saw evidence of long-lost Christian communities.[35] Ceylon was a fertile, well-watered land so rich and
beautiful that they thought it could have been the Garden of Eden.[36]
When they eventually reached China, they found that to the advantages of climate and natural fertility was added the extraordinary
industry of the cultivators that made possible the double and even
triple cropping of the soil — a practice unknown in contemporary
Europe.[37] Even in Japan, where wealth was less obvious and the
climate and agriculture were less luxuriant, the Portuguese missionaries
commented on the longevity and wonderfully healthy appearance of
the people.[38]

The Europeans in Asia thus found themselves in a curious position.
By skilful strategy and the application of a small group of technological
advances, they had succeeded in arriving in Asia for trade and other
purposes. Nonetheless, it seems unlikely that the general level of
incomes in Europe and Asia differed significantly, and amid all this
evidence of Asian abundance and variety it was hard to see what
could be the underlying rationale for serious economic exchange over
such long distances. As Pietro Maffei wrote of the Chinese, 'they sell
everything and buy nothing.'[39]

European interest in trade arose primarily from demand for spices
and other tropical products. These were goods that Europe could not
supply for itself and for which the gap between the prices for purchase
in Asia and sale in Europe was often astronomical. The European
demand for spices was by no means simply a quest for luxuries: spices
were an important food resource which in southern Europe made the
preservation of food possible, and in the cold north made it more

34. de Barros, *Da Asia*, dec. II, liv. II, cap. 1; *ibid.* dec. I, liv. IV, cap. VII.

35. de Barros, *Da Asia*, dec. II, liv. V, cap. I.

36. 'In essa [Ceylon] e tanta dolcezza d'aria, tale fertilità di terra, e copia di fiumi,
e acque perpetua, que si dice questa esser gia stata la stanza de primi nostri padri',
Maffei, *Le Historie*, p. 37. Here, as in his description of China, Maffei and his translator
allow their Italianate eloquence to run wild. This view echoed the tradition reflected
in Dante, who also placed Eden in Ceylon. Lach, *Asia*, vol. 1, book 1, p. 75.

37. Chapter 6 of Maffei's work is one of the earliest western accounts of China,
substantially pre-dating first-hand Jesuit descriptions. The passages referred to here
are on pp. 95–6.

38. Boxer, *Fidalgos of the Far East*, p. 39.

39. Maffei, *Le Historie*, p. 96. The question of relative living standards is discussed
in Braudel, *The Perspective of the World*, pp. 533–5, but although average standards
may have been similar, inequality in Asia is thought to have been greater than in
Europe, Jones, *The European Miracle*, pp. 4–5.

palatable. They were thus a critical necessity after the decline in the availability of meat in the mid-sixteenth century.[40] The incentives for trading were therefore strong. To satisfy the demand, an extensive system of distribution was established, much of it eventually concentrated in Amsterdam, from which the 'prodigious' markets of Poland and Russia could be satisfied. Medicinal products were another commodity of great importance in Euro-Asian trade.

The problem for Europe was to find products and trading mechanisms to acquire these goods. One of the keys to this was to be the insatiable appetite of the Chinese for silver; hence their goods could be acquired for bullion. So great was this appetite and so large the Chinese favourable trade balance to be financed that up to half of all the silver mined in the New World is thought to have found its way to China in the seventeenth century.[41] The other payment mechanism arose from the discovery by the Portuguese and others that they could purchase Asian goods with the profits made by facilitating trade within Asia, which was often constrained by local political barriers and for which the delays of the voyage, dictated as they were by the monsoon seasons, gave ample time. The chief characteristic of the first phase of European trade with Japan was that it combined both of these elements.

The Portuguese in Japan. To the Portuguese, Japan became the final destination of the three-year Asian trading voyage that was part of the *Carreira da India*. The Asian voyages of the *Carreira* started in Goa in April or May, and proceeded via Malacca and Macau, where it often stopped for ten to twelve months. The final stage of the outward voyage was the crossing of the South China Sea to Japan, a journey which, depending on the weather, took two to four weeks.[42] From Goa the Portuguese left loaded with woollens, cloth,

40. Fernand Braudel, *Civilisation and Capitalism 15th–18th Century*, vol. 1, *The Structures of Everyday Life*, London: Collins, 1984, pp. 194–220 and *Capitalism and Material Life, 1400–1800*, New York: Harper and Row, 1967, pp. 152–3.

41. Frederic Wakeman, Jr., *The Great Enterprise The Manchu Reconstruction of Imperial Order in Seventeenth Century China* (2 vols), Berkeley: University of California Press, 1985, vol. 1, pp. 2–7.

42. The standard account of the Macau-Japan trade is C. R. Boxer, *The Great Ship from Amacon: Annals of Macao and the Old Japan Trade 1555–1640*, Lisbon: Centro de Estudios Historicos Ultramarinos, 1959. A great deal of material on the *Carreira* is also provided by Schurhammer in *Francis Xavier, passim.*

crystal, clocks and wine from Europe and with textiles purchased in India. At the first important stop, Cochin, European and Indian goods were traded for gems, cinnamon and pepper. Further on in Malacca, the fleet obtained aromatic woods, shark skins and deer hides. The lengthy stay in Macau was required not only to avoid the typhoon season but also to allow for the purchase of finished and unfinished silks from the half-yearly sales at Canton. Finally, on arrival in Japan, the Portuguese traded silks and other goods from China, together with Indian and European commodities of interest to the Japanese. These were traded mainly for silver but also for lacquer boxes, painted screens and other curios with great rarity value in Europe. On the return trip the Japanese silver was used first in Macau for the purchase of gold, porcelain and other commodities, and later as capital for the next round of Canton silk purchases.[43]

The immense profitability of the Macau-Japan trade depended on two factors. One was the Chinese policy of Seclusion, which led to direct trade with Japan being forbidden because of piracy.[44] The other was the relative undervaluation of gold in China *vis-à-vis* silver compared with the exchange ratios of the two metals in Japan, India and Europe.[45] The silk trade was the mechanism by which the Portuguese could profit from this arbitrage opportunity, and the profits could be used both as capital for the following year and for the direct purchase of Chinese gold and other commodities for disposal in other parts of Asia. For the Portuguese this basic pattern of exchange lasted from the 1560s until the suppression of their trade in Japan at the end of the 1630s. The scale and profitability of these exchanges transformed Macau and Nagasaki, the final ports of call in the trading chain, into substantial cities which would retain their economic significance through the vicissitudes of centuries.

The Japanese were extraordinarily interested in the goods brought by the Portuguese. Apart from the obsession with Chinese silk,

43. Gray, *The Voyage of François Pyrard*, pp. 173–7; Boxer, *Fidalgos of the Far East*, pp. 15–17. There are also vivid details of these voyages in Linschoten, *His Discours of Voyages, passim*.

44. In addition to the key works of Boxer, there are many references to the problems of seaborne piracy and to Sino-Japanese and Portuguese relations in Pasquale M. D'Elia, *Fonti Ricciane. Storia dell'Introduzione del Cristianesimo in Cina, scritta da Matteo Ricci* (3 vols), Rome: Libreria dello Stato, 1942–49.

45. The exchange ratio in Japan was different from that in China by a factor of two, Umemura Mataji *et al.* (eds), *Nihon keizaishi* (Economic history of Japan) (8 vols), Tokyo: Iwanami Shoten, 1988– , vol. 1, p. 137 (hereafter *EHOJ*).

the Jesuit missionaries noted that sophisticated Japanese, completely sceptical over the existence of a world to come, were eager to create a paradise of consumption and pleasure in the present. When Father Luis Froës visited the great warrior Oda Nobunaga, he was shown fifteen Portuguese chests filled with 'scarlet capes and cabaias, velvet capes with feathers and medallions of Our Lady of Grace, many pieces of crimson satin ... hourglasses and sundials, candlesticks and tapes ... and many other different kinds of things ... so that I cannot for the life of me imagine what can be brought thence [from Portugal] that will still be a novelty for him.'[46] This Japanese enthusiasm for novelties was confirmed by later observers, including the German physician to the Dutch settlement in Nagasaki in the late seventeenth century, Engelbert Kaempfer, who remarked that the Japanese competed with each other to buy foreign rarities for which 'being unacquainted with their intrinsic value, they willingly paid whatever price was exacted'.[47]

On another level the Japanese were seriously impressed with the prodigious knowledge and technology that had brought the Portuguese to Japan, as well as with their arms. One source, perhaps exaggerating a little, claimed that within six months of the European arrival, no less than 600 copies of the Portuguese arquebus had been made.[48] So important was this early example of technology transfer that Japanese historians regard Nobunaga's organised use of military firearms (*teppo tai*) in 1575 as the beginning of a new historical era. In fact, Dutch weapons, taken from the first Dutch ship to reach Japan, actually played a part in the foundation of the Tokugawa dynasty (1603–1868), being used at the decisive battle of Sekigahara in 1600.[49]

The founder of the Tokugawa dynasty, Tokugawa Ieyasu, was

---

46. Froës was the keenest and most interesting Jesuit observer of sixteenth-century Japan and influential with Alessandro Valignano, the Order's strategist and Visitor as well as being the author of substantial writings himself. This quotation is from C. R. Boxer, *The Christian Century in Japan, 1549–1650*, Berkeley: University of California Press, 1974, pp. 62–3, 95.

47. Engelbertus Kaempfer, *The History of Japan*, trans. J. G. Scheuchzer, FRS, (2 vols), London, 1727–28, with appendices, p. 311. The important appendices are missing from the early printing of the first edition.

48. Boxer, *The Christian Century*, p. 28.

49. *EHOJ*, vol. 1, p. 7; C. R. Boxer, *Jan Compagnie in Japan, 1600–1817*, The Hague: Martinus Nijhof, 1936, p. 25.

particularly interested in the technological aspect of trade, and the Europeans observed that the Japanese could match their curiosity with the practical skills needed to replicate European devices. Jan Huighen Linschoten, a Dutch spy who provided Europe with one of the first detailed accounts of Asia from a non-Portuguese since Marco Polo, commented that the Japanese were 'cunning workmen in all kinds of handy works, they are sharp witted, and quickly learn anything they see'. This admiration for Japanese skill and craftsmanship was shared by his Portuguese contemporary, Rodrigues, and was confirmed in similar terms a century later by Christopher Fryke. Kaempfer also remarked that 'no nation in the East is so dextrous'.[50]

One major difficulty in the early Japanese exchanges with Europeans was the barrier of language. Francis Xavier despaired of its diabolical difficulty, and the Jesuits at first resorted to communicating through theatrical presentations known as 'holy comedies' rather than the lengthy sermons commonplace in contemporary Europe. However, the Portuguese were fortunate in the presence of the Jesuits, who came to admire the linguistic subtlety of Japanese, which was in any case essential not only for religious purposes but also to facilitate the management of the Jesuit stake in the Macau-Nagasaki trade.[51]

The arrival of the Dutch and English. During the latter part of the sixteenth century, the centre of gravity of European trading power shifted to Amsterdam and the United Provinces of the Netherlands. The arrival and ultimate triumph of the Dutch in the Far East reflected

50. Linschoten, *His Discours of Voyages*, p. 45; Michael Cooper (trans. and ed.), *This Island of Japan: João Rodrigues's account of 16th Century Japan*, Tokyo: Kodansha, 1973, p. 299; Kaempfer, *The History of Japan*, appendix, p. 61. M. Paske-Smith, *Western Barbarians in Japan and Formosa in Tokugawa Days, 1603–1868*, New York: Paragon, 1968, p. 124.

51. Boxer, *The Great Ship*, pp. 37–8. The Jesuits had a small share of the silk carried on the annual voyage, the amount of which was determined by the Macau Senate. See Michael Cooper, *Rodrigues the Interpreter: An Early Jesuit in Japan and China*, New York: Weatherhill, 1974, pp. 243–4. The most notable result of the Jesuit linguistic efforts was Rodrigues's *Vocabulario da Lingoa de Japoa*, a vast work of 401 folio volumes. In addition to their linguistic work, Jesuit historical writings and their letters to colleagues in Europe and other parts of Asia became the foundation of European knowledge of Japan, much relied upon by the Dutch and others in the seventeenth century.

and contributed to this development.[52] To justify their new role in Asia, the Dutch developed the theory of international law and the freedom of the seas,[53] and in 1655 the Governor-General of Batavia * justified their worldwide activities with a theory that explained international trade by reference to divinely ordained differences in natural endowment and manufacturing skills:

The Omnipotent God who created the Heavens, the Earth, and whatsoever is in them ... hath ordained by eternal wisdom, that no one place should be stored with all manner of things; but whatsoever is either necessary for the life, or convenient for the ornament of mankind, whether production of Nature, or invention of Art, should be found partly in one Countrey, and partly in another; Divine Providence so disposing it, that the wants of this Land should be supplied by that ... This is the reason which moved our Nation, above all others, wholly to apply and devote itself to Trade and Commerce through the utmost parts of the Sea.[54]

After 1639, the Dutch were the only European traders allowed access to Japan, and Japan thereby came to be linked to the Dutch trading system that incorporated everywhere of importance from the Red Sea to the Far East, with the sole exception of China — an exception that was significant to the Dutch, whom the Chinese occasionally described as 'cantankerous and unpleasant',[55] but less so to the Japanese, who

* Batavia (derived from the ancient name of the Dutch homeland): the island of Java. It also became the name of the capital of the Dutch East Indies, known today as Jakarta.

52. The origins and controversy surrounding these trends are discussed in Jonathan I. Israel, *Dutch Primacy in World Trade 1585–1740*, Oxford University Press, 1989. See also Cordier, *Histoire Générale*, vol. 3, chs. 17–9, *passim*; Braudel, *The Perspective of the World*, pp. 211–20; and C. R. Boxer, *The Dutch Seaborne Empire*, London: Penguin Books, 1990, for a general history.

53. The theories of the great Dutch jurist Grotius were closely linked to the Far East. Grotius was retained by the VOC to defend the right of one of their captains to seize a Portuguese vessel in the Malacca straits. He did this by elaborating his theory of the freedom of the sea, hence denying the Portuguese claim to *own* the South-East Asian oceans. See the entry on Grotius in the *Encyclopaedia Brittanica* (11th/12th edn), New York, 1910–22 (hereafter *EB*). But see also Boxer's comments on the hypocrisy of this Dutch legalism in *The Dutch Seaborne Empire*, pp. 101ff.

54. Extract of a letter to the Emperor of China and the 'King of Canton', quoted in *A Narrative of the success of an Ambassage sent by John Maatzukyer de Badem, General of Batavia, unto the Emperour of China and Tartary*, London: John Maycock for John Nieuhoff, 1669, p. 12.

55. Boxer, *The Dutch Seaborne Empire*, p. 266.

were already part of the Chinese trading system through Nagasaki merchants and other intermediaries.

The Dutch achieved their position in Japan first through successful intelligence operations that unlocked the secrets of Japanese navigation and trade. They then capitalised on this with their naval and strategic strengths and with a relentless, single-minded materialism that seemed to negate the moral foundations of their success in their austere home environment.[56] This lack of religious, cultural or purely political elements in the Dutch penetration of Asia was perceived unfavourably at the time and later, but it may well have been a factor in their success.[57]

The first Dutch ship arrived in Japan in 1600 and the scale of activity in the East is indicated by the fact that no less than fourteen fleets left the United Provinces for the East Indies in 1602. The original intention of the Dutch had been to confine their Asian activities to commercial matters but clashes with European rivals and the difficulty of handling intense competition in Asia between different Dutch provinces led to the establishment in 1602 of the Dutch East India Company (Verenigde Oost-Indische Compagnie, hereafter the VOC). This was an extraordinary institution. Devised by a federal polity, it sought to develop, regulate and share among the companies from the

56. Although written from a particular political viewpoint, a useful analysis of the interplay between the harsh environment of northern Europe and the finer qualities of Dutch commercial culture is Elie Luzac's anonymous work *La Richesse de la Hollande* (2 vols), London: Aux Dépens de la Compagnie, 1788, esp. vol. 1, pp. 283ff. On their Asian activities, however, even a historian as sympathetic as Pieter Geyl expressed disgust at the Dutch behaviour; and the French historian Cordier commented: 'Les Hollandais ne leur cédèrent en rien dans leur âpreté au gain et jamais nous ne voyons dans leurs conseils de direction percer une idée noble ou simplement désintéressée; ils sacrifient tout, amis comme ennemis . . . même la religion . . . pour ménager leur crédit. L'histoire coloniale des Hollandais est une belle page de l'histoire du developpement commercial de l'Europe, mais une vilaine page de l'histoire de l'humanité', *Histoire Générale*, vol. 3, p. 231. Geyl's comments are to be found in his *The Netherlands in the 17th Century*, part II: *1649–1715*, London: Ernest Benn, 1964, esp. pp. 181ff.

57. Recent research suggests that Cordier may have been a little hard. In Holland, the participants in the eastern trades were liable to arraignment in the ecclesiastical courts and the Dutch, like the Portuguese, developed a moralistic literature of sea catastrophes. Thus when Willem Ysbrantsz Bontekoe watched his burning ship sink in the Sunda straits off Java, his Reformation conscience could be heard in his cry, 'Oh God how is this fine ship undone, yea even as Sodom and Gomorrah', quoted in Simon Schama, *The Embarrassment of Riches: An Interpretation of Dutch Culture in the Golden Age*, London: Collins, 1987, p. 32.

Dutch provinces the proceeds of an enormous and growing trade.[58] To do this it brought Dutch trade and shipping in Asia under unified control and prosecuted vigorous military and diplomatic policies.[59] It established a central fortified land base at Batavia (modern Jakarta) in 1619 and in 1624, having been repeatedly rebuffed by the Chinese, built Castel Zelandia on Taiwan. Finally, in 1640, the Dutch took Malacca, which gave them control of both the Malacca and Sunda straits through which rival western shipping was bound to pass.

Like the Portuguese, the Dutch sought complete monopolies and reinforced controls on trade. For example, they established contracts to ensure that local rulers burned spice trees surplus to the Dutch requirements.[60] And although in their early voyages they were primarily concerned with long-distance trade in spices, they were also to prove extraordinarily successful later in exploiting the potentiality of intra-Asian trade — the *inlandhansel*. This success was not surprising, since the rise of the Dutch in Europe had been based precisely on their development of the specialised shipping and trading services that linked the grain, fisheries and timber markets of the north European economies to the olive oil, textiles and colonial wealth of the south, and which also exploited the dominant position of the United Provinces at the mouth of the Rhine and the great river systems of Germany.[61]

Over the next two centuries the Dutch elaborated an Asian trading network stretching from Aden to Nagasaki, linking both Europe and the Dutch colonies in South America. The power and effectiveness of the Dutch global system was illustrated in the 1630s when the

58. The origins of the company are explained in Israel, *Dutch Primacy*, pp. 68–73. An admiring and informative analysis of it is in John E. Wills Jr., *Pepper, Guns and Parleys. The Dutch East India Company and China, 1622–1681*, Cambridge, MA: Harvard University Press, 1974, pp. 17–20.

59. The militant policy was associated first with Oldenbarneveldt, the Advocate of Holland, who supported it, and later with Jan Pietersz Coen who, as Governor General of the Dutch East Indies, implemented it with ferocity.

60. This and other aspects of commercial strategy are elaborated in Rear Admiral John Splinter Stavorinus, *Voyages to the East Indies* (3 vols, trans. Samuel Hull Wilcocke), London: G. G. and J. Robinson, 1788, vol. 1, pp. 329–84. Data on the VOC voyages from 1597–1724 are listed in vol. 3, pp. 526–31, and confirm that between 1599 and 1611 they were primarily concerned with bringing spices to Europe. Stavorinus's account, together with his comments based on careful reading of contemporary materials, gives a vivid and objective account of the Dutch seaborne empire in Asia in the late eighteenth century.

61. *La Richesse de la Hollande*, vol. 1, *passim*.

failure of their Brazilian sugar plantations prompted them to ship more than 1 million pounds of Chinese sugar through Taiwan to the Middle East and Europe.[62] So sophisticated did their Asian trading system become that most of the 3 million tons of tin taken annually from Palembang (Sumatra) was shipped to China; two-fifths of the camphor exported from Japan was sold in India, and as much as four-fifths of the copper exported from Japan was sold to Dutch markets in Bengal, Surat, Coromandel, Malabar and other parts of Asia.[63] It was within the working of this broader system that the Dutch activities in Japan became so profitable that in their best years they were exceeded in Asia only by the Dutch profits earned in Ceylon and Batavia.[64]

The Dutch established their first Japanese base in 1609 at Hirado in Hizen province. Within four years they were joined by the English, who had made an appearance in the Far East when Drake visited the Moluccas in 1579. In 1600 they responded to rising European pepper prices by establishing the East India Company, which despatched John Saris to the Far East in 1611. Using Linschoten's map and guided in by Japanese pilots, Saris arrived in Japan in 1613.[65] Japan was not the major destination of Saris' voyage but he did succeed in obtaining a charter allowing the English to visit the country for trading purposes, to build houses in Edo (modern Tokyo), and to be responsible for their internal discipline. While in Japan Saris met Will Adams, who had come with the Dutch, and left behind on his departure Richard Cocks as the captain of the English trading settlement.

The English never achieved the success of the Dutch in Japan. They had no demand for a major Japanese export of the time, copper, and seemed to have neither the skills nor the resources for the *inlandhansel*.

---

62. The coasting trade — 'la base de la fortune Neerlandaise' — is described in Louis Dermigny, *La Chine et L'Occident. Le Commerce à Canton au XVIIIème Siècle, 1719–1833* (4 vols), Paris: SEVPEN, 1964, vol. 1, pp. 114–20. Despite its title, this vast study contains much information on Japanese and Asian trade in the seventeenth and eighteenth centuries. See also Israel, *Dutch Primacy in World Trade*, p. 174.

63. Data on the Japan-based *inlandhansel* are from Stavorinus, *Voyages*, vol. 1, ch. 6 and Kristoff Glaman, *Dutch-Asiatic Trade, 1620–1740*, The Hague: Martinus Nijhoff, 1981, pp. 175–9. See also Israel, *Dutch Primacy, passim*. Dates vary for these examples of the *inlandhansel* but Stavorinus' information is from the late eighteenth century.

64. Estimates of the Dutch trade and its profitability are to be found in Glaman and Israel and also in Boxer, *The Great Ship*, pp. 170–1 and Cordier, *Histoire Générale*, vol. 3, p. 224.

65. James Murdoch, *A History of Japan* (3 vols), London: Kegan Paul, 1925–6, vol. 2, p. 585; Cordier, *Histoire Générale*, vol. 3, p. 199; Sir Ernest M. Satow, *The Voyage of Captain John Saris to Japan, 1613*, London: Hakluyt Society, 1900, esp. the intro.

They also had little success in interesting the Japanese in English broadcloths, which were inappropriate for Japanese garments and altogether too dull for the Japanese taste, stimulated as it was by gorgeous Chinese fabrics.[66] The width of English fabric also precluded its use in traditional Japanese clothing.

In the early seventeenth century the domestic situation in Japan began to shift in ways unfavourable to trade, especially to that of the Portuguese. Unlike Tokugawa Ieyasu, the Shogun* Hidetada was hostile to trade, regarded merchants as essentially corrupt, and strongly distrusted foreign intervention in Japanese domestic politics.[67] In 1624 the Spanish, who had been allowed an annual galleon from Manila, were forbidden to trade, but even so the scale of Japanese-Portuguese trade remained substantial as late as the 1630s.[68]

In 1635 the government policy of Seclusion (*sakoku* — 'closed country') was manifested in an edict that forbad Japanese to travel abroad. In 1636 further edicts stipulated that no Japanese vessel was to be allowed beyond coastal waters and that nationals returning from abroad be executed. This policy was not intrinsically anti-trade but directed rather towards the control of European trade and the stabilisation of the Japanese political system within a new East Asian framework of international relations. Its implementation was reinforced by limits on the size of boats and by the construction of large holes in the stern of ships that would make swamping in open seas a certainty.[69]

In 1638 the involvement of the Portuguese in the unsuccessful Christian revolt of Shimabara sealed their fate. In the following year

---

* *Shogun*: 'military general': effective leader of Tokugawa Japan.

66. Saris was instructed to find out what English goods the Japanese would be interested in, Satow, *op. cit.*, p. xiii; see also Paske-Smith, *Western Barbarians in Japan*, pp. 25ff.

67. Hidetada told the King of Siam that merchants were 'abominable fellows'. Cooper, *Rodrigues the Interpreter*, p. 245.

68. The 'eastward' orientation of sixteenth-century Japan and Asia to the Philippines and the Americas tends to be overlooked. Among contemporary western accounts, that of Gonzalez de Mendoza usefully illustrates this outlook. *Histoire du Grand Royaume de la Chine, Situé aux Indes Orientales*, Lyon: François Arnouilet, 1609. Chs. 19–20 in book 6 deal specifically with Japan.

69. Kaempfer discusses many of the strange results of the policy of Seclusion and his book includes a fine print of a ship with a hole in the rear (p. 410, and plate xxi). Early Tokugawa ships were up to 120 feet long and carried 300 men. Miyamoto Mataji et al. (eds), *Nihon boekijin no keifu* (The lineage of Japanese merchants), Tokyo: Yuhikaku, 1980, p. 42.

the captain of the great ship from Macau was given a copy of the edict certifying that 'all future ships [are] to be burned, and their cargoes, and all on board to be executed'. In 1640 the unbelieving Portuguese returned and the Japanese carried out the edict, almost to the letter. From that year Japan moved into 'that state of seclusion which presents some of the strangest phenomena in the history of the world'.[70] When it re-emerged from Seclusion in the mid-nineteenth century, it was to find itself in a state of military and technological inferiority to Europe and America from which it took a century to recover.

It is remarkable that the Portuguese survived in Asia despite the devastating loss of the Macau-Nagasaki trade. They had lost both their most lucrative trade and their power and strategic vision for worldwide dominion. However, they retained their localised trading skills, their close ties with indigenous Asian communities through intermarriage, and the unique political and charitable institutions which enabled them to bind all these together. With these resources, not only did they hold their positions in established settlements such as Goa and Macau but a new diaspora of Portuguese merchant communities also settled in Bantam, Batavia, Cochin China, Malabar and Macassar, continuing an active role in the Asian trading system. The Portuguese language not only remained the *lingua franca* of Asian commerce but was used in Japan for generations after the Portuguese expulsion.[71]

The Seclusion: the Nagasaki and Dutch trade

The policy of Seclusion did not stop all trade between Japan and the outside world. Chinese trade remained on a large scale, and commercial contacts throughout South-East Asia were maintained by Japanese shipping and merchant communities in Batavia, Malacca and the Philippines.[72] The Asian trading system was essentially a Chinese-

70. Murdoch, *A History of Japan*, vol. 2, p. 713.

71. George Bryan Souza, *The Survival of Empire, Portuguese Trade and Society in China and the South China Sea, 1630–1754*, Cambridge University Press, 1986; Ljungstedt, *Historical Sketch*, passim.

72. Hamashita Takeshi and Kawakatsu Heita (eds), *Ajia koiken to Nihon kogyoka, 1500–1900* (The Asian trade sphere and Japanese industrialisation, 1500–1900), Tokyo: Libro Porto, 1991; Boxer, *The Christian Century*, pp. 296–7, 301; Murdoch, *A History of Japan*, vol. 2, p. 487ff.

centred phenomenon, based on the practice of 'tributary trade', whereby the Chinese allowed trading relations to be maintained under the guise of tribute payment from the known world to the Chinese court. This trade was controlled by various conventional practices and also by limiting access to China to a number of key points of entry, which included Macau and Canton. Radiating out from Canton and from the Chinese coastal provinces of Kiangsu, Chekiang, Fukien and Kwangtung were trading networks, serviced by fleets of junks, that extended from the Bay of Bengal and Burma, through most of South-East Asia, and on to Taiwan and Japan.[73] This external system was in turn connected to the most extensive waterborne system of internal trade that the world has ever known, based on the spine of the Grand Canal.[74]

The integration of the Asian and European systems was achieved between the sixteenth and the eighteenth centuries by foreign presence in Malacca, Batavia, Taiwan, Macau and Canton; and in the nineteenth century by western control of Singapore, Hong Kong and the Chinese treaty ports. Macau was the first point at which Europeans successfully inserted themselves into the heart of this system and,

73. Modern accounts of these networks include Dermigny, *Le Commerce à Canton*, vol. 1, pp. 289–310 and Hamashita and Kawakatsu, *The Asian trade sphere*, pp. 38–41. Contemporary European observation on the liveliness and importance of China's role in intra-Asian trade is found in the multi-volume encyclopedia of Chinese affairs compiled by the French Jesuits, *Mémoires concernant l'histoire, les sciences, les moeurs, les usages &c. des Chinois, par les missionnaires de Pékin*, Paris: Nyon L'aîné, 1776–81 (14 vols). 'C'est une erreur assez répandue parmi nous de croire que les Chinois ne peuvent sortir de leur Empire pour commercer: mais il suffit pour détruire ce préjugé de voir la mer couverte des Joncques Chinoises, allant & venant du Japon aux Philippines, à Siam & aux Molucques, ou ils font un commerce immense', *ibid*, vol. 5, p. 42. Stavorinus describes a vivid example of this trade undertaken by the three-masted, 140-foot Chinese junk that the Dutch allowed to make an annual trip to the Celebes. Its outbound cargo included brass, iron, textiles, silk and one million pieces of porcelain. *Voyages*, vol. 2, pp. 283–6.

74. As Magaillans remarked, 'There are two Empires in China, the one upon the Water, the other upon the Land', *A New History of China*, p. 129. Magaillans himself went by boat from Peking to Macau in 1656 with only *one* day taken on land to cross a mountain — having previously travelled up the Yangtze from Hangchow in the east, to modern Chengtu in the far west. These waterborne journeys amounted to a total distance of 1,000 leagues, i.e. about 3,000 miles, p. 131. Marco Polo had earlier estimated that the commerce carried on the Yangtze in the Mongol period exceeded the commerce on all the European rivers put together.

Macau together with Taiwan and Canton, formed part of the network of triangular trades that enabled the Europeans to act as intermediaries between China and Japan.[75] This system, though effective, was far from perfect since according to Dutch accounts the volume of goods offered to the Portuguese through the Macau system often far exceeded their ability to finance it.[76]

Japanese contacts with this sinocentric trading system were of long standing, and they remained active even after the formal breach with the Chinese court and the imposition of Seclusion decrees against Europeans. In the sixteenth century substantial Chinese trading communities settled in southern Japan, and in 1616, Tokugawa Ieyasu strengthened his control of these burgeoning activities by putting the entire trade under official control in Nagasaki.[77] The city thus became the site of a large Chinese quarter and from this territorial base Chinese merchants retained an important role in the Japanese economy up to the early part of the twentieth century. In the 1650s, as many as 200 Chinese junks a year were arriving at Nagasaki, and Chinese exports to Japan included a wide range of products including silks, textiles, brown and white sugar, aromatic woods, nuts, hides, spices and Chinese books and paper.[78] Another important group of imports from China was that of medicinal products, which the Japanese needed despite their efforts to achieve self-sufficiency by the establishment of special herb gardens in Edo and Kyoto.[79]

Trade with China was disturbed in the final years of the Ming dynasty and during the turbulent time when the new dynasty of the

75. The role of Taiwan in the Dutch trading system is fully discussed in Hamashita and Kawakatsu, *The Asian trade sphere*. Of especial interest is their Table on p. 118. Canton is dealt with in Dermigny, *Le Commerce à Canton, passim*. An earlier account of the role of Taiwan as the base for the Dutch trade with Japan and Asia is 'A History of the Dutch Trade' in William Campbell, *Formosa under the Dutch, described from Contemporary Records*, London: Kegan Paul, 1903, repr. Taiwan, 1987.

76. Campbell, *Formosa under the Dutch*, p. 55.

77. Marius B. Jansen, *China in the Tokugawa World*, Cambridge, MA: Harvard University Press, 1992, ch. 1. This book includes a valuable bibliographical guide to recent Japanese scholarship on this subject.

78. Kaempfer, *The History of Japan*, pp. 374–81.

79. Details of Japanese efforts to supply themselves with medicinal herbs from special gardens in Kyoto and Edo are in Miyamoto Mataji (ed.), *Shohin ryutsu no shiteki kenkyu* (Historical research into the circulation of commodities), Kyoto: Minerva Shobo, 1967, pp. 213–30.

Ching was being established. However, in the 1660s and 1680s there were major booms, and trading relations remained active at a lower level in the eighteenth and early nineteenth centuries. One curious feature of this trade was that although the Chinese were allowed spring and autumn visits, prices were only fixed in the spring, a practice that naturally led to large fluctuations in the autumn sale.[80]

With strong elements of seclusion in both Japanese and Chinese trading policies and the loss of the Portuguese intermediaries, much trade was in practice conducted through intermediaries in Taiwan, Korea and the Ryukyu Islands. The latter occupied a unique position in Japan's triangular trades, being simultaneously a tributary of both China and Japan. This curious anomaly required the Ryukyuans to use two calendars, to feign ignorance of the Japanese language to the Chinese and to allow the lords of Satsuma to oversee their relations with China.[81] One other element in the Japanese trading pattern was the role played by the long tradition of secret traders — the *hakatajin*. The city of Hakata 'was the oldest, richest and most beautiful port in Southern Japan', and its merchants had traded immemorially not only in Korea and China but throughout South-East Asia.[82] During the Seclusion, the Hakata often disguised themselves as Chinese and their trading networks played an important role in maintaining Japanese trade in the seventeenth and eighteenth centuries.

For the Europeans, however, Seclusion drastically constricted trade, and in spite of several attempts the Portuguese and the English both failed to return. A Portuguese embassy in 1647 claimed not to have

80. Based on material on the China trade in Hamashita and Kawakatsu, *The Asian trade sphere, passim*; Kaempfer, *The History of Japan, passim*; Uehara Kenzen, *Sakoku to han boeki* (Seclusion and *han* trade), Tokyo: Yaegaku Shobo, 1981; Miyamoto, *The lineage of Japanese merchants*. The fact that a turbulent period of Chinese history was associated with the general flourishing of Japanese trade is curious. One explanation may be that the economic impact of Chinese upheavals will have been shortlived and localised and that recovery from the Ming collapse was generally rapid. Also, the evidence of the Macau trade reveals that the potential supply of exports was consistently far larger than the Portuguese could handle. Trade was therefore determined by foreign demand rather than Chinese supply conditions. For the post-Ming recovery, see Ray Huang, *China: A Macro History*, Armonk, NY: M. E. Sharpe, 1990, ch. 16.

81. The complex relationships of China with Asia neighbours are the theme of John K. Fairbank (ed.), *The Chinese World Order. Traditional China's Foreign Relations*, Cambridge, MA: Harvard University Press, 1968.

82. The quotation and a minute description of the city are in Schurhammer, *Francis Xavier*, vol. 4, pp. 141–8.

known of the death edict and approached the Japanese with the prodigious gift of a piece of coral weighing 545 pounds.[83] A seventeenth-
century English embassy was treated politely, but was unacceptable to
the Japanese because of English links with the Portuguese crown.[84] In
the early nineteenth century, Stamford Raffles took advantage of the
Napoleonic wars to try and oust the Dutch from Deshima, but although
he learned enough to make some prescient observations on the potential
of the Japanese for modernisation, he never got the support from home
necessary to make the decisive breakthrough. Thus for over 200 years
the Dutch maintained their monopoly.

The circumstances of the Dutch trade were bizarre and humiliating,
especially in the seventeenth and latter part of the eighteenth centuries.
But as Kaempfer observed, 'So great was the covetousness of the
Dutch and so great the alluring power of the Japanese gold, that rather
than to quit the prospect of a trade, indeed most advantageous, they
willingly underwent an almost perpetual imprisonment, for such in
fact is our stay in Deshima.'[85] This was no exaggeration. From 1641
the Dutch were confined to Deshima, a small, fan-shaped island off
Nagasaki measuring 82 by 236 paces. The island was surrounded by
a sea-wall and joined to the mainland by a bridge surmounted by
a guardhouse. On their island the Dutch constructed about forty
buildings of various sizes. These included a Japanese-style guesthouse,
kitchens, a cellar, a large house for the Dutch director (the *opperhooft*),
and a Japanese-style hall for doing business. Space was also found
for two gardens, one in formal Dutch style, the other possibly for
vegetables. Seventeenth-century Dutch engravings of Deshima show
no buildings on the bank opposite the island, but eighteenth-century
Japanese prints show that a small and busy settlement had grown up
in response to the work and the trading opportunities the Dutch
presence had created.[86]

83. C. R. Boxer, *A Portuguese Embassy to Japan (1644–1647)*, London: Kegan Paul,
1928, pp. 63–4.

84. *A Copy of the Japan Diary Received per a Danish Ship, July 18, 1674*, appendix
to Kaempfer, *The History of Japan*.

85. Further details of life in Deshima are in Boxer, *The Dutch Seaborne Empire*,
pp. 232–3; for a French account by hearsay but full of insights, see *Voyages de
Mr. De Thevenot*, Paris: La Veuve Biestkins, 1694, pp. 325–33.

86. Isaac Tirion published a fine, detailed sketch of Deshima in 1736 and Van
Siebold an even later one in 1828. Both of these are illustrated in the catalogue of
Paulus Swaen, *Zipangu: The Mapping of Japan*, Geldrop, 1993.

Deshima was home to the Dutch director and a small group of between seven and twenty company men. The director and his colleagues were closely guarded and spied upon; at dinner it was normal for Japanese cooks and waiters, who included spies, substantially to outnumber the diners. The Japanese who served the Dutchmen took blood-curdling oaths to guard against any defections of sentiment or loyalty. The general attitude of the Japanese was that 'to cheat and defraud [were the] unquestionable proofs of a patriot'.[87] When the annual visit was made by the Company's trading vessels, its officers were liable to be 'beaten with sticks . . . as if they were dogs'.[88] In the early days of the settlement, the Dutch were even forced to bury their dead at sea, although a small piece of waste ground was later given them for that purpose.

Whereas in the sixteenth century, language problems had been an inhibiting factor in Japanese relationships with Europeans, by the seventeenth the Japanese had control of this issue. Thus although at least one Dutch director, François Caron, learned some spoken Japanese, translation was effectively in the hands of the specially trained Nagasaki interpreters. The languages known by the interpreter corps included Dutch, Portuguese, Tonkinese, Siamese and Chinese. Kaempfer reports that, in his time, the full establishment of the corps was 150, but that only 123 were in post.[89] These interpreters, with their fragmentary but highly privileged access to westerners and their knowledge, were to play an important role in the intellectual history of Japan and its relations with the West.

In the dreary life of Deshima there were two great events: the annual visit by the Dutch ships from Batavia and the ensuing sale of goods, and the periodic visit by the Dutch ambassadors to Edo. The visit to Edo was an extension of the Japanese system of *sankin kotai* ('alternate attendance'). This was the political control system whereby the Japanese feudal nobility spent part of the year in residence at Edo and for the rest of the time left their families as hostages to the Bakufu, the shogunal government.[90] To participate in this system at all was

87. Kaempfer, *The History of Japan*, pp. 340–1.
88. Murdoch, *A History of Japan*, vol. 2, p. 678.
89. Kaempfer, *The History of Japan*, p. 273.
90. This account is based mainly on the reports of Kaempfer and of Montanus in *Ambassades Memorables de la Compagnie des Indies Orientales des Provinces Unies, Vers les Empereurs du Japon contenant plusieurs choses remarquables arrivées pendant le voyage des Ambassadeurs*, Amsterdam: Jacob de Meurs, 1680. Kaempfer made the journey to

clearly regarded as something of an honour, since it was denied to the Chinese community at Nagasaki, who could deal only with local officials. The Dutch journey to Edo started in February, when the main party set off overland, but they were preceded by a costly and specially equipped barge bearing their gifts. At Shimonoseki the two groups joined up to continue the journey to Osaka, Kyoto and Edo. At Edo the Dutch were treated as Japanese daimyos (feudal lords) and received in a series of formal audiences. They were entertained by their hosts with tea, tobacco and sweetmeats, and in Kaempfer's time they were required to dance, sing and speak in broken Japanese for the amusement of the court. More seriously, the ambassadors were questioned about geography, science and technology and the state of the outside world, and their physician was expected to give medical advice.

To the Japanese, the main purpose of the visit was the renewal of Dutch submission to Japanese authority. Although the journey was costly and often seemed humiliating, it enabled the Dutch to learn something of Japan outside Deshima and Nagasaki; it also offered opportunities, especially for the director, to engage in 'private trade'.[91]

The main venue of trade, however, was the annual sale of goods at Deshima. This was organised by Dutch and Japanese officials in a highly formal way. Before it began, a list of the goods available was displayed in large Japanese characters, and at the same time, the Japanese officials published the level of local taxes that would be levied on them. The wares were then laid out in the special hall, in groups, on silver plates. After inspection, prospective buyers made bids at various levels and were committed to buy only at the lowest bid that would secure the goods against their competitors. At the end of the day Japanese officials placed seals on the doors of the hall, and representatives of both sides dined together. At Dutch insistence, no business was transacted on Sundays.

According to Montanus, based on VOC sources, the goods on offer at a typical late seventeenth-century sale included silks, yarn, skins,

---

Edo twice while Montanus based his writing on documentary materials. A valuable secondary account is Grant K. Goodman, *Japan: The Dutch Experience*, London: Athlone Press, 1986, ch. 4.

91. The private trade of the VOC employees tended to be in rare and relatively specialised articles. In the late eighteenth century, private trade imports to Japan included looking glasses, spectacles, watches, Spanish liquorice and Venetian treacle (a popular medicinal compound for treating poisons). Private exports included silk, fine rice, nightgowns, lacquer, china and fans. Stavorinus, *Voyages*, vol. 1, p. 360.

spices, sugar, textiles, mirrors, aromatic woods and quicksilver.[92] Data
from records in Taiwan illustrate the wide variety of European goods
for which the Japanese merchants placed orders with the Dutch.[93]
The principal commodity bought by the Dutch was various forms
of copper, the best of which was reported to be of very fine quality,
intermixed with traces of gold. Other purchases included gold,
camphor, lacquered boxes, furniture, umbrellas, screens, the finest
quality rice, *sake*, tea and 'marmalade'. Many of these products were
sold later in other parts of Asia. There were strict regulations forbidding the export of certain items, including models of military or
naval significance, maps, arms, and pictures of the Emperor.

The costs of trading in Japan were exceptionally high. The VOC
lost one ship of every two that attempted the dangerous waters off
Japan, while in the late eighteenth century, a complement of ten to
twelve men on Deshima cost the VOC 100,000 guilders a year —
almost exactly the amount needed to support a 500-man establishment
in Batavia; about half of this sum was taken up by the cost of the
embassies and gifts taken to Edo. For most years the profits justified
these sums and shipping losses[94] — a remarkable feat in the seventeenth century, since neither the Ming nor Ching dynasties allowed
the Dutch direct access to the Chinese silk that was needed for the
basic trade, and the Japanese banned exports of silver in 1668.[95]

92. Montanus, *Ambassades Mémorables*, vol. 2, pp. 70–6; Kaempfer, *The History of
Japan*, pp. 363–72.

93. In the late 1620s the Dutch agent in Japan had standing orders for nine types
of European textiles as well as an array of textiles, spices and other products to be
sourced from Dutch trading contacts in South-East Asia. Campbell, *Formosa under
the Dutch*, p. 58.

94. Stavorinus, *Voyages*, vol. 1, p. 359, illustrates with profit data for 1779.
Kaempfer provides data from a late seventeenth century perspective and estimated that
taking into account both direct and *inlandhansel* trade, the rate of profit on goods
purchased for sale in Japan was 90% of their cost — enough to justify the substantial
overheads of the Asian system, including military and shipbuilding expenses and the
salaries of company officials. In addition, the system was supported by the benefits
of the 'private' trade, especially that of the Directors, who were limited to a maximum
of three terms on Deshima.

95. Israel, *Dutch Primacy*, pp. 171–3. The problems of access to China baffled the
Dutch and ultimately led to their failure to establish themselves in the tea trade in the
eighteenth century. The seventeenth-century embassies are the subject of Wills, *Pepper,
Guns and Parleys*, and may also be studied directly from the accounts of three embassies
by Nieuhof and Montanus, whose books brought to European readers the first authentic
pictures of China and Japan.

However, control of Taiwan enabled the silk problem to be solved by indirect trade between the 1620s and 1662, and by the late seventeenth century the Dutch had switched from the export of silver to that of copper — a commodity of great value for both the European and *inlandhansel* trades. Porcelain was another commodity sent to Europe in large quantities.[96] Maintaining profitability in the eighteenth century was even more difficult. British advances in India contributed to the decline of the entire Dutch system, while in Japan the authorities placed increasing restrictions on trade, culminating in 1775 with the abolition of the Dutch director's private trade. Declining profits, domestic revolution and humiliation in the Napoleonic wars all combined to make the preservation of the Deshima link increasingly difficult; but even in their darkest hour the Dutch maintained something of their role in Japanese trade and ultimately held on there until the Ansei treaties in the mid-nineteenth century.[97]

The significance of the Dutch trade went well beyond the mutual benefits of the exchange of goods. From the European viewpoint the Dutch centuries represented a second phase of European learning about Japan, a phase in which there was a major shift of perspective. In the sixteenth century typical European comments came from a Portuguese Jesuit and in the seventeenth and eighteenth centuries from someone connected with the Dutch trading settlement. And although Asia remained for all Europeans a '*terra incognita* — another planet [where] even the plants and animals were different', the Dutch, with their

96. Between 1602 and 1657 the Dutch shipped 3 million pieces of Chinese porcelain to Europe; between 1659 and 1682 they shipped a further 190,000 pieces of Japanese ware. Boxer, *The Dutch Seaborne Empire*, p. 195. Japanese exports were, however, very modest by comparison with the millions of pieces exported annually by the Chinese. See ch. 10 on the export and provincial wares in Soame Jenyns, *Ming Pottery and Porcelain*, London: Faber and Faber, 1953.

97. Data on the Dutch decline between the late seventeenth and eighteenth centuries is in Hamashita and Kawakatsu, *The Asian trade sphere*, p. 314. A near contemporary British account that supplements Stavorinus' analysis of the growing unprofitability of the VOC is included in William Milburn, *Oriental Commerce*, London: Black Parry, 1813. However, it is interesting to note that when Napoleon's Empress Josephine toured the Netherlands during the Imperial progress of 1811, she left the imperial barge to buy Japanese porcelain in Amsterdam. Simon Schama, *Patriots and Liberators: Revolution in the Netherlands, 1780–1813*, London: Fontana Press, 1992, p. 612.

geographical, religious and intellectual formation in northern rather than southern Europe, looked at Japan with new eyes.[98]

The view of Japan and its economy that emerged during the Dutch phase did not emphasise prodigal endowments of nature as earlier European accounts of India,the East Indies and South China had done. Nevertheless, agriculture, especially the cultivation of rice and tea, was seen as a pursuit in which the Japanese had invested exceptional skill, energy and learning effort.[99] Kaempfer was amazed at the varieties of rice and commented that Japanese rice fields were 'by much the finest one could set his eyes on in any part of the world'. The Dutch were also impressed by the people's liveliness, mobility and frugality and the general dynamism of the urban economy. Roads were well built and busy, and the towns and villages neatly laid out with degrees of internal complexity reflecting their importance in the economic and political hierarchy, both local and national. In every town of any size there was a variety of houses, inns, official post houses, temples and bawdy houses — of which Kaempfer remarked that, 'the concourse of people [was] as great at the latter as at the former'.[100]

A distinctive feature of the Dutch view of Japan was its strong emphasis on the differences between European and Japanese tastes, values and practices. For although the Portuguese and other early observers had noted characteristic Japanese behaviour with clinical accuracy and expressed some moral reservations, they believed there was much in the Japanese for Europeans to admire and emulate.[101] The Dutch, however, found aspects of Japan very disconcerting. They strongly disapproved of Japanese cruelty (judicial and otherwise), and

---

98. Braudel, *The Perspective of the World*, p. 488. Braudel's comment is illustrated by the strange engravings in the first European academic study of China's plants, animals and other phenomena: Athanasius Kircher, *China Monumentis qua Sacris qua Profanis, nec non variis Naturae & Artis Spectaculis*, Amsterdam: Waesberge en Weyerstraat, 1667.

99. Montanus described Japan as 'little fertile', but Kaempfer emphasised its endowment of minerals and the significance of the combination of human effort and natural resources in agriculture. Montanus, *Ambassades Memorables*, vol. 1, p. 43; Kaempfer, *The History of Japan*, pp. 107–8.

100. Kaempfer, *ibid.*, p. 260, pp. 402–29.

101. Valignano listed the 'five bad characteristics' of the Japanese but nonetheless wrote that they 'excel not only all the other Oriental peoples, they surpass the Europeans as well'. Alessandro Valignano, *Historia del Principio y Progresso de la Compania de Jesus en las Indias Orientales (1542–64)*, ed. Josef Wicki, Rome: Institutum Historicum SJ, 1944, pp. 127–54 and Lach, *Asia*, vol. 1, book 2, pp. 684–5.

of what they described as deviousness and malice in business dealings. They were staggered by the prices the Japanese would pay for old tea-bowls, swords and western novelties, and remarked on the diametrical differences from their own tastes in food and drink.[102]

Despite such reservations, the overall judgement on Japan's social and economic system was favourable. In the earlier part of his history, Kaempfer said of Japan 'that as a particular World, which Nature seems purposely to have separated from the rest of the Globe, by encompassing it with a rocky and tempestuous Sea, it can easily subsist of it self without any assistance from foreign countries, as long as Arts and Agriculture are follow'd by the Natives.'[103] In the famous sixth appendix to his work he further analysed at length the political economy of Seclusion. Here he argued that the remote location of Japan, its particular resource endowment, the skills of its people and their ability to exploit the internal division of labour, all meant that Seclusion was a rational policy. In discussing these matters Kaempfer showed awareness of the problem of demographic pressures but suggested that these provided the necessary stimulus to continued agricultural innovation. On balance, he therefore concluded that under the leadership of a Confucian shogun, 'their country was never in a happier condition than it now is, governed by an arbitrary Monarch, shut up, and kept from all Commerce and Communication with foreign nations'.[104] This was a somewhat mercantilist conclusion, and one that came strangely from an employee of a worldwide trading organisation in the age of Grotius. However, it illustrates the high, if selective European regard for Japanese economic, technical and social strengths in the late seventeenth century.

The intellectual transfer from Europe

The Japanese, for their part, also gained more from the Dutch trade than commerce. This intellectual contact had an Asian — and particularly Chinese — context. Up till the fifteenth century Chinese

---

102. 'Pour le gout ils rejettent toutes nos délicatesses, et leurs meilleurs potages nous servirent vomir', Montanus, *Ambassades Memorables*, vol. 1, p. 45.

103. Kaempfer, *The History of Japan*, p. 103.

104. '*An Enquiry, whether it be conducive for the good of the Japanese Empire, to keep it shut up, as it now is, and not to suffer its inhabitants to have any Commerce with foreign nations, either at home or abroad*', App. VI to Kaempfer, *op. cit.*

science had benefited both from indigenous development and from significant contact with the mathematics and astronomy of the Muslim world. Thus at one time Muslims, who were an important factor in the early stages of the European scientific renaissance, constituted a link between Asian and European intellectual expansion. But while in sixteenth-century Europe science leapt ahead, in China it stagnated, being replaced with a self-centred, almost exclusively literary culture. When the Jesuits arrived in China in the late sixteenth century, they brought with them new developments in mathematics, astronomy, cosmography and cartography, all subjects covered by the Jesuit training of the time. Outstanding work was done in geography and cartography, and especially important was the information about the outside world provided in the amazing world map (based essentially on the atlas of Ortelius) prepared by Matteo Ricci at the request of the Chinese.[105] In the 1640s Father Martini, a mathematician who had studied under the scientific polyglot Athanasius Kircher, began the mapping of China itself. Although partly derivative, his enterprise culminated in the first European atlas of East Asia and was the foundation of modern geographical understanding of the Chinese empire.[106] The other key figure in this transfer of knowledge was Adam Schall, who became President of the Chinese Tribunal of Astronomy in 1644. In addition to geography, astronomy and the calendrical sciences, he instructed the incoming Manchu dynasty on civil and construction engineering, including the rebuilding of Peking and the mounting of huge bronze cannons.[107]

105. A copy of Ricci's map is provided as the frontispiece in D'Elia, *Fonti Ricciane*, vol. 2. A standard general survey of Tokugawa science is David L. Swain, *Science and Culture in Traditional Japan*, Cambridge, MA: MIT Press, 1978.

106. This atlas, published by Blaeu in 1655, was a book of rare beauty; it contained fifteen provincial maps, complete maps of China and Japan and a long descriptive text described by Sir Henry Yule as infinitely quotable. So accurate was it that as late as 1838 a German Protestant pastor identified the latitudes and longitudes of some 750 place-names as established by Martini and later Jesuit cartographers, all of whom worked with Imperial approval. M. Martini and J. Blaeu, *Novus Atlas Sinensis*, Amsterdam: Blaeu, 1655.

107. Henri Bernard (ed.), *Lettres et Mémoires d'Adam Schall SJ. Relation Historique*, Tientsin: Hautes Études, 1942, esp. part 2, ch. 12. By application of sophisticated hydraulic techniques, Schall also succeeded in mounting three fifty-four ton bells on a tower over 100 feet high. The bells had lain unused since their casting more than 300 years earlier, because the Chinese could not raise them. *A New History of China*, pp. 127–8.

Much of this new knowledge reached Japan. For example, Ortelius's world atlas and a printing press were brought back to Japan by the first Japanese embassy to Europe in 1590. More important, however, was the transmission of knowledge and technique through the Jesuit relationships that linked China and Japan through Macau. By this route Ricci's map, together with his calender, the study of astronomy, geography and the use of the astrolabe were all conveyed to the Kyoto 'academy' for princes as late as 1605.[108] These links were broken by the expulsion of the Jesuits and by a ban on the import of Christian literature and Jesuit scientific works from China imposed in 1630. Thus at a critical moment Japan excluded itself from the whole of the Martini-Schall phase of western intellectual transfer to Asia. That the Chinese failed to take the fullest possible advantage of what they learned at this time is certainly not to say that the Japanese would have done the same.

By the early eighteenth century, however, the Japanese leaders had learned to distinguish subversive from nationally advantageous reading. Not only did they renew efforts to learn about the world through China; they also began to encourage the learning of Dutch, banning only Christian literature. In 1719 Shogun Tokugawa Yoshimune lifted the ban on European books in general, and by 1788 the preparation of the first Japanese philological study of a European language had been allowed.[109] While banning the foreign study of Japanese, proficiency in Dutch was reported to be high by the late eighteenth century and was accompanied by a growing interest in western knowledge. At no time could the Dutch relationship have been more useful. In 1700, income per head in the United Provinces was 50% higher than anywhere else in Europe and the Dutch were pre-eminent in almost every field of endeavour, both intellectual and practical.[110] As Cipolla remarked, 'What a pope said of the

108. See references to Japan in Henri Bernard, *Matteo Ricci's Scientific Contribution to China*, Peking: Henri Vetch, 1935, pp. 70–1. The academy was established by Fr Spinola with the approval of Hideyori, son of Toyotomi Hideyoshi. It had a distinguished noble membership and is likened by Murdoch to an Asian equivalent of the Royal Society for Scientific Research. Murdoch, *A History of Japan*, vol. 2, pp. 625–6.

109. 'The Nagasaki interpreters and the study of Dutch in Japan' in Boxer, *Jan Compagnie*, pp. 57–65.

110. Estimate of income quoted in Angus Maddison, *Phases of Capitalist Development*, Oxford University Press, 1986, p. 29.

Florentines in the Middle Ages can be applied to the Dutch of the seventeenth century: they were the fifth element of the world.'[111]

To intellectual pre-eminence was added the absence of censorship, which made Amsterdam the natural publishing capital of Europe and enabled the Dutch to be the first to realise the full potential of the fact that, as Voltaire noted at the time, the thoughts of men had finally become the objects of commerce.[112] Geography, cartography, astronomy, botany, medicine, physiology and the manufacturing arts were among the subjects studied by the Japanese *rangakusha* ('Dutch scholars') in Dutch books in the eighteenth and early nineteenth centuries – books which sometimes cost their weight in gold, and which left some of their vocabulary embedded in modern Japanese.[113] This knowledge was cleverly combined with Chinese and even with century-old Jesuit sources which, being written in classical Chinese, were at first more comprehensible to the Japanese than the Dutch books. This mixture produced, among other works, Nishikawa Joken's remarkable illustrated study summarising Japanese knowledge of all the peoples and countries known to them in the late seventeenth and early eighteenth centuries.[114]

111. Cipolla, *Before the Industrial Revolution*, pp. 263–76; Paul Hazard, *The European Mind, 1680–1715*, Harmondsworth: Penguin Books, 1964, *passim*.

112. Lucien Febvre and Henri-Jean Martin, *The Coming of the Book: The Impact of Printing, 1450–1800*, London: Verso, 1984, pp. 244–7. A description of the Netherlands as 'La Librairie [bookshop] la plus riche de L'Europe', the reference to Voltaire and other materials on publishing are in *La Richesse de la Hollande*, vol. 1, p. 372 and vol. 2, pp. 304–8.

113. F. Vos, 'Iets over Nederlandse woorden in het Japans' in *350 jaar Nederland-Japan*, Rotterdam: Maritiem Museum 'Prins Hendrick Museum', 1959, pp. 40–2.

114. Nishikawa Joken was a geographer, astronomer and student of foreign learning who lived for many years in Nagasaki. His *Yonjunikoku jinbutsu zusetsu* (Illustrations of the people of forty-two countries), Edo, 1720, was completed in 1714 and published in 1720, the year after Yoshimune's lifting of the ban on European literature. Based partly on an earlier work, it starts with an analysis of the five great geographical divisions of the world, which is based on Ricci's world map. It then proceeds to drawings of people from the forty-two countries, together with text providing some account of the geography, climate, and history of those countries. Although this is the work of a great *rangakusha*, the contemporary Chinese influence is also clear, notably from the editor's foreword, which is written in *kanbun* (the Japanese version of classical Chinese) and justifies the study of foreign things with an appropriate Confucian quotation: 'The Master said: "Even when walking in the company of two other men, I am bound to be able to learn from them. The good points of the one I copy; the bad points of the other I correct in myself."' (This

In practice, only a fraction of this imported knowledge was applied and used at the time. Part of the problem was national security, for while the Tokugawa leadership were willing to acquire from the West its medical knowledge and techniques such as copper-engraving, the applied sciences and defence-related knowledge could not be acquired without allowing foreigners unacceptable access to Japan. Thus, even in astronomy and cartography new knowledge was largely curiosity and book knowledge; it was an advance, but still circumscribed by traditional Chinese learning because the westerners had no opportunity to demonstrate and transmit their scientific techniques as they had done in China.[115] Thus Dutch learning arrived in random fashion and was imperfectly understood. While curious about the practical aspects of guns, clocks and calendars, the Japanese failed in general to understand

---

translation is from D. C. Lau, *Confucius: the Analects (Lun yü)*, Hong Kong: Chinese University Press, 1983, pp. 60–1). Nishikawa's book is discussed by Boxer in *Jan Compagnie*, pp. 17ff. Boxer's view is that almost all of the figures are imaginary, although of fine artistic quality. This view, which implies a very limited Japanese knowledge of the outside world, could be incorrect. Recent scholarship emphasises the range of Japanese trade, cultural and intellectual contacts with *all* of Asia, especially through Nagasaki. I believe that more than half of the sketches of people and costumes could have a foundation, either in observation, or in firm Chinese knowledge; since sixteen of them are of East or South-East Asian peoples and four each are from the Middle East and Muscovy regions. Of the European sketches, the Dutch ones are drawn from life, and only in the English, Italian, Spanish and German ones are we clearly looking at knowledge that may have come through the Dutch, although even the Spanish and South American sketches could have been based on Japanese trading links with Manila. The influence of Ricci in the geographical part of this book is noted by Ayuzawa Shintaro and Okubo Toshiaki in *Sakoku jidai Nihonjin no kaigai chishiki* (The Japanese understanding of the outside world in the era of the Seclusion), Tokyo: Kengensha, 1953, pp. 325–6.

115. In astronomy, Nishikawa Joken attempted to transmit Copernican learning but without breaking decisively with the Chinese past. See Shigeru Nakayama, *A History of Japanese Astronomy*, Cambridge, MA: Harvard University Press, 1969, *passim*. The problems of Japanese cartography can be illustrated by contrasting the scientific Jesuit mapping of China with a map such as Shiba Kunihiko's *Kaisen Nihon yochi rotei zenzu* (revised map of all Japan and its main routes). Printed in 1775, this contained much detail and is the first example of a map with meridians and parallels. Unfortunately the author simply drew the latter without understanding them, and all the information in the map was derived from other sources rather than from direct surveys. A copy of this map was sold at Sotheby's on December 7, 1989, and the catalogue contains a lengthy analysis and description: *Atlases, Travel, Natural History and Topographical Prints*, London: Sotheby's, 1989, p. 171.

the significance of either the basic sciences or even the concepts of linear progress and discovery that underlay them.[116] Nonetheless, access to Dutch knowledge, however opaque it might be, did mean that Japan kept some contact with the explosion of the European mind from the seventeenth century onwards and maintained a channel of intellectual communication that could be developed when circumstances required and allowed it to do so.

Trade and development before 1853: a summary of long-term trends and results

Japanese trading links in Asia extend back at least to the ninth century. Through these contacts came a variety of new goods and technologies, including textiles, metalware, books and medicines, many of which the Japanese copied or, more typically, adapted to their own taste and technologies. In the fifteenth and early sixteenth centuries, however, the direct link with China was ruptured by the Ming government's policy of Seclusion, a policy occasioned by the experience of Japanese piracy in the China seas.

The trading scene was significantly affected by the arrival of the Portuguese in the mid-sixteenth century and of the Dutch and other Europeans somewhat later. Most Europeans travelled to China from the west, but important links with Japan were also established from the east through the Philippines and Spanish America. The expansion of trade with Japan in these years was part of a general expansion of western trade with Asia.[117] The main contribution of the Portuguese was their success in recreating a Sino-Japanese trade flow, with themselves earning profits from their intermediary role. The core of this trade was the exchange of silk for silver, and its scale and expansion is indicated by the fact that between the late sixteenth century and the 1630s silk imports to Japan increased from 100,000 to 400,000 kg. per annum. In this earlier period, the counterpart to this trade was an export of 18,000–20,000 kg. of silver. This outflow was part of a wider bullion outflow from Japan, which constituted its major contribution to the Asian regional economy in the sixteenth and

116. Goodman, *The Dutch Experience*, ch. 15.
117. For details of the seventeenth-century peak, see Dermigny, *Le Commerce à Canton*, pp. 120–1.

Fig. 1.1. THE MAIN PHASES OF JAPANESE FOREIGN TRADE, 1580s–1840s

	1580s–1620s	1620s–1660s	1660s–1720s	1720s–1840s
Trends	Rapid expansion and technology transfer from Europe	High levels maintained Boom in China trade from 1640s	Decline in trade and rise of import substitution and technology transfer from Asian neighbours	Trade falls a further 60% Import substitution continues
Mechanisms and policies	Open policies of Hideyoshi and Ieyasu Trade through local daimyo (Satsuma and Arima) before national unification Bakufu takes control of silk trade in 1604	English leave, 1623; Spanish expelled, 1624 Portuguese expelled, 1639 Seclusion enforced on Japanese in 1633 Bakufu establishes controls through Deshima and Nagasaki	Silver exports banned in 1668	Tight controls and anti-trade ideology followed by han initiatives
Partners	Portuguese/Macau trade followed by Spanish, Dutch and English arrivals East Asian local trades continue	Dutch and Nagasaki (Chinese) trades dominate	Dutch, Chinese and East Asian flows	Dutch, Chinese and East Asian flows
Commodities	Silk for bullion (silver) Weapons and textiles from Europe	Silk for silver/gold Local specialisation in the East Asian trades with imports of textiles and sugar	Copper replaces bullion as staple export	Copper and East Asian specialisation Renewed interest in western technology

seventeenth centuries.[118] Silver flows also serve as a useful measure of the rise of the Dutch as they supplanted the Portuguese in Japan. Between 1622 and the late 1630s, for example, the volume of silver shipped from Japan by the VOC was growing at between 14% and 18% per annum.[119]

The continued expansion of Japanese trade after the closure of the country in the seventeenth century was partly attributable to growth in the Nagasaki trade. This was mainly controlled, direct trade with the Chinese and others, and the silk and silver data both confirm that the Chinese trade reached a remarkable peak around 1660.[120] The key to this continuing expansion was the ability of the Japanese to supply partners with bullion rather than other tradeable commodities. As the seventeenth century progressed, however, mines became harder to work, domestic metal requirements for coinage and other purposes rose, and the bullion supply declined. In 1685 Dutch and Chinese copper exports were limited to 6,000 *kanme* (= 5,232 lb.) and 3,000 *kanme* per annum respectively.[121] By 1688 it became necessary to curtail silver exports, and these restrictions initiated a long-term decline in Japanese foreign trade, although continuing exports of copper to some extent replaced those of silver. All the indicators show trade to have been at low levels in the eighteenth century, with some revival at the *han* (fief) level in the nineteenth.[122]

The importance of international trading activities for the Japanese economy in the period 1549–1853 is illustrated in the summary of trading trends for the whole period presented in Fig. 1.1. Through the European trade, the Japanese gained insights into new technologies as well as western textiles and other goods, especially in the sixteenth century. As we have seen, new techniques were immediately studied and copied, and although by the mid-nineteenth century, the Japanese had fallen far behind the best western techniques, the traditional metallurgical crafts were eventually to prove a surprisingly efficient basis for the rapid development of modern metallurgy and engineering in the late nineteenth century.

118. *EHOJ*, vol. 1, pp. 132–43.

119. *EHOJ*, p. 140, and Israel, *Dutch Primacy*, p. 173.

120. *EHOJ*, vol. 1, pp. 145–6; Dermigny, *Le Commerce à Canton*, p. 156.

121. Jansen, *China in the Tokugawa World*, p. 29.

122. Dermigny's data on the numbers of Chinese junks at Nagasaki suggests a 75% decline from mid-seventeenth century peaks to less than fifty vessels each year by 1719–26.

In terms of commodities, Asian trade enabled the Japanese to engage in a regional division of labour and through this to obtain goods that their traditional economy could not supply. These included spices, tea, medicines, sugar and, above all, cotton and silk textiles. The import of commodities and the physical presence in Japan of the Chinese merchant community were also important for their dynamic effects on Japanese learning. In terms of scale, the expanding outflow of the bullion-for-silk trade in the late sixteenth and early seventeenth centuries was so large that it is estimated to have raised the volume of exports to more than 10% of national output.[123] The immediate impact of these silk imports was to improve the welfare of only the richest tenth of the population. However, the long-term domestic importance of the silk trade was considerable. One reason for this was that from an early stage the Japanese took their imports of Chinese raw and semi-finished silks and, by dyeing and elaborating them with precious metals, made fabrics of legendary beauty. This industry, with its centre in Kyoto, survived several technological revolutions and still flourishes today.[124] Secondly, the development of the import trade and of domestic textile industries serving the rich laid the technical and commercial foundations on which it was possible to build a large-scale textile industry by the later Tokugawa period. This used both cotton and silk and served the needs of a much greater part of the population. Finally, as imports of foreign raw silk declined, domestic sericulture developed, replacing imports with Japanese raw silk production.

As bullion-based trade contracted in the late seventeenth and eighteenth centuries, this pattern of learning and import substitution was to be found not only in textiles, but also in other commodities, including tea, sugar and porcelain.[125] Under official influence, especially that of the Shogun Tokugawa Yoshimune, the necessary skills were acquired from China, Korea and elsewhere; localities suitable for the production of the appropriate raw material were identified,

123. This estimate is made by comparing the value of silver exports with the value of agricultural production, *EHOJ*, vol. 1, p. 234.

124. The role of the *Nishijin* industry and its later transformation is illuminatingly discussed (with many valuable references) by Nakaoka Tetsuro *et al.* in 'The textile history of Nishijin (Kyoto): East meets West', *Textile History*, 19 (2), 1988, pp. 117–41.

125. Fully discussed in Hamashita and Kawakatsu, *The Asian trade sphere*, pp. 157–93.

and substantial self-sufficiency was eventually achieved.[126] Further, of the four industries noted above, tea, sugar and porcelain were to be important export industries after the opening of Japan in the nineteenth century, while textiles in varying forms and states of technical modernisation were to be the mainstay of Japanese export expansion till the 1930s.

With its decline in the eighteenth century, foreign trade lost much of its direct impact on Japan, and this was accompanied by a growing suspicion that trade 'devoured the bones of the Japanese people'. Thus while Seclusion had originally been a matter of prudential statecraft, it began to gain a new ideological basis. Yet at the same time, out of the torrent of contemporary intellectual and practical innovation in the West, a trickling stream was reaching Japan both through direct contact and through the *rangakusha* learning. The clash between anti-trade sentiments on the one hand and the technology-driven need for western economic relations on the other was explosive. It was to make the opening of Japan a mortally dangerous process and it established resonances that echo in Japanese attitudes to foreigners and their trade in the late twentieth century.[127]

126. In 1720 Yoshimune ordered the acquisition of a Chinese botanical work of 1,000 volumes; two years later he invited a Chinese botanist to analyse Japanese plants and advise on agricultural development. Jansen, *China in the Tokugawa World*, pp. 36–7. Details on the early history of Japanese sugar production are provided by Takahashi Kamekichi, *Tokugawa hoken keizai no kenkyu* (Research into the Tokugawa feudal economy), Tokyo: Toyo Shokan, 1941, part 6, 'The development of sugar cane cultivation and sugar manufacture in the Tokugawa era'.

127. A newspaper survey in 1988 reported that 38% of Japanese had not only never met a foreigner but *had no wish ever to do so*.

2

THE WEST AND JAPAN BEFORE
THE OPENING OF THE PORTS

Put forth your force, my iron horse, with limbs that never tire!
The best of oil shall feed your joints, and the best of coal your fire;
Like a train of ghosts, the telegraph posts go wildly trooping by,
While one by one the milestones run, and off behind us fly!
— Prof. Rankine

'Well, a customer is a customer, whether he is a samurai or a townsman.' — Chikamatsu, *The Love Suicides at Amijima*[1]

The opening of the Japanese ports in the 1850s led to the collapse of Seclusion with far-reaching political, economic and cultural consequences. Perry's successful negotiation of a treaty on behalf of the United States in 1854 was followed by a series of treaties negotiated by the West European powers and by Russia. These established a framework for Japan's international economic relations that lasted till the treaty revision of 1899. The opening of Japan — *kaikoku* — also played an important role in the events that led to the Restoration of imperial rule in 1867, when Japan began its transition to a modern form of statehood, modelled in its early stages on European and American examples.

Japanese economic development between the opening of the ports and the 1890s was formed by a subtle interplay between an internal system that had been changing over a long period and an external environment that was itself undergoing revolution. Thus to understand the economic impact that renewed contact with the outside world had on Japan, we need to know something of the basic structures of both the international and Tokugawa economies before they collided with each other in the mid-nineteenth century.

---

1. Rankine quoted in Alfred Russell Wallace, *The Wonderful Century: The Age of New Ideas in Science and Invention*, London: Swan Sonnenschein, 1908, p. 3. Chikamatsu quoted in Masao Maruyama, *Studies in the Intellectual History of Tokugawa Japan*, University of Tokyo Press, 1974, p. 124.

The world environment

There were four striking features of the world economy in this period: accelerating growth and transformation in the West European and American economies, a revolution in industrial and transportation technology, shifting patterns of world economic leadership and an increase in economic integration as a result of the expansion of trade and of major flows of capital and labour.[2]

The pace of growth and transformation is most dramatically illustrated by the performance of individual industries, among which cotton textiles and metallurgy were pre-eminent. In the case of textiles, between the periods 1710–75 and 1775–1815 the rate of growth of British output quadrupled from 2% to 8% per year. A similar acceleration in the output of pig-iron first raised the annual growth-rate from 2% to 6% between 1740–80 and 1785–1840, and then between 1870 and 1914 the world annual growth-rate in steel output rose to 14% per year. At the same time the British income per head grew by .17% annually between 1760 and 1800, by .52% between 1800 to 1830, and by 1.98% between 1830 and 1870. Thus the contrast between the accelerating sectors and the whole economy was sharp, but at the same time the rate and spread of the industrial revolution was levering the general growth-rate upwards.[3]

Industrial progress was closely related to technical innovations. These served first to increase supply and lower costs in established trades and later to create completely new industries. The acceleration in textile output would have been impossible without a group of inventions in the late eighteenth century that radically increased

2. The principal sources for this section are James Foreman-Peck, *A History of the World Economy: International Economic Relations since 1850*, Brighton: Wheatsheaf, 1983; Clive Trebilcock, *The Industrialization of the Continental Powers, 1880–1914*, London: Longman, 1981; David S. Landes, *The Unbound Prometheus: Technological Change and Industrial Development in Western Europe from 1750 to the Present*, Cambridge University Press, 1969; Carlo M. Cipolla (ed.), *The Fontana History of Europe*, vol. 3: *The Industrial Revolution*, London: Collins, 1973. An excellent survey of the controversies in this field is Joel Mokyr (ed.), *The British Industrial Revolution: An Economic Perspective*, Boulder, CO.: Westview Press, 1993.

3. Cipolla, *The Industrial Revolution*, pp. 192–202 and 238; Simon Kuznets, *Modern Economic Growth: Rate, Structure and Spread*, New Haven: Yale University Press, 1967, Table 2.5, pp. 64–5. The debate on the British growth rate is analysed in Mokyr, *The British Industrial Revolution*, chs. 1–4. National Income data are by Crafts and quoted in Mokyr, *op. cit.*, p. 9.

mechanisation and enabled the industry to satisfy rising mass demand. Similarly, the first upward turning-point in the metallurgy growth-rate (the Bessemer process) reflected the switch from wood to coke as the basic metallurgical fuel; the second spurt of growth followed the introduction of the Thomas process in 1879, which made previously unusable phosphoric ores available for high-quality steel production.[4]

Advances in metallurgy and coal-mining were closely linked to improvements in machine-tool making, the internal combustion engine and shipbuilding, and the building of railways. By mid-century, these industries were transforming the physical and economic landscapes of Western Europe and the United States. In shipbuilding, the combination of iron hulls and steam power were the first steps in a revolution that was to transform relations between the West and the Far East. The first ship to exhibit the potential of long-distance steam travel was *The Great Western*, which crossed the Atlantic in fifteen days in 1838. Six years later *The Great Britain* made an even more impressive Atlantic crossing using screw rather than paddle propulsion. And in 1854 construction began on one of the century's most colossal engineering enterprises, *The Great Eastern*. This ship was never actually in service in the eastern trades although, as its name suggests, it was built for them.[5] Thus even before the opening of the Suez Canal in 1869, Rutherford Alcock, the first British consul in Japan, observed that whereas in the era of the grandfather of the current Chinese Emperor officers of the East India Company had needed twelve months to get a reply to a letter from Canton, their successors complained if the gun at Hong Kong did not announce the arrival of mailships within forty-two days of their leaving Marseille.[6]

In the second half of the century, progress shifted from the dirty to the cleaner technologies, especially electricity, chemicals, tele-communications and wireless. Electricity created new possibilities for

---

4. The Bessemer process converted purified liquid iron by blowing air through it. It was first demonstrated in 1856 and it led to a reduction in the cost of steel by four-fifths. The Thomas process allowed the use of phosphoric ores by lining the Bessemer converter with dolomite; lime added to the ores then formed a slag that could be separated and used for fertiliser. J. H. Chesters, *Iron and Steel*, London: Nelson, 1951, ch. 6.

5. Foreman-Peck, *A History*, pp. 35–6; W. H. G. Armytage, *A Social History of Engineering*, London: Faber and Faber, 1961, pp. 134–6; entry on 'Ships', *EB*, 11th edn.

6. Sir Rutherford Alcock, *The Capital of the Tycoon: A Narrative of Three Years' Residence in Japan* (2 vols), London: Longmans, Green, 1863, vol. 1, p. 42.

mechanisation that were to be crucial to Japanese industrialisation, and telecommunications contracted the world economy even more remarkably than steamships and the railway had done. The first transatlantic cable was finally laid in 1866 by *The Great Eastern*, and in 1870 the telegraph reached Bombay.

The timing, pace and institutions of economic progress differed widely. In the late eighteenth and early nineteenth centuries, the lead was taken by Britain. In the 1830s the United States experienced a boom based on the opening of the west and the railway, and the economy accelerated again after the Civil War (1861–65) by combining its abundant natural resources with population inflows from Europe.[7] Meanwhile the continental economies emulated British progress and by the 1870s were closing both the technological and income gaps. Thereafter, in the decades before 1914, intense rivalry between the British and German economies, with Germany developing cartels and highly concentrated forms of industrial organisation in preference to competitive institutions, basing its economic power in the newer industries, especially chemicals and electrical engineering, where investment in science and human skills was crucial.[8]

The other economy where there was significant change between 1890 and 1914 was Russia. Here, despite the handicaps of severe social and political backwardness, Witte, the Finance Minister, achieved major industrial advances by using the gold standard to attract foreign capital and state capitalism as a substitute for the lack of a vigorous private sector.

The precise sequence and pattern of each of these strands in the history of the industrialising economies was to be important to Japan, either because they led to direct economic or technological involvement with the Japanese or because they furnished ideas for the Meiji policymakers, men who were constantly groping for policies and institutions that promised to help them achieve their overriding economic goals.

The eastward thrust of British and American trade policies. At mid-century, it is estimated that Britain accounted for only 2% of the world's

7. Douglass C. North and Robert Paul Thomas (eds), *The Growth of the American Economy to 1860*, New York: Harper and Row, 1968, pp. 1–13, part 7; Frank Thistlethwaite, *The Great Experiment. An Introduction to the History of the American People*, Cambridge University Press, 1955, ch. 5.

8. See esp. Armytage's chapter 'The German Exemplar' (ch. 17) in *A Social History*; Trebilcock, *The Industrialization*, p. 64.

population, but 70% of world trade.[9] Asia played an important and growing part in this extraordinary domination, first through the growth of trade with India, and subsequently by the British acquisition of interests in Singapore, South-East Asia and China. Britain, India and China constituted a 'triangular' trading pattern in which the main flows were British textile exports to India, Indian opium exports to China and Chinese tea exports to Britain. The political foundations of these trades were very different. Whereas India had been fully annexed by force, trade with China was at first without a firm political framework. This changed after the Opium and Arrow wars (1839–42 and 1856–58), when trade came to be based on Treaty arrangements that gave Britain a permanent base in Hong Kong and extraterritorial rights in the Chinese treaty ports. The Treaty of Nanking (1842) gave rights in five ports, including Canton and Shanghai, and later treaties extended this number.[10]

However, during the 1840s and 1850s, at the very moment when attention was turning towards Japan, British economic policy in the Far East was becoming more cautious. One reason for this discretion was the scale of the direct costs of ruling India, especially after the Mutiny of 1857. Further, an alternative, more limited approach had developed for China, in which short-term force was used to extract long-term concessions and strategic commercial footholds. This, in fact, had not been a strikingly successful alternative to full imperial control. A key actor in British thinking at this juncture was Rutherford Alcock, whose career illustrates the interconnectedness of British diplomatic experience and policy in the Far East. As a young man, Alcock had served in Amoy, Shanghai, Foochow and Kwangtung, and seen at first hand the circumstances and effects of the Opium and Arrow wars. Reflecting particularly on the Opium War and the catastrophic Taiping rebellion that followed it, he became convinced that armed

---

9. Foreman-Peck, *A History*, p. 3.

10. General sources for this section include G. C. Allen and Audrey Donnithorne, *Western Enterprise in Far Eastern Economic Development. China and Japan*, London: Geo. Allen and Unwin, 1954; H. B. Morse and H. F. MacNair, *Far Eastern International Relations*, Shanghai: Commercial Press, 1928; H. F. MacNair, *Modern Chinese History Selected Readings*, Shanghai: Commercial Press, 1923; Grace Fox, *Britain and Japan, 1858–1883*, Oxford University Press, 1969; Ishii Kanji and Sekiguchi Hisashi (eds), *Seikai shijo to Bakumatsu kaiko* (The world market and the opening of the ports at the end of the Tokugawa period), Tokyo: Tokyo Daigaku Shuppankai, 1982.

intervention easily led to serious internal dislocation with the result that its costs outweighed any likely benefits.

Alcock took this lesson with him to Japan where he served as Britain's first official representative from 1859 to 1866, after which he returned to China as ambassador. In the 1840s the practical experience of men like Alcock was reinforced by strong tides of liberalism and free trade at home. Thus in place of annexation or the limited use of force, Alcock favoured opening foreign trade by the skilful use of prestige combined with an implied threat of direct intervention. It was for this reason that Japan became more important in British policy than its short-term trading promise justified. In a wonderfully informative account of his first three years in Japan, Alcock summed up the economics of his policy with characteristic frankness:

Putting trade with Japan aside . . . our prestige in the East is a power which supplies without cost the place of fleets and armies. We cannot *afford* [Alcock's emphasis], therefore, by any ill considered backward steps, to damage or jeopardize this, seeing it is the great economiser of our national resources. . . . In this Chain [of influence] not a link can be broken or damaged, even in such an outlying and distant region of the East as Japan, without some danger and prejudice to the whole.[11]

Although these policies were to change dramatically towards the end of the century when Britain joined the race to partition the under-developed areas, they were sufficient at mid-century to ensure that the United States rather than Britain would arrive to open Japan in 1853.

The United States had a considerable history of concern with the Far East, and like Britain, its early concern with Japan was at first a by-product of relations with China. Before independence, the American colonists had imported tea from China and their exclusion from the West Indian trade that followed it added strong pressure for the development of direct trade with China. The first American ship arrived in China in 1784 and in the latter part of the eighteenth century a variety of American contacts with China developed, including a fur trade in which sealskins obtained by New Englanders in the Falklands were taken for trade in Canton. By the early nineteenth century the Americans were active participants

---

11. Alcock, *The Capital of the Tycoon*, vol. 2, p. 218.

in the 'Canton trade', the system whereby the Chinese allowed foreigners limited trading opportunities without breaching either their own policy of seclusion or their concept of Chinese universal sovereignty. Sino-American contacts were at first based in Salem and Boston, using clippers that rounded Cape Horn. Later, however, important contacts with the west coast developed. The settlement of California in the 1840s and the development of trans-American railroads and trans-Pacific steamships united to give America a great potential advantage in trade with China.[12]

In its first phase Sino-American trade consisted mainly of exports of ginseng, opium, woollens, cottons, metals and spices to China, and imports from China of tea, silk, cassia, rhubarb, camphor and 'nankeen' textiles. By mid-century, however, it was the potential of textile exports that provided a new and urgent note of aggressiveness in the Anglo-American rivalry in China. Between 1820 and 1840 cotton spindles installed in American factories increased tenfold. This tremendous growth of textile output and productivity meant that supply was outstripping the needs of domestic markets and, with Lancashire entrenched in India, China, with its 400 million potential customers became a vital target for American exporters. In 1845 some 80% of China's imports were woollen or cotton goods in various forms, and in that year the Chinese market accounted for 35% of American textile exports, a figure estimated to have risen to 50% by the eve of the Civil War.[13] Effective development of the China market required that the advantage of proximity via the west coast ports be fully exploited. The Americans were confident that they had the combination of commercial strengths and shipping skills to succeed in China and this commercial interest was reinforced by the American strategic concern at Britain's rapid expansion in the area, undertaken by the 'annexing' of a chain of fortified ports in Asia.[14]

12. K. S. Latourette, 'The History of Early Relations between The United States and China, 1784–1844', Transactions of the Connecticut Academy of Arts and Sciences, vol. 22, 1917, and Ljungstedt, *An Historical Sketch*, p. 225.

13. An estimate of the structure of China's imports is in S. Wells Williams, *The Middle Kingdom* (2 vols), 3rd edn, New York: Wiley and Halstead, 1857, vol. 2, p. 412; Landes, *The Unbound Prometheus*, p. 215. This shows that while world cotton spindleage doubled between 1834 and 1852, American spindleage tripled. American cotton export data are quoted in Ishii and Sekiguchi, *The world market*, p. 99.

14. The importance of the combination of industrial confidence and seamanship is

In the 1840s, however, both commercial and strategic objectives in the Far East had to take account of the precise state of marine technology. Although the development of iron, steam-powered ships had made trans-Pacific voyages a reality, mastery of the China routes was not possible till the more fuel-efficient expansion and triple-expansion engines had been developed in the 1860s and 1870s.[15] In the interval between these peaks of marine innovation Japan, which had for some time been an important potential port of call for distressed whalers, assumed critical significance as a re-fuelling point on the San Francisco–Shanghai run. In the United States, therefore, the demand to open up Japan was a policy that combined trade and naval strategy, aroused the enthusiasm of industrialists, merchants and shippers and united both East and West Coast interests. It is against this background of economic, technical and political change that we must consider the nature of the Japanese economy with which the westerners came in contact after 1853.

The Tokugawa economy, 1600–1868

Quantitative trends. The absence of reliable material makes impossible the construction of a comprehensive statistical assessment of the Japanese economy before 1853 and, in most respects, before the 1890s. We know, however, that in the period between the late 1880s and the present, Japanese output and trade grew at approximately double the rate of what are now classified as the advanced (i.e. OECD) economies. When taking into account Japan's poor endowment in natural resources, one is forced to conclude that behind this exceptional performance must lie significant development in the pre-modern, pre-statistical age — a vast accumulation of social, commercial and technical skills that found new outlets when conditions were ripe for the economy to be modernised and internationalised. We must therefore make some effort to identify the characteristics of this earlier progress.

discussed by Kinley J. Brauer, '1821–1860: Economics and the diplomacy of American expansion' in William H. Becker and Samuel F. Wells Jr., *Economics and World Power. An Assessment of American Diplomacy since 1789*, New York: Columbia University Press, 1984, pp. 55–118.

15. 'Evolution of the engine' (ch. 9) in W. J. Bassett-Lowke and George Holland, *Ships and Men*, London: George G. Harrap, 1946.

Table 2.1. INDICATORS OF DEVELOPMENT, 1600–1872

	Population (millions)	Cultivated land (millions of cho)	Agricultural output (millions of koku)
1600	12	2.065	19.731
1720	31.28	2.927	32.034
1872	33.11	3.234	46.812

	Population growth % p.a.	Cultivated land growth % p.a.	Output growth % p.a.	Output per head growth % p.a.	Yield per unit of land % p.a.
1600–1720	.8	.29	.4	-.51	.11
1720–1872	.04	.07	.25	.21	.18

Sources: derived from data in *EHOJ*, vol 1, p. 44. Although similar to previous estimates, this work by Miyamoto and Hayami incorporates many new refinements.

Notes:

1. The table is designed to show the long-term contrast between the early and late Tokugawa trends. The data in Fig. 2.1 are a more detailed time series.

2. The data of *per capita* income in Fig. 2.1 are very rough estimates which use the series for per capita agricultural output, adjusted to take account of an estimated fall in agricultural output as a proportion of total output from 80% to 60%, with this change being most pronounced in the sixteenth and nineteenth centuries, as indicated by fragmentary statistics and qualitative materials.

3. Population data for 1720 and subsequent years are based on official population censuses. Earlier data are more speculative.

4. It may seem surprising that *per capita* incomes in 1600 were well above the subsistence level and declined before recovering. However, there are parallels with European history, for Braudel has argued that in some parts of Europe income declined from the Black Death (after which the ratio of population to agricultural resources was favourable) right down to the early nineteenth century.

Although the problems posed by such an enquiry are formidable, Japanese scholars in recent years have provided enough insights into the quantitative changes in the Tokugawa economy through painstaking work to enable us to discern overall trends and even to illustrate these and accompanying institutional changes with meaningful partial statistics of various kinds.[16] In this section we focus on the long-run trends of population, grain output and land utilisation to demonstrate these changes. These data, in the form of absolute figures and annual growth rates, are presented in Table 2.1. and Fig. 2.1.

16. Of particular help is the comprehensive summary of Tokugawa economic scholarship in *EHOJ*, vols 1–3 and material in Miyamoto Matao, *Kinsei Nihon no shijo keizai. Osaka kome shijo no bunseki* (The market economy of early modern Japan: A study of the Osaka rice market), Tokyo: Yuhikaku, 1988. The best overall analysis of Tokugawa society in English is Chie Nakane and Shinzaburo Oishi (eds), *Tokugawa Japan: The Social and Economic Antecedents of Modern Japan*, University of Tokyo Press, 1990.

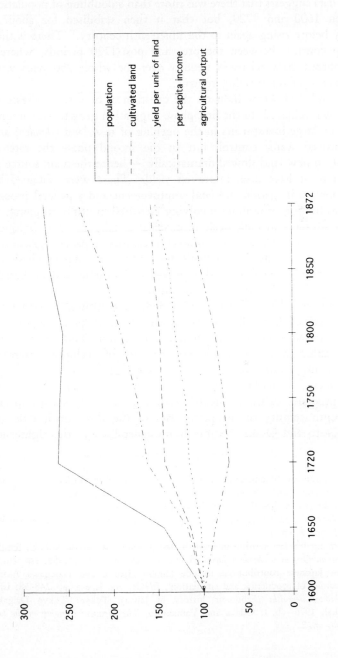

Fig. 2.1. LONG-RUN TRENDS IN TOKUGAWA ECONOMIC INDICATORS, 1600–1872

The data suggests that there was more than a doubling of population between 1600 and 1720, but that it then stabilised for about a century before rising again in the nineteenth century.[17] There is thus a sharp contrast between the pre- and post-1720 periods, whereas grain output grew relatively steadily over the whole 250 years with no evidence of diminishing returns.

The land data throw light on the question of how this increase of output was achieved. In the first phase population growth was accompanied by large investments in the opening of new land (*shinden*) and in improved water control, but in the second phase the rate of addition to new land slowed dramatically — hence the main source of growth must have been improved yields. These were obtained by investment in irrigation and land improvement and a general process of intensification of farming involving increased multiple cropping, as well as advances in biological, mechanical and hydraulic techniques. As a result, by the end of the eighteenth century, Japanese agriculture had achieved considerable sophistication, with growing emphasis on the application of fertilisers and improved seed varieties and a generally impressive display of technological vitality.[18]

During the later Tokugawa period, agricultural output and incomes gained from diversification and the widespread appearance of commercial crops such as tobacco and cotton. This growth and diversification was not simply the product of technical progress, but was also related to changes in farm organisation and to the development of markets for both output and agricultural labour. These processes varied considerably by region. They started in the seventeenth century in the peripheries of the three great cities of Edo, Kyoto and Osaka, became more generalised in the eighteenth

17. Saito Osamu, 'Population fluctuation, east and west' in Odaka Konosuke and Yamamoto Yuzo (eds), *Bakumatsu Meiji no Nihon keizai* (The Japanese economy in the late Tokugawa and Meiji periods), Tokyo: Nihon Keizai Shimbunsha, 1988, ch. 1; Hayami Akira and Sato Hiroshi, 'The historical demography of the common people', in *EHOJ*, vol. 2, ch. 6.

18. Among scholars writing in English, the pre-eminent author is T. C. Smith, *The Agrarian Origins of Modern Japan*, Stanford University Press, 1959, esp. ch. 7. Important Japanese contributions include Shinbo Hiroshi and Hasegawa Akira, 'The dynamics of production and circulation', *EHOJ*, vol. 1, esp. pp. 248–58; Ishii Kanji, *Nihon keizaishi* (Economic history of Japan), Tokyo: Tokyo Daigaku Shuppankai, 1976, ch. 1; Odaka and Yamamoto, *The Japanese economy in the late Tokugawa*, ch. 2.

century, and by the nineteenth had taken the more advanced parts of Japan to high levels of commercialisation and economic specialisation.[19]

Trends in output and population were crucial determinants of changes in living standards, which are reflected in the figures for agricultural output and income roughly estimated *per capita*. Here, we need to remember that the original concept of the *koku* was that it represented the volume of grain necessary to sustain one person for one year.[20] Thus a daimyo with 10,000 *koku* could support a population of 10,000 people. Bearing this in mind, the figures suggest three points. First, in 1600 nearly two *koku* per person were available — a level well above subsistence. Secondly, this level of consumption was never fully regained in the period we are considering. Thirdly, while there was a sharp decline in output *per capita* in the earlier period, there was steady long-term improvement in both food and income in the later one. The credibility of this pattern is reinforced by the fact that, at the low-point in the eighteenth century, consumption fell to around one *koku*. While it appears that food was, on average, available in viable quantities, in practice regional and year-to-year climatic fluctuations must have meant that living standards for many people were falling below subsistence level, and that Malthusian limits on total population were being reached. This interpretation is confirmed by such historical evidence as that from the Tenmei famine in the 1780s, when up to half of the population in parts of northern Japan died.[21]

To get a fuller picture of the income and living standards reached by the mid-nineteenth century, we need data not only on agricultural output other than grain, but on services and non-agricultural output. This is not available in detail, but we have some information on the

19. E. Sydney Crawcour, 'The Tokugawa heritage' in William W. Lockwood (ed.), *The State and Economic Enterprise in Japan*, Princeton University Press, 1965, pp. 36–42; *EHOJ*, vol. 1, pp. 218–9, pp. 229–34.

20. Miyamoto estimated normal rural consumption at .7 and urban consumption at 1.2 *koku* per year. Miyamoto, *The market economy of early modern Japan*, p. 21. The *koku* is 5.12 bushels. By using volume to weight conversion ratios and estimating the structure of grain output (i.e. rice, coarse grains etc.) we can estimate the *per capita* weight and calorie equivalents represented by these data. This produces an estimate of 315 lb. of grain per head, a figure consistent with modern estimates of minimum food requirements in contemporary Asia.

21. Odaka and Yamamoto, *The Japanese economy in the late Tokugawa*, p. 15; Takao Tsuchiya, *An Economic History of Japan, Transactions of the Asiatic Society of Japan*, 2nd series, 15, 1937, pp. 160–1.

Table 2.2. STRUCTURE OF NATIONAL OUTPUT IN THE
LATE TOKUGAWA—EARLY MEIJI PERIOD *(% shares)*

Agricultural share of output	58.2
of which: (rice)	(38.4)
Industrial share of output	33.7
of which: (textiles)	(8.3)
(food processing)	(14)
Share of other output	8.9
Total	100

Source: Estimates for 1874 by Ishii Kanji, *EHOJ*, vol. 1, p. 250.

non-agricultural income of farmers and on occupational structures. We also have fairly firm data — see Table 2.2 — on the structure of national output in 1874, which cannot have been too different from that in the late Tokugawa era. Taken together, they suggest that agricultural output had fallen to a modest proportion of total output by the late Tokugawa period and that the combined contribution of services and non-agricultural output to national income in the mid-nineteenth century was 40% to 45% of the total, a high figure reflecting the development and sophistication of the economy.[22]

Western observers who arrived in Japan after 1853 were able to compare circumstances in Japan with the situation in their own and other Asian countries and their testimony confirms that widespread, visible and distressing poverty was not normal. Alcock, for example, commented:

The evidence of plenty, or a sufficiency at least, everywhere meets the eye; cottages and farmhouses are rarely seen out of repair — in pleasant contrast to China where everything is going to decay . . . there is no sign of starvation or penury . . . if little room for the indulgence of luxury or the display of wealth.[23]

By the nineteenth century the Tokugawa economy had developed markets for distinctively Japanese household consumer goods, even for

22. Data on occupational structure is in Ishii, *Economic history* pp. 28–9. An early estimate of national income and its sources and use is E. Sydney Crawcour, 'The Tokugawa heritage', p. 21.

23. Alcock, *The Capital of the Tycoon*, vol. 1, pp. 300–1. An expert comparative impression of Japan and China that greatly favours Japan may be found in Robert Fortune, *Yedo and Peking: A Narrative of a Journey to the Capitals of Japan and China*, London: John Murray, 1863. In remoter parts of northern Japan, however, travellers such as Isabella Bird were shocked by evidence of low living standards.

the poorer strata of society, and evidence of luxurious consumption by the more privileged is abundant. For example, the daughter of a rich Tokugawa merchant could have a wedding chest filled with more than 200 items of household and personal goods. In theory the consumption in all classes was controlled by sumptuary laws, but these were not always effective although they did influence the *forms* of consumption, encouraging the market for small but exquisite objects that could be enjoyed by the rich in houses that were modest in size and appearance.[24]

Two main conclusions can be drawn from the data reviewed so far: first, that Japanese national income per head grew steadily from the early eighteenth to the mid-nineteenth century, and secondly that average incomes by the latter date were significantly above subsistence. However, it must be re-emphasised that these conclusions are compatible with severe poverty among some segments of the population and great economic insecurity arising from climatic variations.

Recent research has illuminated not merely the size of total population but also the scale of urbanisation and its interaction with non-agricultural development. The urban population is estimated to have grown rapidly in the seventeenth and early eighteenth centuries as production and service activities expanded, first on the basis of demand in the castle towns, and subsequently on that created by the transport arteries between Edo and Osaka on the one hand and the larger castle towns on the other. By the mid-eighteenth century the urban population stabilised, with some absolute decline in the very large cities and a corresponding rise in the small and medium towns where new markets and productive activities were appearing.

At its Tokugawa peak, Edo is estimated to have had a population of 1.3 million, and by 1800 15% to 20% of the Japanese population

---

24. Odaka and Yamamoto, *The Japanese economy in the late Tokugawa*, pp. 11–13. The development of purely Japanese consumption goods, their production and marketing is the subject of a vast and informative life work by Isobe Kiichi, *Dento sangyoron* (The theory of traditional production), Tokyo: Yuhikaku, 1985, esp. pp. 284ff. A note on upper class consumption is 'The gorgeous life of merchants', in Yosaburo Takekoshi, *Economic Aspects of the Civilisation of Japan* (3 vols), London: Geo. Allen and Unwin, 1930, vol. 2, p. 222. Information on bridal furnishings is from Kazuko Koizumi, *Traditional Japanese Furniture*, Tokyo: Kodansha, 1986, pp. 172–3. For the continuing concept of 'small' in Japanese industry see Lee O-Young, *The Compact Culture. The Japanese Tradition of 'Smaller is Better'*, Tokyo: Kodansha, 1991.

is thought to have lived in towns. Apart from Edo, there were other very substantial centres, notably the southern cities of Osaka, Kyoto and Sakai as well as Fukushima,[25] all of which supported vigorous economies. Moreover, recent research suggests that although the total Japanese population was relatively stable in the late Tokugawa period, there were local variations, and upward variations were associated with both agricultural improvement and the growth of non-agricultural output, notably of textiles.[26] This suggests that by the nineteenth century Japan had reached a point of development where its society could both restrain fertility by controls such as late marriage and could adapt localised population growth-rates to local economic opportunities. As we see later, it was precisely those industries which seem to have developed in this way that became the foundation of the export sector after the opening of the ports in the 1850s.

One other feature of the Tokugawa economy was the combination of centralising and decentralising influences. The *han* system tended to be decentralising; with each *han* substantially self-sufficient and strict penalties being imposed for illegal cross-border movements of goods. This undermined the efficiencies to be gained from specialisation and trade. According to an analysis of 252 *han*, while the largest twenty-three had populations averaging 381,000, the other 116 averaged only 16,000.[27]

In contrast, two political mechanisms worked to reduce fragmentation. One was the system of *sankin kotai*, which concentrated population and economic activity in Edo and encouraged mobility between it and other parts of Japan. The other was the operation of the shogunal domain, known as *tenryo* ('heavenly domain'). The *tenryo*

25. Shinbo and Hasegawa in *EHOJ*, vol. 1, esp. pp. 227–8; Gilbert Rozman, *Urban Networks in Ching China and Tokugawa Japan*, Princeton University Press, 1973, ch. 6. Takahashi Kamekichi, *Nihon kindai keizai keiseishi* (The history of the formation of the modern Japanese economy) (3 vols) (hereafter *Formation*), Toyo: Tokyo Keizai Shimposha, 1968, vol. 1, p. 47.

26. This is the thesis in Saito Osamu, *Puroto kogyoka no jidai* (The age of proto-industrialisation) Tokyo: Nihon Hyoronsha, 1984. Variations in population growth are explored in Susan B. Hanley and Kozo Yamamura, *Economic and Demographic Change in Pre-Industrial Japan, 1600–1818*, Princeton University Press, 1977. The role of internal controls in Tokugawa Japan is elaborated in Irene B. Taeuber, *The Population of Japan*, Princeton University Press, 1958. See also note 21 above.

27. Takahashi, *Formation*, vol. 1, p. 71.

was the economic basis of shogunal power and on the eve of its abolition in 1865 produced 27% of national agricultural output. If the output of fiefs closely allied by tradition to the Shogun (*shinpan*) are added, the share rises to 35%. Including the next rank of closely allied fiefs (*fudai*), it would probably rise to 50%. The *tenryo* included not only Edo but also the cities of Kyoto, Osaka and Nagasaki and in all about one third of the nation's population. The inclusion of these large urban populations, with their dense transport and commercial links and key enterprises such as gold and silver mines, meant that the economic preponderance of the *tenryo* was overwhelming.[28] Moreover, quantitative dominance was reinforced by a concentration of institutions that in their early history provided the Bakufu with economic influence far beyond the borders of the *tenryo* itself. Economies of scale and concentration and the integration of political, financial and productive power provided regional comparative advantages to *tenryo* that have ensured that the old shogunal domain retains its dominant place in the Japanese economy to this day. The heart of *tenryo* was the Tokaido — the road from Osaka to Edo — and along it there now runs a continuous belt of activity that has been estimated to produce 8% of the world's economic output.

Institutions and organisation. The two institutions crucial to an understanding of the Tokugawa economy are those relating to class and taxation.[29] The class system was a hereditary occupational structure created by Tokugawa Ieyasu to stabilise and control society. Ieyasu's

28. Takahashi, *Formation*, pp. 24–5, estimates shogunal control in 1842. The political significance of *tenryo* as the material base of shogunal power is emphasised in Maruyama Masao, 'Kaikoku', *Koza gendai rinri* (Contemporary ethics) Tokyo: Chikuma Shobo, 1959, p. 285.

29. This section relies heavily on materials in *EHOJ*, vol. 1, esp. pp. 37–42, 217–70; Ishii, *Economic history*; articles by Miyamoto Mataji and others in *Nihon keizaishi jiten* (A dictionary of Japanese economic history) (3 vols), Tokyo: Nihon Hyoronsha, 1940; Fujita Teiichiro *et al.* (eds), *Nihon shogyoshi* (A history of Japanese commerce), Tokyo, 1978; Ishii Kanji, *Kaikoku to Ishin* (The opening of the ports and restoration), Tokyo: Shogakukan, 1989; Miyamoto Mataji, *Kamigata konjyaku*, (The Kyoto-Osaka district: today and yesterday), Tokyo: Isseido, 1972. Exceptionally helpful secondary sources are W. G. Beasley, *A Modern History of Japan*, London: Weidenfeld and Nicolson, 1963, ch. 1; Marius B. Jansen (ed.), *The Cambridge History of Japan*, vol. 5: *The Nineteenth Century*, Cambridge University Press, 1989. Jansen's introduction and chapter in this work summarise recent scholarship readably and in a masterly manner; the other papers are all reliable.

system divided the population into four broad 'Confucian' categories (samurai, artisans, peasants and merchants), and then into hundreds of occupational divisions within these categories, divisions that were reflected, for example, in a method of town planning that allocated places of residence by trade.[30] While these arrangements were of course economically inefficient because of their inflexibility, they had two positive effects. First, by dividing the population into producers and non-producers, into producers of different kinds of goods and into urban and rural-based populations, the system necessitated not only methods of taxation by which the economically inactive could be supported by the economically active, but also mechanisms to enable peasants and urban producers to exchange their output. Thus the class system tended to undermine the household self-sufficiency typical of undeveloped economies, and sophisticated fiscal arrangements, markets and large flows of resources between different sectors of the economy were all natural outcomes of its development. Further, the class system also provided a basis for occupational identity and morale and hence gave incentives to households to make long-term commitments to the accumulation of skills.

The Tokugawa fiscal system was based on land and provided parallel flows of tax income from the *han* to the daimyo and from the *tenryo* to the Bakufu. Apart from relatively small contributions to public works, military activities and other miscellaneous expenditures, there was no direct transfer of resources from daimyo to Bakufu. Tax collection was based on detailed cadastral surveys and although normally standardised and paid in rice, *nengu*, as it was called, could be paid in cash or a wide variety of other products. Since a great deal of daimyo and Bakufu expenditure consisted of stipends paid in kind, a corresponding share of the economy's exchange was real rather than monetary. Nonetheless, there was always a residue of expenditure that required the use of cash. To obtain this, rice or other produce had to be regularly marketed: this mostly took place in Osaka, and because of the scale of Bakufu-related business, it created a broad corridor of economic interaction between Osaka and Edo. The daimyo and residents of the *han* also required access to Osaka, and for this purpose usually maintained warehouses (*kurayashiki*) for their products, as well

---

30. In the late Tokugawa period peasants made up 85% of the population, merchants and artisans 8% and samurai (*bushi*) 6%. Miyamoto, *The market economy of early modern Japan*, p. 21.

as officials responsible for managing their economic interests in the market-place.[31] The flows of agricultural consumption and use in the late Tokugawa period are illustrated in Fig. 2.2.

Although simple in principle, the mechanisms for converting *nengu* into cash grew in complexity as the Osaka merchant community offered increasingly sophisticated services, including margin and futures contracts, banking, transport and insurance.[32] To handle such a range of options, the merchants developed complex methodologies of calculation and accountancy, which they recorded in manuals, while families such as the Mitsui established systems of 'house' and trade regulations. These regulations provided guidance to sound and acceptable business practice and enabled the head office of a business to establish branches that would operate according to house principles, without detailed supervision.[33]

The economic power of Osaka rested not only on the city being a provider of commercial and financial services, but also on its role as a centre of production. It had the advantages of proximity to raw materials for textile and other craft production, and to the market of the imperial court at Kyoto. Thus the Kinai region (Osaka, Kyoto and Sakai) became the centre of a regional network serving Edo and other markets, largely by coastal and water transport and often in ships of substantial size.[34] It is difficult to quantify Osaka's role precisely but one set of mid-Tokugawa data identifies centres of production throughout the whole economy for eleven categories of output. This shows that while the five Kinai *han* accounted for 706 of these centres,

31. See esp. materials in Miyamoto, *The Kyoto-Osaka district.*

32. When a market in stock market futures opened in Osaka in 1987, an article appeared in the Japanese press tracing the history of futures trading back to the legitimisation of the Osaka rice futures market in 1730. *Look Japan*, July 1988, p. 9.

33. Sakudo Yotaro, 'The management practices of family businesses' in Nakane and Oishi, *Tokugawa Japan*, pp. 147–66; Miyamoto, *The Kyoto-Osaka district*, esp. pp. 145 and 160; Takahashi, *Formation*, vol. 1, ch. 9. Takahashi notes that one famous handbook of commercial calculation, originally published in 1627, had been reprinted 400 times by the early Meiji.

34. Moriya Katsuhisa, 'Urban networks and information networks', in Nakane and Oishi, *Tokugawa Japan*, pp. 97–123; Takahashi Kamekichi, *Nihon kindai keizai hattatsushi* (The development of the modern Japanese economy) (3 vols) (hereafter *Development*), Tokyo: Toyo Keizai Shimposha, 1983, vol. 1, ch. 1 and Fujita, *A history of Japanese commerce.* By the end of the Tokugawa era, larger ships could carry up to 10,000 bushels of grain.

Fig. 2.2. THE STRUCTURE OF RICE CONSUMPTION AND DISTRIBUTION
IN THE LATE TOKUGAWA/EARLY MEIJI PERIOD

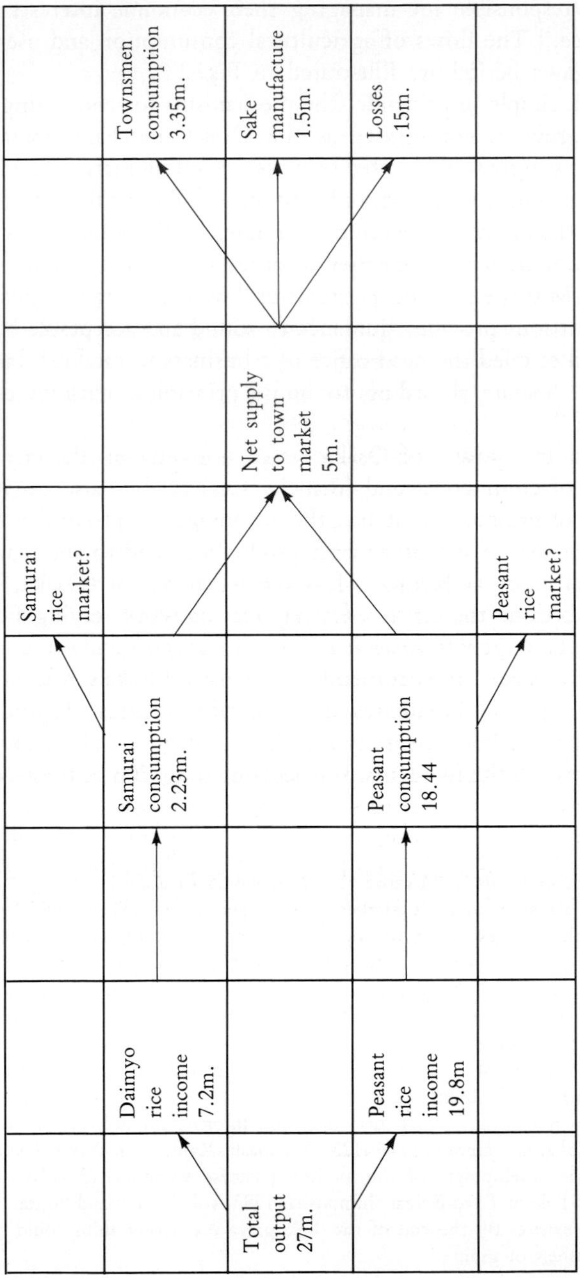

Total output 27m.

Daimyo rice income 7.2m.

Samurai consumption 2.23m.

Samurai rice market?

Peasant rice income 19.8m

Peasant consumption 18.44

Peasant rice market?

Net supply to town market 5m.

Townsmen consumption 3.35m.

Sake manufacture 1.5m.

Losses .15m.

Source: Miyamoto, *The market economy of early modern Japan*, p. 22.
Note: This estimate is for the mid-nineteenth century. It is based on a total crop of 27 million *koku* and a population of 31 million. The volume of business in peasant and samurai markets is unknown.

fifty-seven other *han* accounted for only 1,101. The dominance of Osaka in distribution is confirmed by data on the origins of textiles, sake and oil imported into Edo. From these it is clear that in the first half of the Tokugawa period, Osaka's position as a centre of *nengu* marketing and of production and distribution, made it the heart of a national market.[35]

One other institution important to Osaka and the national system was the *kabu nakama*, which is best understood in relation to the class system. A *kabu* was essentially a right to practise an occupation, which might be a social or political office (e.g. village headman) or an economic trade or function. Originally a *kabu* could be held by virtue of informal social assent, but increasingly it came to be a right granted by a political authority that might be bought and sold. The *kabu nakama* was an association of *kabu*-holders.[36]

Early in the Tokugawa period, the wholesale merchants (*toiya*) and the *kabu nakama* were regarded as undesirable restraints on trade, working against the interests of consumers and the government. However, the attitude of officials to the market changed as they increased their understanding of the mechanism through which the real value of their *nengu* revenues were ultimately determined. Moreover, as expenditures outran incomes and as the demand for commodities purchased with cash grew, both daimyo and Bakufu became indebted to the *kabu nakama* and *toiya*. There thus developed a mutuality of interest between the authorities and these groups, with traders seeking formal authority to exercise their market power more effectively, and the authorities seeking to use them to ensure the stability and predictability of their tax revenues. Both groups could also be taxed and so used to police the enforced circulation of debased currency.[37] Out of these relationships came the bias in favour of both restrictive practices and the establishment of close links between officials and merchants, both of which have persisted as important elements in the post-Tokugawa economy.

35. For these and similar data see Fujita, *A history of Japanese commerce*, pp. 26, 42, 52, 56.

36. Based on articles in *Nihon keizaishi jiten* and Takekoshi, *Economic Aspects*, vol. 2, chs. 58–61.

37. Miyamoto, *The Kyoto-Osaka district*, pp. 235ff.; Miyamoto, *Research into the circulation of commodities*, contains valuable materials on the system and its reform in the Saga domain, pp. 326–47.

As this story of evolution implies, although the Tokugawa attempted to create static and mutually supportive social and economic mechanisms, institutional equilibrium was eventually disturbed by economic progress. By the middle of the eighteenth century there had been two important changes: the growth and diversification of output, and widening markets. The consequent rise in incomes partly reflected the growing unreality of a tax-base that used traditional quotas rather than a realistic estimate of capacity to pay. This therefore provided incentives for both additional agricultural and non-agricultural output. Ironically, the system also contributed to a crisis in public finance as the Bakufu's control over production progressively slipped away.[38] The Bakufu tried to meet its fiscal problems by economies in expenditure, market control, direct taxation of merchants and associations, and currency debasement.

At the *han* level, where the seriousness of the fiscal problem was even greater (as is indicated by the rising share of income accounted for by loans), the response to difficulty was more creative. The daimyo attacked their deficits by reducing their dependence on Osaka, both as a market in which they sold *nengu* and as a place where they acquired non-agricultural goods. They did this by selling their tax revenues in local markets, which they developed by official 'nurture' (*ikusei*), and by expanding the production not only of goods needed to increase *han* self-sufficiency (*issai no bussan*), but also of those in which they had some comparative advantage and could 'export' to other regions. Such exports were doubly advantageous to the *han* since they gained both economic expansion and the fiscal benefit of the control of marketing.[39] As these strategies succeeded, the development of *han* 'export' production became an object of financial policy through currency issue and debasement and came to be known as *shokusan kogyo* ('increase in production and founding of industry'). This name

38. Oguchi Yujiro, 'Bakufu finances', in *EHOJ*, vol. 2, pp. 128–71. The *nengu* were originally based on realistic assessments of village capacity to pay, and were a heavy burden. But as assessments became outdated, *nengu* amounts tended to be fixed at customary levels, and hence the burden of the *nengu* form of tax fell. Moreover, insofar as *nengu* was used for infrastructural construction, its economic benefit could be substantial. See also, Thomas C. Smith, *Native Sources of Japanese Industrialization, 1750–1920*, Berkeley: University of California Press, 1988, ch. 2, esp. p. 69.

39. At one point only 57% of Saga revenues were supplied by *nengu*. Miyamoto, *Research into the circulation of commodities*, pp. 326–47.

and strategy were to become the core of early Meiji industrialisation policy.[40]

As these changes succeeded, they reduced *han* dependence on Osaka and created new channels of economic interaction revolving around three levels of markets: those in the three large cities, those in the castle towns, and new lower-level ones. These changes in the flow of interaction are summarised in Fig. 2.3.

One important result of the new system was to create additional stabilisation problems for the Bakufu. Under the old system the Osaka market was controlled in the Bakufu interest and economic fluctuations tended to destabilise local economies, but under the new one Osaka became the residual market in which the Bakufu had to convert its revenues. Thus attempts to solve *han* fiscal problems worsened the financial crisis at the centre, thereby generating serious domestic political frictions.[41]

The long-run economic pattern. The long-run evolution of the Tokugawa economy may be summarised as follows. Between 1600 and the early eighteenth century, there was rapid and extensive growth as population and land resources expanded and urban populations increased. From the outset Osaka acquired a key economic role as a continuing centre of traditional production and as the market in which the Bakufu exchanged its *nengu* revenues for cash.

During the eighteenth century, population growth slowed, extension of arable land ceased, output diversified, and economic interactions became more intense. Thus in addition to the Edo–Osaka axis, *han* economies and small towns flourished in new market relations, and increasingly sought specialisation in production and exchange. By the nineteenth century the *han* authorities, now pursuing political as much as purely economic goals, continued to develop independent financial, commercial and industrialisation strategies. The growing economic complexity and strength in the *tenryo* were putting it so far beyond direct control of Bakufu officials that it was becoming 'the lordless domain'.

40. Odaka and Yamamoto, *The Japanese economy in the late Tokugawa*, pp. 11–13; *EHOJ*, vol. 2, introduction, p. 37, and Nishikawa Shunsaku and Amano Masatoshi, 'Han industrial and economic policies', *EHOJ*, vol. 2, pp. 173–218.

41. Ishii, *Economic history*, ch. 1. Bakufu economic policies engendered serious friction in Satsuma, Choshu and Hizen. E. H. Norman, *Japan's Emergence as a Modern State, Political and Economic Problems of the Meiji Period*, New York: Institute of Pacific Relations, 1940, p. 67.

Fig. 2.3

(*a*) EARLY TOKUGAWA ECONOMIC STRUCTURE/FLOWS

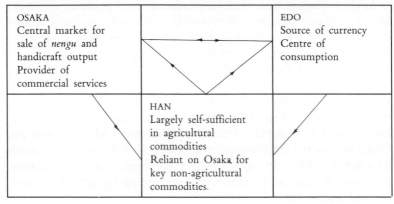

OSAKA Central market for sale of *nengu* and handicraft output Provider of commercial services		EDO Source of currency Centre of consumption
	HAN Largely self-sufficient in agricultural commodities Reliant on Osaka for key non-agricultural commodities.	

(*b*) LATE TOKUGAWA ECONOMIC STRUCTURE/FLOWS

OSAKA Central market and provider of sophisticated commercial services Centre of handicraft output Surrounded by belt of specialised producers		EDO New central market surrounded by belt of specialised production Source of currency
	HAN Growing diversification Active industrial and financial policies interacting through new local and central markets with all parts of the system	

Source: Adapted from Miyamoto Matao and Uemura Masahiro, 'The structure of fluctuations in the Tokugawa economy', *EHOJ*, vol. 1, pp. 278–85.

Thus it was the strange paradox of Tokugawa economic progress that the key political, social and fiscal institutions of early Tokugawa society appear at first to be monolithic and inimical to economic efficiency and progress. They impeded economic flexibility of all kinds, they undermined rural incentives with harsh taxation and they were appropriate to a primitive economy in which resources were allocated directly, with no role for money and a commercial system. By the nineteenth century, however, we find a complex, multi-sectored society in which decentralised choices were possible and in which savings, investment, innovation and responses to emerging 'markets' of various kinds were all to some extent rewarded. In a comparative perspective, what was absolutely critical here were the resources released by the long-term failure of the taxation policies to press as hard as might have been possible on the increasingly anachronistic tax-base. This left a growing margin of resources for incentives, consumption and economic diversification.

The reason for this 'failure' in taxation lies in the genius of the Tokugawa *political* arrangements. Internally, these worked by forbidding significant local military expenditure by the daimyos, and as the system established itself successfully they also limited the need for central military expenditure. In relation to the outside world, the costs of defending Japan through the Seclusion system did not become significant till the middle of the nineteenth century. Had the Japanese been obliged to control and defend a vast, far-flung, racially heterogeneous and frequently threatened empire as the Chinese had to do (an exercise involving hundreds of thousands of men and the logistical support for travelling and fighting over thousands of miles), the pressure for tax revenues would probably have kept the economy at a primitive level and subjected the political structure to periodic upheavals, parallelling the dynastic collapses that took place in China when financial pressures and the backlog of insoluble problems became unbearable.[42] But in the more compact, isolated and increasingly pacific Japan, this pattern was avoided. In spite of deepening class, regional, and ideological tensions and the growing burden of a samurai (warrior) class whose function in society was disappearing, the real economy progressed.

---

42. For the Chinese case, see the recent arguments of Ray Huang, *China: A Macro History*.

The evolution of ideas

Up to this point we have looked at economic change within the broad framework of the Tokugawa system. We must now turn to the interaction between these developments and trends in thinking, economic culture and understanding of the outside world.

At the turn of the sixteenth century the dominant intellectual influence on Japan was China. From the Chinese, the Japanese had acquired Buddhism and the wider heritage of the Confucian and historical classics. Thus when Toyotomi Hideyoshi, the most powerful warrior in the period 1582–98, adopted the 'sword hunt' as an instrument of pacification, he was consciously following the example of the legendary Chinese Emperor Yao. His successor, Tokugawa Ieyasu, not only maintained a Confucian academy at the important Buddhist Nanzenji temple in Kyoto, but spent many hours listening to readings of the *Four Books* of the Confucian canon and the classical Chinese histories.[43]

Buddhism provided some elements of an ideology favourable to economic progress; it called for thrift in rulers and taught its followers that work should be regarded as a serious, universal vocation, a thank-offering for the abundance of the natural world.[44] But against this view the other-worldliness inherent in Confucian philosophy and its emphasis on the irretrievable loss of a golden age pointed in another, less economically favourable direction.[45] This dichotomy and its inherent strains were reflected in the frequency with which figures in public life abandoned their careers in mid-stream and disappeared forever into monastic communities or lives of eccentric, solitary pilgrimage.

Further, from the standpoint of government, Buddhism's emphasis on the individual and his subjective state failed to provide adequate guidance to rulers. In the aftermath of a century of civil war, they needed to demarcate the public from the private domain of action and find a role in civil society for a turbulent warrior class. In

---

43. Ryusaku Tsunoda, Wm. Theodore de Bary and Donald Keene (eds), *Sources of Japanese Tradition*, New York: Columbia University Press, 1958, pp. 339–42.

44. This summary is based particulary on Robert N. Bellah, *Tokugawa Religion*, Glencoe: Free Press, 1957 and Maruyama, *Studies in the Intellectual History*.

45. Masaharu Anesaki, *History of Japanese Religion, With Special Reference to the Social and Moral Life of the Nation*, London: Kegan Paul, 1963. On Buddhist transcendentalism, see esp. pp. 7–8.

response to these problems we find that although Tokugawa Buddhism developed its own Japanese form that put new emphasis on social responsibility, it was progressively supplemented and displaced by schools of Confucianism and of Shintoism, the indigenous form of Japanese 'religion'.[46]

As we previously noted, one of the main contributions of Tokugawa Confucianism was its system of social and occupational stratification.[47] Economically this restricted labour flexibility but it did have its positive aspects. As economic issues emerged, the Japanese Confucian schools began the process of evolving ideologies that were more worldly, empirical and humanistic. Compared to Chinese Confucianism, they were also very nationalistic. Their leading thinkers, dismissing the superiority of the golden age, confronted the realities of human behaviour, emphasised the importance of historical and other forms of pragmatic investigation and began to seek solutions to the structural problems of Tokugawa society and economy.[48]

By the eighteenth century the traditional Confucian class system and its agrarian bias were increasingly anachronistic. Japanese thinkers were deeply worried by the crisis of the fiscal system and by the visible distress of the samurai class who had no economic function in society, and whose means of support were becoming progressively inadequate. It is true that some *han* leaders attempted to solve their economic problems, but the Bakufu, while often courageous, was usually conservative. Even the enlightened early eighteenth-century shogun Yoshimune, who sought to expand the area of cultivated land and introduced both sugar cane and the sweet potato into Japan, believed that the Seclusion policies should be tightened rather than relaxed.

To grapple with these issues, thinkers such as Hirata Atsutane (1776–1843) broadened the map of knowledge to include not only the seven major branches of Japanese and Chinese learning but also astronomy, geography, and the scientific methodology of the Dutch.

46. Anesaki, *History of Japanese Religion*, pp. 270–1; Tsunoda, *Sources*, part 4.

47. This system and its translation into city planning is explained in James L. McClain, *Kanazawa: A Seventeenth Century Japanese Castle Town*, New Haven: Yale University Press, 1982. Within a small clan, the single class of samurai might have more than 100 distinctions.

48. A key figure was Motoori Norinaga who wrote: 'There are many instances when later ages have been superior to antiquity.' Maruyama, *Studies in the Intellectual History*, p. 164.

The last of these was particularly important, and on this subject Hirata remarked:

The Dutch have the excellent national characteristic of investigating matters with great patience until they can get to the very bottom. For the sake of such research they have devised surveying instruments as well as telescopes and helioscopes with which to examine the sun, moon, and stars. It may take five or ten years or even a whole lifetime for such research to be completed; when problems cannot be solved in one lifetime, scholars write down their own findings and leave the solution for their children, grandchildren, and disciples to discover, though it may require generations.[49]

In Hirata's thought, all sources of knowledge were welcome, but they had to be understood within the unique framework of Japanese religion. Thus although Hirata praised *rangakusha* such as Nishikawa Joken for introducing the study of the outside world into Japan, the intellectual breakout was incomplete, since Hirata not only regarded Dutch as 'the language of monkeys', but also put western learning back into a theological framework of the kind from which it had been escaping in Europe since the Renaissance.[50]

Outstanding among those who addressed the problems of understanding the outside world and economics directly was Ogyu Sorai (1666–1728). He realised that although acquiring foreign languages was vital, it was not enough, since there was always the danger that without the dimensions of practical or direct knowledge, linguistic skill alone could allow the Japanese to maintain their illusions about the outside world.[51] In economics, Ogyu argued that

49. Tsunoda, *Sources*, p. 546.

50. Of Nishikawa, Hirata said: 'Before him people knew nothing whatsoever about astronomy, geography, or the ways of foreign countries.' Tsunoda, *Sources*, p. 542; Donald Keene, *The Japanese Discovery of Europe, 1720–1830*, Stanford University Press, 1969, p. 161.

51. The Japanese had traditionally used Chinese, first by constructing *wakun* texts (i.e. texts in which the Chinese characters had been supplemented with Japanese *kana* (syllabary) that made the texts intelligible, in spite of the fundamental differences in grammar); and then by pronouncing the amended text in Japanese (a practice known as *yomikudashi*). After all this, Ogyu argued, the original had been so transformed as to make the grasping of the reality behind language impossible. He therefore instructed his pupils to learn the original Chinese phonology first and then translate into 'the language of the peasants'. He called this revolutionary process *kiyo no gaku* (the learning of the Nagasaki translators). Naoki Sakai, *Voices of the Past. The Status of Language in Eighteenth-Century Japanese Discourse*, Ithaca, NY: Cornell University Press, 1992, ch. 7.

'the fundamental policy in governing the state and the world should first of all be to increase wealth', and he pointed out that the problem of the samurai in society was like that of having a guest at an inn who did not realise that 'even a single chopstick had to be paid for'.[52] A slightly later thinker, Kaiho Seiryo (1755–1817), advanced the proposition that 'all things in heaven and earth are commodities', and he pointed to the hypocrisy of Japanese critics of the commercialism and worldliness of the Dutch. 'People burst out laughing', he wrote, 'when told that the King of Holland engages in trade. But they themselves buy and sell things.'[53]

Although by the early part of the nineteenth century the Chinese influence was still enormously powerful,[54] in Japan a gradual expansion of intellectual horizons was beginning, which introduced new ideas and gave it some awareness of facts and systems of thinking in the 'outside world'. These ideas were debated more fiercely as domestic problems intensified and as the country experienced serious pressures from the outside world, parts of which had now opened up a very significant lead over Japan in their economic and technological development. This trend was summed up by the emergence of Honda Toshiaki (1744–1821), who had absorbed something of the world as a ship's captain and mastered much of the Dutch learning. He thought problems through in statistical terms, and then went on to propose ways in which Japan could come to terms with the outside world. Honda asked the question, by no means modest, that was to be repeated later by others: 'How may Japan become the greatest nation in the world?' He answered this query with a view of the future that was extraordinarily prescient: Japan would break out of economic difficulties by acquiring its own colonies and developing gunpowder,

---

52. Maruyama, *Studies in the Intellectual History*, p. 131.
53. *Ibid.*, pp. 295–7.
54. Rising literacy in Japan made Chinese writings increasingly accessible. A good example of the persistence of the moral and literary influences of Chinese into the early twentieth century can be found in the early life of the great Meiji businessman, Shibusawa Eiichi, whose career is touched upon in later chapters. This intellectual influence was also associated with aesthetic concerns, as in the careers of the great businessmen art collectors such as Takashi Masuda (Mitsui Bussan), Okura Kihachiro (Okura Zaibatsu), Yasuda Zenjiro (Yasuda Ginko) and Fujita Densaburo (Fujita Gumi). See Christine M. E. Guth, *Art, Tea, and Industry: Masuda Takashi and the Mitsui Circle*, Princeton University Press, 1993.

metal and shipping industries. Above all, Honda argued that fundamental thinking was needed to define a new role for foreign trade in
Japan. Aware of population pressure, he saw that Japan would eventually have to import food paid for by exports. To achieve this he
argued for an early opening of trade with Russia and for the creation
of 'institutions which will produce a large amount of expertly made
novel objects and specialty goods'. Although isolated in his day, Honda
anticipated the problems that would beset Japan more than a century
ahead. At the same time, he was providing the building-blocks for
those who had to handle the domestic and foreign crisis precipitated
by the arrival of Perry in Japan in 1853.[55]

The state of the Japanese economy on the eve of the ports being opened
was complex and paradoxical. On the positive side, long-run growth
and gently rising output per head had been achieved. In agriculture,
this was the result of sustained improvement in techniques, evolving
farm organisation and investment in land, irrigation and infrastructure. Output and the market for non-agricultural goods had also
expanded. The Seclusion had provided an environment in which
distinctively Japanese tastes and skills could flourish, and markets
developed accordingly both for ordinary necessities and for the
luxury goods consumed by the Bakufu, court and daimyo, as well as
the merchant class. Both output and services were supported and
delivered by a sophisticated tertiary sector. What the economy lacked
technically were advances based on the exploitation of physical
science and a source of fuel that would release production and transport
from the limitation of dependence on wood. By the mid-nineteenth
century these deficiencies would be remedied by coal-mining and the
transfer to Japan of newly-created western technologies. But for this
to happen, fundamental changes were needed: although the Japanese
had some striking organisational, intellectual and technical achievements, the impact of these on its capacity to participate in the new
world of nineteenth-century economic organisation and technology
depended ultimately on institutional and ideological factors, many of
which remained unfavourable.

As we have seen, *Bakuhan* — Bakufu rule of *hans* — and status systems, and the policy of Seclusion, had unsatisfactory economic effects:

55. Honda is the main subject of Keene, *The Japanese Discovery of Europe.*

they impeded the integration of the national economy, which was a pre-requisite for economies of scale and specialisation, and they inhibited economic flexibility and the transfer to Japan of western knowledge. Furthermore, they wrapped society in an ideological orthodoxy so powerful that it prevented individuals and groups from acting with true creativity or independence, and for all but a small number of eccentrics on the margins of normal life, they made alternative ways of thinking unimaginable.[56] Thus for all its achievements, traditional Japan failed to maximise the economy's indigenous potential or to benefit from increasing opportunities created by progress in the West. Only the physical intrusion of foreigners could shift these obstacles and allow the prodigious accumulated skills of the Japanese to unfold in the new world of industrial revolution and international trade.

56. This is a theme of the extraordinarily penetrating study by H. D. Harootunian, *Toward Restoration: The Growth of Political Consciousness in Tokugawa Japan*, Berkeley: University of California Press, 1970.

3

KAIKOKU: THE OPENING
OF JAPAN, 1853–1867

'The exchange of goods is a universal practice. This we we should explain to the spirits of our ancestors.' — Ii Naosuke (1853)[1]

Will it make us rich if we sell ourselves
at a good price,
Heaping up dollars like mountains of dirt?
How cruel it is to convert into dollars
the labours of the people of the gods!
— Hanzo's poem (1861) in Shimazaki Toson, *Before the Dawn*

Contacts, treaties and treaty ports

The Russians, British and Americans each made sporadic attempts to penetrate the Japanese Seclusion in the late eighteenth and early nineteenth centuries. Interest quickened perceptibly after the British imposed the treaty of Nanking on China in 1842, and in 1844 the Dutch warned the shogun that western industrialisation was radically changing the world and, with it, the international acceptability of Japanese anti-foreign policies. Japanese attitudes, however, remained uncompromising. As late as 1825 orders had been given to fire on foreign vessels without warning and to arrest and kill foreigners intruding into Japanese waters. These policies were maintained until external influences forced them to change.[2]

---

1. Ii Naosuke was a *fudai* daimyo, a shogunal counsellor and a famous master of the tea ceremony. He struggled desperately with the problems of Japan's transition from the Tokugawa to the modern world and was assassinated for his views in 1860 at Sakuradamon — today a stop on the Tokyo subway. For Shimazaki Toson, see note 43. Ii Naosuke's statement is in his advice to the Bakufu of October 1853, a translation of which is in W. G. Beasley, *Select Documents on Japanese Foreign Policy, 1853–1868*, Oxford University Press, 1955, pp. 117–19.

2. This was the policy of 'don't think twice [about firing on foreign ships]' (*ninen naku uchiharau*). Jansen, *The Nineteenth Century*, ch. 1, pp. 102–3. The edict was subsequently translated and reprinted in the British Diplomatic papers: Foreign Office,

The American expedition to open Japan was undertaken at the suggestion of its leader, Commodore Perry. The key document carried by Perry to Japan was a letter to the Emperor from President Fillmore, in which the President requested Japan to open relations, cooperate in the development of trade, assist distressed whalers and provide bunkering and supplies for ships on the California to China run. However, an unpublicised part of the expedition's task is revealed in Perry's letter to the United States Secretary of the Navy in 1852, where he noted British naval dominance in the Far East and South East Asia and argued that this enabled Britain to 'have the power of shutting up at will and controlling the enormous trade of those seas'.[3]

Perry and the Americans approached Japan surprisingly well briefed on Asian affairs. Having studied the errors of other westerners, Perry was convinced that the ingredients for success in handling the Japanese were firmness, openness and consistency of word and action. This was a method which the subsequent official record of the expedition described as having 'triumphed over a system which admitted of no truth but for the purposes of deception'.[4]

Communication with the Japanese in the 1850s was extremely difficult, partly for linguistic reasons. The interpretation of exchanges was triangular, with both English and Japanese being expressed through the common medium of Dutch. Even the American Treaty of Amity and Commerce (1858) was drafted in all three languages, with the Dutch as the definitive version. Even so, the use of Dutch had its difficulties, since the version of the language understood by the Japanese interpreters was that of seventeenth-century sea captains. The Japanese negotiators even tried to insist that the Dutch text of the treaty should follow Japanese word order.[5]

The original Treaty of Friendship (1854) negotiated by Perry provided for 'perfect, permanent and universal peace', and it contained

---

'Proclamation formerly issued in Japan with respect to foreign vessels.' Repr. in *British Parliamentary Papers, Japan* (10 vols) (hereafter *BPPJ*), Shannon: Irish University Press, 1971, vol. 2, pp. 375–6.

3. Sidney Wallach (ed.), *Narrative of the expedition of an American Squadron to the China Seas and Japan*, London: Macdonald, 1954, pp. 9–12, 82–4.

4. Ishii and Sekiguchi, *The world market*, p. 91; Latourette, *The History of Early Relations*, pp. 122–4. The quotation is from Wallach, *Narrative*, p. 34.

5. M. E. Cosenza (ed.), *The Complete Journal of Townshend Harris*, New York: Doubleday, 1959, pp. 374–5.

assurances that the Japanese would meet the demands of the United States for safe haven and access to naval supplies.[6] Two ports, Shimoda and Hakodate, were to be opened for this purpose, and Americans using them were to be allowed to exchange gold and silver for goods 'under regulations for this purpose', and were not to be subject to restrictions on movement as stringent as those applied to the Dutch and Chinese. The treaty did not include provisions for the development of normal foreign trade, but it did provide for the stationing of an American consul at Shimoda.

The first American consul, Townshend Harris, was a remarkable man. An avid student of Kaempfer and well versed in contemporary economic thought, he had succeeded by 1857 in negotiating the Treaty of Shimoda, which granted the Americans extraterritorial rights, and the Treaty of Amity and Commerce the following year. The latter opened Japan for trade and made provision for four more open ports. Harris's principal tactic was to persuade the Japanese that by negotiating model agreements with the Americans they could forestall more unfavourable treaties of the 'gunboat' type such as the European powers had imposed on China.

Harris played an important part in the early economic education of the Japanese leadership. He reinforced the Dutch advice that steam technology had created a world in which Seclusion would not be acceptable, although he simultaneously emphasised the positive point that trade would create opportunities for Japan to play a new and powerful role in the world. This argument was not easily accepted because most Japanese still saw foreign trade as implying the loss of finite and valuable Japanese resources for no significant return. Harris, however, argued: 'Commerce has become very extensive since the invention of steam, and the countries of the West have in consequence become rich. The nations of the West hope that by means of steam communication all the world will become as one family . . . No nation has the right to refuse to hold intercourse with others.'[7] A further message that Harris took to Japan was that taxation of foreign trade

6. The texts of the major bilateral and multilateral treaties, in all relevant languages, are in Gaimusho Joyakukyoku, *Kyu joyaku isan* (Compendium of old treaties) (3 parts in 4 books), Tokyo: Gaimusho, 1930–36. The best documentary survey of the period in English is Beasley, *Select Documents*.

7. 'Statement made by Townshend Harris at his interview with Hotta Masayoshi, 12 December 1857', Beasley, *Select Documents*, pp. 159–65.

(i.e. tariffs and export taxes) could produce revenues which would enable Japan to support a 'respectable navy' and develop the means to ward off foreign interference. This argument held a decisive attraction.[8]

The Shimoda and Harris treaties and those with Britain and the other powers that followed radically altered Japan's international economic position. The basic premise of the treaties was an obligation to encourage and regulate trade.[9] They provided for the establishment of treaty ports with defined rights for foreigners in Japan, laid down both the level of trade taxes (implicitly admitting the right of foreigners to determine the level of such taxes in Japan) and contained provisions concerning the acceptability of coinage which were to have important implications for the Japanese monetary system. They were known collectively as the Ansei treaties (after the contemporary Japanese reign name) and they were clearly 'unequal' in the sense that they contained provisions that were not fully reciprocal. However, the Japanese obtained important rights abroad, including a guarantee of the right to hire foreign technicians and specialists and even to purchase and construct warships in foreign shipyards.

The treaty port system and extraterritoriality. The treaty port system and the principle of extraterritoriality were central to Japanese economic and trade development after the opening of the ports — not only because of their immediate economic implications but also because they formed the background to Japan's military and economic expansion into Taiwan and Korea in the late nineteenth century, and into Manchuria and China during the first half of the twentieth. As applied to Japan in the 1850s, these systems were at first an extension of practices evolved over a long time in China and which had taken their modern form between 1842 and 1876. They were modified by Japan's dual determination to give no more than was essential in the face of overwhelming power and to preserve as far as possible the benefits of the old Deshima system.

---

8. Cosenza, *The Complete Journal*, p. 485.

9. The American view on this is explained in Becker and Wells, *Economics and World Power: An Assessment of American Diplomacy since 1789*, pp. 55–118, and a similar, nineteenth-century French philosophy is outlined by Lewis M. Chère in *The Diplomacy of the Sino-French War (1883–1885): Global Implications of an Undeclared War*, Bloomington, IN: Crossroad Books, 1988, pp. 3ff.

As we saw in Chapter 1, the Chinese tradition of dealing with foreigners went back at least to the Tang dynasty, when foreign merchant communities were resident in the great northern cities at the Chinese end of the trans-Himalayan silk route, in the Yangtze valley, along the Grand Canal and, above all, in Canton.[10] Particularly remarkable was the penetration of Muslims, of whom 10–15,000 were reported to be living in Canton in the ninth century and who were found in the same city by the great fourteenth-century Arab traveller, Ibn Battuta, living in their own quarters with a mosque and bazaar, all under the jurisdiction of a *cadhi* (Islamic judge).[11] The Chinese authorities valued the goods brought by these foreigners, but they nonetheless interfered with trade, which they thought of as a convenient, taxable monopoly. Equally, it was impossible in practice for the Chinese to differentiate trade from the political tribute system through which the court received goods and homage from the known non-Chinese world, including at one time Japan.

By the eighteenth century the Chinese foreign trade system was a sophisticated, time-honoured and essentially defensive system, into which Europeans if they wished to enter the burgeoning trade in tea and other commodities had to insert themselves as skilfully as they were able. Thus when the East India Company was allowed to operate in Canton in the eighteenth century, it was subject to these standard controls and had at first to deal with the officially-approved dealers known as the 'co-hongs'. By the early nineteenth century east-west trade in its Chinese form consisted of selected trading monopolies interacting in a highly controlled and geographically confined space. Within this space elements of extraterritorial jurisdiction were ceded

10. Extraordinary details of the Tang system are described in ch. 1 of Edward H. Schafer, *The Golden Peaches of Samarkand*, Berkeley: University of California Press, 1963. Further accounts of early Chinese thinking are in Fairbank, *The Chinese World Order*. The fullest western descriptions of the eighteenth-century system and its early nineteenth-century evolution can be obtained from Dermigny, *Le Commerce à Canton* and J. K. Fairbank, *Trade and Diplomacy on the China Coast: The Opening of the Treaty Ports, 1842–1854*, Cambridge, MA: Harvard University Press, 1953. Even today the western silk road capital of Xian has a *registered* population of over 100,000 Muslims, Catholics and other Christians. This figure must greatly underestimate the lingering extent of China's medieval open-door policies.

11. Dermigny, *Le Commerce à Canton*, pp. 297–8. See also the references in D'Elia, *Fonti Ricciane*, vol. 1, p. 110. The functions of the *cadhi* (today spelt *qadi* or *cadi*) are explained in D'Herbelot's, *Bibliothèque Orientale ou Dictionnaire Universel*, Maestricht: Dufour et Roux, 1776, p. 209.

to the British company, which was expected to discipline its own officials.

The 'Canton system', with its limited form of extraterritoriality, had ceased to be acceptable to the British and other foreigners by the late 1830s. Westerners were ignorant of the details of Chinese law, disliked what they did know, and were disgusted by Chinese judicial torture and punishments. After the abolition of the East India Company monopoly in 1834, western merchants would no longer accept the arbitrariness of officialdom or the fact that Chinese law did not recognise individual rights and responsibilities, since it thus made effective bankruptcy proceedings, among other things, impossible.[12] It was in these circumstances that Britain and other European powers introduced extraterritoriality into China by force, and a system that had not historically been seen as intrinsically demeaning and which had largely been a device in both medieval China and Europe to make honourable commercial interaction possible between non-Muslim and Muslim civilisations, had now become, under these new conditions, an affront to national dignity.[13]

One of the most important economic aspects of the new Chinese treaty ports was that goods imported into them had an initial tariff levied and were then exempt from further payment. In contrast, goods imported into non-treaty port cities were subject to an indefinite number of local taxes as they were moved from place to place. The system therefore effectively divided the economy into a customs union, comprising the treaty ports, and the 'inland' up-country areas where trade was subject to a morass of restrictions. The conflicts caused by this duality led Westerners to demand successfully a continuous expansion in the number of treaty ports.

This then was the Chinese system which the western powers wished to extend to Japan, and which was already being used as the basis for achieving economic benefits in Japan. As Alcock observed, 'The Chinese [through the system] formed a natural and, to all appearance,

---

12. A contemporary source that vividly reflects European views is Charles Gutzlaff, *China Opened* (2 vols), London: Smith, Elder, 1838, esp. vol. 2, ch. 14.

13. Based on G. C. Allen, *Western Enterprise*, esp. Appendix D; H. B. Morse, *The Trade and Administration of China*, London: Longmans, Green, 1921, chs. 7–9; N. B. Dennys, *The Treaty Ports of China and Japan Guide Book and Vade Mecum*, Hong Kong, 1860, repr. San Francisco: CMRC, 1977, and Seiji G. Hishida, *The International Position of Japan as a Great Power*, New York: Columbia University Press, 1905, pp. 133ff.

a necessary link in the first development of any large trade between Europe and Japan.'[14]

Foreign activities and contacts in the 1860s. The foreign population of Japan expanded rapidly in the 1860s. Early arrivals included business houses such as Jardines and Dents and banks such as the Chartered and Hong Kong and Shanghai, while the Peninsular and Orient Shipping Company opened a service from Shanghai to Yokohama.[15] Thus Nagasaki, where in 1860 there had been only 100 foreigners of whom twenty-five were British, was home by 1864 to 200 British citizens. Indeed, when the harbour was full, up to 7,000 Europeans altogether were resident.[16] The Europeans and their companies quickly established an active civic and social life in the treaty ports as they had done in China. They came to concern themselves with law and order, and introduced tramways, electricity, balls, tea parties, the Kobe races and the notorious Yokohama hunt, which ran night and day, employing a motley pack of beagles and dwarf foxhounds imported for the purpose from Shanghai.

The composition of the foreign business classes in the ports was varied, including many whose behaviour caused concern to the consular officials. This floating population of adventurers made a poor impression on the Japanese and was described by compatriots as a band of 'greedy vultures' and 'the moral refuse of Europe'. Even Alcock, finally exasperated beyond measure, described them as 'the scum of the earth' for which indiscretion he was banned from the Yokohama Club.

Early commercial relations were also coloured by a new type of Japanese trader lured to the ports by the opportunities created. Far removed from the urbane and civilised traditional merchant families of Osaka, the newcomers were described as *ikkaku senkinjin* ('one grab — a thousand pieces of silver men') and they rapidly gained an

14. Alcock, *The Capital of the Tycoon*, vol. 1, p. 39.

15. Fox, *Britain and Japan*, ch. 12.

16. These data and much of the following are drawn from Harold S. Williams, *Tales of the Foreign Settlements in Japan*, Tokyo: Charles Tuttle, 1958, and John R. Black, *Young Japan. Yokohama and Yedo: A narrative of the settlement and the city from the signing of the treaties in 1856, to the close of the year 1879* (2 vols), Yokohama: Kelly and Walsh, 1880, 1881.

equally bad name with foreigners and with the Japanese authorities.[17] Economically, the function of the new merchants was to destroy the old trading monopolies of the political authorities.

The other important group of foreigners engaged in Japanese trade at this time remained the Chinese. The Dutch had always found their competition a problem and they remained a dominant force long after the opening of the ports, controlling Japanese trade through networks of regional contacts. Even in the late 1860s, when the formal monopolies in the export of aquatic goods and drugs had been surrendered on western insistence, the Chinese are estimated to have controlled more than half of the Nagasaki trade. They were frequently employed by westerners who could not handle Japanese merchants directly, in part because of the language barrier. There were also many examples of Japanese trade organised through joint contractual Sino-western alliances, usually based in Shanghai. The Chinese influence persisted well into the 1920s, reflecting the activities of the Chinese merchants in Osaka and Kobe who handled exports of Japanese textiles destined for Chinese and South East Asian markets. This tradition ensured that while the pattern of Japanese export expansion was mainly the product of Japan's gradual emancipation from Western commercial hegemony, it was also a reflection of the enduring influence of Chinese international merchant relationships.[18]

As long as the Ansei treaties were in force, foreign travel in Japan was tightly restricted, except for the consuls. The 'inland' trade was not allowed. Nonetheless, the westerners did all they could in the absence of official materials and statistics to learn about the country and were generally much impressed by what they saw. Perry's officers and men 'were in raptures' and, echoing Kaempfer, noted '. . . the high cultivation of the land everywhere . . . the innumerable thrifty villages', and the 'sense of beauty, abundance, and happiness which

17. Alcock, *The Capital of the Tycoon*, vol. 2, p. 243. Similar phrases were to be used pejoratively again in the early twentieth century to describe the growing culture of money making and the weakening of traditional morality. Carol Gluck, *Japan's Modern Myths. Ideology in the Late Meiji Period*, Princeton University Press, 1985, ch. 6.

18. On the general question of Chinese merchants see Sugiyama Shinya, 'The international environment and foreign trade', *EHOJ*, vol. 3, pp. 185–7. Alcock's account of the Chinese monopoly situation in 1859 is in Foreign Office, 'Extract from a despatch from Mr Alcock', June 18, 1859, *BPPJ*, vol. 4, pp. 49–50. Cases of joint Sino-British arrangements are described in Hao Yen-p'ing, *The Commercial Revolution in Nineteenth Century China. The Rise of Sino-Western Capitalism*, Berkeley: University of California Press, 1986, pp. 232–3.

Table 3.1. EXPORTS, IMPORTS AND TRADE BALANCES, 1860–67
(× 1,000 yen)

	Exports	Imports	Balance
1860	7,457	3,116	4,431
1861	4,911	3,318	1,593
1862	10,662	6,891	3,771
1863	13,283	7,278	6,005
1864	12,545	10,129	2,416
1865	20,800	17,922	2,878
1866	18,692	18,664	28
1867	13,638	23,649	− 10,011

Source: These data are controversial. The estimates here are those of Shinya Sugiyama
in *Japan's Industrialization in the World Economy, 1859–1899: Export Trade and Overseas
Competition,* London: Athlone Press, 1988, p. 46. These data differ slightly from
those in Ishii, *Economic history,* p. 41, while other data for 1866 and 1867 suggest
a deficit in those years. See *Nihon boeki seiran* (Foreign trade of Japan: a statistical
outline) Tokyo: Toyo Keizai Shimposha, 1975, p. 16.

everyone delighted to contemplate'.[19] Townshend Harris recorded
similar opinions about both the Japanese and their agriculture, and
Alcock, who travelled widely in an attempt to test Japanese claims
that foreign trade was unpopular, made some prescient remarks about
Japanese technological skills, which he considered had achieved 'as
great perfection [of the industrial arts] as could well be attainable
without the aid of steampower and machinery'.[20]

Trends in trade and the economy, 1859–1866

The American arrival in Japan was prompted by a mixture of economic
and strategic ambitions and international rivalry ensured that the
signing of one treaty was followed by others on equal or better terms.
Once foreigners had arrived there, commercial considerations quickly
became paramount to them, for even after 500 years, Marco Polo's
images of a (literally) golden Japan still lingered.[21]

The growth of trade after the opening of the ports is shown in
Table 3.1. and its commodity structure in Table 3.2. The most
representative data for the period are those for 1860–65. These

19. Wallach, *Narrative,* p. 97.
20. Alcock, *Capital of the Tycoon,* vol. 2, p. 301.
21. Black, *Young Japan,* vol. 2, p. 334.

Table 3.2. THE COMMODITY STRUCTURES OF EXPORTS
AND IMPORTS (YOKOHAMA TRADE), 1860–65

Exports (% of total)

	Silk	Tea	Cotton	Oil	Copper
1860	65.6	7.8		5.5	
1861	68.3	16.7			3.6
1862	86	9			1.2
1863	83.6	5.1	8.9		
1864	68.5	5.2	19.9		
1865	83.7	10.2			

Source: Ishii, *Economic history*, p. 41.
Between 1860 and 1865 Yokohama accounted for between 70% and 95%
of total trade.

show that trade grew rapidly. Exports were initially far higher than
imports and grew at 33% per year. Imports, from a lower base,
grew at 49% per annum. Thus by 1866 67, years of disturbance, a
trade deficit had appeared. Table 3.2 reveals the dominance of silk
in exports; other exports included coal, copper, handicrafts, wax,
tobacco, camphor and a variety of fish products – the latter much
appreciated by the Chinese. Imports were mainly cotton and woollen
goods, although there were also significant imports of ships, arms and
capital goods.[22]

There are no data that make possible a satisfactory quantitative
analysis of the impact of trade on the domestic economy. Contemporary descriptions confirm that in the silk and related trades there
were technical and organisational changes, output rose rapidly and
much prosperity was generated. In the silk district of Oshu, Fukuzawa
Yukichi reported that incomes were rising, employment patterns
changing and that 'the whole fief is on a boom'.[23] However, it is

22. A full account of the commodity composition and other aspects of *kaikoku* trade
are in Sugiyama Shinya in *EHOJ*, vol. 3, pp. 173–221. See also Keizo Shibusawa (ed.),
Japanese Society in the Meiji Era, Tokyo: Obunsha, 1958, ch. 1.

23. *Nihon boeki seiran*, p. 17. Fukuzawa Yukichi (1835–1901) was of fairly humble
samurai origin and his father was in charge of his domain's warehouse (*kurayashiki*)
at Osaka. He studied Dutch before the Restoration and went on memorable visits
to America and Europe. A thinker and a prolific writer, he was a dominant intellectual
influence in the Meiji era and the founder of what is today Keio University. His
autobiography is one of the most illuminating sources for the period available in
English.

clear at the same time that the rapid expansion of demand for agriculturally-based exports caused severe dislocation to which, in an economy still subject to customary forms of resource allocation and highly artificial arrangements for the distribution of key commodities, it was difficult to adjust.[24]

The *kaikoku* boom and its problems had important implications for the traditional Tokugawa system. It led to further erosion both of Bakufu control and of the commercial hegemony of Osaka, and to a further rise in the economic strength of the great and potentially rebellious domains. The Bakufu deliberately tried to minimise the domestic impact of foreign trade by isolating Osaka from foreigners, keeping them restricted to carefully chosen, less important locations. It also tried to maintain its economic influence both by direct administrative control of prices and key export commodities and by sending established Edo merchants to handle the trade at the new ports.[25] But as opportunities expanded, the new class of opportunistic merchants consistently undermined the traditional economic institutions by bidding against the Osaka merchants for silk and export commodities and by travelling inland to buy raw materials directly from the farmers.[26]

The influx of imports and the explosive foreign demand for Japanese agricultural products, especially silk, had severe effects on domestic producers who suddenly found themselves without the raw materials they needed to work. So powerful were these effects on the craftsmen of Kiryu that workers were described as: '. . . on the verge of starvation. Overcome with grief, they have formed themselves into neighbourhood groups for mutual help, which will surely develop into mobs.'[27]

Another major effect of *kaikoku* was the further deterioration of the central fiscal system. To respond to the foreign challenge, the Bakufu had to provide the diplomatic, defence and other services expected of a modern state. As a proportion of total expenditure, ports, guns, ships and similar outlays rose from 5% to 70% during the *kaikoku* period.

---

24. Shibusawa, *Japanese Society in the Meiji Era*, ch. 1; Takahashi, *Research into the Tokugawa feudal economy, passim.*

25. Shibusawa, *Japanese Society in the Meiji Era*, ch. 1.

26. Ishii, *Economic history*, p. 40; Miyamoto, *Research into the circulation of commodities*, pp. 115–31.

27. Shibusawa, *Japanese Society in the Meiji Era*, p. 20.

Failing any major change in its traditional revenues, the Bakufu responded with largely impracticable schemes to raise money through such methods as wine taxes, land development, canal building and night soil collection.[28] In consequence, the Bakufu relied increasingly for its income on currency depreciation, which was itself a cause of inflation — the third substantial economic result of *kaikoku*.

Inflation was not a new phenomenon in Japan. The long term trend of prices had shifted markedly upwards from around 1820, largely in response to *han* and Bakufu fiscal and monetary policies. Many scholars believe this inflationary process played a positive role in the expansion of the late Tokugawa economy. But after 1859 the rate of inflation was also strongly influenced by the adaptation of Japan to the world monetary system and by the demand transmitted from the export sector, which took the novel form of open price competition between domestic merchants for the control of exportable products. This acceleration in prices is illustrated in Fig. 3.1, while the increase in the price of exportables may be illustrated from the fact that in the three periods demarcated by the years 1853, 1860, 1863 and 1867, the annual rate of price increase of vegetable oil products rose from 4.2% to 11.6%, and then to 40%.[29]

The unresolved issues of the kaikoku period

Against this background of rapid but unstable economic change, three groups of problems arose. These related to the freedom and viability of trade and access to the Japanese economy, Bakufu policies towards foreign trade, and problems created by institutional misunderstandings and inadequacies.

Because most westerners were merchants, bankers or shippers, they were interested in Japan as a market in which they could both sell and buy. In the early years, both Harris and Alcock had anxieties about the prospects for Japanese trade, and although Alcock saw possibilities for Japanese exports, both men recognised that the ethos of restraint

---

28. Military spending is discussed in Nakamura Takafusa, *Meiji Taishoki no keizai* (The economy of the Meiji-Taisho period), Tokyo: Tokyo Daigaku Shuppankai, 1985, p. 7, and *EHOJ*, vol. 3, pp. 118–9; Eiichi Kiyooka (ed.), *The Autobiography of Fukuzawa Yukichi*, Tokyo: Hokuseido Press, 1948, pp. 180–1.

29. Miyamoto, *Research into the circulation of commodities*, pp. 118, 121, 127. See also Harris, who commented: 'They appear to raise [prices] at each new arrival of a ship here.' Cosenza, *The Complete Journal*, p. 210.

Fig. 3.1. PRICE INCREASES, 1856–67

Source: EHOJ, vol. 3, p. 124.

in consumption and the prevailing sumptuary laws were serious obstacles to any large increase in imports of consumer goods. As Harris noted in a diary entry for 1857:

Simplicity and frugality is the great maxim of this country, and it is enforced in a most surprising manner. It would be an endless task to attempt to put down all the acts of a Japanese that are regulated by authority. This is no country for modistes, tailors, jewellers and the whole army that batten on the imaginary wants of the West.[30]

These views proved too pessimistic and western textiles were among the first products to be imported, quickly achieving popularity. By the mid-1860s the British consular reports were much more optimistic and Locock, the British Embassy secretary, summed up market prospects in a report on Osaka as follows:

... Young Japan is eager to cast off its old clothes along with its old restraints. There is ahead a furor at Osaka for everything foreign, from a pair of top boots to a Geneva watch, from a cake of old Windsor to a bottle of Champagne.[31]

Alcock too became increasingly sanguine, although he had more insight into the social implication of what was happening.

Nothing but opportunity is wanting to make the Japanese generally consumers of European luxuries — to the great detriment, it is to be feared, of the frugality and temperance so earnestly inculcated in the habits of their fisherman ancestors.[32]

There were other potential problems with this trade. When the Japanese opened their ports, western ships queued to enter but there was genuine alarm over whether Japan could satisfy the demand for ships' provisions, let alone for the tea, silk and other exportable commodities sought by foreign merchants.[33] To these difficulties of

30. Cosenza, *The Complete Journal*, p. 360.
31. Foreign Office, 'Report by Mr Locock, Her Majesty's Secretary of Embassy, on the Ports of Osaka and Hiogo', Yokohama, June 10, 1867, *BPPJ*, vol. 4, pp. 271–84. See also, 'Sir H. Parkes to the Earl of Clarendon', Yokohama, May 16, 1866, *BPPJ*, vol. 4, p. 241, where Parkes argued that the absence of surplus labour in Japan, compared to China, made local handloom costs sufficiently high to be undercut by European manufactures.
32. Alcock, *The Capital of the Tycoon*, vol. 1, p. 393.
33. When the first British consul arrived at Nagasaki in 1859, fifteen ships were lying idle in the port awaiting return cargoes. Paske-Smith, *Western Barbarians in Japan*, p. 199.

physical supply were added the organisational problems created by the Bakufu's attempts to restrict and control trade and even to make the treaties inoperable.

Trade policy remained highly controversial in Bakufu politics. Confucian statesmen continued to argue that trade was an intrinsically harmful process in which Japan exchanged its lifeblood for trinkets. For example, during the Perry crisis (i.e. when Perry virtually forced the opening of Japan) Matsudaira Keiei advised the Bakufu that 'we could, by using up our resources in trade, satisfy the insatiable greed of foreigners, [and] bring daily nearer the collapse of our country.'[34]

There was a change of attitude in Japan after 1856, reflecting the realisation that development of trade and shipping were indispensible to the strengthening of Japan's ability to resist foreigners and survive in the modern world. As a result, trading companies were set up, steps were taken to sound out Japanese prospects in Heilungkiang and Shanghai, and plans were made for official purchases of coal, cloth, fish and other products to sell to foreigners.[35] But in spite of this shift of policy, fundamental difficulties remained, difficulties that the Bakufu was ultimately unable to resolve.

The underlying institutional problem was that in the West the framework for economic activity was largely understood and had begun to take its modern form. This framework consisted of sovereign states, individuals and, increasingly, modern joint stock companies. Each entity had acknowledged functions, responsibilities and rights. The role of the state in this system was to encourage, protect and regulate trade in which individuals and companies had rights to participate. Analogous rights and duties existed at the international level, where commercial relations were governed by emerging concepts of international law and regulated by treaties binding on sovereign states.[36]

When the westerners, working and thinking within this frame-

34. Beasley, *Select Documents*, p. 114. See also Nariaki's third (of ten) reasons for opposing peace with the foreigners in which he emphasises the outflow of precious metals which 'incur a great loss while not acquiring the smallest benefit'.

35. Yamaguchi Kazuo, *Bakumatsu boekishi* (A history of foreign trade in the late Tokugawa period), Tokyo: Chuo Koronsha, 1943, pp. 328ff.

36. A contemporary western discussion of the Roman and Grotian contributions to international law is Henry Sumner Maine, *Ancient Law: Its Connections with the Early History of Society, and its Relation to Modern Ideas*, London: John Murray, 1861, ch. 4. See also materials cited in note 9.

work, arrived in the Far East, they found little that corresponded to it. In China, as we have seen, the basis of domestic law was completely different and the Chinese state maintained its claims to universal empire — claims that were not thought to be inconsistent with accommodating foreigners within the isolation of the treaty ports.[37] In Japan, Harris could find neither a concept of 'the law of nations' nor a unified sovereign state because power was shared between daimyo and Bakufu, with the Emperor exercising a shadowy sovereignty in the background.[38] The main practical question arising out of this was: who could represent Japan in international relations and take responsibility for the Ansei treaties? In drafting these the western powers had mistakenly equated the shogun ('the tycoon'), with the sovereigns. Eventually they realised this error, and in 1866 the British minister was obliged to press the Emperor to formally endorse earlier treaties.[39] Further, even if it had been appropriate for the Bakufu to represent Japan externally, the western treaty-makers did not understand that the feudal system left most domestic law as a *han* responsibility. Hence the Bakufu had no right to cede extra-territoriality provisions, and certainly no power to enforce them.

Friction also arose from the Tokugawa practice of occupational classification. Whereas the westerners assumed that all citizens had rights to trade and engage in the economic activities of their choice, such freedoms were unheard of in Japan and contrary to prevailing law.[40]

Finally, the opening of the ports sharpened the existing political

37. The universality of Chinese claims was encapsulated in the theory of *shih wu wai* (lit. 'nothing left out'). Chinese maps and gazetteers included as 'Chinese' the mountain and river deities of South-East Asia, Korea, the Ryukyus and Japan. Fairbank, *The Chinese World Order, passim.*

38. Hishida, *The International Position of Japan*, p. 346. A general discussion of these issues is in MITI, *Shoko seisakushi* (A history of policy towards commerce and industry), vols 5–6, *Boeki* (Foreign trade), Tokyo: 1965, 1971 (hereafter MITI, vol. 5, *Foreign trade*). In spite of the wealth of more recent scholarship, the Introduction to these volumes remains unsurpassed in its usefulness as an account of *kaikoku* and for insight into the relations between economic, social and political change.

39. Dennys, *The Treaty Ports*, p. 553.

40. These rights were developed and justified by European economists (mainly French) only in the eighteenth century. The terms *laissez-faire* and *laissez-aller* referred to the post-feudal/mercantilist right of individuals to enter any trade, to make any product and to send their goods to any market. 'Free trade' as a concept to regulate international economic relations did not develop till the nineteenth century, when it was applied in Asia.

conflict between the Bakufu and *han* interests. While the Bakufu had sought to develop trade through its traditional monopolistic devices, *han* governments had been undermining central control by developing 'exports' for more than a century, and in some cases had even extended their reform policies to foreign trade. The *han* thus saw the opening of the ports as a new opportunity to further their interests, thus bringing them into direct conflict with the central authorities.[41]

We can therefore see that the opening of the ports also opened a Pandora's box of problems based partly on differences of fundamental principle and partly on conflicts of domestic interest suppressed by the traditional system. It thus precipitated an insoluble crisis for the Japanese state. For more than a century before 1853 important changes had been taking place in the traditional system, and after 1853 the speed of this transformation increased dramatically. The opening of the ports accelerated domestic economic change, made the expansion of exports essential for national survival, sharpened the crisis of the ruling class, disturbed traditional ideologies, and made the fundamental constitutional reform that would allow Japan to participate in the world political and economic system inescapable.[42]

Thus behind what foreigners often described as a calm and placid scene, was a society in turmoil. The most striking quantitative indicators of this were the exponential inflation rate; the eleven peasant uprisings based on economic grievances in the first eight months of 1866 alone; and the assassinations of sixteen foreigners between 1859 and 1867.[43] As time passed, the problem grew more acute. Western demands in China escalated in the 1860s and Britain was acquiring a taste for a more bellicose style of foreign policy highly reminiscent of attitudes to China on the eve of the Opium War. Even the gentle British naturalist, Robert Fortune, saw war

41. Details of Satsuma–Ryukyu trade and its effects are in Ishii and Sekiguchi, *The world market*, p. 54.

42. The nature of the social and intellectual crisis caused by the Ansei treaties is described in Maruyama Masao, *Bunmeiron no gairyaku o yomu* (On reading *An outline theory of civilization*), Tokyo: Iwanami Shoten, 1986, vol. 1, ch. 1.

43. See also material by Marius B. Jansen, 'The Meiji Restoration', ch. 5 in Jansen, *The Nineteenth Century*, esp. pp. 340–2. An exceptionally vivid description of late Tokugawa society, the agony of *kaikoku* and the disillusionment of some people with the early Meiji era may be found in a novel by Shimazaki Toson, who tells his story through the eyes of an idealistic disciple of Hirata Atsutane (see ch. 2 above). Shimazaki Toson, (trans. William Naff), *Before the Dawn*, Honolulu: University of Hawaii Press, 1987.

with Japan as almost inescapable;[44] and after the international shelling of Shimonoseki in 1864, a British consular report remarked that the event had 'greatly improved the state of this market'.[45]

Some western observers did grasp the nature of the Japanese crisis. They realised that extraterritorial rights were unenforceable as the Japanese political system then stood, and that because trade threatened the traditional élite and the class structure supporting it, neither logical argument nor promises of prospective Japanese gains from trade would ever make it acceptable.[46]

To those Japanese who understood the situation, the opening of the ports had taught two lessons: that national self-preservation required an urgent programme of technical modernisation and an expansion of international trade to pay for it; and that the Bakufu was incapable of implementing such a policy. Indeed, the new government's declaration of the Restoration of imperial rule openly stated: 'Owing to the recent high prices, the rich get ever richer, while the poor are driven to dire destitution. All this comes from the incompetence of the Shogunate.'[47] Thus, there was a need for fundamental political change, which by guaranteeing the promotion of men of ability and the achievement of a national consensus could lay the foundations for a modern state. In his formal letter of resignation the last shogun wrote: 'Now that foreign intercourse becomes daily more extensive, unless the Government is directed from one central authority, the foundations of the state will fall to pieces.'[48] It was against the threat of such collapse that the active struggle for Restoration of the imperial system began in 1867.

44. '. . . Owing, no doubt, partly to our wide-spread dominions and to our extensive commerce — we have war always forced upon us against our inclinations; and that this will be one of the results of our new treaty with Japan, there is, as I have already said, but too much reason to anticipate.' Fortune, *Yedo and Peking*, p. 296.

45. Foreign Office, 'Acting consul Flowers to Mr Winchester', April 21, 1865, *BPPJ*, vol. 4, pp. 103–11.

46. Alcock, *The Capital of the Tycoon*, vol. 2, p. 35; and Dennys, *The Treaty Ports*, p. 551: 'They [the samurai] naturally fear that with foreign cotton and mule twists may come in dangerous doctrines of equality and freedom.' These fears were to be echoed more than a century later in Communist China, under similar internal and external pressure to expand trade and modernise the economy.

47. Shibusawa, *Japanese Society in the Meiji Era*, p. 51.

48. Quotation from W. W. McClaren, *Japanese Government Documents*, Transactions of the Asiatic Society of Japan, Yokohama: Kelly and Walsh, 1914, pp. 1–2. See also Harootunian, *Toward Restoration*, p. 10.

4

EARLY MEIJI MODERNISATION AND THE DEVELOPMENT OF THE TRADITIONAL EXPORT SECTOR

'1870–71: Great progress of internal improvements, and assimilation to European civilisation; proposed establishment of railways, telegraphs etc. 1877: Progress in Japan: 3,744 post offices; 22,053,430 letters and 7,372,566 domestic newspapers sent by post; 2 railways in operation; 34 lighthouses; ample religious freedom and virtual free trade.' — Entries on 'Japan' in Benjamin Vincent, *Haydn's Dictionary of Dates relating to all Ages and Nations* (1878)

During the first two decades of the Meiji period the government began a far-reaching transformation of Japanese society, a transformation calculated to make as effective a response to the challenge from the western nations as possible. This policy was summed up in the phrase *fukoku kyohei* ('rich country, strong military'), a slogan shared by Japanese and Chinese reformers alike.

An immediate priority in this process was the abolition of the *han* administration and the centralisation of power. This was followed by the removal of restrictions on movement and occupational choice. Combined with the establishment of the legal infrastructure necessary for private property, these measures laid the foundations for a market economy. Although there was at first much direct government intervention in the economy, by the mid-1880s the Finance Minister, Matsukata Masayoshi, was able to extricate the government from its direct role in modernisation. He did this by establishing a fiscal and monetary environment in which private enterprise could begin to flourish both at home and abroad.[1] The economic possibilities he created were reflected in the establishment in 1883 of the Osaka Spinning Company (Osaka Boseki Kaisha), Japan's first large-scale private industrial enterprise and a future leader of the textile industry.

---

1. Matsukata Masayoshi (1835–1924) was the dominant figure in laying the institutional and policy foundations of the Meiji era. From a distinguished family, he served as Minister of Finance from 1881. He created Japan's supply-side philosophy, established a central and commercial banking system and put Japan on the gold standard. Modern Japan is still influenced by his economic philosophy.

Table 4.1. EXPORTS, IMPORTS AND THE TRADE
BALANCE, 1868–89
(millions of yen, current prices)

	Exports	Imports	Balance
1868–73	17	28	−11
1874–78	23.5	35.4	−11.9
1879–86	35.9	40.6	−4.7
1887–89	64	69.1	−5.1

Source: Ohkawa Kazushi *et al.* (eds), *Choki keizai tokei*, vol. 14: *Boeki to kokusai shushi* (Long-term economic statistics. Foreign trade and international payments), Tokyo: Toyo Keizai Shimposha, 1979 (hereafter, *LTES*).

This industry was to transform Japan's domestic economy and foreign trade.

As the 1880s drew to a close, shifts in the character of the economy were accompanied by political consolidation. The Meiji phase of radical, westernised openness came to an end and the competing elements in the Restoration began to coalesce into an authoritarian rather than a liberal entity. This was a shift in which constitutional, educational, military and economic change each played a role.[2]

Trade trends

Reliable data on trade and payments in the early Meiji period are limited, and because we have no national income data from before 1890, only an incomplete analysis of the relationships between trade and the domestic economy is possible. We see in Table 4.1 that after 1868, the unfavourable trends in the trade imbalance of the late *kaikoku* period got worse and the trade account went into deficit. This reflected both domestic supply and exchange-rate problems that limited export

2. The Restoration literature is vast. These comments draw principally on W. G. Beasley, *The Meiji Restoration*, Stanford University Press, 1973, and two works by Toyama Shigeki, *Meiji Ishin* (The Meiji Restoration), Tokyo: Iwanami Shoten, 1951 and *Meiji Ishin to jindai* (The Meiji Restoration and today), Tokyo: Iwanami Shoten, 1968. A subtle account of the Japanese transfer of organisational models is D. Eleanor Westney, *Imitation and Innovation: The Transfer of Western Organizational Patterns to Meiji Japan*, Cambridge, MA: Harvard University Press, 1987.

Table 4.2. RATES OF GROWTH OF EXPORTS AND
IMPORTS: VOLUME AND VALUE, 1874–89

| | EXPORTS | | IMPORTS | |
	Volume	*Value*	*Volume*	*Value*
1874–78	11.6	6.5	2.4	4.7
1879–86	8.8	7	.3	−1.3
1887–89	12.2	10	10.1	20
1874–89	9.6	9.9	6	4.5

Source: L TES, *Foreign trade*, pp. 184–9 and 214–15.
Growth rates estimated by regression from raw data.

growth, and a high demand in Japan for imports of foreign consumer
and capital goods. In general, foreign goods were of high quality, competitive in price and, in the case of capital goods, embodied technologies beyond Japanese capacities.

The trade imbalance peaked in the 1870s and it is clear from the
table that there was a generally improving trend in the 1880s. One
of the keys to these trends was a change in monetary policy and the
exchange rate.[3] After 1868, the government had been forced to rely
heavily on currency expansion to finance public expenditures, as a
result of which the external value of the yen fell erratically but
persistently. The Matsukata deflation of 1881–84 was designed to
stabilise the currency, and by depressing internal demand it contributed
to a sharp reduction in imports. Moreover, between 1886 and 1889,
exports benefited from the establishment of a silver standard (this was
a time when silver was depreciating against gold).

In Table 4.2 value and volume trends are separated, and these data
bring out the point that Japanese exports grew in volume at a brisk
pace throughout the whole period. The relatively stable commodity
structure of trade between 1868 and 1882 is shown in Table 4.3, where
we see that over four-fifths of exports were primary products, of which
silk and tea were the staples. On the import side, textile products
and sugar accounted for 50% to 60% of the total, although there
were also imports of capital goods and ships and armaments that are
accounted for within the category of 'other' goods.

The scale of the trade deficit for most of this period reveals the structural nature of the Japanese trade problem under conditions of enforced

3. More detailed discussion of the currency and exchange issues is presented in
ch. 5.

Table 4.3. THE COMMODITY STRUCTURE OF
FOREIGN TRADE, 1868–82
(% shares)

	EXPORTS		
	1868–72	*1873–77*	*1878–82*
Silk products	56.9	46	43.2
Tea	24.5	25.9	22
Marine products	5.9	5.5	6.3
Grains	–	3.9	5.5
Minerals (coal)	1.6	3.4	3.3
Metals (copper)	3.5	2.6	2.6
Other (handicrafts)	7.6	12.7	17.1

	IMPORTS		
	1868–72	*1873–77*	*1878–82*
Grains	21.1	.5	1.4
Sugar products	9.4	100.7	11.3
Cotton thread	18.3	16.7	22.7
Textile products	16.4	18.9	15.7
Woollens	16	18.7	14.4
Metal products	2.3	4.6	6
Other (capital goods)	16.5	29.9	28.5

Source: Takahashi, *Development,* vol. 3, pp. 218–19.

free trade. On the import side, Japan had urgent requirements for
capital goods and arms, while it also experienced a wave of interest
in western consumer goods. The adoption by the court of western
clothing for formal occasions, the abolition of samurai sword-bearing,
and freedom to travel abroad all fuelled a booming appetite for
western textiles, clothing and other goods.[4] Detailed analyses of
import penetration undertaken by the government in the late 1870s
and early 1880s confirmed that in the key areas of textiles and sugar,
the price and quality advantages of imports reinforced the influence
of fashion.[5]

The rapid penetration of imports also reflected the effectiveness of
the Japanese domestic distribution system. The comparison with China

4. Takahashi, *Formation*, vol. 2, pp. 154ff.
5. MITI, vol. 5, *Foreign trade*, pp. 252ff.

on this point is very instructive. In nineteenth-century China, vast distances, poor communications and internal trade barriers all provided substantial non-tariff protection against imports. In Japan, however, the more sophisticated and close-knit distribution system of the late Tokugawa period was sufficient to provide western goods with an initial penetration of the market. Subsequently the abolition of the *han* and the large Meiji investment in transport and communications gave dramatic impetus to the unification of the national market and the efficiency of distribution. As a result, as early as 1865 *per capita* imports of cloth were higher in Japan than in China, and by 1871 Japan, with a population less than a tenth the size of China's, was importing a larger total volume of cotton thread.[6]

The impact of trade on the domestic economy was varied. Outside agriculture, declining activities tended to be trades that had served the specialised needs of the feudal system. Although the main non-agricultural industry — textiles — did have its structure modified by imports, it nonetheless survived, as we see later, by technical adaptation and the use of imported yarns for weaving. However, the impact of foreign trade on agriculture was substantial. Changes in agricultural structure were inevitably rapid at this time because of the unification of the domestic market and the abolition of traditional limitations on peasants' choice of crops to plant. To these changes were added the further adjustments called for by large imports of vegetable oil, sugar, cotton, salt and wool on the one hand, and rising exports of silk, tea, rice and other agricultural products on the other.

Exports from the traditional sector

What is so striking about the growth of exports in the early to middle Meiji period is the dominant role played by manufacturing activities that were well established in the traditional economy, and had generally responded vigorously back in the 1850s to the opportunities created by opening the ports. These included the silk, tea and handicrafts industries, to which must be added coal, copper and other products from the agricultural and fishing sectors. The success of these export commodities reflected experience acquired in the traditional economy, continued learning and adaptation of new mechanical and commercial techniques, and active government policies. Discussion

6. Ishii, *The opening of the ports*, p. 296.

will be limited in this chapter to a brief account of the silk, tea and handicrafts trades and to analysis of the evolution of government trade policy and institutions.[7]

Silk. The basic ingredients of this industry — silkworms and the mulberry plant — are believed to have been brought from the Asian mainland to Japan in the third century. Thereafter the production of thread and the crafts of weaving and dyeing developed into one of the most sophisticated of the Japanese industrial arts, arts that flourished particularly well when they were located close to the court societies such as those at Kamakura and Kyoto.[8] We saw in Chapter 1 how the Japanese craving for Chinese silks was a key to the development of foreign trade in the sixteenth century. After the closure of the country, the domestic industry developed, diversified and flourished. This occurred especially in the Genroku era (1688–1705), when the samurai were allowed garments of gorgeous crepe and *habutae* silks, and even craftsmen wore padded silk and cotton jackets. In the late eighteenth and early nineteenth centuries, the tightening of sumptuary laws against extravagant consumption put the industry into decline. But the silk sector quickly responded after the opening of the ports and became the staple Japanese export.

The nature and changing structure of the international silk industry are illustrated in Table 4.4, which demonstrates the remarkable fact that, between them, France and China in 1874 accounted for approximately half of the world's output, consumption and exports of silk. It is also clear that Europe alone accounted for half of the world's silk consumption. Initially then, Europe was the key market and China was Japan's key competitor. However, in the longer run it was the phenomenal growth of American consumption that proved to be the crucial factor in the world silk trade; thus whoever succeeded in the American market would be bound to become a world industry leader.

This was the route that Japan followed. In 1866–67 Britain was

---

7. The best account of the development of individual export trades in this period is Sugiyama, *Japan's Industrialization*.

8. This section is based on Ishii Kanji, *Nihon sanshigyoshi bunseki* (An analysis of the history of the Japanese silk industry), Tokyo: Tokyo Daigaku Shuppankai, 1971; Sugiyama, *Japan's Industrialization*, ch. 4; J. J. Rein, *The Industries of Japan*, London: Hodder and Stoughton, 1894, pp. 185ff; Keishi Ohara and Tamotsu Okata (eds) *Japanese Trade and Industry in the Meiji–Taisho Era*, Tokyo: Obunsha, 1957, part 4; and British Consular Records for 1872 and 1876.

Table 4.4. WORLD OUTPUT, CONSUMPTION AND
TRADE IN SILK, 1874–1910

	Output (% shares in 1874)	Exports (% shares in 1874)	Consumption (% shares in 1874)	Growth rate of consumption (1874–1907/ 1910)
France	9	5	31	−1.78
China	40	39	25	+0.31
India	15	5	13	−5.57
Italy	17	33	7	−1.31
Japan	8	7	6	+3.24
Great Britain	–	–	6	−2.66
United States	–	–	2	+8.57

Source: Ishii, *An analysis of the history of the Japanese silk industry*, p. 20.

Japan's main customer, accounting for 64% of total silk exports, but by 1878 its place had been taken by France which accounted for 55% of the total. By 1884 America had become the main customer and by 1920 that market took 84% of all Japanese silk exports. The extent of Japan's success against the Chinese competition is evident from the fact that between 1870 and 1920, while China's share of the American silk market fell from 26% to 20%, that of Japan rose from 1% to 78%.[9]

An important reason for the early Japanese success in Europe was that production in France and Italy was seriously affected by the corpuscular disease which affected silkworm eggs. This started in the 1850s but the highest mortality was in the 1860s, and as a result European raw silk prices doubled between 1863 and 1865. The timing of this catastrophe meant that profits in the export trade reflected an effective difference between Japanese and European raw silk prices of, respectively, threefold to fivefold. Half of this difference could be accounted for by merchants taking advantage of the difference between the Japanese and world silver-to-gold price ratios (merchants could trade in silver and then exchange it for gold at home at a higher ratio than prevailed outside Japan).

However, apart from government support in marketing and quality control, the main reasons for success in the silk trade were continuous technical innovation (see Chapter 11) and the fact that, as an exporter, Japan responded to international markets in ways that progressively

9. Ishii, *An analysis of the history of the Japanese silk industry*, pp. 22, 41.

gave it the price and quality advantages to compete successfully against not only the low-quality output of the Chinese but also the sophisticated products of the Europeans.[10]

The traditional and highly competitive nature of the industry helps to explain its initial sophistication as well as its subsequent technical and commercial progress, yet the government's role can scarcely be overestimated. During the *kaikoku* period, the silk trade had been concentrated in Yokohama where the traditional network of producers and wholesalers was concentrated. Much trade was done through Chinese intermediaries who worked with western merchants such as Jardines and Dents.[11] But despite its profitability, the organisation of the trade presented serious problems. For while the Bakufu was attempting to control and tax the trade through the traditional system of *kabu nakama*, popular anti-foreign movements, inflamed by inflation and economic dislocation, disrupted the silk supply by violence and murder.

The Meiji leaders were agreed that the development of silk exports was crucial for Japanese trade, but in the early 1870s they faced a sea of difficulties.[12] Pasteur's discovery of a solution to the problem of the corpuscular disease led to a decline in the demand for eggs. It was also found that European demand for silk thread suitable for machine-driven weaving required levels of quality and consistency which, if they were not met, led to very poor prices. The government responded to these commercial and technical challenges by investing in research, technical study visits to France, Italy and Austria, participation in international exhibitions, the production of technical literature, and the establishment of a model filiature, the Tomioka Spinning Company.

The central problem, however, was that even if supply could be enlarged and quality enhanced, the Japanese had no control of international marketing, since this remained in the hands of foreign merchants in the open ports. In 1870 Hayami Kenso, a leading Japanese

10. This is exhaustively discussed in the writings of Ishii and that of Sugiyama cited in notes 7 8.

11. In 1878 there were 2,500 Chinese in Japan, of whom 1,100 were in Yokohama. Williams, *Tales of the Foreign Settlements in Japan*, p. 128.

12. Haru Matsukata Reischauer, *Samurai and Silk: A Japanese and American Heritage*, Cambridge, MA: Belknap Press, 1986, pp. 222–4; Kyugoro Obata (ed.), *An Interpretation of the Life of Viscount Shibusawa*, Tokyo: Daiyamondo Jigyo Co., 1937, pp. 70–1.

Table 4.5. ANNUAL GROWTH RATES OF TEA OUTPUT
AND EXPORTS (VOLUME AND VALUE), 1871/75–1891/95

Output	Exports	Value of exports
5.14%	4.27%	1.74%

Source: Sugiyama, *Japan's Industrialization*, p. 142.

expert in the trade, found details of European silk prices in a copy of a London newspaper. It was only then that he grasped for the first time the enormous profits being made by foreign merchants purchasing silk in Japan. By the mid-1870s this kind of information was regularly available in Japan through the telegraph. The Japanese responded partly by initiating direct sales to export markets and partly by establishing collective organisations to control sales to foreign merchants in Japan. A pioneer of direct sales was Arai Rioichiro who was born into the Hoshinos, a famous traditional family of silk merchants. Arai started to learn English in 1871 and in 1876 sailed for New York. His early career in America was fraught with difficulties, but by the time he retired in 1927, his Morimura Arai Company was the largest exporter of Japanese silk, having profited enormously from the silk stocking boom of the 1920s. Arai himself became a respected figure in New York, with a mansion in Old Greenwich and membership of two exclusive golf clubs.[13]

But this is looking ahead, for none of these attempts to break the hold of the foreign merchants produced significant results in the early Meiji period, and it was not till the First World War that Japan's traditional export trade was basically brought under Japanese control, although by this time it was declining in significance due to the rise of cotton and other manufactures.

Tea and handicrafts. Tea accounted for a quarter of Japanese export earnings at the time of the Restoration, but this had declined to one-fifth by 1890 (Table 4.3). In Table 4.5 we see that this result was a reflection of brisk growth in the volumes of both total output and

---

13. Arai and Matsukata were the grandfathers of Haru Reischauer and are the subject of her beautiful and indispensable memoir, *Samurai and Silk*.

exports. However declining prices kept the increase in the value of exports growing at a much more modest rate.[14]

Traditional Japanese tea is of the green variety and undergoes a process in which leaves are stewed in iron kettles, fired, sorted and dried. The highest-quality teas are then reduced to powder. However, in the largest markets at this time — notably Britain and Russia — consumers preferred black teas and these required fermentation processes for which the native leaves were not suitable. In the long run, this limitation and the growing success of tea plantations in India and Ceylon, which specialised in black teas, restricted the growth of Japanese exports.

Many of the problems in the tea sector were similar to those in silk. Prices were sensitive to quality and adulteration, and tackling this required the government to introduce a mixture of technical and organisational reforms.[15] Another parallel was the importance of China as a competitor and of America as a market. China was important as an exporter of green teas and America was the only major market where these were popular. For most of the period between the Restoration and 1890, America accounted for 80% to 90% of Japanese tea exports. In the 1890s American tastes began to move towards the black teas, and this, combined with continuing problems over quality and competition from China and other new producers, added to Japanese difficulties. Nonetheless, because rising incomes in Japan led to increasing domestic consumption of tea, the success of the industry in increasing output (by extending the tea acreage and technical progress) at least ensured that significant imports were not required. Although tea was only directly important to Japanese export earnings for the thirty to forty years following the opening of the ports, these were critical years in which tea played an indispensable role as a traditional export that was successful in world markets.

Although not large in total export value, handicrafts played a

14. Rein, *The Industries of Japan*, pp. 110ff; Ohara and Okata, *Japanese Trade and Industry*, part 3; Kaempfer, 'A natural history of the Japanese tea', Appendix to *The History of Japan*. The tea sown area data are in Ohara and Okata, *Japanese Trade and Industry*, p. 180.

15. Adulteration and quality problems are persistent themes in the Consular Reports. For example, see Foreign Office, 'Report on the Trade of the Ports of Hiogo and Osaka for the year 1880', *BPPJ*, vol. 6, p. 679.

distinctive role in early trade expansion, and the small-scale manufacturing sector in which they were produced remained an important part of the economy right up to 1937. Handicraft products included lacquer, bronzes and other metalware, carvings in wood, ivory, stone and semi-precious materials, and porcelain. Many of these objects were traditionally produced by craftsmen serving the markets created by the court, temples and rich households; but handicrafts were also found in ordinary homes and were often charmingly small and attractive. The skills of these crafts survived the Restoration, and magnificent specimens were exhibited at the great international exhibitions, where they were much admired and purchased.[16] Partly because the arrival of these pieces in Europe coincided with a wave of interest in the 'industrial arts', these Japanese pieces played an influential role overseas, not only by providing favourable publicity for Japanese skills but also by contributing to the development of European taste and the craft industries. Indeed, according to Caroline Mathieu, 'Japan began increasingly to dominate the artistic scene [of the decorative arts] especially after the 1867 Universal Exhibition, at which the Japanese arts section caused a sensation.'[17]

Trade policies and institutions

Early Meiji policies. The first twenty years of Meiji economic policy was a period of considerable confusion. Although the requirements of trade and technological modernisation were an important element in élite calls for the Restoration, much popular support for the movement was based on hatred of foreign merchants. What had unified the Japanese was the Bakufu's incapacity to resolve, in any way at all, the inter-

---

16. These products have appreciated well. A Japanese bronze garden fountain was purchased by the Earl of Lonsdale for an unknown sum at the Paris Exposition of 1889. It was auctioned at Sotheby's for £50 in 1947 and for £35,000 in 1990 (*Country Life*, December 1990).

17. The European consumer taste for Japanese items is illustrated by the comment of the Misses Garnet: 'To the appreciative mind, not spoiled by the luxury of wealth, what keen pleasure there is in the possession of one new treasure: A Persian tile, an Algerian flower-pot, an old Flemish cup ... an Icelandic spoon, a Japanese cabinet ...', the Misses Garnet, *House Decoration*, quoted by Asa Briggs in *Victorian Things*, London: Batsford, 1988, p. 246. The quotation is from Caroline Mathieu, *Guide to the Musée d'Orsay*, Paris, 1987, which also has details of some of the fantastic pieces of French industrial art influenced by Japanese taste.

related problems of Japan's internal and external order (*naiyu gaikan* — 'troubles within; disaster without').

A primary task of the Meiji statesmen was thus to secure a broader consensus on the necessity for foreign trade. By the 1870s the urgency of the issue was accentuated by monetary problems. The outflow of bullion to cover the trade deficit and the large issues of domestic paper to cover budget deficits combined to cause serious inflation and currency instability. Although the government was beginning the work of fiscal reconstruction based on a land tax, Matsukata Masayoshi (who was to become Japan's most distinguished Finance Minister) realised that, because the country was linked to the world economy through trade, internal and external monetary policies had to be mutually reinforcing. Okuma Shigenobu argued that the external balance had become the most important constraint on the internal rate of growth.[18]

Popular dislike of foreign trade after 1867 rested on two foundations: inherited ideological values and the economic dislocation caused by inflation and the dismantling of the feudal economy. A striking insight into nineteenth-century attitudes to commerce and trade is provided by the views of Fukuzawa Hyakusuke, father of the reformer and traveller, Fukuzawa Yukichi. Although a clan official in charge of a *kurayashiki* in Osaka, contact with merchants and bankers did nothing to diminish his Confucian contempt for commercial values, to the extent that he took his son away from a school where the teacher included arithmetic among his lessons, saying: 'It is abominable that innocent children should be taught to use numbers . . . the instrument of merchants.'[19]

The Confucian debates on trade continued in the 1870s. Critics emphasised the natural self-sufficiency of Japan, the evils of trade-induced inflation and the danger of allowing foreigners into Japan under the pretext of commerce. Remarkably, the counter-arguments for trade and expanded contact with foreigners were made largely by advocates who continued to put at least the foundations of their

18. Takahashi, *Formation*, vol. 2, p. 175. Okuma Shigenobu (1838–1922) studied 'western learning' and was involved with the administration of foreign trade before the Restoration. He subsequently became a key figure in shaping Meiji economic policy, particularly as Minister of Finance, 1873–80.

19. Kiyooka, *Autobiography*, p. 3.

case within the framework of traditional Japanese values.[20] Thus one author put his pro-trade case in the following fictitious Confucian dialogue: Japan has unrivalled moral superiority over the rest of the world, and its wealth and self-sufficiency reflect this. Trade is therefore not absolutely necessary for Japan, but to prohibit the export of 'surplus' Japanese commodities would be to waste them and thus violate the Confucian duty of universal benevolence. With some sophistry, the author went on to suggest that 'gain' and acquisitiveness are consistent with natural ethics and, moving to newer ground, he emphasised that the steamship had transformed the possibilities for the international division of labour and was creating a world in which Japan had to participate successfully in order to sustain its independence and national destiny:

In a world where free intercourse is making such rapid strides, Japan must not be left alone. The development of commerce is in obedience to a law of nature, and its course can neither be delayed or arrested.

In conclusion, the Confucian protagonist Mr Clever (*saisuke*) finally won over Mr Obstinate (*guanroku*) by pointing out the connections between trade, technology and national defence:

If, on the one hand, we persistently refuse to engage in commerce, foreigners, of course, learn nothing about Japan, but we should be equally ignorant of western civilisation. We could not buy their ships and guns, nor could we [learn to] manufacture them in Japan.

The moral and nationalistic approach to foreign trade and the tradition of loyally subordinating personal advantage to the wider collective gain have persisted in various guises ever since their early articulation in the Meiji period. As Japan became a more self-conscious actor in the world economy, these elements grew less visible, but they remain important, and without some awareness of them one cannot fully understand either Japanese public policy or private sector behaviour.[21]

20. This section is based on two lengthy 'inclosures' to the consular *Commercial Reports*, for 1869–70, Foreign Office, 'Scattered remarks on commerce by Kato Sukeichi' and 'Conversations on commerce: A dialogue between Gwanroku and Saisuke', *BPPJ*, vol. 4, pp. 500–24.

21. The thesis of the secret undercurrent of Japanese nationalistic economic behaviour is the subject of an important, detailed study by Morikawa Hidemasa (ed.), *Nihongata keiei no genryu* (The sources of the Japanese style of management), Tokyo: Toyo Keizai Shimposha, 1973.

In its attempts to translate the broadening consensus on national objectives into effective policies, the Meiji leadership encountered three groups of problems. The first was Japanese ignorance of contemporary technology and of the specific commercial skills relating to international trade, especially in shipping, insurance and finance. The second was the absence of appropriate institutions to acquire and deploy these skills: although the traditional economy had generated its own forms of organisation, many of these had either been swept away in the reforms following the Restoration or were not immediately appropriate to the functions they now had to perform. The third problem was the Ansei treaties, negotiated by the Bakufu, but inherited unchanged by the Meiji leaders. The provisions in these treaties for very low tariffs and foreign extraterritorial rights were crucial constraints on Japanese economic policies. For example, the tariff conditions not only precluded protection of infant industries but also had implications for domestic fiscal and commercial policies. Further, the combination of Japanese commercial ignorance and extraterritoriality made the shifting of any of the trade controlled by westerners into Japanese hands difficult, thus limiting the power of the authorities to influence the level or structure of trade by direct controls.

In the face of these issues, opinions polarised. The Foreign Ministry, nervous of the power of foreigners, took the view that the prospects for an active trade policy were poor and advocated a passive, *laissez-faire* approach.[22] Others, notably in the Ministry of Finance, wanted active, interventionist and eventually protective policies. Further, since all groups recognised that the treaties could not be changed in the short term, differences on external policy had implications for the options of internal policy. If the Japanese economy could not be protected by external tariffs, it had to be protected by internal assistance and subsidy, and if tariffs could not be used to raise income, then subsidies for one sector had to be paid for by the taxation of another. These issues led eventually to a crucial debate on the nature of the private sector and the limits of government activity. Thus the external imposition of treaties on Japan in the 1850s not only influenced the balance and commodity structure of trade in the early Meiji period but also set the agenda for discussions about domestic institutions and policy.

22. Except as noted, this section relies on MITI, vol. 5: *Foreign trade*, which deals in great detail (including long documentary quotes) with early Meiji trade policy.

Meiji trade policy evolved and was implemented in three phases. In the first, 1867–75, the government intervened directly in the establishment of enterprises and the transfer of technology necessary for import substitution and export development. This was the policy of *shokusan kogyo* which, in using taxes to promote trade-oriented enterprises, was in direct succession to the eighteenth- and nineteenth-century *han* policies.[23] The government also established new companies to handle trade and foreign exchange. The main objectives of these were to replace the *kabu nakama* and the old *han* monopolies by controlling foreign exchange and the supply and pricing of export goods for sale to foreign merchants. The foreign merchants strongly opposed both the companies and the newly-developed chambers of commerce. They complained that the restrictive monopolies of the Tokugawa regime had been replaced by organisations that were superficially private but actually 'a gigantic monopoly in the hands of the Japanese government'.[24]

These early companies were not successful, partly because they had insufficient financial resources to manage supply effectively, especially under conditions of falling prices, but also because they implied acceptance of the dominant role of the foreign merchant. In 1875–76 the government embarked on a new approach to the export sector. Pioneered by Okubo Toshimichi and Okuma Shigenobu, it recognised the need to enhance the role of a more genuinely independent private sector.[25] Private companies were encouraged to sell directly in foreign markets and to investigate the opportunities for export diversification. In this new scenario, government was to provide fiscal and monetary stability, a supportive banking system, physical infrastructure, assistance in seeking and disseminating information, participation in inter-

23. Nakamura, *The economy of the Meiji–Taisho period*, p. 10, Morikawa Hidemasa *et al.* (eds), *Kindai Nihon no keieishi no kiso chishiki* (Basic knowledge of the history of modern Japanese management), Tokyo: Yuhikaku, 1974, pp. 22–3.

24. See esp. Foreign Office: 'A Report by Mr Mounsey on Rice and the Rice Trade of Japan', April 12, 1878, *BPPJ*, vol. 6, pp. 189–201, and the Consular *Commercial Report* for 1872. In the *Report*, the author notes that the treaty provisions designed to deliver the Japanese merchants from 'subjection and servile dependence' are 'as a matter of fact, a dead letter'. Much information on the transition and the early Meiji companies is contained in Honjo Eijiro (ed.), *Meiji Ishin keizaishi kenkyu* (Research into the economic history of the Meiji Restoration), Tokyo: Yamamoto Sansei, 1931.

25. Okubo Toshimichi (1830–78) served as Minister of Finance in 1871, moving to the Ministry of Home Affairs in 1873.

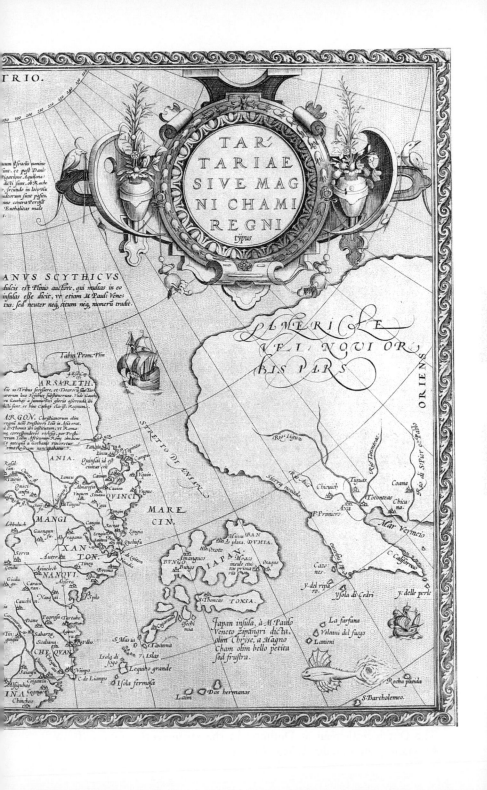

The Dutch settlement at Deshima in the seventeenth century (from Montanus, *Ambassades Mémorables*, 1680).

dans l'Isle de Disma .
ACKI op 't Eylandt.

AQUE on the Iland

1. Lieu où l'on charge et decharge
les marchandises .
2. Maison des Visiteurs Iaponois .
3. Maison de l'Intendant .
4. Sommeleric .
5. Lieu où les marchandises sont
exposées en vente .

阿
蘭
陀

The Japanese view of the Dutch (from Nishikawa Joken, *Yonjunikoku jinbutsu zusetsu*, 1720).

A tribute-bearing junk visiting Japan from the Ryukyu Islands, from a contemporary French print, probably nineteenth-century. It shows the massive scale of these junks, which were clearly engaged in intra-Asian trading under the guise of tribute-bearing.

The stranglehold of foreign merchants in the *kaikoku* period. This Yokohama print by an unidentified artist was published around 1860. It shows a Japanese merchant captured in a stranglehold by American, Dutch and Chinese merchants.

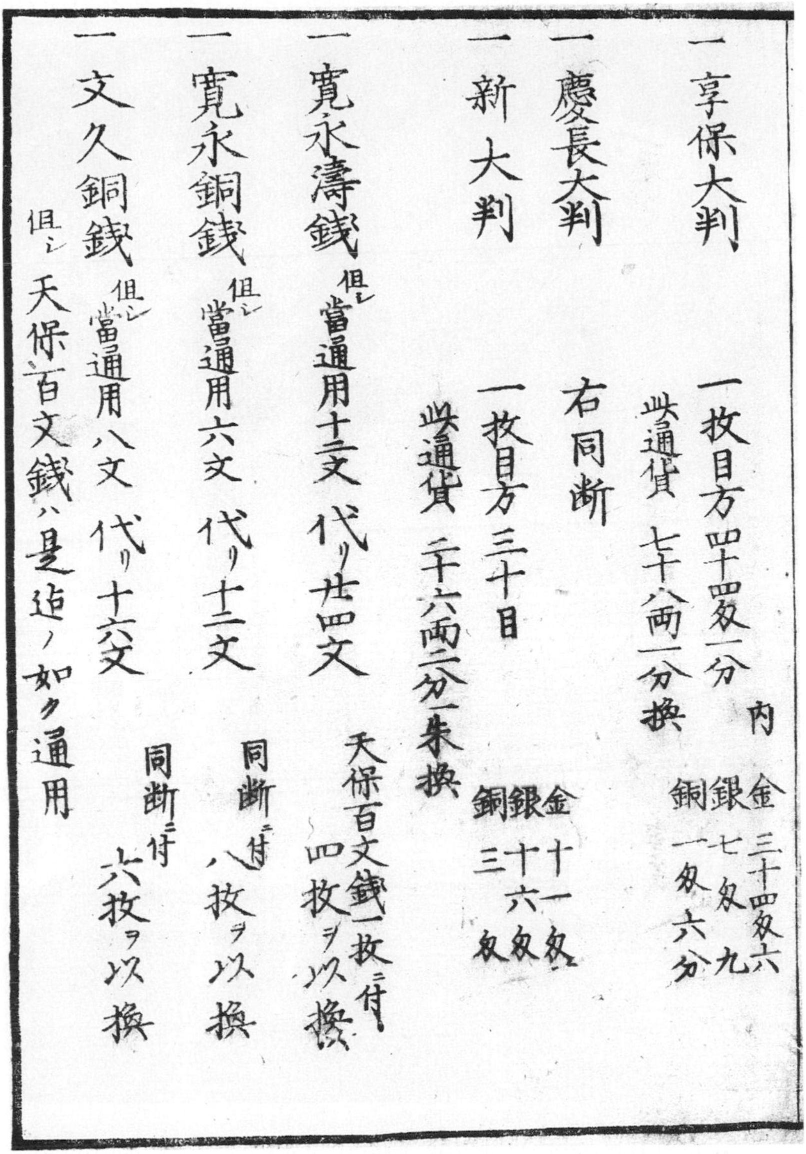

一　享保大判
　一枚目方四十四匁一分
　此通貨　七十八両一分換
　　内　金三十四匁六
　　　　銀七匁九
　　　　銅一匁六分

一　慶長大判
　右同断
　一枚目方三十目
　此通貨　二十六両二分一朱換
　　　　金十一匁
　　　　銀
　　　　銅三十六匁

一　新大判

一　寛永濤錢
　但シ當通用十二文　代リ廿四文
　天保百文錢一枚ニ付
　四枚ヲ以換

一　寛永銅錢
　但シ當通用六文　代リ十二文
　同断ニ付
　八枚ヲ以換

一　文久銅錢
　但シ當通用八文　代リ十六文
　同断ニ付
　六枚ヲ以換

但シ天保百文錢ハ是迄ノ如ク通用

A late Tokugawa currency manual. A page from the *Kahi torishirasho* (Currency investigation book), published by the Daijokan (State Council) in 1867. The book reports the precise bullion content of contemporary domestic and foreign monies, illustrating both the complexity of the monetary situation and the growing determination of officialdom to get to grips with it.

The Mikado (Emperor) visits the Yokosuka arsenal in the late 1860s. A contemporary French print published in the journal *L'Illustration*. The Mikado is being given a demonstration of iron casting by the French technicians as part of a general tour of the Yokosuka facility.

The bombardment of Kagoshima by the British fleet, 1863, from a contemporary French print. The key to the numbers gives details of individual ships and events.

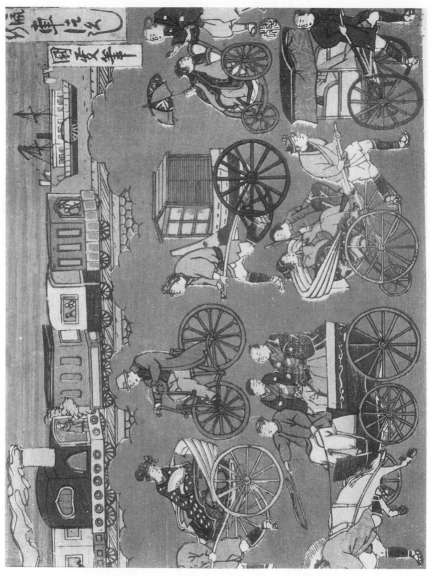

The Meiji transport revolution (the top half of a print by Kunimasa, published in 1871). The artist has shown jinrikshas, carriages and steamboats and even a train and steam-engine. The latter must have been drawn from eyewitness reports, since no railway ran in Japan till 1872.

national fairs and exhibitions, and diplomatic support. Although Okubo and Okuma acted jointly in this initiative, there was a significant difference of emphasis between them. While Okuma wanted companies to react to price signals and careful calculation, Okubo urged a policy that would be less concerned with short-term factors and concentrate on the main strategic thrust of an export-based development.[26] Of course, none of this was easy to implement, partly because the cultural and psychological preconditions for aggressive capitalism were still lacking. Okuma and Matsukata both complained endlessly of the passive and dependent character of the Japanese, and Matsukata's policies were designed to provide the incentives that would change this. A summary of these early Meiji policies and institutions is shown in Table 4.6.

In 1880 a treasury official, Maeda Masana, presented Okuma with a new set of proposals for export expansion. While Maeda focused first on the need to revise the treaties and eliminate the unfair advantages of foreign merchants in Japan, he also recognised that export growth depended on the further development of the productive sector and that the problems of making direct exports profitable had not yet been solved. Maeda's strategy involved a 'tripod' of institutional developments. These consisted of establishing a specialised foreign exchange bank to promote export expansion; direct support through fiscal policy and through this bank for individuals and groups of export producers; and intensified direct marketing efforts using specialised trading companies, which were also to be assured of banking support and were expected to relate directly to producers.[27]

Stated in more general terms, what Maeda saw was that success in export promotion called for an efficient private productive sector, supported both by strong financial institutions and by companies specialised in the skills necessary to develop foreign markets and capable of acting as an intelligence service to domestic producers cut off by distance, language and culture from both potential markets and technological developments in the outside world. Significantly Maeda insisted that in order to accumulate and sustain their financial strength, these trading companies should be restricted in number to seven and should not compete on market principles. Thus in place of reliance on direct action to develop industry and promote exports, the

26. MITI, vol. 5, *Foreign trade*, p. 152.
27. *Ibid.*, pp. 187ff.

Table 4.6. EARLY MEIJI TRADE INSTITUTIONS AND POLICIES

	Institutions	*Functions*
1867–76	Commerce Bureau (Shohoshi)	Control foreign trade by traditional techniques
1869	Succeeded by Trade Bureau (Tsushoshi)	1. Promote trade 2. Balance exports and imports 3. Control imports made by government departments
1873	Home Office (Naimusho)	1. General economic responsibilities
1876	Trade Encouragement Bureau of Home Office (Kanshokyoku)	1. Analyse and develop trade policies 2. Study foreign markets 3. Devise regulatory frameworks for activity
1876	Establishment with government support of Mitsui Bussan and Mitsui Bank and private sector companies	1. Promote foreign trade 2. Develop China market 3. Begin the recovery of trade control from foreign hands
1870–78	Establishment of consulates in America, China, Europe and Russia	Support Japanese trade expansion with intelligence and diplomatic techniques
1881	Ministry of Agriculture and Commerce (Noshomusho)	1. Take responsibility for all economic affairs 2. Manage the transfer of state enterprises to private sector 3. Control and encourage Japanese foreign trade to enable it to match western standards
1890	Chambers of commerce (*shogyo kaigisho*)	1. Develop systems and rules for commercial development 2. Disseminate international commercial intelligence

government was now to implement its objectives by fostering private output and by creating infrastructural backing in the form of a tightly controlled private financial sector and a government-supported oligopoly of trading houses. Although Maeda's proposal was a culmination of several years of official thinking about trade, and Matsukata's deflation had limited the direct financial role that government could play in the 1880s, it was nonetheless prophetic, and a blueprint with an influence on Japanese foreign trade policy that is still visible more than a century later.

Maeda's proposal coincided almost exactly with the Matsukata reconstruction of the Japanese financial system and the deflation that followed it. Thus government policy towards the private sector was immediately confronted with a serious dilemma, because opinion in Japan was hardening in favour of industrial protection. In their move towards protection, the Japanese had been influenced by a world-wide trend in favour of tariffs and many became convinced of the general rule that an economy's need for protection depended directly on the technological gap between itself and Britain.[28] Yet as long as the Ansei treaties remained in force, tariff increases were inadmissible and Japanese protection could *only* take the form of internal support and subsidy. Since the discriminatory character of such subsidies inevitably kept the government and individual firms at close quarters, the subsidies would tend to postpone the time when the private sector could develop a genuine independence and cease to look to the government as the source of universal support and guidance. Only an external tariff could give protection that was non-discriminatory. Hence trade policies down to the 1890s were regarded as provisional, pending revision of the treaties and the re-establishment of tariff autonomy.

Despite the internal and external obstacles to trade development, by 1890 much had been accomplished both by the government and the private sector. The government attacked the problems of ignorance both by a thoroughgoing educational reform and by hiring foreign specialists to work in new and modernising industries, in education

---

28. The average tariff rate in 1867–98 was 3% to 3.8%. See Takahashi, *Formation*, vol. 2, p. 173; MITI, vol. 5, *Foreign trade*, p. 212; Umezu Kazuro, *Nihon no boeki shiso* (Japanese foreign trade thinking), Kyoto: Minerva Shobo, 1963, pp. 23, 48, 173ff., and comments by Matsukata and Inouye in Alfred Stead (ed.), *Japan by the Japanese: A Survey by the Highest Authorities*, London: William Heinemann, 1904, pp. 307, 354.

and in government departments. It also embarked on a programme of high-level foreign visits. These had started in the Tokugawa period, with expeditions to America in 1860 and to Europe via the Suez Canal in 1862. On Meiji tours, Okubo had been impressed by the example of Prussia as a late industrialiser; Shibusawa Eiichi was lectured by the King of the Belgians on the economic significance of the iron and steel industries; and Matsukata astonished the French with his sophisticated understanding of financial policy.[29] These visits were paralleled by a flow of more specialised technical delegations, all following the injunction in the Emperor's Charter Oath to 'seek wisdom throughout the world'.

We have already seen the government's direct involvement in the tea, silk and other export sectors. Indirectly it also supported exports by investing in transportation and in physical and services infrastructure. In the railway industry it not only directed and supported development through a mixture of public and subsidised private investment, but insisted on preferential rates for exports. Shipping was another pivotal export-oriented policy. After experiments with various combinations of private and public-sector market structures, the government settled on a policy of official backing for one key private company — the Nippon Yusen Kaisha (NYK), which had been established in 1885: so close were the links between them that not only did the NYK receive direct subsidies and guaranteed rates of return on capital, but Matsukata personally controlled its staffing and expenses. The company's fundamental corporate objective was summed up in a statement made in 1893: 'The basic strategy of managing [the NYK] is to contribute to the development of [Japan's] foreign trade.'[30] At a more humdrum level the government also supported exports by developing foreign market intelligence systems, distributing samples and making arrangements for information about Japan and Japanese goods to be seen at the great international exhibitions of the age.

Japan's use of exhibitions was remarkable, given the fundamental

---

29. The 1860 trip was accompanied by Fukuzawa Yukichi as translator. Kiyooka, *The Autobiography of Fukuzawa Yukichi*, ch. 6; Paske-Smith, *Western Barbarians*, p. 188; Reischauer, *Samurai and Silk*, 1987, pp. 75–6; Obata, *An Interpretation of the Life of Shibusawa*, pp. 48, 69.

30. `*Nihon yusen kabushiki kaisha nanajunenshi* (The seventy-year history of the NYK), Tokyo, 1956, p. 35.

European philosophy of western promoters of these events. This philosophy was most obvious in the original Great Exhibition at the Crystal Palace in London in 1851, an event designed to sum up the state of the world and all its forms of physical production in the three dimensions of time, geography and the world's hierarchy of civilisation and development. The message of the Great Exhibition was that the peak of world evolution had been attained by Britain in 1851. Continental Europe and America were a little behind, and the rest of the world was at a different level altogether, only developing at all because of the rising demand for raw materials and handicrafts from the advanced economies. Japan was almost the only large country that did not take part; China, India, the Dutch East Indies, parts of Africa, Persia and most other Middle Eastern countries were all represented, and the message of the Exhibition to them was that free trade, parliamentary monarchy and the Anglican Church were the keys to success. Moreover, they were encouraged to remain loyal to their allotted places in the world hierarchy. That is to say, they should respond to demand through trade and *not* try to sidestep this by, for example, moving from handicraft to machine manufacture.[31]

Although such formulae were anathema to the Japanese, they nonetheless made avid use of the exhibitions both to learn about the outside world and to educate the world about Japan. Their representatives attended the Paris Exposition of 1867 and exhibited a major display at the Vienna Exposition of 1873. At the 1878 Paris Exposition, Matsukata found it necessary to counter almost total ignorance of Japan with a display of maps, charts and statistical

31. A general account of the Exhibition may be obtained from Asa Briggs, *Victorian Things*, *passim*, and the same author's *Victorian People*, London: Penguin Books, 1967, ch. 2. These comments about the role of the periphery and Asian economies are based on the introductory matter and the sections on India and Turkey in the Exhibition's special journal, *The Illustrated Exhibitor*, nos 1–30, June–December 1851. Exhibits from China included a piece of raw silk sent by Kung Yee of Shanghai (which won a prize medal — the second highest class of award) and a bedstead sent in by Rutherford Alcock, then still in the early Chinese phase of his career before the transfer to Japan. The journal noted that the Turkish exhibitors in particular should learn from comparison with superior western products that they could never compete with factory-made western textiles. As M. Blanqui, Member of the Institut de France, wrote, 'It is useful for [the Turks] as well as for ourselves to tell them that they would take a wrong course in neglecting their natural productions, for which they have a certain market, in the pursuit of a more than doubtful manufacturing course.' (No. 18, Oct. 4, 1851, pp. 329–30.)

table, and he contributed a foreword to the special Japanese catalogue prepared for the event. Official Japanese interest in these exhibitions continued up to the Columbus World Fair at Chicago in 1893.[32]

At the same time as promoting exports, the Japanese government also began an active process of import substitution. To improve the trade balance without disturbing national priorities, consumer goods clearly had to be the main objective of this policy. Most important of all was the textile market. On one famous occasion Matsukata addressed a meeting of Osaka manufacturers and, holding up a piece of imported cotton, he bluntly told his audience that the textile trade deficit was endangering the economic stability of Japan, and promised technical support for the industry if it moved promptly to eliminate it. By the late 1880s these efforts were beginning to show results. Some direct export sales had been achieved in silk, tea, rice and coal. Mitsui and other trading houses were becoming active both on government and private account. The foreign exchange bank envisaged by Maeda — The Yokohama Specie Bank — was established in 1880 and substantial progress was made in import substitution in textiles, matches and cement.

From the foreign point of view, however, other factors were also influencing the level of imports into Japan. For example, by strict application of the treaty provisions, the Japanese stopped foreigners gaining access to any parts of Japan outside the treaty ports, thereby limiting their ability to expand their knowledge of the Japanese market and participate directly in it. Foreigners also complained of bureaucratic non-trade barriers in the form of delays and the imposition of impossibly high technical standards for imports.[33]

Most serious of all, however, was the failure of foreign manufacturers to invest in linguistic and intelligence skills and to make the other commitments necessary for their success in Japan. The French provide a good illustration of this problem. France had invested much diplomatic and military effort in its Asian expansion and at the time

32. *Le Japon à l'Exposition Universelle de 1878*, Paris: Commission Impériale du Japon, 1878. A copy of this may be found in the library of the Economics Dept. in the University of Tokyo.

33. Pharmaceutical imports faced a combination of import substitution, official procrastination and the use of unrealistic technical standards by the Japanese authorities in deciding the acceptability of imports. See Foreign Office, '*Commercial Report, 1883*', *BPPJ*, vol. 7, pp. 178–9.

of the Meiji Restoration, its officials, especially the minister Léon Roches, planned to establish a series of unique commercial and military links that would secure France a dominant foreign role in Japan. These hopes were based partly on important common interests in the silk trade, partly on plans to sell ships and arms to the Japanese, and partly on ambitions to 'make Japan for France what China is for the British — that is to say, a French market'.[34] But in spite of these plans and hopes a perceptive critic of Meiji-period French policy complained in the early 1900s that although some promising initiatives had been undertaken, French businessmen refused to take Japan seriously. The French middle classes, he noted, are so attached to their own country and to the 'happiness of family life' (*'douceur de la vie familiale'*) that they will not commit themselves to a lifetime in such an unfamiliar and remote land as Japan — 'which is why we are beaten there' (*'pourquoi nous sommes battus'*).[35]

British diplomatic officials also became deeply unhappy as the Meiji period advanced, viewing the failures of their compatriot businessmen with foreboding. In the 1880s consular officials complained scathingly that complacent British firms had made no effort to understand the market or to send technical experts; that they could not find a single businessman with even basic skill in speaking Japanese; and that catalogues in English with no prices were 'so much waste paper'. By the turn of the 1890s they observed and described in vivid detail the first signs that Japanese industry was entering the machine age, threatening not only to displace imports into Japan but even — incredible as it seemed at the time — to emerge as a potential threat to British-manufactured exports in Asia.[36]

---

34. These comments are partly based on the important unpublished Ph.D. thesis of Dr Richard Sims, 'French Policy towards Japan, 1854–1894', University of London, 1968, esp. pp. 77ff. The optimism of France over Japan on the eve of the Restoration (Spring 1867) is vigorously reflected in Comte de Beauvoir, *Pékin, Yeddo, San Francisco. Voyage autour du Monde*, vol. 3, Paris: Plon, 1872. In this, the author describes the Japanese as the 'French of the East'. Informed observations of a contemporary British diplomat on Roche's ambitious plans to secure monopoly positions for French activities in Japan are in Lord Redesdale, *Memories* (2 vols), London: Hutchinson, n.d., vol. 1, ch. 18.

35. Leo Byram, *Petit Jap Deviendra Grand! L'Expansion japonaise en Extrême-Orient*, Paris: Berger-Levrault, 1908, p. 317.

36. See, for example, Foreign Office, 'Report on the Import Trade of Great Britain with Japan (1886)', *BPPJ*, vol. 7, pp. 525–36; 'Foreign Trade of Japan (1896)', *BPPJ*, vol. 10, p. 255.

Part II
TRADE AND THE TRANSITION
TO A MODERN ECONOMY

5

GROWTH AND TRANSFORMATION IN JAPAN'S TRADE AND PAYMENTS, 1890–1937

The long view

In the traditional Japanese economy, foreign trade was largely a marginal activity. Through it, Japan acquired luxury goods, sugar, medicines and a small number of manufactures, and exported in return copper, bullion and a range of exportable goods produced by handicraft technologies. Geographically, Japan's direct and indirect trade shifted from a worldwide phase in the sixteenth and early seventeenth centuries, to one largely restricted to regional Asian partners by the late eighteenth century.

The arrival of westerners after 1853 led to rapid trade expansion. Their demand for silk and tea was strong and was increasingly matched by Japanese requirements for cotton goods, arms, ships and capital equipment. These trends continued under conditions of enforced free trade in the early Meiji period, when Japan began to exhibit a tendency towards chronic trade deficit and balance of payments problems.

A turning-point in this long-run development was reached in 1890 when Japanese cotton yarn, now produced by factory methods, began to be exported. By the mid-1930s Japan had become the largest exporter of cotton piece goods in the world; yet even this success was insufficient to close the overall trade deficit.

In the 1950s trade entered another phase of expansion and change. In 1955 heavy industry displaced textiles and light industry as the largest exporting sector, and in the 1960s Japan at last began the transformation to a trade-surplus economy. The surplus grew almost exponentially during the 1970s and 1980s and was still increasing in the 1990s, by which time the traditional heavy industry sector had been replaced by automobiles, electronics and other technology-intensive industries as the main export earners. In addition, Japan had by this time become engaged in a complex division of labour through a combination of trade and direct investment.

The growth of the post-war trade surplus was accompanied by increasing outflows of all forms of capital. This process peaked in 1986–88 in the sense that capital exports substantially exceeded trade

115

Table 5.1. BALANCE OF PAYMENTS, SELECTED PHASES, 1890–1986
(annual averages, millions of yen 1890–1939; billions of US$ 1955–86)

	Exports	Imports	Merchandise balance	Current account balance	Long-term capital	Basic balance
1890–94	88	94	−6	−1	−1	−2
1895–1914	366	413	−47	−45	70	25
1915–19	1,692	1,425	267	618	−347	271
1920–31	2,118	2,513	−395	−190	−148	−338
1932–36	2,779	2,857	−78	116	−335	−219
1937–39	4,436	4,241	195	−323	−834	−1,157
1955	2	2	0	0.2	0	0.2
1968	13.5	10.5	3	1.5	−0.1	1.4
1986	206	113	93	86	−131	−45

Source: LTES, *Foreign trade*, pp. 214–17; MITI, *Tsusho hakusho* (Trade white paper), Tokyo: MITI, various years.

surpluses. Capital exports in the form of purchases of financial assets and property, as well as of direct industrial investment, meant that Japan's world economic status came to be reflected not only in merchandise trade but also in prominent involvement in almost every aspect of the world economy. Thus by the 1980s it found itself thrust into a position of world financial and industrial leadership, a role analogous to that of Britain before 1914 and of the United States after the Second World War.

This chapter examines the outline of this process through to 1937 in terms of both the balance of payments and the growth and structure of commodity trade. The major issues suggested by the data and the role played by economic policy in these outcomes will be examined in subsequent chapters.

The balance of payments

Data of the main components of the balance of payments are shown in Table 5.1. In this and the other tables, the turning points and periodisation have been chosen as far as possible to illustrate both clear movements in the data themselves and major events and changes in policy. Thus in Table 5.1 we see a series of turning points: 1894–95 (coinciding with the Sino-Japanese war of those years, which opened Asian markets to Japanese manufactures); 1915–19 (the First World

Table 5.2. EXPORTS AS % OF IMPORTS,
1890–1986

1890–94	94
1895–1914	89
1915–19	119
1920–31	84
1932–36	97
1937–39	105
1940–44	113
1955	100
1968	129
1986	182

Source: as Table 5.1.

War boom in Japan); and 1931 (the year in which Japan went off the gold standard into a fully independent, managed currency system). Finally, 1937, when the later Sino-Japanese war began, also marked for Japan the beginning of the Second World War, a period when the economy and foreign trade assumed abnormal characteristics.

The merchandise balance and the current account. The most important column in Table 5.1 is that for the merchandise trade balance. From the pre-1937 data it is clear that, excluding the First World War, the merchandise imbalance rose from a modest negative figure in the early 1890s to a peak in the 1920s. The worst years are 1923 and 1924, when a deficit of ¥851 million was recorded. In the 1930s, however, the trend improved: during the five years 1932–36 the imbalance fell by four-fifths, and in 1937–39 the balance becomes positive.

To place these figures in a long-term perspective it is necessary to look at the post-war period. These data are also shown in Table 5.1 for three selected years: 1955 (when heavy industry first achieved dominance in the export structure), 1969 (the peak of post-war high-speed growth), and 1986 (when capital outflows exceeded the trade surplus and Japan reverted to a policy of growth through the expansion of internal demand).

Price changes and the use of yen and dollars make direct comparison of the pre- and post-war years difficult. Thus in Table 5.2 exports are expressed as a percentage of imports for the same periods and years. This Table shows that the pattern suggested by the basic statistical series is correct but somewhat modified in scale when expressed in these terms. The years before the First World War and the 1920s are still shown as periods of deterioration and the improvement in the 1930s is clearly indicated. The effect of the world inflation in the 1970s is to heighten excessively the contrast between the 1968 and 1986 surpluses. The progress towards trade surplus suggested by the post-war data is, in fact, fairly steady. It is of course not surprising that the pre-war pattern of visible trade improvement was powerfully disrupted by war and recovery, because the war destroyed not only Japan's physical industrial base but also its pre-war regional pattern of export markets and import sources.

The data in the columns to the right of the merchandise balance in Table 5.1 represent that balance adjusted for services such as shipping and insurance, and then for transfers of government funds. The latter were particulary important in the 1890s because they included the Chinese war indemnity, amounting to ¥358 million, which was paid in gold and sterling between 1895 and 1898 and was therefore a sum equal to the entire cumulative merchandise deficit between 1895 and 1902.

Long-term capital and the basic balance. Despite the Chinese windfall, Japan could not finance its international payments without capital flows. In the long and difficult period between 1895 and 1914, long-run net inflows were significant, totalling over ¥100 million in each of the years 1906, 1909 and 1910. This inflow represented a combination of official loans and private direct investment (discussed in Chapter 6). The long-term outflow during the First World War represented the investment of the current account surplus abroad. There were then substantial long-term outflows in the 1920s and 1930s, representing Japan's investment in her colonial empire.

The final column in Table 5.2, the basic balance, combines the current account with long-term capital flows. The rationale for looking at this combination is that it is an indicator of balance of payments health in the sense that while large trade imbalances can persist over long periods, a large negative basic balance will at some point require major policy action to correct it. No country can remain financially viable on indefinite short-term capital flows. These data show that because of the capital inflows and the exceptional circumstances of the First World War, the basic balance is positive from 1890 to 1919 while that from 1919 to 1937 is negative. This implies that Japan's inter-war combination of capital outflows and serious

Table 5.3. LONG-TERM TRENDS IN THE SHARE OF EXPORTS PLUS
IMPORTS IN NATIONAL PRODUCT, JAPAN, UNITED STATES AND
DENMARK, VARIOUS YEARS 1834–1936 (%)

	Japanese trade share		U.S. trade share		Denmark trade share
1887–96	9.2	1834–43	12.9	1870–79	45.6
1897–1906	16.8	1904–13	11.0	1910–14	61.6
1907–16	23.1	1919–28	10.8	1921–29	57.3
1917–26	27.0				
1927–36	33.7				

Source: Ippei Yamazawa, *Economic Development and International Trade: The Japanese Model*, Hawaii: East-West Center, 1990, p. 4; Kuznets, *Modern Economic Growth*, p. 312.

merchandise trade imbalance required active international financial management to acquire the short-term capital inflows necessary for national solvency. After the Second World War, net long-term capital outflows did not re-emerge till the 1980s, but by 1986 a new pattern had become established in which Japan was again a substantial long-term capital exporter, although this time the role was supported by the strength of the merchandise balance.

Trade and the economy

An important measure of the overall relationship between trade and the economy is the changing share of imports and exports in national income. These trends and a comparison with other economies are estimated in Table 5.3. This reveals that as a percentage of gross national product (GNP) trade approximately quadrupled over seventy years. Nonetheless, even the share reached in the 1930s was not exceptional by international standards. It was higher than the 11% recorded in 1904–28 by the United States, which was a large, richly-endowed and naturally self-sufficient economy. Compared to the 40% to 60% range found in the small, geographically central, trade-oriented economy of Denmark, the Japanese figures are modest, and they appear even more so if compared with the post-1945 data for the Asian Newly Industrialising Countries (NICs), where ratios in excess of 100% are found.

What is especially remarkable about Japan's trade is the long-term

Table 5.4. REAL GROWTH OF OUTPUT AND EXPORT VOLUME,
JAPAN AND THE WORLD, 1870s–1937
(% per annum)

	1872–1913	*1913–29*	*1929–37*	*1872–1937*
World GDP	2.7	2.2	0.9	2.3
Japan GDP	2.5	3.7	4.8	3.0
	1872–1912	*1912–30*	*1930–37*	*1878–1937*
World export volume	3.3	0.8	−0.6	2.1
Japan export volume	7.2	4.3	9.3	6.6
	1912–23	*1923–30*		
World export volume	−1.5	4.5		
Japan export volume	4.9	3.4		

Source: Kanemori Hisao, *Nihon no boeki* (Japanese foreign trade), Tokyo: Shiseido, 1965, p. 273;
Angus Maddison, *Phases of Capitalist Development*, Appendix A; Solomos Solomou, *Phases of
Growth, 1850–1973: Kondratieff Waves and Kuznets Cycles*, Cambridge University Press, 1990,
p. 148.

rate of growth of exports and imports. Table 5.4 details Japanese and
world rates of growth for total output and foreign trade from the
1870s to the 1930s. Long-term estimates of this kind are obviously
subject to margins of error and the periods for estimating output and
trade shown here do not match precisely. Nonetheless, the underlying
patterns are clear. Consider the very long run. The world data show
that trade volume grew slightly more slowly than output — or, allowing for some error, at about the same pace. However, the Japanese
long-run data show that while output grew somewhat faster than the
world rate, export growth was three times faster. The faster growth
of Japanese domestic output would not be surprising, since within the
group of countries defined here as 'the world', Japan was a newcomer
and thus might be expected to have had a higher growth-rate than
the more mature economies. However, when the data are broken up

Table 5.5. SHARES OF WORLD EXPORTS OF MANUFACTURES, 1899–1937

	1899	*1913*	*1929*	*1937*
U.S.A.	11.7	13	20.4	19.2
Great Britain	33.2	30.2	22.4	20.9
Germany	22.4	26.6	20.5	21.8
Japan	1.5	2.3	3.9	6.9

Source: Giovanni Dosi, Keith Pavitt and Luc Soete, *The Economics of Technical Change and International Trade*, New York: Harvester, 1990, p. 65.
Note: For 1899 and 1913, 'world' data exclude the Netherlands.

into three time periods, it becomes clear that Japan's growth-rate was accelerating between 1872 and 1937 and achieving its highest growth and greatest superiority over the world rate in the final eight years of that period, during the world depression. What the data reflect is a pattern of development in which Japan achieved a high growth of output based on domestic demand. This growth generated rapid increases in demand for imports, initially for consumer and capital goods and later for capital goods, raw materials and food. To sustain domestic growth, therefore, a high rate of growth in exports was required to pay for imports. This virtuous circle was only achievable to the extent that there was a strong bias in domestic growth towards potentially exportable goods such as textiles, and that this potential was realised in actual competitiveness by trade and exchange rate policies as well as long-run industrial performance. If the virtuous circle was not achieved, imports had to be covered by capital inflows or bullion outflows.

In spite of Japan's relatively superior export growth, its share of world trade in manufactures was still relatively low, even at the end of the 1930s when it had become so important in some branches of trade.

Table 5.5 demonstrates the reversal of the relative importance of Britain and the United States, the consistently dominant position of German industry, and for Japan a sharp improvement albeit only to a still modest trading status. While in terms of all goods, the Japanese share was less than half that shown here for manufactures alone. What this status implied was that in most industries, Japan was a price-taker that had to rely on competitive performance to make its way in world markets. However, because Japan's trade was so concentrated in textiles, its role in the silk and cotton trades was highly significant for competitor economies; hence the Japanese expansion in these sectors required competitors to make a vigorous response or major internal adjustment.

The growth and structure of commodity trade

Productivity and the terms of trade. Further insight into the mechanisms of Japanese trade and growth are provided by two other series of data: the long-run growth-rate of industrial productivity and the terms of trade (here, the net barter terms of trade is defined as the export price index divided by the import price index). Productivity data are inevitably problematic, but one estimate for Japan, the United States and Britain suggests rates for the period 1899–1937 of 3.8%, 1.8% and 1.6% respectively. These data confirm that productivity growth, reflecting technology transfer, learning and investment, was an underlying factor in export expansion and competitiveness.[1]

The interaction between trends of industrial output, exports and the terms of trade is shown in Fig. 5.1, which illustrates two points: first, the persistent long-run upward trends of output and exports over the whole seventy-year period, despite widely differing stages of Japanese development and world trade conditions, and, secondly, the exceptional shift in the terms of trade that took place in the 1930s. If these data are grouped into three main periods, the *average* values of the terms of trade are as follows:

Meiji phase	1880–1912	131
Taisho-Showa phase A	1913–29	150
Showa phase B	1930–37	103

This measure of the terms of trade is in fact a close proxy for Japanese international price competitiveness, and the trends may be interpreted in the following way. Between the 1880s and 1908 the terms of trade fluctuated under various influences with no major improvement in price competitiveness for Japanese exports, which

---

1. Kanemori, *Japanese foreign trade*, p. 153.

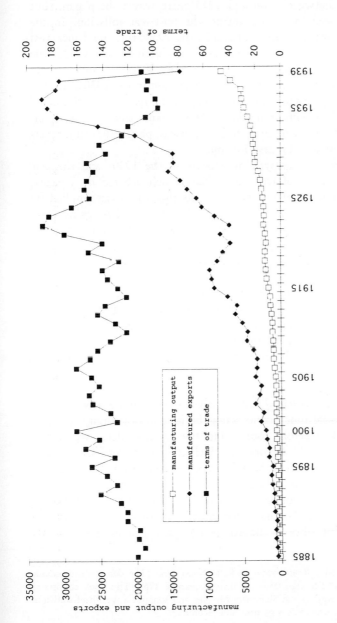

Fig. 5.1 MANUFACTURING OUTPUT, MANUFACTURED EXPORTS AND THE TERMS OF TRADE, 1885–1939

Source: Kazushi Ohkawa and Miyohei Shinohara (eds), *Patterns of Japanese Economic Development A Quantitative Appraisal*, New Haven: Yale University Press, 1979, appendix tables.
The series for manufactured output and exports are at constant 1934–36 prices. Terms of trade data take the same years as equal to 100.

at the time were largely primary products with internationally determined prices. Between 1908 and 1915 there was a sharp gain, but this was followed by a loss during the post-war inflation. In the 1920s competitiveness improved and in the 1930s this trend increased dramatically, reflecting both Japanese productivity gains and the impact of a yen devaluation of approximately 50%. Devaluation and price-cutting were essential to export expansion in the 1930s, because while Japan was growing, the world depression reduced or eliminated income growth in export markets. At the same time it made consumers more than ever sensitive to lower prices, particularly in markets with the lowest and highest incomes.

The extraordinary growth of exports in the 1930s and the role in this of the terms of trade have been much debated by Japanese economists, some of whom have argued that the losses implied by deterioration in the terms of trade offset the welfare gains from growth.[2] However, the performance of Japanese exports in the 1930s clearly foreshadowed the post-war era of high speed growth, and by keeping the momentum of growth brisk, the economy made gains other than those reflected in immediate levels of consumer income. The difference between pre- and post-war export growth was that while in both periods Japanese gains reflected relative gains in productivity and powerful supply-side responsiveness, in the post-war period Japanese exports expanded on a tide of world income expansion and trade liberalisation and did not need to rely on price-cutting and currency devaluation.

The commodity composition of trade. Analysis of the commodity structure of trade can reveal much concerning the function of foreign trade in an economy, but before considering the Japanese data, we should briefly recapitulate the factors on which the commodity structure of an economy's foreign trade may be expected to depend. First, there is its endowment of land and other natural resources and, secondly, the relative availability of unskilled and skilled labour and capital and the efficiency of the markets that price and allocate these. Thirdly, arising out of this availability is the competitive strength of the economy

---

2. Kojima Kiyoshi, *Ronso keizai seicho to Nihon boeki* (The debate on economic growth and Japanese foreign trade), Tokyo: Kobundo, 1960. This book consists of a debate between Kojima and Shinohara Miyohei and contains a wealth of statistical material on trade, economic structure and incomes.

within a hierarchy of industries, at the bottom of which are industries using unskilled labour relatively intensively and with low requirements for skills and capital, while at the top are industries with the opposite resource requirements. (It is not a large step to redefine this hierarchy as a scale in which comparative advantage is created by the differing degrees of technological difficulty required for each industry, and by differing national abilities to meet such requirements. Fourthly, we have the influence of the size and character of the domestic market, as determined by the consumption behaviour of private households, the demands of the public sector, the structure of economic institutions and the nature of government intervention in the economy, e.g. through taxation and tariff policy. Finally, there is the role in the economy of direct foreign investment, which may be expected to influence both imports and exports.[3]

Of these factors, the second and third have been the subject of much debate, relating on the one hand to the criteria for defining resource patterns and positioning industries in the hierarchy, and on the other to the statistical evidence for the different kinds of comparative advantage these factors generate in the real world. These inquiries often produce confusing results, with evidence of countries in the early stages of development apparently showing competitive advantage in high-level industries and of advanced economies still strong in the 'lower-level' ones. Nonetheless, the case for a hierarchy of industries and a corresponding pattern of natural, comparative trading advantage is broadly convincing. Exceptions can often be explained by special factors such as the linkages between manufacturing and natural resources, transport costs and the impact of government policies.

One reason for apparent anomalies — and this is particularly important for understanding Japanese trade — is the problem of defining 'an industry'. This is because many 'industries' are best thought of as agglomerations of activity producing a variety of products which, from the consumer's point of view, might appear to be in common families but are actually very different in manufacturing method and resource requirements. Textiles and clothing exemplify this *par*

---

3. Valuable recent discussions of these issues that focus on the relationship between theory and experience include Hans Linnemann (ed.), *Export-Oriented Industrialization in Developing Countries*, Singapore University Press, 1987, and Dosi, *The Economics of Technical Change and International Trade*.

excellence. Here is an industry grouping that has within it an immense range of branches and sub-branches, ranging from the labour-intensive, technologically standardised cotton manufactures produced by economies at the lowest level of development to the highly sophisticated products for which the key resources are the flair of Italian designers or the brains of Austrian textile machinery makers.[4] It is this range in elements that explains why the industry is still one in which apprentice industrialisers can compete at the lower end while the most advanced economies, such as Germany and Japan, retain significant domestic textile capacity while simultaneously conducting a large two-way foreign trade in textile products. Another industry that defies easy classification is machinery. This again is an activity where economies with widely differing resource endowments can find segments in which they are competitive. It is against this background that the Japanese data can best be considered.

Table 5.6 breaks imports down into seven broad categories and into the still broader categories of manufactures and non-manufactures. In the earliest period, imports of manufactures predominated. Textiles (consumer goods) were the largest category, followed by machinery of all kinds. This structure was then rapidly transformed. First, imports of raw cotton for the domestic textile industry increased and, combined with food imports, accounted for nearly 50% of imports by the 1930s, at the end of which imports of metal ores and fuels, though still proportionately small, began to grow very rapidly. Taking into account the pre-1890 data (see Chapters 3 and 4), it is clear that by the 1930s the functions of imports had become those of providing the food and raw materials for an economy that was relatively poorly endowed to produce them, as well as access to advanced capital equipment for an economy where, relative to the more advanced economies, skills and capital were scarce. This pattern re-appears in the post-

---

4. In a modern world bazaar such as Hong Kong, the purchaser of shirting material can choose between three basic types: cheap, simple cottons from low-income economies, superfine cottons from Switzerland and Austria and intermediate qualities from Japan, not as good as the former but close to it and costing two-thirds of the price in made-up form. The price-range for finished products is *ca.* HK$350–$1,300, which suggests that material costs alone must range from about $60 to $800. Apart from these choices, there are also super-expensive readymade shirts embodying fashion flair, notably from Italy, costing $10,000 in finished form. Thus there is an overall range of cottons and shirts that still enables economies at every level of development to remain competitive.

Table 5.6. STRUCTURE OF IMPORTS, 1890–1939
(% shares at constant prices)

	Textiles	Metals	Machinery	All manufactures	Crude foodstuffs	Textile raw materials	Metal ores	Coal petroleum	All non-manufactures
1890–1900	23	8	14	64	11	20	0	4	36
1901–14	8	9	18	54	13	27	0	3	46
1915–19	2	12	8	39	13	39	2	1	61
1920–31	4	12	11	47	15	29	1	3	53
1932–36	2	10	4	35	18	33	2	6	65
1937–39	2	21	7	46	14	22	4	7	54

Source: LTES, *Foreign trade*, pp. 188–91

Second World War period and persists till the late 1980s, when the combination of a decline in the raw material intensity of the economy, very favourable trends in the terms of trade and pressure from trade partners to open Japanese markets shifted the import structure back towards the early Meiji pattern. Once again a predominant share of imports was in manufactures, including consumer goods embodying skills unavailable domestically.

These statistics suggest that although the share of imports in the national product was quantitatively modest, their role was crucial. In the first phase, imports supplied the manufactures that stimulated Japanese consumer interest in machine-made consumer goods and enabled Japan to begin the process of technology transfer. By the 1930s the whole new structure of industrialisation rested on a foundation of imported raw materials and food.

The major function of exports in this scenario was to supply the foreign exchange to pay for imports and to provide opportunities for Japanese industry to achieve a scale of operation and a degree of modernisation otherwise unattainable. The fact that the structure of imports became so closely attuned to industrial expansion and that trade was unbalanced for almost the whole period up to 1937 clearly implies that export performance was a crucial factor in the capacity of the Japanese economy to industrialise. Thus although export growth was by world standards exceptionally high, Japan found itself up till the breakthrough to trade balance in the 1960s in a syndrome where growth and trade were highly interdependent, with progress vulnerable to unfavourable shocks. These included those created by fluctuations in other countries, or by domestic events such as major policy errors, political upheavals and even natural catastrophes such as the Kanto earthquake of 1923.

The export structure shown in Table 5.7 can now be considered. Two important changes in the broad categories can be seen here. First, there is the decline of primary products, which were extremely important in the 1860s and still accounted for 36% of all exports in the 1890s. By the end of the 1930s, however, their share had declined to 7%. Agricultural exports passed a significant downward turning-point around 1900, at which point Japan began to think seriously about its future as a food importer.

The converse of these figures are those for manufactures. By the 1930s these accounted for 90% of exports and, within this total, textiles, including silk and cotton goods, bulked large. By the 1920s

Table 5.7. STRUCTURE OF EXPORTS, 1890–1939
(% shares at constant prices)

	Textiles	Metals	Machinery	All manufactures	Agricultural products	All primary products
1890–1900	38	6	0	64	20	36
1901–14	47	5	1	80	8	20
1915–19	46	6	6	87	7	13
1920–31	57	5	3	91	5	9
1932–36	52	7	7	93	3	7
1937–39	43	7	13	93	3	7

Source: LTES, *Foreign trade*, pp. 184–7.

this group accounted for more than half of all export earnings. They remained important in the 1930s, although the relative significance of silk declined sharply while that of cotton goods rose. The same period saw significant diversification into new commodities, including machinery, electrical and other goods. These all reflected the diversified progress of industrialisation and a widening range of succesful technology transfer.

Looking ahead, the post-war data show the completion of this transformation. Heavy industry, where domestic growth accelerated in the 1930s, became the principal export sector by 1955. Steel, chemicals and shipbuilding then gave way in the 1970s and 1980s to automobiles, electrical and electronic goods and machinery, the last-named a sector in which great qualitative improvements took place as it moved from mechanically to electronically controlled manufacturing systems and embodied increasing levels of metallurgical sophistication.

In spite of all these changes, the most striking feature of the commodity composition of exports between the early Meiji period and the Second World War is how dependent it was on a very small group of commodities. Between them, tea, raw silk, silk fabric and cotton yarn accounted for 60% of exports in the first Meiji decade (1868–77). This same group accounted for a slightly higher proportion in the 1920s and only declined marginally in the 1930s as a result of the collapse of the American silk market. Thus the dependence of this group of industries on foreign trade was significant, but its ability to achieve modernisation was correspondingly enhanced.

Table 5.8 illustrates the significance of exports for individual Japanese industries. Here we find that for the manufacturing sector

Table 5.8. SHARE OF OUTPUT EXPORTED IN
MANUFACTURING INDUSTRIES, 1880–1935
(*five-year averages*)

	Textiles	Chemicals	Metals	Machinery	Other manufactures	All manufactures
1880	14.3	2.9	12.7	0.0	6.9	5.6
1900	28.2	12.7	45.3	2.3	32.8	15.5
1915	42.6	20.2	29.4	5.7	38.8	23.5
1920	35.2	15.3	14.3	5	26.3	19
1930	37.5	12.8	11.5	8	19.9	19.2
1935	35.8	13.6	12.4	10.3	25.5	19.4

Source: Kazushi Ohkawa and Hirohisa Kohama, *Lectures on Developing Economies Japan's Experience and its Relevance*, Tokyo University Press, 1989, p. 299.

as a whole the share of output exported rose from 5.6% in 1880 to a peak of 23.5% in 1920; thereafter it declined to 19.4% in 1935. The pattern of individual industries displays the rise of textiles and the subsequent relative improvement of steel and the heavier industries in the 1930s. The phenomenon of increasing specialisation within the cotton textiles sector as Japan's comparative advantage shifted from lower- to higher-quality goods is discussed later.

The way in which Japan's pattern of trade fitted into the evolving world wide pattern of specialisation is shown in Table 5.9. Here the relative competitive position of Japan and the key world economies in terms of their 'revealed comparative advantage' in different industries can be seen.

Finally, we can observe the famous phenomenon of Akamatsu's flying geese when relating changing patterns of imports, exports and domestic output. This pattern maintains that an industry moves through the following stages: first, domestic consumption is initiated on the basis of imports; secondly, domestic production begins using imported capital goods; thirdly, domestic production displaces imports and exports begin; and fourthly, the industry becomes a major exporter, depending on imported raw materials but using domestically developed (and adapted) capital goods.[5] Cotton textiles were the first

5. Akamatsu's analysis has been fully developed by Yamazawa and others of the Hitotsubashi school. This theory, combined with a theory of foreign investment, provides a rationale for the evolving trade and domestic structure of Japan and its Asian partners. A useful collection of Akamatsu's papers in Japanese, English and German is Kojima Kiyoshi (ed.), *Gakumon henro* (A pilgrimage of learning), Tokyo: Seikai Keizai Kenkyukai, 1975. See also ch. 13, below.

Table 5.9. INTERNATIONAL REVEALED COMPARATIVE
ADVANTAGE IN THREE INDUSTRIES, 1899–1937

	1899	*1913*	*1929*	*1937*
Textiles/clothing				
Britain	1.27	1.42	1.48	1.56
U.S.A.	0.21	0.23	0.27	0.21
France	1.05	1.25	1.38	1.14
Germany	0.74	0.55	0.58	0.49
Japan	1.67	1.79	2.45	2.7
Machinery/electrical equipment				
Britain	1.19	0.93	0.80	0.93
U.S.A.	2.32	1.85	1.72	1.65
France	0.39	0.34	0.46	0.43
Germany	0.86	1.28	1.31	1.29
Japan	0.00	0.04	0.15	0.34
Transport equipment				
Britain	1.68	1.19	0.92	0.96
U.S.A.	1.17	1.37	2.07	2.20
France	0.47	1.25	0.68	0.72
Germany	0.49	0.70	0.40	0.75
Japan	0.00	0.13	0.13	0.39

Source: Dosi, *The Economics of Technical Change and International Trade*, p. 70.
Note: Revealed comparative advantage is defined as a country's share in the world exports of
a particular manufactured commodity, divided by its share in world manufacturing exports. Thus
if Britain has 50% of the world textile trade and 25% of total manufactured trade, the index
of revealed advantage is 2.

industry in which this sequence was observed, and other manufacturing industries, including iron and steel, textiles and other kinds
of machinery, followed the same sequence as Japan's comparative
advantage evolved.

The regional composition of trade. The evolution of Japan's export and
import patterns was closely related to changing trade partners, and,
as we shall see in later chapters, the geography of Japanese foreign trade
was to pose important issues for policy. The main shifts in regional
trade patterns are summarised in Tables 5.10 and 5.11. In 1890 export
markets were divided fairly equally between Asia, North America
and Europe. Thereafter the Asian share of Japanese exports increased

Table 5.10. THE MAJOR DESTINATIONS OF JAPANESE EXPORTS,
SELECTED YEARS, 1890–1940
(% shares)

	Asia	North America	South America	Europe	Africa	Other
1890	31	38	0	28	0	3
1900	50	27	0	21	0	2
1914	53	30	0	14	0	3
1919	58	25	1	8	2	7
1929	53	36	1	6	2	3
1936	63	17	3	9	6	2
1940	79	11	3	3	2	2

Source: LTES, *Foreign trade*, pp. 206–9.

Table 5.11. THE MAJOR SOURCES OF JAPANESE IMPORTS,
SELECTED YEARS, 1890–1940
(% shares)

	Asia	North America	South America	Europe	Africa	Other
1890	38	9	0	52	0	1
1900	34	22	0	44	0	0
1914	57	15	0	24	1	3
1919	57	31	1	7	2	2
1929	51	26	1	15	2	5
1936	53	25	4	9	3	6
1940	58	28	5	4	2	3

Source: LTES, *Foreign trade*, pp. 210–13.

rapidly, reaching 79% by 1940. During the 1930s the declining
western share reflected not only the rise of Asia but also the emergence
of export markets in Africa and Latin America. The individual components of the increasingly dominant Asian trade are shown in
Tables 5.12 and 5.13. The Japanese data distinguish seven key areas,
five of which (Taiwan, the Kwantung Leased Territory, Manchuria,
China and Hong Kong) can be considered as 'Chinese', and this group
is aggregated accordingly. The Hong Kong data are a problem because
for many exports Hong Kong was an entrepôt and not a final destination, with many Hong Kong imports being re-exported to other parts
of Asia. Apart from the data for China and 'Chinese' destinations, two

Table 5.12. SHARES OF MAJOR ASIAN COUNTRIES IN JAPANESE EXPORTS TO ASIA, SELECTED YEARS, 1890–1940

	Korea	Taiwan	Kwantung Leased Territory	Manchuria	China	Hong Kong	Greater China	S.E. Asia	Other
1890	8				31	56	87	1	4
1900	10	8			30	38	76	2	12
1914	11	11	6		46	9	72	6	11
1919	15	7	12		36	5	60	9	16
1929	23	10	9		25	4	48	12	17
1936	29	11	15	7	7	3	43	13	15
1940	31	10	14	14	16	1	55	7	7

Source: LTES, *Foreign trade*, pp. 206–9.
Note: Blank spaces indicate no data available.

Table 5.13. SHARES OF MAJOR ASIAN COUNTRIES IN JAPANESE IMPORTS FROM ASIA, SELECTED YEARS, 1890–1940

	Korea	Taiwan	Kwantung Leased Territory	Manchuria	China	Hong Kong	Greater China	S.E. Asia	Other
1890	15				30	19		2	34
1900	9	5			31	11	47	14	30
1914	8	12	8		15	0	35	14	43
1919	14	10	11		23	0	44	19	23
1929	21	16	11		14	0	41	11	27
1936	27	19	2	11	8	0	40	14	19
1940	27	17	2	13	12	0	44	18	11

Source: LTES, *Foreign trade*, pp. 210–13.

Table 5.14. MARKET DESTINATIONS OF 'NEW' AND 'TRADITIONAL'
INDUSTRIAL EXPORTS, 1900
(% shares to each type of market)

	To developing economies	To advanced economies	Other
'NEW' INDUSTRY EXPORTS			
Cotton thread	100	0	0
Cotton blankets	100	0	0
Matches	99.8	.1	.1
Western-style umbrellas	99.6	.3	.1
Watches	99.6	.4	0
Beer	99.4	.4	.2
Metal products	95.8	4.2	0
Other cotton goods	99.4	.5	.1
'TRADITIONAL' INDUSTRY EXPORTS			
Silk goods	38.6	57	4.4
Pottery	33.4	61.3	5.3
Toys	23.9	70.7	5.4
Silk handkerchiefs	21.7	69.8	8.5
Carpets	14.0	77.3	8.7
Raw silk	0	99.6	.4

Source: Takahashi, *Development*, vol. 3, p. 399. Takahashi is here quoting a MITI study.
Note: The 'developing' economies are all in Asia; the 'advanced' in Europe and America; 'other'
denotes Canada and Australia.

other significant import trends are those for Korea and South-East
Asia. The economic, marketing and political realities behind these data
will be examined later.

The broad pattern of country/commodity flows behind these figures
was as follows: silk and tea exports went to America and Europe,
textiles and labour intensive manufactures were sent to Korea, China
and South-East Asia and capital goods to Manchuria. Or, one could
say that in the early stages of industrialisation Japan could sell primary
products and traditional exports to advanced economies, but manufactures produced by newly-acquired manufacturing technology proved
far more successful in Asian markets. This was because in these markets
either the trade-off between price and quality levels embodied in
Japanese goods was attractive to local consumers or Japan had the
political power to obtain access to the market, or a combination
of both factors was at work. This dichotomy of export markets is
summarised in Table 5.14.

Table 5.15. EXPORT AND IMPORT SHARES OF ASIA, NORTH AMERICA
AND EUROPE, SELECTED YEARS, 1890–1940

| | Asia | | North America | | Europe | | |
	Export share	Import share	Export share	Import share	Export share	Import share	Average difference
1890	31	38	38	9	28	52	20
1900	50	34	27	22	21	44	15
1914	53	57	30	15	14	24	10
1919	58	57	25	31	8	7	3
1929	53	51	36	26	6	15	7
1936	66	53	17	25	9	9	7
1940	79	58	11	28	3	4	13

Source: As Tables 5.12 and 5.13.

Finally, if the geography of imports and exports is viewed in tandem, a three-stage pattern emerges. In the first stage Japan's trade was essentially multilateral: i.e. the geographical structures of export outlets and import sources did not coincide. In the second stage up to 1936, the trend — subject to a slight disturbance during the First World War — was one of increasing convergence of import sources and export destinations. As war approached, this trend was reversed because of rising Japanese demand for the fuels and high-level industrial products needed for armaments. However, when looking at these data we should remember that many individual products bucked the trends in significant ways.[6]

In the perspective of more than a century, the Japanese were remarkably successful in achieving mutually supportive patterns of external and internal expansion. How can we explain this? The theories referred to earlier distinguish three major explanations of trade flows. First, there were those based on the uneven worldwide distribution of natural resources. Secondly, there were those occurring in products where the technology of production was relatively stable and widely known, so that international competitive advantage tended to reflect the comparative endowment of an economy in labour, skills

6. A variant on this regional approach to the balance of trade is the country-by-country bilateral analysis of Kanemori. According to Kanemori's estimates, bilaterally balanced trade rose from 47.6% of trade in 1880 to 80.2% in 1930, and then fell to 67.8% in 1940. Kanemori, *Nihon no boeki*, p. 108.

and capital. Finally there were those based on competitive advantage achieved by technical innovation or by inequalities of access to existing techniques. While these theories explain the structure of trade in terms of commodities, the overall weight of a country's trade in the world system depends on domestic growth and productivity. The economy in which output and productivity grow relatively fast tends to increase its importance in world trade through a wide range of industries.

These explanations are not mutually exclusive, and the power of each has been demonstrated in empirical studies of world trade. Further, inequalities of either natural resources endowment or technology are likely to stimulate international flows of capital and other resources to exploit the potential gains that these create, and these resource flows will have secondary effects on trade in goods and services. In the case of Japan, these three broad explanatory categories correspond roughly to the three distinct phases of export development in the modern era, namely the 1860s to the 1890s, the 1890s to the 1970s, and the 1970s to the 1990s. Before 1890 export competitiveness was based on the combination of natural resources and traditional skills that produced silk, tea, handicrafts and primary products. Between 1890 and 1937 Japan's exports were increasingly the output of the classic labour-intensive industry — textiles. Even so, as labour costs rose relative to capital, comparative advantage began to move on to more skill- and capital-intensive industries and, within textiles, to the higher branches. Even in the inter-war phase, trade also began to reflect the outflow of textile (and other) Japanese capital. In the 1960s heavy industrial goods became the dominant exports and finally, from the late 1970s, there have been increasing contributions from exports based on Japanese technological advance and on large-scale Japanese direct overseas investment influenced by a variety of motives. Import development has been a mirror image of this pattern, reflecting natural resource shortage and a relative lack of skills. In short, what has underpinned Japan's rise in the world trading economy has been its domestic growth, which was structured in favour of goods that could be and were exported.

Set out in this way, the story sounds evolutionary, market-determined and rather mechanical, but of course this was not so. Not only did trade expansion relate closely to Japan's involvement in five major wars and the creation of an overseas empire, but the achievement of competitiveness at each stage of development depended on public and private sector behaviour, on the relationship between the two, and on Japanese global economic strategies.

Thus the fact that mid-nineteenth-century Japan had the capability to produce tradeable goods did not guarantee either the expansion of their supply or their penetration of international markets. This required major efforts to improve resource allocation, ensure control of quality, improve marketing intelligence and gain entry and acceptance in foreign markets. The shift to competitiveness in factory-based exports was even harder, since it involved complex strategies, first to acquire and adapt contemporary industrial technologies and set Japan on the path of rising industrial productivity, and then to solve the equally difficult continuing problems of marketing in a world where there were serious linguistic and cultural barriers to Japanese advances, not to mention foreign vested interests protected by political power.

In a world of changing trade and payments regimes and of shocks created by war and economic fluctuations, all this was extraordinarily difficult, and certainly the Japanese made mistakes and took wrong turnings. The nature of the Japanese trade achievement is to be understood not only by the ways in which they developed their comparative advantage in production, but also by the contributions of the service sector and the role of government in welding these different sources of economic strength into comprehensive forms of trade competitiveness.

6

THE ROLE OF PUBLIC POLICY

'The strength or weakness of a nation depends on the wealth or poverty of its people; the wealth or poverty of a people depends on the volume of production'. — Okubo Toshimichi, *Memorial to the Emperor on the Encouragement of Industry* (1874)

The omnipresent role of government in trade affairs in the early Meiji period has already been noted. This chapter explores the further development of public policy and action in three distinct arenas: currency and exchange rate management, inward flows of foreign capital, and trade promotion in the public sector. All these activities promoted and supplemented the expansion of the private sector, which the case-study in the following two chapters discusses in detail.

Currency and exchange rate management

The specie components of the traditional Japanese currency system were gold, silver and copper. Because these all had international values and monetary functions, the opening of the ports initiated a complex monetary interaction between Japan and the outside world that lasted through to the 1930s. This interaction took place in an international monetary system that itself underwent profound changes between the 1860s and 1930s. The main events in this transformation were the widespread European conversions from silver and bimetallic standards to the gold standard in the 1870s and 1880s; the operation of the gold standard in the period leading to the First World War; wartime gold inconvertibility; and the attempt to re-establish the gold standard in the 1920s. This was followed by the final departures from gold in favour of managed monetary and exchange-rate systems in the 1930s.

For much of this period Japan's freedom of choice in monetary matters was severly circumscribed. It was initially limited by treaty obligations and other conditions imposed by the western powers, as well as by an important fact of commercial life in the Far East: the prevailing supremacy of the Mexican silver dollar. Subsequently, although the Meiji government gradually regained autonomy in most spheres of economic policy, the structural weakness of visible trade and the need for capital imports meant that Japan had difficulty in remaining off the gold standard — which, after a long struggle, was finally established there in 1897. Once on the standard, however, reconciling domestic policies with the need to remain on it presented Japan with a new set of obligations and difficulties.

Although Japan's visible trade balance was transformed during the First World War, external policy options were limited by the physical impossibility of moving gold and by the suspension of the gold standard. The situation eased somewhat in the 1920s, but Japanese currency policies continued to be influenced by what had then become a well-established traditional approach to international monetary policy. Only in 1931 did the government finally abandon its preference for the gold standard established by Matsukata and others in the previous century.

Despite the paucity of room for manoeuvre, Japanese financial policies were crucial to the performance of trade and payments. Internally, the growth of industries with export potential required a financial system that mobilised capital and provided incentives for expansion. Externally, financial policy determined the exchange rate (and hence the foreign prices of Japanese goods) which, in an era when exports were largely standardised commodities, was the major determinant of their competiveness. Financial policy and institution-building were therefore indispensable ingredients of any strategy of economic transformation through trade.

The monetary system of the Tokugawa period had been under pressure from the mid-eighteenth century onwards because fiscal deficits encouraged both the debasement of coinage and the issue of non-convertible paper money by the *han* governments — who had effectively moved Japan on to a managed monetary system in the late Tokugawa period.[1] During the nineteenth century this led to expansion of the money supply and inflation, and while inflation may have had positive effects on growth, it did not provide a sound basis for international monetary relations in the 1850s.[2]

When foreigners began to trade in the open ports, their most

1. Nakamura, *The economy of the Meiji–Taisho period*, chs. 1–4; Hiroshi Shinjo, *History of the Yen*, Tokyo: Kinokuniya, 1962, ch. 2.
2. A model account of these issues is in Peter Frost, *The Bakumatsu Currency Crisis*, Cambridge MA: Harvard East Asian Monographs, 1970.

important monetary discovery was the enormous disparity between international and Japanese relative valuations of copper, silver and gold. The world price ratio between silver and gold was *ca.* 16:1 as against the Japanese ratio of 3:1. Copper was also hugely overvalued in relation to ratios prevailing across the sea in China. The silver/gold discrepancy created a stampede of foreigners trying to acquire Japanese silver which they could exchange for gold. As Alcock remarked,

No wonder a sort of delirium came upon them. Trade! what were the miserable profits upon transactions in buying and selling of foreign and Japanese produce compared to this? Who would look at tea and silk, with all the risks of falling markets, in face of a steady and certain exchange of silver against Japanese gold, with never less than a 100 per cent gain?[3]

This problem, and the outflow of gold it caused, ultimately forced Japan to assign new notional values to silver and adapt its own price ratios to those in the world at large. However, this was a difficult inflationary process and, as Alcock again perceptively noted, 'so sudden and violent a rending of the monetary arrangement of a country produced by the interference of foreigners, is without precedent in modern times.'[4]

The chaotic political and economic conditions of the final years of the shogunate and the first Meiji years brought further problems. The trade deficit from 1866 required gold outflows to pay for it, while the fiscal problems of the new Meiji government resulted in further issues of *kinsatsu* ('gold notes') and other paper obligations. After the government's recourse to foreign loans in 1870 and 1873, inability to repay these and consequent national bankruptcy were a real possibility unless internal monetary stabilisation could be achieved.[5]

The first attempt to stabilise the yen took the form of the adoption of a bimetallic system in which silver was made the main unit of value and gold was subsidiary. But in 1870 the government was persuaded to reverse this. It adopted a gold standard system, with a subsidiary role for silver allowing it to serve as a trading currency in the

3. Alcock, *The Capital of the Tycoon*, vol. 1, p. 283.
4. *Ibid.*, vol. 2, p. 426.
5. MITI, vol. 5, *Foreign trade*, pp. 30ff., 171–2, 195. The interaction of internal and external problems was particularly emphasised by Finance Minister Okuma, Takahashi, *Formation*, vol. 2, p. 175.

treaty ports in competition with the Mexican silver dollar.[6] This early attempt to establish a gold standard failed, partly because excessive issues of paper money by government and by the national banks (established after 1871) caused paper to depreciate continuously against nominal specie values, and partly because the decline of the world silver price relative to gold accelerated gold outflows from Japan where an inappropriate rate had been specified under the bimetallic system. By 1878 outstanding paper obligations were seven times higher than those of 1868 and nearly ten times as large as the specie reserve. Expenditures rose with the money supply and were reflected in trade deficits and outflows of bullion in almost every year between 1869 and 1880. In 1878 the government allowed internal circulation of the silver coins intended for the treaty ports, but the depreciation of paper against silver continued till 1881.

Japan's financial difficulties at this time have to be seen in the context of important changes in the world monetary system. During the 1870s world production of silver increased rapidly and, in 1873, Germany went on the gold standard. This decision was both economic and political, and it forced a group of eight European countries to abandon bimetallism in favour of the gold standard.[7] These conversions to gold-based money added to the world silver supply and the increasing depreciation of silver against gold. Although Japan was in no position to move to the gold standard at that time, Matsukata became convinced that it had to adopt deflationary fiscal policies and establish a banking system that would be directly responsible to government and able to control the money supply. Only if underpinned by such a system could confidence in paper money and a financial infrastructure conducive to domestic expansion and exports be established. In framing his regulations for the new central bank (the Bank of Japan),

6. A valuable English-language source for Meiji monetary history is Masayoshi Matsukata, *Report on the Adoption of the Gold Standard in Japan*, Tokyo: Government Press, 1899. A massive recent history with reworked statistics and other materials is *Nihon keizai no kahi teki bunseki, 1868–1970* (An analysis of currency in the Japanese economy: 1868–1970), Tokyo: Sobunsha, 1984. I have also benefited from Kanji Ishii, 'International Factors in the Formation of Banking Systems, Japan 1870–1914' (mimeo).

7. The political dimension of the gold standard and the relationships between internal *laissez-faire*, free trade and the gold standard in the late nineteenth century are themes of Karl Polanyi, *The Great Transformation. The Political and Economic Origins of Our Time*, Boston: Beacon Press, 1957.

Matsukata emphasised the external significance of these changes. Basing his view on a study of European central banking practices, he argued that a central bank would be able to influence the balance of payments by both establishing a worldwide network of banking relationships and by varying the rate at which the bank discounted trade bills to attract short-term credit.

Matsukata's determination to establish confidence in banking systems and paper money was rewarded in the early 1880s as prices fell and the ratio of bullion to paper money rose.[8] Finally, in 1886, the yen achieved parity with its nominal silver value. During the process of eliminating the discount on paper against silver, Japan was effectively running a 'managed currency,' in which there was no direct link between internal and external prices. Thereafter it became a silver standard economy, in company with other Asian and Latin American economies and in contrast to the gold standard group of advanced economies.

What was the net effect of all these changes? During the early *kaikoku* period Japan's domestic monetary system had been forced to adapt to the world valuation of precious metals. This was an inherently inflationary process, involving large outflows of gold (between 1857 and 1866 the yen price of gold quadrupled). This adaptation affected trade and competitiveness in several ways: it raised domestic price levels, it diverted effort from the production and trade of *goods* to speculation in *money*, and it depressed trade generally by increasing its uncertainties. The problems and behaviour of foreign businessmen were of course determined by the fact that they were undertaking transactions in a remote corner of the world, still without the aid of the telegraph, and in trades where American and European prices were notoriously volatile. Uncertainties in Japan were a serious deterrent, compounding the riskiness of business decisions.

In 1886, internal and external prices were finally linked through silver. Japan's trading competitiveness depended thereafter on domestic productivity and prices on the one hand, and the changing inter-

---

8. Between 1882 and 1886 industrial prices fell by 41% while between 1880 and 1885, the ratio of specie to paper liabilities rose from 5.7% to 47.8%. See data and discussion in Nihon Ginko Hyakunenshi Iinkai (ed.), *Nihon ginko hyakunenshi* (The hundred-year history of the Bank of Japan (7 vols), Tokyo: Nihon Ginko, 1982–86, vol. 1, pp. 116–17.

national price of silver relative to gold on the other.[9] During the early 1880s, the trend in bullion prices was strongly favourable to gold, a factor which probably accounts for the stagnation in some of the gold standard economies. This stagnation and the reduction in incomes that accompanied it reduced the demand for imports in the gold standard economies. In Japan, therefore, it had the effect of intensifying the effects of Matsukata's fiscal and monetary deflation, but because the deflation was *so* severe, the fall in Japanese import demand was accompanied by a fall in export prices, and this gain in price competitiveness offset the lack of demand in Japan's trade partners. Thus the net effect on the Japanese visible trade balance was positive. In some respects this achievement foreshadowed the experience in the 1930s, when Japan increased exports and improved its trade position during a world depression.

The problem of the gold standard, 1886–1914

In spite of the success of Matsukata's stabilisation on the silver standard, the problem of the gold standard remained. During the late nineteenth century it became established as the dominant system in world trade.[10] The system required that currency values were fixed in terms of gold and that exports and imports of gold flowed freely. Under conditions of domestic *laissez faire* and international free trade, the theoretical attraction of the gold standard was its automatic capacity for regulating the internal and external balances of members of the system. It could do this because gold was both the basis of domestic money and the means for international settlement. Hence trade surpluses and deficits were reflected in flows of gold, which in turn expanded or contracted domestic money supplies, inflating or deflating domestic incomes and prices and thereby ensuring movement towards a balance of external trade. The gold standard, in other words, was the mechanism that integrated domestic economies into a world market.

---

9. Price linkages are clear from diagram 2.3 in Nakamura, *The economy of the Meiji–Taisho period*, p. 51.

10. A recent collection of classic papers on this subject is Barry Eichengreen (ed.), *The Gold Standard in Theory and History*, New York: Methuen, 1985. A valuable summary of international developments and British thinking in the 1920s is the 1931 *Report of the Committee on Finance and Industry* (the Macmillan Report), repr. London: HMSO, 1961. This contains an analysis of the gold standard by J. M. Keynes who had spent half a lifetime thinking about the issues, starting with his work on the Indian currency question, a matter crucial to Japan.

Corrections made by this mechanism could be reinforced by changes in the bank rate, which both signalled the direction of policy and attracted short-term loans to cover the adjustment period. As long as there was confidence in adherence to the gold value, lenders were willing to transmit funds to take advantage of quite small interest differentials, hence the system could work with relative smoothness. Further, the gold standard was supported by the unique role played in the world economy by the Bank of England, which operated as the hub of an international network of co-operative financial relationships and managed the London capital market. It could thus ensure that flows of capital from London offset trade deficits and alleviated balance of payments problems.

During the 1890s the silver economies felt the consequences of a continuous decline in the value of silver, and in Japan this decline was mirrored by the decline of the yen against the dollar and the pound. The domestic impact of this devaluation was strong: foreign imports into Japan were increasingly replaced by cheaper domestic products while Japanese exports of cotton and other goods rapidly penetrated Asian and other markets, providing strong growth in the incipient private company sector. It was especially crucial in this situation that in 1893 India, which was important to Japan both as an export market and as a competitor in third-country markets, went on the gold standard, a move that took account of British imperial interests and the need to protect the value of the pensions and savings of British expatriate civil servants more than of the Indian need for export competitiveness.[11] Japan's other potential competitor in Asia was China, which was still on the silver standard but severely hampered as a trade competitor by political instability and inefficient administration.[12]

Nowhere was the incipient industrialisation of Asia and the silver question and its trading implications more carefully followed and debated than in Shanghai. In Shanghai the powerful Bimetallic League and its propagandists claimed that with free enterprise and a proper

11. By contrast, when presented with a similar choice in the 1980s, the government of Hong Kong did not hesitate to allow the Hong Kong dollar to fall, thereby benefiting trade and growth at the expense of the short-term anxieties of expatriate civil servants whose savings and pensions were denominated in the local currency.
12. Nakamura, *The economy of the Meiji–Taisho period*, p. 49.

bimetallic system, Shanghai would become a 'forest of chimneys', an argument illustrated by the brilliant progress of Japan.

Now it must be evident that this state of things [the silver depreciation] gives an enormous stimulus to Japan to produce as much as they can for sale in other lands, and accordingly that country is very prosperous and every year arise fresh industries. During six weeks spent there I do not recall once being solicited for charity; the people appear to be contented, happy and fully employed. . . . Instead of the wretched return that joint stock companies appear by their printed returns to yield in Lancashire for the making of cloth and yarn, a long list was published last Autumn showing from 10 to 15 per cent profit yielded by similar industries in native hands in Japan.[13]

In these circumstances it is hardly surprising that a move from silver to gold was controversial in Japan. Textile and other manufacturers were well aware that silver depreciation had been crucially helpful in India and other markets; the gold standard was described as 'a black cloud' hanging over the industry, and Shibusawa Eiichi, the leading spokesman for the Japanese private industrial sector, argued strongly with Matsukata for maintaining silver.[14]

The matter was exhaustively analysed by the Coinage Investigation Commission which sat from 1893 to 1896 and was the Japanese variant of a long line of late nineteenth-century currency commissions. It was required to answer the following main questions: What were the general causes of fluctuations in the price of silver and what were their effects? What was the impact of such fluctuations on Japan? And was it necessary to change Japan's currency system? The Commission's report was highly detailed and reflected the deep divisions in Japan on this issue. In a compromise judgement it advocated change in the system at some future date. In fact, only six of the fifteen members actively supported the gold standard; two others advocated bimetallism and seven — the largest single group — wanted to stay with silver.[15]

Armed with this compromise and with the gold and sterling indemnity payment for the Sino-Japanese war of 1894–95, Matsukata pressed ahead, and in March 1897 he elaborated the case for the gold standard and a new coinage system in a speech to the Imperial Diet.

13. See the arguments of 'Bimetallist', *North China Herald* (hereafter *NCH*) July 6, 1894.
14. Takahashi, *Development*, vol. 1, p. 103. See also anti-gold arguments reported in 'Silver's position in China and Japan', *NCH*, Aug. 18, 1893. The quotation is from Miyamoto, *The lineage of Japanese merchants*, p. 102.
15. Matsukata, *Report on the Adoption of the Gold Standard*, ch. 2.

He emphasised, first, that silver was an inherently unstable and speculative medium that provided an unsatisfactory environment for the long-term expansion of trade in commodities. Secondly, he pointed out that much of the recent improvement in trade reflected Japanese supply-side and transportation advances rather than price gains through silver devaluation, and that any competitive gains that had arisen from the silver devaluation would prove transitory, since they would in due course be dissipated by domestic wage and price rises; and, further, that long-run growth and competitiveness would depend on supply-side efficiency, which would be harmed by adherence to the soft silver standard.

There was one other immediate factor in the decision for gold which Matsukata well understood but did not fully spell out: this was Japan's need for capital imports. Economies that were not on the gold standard had difficulties in attracting capital from those that were. This was because investors in gold standard economies were in effect being asked to bear not only the political or commercial risks of loans and investments but a currency risk as well. This was a serious factor in China's failure to attract western investment in the late nineteenth century and a crucial issue for Japan. Immediately after the Sino-Japanese war, Japan embarked on a programme of economic and colonial development that required massive expansion of the state budget and of imports of capital goods. Even with the help of silver devaluation, Japan had been unable to balance visible and current account trade, and with investment programmes for transport and military modernisation that had a high import content, the prospects for balancing trade in the immediate future were not good. Access to international capital markets was therefore essential to relieve both the external payments problem and domestic budgetary tensions. For access to international capital markets on favourable terms, investors needed the gold guarantee. Indeed, it is arguable that by committing the country to a huge ten-year financial plan (1896–1905) with a borrowing requirement equal to nearly a quarter of all expenditures, Matsukata must have realised that, whatever his colleagues believed, a return to the gold standard was inevitable.[16]

At the end of his speech Matsukata alluded without elaboration to

16. Takahashi, *Development*, vol. 1, pp. 103ff., p. 472. Data on budgets and financial strategy are in Nihon Ginko Hyakunenshi Iinkai, *The Bank of Japan hundred year history*, vol. 1, pp. 494–9; Masayoshi Matsukata, *Report on the Post-Bellum Financial Administration in Japan 1896–1900*, Tokyo, 1901; Koichi Emi, *Government Fiscal Activity and Economic Growth in Japan 1868–1960*, Tokyo: Kinokuniya, 1963.

a point underlying the pro-gold thinking in Japan and elsewhere. This was the fact that all the world's leading countries were on the gold standard and that to join this group, economically and politically, a country would have to adopt the same monetary standard. A typical contemporary summing-up of this point was:

The civilisation of a country may be gauged in many ways and by many standards. But one of the surest ways of gauging it is by the standard of money used. The passing from copper to silver marks one stage. The passing from silver to gold marks a more perfect stage in the progress of civilisation.[17]

The performance of Japanese trade and payments after the return to gold vindicated some but not all of Matsukata's judgements. In the short run his foreign admirers were impressed: 'Many were the prognostications of failure when Count Matsukata undertook the disestablishment of silver there [in Japan], but he was right and his critics were wrong.'[18] In fact, there was some loss of competitiveness to China, which remained on silver, but the Japanese price difficulties in China were offset by the vigorous development of other instruments of trade policy. Moreover, the gold standard *did* lead to a strong inflow of foreign capital, which supported the balance of payments and accelerated the transfer to Japan of industrial technology. Capital flows were also both a consequence and a cause of Japan's success in the Russo-Japanese war of 1904–5. During that war the Russians were at one stage so desperate to obtain a further £25 million loan from Berlin that they were reduced to making a disastrously unwise military offensive in their efforts to impress foreign observers and ultimately failed, both militarily and financially.[19] The Japanese on the other hand were in an upward spiral of esteem in which success in the war made capital inflows easier, since battlefield success 'not only enhanced the reputation of Japanese arms but also amply testified to the solidity of Japanese financial conditions'.[20]

17. 'The currency question', *NCH*, Jan. 27, 1903.
18. 'The Gold Standard for Siam', *NCH*, Dec. 3, 1902.
19. Lord Brooke, *An Eyewitness in Manchuria*, London: Eveleigh Nash, 1905, p. 283.
20. 'Japan: The New Loan', *NCH*, April 7, 1905. The financial implications of this pro-Japan fervour were illustrated by events surrounding the Japanese £30 million 4.5% loan offered in March 1905. So great was the rush of investors to subscribe to this offer that they overwhelmed the City of London police and forced the Hong Kong and Shanghai Bank (who were handling the issue) to call in their rugby football team to restore order. Frank H. H. King, *The History of the Hong Kong Banking Corporation: The Hong Kong Bank in the Period of Imperialism and War, 1895–1918*, Cambridge University Press, 1988, p. 99.

Nonetheless, by 1912–14, after the euphoria of the war and war-related loans, the fundamental problem of the balance of payments resurfaced. The trade balance remained negative and capital inflows and the gold standard supported each other in an unstable alliance that any major shock or setback might sweep away. In the 1908 domestic boom the Bank of Japan was forced to conserve its gold stock by borrowing at excessive cost in London, and by 1913 the Bank had formed the view that severe domestic deflation would be necessary to remain on the gold standard. Indeed, had the First World War not transformed Japan's foreign trade performance for the better, both the data and contemporary opinion suggest that maintenance of the gold standard would have proved impossible.[21]

The gold standard and exchange rate policy from the First World War to 1937

The outbreak of the First World War caused severe problems for Japan's external finances. Trade at that time was financed largely by discounting bills which had to be sent to London, but the suspension of the Trans-Siberian Railway made transmission of these bills impossible. Further, pre-war payment difficulties had led to the running down of foreign balances on which Japan could otherwise have drawn.[22] By early 1915, however, the situation began to improve. Vigorous export expansion began as Japan supplied war demand from Europe and the United States. It also expanded exports to India, South-East Asia, South Africa and Latin America, all markets temporarily unable to obtain supplies from normal western sources. As a result of this boom, Japan achieved in 1915–20 a large cumulative visible trade surplus. There was a similar transformation in invisibles, with net receipts from shipping showing a particularly large improvement. Indeed, the expansion of the Japanese shipbuilding and

---

21. Nihon Ginko Hyakunenshi Iinkai, *The Bank of Japan hundred year history*, vol. 2, pp. 278–83; Takahashi, *Development*, vol. 1, p. 455; Junnosuke Inouye, *Problems of the Japanese Exchange 1914–1926*, Glasgow: Robert Maclehose, 1931, pp. 7–8. See also an informative (unsigned) analysis, 'The First World War and our Country's Foreign Exchange', parts 1–3 in *Tokyo Ginko geppo* (Bank of Tokyo Monthly), no. 2, 1954, pp. 28–39; *ibid*, no. 4, 1954, pp. 24–38; no. 9, 1954, pp. 12–28.

22. Inouye, *Problems*, contains the authoritative account of the wartime financial problems, supplemented by the material in *Bank of Tokyo Monthly* referred to above.

shipping industries during the First World War marked the emergence of Japan as a world-class competitor in these sectors, and in the successes of these years the Meiji policies of subsidisation, protection and intense efforts in technology transfer all bore fruit.

As a result of the war Japan's international net indebtedness of ¥1.1 billion was changed into a net credit position of ¥2.7 billion with gross gold and foreign exchange holdings in 1920 amounting to ¥4.37 billion. However, the internal expansion of the money supply during the war had raised Japanese wages and prices far above their 1914 levels. The war also created acute difficulties for the foreign exchange banks because wartime interest rates in Japan were higher than those in New York and London, which meant that the interest differential between funds borrowed in Japan and funds the banks were forced to hold and lend abroad was 3% to 4%. When America finally suspended gold payments in 1917, Japan was forced to follow suit and hence lost the use of reserves accumulated in New York.

Looking at this history retrospectively, the great Japanese banker Inouye Junnosuke argued that toleration of an uncontrolled export boom had been a mistake, because its inflationary effects were responsible both for a serious maldistribution of income within Japan and for the unmanageable problems of post-war readjustment. However, Inouye acknowledged that as the result of the many decades of trade deficits and anxiety over the stability of capital inflows, Japan, given the opportunity, would inevitably encourage vigorous export development and attempt to build up gold and foreign currency reserves in anticipation of a return to pre-war problems.

The rapid American return to the gold standard in 1919 took Japan by surprise. Despite their accumulation of reserves, the Japanese authorities were aware that Japanese price levels were not competitive enough for a return to gold at pre-war parity. They also correctly foresaw that further sharp post-war price declines abroad were imminent. These indeed took place in 1920, adding to Japanese adjustment problems.[23]

Between 1921 and 1929 official Japanese thinking continued to favour a return to gold at the old rate but this proved difficult.

---

23. A comprehensive account of financial and exchange rate policy in the 1920s is Hugh T. Patrick, 'The economic muddle of the 1920s' in James W. Morley (ed.), *Dilemmas of Growth in Pre-War Japan*, Princeton University Press, 1971, pp. 211–66.

Table 6.1. WHOLESALE PRICES AND COMPETITIVENESS IN JAPAN
AND THE UNITED STATES, 1913–39

	United States price index	Japan price index	Japan (adjusted for exchange rate)	Index of yen value	Level of Japanese prices above (+) or below (−) US price
1913	100	100	100	100	0
1920	220.8	259.3	260.6	101	+18
1921	139.9	200.3	194.7	97	+39
1922	138.9	195.8	189.9	97	+37
1923	143.9	199.2	197.2	99	+37
1924	140.8	206.5	175.7	85	+25
1925	147.9	201.7	166.5	83	+13
1926	142.9	178.7	169.7	95	+19
1927	137	169.8	162.9	96	+15
1928	139.9	170.9	160.9	94	+15
1929	137.9	166.1	155	93	+12
1930	125.1	136.7	136.7	100	+9
1931	105.7	115.6	114.4	99	+8
1932	93.8	128.2	73	57	−22
1933	95.4	147	75.1	51	−21
1934	108.4	149.8	89.5	60	−17
1935	115.7	153.7	88.9	58	−23
1936	117	160.1	93.9	59	−20
1937	150.5	194.4	113.4	58	−25

Source: Morley, *Dilemmas of Growth in Prewar Japan*, p. 233.

Deflationary policies were never sufficiently strong to reduce Japanese wages and prices to competitive levels, and the Japanese did not wish to hazard their gold reserves on a risky return to the gold standard. Indeed, they wished to use these reserves as ammunition in a war of commercial aggression against Britain and the United States for control of the Chinese market.

In 1923 Japan's balance of payments problems were exacerbated by the Kanto earthquake, which affected over 3.5 million people and caused damage estimated at ¥2.5 billion — more than three times the level of total government expenditure.[24] The earthquake led directly to a 22% fall in the value of the yen at a time when short- and long-term foreign capital was needed to aid reconstruction. The yen began

24. The Bank of Japan's handling of this disaster is described in Nihon Ginko Hyakunenshi Iinkai, *The Bank of Japan hundred year history*, vol. 3, pp. 48–54.

to recover after 1924, and under the influence of Inouye and others opinion hardened in favour of a return to gold. Inouye's arguments for gold echoed those of Matsukata and focussed on two points. First he noted the de-stabilising impact on the yen of silver speculation originating in Shanghai, in which 'the yen had been treated as a gambling counter'.[25] Such instability, he believed, was damaging to output and trade, and the evidence of contemporary events in France, Russia and Germany all suggested to him that failure to return to gold was the path to hyper-inflation, exchange collapse and exclusion from the mainstream of international trade. Secondly, Inouye made explicit the point that Matsukata had preferred merely to imply: namely, that Japan's economic transformation had not yet reached the point where a balance of visible trade was possible. On the contrary, he said:

Year after year Japan has been importing more than she has been exporting: year after year her invisible expenditure has tended to exceed her invisible revenue, and this has meant for her a perpetual shortage of money wherewith to pay her bills abroad. That, gentlemen, is our position today. . . .[26]

In these circumstances, Inouye argued, Japan had few options available. One suggestion was the more vigorous use of tariffs to control imports, but this was no longer likely to be generally helpful because most imports were now either the raw materials or capital goods needed for industry or food consumption. In 'the far distant future' Inouye foresaw that export expansion would solve the problem. In the short run, however, he believed that Japan had to have access to rationally motivated short- and long-term capital, and this still required the gold standard. As one involved in the precarious management of Japan's capital account, with its requirement of borrowing short to lend long, Inouye believed that there was no alternative to continuing the policies of deflation and fiscal prudence so that prices could be brought down to a level where the return to the gold could be made.

While Inouye's views were not shared by many economists outside official circles, in 1928 the deputy governor of the Bank of Japan reiterated the view that since all the major economies in the world were on or going back to gold, Japan must follow suit and handle

25. Inouye, *Problems*, p. 157
26. *Ibid.*, p. 204

the problems as they arose.[27] But it was not till 1929, when the incoming Hamaguchi government was faced with the problem of re-financing a large sterling loan in 1930, that Japan committed itself to a return to the gold standard, and on 1 January 1930 the gold embargo was lifted.[28] In view of the fact that this decision was taken *after* the Wall Street crash of September 1929 — seen in retrospect as the start of the great depression — and in view also of the danger of Japanese private speculation against the yen, the move to gold seems extraordinary. But it was a decision in line with a series of international conference discussions at Brussels, Locarno, Geneva, Genoa and Lausanne, and was consistent with a tradition of Japanese thinking on international monetary affairs that went back to 1870. Also, it must be appreciated that the decision was taken at a time when Japanese leaders still believed world economic prospects to be highly favourable.[29] In any event, Britain went off the gold standard only eight months later and when Japan followed suit in December 1931 its policy-makers did so in the growing conviction that the nineteenth-century world of free trade and unrestricted capital flows had come to an end, and that the age of regulated economies and trading blocs had arrived.

During the 1930s capital movements were restricted and the yen was allowed to fall precipitately in value. This again allowed a phase of price competitiveness. However, it was because the supply-side and export development efforts were in place and able to respond to this opportunity that Japan was at last able to expand exports rapidly and to demonstrate potential for an eventual trade balance.

Foreign capital

Foreign capital had begun to enter Japan during the *kaikoku* period. Individual *han* with fiscal problems and urgent requirements for ships, arms and industry borrowed from foreign sources in order to obtain them. A good example of this type of initiative was the establishment

27. The continuation of the 'hundred-year debate' is discussed in Nihon Ginko Hyakunenshi Iinkai, *The Bank of Japan hundred year history*, vol. 3, pp. 159–67.

28. In addition to Patrick, cited above, the return to the gold standard is described in MITI, vol. 5, *Foreign trade*, pp. 46ff. and 142ff., and by Sumiyami Kiyo, *Showa kyoko* (The Showa depression), Tokyo: Yuhikaku, 1974, part 3.

29. Sumiyami, *The Showa depression*, pp. 20–1.

of the iron foundry that later became the Japanese naval arsenal at Yokosuka. Foreign capital also entered Japan through the private sector, where foreign banks had assumed an important role in financing Japan's international trade. Notable arrivals in the 1860s included the Oriental Bank and the Hong Kong and Shanghai Bank, together with banks from Germany and France.[30]

After 1867 the Meiji government took responsibility for the foreign obligations incurred by the *han*, repaid them promptly, and then borrowed again to re-purchase the rights in coal-mining and railway construction that had been sold to foreigners. The government also financed the railway concession for a line from Tokyo to Yokohama with a £1 million loan at 9% and in 1873 took a further loan of £2.4 million at 7%. Thereafter official borrowing ceased till 1897, and official policy forbad borrowing by the private sector as well.[31] There were two reasons for this hostility to foreign capital. One was the belief that foreign capital would coalesce with treaty port rights to create an unbreakable network of foreign economic control over Japan (Egypt provided a striking contemporary example of this danger). The other reason was anxiety over the severe debt repayment problem that might arise if fiscal and trade deficits were large and erratic and the external value of the yen was declining. Nonetheless, until firm central bank control was established in 1882, private businesses continued to attempt secret borrowing operations from western firms in Japan.

By the time the currency situation had stabilised in the late 1880s, the debate over the role of foreign capital in Japan had been

30. A list of foreign loans made to *han* governments in the Tokugawa is in Takahashi, *Formation*, vol. 3, p. 730. See also important materials in Ishii, *International Factors*, pp. 2–4. A still useful account of the role of foreign capital in Japan is G. C. Allen and Audrey G. Donnithorne, *Western Enterprise in Far Eastern Economic Development*, part 2.

31. Comprehensive data on Japanese loans and domestic finance was published by the Ministry of Finance in their *Annuaire Financière et Economique du Japon* (various years). I have used the English-language edition of this (*Financial and Economic Annual of Japan*) for 1905, esp. ch. 4. A similar list of foreign loans is in Inouye, *Problems*, Appendix V; and W. F. Spalding, *Eastern Exchange. Currency and Finance*, London: Pitman, 1918. Also worth consulting in English are materials on finance in Count Okuma (ed.), *Fifty Years of New Japan*, London: Smith, Elder, 1909, ch. 15 and Alfred Stead, *Japan by the Japanese*.

The Role of Public Policy

revived.[32] On one side was a virulent anti-foreignism which fuelled the 'movement to recover commercial autonomy' and abolish extraterritoriality, and which spilled over into generalised hostility to foreign private investment. In particular, patriots sought to forbid foreign ownership of land, mines, shipping, docks and all key industrial activities, arguing that such ownership would constitute an extension of extraterritoriality.[33] Against this position Fukuzawa Yukichi and others wrote influential works in favour of supplementing the domestic capital shortages of private firms with foreign capital. But only in the latter half of the 1890s were arguments for foreign investment converted into offical policy, and on the basis of the Chinese indemnity the late Meiji era turned into the golden age of capital imports.

There were in fact strong reasons for seeking additional funds after 1895. The Sino-Japanese war had been financed internally but, as we have seen, subsequent plans for domestic modernisation, together with plans to open up Hokkaido and Manchuria, called for resources beyond the scope of domestic taxation. The role played by the capital sector in financing the balance of payments is seen in Table 6.2. The different forms of foreign investment are summarised in Table 6.3.

Up till 1905, national overseas loans were by far the largest item in the capital inflow account. The loans shown include those taken out on the strength of the return to gold and the Anglo-Japanese Alliance. The six loans concentrated in 1904–5 were used to finance the Russo-Japanese war. Two of them were conversions, reflecting the fact that as Japan's credit rating rose, loans at 6% and 5% could be refinanced at 5% and 4%.

As is clear from the data for 1905, the central government was the largest single foreign borrower and by that year, over half of the Japanese government long-term debt was held abroad.[34] Nonetheless, local government, private sector bond issues and direct foreign investment all continued as significant elements in the capital account. Local

32. A full account of these debates and other material on foreign financial and industrial capital in Japan is in Takahashi, *Development*, vol. 1, pp. 123ff.

33. In 1891 the *Jiyuto* (Liberal Party) was campaigning to link treaty revision with laws forbidding foreign ownership of a wide selection of Japanese assets. In the same year, foreigners in Japan and Asia were alarmed by the anti-foreignism expressed in the attempted assassination of the Russian Crown Prince; see 'The departure of the Czarevitch', *NCH*, May 22 and 29, 1891.

34. Takahashi, *Development*, vol. 1, p. 155.

Table 6.2. FOREIGN CAPITAL AND ITS SIGNIFICANCE, 1886–1936
(millions of yen)

	Net long-term capital balance. Outflows of Japanese capital ( )	Net short-term capital balance	Commodity trade balance	Transfers and long-term capital as % of gross domestic capital formation
1886–93	−6.6 (0)	24.9	−24.8	1
1894–1903	156.4 (28.4)	−165.7	−399.1	17.2
1904–13	1254.5 (194.4)	−97.2	−552.6	20.2
1914–19	−1668.5 (1326.8)	343.3	1333.7	−15.1
1920–31	−1720.2 (1435.0)	2726.5	−4737.3	−4.5
1932–36	−2850 (1511.4)	1712.5	−818.9	−8.1

Source: Estimates by Yamazawa in *Development*, p. 4 and as Table 5.1.
Notes:
1. Amounts are cumulative for periods shown.
2. The value of the Chinese war indemnity paid in 1895–98 was ¥357.8 million.

Table 6.3. YEAR-END FOREIGN DEBT, BY CATEGORIES, 1905 AND 1913

	1905	1913	Net addition 1905–13
National bonds for overseas subscription	1142.2	1524.6	+382.4
Domestic bonds purchased overseas (face value)	93	—	−93
Bonds issued domestically but subsequently bought by foreigners	160	74.5	−85.5
Local government bonds	4.1	177.1	+173
Company bonds	9.7	166.8	+157.1
Direct foreign investment	5	26.4	+21.4
Total	1414.3	1969.6	+555.4

Source: Kamekichi Takahashi, *The Rise and Development of Japan's Modern Economy: The Basis for Miraculous Growth*, Tokyo: Jiji Press, 1969, p. 301.

Table 6.4. THE RANKING OF FOREIGN INVESTMENT
BY SECTORS AT YEAR-END, 1911

1	Gas and electrical supply
2	Oil and mining
3	Textiles
4	Electricals
5	Electric railways
6	Insurance
7	Fertiliser manufacture
8	Paper manufacture
9	Shipbuilding and transport
10	Banking

Source: Takahashi, *Development*, vol. 1, p. 152.

government borrowings were used to finance utililities, gasworks and docks, while the most significant private sector borrowings were those associated with direct investment, usually in the form of joint ventures between foreign and Japanese industrial firms. The ranking of foreign investment by industrial sectors for 1911 is shown in Table 6.4.

The motives for foreign investment in Japan at this time repay investigation. The willingness of foreigners to subscribe to and deal in national bond issues reflected the dramatic change in western sentiment concerning Japan between 1894 and 1914. This change was based on foreigners' observation of Japan's success in two foreign wars, its visible industrial and trading progress and the establishment of sound fiscal and financial systems. These favourable sentiments were assiduously cultivated by the Japanese' government, and investment in Japan was further encouraged by an outpouring from Tokyo of foreign-language statistical and other publications.[35] Foreign diplomats in Japan, many of them enthusiastic Japanophiles, also urged their compatriots to develop business relations with Japan, frequently mentioning that working in Japan was cheap. Indeed, as

35. See esp. the *Annuaire Financière* and other sources cited in note 30 and, above all, Department of Agriculture and Commerce (Japan), *Japan in the Beginning of the Twentieth Century*, London: John Murray, 1904. The latter was an 828-page compendium of data and facts concerning every aspect of Japan's economic, legal and political systems.

one wrote, 'There can, in fact, be no country in the world in which visitors can live luxuriously at so small an outlay . . . .'[36]

The revision of the treaties and the move towards tariff autonomy were also important encouragements to foreign investment. The former gave new freedoms to foreign businessmen, and the latter not only provided revenues from which national borrowing could be repaid but also, with the development of tariff protection of Japanese industry, strengthened the incentives for firms to invest within the tariff wall before it was too late. As in the 1850s, the Americans played an important role in this new foreign invasion of Japan, partly because American companies were at that time forming a view of the world in which China, India and the United States would be the three great Pacific powers. In this new Pacific scenario Japan was crucial since it was the only effective location for American capital.[37]

The flow of foreign capital into Japan in the years before 1914 was substantial, and as we see from Table 6.2 these inflows were a valuable supplement to domestic savings as well as having favourable balance of payment and technology transfer effects. Inflows before the First World War were equal to one-fifth of domestic investment and in some years they were estimated to be equal in size to the entire investment made by the private corporate sector.

In industrial investment the benefits were qualitative as well as quantitative. The Japanese carefully selected foreign partners to maximise the favourable effects of technology transfer in Japan, and structured their activities in ways that minimised foreign interference in the economy. So much so that foreigners sometimes complained bitterly of the Japanese sharp practice of taking over foreign investments once the key technologies had been mastered.[38]

36. The first class fare to Yokohama was £70 and a room in the best class of hotel cost £25 per month. For a further £14 a month an English businessman could expect to hire a brougham with two horses, a coachman, a groom, a servant and an English-speaking clerk. Details from 'Report for the Year 1895 on the Foreign Trade of Japan', *BPPJ*, vol. 10, pp. 11–62.

37. See an important quotation from Masuda Takashi in Takahashi, *Development*, vol. 1, p. 149. Masuda was a former samurai who became a leading director of Mitsui Bussan. He pioneered the company's development in Shanghai and later developed the company's business in Taiwan and Manchuria.

38. See for example the experience of the Oriental Compressol Company, which had a majority foreign ownership and a business in a new form of concrete patented by the French. When the president of the company left Japan the newspaper reported that a 'chattering mob of Japanese' forced their way into the company offices

　　The impact of foreign capital on import substitution and export expansion ranked high as criteria for encouraging foreign investment, with shipping a good example of an industry that received major benefits from foreign relationships, with important results for both visible and invisible trade. However, the benefits of foreign investment on the trade balance were not immediate. In the short term, the high import content of public and private domestic investment, high levels of aggregate demand and the constraints of the gold standard all made the management of the external sector difficult. But the industries that grew particulary rapidly during the First World War and even began to export for the first time on a significant scale — electricals, shipbuilding and metallurgy — were precisely those that had benefited from foreign direct and indirect investment before the war.[39]

　　In the inter-war period the major outflows of investment shown in Table 6.2 were mainly to the colonial empire, while inflows of direct investment remained important in new industries such as chemicals and electricals. With cars, the conflict between Japan's protectionist ambitions and American plans to use joint ventures and direct investment as a means to penetrate the Japanese market created serious economic friction. We can also observe that for most of this period, and especially in the 1920s, the maintainence of balance of payments' equilibrium depended on short-term inflows. Before 1930 it had been argued that the volatility of capital flows and the problems of managing them would be solved by the return to gold, an argument analogous to Matsukata's view that the gold standard would simplify Japan's payments policies. But this time the expectation proved false, for whereas the pre-war gold standard based on London had proved helpful on the capital account, the post-war bi-polar gold standard based on London and New York was hampered in its operation by growing domestic inflexibilities, political unwillingness to pay the social costs of deflation, trade restrictions and the failure of New York to support the system with outflows of investment in 1928 and 1929. The system, therefore, did not prove viable, and speculation and volatile capital flows became worldwide and not simply Japanese

---

and attempted to take over the company by means of unauthorised meetings of shareholders. See 'Foreign Capital in Japan: Alleged attempt to oust foreigners', *NCH*, Sept. 4, 1909.

　39. Nakamura, *The economy of the Meiji–Taisho period*, ch. 6.

problems. Thus while Japan continued to have a policy of importing capital right up to the outbreak of the Pacific war, it also responded to the international economic breakdown by restraints on capital movements and unorthodox methods of trade diplomacy.[40]

Tariff policy

Tariffs, as devices either to raise revenue or to protect domestic industries, were unknown to Tokugawa governments but in the attachment to the Treaty of Amity and Commerce of 1858, four classes of dutiable goods were defined. Class 1 was duty-free and included household goods and books. Class 2 carried a 5% duty and included supplies, coal, rice and goods for provisioning foreign ships. Class 3 was rated at 35% and included intoxicating liquors. All other goods were placed in Class 4 and rated at 25%. Exports other than gold or bullion were charged at 5%. This structure provided the Tokugawa government with useful revenue without a serious distortion of the domestic economic structure. In 1866, however, the Five Powers insisted on a new tariff convention that deprived Japan of tariff autonomy and imposed a maximum rate of 5% on imports. These import tariffs remained till the revision of the treaties in 1899, producing an average actual tariff rate during this period of less than 4%.[41]

In the years leading up to revision, the question of tariffs was strongly debated. A major inquiry in 1873 noted the urgent need to eliminate the trade deficit in manufactured goods, and proposed a combination of tariff protection and abolition of export taxes. At this stage, the main official concern was to control the balance of trade and raise revenue, as well as giving protection to import-substitute industries.[42] But, as noted in Chapter 4, the Foreign Ministry was unwilling to confront the foreign powers on treaty revision; hence

---

40. Capital outflows were subject to the 1931 Capital Flight Prevention Law and the 1933 Foreign Exchange Control Law, MITI, vol. 6: *Foreign trade*, pp. 216ff.

41. The Treaty of 1858 and appendages are in Gaimusho Joyakukyoku, *Compendium of old treaties*, vol. 1, part 1, pp. 13–42. The 1866 Tariff Convention can be found on pp. 45–78. Useful material on Meiji tariff history from the viewpoint of international law is to be found in Hishida, *The International Position of Japan*, pp. 136ff. and 146ff. See also Hori Tsuneo, *Meiji keizai shisoshi* (A history of Meiji economic thought), Tokyo: Meiji Bunken, 1975, esp. ch. 5.

42. MITI, vol. 5: *Foreign trade*, pp. 476, 485–6, discusses the internal Japanese debates on the issue.

Japan was forced to provide protection through subsidies of various kinds. Such a policy was incompatible with the development of a vigorous independent system of free enterprise.

As the Meiji era progressed, the calls from business for protection were gradually accompanied by increasingly sophisticated academic analyses of the problem. In the intellectual debates the division between the free traders and the protectionists was not simple. Those that supported the combination of free trade and *laissez-faire* often did so within the framework of a 'historical' approach. In other words, they took the view that whereas *laissez-faire* and free trade were the best policies for the advanced economies, for the relatively backward economies such as Japan, transitional protection and government intervention could be justified. This theory found an echo in the literature of official policy, which held that tariffs could be justified in exact proportion to the technological gap between Britain and the country in question. Against these views, however, was a more intransigent school of protection which had read deeply (and translated) the leading theorists of protection in Europe and America, particularly the American Henry Charles Carey.[43] The Japanese conversion to protectionism also had much to do with agriculture, a linkage found in several contemporary western theories which emphasised the uniqueness of economic activities dependent on non-renewable resources. In Japan, arguments for agricultural protection echoed the traditional neo-Confucian ranking of agricultural activities, and this may well have been a factor in the easy acceptance of protectionist arguments. Other strands in contemporary protectionsm that appealed to the Japanese were collectivism and nationalism. For example, Fukuzawa Yukichi, who had embraced both domestic *laissez-faire* as a means of destroying feudalism and free trade as its logical corollary, later abandoned the latter for nationalistic reasons while basically holding to the former.

During the 1890s the pressures for tariff reforms, not simply from theorists but also from manufacturers, became intense. A first result

43. The productivity of the Japanese translators of modern and contemporary European and American economists and philosophers was prodigious. They started with Smith, Ricardo, Malthus, Mill and Senior and went on to Jevons, Sidgwick, Bagehot, Bastable and J.M. Keynes. Among continental Europeans they covered were List, Roscher, Schönberg, Stein, Wagner, Cossa, Bastiat, Beauregard, Say and Laveleye. A comprehensive account of this work with details of the translations is Hori, *A history of Meiji economic thought*, esp. ch. 5.

Table 6.5. AVERAGE TARIFFS LEVIED ON
DUTIABLE GOODS, 1867–1913

1867	3.7
1898	3.8
1903	9.7
1908	15.9
1913	20

Source: Takahashi, *Formation*, vol. 2, p. 173.

of this pressure was the abolition of export and import taxes on raw cotton. However the active raising of tariffs to protect Japanese industries was not possible before 1899. In negotiations with the foreign powers over treaty revision, protection was a particulary sensitive subject. For while these powers could see that the days of extraterritoriality were over, the British in particular used all their remaining influence to maintain ease of access to the Japanese market. Thus in order to secure the greater goal of treaty revision, Japan made substantial short-term concessions on tariffs to Britain, France and Germany. Under the final arrangements, imports from these countries were subject to tariffs in a range of 5% to 15% compared to a general range of 5% to 45%. No reciprocal reductions were granted on Japanese goods. These negotiations, which continued from the late 1890s through to 1911, were greeted with popular hostility both in Japan, where any concessions to foreigners were unpopular, and in Britain, where the government had great difficulty justifying acquiescence before the House of Commons.[44] The course of average tariff levels is shown in Table 6.5. After the final settlement involving foreign negotiation was reached in 1911, both average tariff rates and the income from tariffs rose sharply. Between 1898 and 1913 the average tariff on dutiable goods rose from 3.8% to 20% and tariff revenue quadrupled. The tariff policy was based on the protection of industries with either strong import-substitution or export potential. Careful

44. The outcry on the issue is illustrated in 'The Japanese Tariff', *NCH*, June 10, 1910. The Birmingham Chamber of Commerce was particularly incensed at the proposed raising of tariffs on iron pipes and coated metals to 20%; machinery rates were to be 15% to 20% higher, while some specialist textiles were to have a rate of 400% imposed. A lengthy defence of the Japanese position by the foreign editor of the *Kokumin Shimbun* is 'The new Japanese tariff and Great Britain', *NCH*, June 17, 1910. This argued that the proposed rates were revenue-raising but not 'protective'.

analysis of four classes of textile products and five other goods shows that changes in tariffs were notably successful in stimulating the output of watches, toys, rails and cars and in achieving self-sufficiency in manufactured sugar — a long-term problem.[45]

Tariffs were revised several times during the First World War and became a serious issue immediately afterwards, when Japan used tariff policy in an attempt to protect wartime gains in the chemical and metallurgical industries from the renewed American competition. Pragmatic tariff revisions continued throughout the 1920s, and this trend was summed up in a major revision of tariffs agreed in 1926.[46] While emphasising the need to lower business costs and protect new industries, the revision raised tariffs on luxury goods and lowered them on goods produced by industries judged sufficiently mature to be capable of benefiting from foreign competition.[47]

The most serious problems in tariff policy in the 1920s were posed by the steel industry. As a major supplier of raw materials to other industries, it could only be protected at the expense of other sectors. In 1929 a solution to this problem was sought through lowering tariffs and providing subsidies for the formation of a new, concentrated organisation of the industry, which was expected to reach a fully efficient state quite quickly.[48]

In November 1936 the final pre-war revision of the tariff structure was undertaken. This attempted both to provide revenue to cover a serious budget deficit and to shape the tariff structure in ways consistent with national priorities and with the new techniques of direct economic planning being evolved to manage a war economy.

Commercial policy and micro-strategies

In 1890 Japan's trade and payments position was weak: exports exceeded imports by 58%, the long accumulated stock of bullion and reserves was substantially exhausted, and the capital account showed a small net outflow of funds. The outlook for the commodity structure

45. Takahashi, *Development*, vol. 1, pp. 212, 217–18.

46. An excellent discussion of these issues is 'Tariff policy and the heavy and chemical industrialisation of the 1920s' in Oishi Kaichiro (ed.), *Senkanki Nihon no taigai keizai kankei* (Japan's inter-war external economic relations), Tokyo: Nihon Hyoronsha, 1992, ch. 2.

47. MITI, vol. 5: *Foreign Trade*, pp. 20–2, 86ff., 90–3.

48. *Ibid.*, p. 96.

Table 6.6. THE STRUCTURE OF EXPORTS BY
DEGREE OF MODERNISATION, 1867–1927

	Raw materials	Raw silk	Factory: small-scale	Factory: large-scale	Other
1867–72	54.2	40.2	0.6	0.1	4.9
1888–93	44	40.1	5.4	1.1	9.4
1898–1902	23	29.4	5.4	12.1	30.1
1912–15	15.3	28	10.3	20	26.4
1920–23	8.4	33.4	10.4	29.1	18.7
1927	7.2	37.9	11.7	31.81	11.4

Source: Takahashi, *Development*, vol. 3, p. 226.

of exports in 1890 could not be described as promising. Raw materials
and agricultural goods were still important, although Japan's resource
endowment was relatively weak. In tea, for example, Japan was facing
serious and ultimately decisive competition from the black teas of India
and Ceylon. The performance of silk, Japan's other raw-material-based
staple export, was still strong, but only because China, despite superior
natural advantages, could not match the Japanese technical and
commercial skills.[49] Apart from silk products, other manufactured
exports still accounted for less than 10% of exports and faced a difficult
and uncertain future in a world economy dominated by the western
powers. The commodity breakdown of trade by degree of modernisation is shown in Table 6.6. As seen in Chapter 5 (especially Table
5.14), 'modern' manufactures found outlets in local Asian markets
while exports to the rich markets of the advanced economies consisted
of silk, raw materials and the output of traditional industries.

To Japanese bureaucrats and businessmen Japan's external problems
must have seemed formidable. They understood that future industrial growth would require imported raw materials — especially raw
cotton — and capital goods. Thus, unless domestic growth was
strongly biased towards exportable products and the commercial sector
succeeded in exporting an appropriate share of these, the long-term
prospects for the balance of payments were poor. Competitiveness
achieved by domestic supply-side and exchange-rate policies was one

49. Materials on tea and silk are reported in 'Japan and her tea customers', *NCH*,
May 4, 1894 and 'Mr Taylor's Report on the foreign trade of China for 1897', *NCH*,
April 4, 1898.

part of the answer, but it alone could not suffice in a situation where access to markets required penetration of high political, cultural and other barriers. The pressure to import increased sharply after the Sino-Japanese and Russo-Japanese wars. Thereafter Japan had to cope with exchange-rate difficulties following the First World War, with the anti-Japanese Chinese boycotts in the 1920s and, finally, with world depression in the 1930s. These problems put intense demands on overall national strategies and on the private sector. The next section examines both the role played in trade expansion by government commercial policies and the detailed work of trade promotion undertaken by the government bureaucracy.

State commercial policies and trade expansion

Responsibility for commercial policy belonged first to the Ministry of Agriculture and Commerce (Noshomusho) and then, after 1925, to the Ministry of Commerce and Industry (Shokosho). Foreign and domestic policies were thus controlled by a single ministry and the general character of industrial policy was an important factor in determining foreign trade policies. Before 1882 industrial policy had been interventionist, with government involvement extending to the creation and management of state-owned enterprises. Matsukata's financial stringency and general philosophy brought this phase to an end in the 1880s, when intervention shifted into a more subtle but still influential mode. In the 'post-bellum' plans after 1894 and 1905, direct intervention was restored for the purposes of establishing a metallurgical industry, developing armaments and rationalising and expanding the railway sector. In the 1920s the government retreated from direct industrial management, although investment in infrastructural activities remained high. In the 1930s direct intervention was revived, this time in the development of practices often seen as forerunners of post-war industrial policy.[50]

Two major tasks for the government in the 1890s were the recovery of autonomy in trade policy and the elimination of the western dominance of Japanese trade and shipping. The reality of this

---

50. This summary is based on Chalmers Johnson, *MITI and the Japanese Miracle: The Growth of Industrial Policy, 1925–1975*, Stanford University Press, 1982 and readings in MITI, *A history of policy, passim*. Data on the role of central and local government public spending are in Nakamura, *The economy of the Meiji-Taisho period*, p. 120.

dominance is revealed not only by the treaty provisions, but also by data on foreign shares of Japan's shipping, export and import trades. Thus the western position in Japan was based first on the old Ansei treaties, which gave extraterritorial powers and a veto on tariff policy to foreigners, and secondly on the superior skills of the foreigners as embodied in their financial and commercial institutions.

The recovery of 'commercial rights' began early, especially in the silk trade, yet initial efforts made slow headway as neither treaty revision nor instant acquisition of western commercial capabilities was possible. As long as trade was in foreign hands, import-substitution and export development policies could never be properly implemented. Well before the treaty revision of 1899 the government began to put in hand infrastructural development designed to assist the private sector move towards level terms with the westerners. Basic technical and commercial education were actively expanded from the 1870s onwards, with emphasis on the combination of training in commercial techniques and foreign languages. Thus elementary school attendance rates rose from 28% in 1873 to almost 100% by 1912, while the costs of school education amounted to a third of all local budgets.

The emphasis on language in education is illustrated by the timetable for middle-school children who, in their third year of study, spent a quarter of their time on language work. As early as the 1880s, the general rise in literacy was reflected in the publication of 550 newspapers and periodicals, of which seventeen dailies and 116 periodicals were published in Tokyo alone. At higher-level institutions and commercial colleges the emphasis on language continued and British observers viewed this orientation towards commercially applicable skills with some concern. One British Foreign Office report commented, 'There is certainly no School in the United Kingdom which can compare with the higher commercial school in comprehensiveness and minuteness of programme.' In the universities, the allocation of chairs gave a clear indication of the priority attached by the government to applied science and technology.[51]

Early infrastructural action was also demonstrated in the development of the Yokohama Specie Bank and Japan's first insurance

51. Emi, *Government Fiscal Activity*, pp. 125–31; Stead, *Japan by the Japanese*, ch. 13; Henry Norman, *The Real Japan*, London: T. Fisher Unwin, 1892, p. 42, and Foreign Office, '*Report on Commercial Education in Japan by Mr A. H. Lay*' (1899), *BPPJ*, vol. 10, pp. 463–77.

Table 6.7. PROGRESS IN SHIPPING AND MARINE INSURANCE, 1892–1903

	No. of marine insurance contracts	Index of value of contracts		Tonnage of foreign steamers purchased	Tonnage of steamers built in Japan
1892	33,944	100	1893	13,036	3,967
1896	374,219	546	1898	44,110	13,929
1899	495,904	559	1903	33,400	33,612

Source: Ministry of Finance, *Financial and Economic Annual of Japan*, pp. 60–1,145.

companies. Insurance was particularly crucial because of its relationship to shipping. By refusing to insure ships captained by Japanese, westerners had deliberately interfered with the growth of a Japanese merchant marine, and this problem was only solved by the establishment of the Tokyo Marine Insurance Company.[52]

In the 1880s and 1890s shipping was an industry which commercial and military factors combined to make a priority candidate for special assistance. The government responded not only by creating and subsidising the Nippon Yusen Kaisha but also by providing a succession of incentives, first to encourage Japanese ownership and management of shipping, and then to establish facilities for the production of large-scale ships built to advanced technical specifications.[53] Progress in shipping and marine insurance is summarised in Table 6.7.

Apart from the legal rights of foreigners in Japan, one of the obstacles to the recovery of commercial rights was their strength in traditional Japanese trades and markets. Thus an important aspect of Japanese exporting strategy was to shift exporting activity to new products and new geographical markets. Thus cotton textiles, coal and soya beans represented the new products which Japan could develop free of outside interference, and after 1895 Korea and China were geographical markets where Japan could establish trading bases on equal or better terms than westerners. The net result of these policies was that by 1914 Japan's freedom of trade policy operation had been substantially enlarged.

We saw earlier how the Japanese used the great international exhibitions to glean information and introduce Japan and its products to

52. MITI, vol. 5: *Foreign trade*, p. 327; Morikawa, *Basic knowledge*, pp. 82–3.
53. Takahashi, *Development*, vol. 3, ch. 1; Morikawa, *op. cit.*, pp. 398–9.

the wider world. After 1890 these objectives were pursued through more sophisticated strategies. Specialists in different trades and industries were sent all over the world to seek out technical and market intelligence, identify market opportunties and locate sources of raw materials. For example, between 1893 and 1897 commercial intelligence visits were made to China, India, South-East Asia, Australasia, Russia, Europe and the Americas, North and South. China was a nation of particular interest. Early reconnaissance in China had provided the information used in framing the commercial treaties signed at the end of the Sino-Japanese war. After the war itself new missions were sent to explore economic prospects in Manchuria and the Yangtze valley. In 1910 the United States was the object of a particulary detailed analysis of its markets, trade law, financial institutions and indeed every aspect of the economy relevant to Japanese commercial interests.[54]

An integral part of trade promotion was the holding of small exhibitions and the sending of samples (*mihon*). In 1896 more than 8,000 samples in nine major product categories and from up to seven different sources of Japanese supply were sent as far afield as Mexico, Singapore, Bombay and Odessa. These activities were increasingly supported by the establishment of consulates, usually set up as a result of pressure from local Japanese chambers of commerce. By 1895 there were fifteen consulates in Britain, the United States, France and Italy, and no less than eight in China. An important function of the consuls was to collect commercial and economic information, and the consular reports were centrally edited, bound in compendia and made available to the business community through local Japanese chambers of commerce.

An important watershed in commercial diplomacy came in 1900, by which year extraterritoriality had been abolished, partial tariff autonomy regained and the gold standard established. In that year too, the Minister for Agriculture and Commerce made an important statement on his ministry's approach to trade policy.[55] First he acknowledged that the commodity structure of Japanese trade would call for increased acquisition of raw materials, to be paid for by the sale of manufactures. The major sources of these, he argued, would be China, Manchuria, India and the United States. To generate more exports, he emphasised the need both to reduce manufacturing costs

54. MITI, vol. 5: *Foreign trade*, pp. 290–370.
55. *Ibid.*, pp. 358ff.

and to increase assistance for foreign marketing. He particularly stressed the role of the Yokohama Specie Bank and the development of aggressive financial policies overseas (e.g. in China). He also supported active development of shipping within Asia, focusing on the building up of networks of 'colonial' lines linking Taiwan, Shanghai, Dairen and Hokkaido.

Domestically, the minister proposed that both government and business should target commodities ready to make the transition from import substitution to exporting, in addition to building up institutions to control quality in the private sector. He also emphasised the overriding importance of language study and of commercial travelling by trading companies, since they would deepen Japanese understanding of consumers who were culturally embedded in foreign societies. The quality-control element of his plans was to be implemented by export associations which would also manage pricing and collective forms of export market manipulation.

The remarkable aspect of this statement was that it not only set out a broad strategy for trade-oriented economic development but also went on to consider the details of immediate measures by identifying strategic products and markets. Paper and figured mats provide just two such examples. Paper was proposed as an import-substitute industry ready for conversion to exporting and in his analysis the minister quoted data illustrating how Japan was failing to match competitors in the Chinese paper market. To sharpen competitiveness he advocated that preferential interest rates be provided by the Yokohama Specie Bank and that differential sea and rail tariffs be made available by the shipping and rail lines. For figured mats the minister examined the problems of exporting the output of decentralised small-scale producers, and especially the problem of quality. Since small-scale enterprises were to retain an important role in the export sector, he proposed various remedies for its problems including the centralisation of dyeing processes, a major cause of inconsistent quality. The success of such measures to help the small-scale sector is shown by export data and reports such as those in the annual British *Trade Report* which noted from Shanghai as early as 1897 that 'in matches and umbrellas, Japan rules the market'.[56]

Up till now we have discussed export promotion. But in the late Meiji period, import substitution remained important and continued

56. 'Mr Rocher's Report of trade of Shanghai 1897', *NCH*, May 2, 1898.

to be an object of official policies. For example, as early as 1879, one detailed analysis of import penetration displayed its results in a table showing sales of ten imported commodities in a sample of no less than thirty-six local Japanese markets. In the 1890s silver depreciation was a major stimulus to import substitution in consumer goods, while the acquisition of Formosa (Taiwan) in 1895 ultimately enabled Japan to cover its long-standing sugar deficit. Colonialism and cost factors apart, the Japanese were also helped in import substitution by the skilful way in which they turned the Ansei treaties to their own advantage; foreign extraterritoriality was converted from a springboard into a prison. At the same time as the Japanese were vigorously exploring the world for new markets, they applied the treaty provisions to prevent foreigners from travelling outside the ports to investigate the inland Japanese market. The continiung ineptitude of foreign firms in Japan is well documented in the British consular reports. In the reports for 1895 and 1896 we find that while British firms observed the rapid advances in Japanese engineering capabilities with alarm, they still sent catalogues to Japan written in English and without price-lists.[57]

The First World War created new opportunities for Japanese exports. Demand from the belligerents expanded while trade contacts between Europe, America and Asia were disrupted due in part to the conversion of the entire British merchant fleet to war purposes and the loan of 2.4 million out of 18.9 million tons of shipping to France and Italy. As a direct result, the Lancashire cotton industry had great difficulty in procuring the American raw cotton it needed to manufacture piece goods suitable for far eastern markets. In response, the Japanese government banned exports of important raw materials and undertook yet another investigation into trade opportunities. This produced in 1915 findings that led to an active policy of attacking traditional western markets in Asia and seeking raw material supplies in China, India, Mongolia and North America.[58]

In the difficult decade of the 1920s, the exchange rate was uncompetitive, anti-Japanese boycotts in China threatened access to a traditional market, and the Kanto earthquake damaged both the domestic

57. Foreign Office, 'Japan Report for the year 1895/1896 on the Foreign Trade of Japan', *BPPJ*, vol. 10, pp. 11–62. Import penetration analysis is in MITI, vol. 5: *Foreign trade*, pp. 226ff., 251–2.
58. MITI, vol. 6: *Foreign trade*, ch. 1.

and external economies. In 1927 and 1928 exports fell below the 1926 levels and the trade imbalance continued to cause anxiety. A significant development in this decade was the passing of the Export Industries Association Law in 1925, designed to help the small-scale sector continue its export development. Remarkably, small companies were still accounting for a rising proportion of exports, but they were seen as 'excessively competitive', short of capital, incapable of maintaining quality standards and lacking in the skills and knowledge needed for further strategic export development. The new Ministry of Commerce and Industry sought to remedy these weaknesses by establishing associations organised on the basis of product types or geographical market concentrations, or occasionally on a mixture of the two. The main principle of association membership was voluntary adherence by individual companies, although associations were to be supported by various types of government action. In 1926 similar arrangements were made specifically for the silk industry.[59]

During the 1930s the task of the Export Associations became even more urgent. Given the relatively inelastic demand by Japan for raw material imports, export *volume* had to increase spectacularly under conditions of worldwide trade depression in order to offset the effect of the exchange-rate depreciation. New regulations for the Associations were developed in 1933–34, under which the previous soft treatment of 'outsiders', i.e. those not in the Associations, came to an end. Associations were required to exercise tighter controls not only over quality but also over supply and pricing. This was indeed the 'era of export control'. In place of self-regulation, the new arrangements provided for a much enhanced role for the Associations in export development, which was clearly intended to lead to the operation of export cartels. In 1937, in the face of unmanageable trade imbalances, a parallel system was set up with great difficulty to control imports.

<hr />

59. A useful survey of Japanese trade organisation as it developed in the 1920s is in Mitsubishi Economic Research Bureau, *Japanese Trade and Industry Present and Future*, London: Macmillan, 1936, ch. 22. See also 'Pre- and post-war Export Associations' in *The Bank of Tokyo Monthly*, no. 8, 1954, pp. 28–41. This comprehensive article discusses the Associations in relation to post Second World War trade policy but is revealing about their history and, in particular, is much more explicit about official intentions with regard to export pricing and the conflict between producers and traders than the contemporary inter-war MITI documents.

Examples of inter-war strategies for export expansion: Africa and the electrical industry

The complexity and meaning of micro-trade policy and regulation in the inter-war period are well illustrated by two case-studies, one geographical and the other industrial.

Africa. Africa, a continent remote from Japan in every way, contained a set of markets which were exceptionally difficult to penetrate. At this time almost the whole continent was under the control of the western colonial powers. It was too important to ignore since it consisted mainly of developing countries with little domestic manufacturing industry and customers with low incomes of the kind that the Japanese had successfully reached in Asia. Further, Africa was contiguous to the Middle East where the cotton economies, notably Egypt, were significant suppliers of raw cotton to the Japanese cotton industry.

The official role in export expansion to Africa had to be central, for without local diplomatic support and the assistance of subsidised shipping routes and other trading infrastructure, there could be no progress. The official strategy was to build up consular strength in Cairo to develop the Mediterranean and East African markets, and in Casablanca to penetrate West Africa.

Shipping was important in these plans. Apart from setting up regular and tramp services, it was used for diplomatic and trade propaganda purposes. As early as 1926 the Osaka Shosen (Osaka Merchant Shipping Company) sent the *Canada Maru* to Durban, whence it cruised up the East African coast on an essentially diplomatic mission. By an extraordinary chance the South African writer Laurens van der Post was invited to accompany this voyage. The *Canada Maru* was a neat though modest ship, but the seriousness of the enterprise was borne in on van der Post, not only by the exceptional character of the vessel's captain and the nature of his instructions from the Osaka Shosen, but also by what he saw at dinner on his first night aboard:

I saw before me a ship's saloon worthy of the highest mail-boat standards. The single long table was covered with a dazzling white cloth and was laid with silver, cut glass tumblers and crystal wine goblets. In front of each pointed, neatly folded napkin was an elegant silver menu holder on which was printed what seemed like an incredible number of courses.[60]

60. Laurens van der Post, *Yet Being Someone Other*, London: Penguin Books, 1984, p. 113.

In 1933, on a similar promotional voyage, the *Alaska Maru* cruised down the West African coast. This voyage, however, was more openly commercial since the ship caused something of a sensation by selling Japanese-assembled Ford cars, bicycles and typewriters at unheard-of prices. Bicycle tyres were offered as loss leaders for a derisory one French franc each.

The impact of the Japanese exporting efforts in Africa in the early 1930s was dramatic, not only for local consumers but also for colonial exporters and local producers. Apart from Algeria, which enjoyed high protection, African markets were invaded first by Japanese trade missions and then by textiles and other goods. In Morocco, for example, Japan appeared in the import statistics in 1930 in the 'other countries' category. By 1932 it was the fourth-largest source of Moroccan imports and by 1934 second only to France. In the same market British textile sales were outselling the Japanese in 1932 by a ratio of 13 to 1, but in January 1934 Japan was outselling the British by 3 to 1. Particularly striking was the Japanese policy of bypassing traditional distribution systems and paying minute attention to the special clothing needs of the indigenous population, who were traditionally supplied by local handicrafts. After only one or two years of market analysis, the Japanese were actively importing such items as the Moroccan 'Belgha' shoe at 60% of the traditional price, thereby threatening the livelihood of thousands of local artisans.

As a result of this export expansion campaign, Africa and the Middle East rose to become significant markets for Japanese manufactures, and African considerations became an important element in the worldwide trade frictions between Japan and the West.[61]

The electric light industry. An excellent industrial example of the impact of official export development activities is that of the Japanese electric light industry, which achieved a rate of growth in export volume of 17% annually between 1928 and 1935.[62]

The light industry as a whole was divided into three parts. At its apex was the Tokyo Electric Company (TEC), created by a joint

---

61. The story of Japanese trade development in Africa is virtually unresearched. I have relied for these comments on a contemporary French monograph: M. Martelli-Chautard, *L'expansion japonaise en Afrique*, Paris: Comité de l'Afrique Française, 1934.

62. This is based on Teijiro Uyeda, *Small-scale industries of Japan: The Electric Light Industry*, Tokyo: Institute of Pacific Relations, 1936.

venture with General Electric of America before the First World War. The company established itself by use of General Electric patents and grew rapidly during the war. It was equipped to high standards, but by agreement with General Electric restricted its exports to Manchuria, China and parts of South-East Asia.

Below the TEC were two other groups of firms: the 'town' and the 'standard' firms. These were known collectively as the 'home-made' manufacturers because they did not hold foreign patents. This sector recruited labour from the TEC in the post-war years, partly because of the decline in the growth-rate of the TEC and partly because of its continued mechanisation. This whole sector benefited greatly from the expiry of the General Electric patent on the tungsten filament in 1927.

The difference between the 'town' and the 'standard' firms was that the latter were medium-sized companies with modern equipment, while the 'town' sector was made up of small, usually family-based workshops. About 90% of the output of the 'town' sector was exported, mainly through specialised merchants in Yokohama who operated a form of putting out by supplying financial and material support. Naturally the 'town' sector suffered from instability, serious variations in quality and ferociously competitive pricing, as a result of which the yen price of exports of household lamps declined by nearly 40% between 1928 and 1934. The official view, therefore, was that regulation was necessary to improve quality, develop export marketing, and encourage the acquisition of labour skills and modernisation. Further regulation through cartelisation would enable Japan to get a higher net foreign exchange return than would be yielded by market forces. This was essential. For example, the combination of domestic price reduction and devaluation had reduced the foreign exchange price of household lamps by more than 75% between 1930 and 1934.

Regulation of the industry involved a variety of bodies. Under the umbrella organisation of the Japan Union of Lamp Manufacturers were the Electric Lamp Manufacturers Association for Exports (run by the merchants), the Association of 'standard' companies, and the Home-Made Electric Lamp Manufacturing Association, representing the 'town' workshops. The first attempt at regulation by the Ministry of Commerce and Industry involved using the 1933 legislation to give the Japan Union the power to inspect export output at a fee which for 'outsiders' was eight times that for members. In 1934 the Ministry tried another tack by giving the 'standard' producers' association exclusive rights to export lamps from Japan. In response to this seizure of power by the 'standard' manufacturers, many 'town' firms either moved offshore to Korea or went underground in Japan. Eventually, the smaller firms succeeded in gaining more favourable treatment for 'outsiders'. Apart from the export growth noted above, the net effects of this regulation were raised prices (e.g. by 10% in 1935) and improvements in quality, technical modernisation and better working conditions in the 'town' workshops.

Trade frictions

Japanese trade expansion in the 1930s reflected not only price advantages and supply-side improvements but also the cumulative effects of micro–strategies developed consistently for more than forty years. In an effort to support exports in the face of the world trade depression, the Export Subsidy Law of 1930 gave special financial assistance to firms selling in North and South America, Russia, Africa and other parts of Asia. The result was the first episode of trade friction created by targeted Japanese export expansion. As detailed in Chapter 8, Britain defended its textile markets in India, Africa and the Middle East, and the Dutch their beer, cement and textiles interests in the East Indies. There were also major disputes with Australia, Canada and the United States. Recurrent themes in the anti-Japanese criticism were the aggressive Japanese devaluation and the 'low [inhuman] wages'. To combat this friction Japan passed a Trade Protection Law in 1934 and used its implicit powers of trade retaliation with good effect, notably in disputes relating to India and Canada.[63]

In spite of this friction, Japanese trade policies were successful in penetrating new markets. The size of the trade deficit in 1937 might be taken as evidence of failure in the strategies of the 1930s but these strategies were not the source of this deficit. The trade imbalance in 1937 reflected a short-term failure to control government spending and domestic demand. This in turn reflected political failures that

63. MITI, vol. 5, *Foreign trade*, pp. 158–74. The trade battle for the Middle East is illuminatingly described in Hiroshi Shimizu, *Anglo-Japanese Rivalry in the Middle East in the Inter-war Period*, London: Ithaca Press, 1986. The trade frictions generated a mass of literature critical of Japan, e.g., Freda Utley, *Japan's Feet of Clay*, London: Faber and Faber, 1937.

ultimately led to catastrophic choices of national strategy. For our purposes the 1930s were significant in showing how, given a competitive exchange rate, Japan had the capacity to organise dramatic expansion of export supply, to develop effective micro-commercial strategies over long periods, to engage in successful trade diplomacy to resolve trade frictions without sacrificing its interests, and to use a combination of public and private sector skills to divert trade into new products and new geographical markets. In the much more favourable international environment after the Second World War, the full implications of this progress were to be manifested in a spectacular way.

7

THE RESPONSE OF THE PRIVATE SECTOR: THE FOUNDATIONS OF THE COTTON TEXTILES INDUSTRY

'The strength or weakness of a nation depends on the wealth or poverty of its people; the wealth or poverty of a people depends on the volume of production.' — Okubo Toshimichi, *Memorial to the Emperor on the Encouragement of Industry* (1874)

The importance of cotton

The cotton textile industry was the foundation of the industrial revolution and the mainstay of world trade in manufactured goods throughout the nineteenth century. The pace of growth and foreign trade expansion in textiles, and Britain's predominant role in this, are all illustrated in Table 7.1. Here the indicator of long-run trends is the physical consumption of raw cotton. During this period, both *mill* and *handspun* cotton were produced, and the data on the latter are included to show the changing importance of the manufactured and traditional forms of production. These data show that in the late eighteenth century the industry was still predominantly a handicraft activity, and heavily concentrated in those parts of the world where cotton is cultivated most easily. However, by the early nineteenth century the impact and pace of the industrial revolution was striking; by the 1880s, while the consumption of handspun cotton had doubled by comparison with 1790, the consumption of mill output had increased by a factor of 160. The growth of the industry eased between the 1880s and 1910–13, and then declined in the inter-war years. By the late 1930s the machine revolution was almost complete and handspun goods amounted to only 4% of total consumption.

The exceptionally large role of international trade in the industry's modern development has several explanations. The most important of these are the early geographical concentration of cotton manufacturing skills, the worldwide demand for cotton clothing to improve living standards, the rapid fall in the prices of cotton goods as

Table 7.1. THE GROWTH OF WORLD CONSUMPTION AND TRADE
IN COTTON AND COTTON GOODS, 1790–1938
(millions of lbs, rate of growth per annum)

	1790–1829/31	1829/31–1882/84	1882/84–1910/13	1910/13–1936/38
Rate of growth of mill consumption of cotton % per annum	7.3	4.3	3.5	1.1

	1790	1829/31	1882/84	1910/13	1936/38
British mill consumption as % of world total	100	57	37	20	9
Raw cotton self-sufficiency rate (%) in manufacturing countries	0	12	30	38	55
British exports of cotton goods as % of world exports	100	70	82	58	28
Exports of cotton goods as % of British production	25	67	85	81	46
World consumption of mill output (m. lbs)	25	420	4,000	10,500	14,000
World trade (m. lbs)	5	229	1,537	2,948	2,170
Trade as % of total output	20	55	38	28	16
Estimated consumption of handspun cotton (m. lbs)	500		1,000		500

Source: Derived from data in R. Robson, *The Cotton Industry in Britain*, London: Macmillan, 1957, p. 2.

mechanisation increased supply, and the enormous expansion in the supply of raw cotton from the southern United States.[1] These factors explain why in 1829–31, for example, over half of the world's production of mill-spun cotton was exported, and although this proportion fell steadily as textile industrialisation spread, the total volume of trade continued to expand up to the First World War.

1. Between 1815 and 1850, yarn and cloth prices fell by 50% and 80% respectively. François Crouzet, *The Victorian Economy*, London: Methuen, 1982, p. 196. The role of raw materials is emphasised by D. A. Farnie, *The English Cotton Industry and the World Market, 1815–1896*, Oxford: Clarendon Press, 1979, pp. 82ff.

The dominant role of Britain in the industry and the importance of textiles among British exports are also shown in Table 7.1. In 1882–84, Britain accounted for an extraordinary 82% of world textile trade, and these exports in turn accounted for 85% of British textile output. In Japan, by contrast, only 1.2% of cotton thread supply was satisfied by domestic mills in the same period. By 1936–38, however, this situation had changed decisively. The British share of the world cotton trade had fallen to 28% and the exported share of British cotton output to only 46%. Japan's role in this decline can be judged by the fact that from negligible beginnings in the 1880s it had surpassed Britain as the major producer of both yarn and cotton piece-goods by 1935, while in trade Japan and Britain together accounted for 71% of the volume and 67% of the value of cotton piece-goods exports. This chapter seeks to explain how this transformation came about and how the Japanese, who received all their early lessons in textile technology and organisation from Lancashire, ultimately became the leading agent in its industrial decline.[2]

For Japan the textile industry presented a crucial industrial challenge, and the consequences of failure to meet it would have been far-reaching. From the 1860s to the 1880s imports of finished textiles for consumption were the chief factor in the trade imbalance. For a country like Japan, with relatively cheap labour, textiles were a potentially important export industry quite apart from the need for import substitution. But given the initial technical and commercial supremacy of the British, European and American producers, achieving the basic goals of viability and competitiveness was to be very difficult, requiring solutions to four basic problems. These were: the choice, transfer and adaptation of western textile technology; establishment of the financial

---

2. The basic secondary sources for the early modern history of Japanese textiles are Takamura Naosuke, *Nihon bosekigyoshi no josetsu* (An introduction to the history of the Japanese cotton spinning industry), Tokyo: Hanawa Shobo, 1971 and MITI, *A history of policy*, vols 15 and 16, *Seni kogyo* (Textiles). For the inter-war period, a valuable recent work is Nishikawa Hiroshi, *Nihon teikokushugi to mengyo* (Japanese imperialism and the cotton industry), Kyoto: Minerva Shobo, 1987. Among English language works, useful sources are K. Seki, *The Cotton Industry of Japan*, Tokyo: Japan Society for the Promotion of Science, 1956, and Jae Koh Sung, *Stages of Industrial Development in Asia: A Comparative History of the Cotton Industry in Japan, India, China and Korea*, Philadelphia: University of Philadelphia Press, 1966. Of great value for the study of world trends are articles on cotton and related subjects in *Encyclopaedia Britannica*, esp. the 11th (1910) to the 1951 editions which between them cover the history of the industry's commercial and technical development from the late nineteenth century to the Second World War.

and other institutional structures needed to enable firms in the industry to grow to the scale necessary for competitiveness; access to adequate supplies of raw materials; and acquisition of the commercial skills needed to supplant the foreigners in the home markets and then compete with them in third countries.

The government was active in all four activities, but the particular significance of textiles here is that it was the first industry in which, after a short phase of government leadership, Japanese private enterprise showed a decisive ability to succeed by combining the most advanced practices from abroad with its own innovations in both technology and organisation.[3]

The evolution of the industry can be seen in the perspective of two major and several minor phases of development. The First World War forms a natural demarcation of the major phases since, by 1914, the industry had matured to the point where it had established modern spinning and weaving branches as well as substantially displacing imported textiles and securing an export beachhead in the adjacent markets of China and Korea. During the First World War, the industry responded to the opportunities created by the temporary difficulties of Britain and other countries and laid the foundations in South-East Asia, Africa, Latin America and the Middle East on which it would later build a worldwide strategy for export expansion. After the war the main issues facing the industry were the struggle for trading supremacy *vis-à-vis* Britain and the problems created by the world depression. In both areas Japan's relationship with India was important.

At a more detailed level the pre-First World War years can be divided into four phases: the phase of direct government intervention in the 1860s and 1870s to transplant modern spinning technology; the foundation and early history of the Osaka Boseki Kaisha (The Osaka Spinning Company) and other private companies in the 1880s; the emergence of these companies in the 1890s as serious competitors in the international thread market; and finally the growing dominance

---

3. Western writers on Japanese textiles have generally been seriously misled about the state's role in the industry. They have taken lack of tariff protection for lack of support and have relied too heavily on Seki, *The Cotton Industry*, an admirable study, but reflecting a very distinct point of view. See, for example, the important study by Lars Sandberg, *Lancashire in Decline: A Study in Entrepreneurship, Technology, and International Trade*, Columbus: Ohio State University Press, 1974, where the author refers to Japanese textile development being achieved 'without the aid of tariff or any other kind of government assistance', p. 174.

in the 1900s of large 'integrated' companies, engaged in both spinning and weaving and increasingly active in the export of cloth.

The foundation of the modern industry, 1867–1900

In the pre-modern era the Japanese enjoyed a striking history both as consumers and producers of textile goods. In early and medieval Japan silk and cotton fabrics were imported from many sources, especially China, but their technologies and designs were quickly absorbed into distinctively Japanese traditions of textile taste and fabrication. In the sixteenth century European fabrics (*namban mono*) were imported and admired, and the domestic textiles produced in the Momoyama period (1568–1600) and later are artifacts of extraordinary beauty.[4] During the Tokugawa era the textile trade had to contend with the depressing influence of sumptuary laws that restricted dress according to the occupation and status of the wearer, but in spite of this the merchant and theatrical classes succeeded in inspiring and supporting the continuation of fine textile production, especially during the Genroku period of the late seventeenth century. Thus by the late Tokugawa period, textile design, production and marketing were widely practised and sophisticated trades, serving all classes of society. The industry relied entirely on domestic raw cotton, and the combination of access to these materials and to major concentrations of population with purchasing power made Osaka a natural point of industry concentration. Even so, by the mid-nineteenth century a number of other centres had emerged as significant producers.

This domestic scene was seriously disturbed in the mid-nineteenth century when Japanese consumers, echoing the behaviour of their sixteenth-century predecessors, began to demonstrate a voracious

4. Materials on the spread of the Tokugawa textile industry are in Odaka and Yamanoto, *The Japanese Economy in the late Tokugawa*, ch. 3. For the transfer and development of traditional technology, see Isobe, *The theory of traditional craft production, passim*. A general account of traditional textiles is Seiroku Noma, *Japanese Costume and Textile Arts*, Tokyo: Heibonsha, 1974. The upper-class market is illustrated in Amanda Mayer Stinchecum, *Kosode: 16th–19th Century Textiles from the Nomura Collection*, New York: Kodansha, 1984 and the lower-class markets in Fifi White, *Japanese Folk Textiles*, Kyoto: Shikosha, 1988. Apart from the levels of technology and the development of production, a fascinating feature of the trade discussed in Noma and Stinchecum is the extent and sophistication of kimono designs, which were recorded in the *hiinagata-bon* (kimono design books).

Table 7.2. THE COMPOSITION OF JAPAN'S CLOTH SUPPLY
BY SOURCE AND TECHNOLOGY LEVEL, 1861–97
(quantities)

	% cloth imported	% domestic cloth using imported thread	Import dependence (cloth and thread)	% domestic cloth using traditional thread	% domestic cloth using Japanese machine-made thread	Index of total consumption
1861	10	1	(11)	89	–	100
1880	23.4	40.5	(63.9)	34.9	1.2	248
1883	18.9	49.1	(68)	25.6	6.4	176
1891	11.4	18.6	(30)	19.3	50.7	328
1897	12.3	10.4	(22.7)	9.8	67.8	546

Sources: Derived from tables in Ishii, *Economic history*, p. 110; Takamura, *An introduction*, vol. 1, p. 30.

demand for the novelties of imported machine-made cloth. It was against this background that a Satsuma prince imported English equipment in 1867 to establish the Kagoshima Bosekisho — a steam-driven spinning mill of 3,648 spindles. After the Restoration, the Meiji government confirmed the high and immediate priority of textiles and adopted in its industralisation policy the principle that, while heavy and armaments-related industries were expected to be in the public sector and heavily subsidised for an indefinite period, the light and textile industries should be transferred to the private sector as soon as possible. Thus on the foundation of the Kagoshima Bosekisho, the basic Meiji policy was to establish two model mills of 2,000 spindles each, and to subsidise machinery imports for ten further mills of the same size.[5] This group of factories constituted Japan's first effort to establish a modern spinning industry and their impact is reflected in Tables 7.2 and 7.3, which show the relative importance of domestic and foreign supplies of thread and cloth up to 1897. These tables illustrate three phases in the evolution of the Japanese cotton market. The initial phase is shown by the 1861 data. During this phase the output of the traditional spinning and weaving sectors predominated, but significant imports of cloth had begun to appear. An intermediate phase (1883) followed, when foreign cloth and yarn accounted for

5. MITI, vol. 15, *Textiles*, ch. 1; Takamura, *An introduction*, vol. 1, ch. 1; Seki, *The Cotton Industry*, pp. 8ff.

Table 7.3. RATE OF GROWTH OF TOTAL
CONSUMPTION FROM ALL SOURCES,
SELECT PERIODS 1861–97 (*% per annum*)

1861–80	5.2
1880–91	2.6
1891–7	8.9

Source: as Table 7.2.

68% of supplies, but cloth imports had declined in favour of the yarn imports used by domestic (handicraft) weavers. The final phase (1897) was one where domestic cloth using domestic factory thread had substantially displaced both thread and cloth imports. This sequence anticipates the pattern of events by which western textiles were eventually driven from almost all the markets of Asia.[6]

What is so striking about the Japanese story recorded here is the speed with which domestic thread replaced imports: its share of consumption rose from 6.4% to 50.7% in a mere eight years from 1883 to 1891. This development did not, however, reflect the direct success of the first group of modern spinning mills. The later 1880s were a difficult time for the industry because movements in the silver price strengthened foreign competitiveness, especially against the 2,000 spindle mills that would have been uncompetitive in their original form under any circumstances. There were several reasons for this lack of viability. One was that the financial foundations of the mills were narrow, clan-based and incapable of the flexibility needed to handle problems such as cost overruns and other financial shocks. Also they were managed largely by local government officials who lacked the necessary training and skills. Technically, the Japanese mills were handicapped by their dependence on water power, by inadequate local raw cotton supplies and by the failure to obtain the economies of scale necessary to be competitive with best practice elsewhere. Although the attempt to make these mills successful in their original form did end in 1886, it would be a mistake to regard the episode as a failure. The early mills made a significant contribution to Japanese learning in a

6. For Britain, the Asian share of the total market peaked as early as 1880 with the market for piece-goods peaking in 1888. See the discussion in Farnie, *The English Cotton Industry*, p. 127.

period when the private sector scarcely existed and had little interest in such a novel and risky mode of production.[7]

The decisive shift to the private sector and commercial viability began in the early 1880s, supported by Matsukata's policy of encouraging private enterprise with a strong government-directed financial system. In textiles the crucial event was the formation of the Osaka Boseki under the leadership of Shibusawa Eiichi. Shibusawa was a model Meiji businessman: technically aware, flexible in pursuit of fixed objectives, deeply nationalistic yet international in outlook.[8] He and his associates grasped the crucial significance of textiles and the need for the Japanese textile industry to become internationally viable. Indeed, as a foreign exchange banker he had observed the declining competitive position of Japanese textiles as early as the late 1870s and understood the consequences of failure to come to grips with this problem. With his associates he studied carefully the lessons of the 2,000 spindle mills and made early efforts to obtain direct access to British and other foreign technical experience.

Shibusawa first developed the idea of establishing a large-scale, technically advanced Japanese textile company in 1879 and 1880, when the Osaka Chamber of Commerce (*Osaka Shogyo Kaigisho*) investigated the problem of uncompetitive Japanese prices for cotton goods and an important government report noted that sugar and textiles still accounted for two-thirds of Japanese imports.[9] For specialist advice, Shibusawa relied on Yamanobe Takeo, a Japanese student in England. The latter's advice was at first transmitted by correspondence but in July 1880 Yamanobe returned to Japan and in the next two years Shibusawa set about raising funds from a broad constituency of backers, which included representatives of both the merchant class and the nobility (*kazoku*). He then took two further important decisions: to base the company in Osaka, and to employ steam- rather than water-driven technology. The spindles for the new plant were ordered from

7. MITI, vol. 15, *Textiles*, p. 142.

8. Obata, *An Interpretation of the Life of Viscount Shibusawa*; articles on Shibusawa and the Osaka Boseki in *Nihon keizaishi jiten*; Kimura Masato, *Shibusawa Eiichi*, Tokyo: Chuo Shinsho, 1991.

9. '1880 Men – to kyoshinkai hokoku' (The 1880 Report of the Sugar and Textile Competitive Exhibition) quoted in MITI, *Textiles*, vol. 15, pp. 8–11; Takamura, *An introduction*, vol. 1, p. 28.

Platt's of Oldham in late 1881; the plant opened in July 1883 and was fully operational by mid-1884.[10]

Measured by all relevant indicators, the early record of the Osaka Boseki was outstanding. Between 1884 and 1890 output increased eightfold and labour costs per bale were reduced by 37%. Quality (measured by the 'count' of yarn) rose, with average counts rising from 14 to a range of 16 to 22. Financially, profits on paid-up capital were 31.6% in 1884, rose to 60.8% in the first half of 1887 and were still 29.5% in the difficult first half of 1889. The company's shares traded on the Osaka Stock Exchange at between 200% and 350% of their placement price.

The main reasons for this success were the company's financial structure, its technical characteristics and the quality and management of its human resources. Financially, the Osaka Boseki drew funds from a much wider and more powerful range of investors than the 2,000 spindle companies did, and the example of its profits, dividend policy and share price performance was important in the early development not only of the private sector spinning industry but also of the Japanese capital market generally. The company's profitability enabled it to combine generous dividend policies with the accumulation of internal reserves for capital investment and raw cotton stockholding, a tradition that was to become a distinctive characteristic of the Japanese textile industry with important consequences for its long-term competitiveness.

Technically, the initial plant of 10,500 spindles was five times larger than the earlier group of modern plants, and in theory it should have reached the economies of scale of foreign competitors. But in spite of these technical and other advances, Japanese working and management skills were still insufficient to secure the final breakthrough to competitiveness. The final element in the Osaka Boseki system and the one that made it competitive was the implementation in 1883 of the double shift. This was greatly eased by Shibusawa's revolutionary use of electric lighting, in 1885, through which a higher degree of plant utilisation was obtained than was normal even for foreign competitors. In essence, the shift system enabled the company to achieve a more

---

10. These and subsequent details are drawn primarily from MITI, vol. 15, *Textiles*, *passim*; *Toyo boseki nanajunenshi* (The seventy-year history of the Toyo Spinning Company), Tokyo, 1953. Toyo was the company formed by a merger with the Osaka in 1914. Takamura, *An outline*, vol. 1, ch. 1, esp. the Table on p. 64.

Table 7.4. THE GROWTH AND SCALE OF COMPANIES IN
THE COTTON-SPINNING SECTOR, 1884–1914

	Osaka Boseki (spindles)	Other large companies	Medium-sized companies	Small companies
1884	10,500	12 (2,170)	–	–
1889	61,320	15 (13,000)	–	–
1914	441,700	5 (245,000)	6 (90,000)	26 (1,700–39,300)

Source: Derived from data in Takamura, *An introduction*, vol. 1, p. 79; vol. 2, pp. 212–13.
Note: Figures in brackets are the average no. of spindles per company.

labour-intensive variant of the British technology.[11] To staff the
two-shift system the company employed a workforce increasingly
recruited from a wide geographical base. By the 1900s, however,
recruitment had become a much more specialised and targeted operation, focused on the organised transfer of young females from the
villages.

The early effect of all these changes is reflected in the detailed
analysis of the 1884 cost structure of the Osaka Boseki. This shows
that relative to the 2,000- 3,000- spindle plants, although physical
productivity per spindle was comparable, the company achieved
substantial cost reduction by skilled labour management and economies
of scale in the use of fuel and raw materials.[12]

Shibusawa's success and the further rise in textile profitability during
a railway construction boom encouraged a wave of textile company
formation. Between 1888 and 1890 spindleage increased sixfold and
cotton spinning finally became a large-scale, concentrated urban
industry. The growth and changing scale of firms in the industry
between 1884 and 1914 are shown in Table 7.4, where we see
that while in 1884 the Osaka Boseki stood alone as a large-scale
company, within five years fifteen other companies with an average
spindleage of 13,000 had appeared. At first there were substantial

11. The two shifts allowed for almost 24-hour working of plant. Data on the early
system may be found in T. Shindo, *Labour in the Japanese Cotton Industry*, Tokyo:
Japan Society for the Promotion of Science, 1961, pp. 61–8. Shindo was a former
chairman of Toyo. The issue is also fully discussed in Takamura, *An introduction*,
vol. 1, pp. 134–44, and in a very critical light by Freda Utley, *Lancashire and the Far
East*, London: Geo. Allen and Unwin, 1931.
12. Data are in Takamura, *An introduction*, vol. 1, p. 79.

Table 7.5. VARIATIONS IN SCALE AND PRODUCTIVITY
IN SPINNING COMPANIES, JUNE 1889

No. of companies in group	Average employment	Average spindleage	Output *	Index of labour productivity based on Osaka Boseki = 100
Osaka Boseki	1,527	32,100	67,648	100
6	501	11,019	18,488	81
6	302	4,840	9,999	64
9	94	2,000	2,702	49

Source: Based on data in Takamura, An introduction, vol. 1, p. 137.
* Output measured by weight in kan where one kan equals $8\frac{1}{2}$ lbs.

variations of productivity between companies, as can be seen in Table 7.5, but as competition matured and learning experiences were absorbed and shared, progress in productivity, quality and cost reduction was rapid and more evenly distributed.

The growth of output and the progress of spinning and weaving towards international competitiveness for the whole period from the early Meiji to the late 1930s may be judged from Figs 7.1 and 7.2, which show that significant import substitution was achieved in the late 1880s and 1890s and that a start had been made in exporting. In the thread sector exports exceeded imports in 1897 and the same watershed was crossed in the cloth sector by 1910. A point not visible in Figs 7.1 and 7.2 is that the important competition in the home thread market was from India, which in 1887–89 had accounted for more than half of all imports and about 40% of domestic supply. By 1898 Indian imports had been eliminated, although substantial British imports of higher-quality thread remained.[13]

Apart from the factors referred to in the discussion of the Osaka Boseki, there are four reasons for the rapid progress of the Japanese cotton industry up to 1900: the management of raw material supply, the evolution of spinning technology, marketing strategies at home and abroad, and the nature of competition and leadership in the industry. To grasp these points and their subsequent development, we have to

13. Japan also gained great advantages from the sharp drop of Indian output that was the result of the bubonic plague epidemic of 1896–97. See V. B. Kulkarni, History of the Indian Textile Industry, Bombay: Bombay Millowners' Association, 1979, p. 59.

consider in general terms both the raw material problem and the issues posed by spinning technology.

The raw material problem. Raw cotton is grown in many parts of the world. Its basic requirements are a growing season of at least six months and adequate moisture in the form of monsoon rains or irrigation systems. Differences in plant varieties, cultivation techniques, climate and other growing conditions give rise to great variations in the character of crops, and the management of these variations is a crucial part of the cotton spinners art. Although grown in more than sixty countries, most commercially traded cotton in our period came from only five sources, and it was the handling of these alternatives that was important to Japan. In 1911–12 the major sources and their respective shares of world output were the United States (68%), India (13%), Egypt (6%) and China (3%). The very large share of the United States was important, since climatic variations made the American crop persistently unstable and the cause of large variations in international prices.[14]

The most important physical characteristic of raw cotton is the average length of staple (cotton fibre) since longer staples generally spin into finer qualities of thread. Indian staples are typically $\frac{3}{4}$ inch, American are up to $1\frac{1}{4}$ inches, while Egyptian and other fine varieties such as Sea Island are $1\frac{1}{2}$ inches and more. Staples in China vary considerably, although they are normally within a range of $\frac{3}{8}$ inch to $\frac{1}{2}$ inch. When spun, these variations in length (and other characteristics) are reflected in variations of quality, of which the most basic measure is the 'count', normally defined by the English standard of the number of 840-yard hanks that weigh 1 lb. 'Low' counts from short staples are typically up to 16. 'Medium' counts range between 16 and 14, while 'high' counts can go above 100.

The blending problem. For the spinner the problems and opportunities created by raw material variation are both technical and commercial, since what he must do is scan the market-place, select raw cottons of varying quality and price, and then blend them in the spinning process to produce a planned quality of yarn at minimum cost. It was the

14. Articles on 'Cotton' and 'The Cotton Industry' in *EB* (11th and 1951 editions); L. C. Tippett, *A Portrait of the Lancashire Textile Industry*, Oxford University Press, 1969, ch. 2.

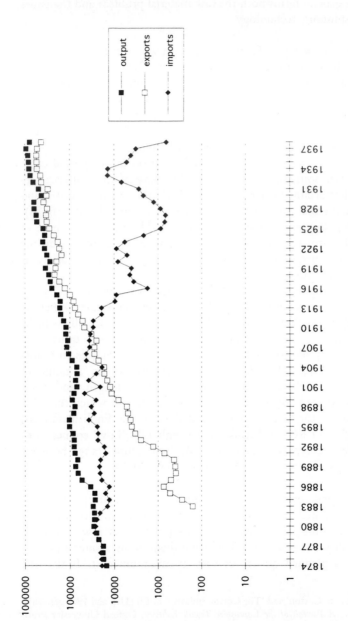

Fig. 7.1. OUTPUT, EXPORTS AND IMPORTS OF COTTON CLOTH, 1874–1938

Source: Yamazawa Ippei, *Nihon no keizai hatten to kokusai bungyo* (Japanese economic development and the international division of labour) Tokyo: Toyo Keizai Shimposha, 1985, pp. 248–9.

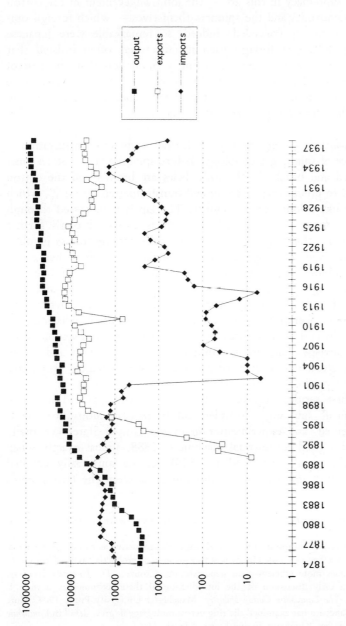

Fig. 7.2 OUTPUT, EXPORTS AND IMPORTS OF COTTON THREAD, 1874–1938

Source: Yamazawa, *Japanese economic development*, pp. 248-9.

Japanese supremacy in this art — the joint achievement of the cotton trading companies and the spinners themselves — which foreign opinion unanimously conceded. Indeed, so remarkable were Japanese blending skills that foreign yarn manufacturers often insisted that Japanese spinners were manufacturing yarn for less than the cost of raw materials. This was not actually the case: what the Japanese were doing was to produce qualities of yarn with cheaper varieties of raw cotton than foreign spinners could conceive of.

The introduction of ring spinning. A further technical consideration is the choice of spinning technology. Before spinning, raw cotton must be ginned and baled. At the mill, bales are broken and the cotton subjected to preliminary cleaning and transformation into 'lap', which is rather like a long, crude blanket. The lap is then passed through rollers to form 'sliver', which in turn is passed through further roller systems that make 'roving'. The final spinning process involves attenuating and twisting the roving to make yarn that is then rolled on to bobbins.[15] Two alternative technologies became available for this final stage in the late nineteenth century: the mule and ring systems. The mule was the first to appear and its use involved an intermittent operation in which the processes of attenuating and twisting the cotton alternated, with the yarn spun from spindles on a moving carriage. The system required complex machinery and skilled male operators, but when used properly it was extremely productive and could produce fine qualities of yarn.[16]

The first serious version of the ring system appeared in 1828, and it made spinning a simpler and more continuous process. It was patented, and experimentation in the United States eventually produced a good commercial machine in 1888, almost exactly when the Roberts mule (patented in 1825) became universally adopted by the British industry.[17] The differences between the two systems

15. Tippett, *A Portrait*, ch. 3 and Robson, *The Cotton Industry in Britain*, pp. xiii–xx.

16. The early Crompton mule was 25 times as productive as handspinning while the Roberts self-acting mule (1825) was fifteen times as productive as the Crompton, i.e. 375 times more efficient than handspinning, Crouzet, *The Victorian Economy*, p. 101. An early discussion of the introduction of these technologies is in S. J. Chapman, *The Lancashire Cotton Industry*, Manchester University Press, 1904. More recently, Sandberg has examined the ring versus mule issue in great detail in *Lancashire in Decline* as has Kiyokawa in works cited in ch. 11.

17. Chapman, *The Lancashire Cotton Industry*, pp. 69–70.

in the late 1880s were that while mule spinning could produce finer yarns, the late nineteenth-century ring machinery was simpler to produce and maintain, and its operation required less skill. Thus if adequate supervision were available, expensive skilled male workers could be replaced by less skilled, younger and lower-paid female workers who were readily available from rural areas.

The commercial availability of the ring system coincided with the upsurge of spinning company formation in Japan and therefore gave the industry the opportunity to equip itself with a technology that was adaptable to Japanese resources in a way that offered significant competitive advantages. This substitution of a new form of machinery for skilled craftsmen was an innovation that went in the direction that full-scale mass production was to take in American industry from the early 1900s. It also shows how, almost from the very beginning, Japanese adaptations of western techniques involved significant innovations in the overall system of factory organisation.

The main problem with the system — its appropriateness to lower counts — was not a serious disadvantage, since low counts produced cloth of quality that was suitable both for import substitution in Japan and for exports to low-income Asian markets. Higher-quality cloth could continue to be woven from imported yarns, and by the 1920s the Japanese had improved cotton blending skills and ring technology to the point where they could ring-spin high-quality yarns while retaining the cost advantages inherent in the system.

Installation of the ring system in Japan provided opportunities to enlarge the scale of operations to the 20,000-spindle level and above. This expansion and the adoption of the ring system went ahead rapidly. In 1880 rings accounted for only 6% of total spindleage. By 1890 spindleage had increased twenty-eight fold, with rings accounting for 65% of the total.[18] The Osaka Boseki, which had originally been equipped with the mule, converted to the ring for its third factory, which was completed in 1887. This enthusiastic adoption of the new system was not simply a passive calculation of the immediately appropriate technology; rather, it reflected a passion for seeking out and adopting technical excellence (a passion which foreign competitors admired but often felt was carried to irrational lengths) and an ability to choose technologies that could be rapidly improved

18. Takamura, *An introduction*, vol. 1, p. 111.

by development in Japan to be integrated into complete factory systems.[19] However, to implement the new technique on the scale needed to take full advantage of it required funds not only for purchase of equipment but also for the employment of expensive foreign textile specialists. Both these costs were serious barriers to entry into the industry for small firms with limited financial resources.[20]

With the variety of sources of raw cotton, the complex evolving technologies available for blending and spinning, the differing quality requirements for yarn and cloth in consumer markets, and the range of accounting, managerial and commercial skills required to manage large companies, the achievement of international competitiveness in textiles was a formidable challenge to newcomers. It was a challenge which initially defeated two contemporary industrialisers, China and India, but which Japan met with phenomenal success.

The Japanese raw material problem and the early development of the Bokyo

The growth of the spinning industry put strains on the Japanese raw material supply. The Meiji leadership initially planned for self-sufficiency in raw cotton, and this was reflected in the low level of imports in the 1880s. But the attainment of this goal proved impracticable.[21] Local cotton was of low and variable quality and its supply subject to crop failures while competitive mill-manufactured yarn required dependable supplies of standardised qualities. Thus in spite of the power of agricultural vested interests, the spinning companies were allowed to embark on policies that were to ruin domestic cotton farmers.[22] In 1877 Mitsui Bussan established offices in Shanghai from where it began to import cotton in the mid-1880s. By 1887, 45% of the raw cotton supplied to Japanese mills came from China. However,

---

19. Admirers of the seemingly irrational include Kulkarni, *History*, p. 57, but Farnie reflects the British aversion for 'technological monomania' in *The English Cotton Industry*, p. 197.

20. Examples of the high cost of foreign experts are discussed in Takamura, *An introduction*, vol. 1, p. 141.

21. Nawa Toichi, *Nihon bosekigyo no shiteki bunseki* (An historical analysis of the Japanese textile industry), Tokyo: Choryusha, 1949, p. 149; Umezu, *Japanese foreign trade thinking*, p. 44.

22. MITI, vol. 15, *Textiles*, p. 249.

quality problems and interruptions in the Chinese supply in 1889
caused a crisis which at one stage left half the spindles in Japan idle.
Price trends at this time suggested that Chinese cotton was becoming
more expensive relative to the better-quality products of American and
Indian competitors.

It was in these circumstances that the Nihon Boseki Kyokai (the
Japan Cotton Spinners Association — known also as *Boren*) began
seriously to examine the possibilities of importing raw cotton of
generally higher quality from India. This was a step that posed many
problems. India was remote from Japan, and Asian shipping routes
were dominated by the P. & O. Line, with the shipping rate conference controlled by it. Further its colonial-style, caste-dominated
business environment was relatively unknown to the Japanese.
Nonetheless, in 1893, as a result of several visits to India by Japanese
business leaders and support from the Foreign Ministry and Ministry
of Agriculture and Commerce, a major shipping agreement was
concluded. Under this agreement the Nihon Yusen Kaisha (NYK)
offered special shipping rates to Japanese raw cotton importers. This
move was accompanied by the establishment of a comprehensive group
of Japanese trading and banking firms in Bombay.[23] By 1896 cotton
imports accounted for 96% of the Japanese mills' supply, and blending
techniques involving Indian, Chinese and American cottons were well
established. The shipping rebates offered by the NYK, which were
supported by government subsidy, were estimated to account for 5%
to 10% of cotton spinners' profits and constituted the key to Japanese
export expansion in China.

This Bokyo inititiative, supported by both government and private
sector, embodied all the features of the model of trade and economic
expansion envisaged by the Maeda proposal thirteen years earlier, and
was its first successful implementation. In the short run, the Indian
agreement served its purpose in providing the raw material base on
which the domestic industry could displace foreign competition at
home and make serious inroads into foreign markets. Over the longer

---

23. The raw material issue is fully discussed in Takamura, *An introduction*, vol. 1,
ch. 2. The key recent source for the history of the Bokyo is *Bokyo hyakunenshi* (The
hundred-year history of the Japan Cotton Spinners' Association), Osaka: Japan Textile
Federation, 1982, esp. pp. 25ff. for the early years. The ministries involved in the
negotiations are discussed in Miyamoto, *The lineage of Japanese merchants*, pp. 100ff.

Table 7.6. DOMESTIC DEMAND, SUPPLY AND SELF–SUFFICIENCY
IN YARN AND CLOTH, 1882–90
(¥ *at constant prices, growth % per annum)*

	1882–90
Rate of growth of domestic demand for yarn	16.2
Rate of growth of domestic supply of yarn	32.2
Rate of growth of domestic demand for cloth	7.5
Rate of growth of domestic supply of cloth	11.6

	1882	1890
Self-sufficiency in yarn	26	72
Self-sufficiency in cloth	57	77

Source: Based on data in Yamazawa, *Japanese economic development*, pp. 248–9.

term it was to have other, unforeseen influences on Japanese commercial development.[24]

In 1889–90 the textile industry suffered its first crisis of over-
capacity. This was partly an international and exchange rate problem
but between 1882 and 1890, as Table 7.6 shows, domestic yarn
was growing at twice the rate of growth of demand, and a similar
imbalance in cloth trends had also appeared. Clearly, as import substitution became harder in the more specialised products, future growth
required the development of other outlets for the grades of yarn and
cloth in which Japan was becoming a competitive producer.

The industry's response to this situation was twofold and followed
a pattern to be repeated in many subsequent crises. First, the Bokyo
organised a *tanshuku*, i.e. a period of planned short-term working
in which reductions in output were allocated to member companies
according to existing spindle capacity. British observers in Shanghai
commented on the unoriginality of this measure, but they missed
the important point that with the *tanshuku* the Bokyo had organised
its first exercise in strategic subsidised exporting. By this arrangement
members committed themselves to making exports to China of 30,000
bales over five years. These exports were to be at prices that subsidised

24. Between 1887 and 1890, domestic raw cotton dropped from 55% to 14% of
total supply and to a negligible figure by the late 1890s. Between 1890 and 1898 the
Chinese share of total imports fell from 70% to 7% (by volume) while the Indian
share rose from 21% to 63%. Takamura, *An introduction*, vol. 1, pp. 129, 193.

exports at the expense of the home market, thus instituting the 'dual price system' that has remained a grievance to Japan's trading partners ever since.[25]

This inititative was the first significant attack on the Asian market by Japanese manufactured exports, and it involved sharp competition with British and Indian exporters. Both competitors were found to have weaknesses. In dealing with the British, Japan focused on its comparative advantage in low-priced but durable goods, popular in a market where the taste for manufactured goods was growing but incomes were still relatively low. Indian exporters, on the other hand, found themselves disadvantaged by the decision to put the rupee on the gold standard in 1893, by inefficiencies in the choice of British textile machinery (and of failure to adapt it), by the high prices paid for coal to run steam machinery, and by transport costs that could not match the subsidised rates provided by the 1893 Japanese shipping arrangements.[26]

In 1894–95 the Japanese domestic market was strongly stimulated by government procurement in the Sino-Japanese war which opened the way after the Japanese victory for further marketing initiatives by Japanese merchants and trading houses in China and Korea. By 1897, however, boom had again given way to depression. Both cloth and thread output had lost the momentum of the 1890s and the trend did not revive until demand was stimulated by the Russo-Japanese war in 1904–5. Thus while the 1890s had seen extraordinary achievements, by the early 1900s demand deficiency and structural imbalances had become serious problems. In the thread market, gains from import substitution were almost exhausted and exports were on a plateau. In cloth, skill barriers made further import substitution difficult, while exports, though promising, were still relatively small.

25. Takamura, *An introduction*, ch. 2; *Bokyo hyakunenshi*, p. 17; Sampei Takako, *Nihon mengyo hattatsushi* (A history of the development of the Japanese cotton industry), Tokyo: Keio Shobo, 1941, pp. 106ff.

26. Sampei, *A history*, p. 77. A detailed analysis of comparative Japanese/Indian costs of supplying the Shanghai market is in Takamura, *An introduction*, vol. 1, p. 235. These show Japanese costs initially marginally higher prior to productivity and currency changes that benefited Japan between 1893 and 1897. Data for small groups of Japanese and Indian companies producing twenty-count yarn in 1898 show higher Indian wages costs and similar labour productivity but much higher capital (spindle) productivity in Japan. The crucial role of intensive capital utilisation is further underlined by data for 1906, Takamura, *An introduction*, vol. 1 p. 339, vol. 2, p. 143.

A recurring topic in our discussion of the industry so far has been the role of the Bokyo. This association was founded in 1882 under indirect government guidance.[27] It played an integral part in the early development of the industry and is still important today in its modern form. Indeed, its role has been so distinctive that it would be entirely misleading to think of the Japanese textile industry as a western-style, competitive structure; it was actually established *before* the emergence of large-scale firms, and its activities have meant that the industry operates in ways that were and are largely without precedent in western economies.

During the 1880s the Bokyo was active in encouraging the establishment of large-scale spinning companies, and from 1889 it organised *tanshuku*, planned exporting, the regulation of labour contracts, dissemination of technical information and coordination of the parties to the agreement that established the Indian raw cotton supply. It also successfully lobbied for abolition of the taxes on raw cotton imports (1896) and yarn exports (1894) which was critical in the achievement of competitiveness in the 1890s. It was also eventually given plenary powers to negotiate textile quota agreements with foreign governments. An excellent early example of the power and willingness of the Bokyo to intervene directly in the domestic market was its instruction to members not to use imported thread where domestic supply was available. This was influential in eliminating foreign thread from Japan after 1890.

The Bokyo's authority was derived from several sources. From the outset it had a distinguished leadership drawn from companies large enough to enjoy directly the benefits of many of its activities, and it benefited from excellent political connections.[28] This authority was augmented by the 1893 Indian shipping agreement whereby the vital rebates were only available to Bokyo members. Thus any firm seeking growth through trade had to be a member. It might be thought that an organisation which controlled export quantities and prices, restricted domestic output and intervened in labour markets must have had a severely anti-competitive impact on the industry. But this was not so.

---

27. *Toyo boseki nanajunenshi*, p. 555.

28. At a Bokyo meeting to discuss tariff and other matters in 1888, participants included the Foreign Minister (Okuma), the Finance Minister (Matsukata) and the Commerce and Agriculture Minister (Inoue) as well as Shibusawa, who is described as representing the First National Bank. MITI, vol. 15, *Textiles*, pp. 248–9.

The association was open and belonging to it was clearly advantageous to firms that had reached a certain size, yet, even after acquiring membership, firms competed fiercely in the domestic market. However, by controlling the terms on which raw materials could be obtained and in requiring members to subsidise exports at the expense of domestic profitability, the Bokyo placed strong financial pressures on small firms and hence created an environment in which only large-scale, low-cost operations could survive. Overall, what was so clearly established at this early stage was the capacity of Japanese business to combine competitive and collaborative behaviour in ways that advanced productivity and technical progress at home, while enabling Japanese firms as a group to succeed in overseas markets.[29]

Compared to the 1890s the development of the industry between 1900 and the First World War was slow and difficult. In the thread sector, other than during the Russo-Japanese war boom, short-time working was in force in nine of the thirteen years between 1899 and 1912; only in 1910 did exports exceed the level achieved in 1898. Cloth output too performed weakly in the early 1900s and the growth of output between the peaks of 1896 and 1914 was less than 3% annually. Even so, there was one significant development in the cloth sector, namely the expansion of cloth exports, mainly from the integrated companies, which by 1914 accounted for half of total output.

However, the Russo-Japanese war had important longer-term implications for the industry since it provided further opportunities for exports into Korea, Manchuria and China proper. The Korean market had been pioneered by the Kanekin Seishoku Kaisha as early as 1893, but real penetration followed with the competitive entry of the Osaka Boseki and the Mie company in the early 1900s. At first, these companies competed with one another, but under the leadership of Mitsui Bussan and Shibusawa they joined forces in 1903–4 to form an alliance known as the Sanei Menpu Yushitsu Kumiai. According to the official history of the Osaka Boseki, 'The rationale for [the Sanei] was that if

---

29. The role of the Bokyo is discussed in all the standard sources. The combination of competitiveness and collaboration is also emphasised in one of the most interesting informal sources on the history of the industry, 'The Japanese textile industry and exports', in Ando Yoshio (ed.), *Showa keizaishi e no shogen* (Testimony on Showa economic history), 3 vols, Tokyo: Mainichi Press, 1965, vol .1, pp. 283–307. This section includes personal recollections stretching back to the earliest days of the modern industry, including the 1933–34 Anglo-Japanese trade negotiations over the partition of British Empire markets.

Table 7.7. BRITISH, AMERICAN AND JAPANESE SHARES OF THE
KOREAN AND MANCHURIAN CLOTH MARKETS, 1903–14
(% shares of the market by volume)

| | KOREA | | | | | MANCHURIA | | |
	Britain	U.S.A.	Japan	Consortium % of Japanese exports		Britain	Japan	Consortium % of Japanese exports
1903	59	0	41	0	1906	66	34	98
1908	48	1	51	71	1909	45	55	31
1912	16	0	84	42	1911	21	79	11
1914	3	0	97	0				

Source: Takamura, *An introduction*, vol. 2, pp. 187–9.
Note: Korean data are quantities of kanekins and coarse cloths. The consortium data for Korea
are the share of sales of the Sanei Menpu.

the three companies completely halted their mutual competition and
unified and strengthened their selling force, they could monopolise
the Korean internal market with Japanese goods.' A similar tactic was
used in Manchuria, again under the leadership of Mitsui and banking
interests, and once again the alliance was dissolved when Japanese
market dominance had been achieved.[30]

One interesting aspect of the industry's expansion into China
was that it illustrated how Japanese strategy divided a market geographically. Manchuria and the Yangtze valley as a whole were defined
as the prime areas of Japanese interest, and individual companies
were encouraged to develop their own regional spheres of influence
within them.[31] The expansion into Manchurian and Korean markets
is summarised in Table 7.7. Although the private sector was clearly
developing independent strengths, the direct role of government in this
expansion was substantial. In addition to subsidised shipping rates,
the nationalisation of the railway system in 1907 gave government
the power to implement supportive but discriminatory rail tariffs as
well. The strength of official financial backing was also reflected in
the rediscounting of the *boseki tegata* (the cotton promissory note)

30. *Toyo boseki nanajunenshi*, pp. 375–99, discusses the overseas policies of the Osaka
Boseki. By 1914 the Osaka had absorbed both of its partners in the original Sanei
grouping in the new Toyo Company.
31. Seki, *The Cotton Industry*, pp. 21–2; Sampei, *A history*, pp. 119ff.

by the Bank of Japan at a special rate, which gave it almost a gilt-edged status in the market.

In this difficult period before the First World War, the industry's structure matured in important ways. First, each trade depression was followed by company mergers. These were usually supported by the banks, which by means of this process eroded the early dependence of the larger companies on stock market financing.[32] Secondly, the growing structural imbalance between spinning and weaving capacities encouraged the spinners to take over the generally much smaller weaving concerns, together with other ancillary processes such as dyeing and finishing. The best of the new 'integrated' enterprises (*keiei kigyo*) were known for their 'active management' (*omowaku keiei*), which served to sharpen Japan's competitiveness in domestic and especially overseas cloth markets. Thus by 1914, the integrated companies, although they accounted for only 34% of cloth output, sold 71% of Japanese cloth exports.

The classic merger was that between the Osaka Boseki and the Mie Boseki in 1914. The first president of the new Toyo Boseki was Yamanobe Takeo. He explained the merger to shareholders in terms that foreshadowed several aspects of post-war industrial policy. First, he emphasised the worldwide trend towards large companies that needed to obtain maximum operational scale, effective policies of technical development and power in financial markets and product markets. Secondly, he argued that the diplomatic problems facing Japanese trade expansion were now extending from the regional (tariff disputes with China) to the international (the opening of the Panama Canal), and that to compete effectively in this environment companies had to represent large concentrations of power. Finally, after a lifetime of management experience in the Osaka Boseki, Yamanobe noted that this particular alliance would be favoured by the even (*mata hakuchu*) matching of management power and the long history of sisterly

32. The 'big six' spinners that emerged from this phase of concentration were the result of mergers of sixteen companies, including the conversion of the Osaka Boseki into the Toyo company. The big six were made up of the Osaka and Mie companies that formed the Toyo Boseki; the Sesshin, Amasaki, Godo and Kanegafuchi companies; and the Tokyo Gasu and Fuji companies that merged to form Fuji Gasu. Takamura, *An introduction*, vol. 1, p. 115.

(*shimai*) relations between the companies, dating back notably to their joint ventures in Korea and Manchuria.[33]

Thus in the period leading up to the First World War, we may sum up the developing structure of the industry as follows. In the first phase the industry's growth reflected one outstanding pioneer spinning company. In the second phase, it enjoyed dynamic, extensive growth, again mainly in spinning, with many companies being formed. Finally, in the difficult conditions of the 1900s, it consolidated into a more concentrated structure where large integrated companies shared leadership with both the financial sector and the Bokyo.[34]

33. *Toyo boseki nanajunenshi*, pp. 147–50.
34. Data from Takamura, *An introduction*, vol. 2, p. 221.

8

THE ACHIEVEMENT OF INTERNATIONAL COMPETITIVENESS IN COTTON TEXTILES, 1914–1937

The First World War

The First World War brought a significant shift in the fortunes of the textile industry. Although *tanshuku* were in force from August 1914 to January 1916, thread output grew during the war and exports in 1915 were nearly twice the level of 1912–14 (see figs 7.1 and 7.2). Cloth made even more rapid progress. Output in 1918 was double and exports were treble the pre-war levels. Thus the war accelerated import substitution at home, and abroad Japan seized the opportunity to break out of its narrow foothold in North-East Asia and make bold initiatives in India, South-East Asia, Africa and the Americas.[1]

This expansion had consequences for the structure, profitability and technical advance of the industry. Structurally its main effect was to provide profitable opportunities for small and medium-sized companies to expand relative to the 'big five' companies. Financially, the combination of inflation and declining real wages led to rises in profit rates for the large and smaller companies, from 17.2% and 6.9% respectively in 1914, to 94.2% and 57.9% in 1918. Dividends rose but did not keep pace with this astonishing rise in profits, so that a rapid internal accumulation of resources took place. Overall, financial reserves as a proportion of fixed capital tripled, and by 1919 the big five companies were holding published reserves 50% larger than the value of their fixed assets, with unpublished reserves in excess. This financial strength and the use made of it were to be decisive in the inter-war struggle for international competitiveness.[2]

---

1. Nishikawa, *Japanese imperialism*, pp. 25ff.; Sampei, *A history*, p. 165; Takamura, 'Capital accumulation' in Oishi Kaichiro (ed.), *Nihon teikokushugishi: dai ichiji dai senki* (The history of Japanese imperialism: The First World War), Tokyo: Tokyo Daigaku Shuppankai, 1985, pp. 153–97.

2. Takamura, *An outline*, vol. 2, p. 264; Nishikawa, *Japanese imperialism*, p. 36. The 'big five' in 1928 (in size order by numbers of rings installed) were Kanegafuchi, Dai Nippon, Toyo, Fuji Gasu and Nisshin. Arno S. Pearse, *The Cotton Industry of Japan and China*, Manchester: International Federation of Master Cotton Spinners and Manufacturers, 1929, pp. 28–9.

Japan in the world textile economy, 1919–1937

The textile sector continued on an expansionary trend throughout the inter-war years. In the case of thread, although export demand declined, internal demand and overall output grew at 5% and 4% annually. Export performance in the 1920s was poor, but this was largely a reflection of the transfer of spinning capacity to Japanese-owned mills in China. Cloth, by contrast, continued its progress, with demand, output and exports growing respectively at 6%, 5% and 9%. By 1937, while thread imports were negligible and cloth imports a mere 2% of the domestic market, thread and cloth exports accounted for 6% and 56% of domestic output. Although Japan had completed import substitution for thread by the 1930s and maintained competitiveness in the home market, this industry had reached the stage where continued international competitiveness required the transfer of output to economies where Japanese managerial and technical expertise could be combined with lower labour costs. For example, the rising imports seen in Fig. 7.1 (p. 188) largely represent the imports into Japan of the Japanese-owned factories in China. On the other hand, by the late 1930s the domestic cloth industry had achieved and was maintaining full domestic and international competitiveness.

The significance of this growth can be seen if we place it in its international context. Table 7.1 (p. 177) shows the extent of growth in the golden age between the early 1880s and the First World War, the erosion of Britain's previously dominant position, and the declining proportion of world textile output traded as second- and third-generation industrialisers established and enlarged their domestic capacity. Nonetheless, despite growing competition, the Edwardian years were almost literally the Indian summer of the British textile industry. Investment, output, exports and profits all advanced, with exports to India performing particularly well.[3] Thus in 1914 Britain still accounted for more than half of world trade in cotton goods and exported four-fifths of the home industry's total output.

However, there were crucial weaknesses in the evolving structure of Britain's overseas markets. Geographically, the share in British exports between 1865 and 1913 of the poorer countries of the Middle

---

3. British cloth exports to India increased from 1 to 2 billion yards between 1870 and 1900 and then from 2 to 3 billion in 1913. British exporters were also notably successful in the Dutch East Indies, Argentina and China. Crouzet, *The Victorian Economy*, pp. 211ff., Sandberg, *Lancashire in Decline*, p. 142.

East, Asia, Latin America and Africa had grown from 68% to 79%, and within this figure the share of China and the rest of Asia had nearly doubled from 16% to 30%. Qualitatively, most of these exports were relatively unsophisticated cloths. Britain's exports were thus increasingly of a kind, and went to markets where Japanese competitiveness posed the greatest potential threat.[4]

Comparison of the First World War data (Table 7.1) with those for 1936–38 shows how this threat was realised and led to a catastrophic decline in the British position. For by the late 1930s British mills accounted for only 9% of raw cotton consumption and only 28% of world exports. This basic statistical description conceals two important dimensions of the story: the transformation in the complexity of the industry that had taken place by the 1930s, and the extent to which competition between the wars transformed British leadership into a dual hegemony of Britain and Japan, with Japan's trading rise itself being part of wider regional changes in Asia.

One measure of the growing complexity of the industry was the increasing intricacy of trade in raw materials and intermediate and finished goods. While the United States, Brazil, China, Egypt, India and Russia remained the largest commercial growers of raw cotton, their relative weight declined and the United States' share of output fell from 68% in 1911–12 to 40% in 1936–37.[5] Variations in cotton quality, price and availability all compounded the blender's task, and the matrix of inter-country imports reveals that to maintain commercial viability in a range of intermediate and finished cotton products, economies with no domestic supply of cotton had to import from a selection of major and minor producers, and that even major raw cotton producers such as China and India had to import higher-quality materials for blending and special purposes.[6]

At the intermediate stage of the industry, yarn production also showed signs of increasingly sophisticated inter-country specialisation, with a distinct regional pattern. The advanced European economies specialised among themselves and supplied yarn to the next-generation industries in the Balkans and Latin America, while China, Japan and India formed an increasingly self-sufficient Asian system, in which

---

4. Data based on Sandberg, *Lancashire in Decline*, pp. 145–6.
5. *EB* (1951 cdn), vol. 6, p. 534.
6. International Labour Organization (ILO), *The World Textile Industry: Economic and Social Problems*, London: P.S. King, 1937, p. 72.

Table 8.1. % SHARES AND RATES OF GROWTH OF WORLD SPINNING
CAPACITY IN THE U.S.A., BRITAIN, JAPAN, INDIA AND CHINA, 1913–38

	Britain	Britain and U.S.A.	Japan	Japan, India and China	Others	Index of growth of total no. of spindles
1913	39	61	2	7	32	100
1920	38	61	2	8	31	108
1930	34	54	4	12	34	115
1938	26	44	9	18	38	103

GROWTH RATE OF SPINDLEAGE (% per annum)

	World	Japan
1913–20	1.1	7
1920–30	.6	6.7
1930–8	− 1.4	7.4

Source: EB (1951 edn), vol. 6, p. 547.

Chinese yarns were used in India and Japan supplied both India and China with higher-quality goods.[7] In the cloth market, variations in quality and specialisation can be measured by comparing the unit value (i.e. the value per square yard) of exports. In 1934, for example, the unit values of Japanese exports were little more than half those of Britain, while within Europe sophisticated Swiss products had unit values three-and-a-half times higher than those found in Italian exports.[8] Thus to complex raw material choices on the input side were added increasing variations in the products required to suit different incomes, national tastes and other market peculiarities. The task of integrating these technical and commercial opportunities presented a formidable challenge to the industry, which was one made all the more difficult by the trade depression after 1931.

Let us now turn to the rise of Japan to joint world leadership in textiles. This is best illustrated by changes in national textile capacity; a key index for this purpose is the number of spindles installed. Table 8.1 shows the changing proportions of world spindleage, accounted for by the United States and Britain on the one hand, and by Japan, China and India on the other. We see that between 1920 and 1938 Japan quadrupled and the Asian group as a whole doubled their shares

7. *Ibid.*, p. 74.
8. *Ibid.*, pp. 76–7.

of capacity, while the western economies' share fell by a third. To focus exclusively on Japan, throughout the two phases of decelerating growth for the world as a whole, covering the years 1913–30 and the third phase of decline from 1930–37, Japan's capacity grew steadily at between 5% and 7% annually, while the United States and Britain were actually scrapping one-third of their capacity.[9] The data for weaving capacity also show a rise in Asia's position, to the point where it accounted for 38% of the world total by 1938.[10]

Turning to foreign trade, the changes are even more surprising. By 1935 Japan and China had become the third- and fourth-largest yarn exporters, though still substantially behind Britain. In cloth, however, Japan was the largest exporter in quantity and had joined Britain in a joint dominion over world markets.

The sources of Japanese competitive strength

The international rise of the Japanese textile industry was highly controversial because although Japan's share of world trade in all commodities in the 1930s was only 2% to 3%, the concentration of its export efforts in one industry and the expansion of that industry through a sequence of carefully selected markets meant that its success required large, rapid and uncomfortable adjustments for competitors. In the mid-1930s world textile employment still accounted for 14 million people, and the United States, Britain, Germany and Japan each had more than a million workers in the industry. In terms of foreign trade, textiles still accounted for one-sixth of world trade in 1935 and a substantially higher proportion of the trade of Britain and the United States.

Moreover, the trade frictions created by Japanese penetration were by no means simply the reactions of exporters losing market share. For consumers, especially those in poorer economies such as Ceylon and the Dutch East Indies, Japanese textile (and other) imports opened new and exciting opportunities for consumption, and they actively resisted these being bargained away by high-cost producer interests. Indeed competitors believed that Japanese attention to markets with

9. *EB* (1951 edn), pp. 546–7.
10. *Ibid.*, p. 551.

poor populations was a deliberate political ploy.[11] All these issues were naturally sharpened by the depression and Japan's intensification of price competitiveness by a 50% devaluation of the yen against the dollar.

The general framework of these developments was discussed in the previous chapter. Clearly the long-run improvement in competitiveness reflected Japan's labour cost advantage in a labour-intensive industry, but this simple statement leaves too much of the inter-war development unexplained: it does not elucidate the significance of either raw material costs or the complexity of the total operation whereby raw material acquisition was ultimately linked to the sale of the finished product. Nor does it explain the extraordinary speed of Britain's relative decline or the failure of India and China to keep pace with Japanese achievements, although they too had the advantages of low labour costs and access to foreign technology, together with the added benefit of domestic raw cotton and huge home markets. It also fails to explain the shorter-run phenomenon of Japan's ability in the early 1930s to take advantage of its currency devaluation, which required not only an enormous expansion of supply but also the capacity to stop domestic costs rising to the point where they eliminated the benefit of the devaluation.

In seeking clues to these latter conundrums, we divide our analysis into two parts, looking first at the importance of 'rationalisation' (*gorika*) and marketing and, secondly, at the special role of relations between Japan and India and the growing significance of international trade management.

Gorika is a Japanese term embracing a variety of activities that include the integration and amalgamation of firms, technical improvement and the raising of managerial and organisational standards. These activities were crucial to the supply side of our story, while marketing and trade management skills were necessary to convert supply and competitiveness into export sales.

---

11. A useful source of English language material on the general subject of Japanese economic penetration in Asia is G. E. Hubbard, *Eastern Industrialization and its Effects on the West, with Special Reference to Great Britain and Japan*, Oxford University Press, 1935. For the Japanese perspective, a voluminous and helpful book is Mitsubishi Keizai Kenkyujo, *Taiheiyo ni okeru kokusai keizai kankei* (International economic relations in the Pacific), Tokyo: Nihon Hyoronsha, 1937.

Amalgamation and concentration. As we have seen, rationalisation was integral to the textile industry's response to short-term crises before the First World War, and this association between crisis and rationalisation remained important in the years after the war. Serious shortfalls of demand in 1920 and 1922–23 were stimulants to rationalisation, and after 1925 the industry's leadership knew that it had to respond not only to the prospect of a rising yen as the return to the gold standard was implemented, but also to the planned abolition of night work which, since the 1890s, had been regarded as one of the secrets of Japanese competitiveness.[12] After 1931 rationalisation processes were reinforced by the provisions of the Important Industries Control Law, which formalised and strengthened the power of trade associations and the role of government leadership in the private sector.

Company integration and amalgamation had been important before the First World War, and market conditions in the 1920s encouraged a resumption of this trend. In the spinning sector the combination of amalgamation and expansion finally raised the capacities of individual companies up to the level of one million spindles — 100 times the original scale of the early stages of the old Osaka Boseki. By 1929 six large spinners accounted for 48% of total spindleage and by 1937 companies with less than 100,000 spindles accounted for only 12.9% of the industry's capacity. A similar process was at work in weaving, where by the end of the 1920s more than 50% of looms were controlled by only seven companies.[13] However, small-scale weaving remained important because its output was sold in segments of the market where lack of scale was not a serious disadvantage.

An equally important trend was the renewed importance of companies that integrated the spinning, weaving and ancillary trades. This process was made easier because, from the outset of the modern industry, spinning had been more concentrated than weaving; hence the big spinners could exercise their market power in the sale of yarn to the weavers and thus obtain significant influence over their profitability and behaviour.

The technical arguments for integration and specialisation in textiles

---

12. Nishikawa, *Japanese imperialism*, pp. 4–5.

13. G.C. Allen, 'The cotton industry' in E. B. Schumpeter (ed.), *The Industrialization of Japan and Manchukuo 1930–1940: Population, Raw Materials and Industry*, New York: Macmillan, 1940, pp. 568–95; Nishikawa, *Japanese imperialism*, pp. 571ff.

have been much debated.[14] During the early modernisation of the
industry in Britain (1825–50) companies tended to take integrated
form, since mechanisation encouraged spinners to develop their own
weaving operations to absorb the rapidly increasing output of yarn.
However, after about 1850 the tide began to flow strongly in the
opposite direction. Companies increasingly specialised altogether, not
only in the main activities of spinning, weaving, finishing and dyeing
but even in different types and qualities of products within these
trades. The tendency for spinning and weaving to be separated was
explained by some in terms of the marketing differences between the
two products, with yarn markets being relatively developed and easy to
sell into, while it was harder to succeed in the more complex cloth
markets. This distinction was used in turn to explain why spinning
companies tended to be joint stock companies, with clear objectives
and standardised managerial skills, while cloth companies were more
likely to be private, with the value of the company depending critically
on individual and idiosyncratic experience and abilities.

A further cleavage in the industry was the division between production and selling. In the traditional industry the role of the merchant
had been very important, and in the late eighteenth-century transition
to modernity it was the foreign merchants based in Manchester who
were largely responsible for the rapid expansion of British textile
exports. During the nineteenth century Manchester and Liverpool
consolidated themselves as the world centres for trading finished and
raw cotton goods respectively, to some extent at the price of keeping
production and selling distinct operations.[15]

This trend towards specialisation in the late nineteenth century was
often seen as an indicator of modernity and thus appropriate for the
world's leading textile industry. By the inter-war years, however,

14. A good discussion of the technical issues is Robson, *The Cotton Industry in
Britain*, ch. 3. A near-contemporary book (written with advice from Alfred Marshall)
which generally emphasises the benefits of specialisation is Chapman, *The Lancashire
Cotton Industry*, esp. pp. 116ff., 152–72. See also Farnie, *The English Cotton Industry*,
pp. 138–9, 157–62, 320; Crouzet, *The Victorian Economy*, pp. 212–13; and Utley,
Lancashire and the Far East, in which there are substantial criticisms of the quality of
the British industry's management and the problems of small-scale disruption and
economic blackmail in inter-company relations.

15. '. . . The most remarkable separation of functions in the cotton goods trade
is the almost complete distinction between the business of manufacturing and
distributing'. Farnie, *The English Cotton Industry*, p. 157.

doubts began to surface as observers and participants in the industry noted the inefficiencies of a structure that was competitive but fragmented and lacked strategic industry-wide leadership; furthermore, its constituent companies were inevitably smaller and less powerful financially than they would have been in a more integrated industry producing the same output. Particular problems were the unfavourable impact of fragmentation on the diffusion of techniques requiring sophisticated multi-sector collaboration, the inadequacy of the contacts between production and selling at a time when world market requirements were changing rapidly, and the costs and inefficiencies generated by cut-throat competition and mutual ignorance among small companies.

In Japan, however, few doubted the efficiency of concentration in spinning and weaving and of integration that enabled companies to combine the dyeing, finishing and other trades.[16] In spinning, a major advantage of concentration and scale was the achievement of greater specialisation by counts, both among plants within individual companies and also between companies. Thus Toyo Boseki, Dai Nippon and Kurashiki became well known for their low counts, Kanegafuchi were active in medium counts and Fuji Gasu and Nisshin specialised in higher counts.

According to industry sources, the benefits of integration and scale also included more effective solutions to the problems of transporting thread to weaving sheds and of matching spinning output to weaving requirements, as well as providing better quality control and faster dissemination of new techniques. They created economies of scale in raw materials purchasing, marketing and market research and engendered an ability to maintain strict commercial secrecy during the development of new products where this required simultaneous improvements in spinning and weaving. Finally, integration and scale fostered the capability to respond to market fluctuations by internal company restructuring rather than by the rise and bankruptcy of entire firms.

An extraordinary acknowledgement of the relative superiority of the Japanese integrated company can be found in the chairman's speech at the annual general meeting of the British Calico Printers' Association in September 1942:

---

16. Frank Japanese statements about their investment policy are not easily found, but clear insights on the matter are set out in Ando, *Testimony on Showa economic history*, vol. 1, pp. 283–306.

Before the war Japan was a menace and a difficulty; she was well organized; she studied the markets; she had no moral scruple about pirating and copying our designs and trade marks; she sold her goods at 30 per cent to 60 per cent below Great Britain's prices and her industries were in receipt of substantial indirect subsidies from currency manipulation and trickery in the interpretation of tariffs ... *Her industry was, in the main, vertical in conception* [emphasis added].

The speaker then went on to outline a future for British industry that in effect required companies to follow the Japanese model.

The essence of success in the cotton export trade is, in my opinion, cooperation, teamwork, first-class salesmanship ... There are firms in Lancashire which have such an organization and are insulated against the ill effects of rivalries and clashes of interest which arise between the different horizontal sections of the trade; their well being is unquestioned. If any one section when fully engaged [i.e. is at full capacity] is able to exact an unduly high price for its products or services, without regard to the ultimate effect which it will have on the dependent horizontal sections or on the finished article, you will have a gradual wasting away, your best men will seek other jobs and your Government other forms of protection and bi-lateral trade.[17]

In this address the speaker simultaneously made a correct analysis of the strengths of the Japanese industry, especially its vertical structure and cooperative spirit and organisation, and contrived to say that the crucial factors in Japanese price competitiveness were commercial and political malpractices. However, in his recommendations for the post-war industry he did not follow the logic of this by simply emphasising the need to eliminate these malpractices, but rather advocated that British firms should conform to Japanese patterns, thereby implying the superiority of the integrated structure.

Technology and management. The scale and timing of what was achieved by Japanese companies in improved supply are illustrated in Table 8.2 which probably understates improvements because the data make inadequate allowance for simultaneous advances in quality. When this progress and the corresponding gains in cost reduction and competitiveness are explained, technical and managerial factors are inextricable. On the technical side, an important underlying source of mechanisation and improvement was the expansion of the electricity supply. This had become important during the First World War

17. *The Times*, 24 Sept. 1942.

Table 8.2. INDICES OF LABOUR PRODUCTIVITY
IN SPINNING AND WEAVING, 1919–39

	1919	1929	1939
Spinning	100	121	157
Weaving	100	218	432

Source: S. Sugiyama, 'The expansion of Japan's cotton textile exports into South East Asia', paper given at the conference on International Commercial Rivalry in Southeast Asia in the Inter-War Period, held at Shimoda, Japan, 1988.
Note: Spinning data are comprehensive but weaving data are probably representative of larger and integrated firms only.

and it progressively enhanced every aspect of mechanisation. By the 1920s Japan was the third-largest producer of electricity in the world and as a power-source for both lighting and the small-scale electric motor, electricity had the advantage of almost infinite divisibility, and therefore benefited small as well as large-scale plants.

In the spinning sector two key improvements were the introduction of the 'high draft' systems that accelerated the final stages of processing before spinning, and the continuing advance in ring technology. The latter enabled the benefits of ring economy to be combined with the standards of quality appropriate for a growing number of markets and income levels, and made the ring increasingly capable of matching the standards obtainable in mule spinning. By 1936 ring spindles accounted for 93% to 100% of spinning capacity in several major producers including India, the United States, Japan, China and Brazil. Apart from Britain with only 27%, no country had less than two-thirds of its spindleage in ring systems.[18]

However, as the data suggest, the more spectacular improvement in the industry was the development of the automatic loom and its various related attachments. This had originated in the United States where the Northrop loom, which was truly automatic in the sense that weft was continually supplied by changing cop or shuttle, had been patented as early as 1894. But by the 1920s the American models were, by many informed judgements, equalled and in some ways surpassed by the Toyoda automatic loom and other Japanese machines, including the Nogami, Enshu, Kanai Traveller and Kanegafuchi

18. ILO, *The World Textile Industry*, p. 51.

models. This development was not sudden. Toyoda Sakichi had perfected his first power loom in 1898 and subsequently made a series of patented improvements. Toyoda financed his activities by running three textile companies, two in Japan and one in China. In 1925 he patented his 'G' model automatic loom, which worked so well that in 1929 Platt's bought the foreign patent rights and advertised the 'Platt-Toyoda' loom in India and elsewhere as 'the Fastest, Simplest and Best Automatic Loom in the World . . . an unequalled loom'.[19] While this language may be typical of advertising hyperbole, the fact of the patent purchase speaks for itself as evidence of the machine-making standards the Japanese had achieved by the end of the 1920s.[20]

The uneven diffusion of this technology internationally is shown by the fact that by 1936 automatic looms accounted for 92% and 88% of looms in the United States and Japan but only 3% and 9% of looms in Britain and Germany.[21] One explanation of this was that automatic weaving had important technical complementarities with ring spinning, and for Britain in particular raising the technical level of weaving would have required a major investment in spinning as well.

This wave of technical improvement and productivity advance in the Japanese industry was a result of a spectrum of practice extending from large-scale direct import and use of foreign equipment, through skilful adaptation (such as Japanese automatic attachments to Northrop and Stafford looms) on to major domestic innovation as exemplified in the mature Toyoda model. As for imports, a British observer in 1928 was impressed to find that machine performance in Japan was consistently higher than the standards specified by the British manufacturers' operating manuals. As the capacity for imitation, adaptation and innovation progressed, the Japanese textile machinery industry made the transition from import substitution to exporting. It did so

19. The full advertisment appears in Arno S. Pearse, *The Cotton Industry of India*, Manchester: International Federation of Master Cotton Spinners' and Manufacturers Association, 1930, p. 323.

20. Toyoda is discussed by Yukihiko Kiyokawa in 'Entrepreneurship and innovations in Japan: an implication of the experience of the technological development in the textile industry', *The Developing Economies*, vol. XXII, no. 3, 1984, pp. 224–8. The Platt-Japan relationship was mediated by the Mitsui Company that had pioneered the early purchases of British textile machinery.

21. *EB* (1951 edn), vol. 6, p. 550.

with extraordinary speed. Whereas in 1929 imports were more than five times the level of exports, four years later Japan had become a net exporter of textile machinery. By 1937 exports were seventeen times the level of imports.[22] Qualified Japanese observers attributed this success to the size and flexibility of their machine-making firms which they contrasted with the smaller, more specialised firms in Britain, and with the scale and active level of investment policies of the cotton combines. They felt that the latter ensured rapid and even transmission of new technical possibilities and quality standards through all stages of the production process.

The divergent technological performance of the Japanese and British industries may be seen partly as the result of the established Japanese drive for technical improvement, the long-run logic of which had been first demonstrated in the ring system and again by the integrated modernisation of the inter-war years. It is especially remarkable how successfully the Japanese appeared to judge the wider issues and the longer-run dynamics. They anticipated both the future appropriateness of technologies and the potential for Japanese adaptation and learning, which would reduce longer-run costs below the figures envisaged by contemporaries. They took decisions that in short-term or narrow perspectives seemed inexplicable. The loom provides a graphic example. Kroese, a Dutch textile specialist sent to report on the industry in 1949, noted that the price differential between standard and advanced looms was much lower in Japan than in Europe. Yet given Japanese labour costs, he concluded that the adoption of the Toyoda and Sakamoto automatic looms was 'a preference which we fail to explain on merely economic grounds'.[23]

The financial history and structure of the two industries were also important factors in their technological paths. Both had profited from the wartime boom in demand, but in Japan flexible depreciation conventions and added gains from shrewd investment in raw cotton stocks allowed the accumulation of the enormous reserves used in the 1920s to promote rationalisation and technical improvement. In Britain, however, the industry capitalised its wartime gains in a programme of company refinancings that left the old owners of the companies rich

22. 'The textile machinery industry' in *Showa sangyoshi* (A history of industry in the Showa period) (3 vols), Tokyo: Toyo Keizai Shimposha, 1925, pp. 427–40.

23. For Japanese insights, see Ando, *Testimony on Showa economic history*, vol. 1, pp. 296ff.

but their industry heavily indebted to the banks. During the 1920s, when trading proved much more difficult than anticipated, the fixed interest charges imposed by the banks left no room for internally financed investment and in these circumstances investors were unwilling to provide new equity capital.[24]

The competitive impact of new and improved technology in Japan was reinforced by changes in labour organisation. In spinning and weaving, manning levels per machine fell, the average age of the workforce dropped sharply, and the proportion of less skilled female workers rose. According to one calculation, new techniques in spinning for the production of 40-count yarn in 400-spindle plants reduced machinery and manpower requirements by a third. In weaving, observers noted that Japanese manning levels were less than half the minimum specified by the Lancashire textile unions.[25]

The net effect of all these changes was to transform an industry which in its British form had become an accumulation of specialised trades and separate companies, often poorly managed and interacting in ways damaging to the overall efficiency of the industry, into a Japanese form where integrated, large-scale yet flexible operations used some of the most advanced technologies available.

Managerial and commercial skills. It would be a mistake to think of Japan's competitiveness simply in terms of physical productivity and technical excellence. The growing effectiveness of the Japanese textile companies also reflected improvement of managerial and commercial skills. For example, the successful organisation of large numbers of plants of varying technical characteristics, specialisations and marketing objectives required new information and accounting systems

24. The British problem is discussed in Robson, *The Cotton Industry in Britain*, ch. 1 and exhaustively in Utley, *Lancashire and the Far East*. Utley was highly critical of the British textile firms and their failure to recognise the nature of the challenge facing them. Data on British equipment was reported in documents of the British Committee of Enquiry of the Textile Spinning and Weaving Industries, cited in Shindo, *Labour in the Japanese Textile Industry*, pp. 7–8. Japanese policies are discussed in Seki, *The Cotton Industry of Japan*, p. 70, and in Nishikawa, *Japanese imperialism*, ch. 3.

25. In spinning, the percentage of the female labour force less than sixteen years old rose from 13.5% to 38.7% between 1927 and 1937. Shindo, *Labor in the Japanese Cotton Industry*, pp. 7–8. See also, Nishikawa, *Japanese imperialism*, ch. 3 esp. Table III–21, and Arno S. Pearse, *Japan and China. Cotton Industry Report*, Manchester: International Federation of Master Cotton Spinners and Manufacturers, 1929, pp. 79 and 129.

and new techniques of management. Commercial strengths were especially evident in the growing efficiency of raw material acquisition and marketing.

Japanese handling of the raw material problem has already been discussed. Between the World Wars, while popular opinion tended to think of Japan's trading advantage in terms of low wages and dumping, informed competitors confirmed that raw materials purchasing through big, specialist companies, together with associated blending and spinning skills, were the decisive sources of competitive advantage. Studies of the textile cost structure estimated that raw material costs were 60% to 70% of total costs; hence economies achieved in buying and blending were bound to be significant for total costs.[26] In the former case, the combination of Japan's large and growing demand for raw cotton and the concentration of buying power in a handful of companies gave the industry exceptional market power in the buyers' market of the 1930s. Japan's gains from cotton trading were also eased by the efficiency and rate structure of the Japanese merchant marine, which enabled the cotton-buying firms not only to supply the domestic market competitively but also to conduct a world wide cotton trading business as well.[27]

The full significance of this combination of industrial restructuring and technical, managerial and commercial advance is only appreciated within the wider context of developments in government policy discussed in previous chapter. In particular the 50% devaluation of the yen clearly offered the Japanese industry an enormous, unanticipated short-term price advantage. But turning that opportunity to more than a temporary benefit called not only for great flexibility of supply but also for the ability to ensure that domestic costs did not rise to offset devaluation. This can easily happen if devaluation causes import prices to rise and organised labour attempts to recoup by wage rises the loss of real income it is bound to suffer. In the case of raw cotton Japan was fortunate that the depression weakened import prices while a succession of good harvests at home caused grain prices to fall, which helped the labour problem. The success of the devaluation is confirmed by a survey of textile industry wages in September 1935, which showed that compared with 1929, real wages in textiles

26. Hubbard, *Eastern Industrialization*, pp. 98, 119–23.

27. Raw cotton from Texas could be transported more cheaply to Kobe than to the mills of New England. Seki, *The Cotton Industry of Japan*, p. 51.

Table 8.3. THE GEOGRAPHICAL DISTRIBUTION OF THE JAPANESE
COTTON CLOTH EXPORT MARKET, 1890–1936

	Taiwan and Korea	China	South-East Asia	Others
1890–92	14.3	68.9	7.5	9.3
1900–2	60.5	37.9	.8	.8
1911–13	33.5	58.4	3.9	4.2
1924–26	12.6	46.7	26.3	14.4
1934–36	9.8	15.4	30.8	44

Source: Yamazawa, *Japanese economic development*, p. 81.

had fallen by 10% in Japan (the rise in eight major competitors was 11%).[28]

It was ironic that the drive to production efficiency undertaken in the late 1920s to enable the industry to accommodate a planned *rise* in the value of the yen as the gold standard was reimposed, actually enabled the industry to take the fullest advantage of the *fall* in the yen that followed the abandonment of gold in 1931.

Markets and marketing

Turning from production to marketing, we now have to ask how and where Japan managed to dispose of such large volumes of cloth output during a depression. Or, looking at the problem in a slightly longer-term perspective, we may state the issue as follows: while between 1910–13 and 1936–38 the world market for textile goods *declined* in volume by 32%, Japanese exports increased thirteenfold and Japan's share of world exports rose from 2% to 39%. How was this accomplished?[29]

The evolution of the Japanese cloth market between 1890 and 1936 is illustrated in Table 8.3, and the principal fact that emerges is the rise and post-war fall of dependence on the markets of China, Korea and Taiwan: the share of Japan's exports absorbed by these three countries declining from over 80% in 1890–1992 to 25% in 1934–36.

28. ILO, *The World Textile Industry*, p. 332. Note, however, that part of this fall in wages reflected the changing structure of the labour force towards younger, female (hence less expensive) workers. I am aware of no estimate of the relative importance of the two effects.

29. Data from Robson, *The Cotton Industry in Britain*, p. 4.

Table 8.4. JAPANESE EXPORTS OF COTTON PIECE-GOODS
BY MAJOR MARKETS, 1924–35
(volume, % shares)

	1924	1935	Change in contribution to export share
Total volume of exports (million sq. yards)	979	2,724	
Index of above	100	278	
British India and Ceylon	15	21	+6
China, Hong Kong	53	12	−41
Dutch East Indies, Malaya, Siam, Philippines	13	21	+8
South America	1	7	+6
Australasia	2	3	+1
Africa (except South Africa)	0	10	+10
Other	16	26	+10

Source: ILO, *The World Textile Industry*, p. 130.

The place of the local East Asian markets in the inter-war period was taken up by diversification into India, South-East Asia and other countries. A more detailed view of these markets, and of Japan's penetration of them in cotton piece-goods, is given in Tables 8.4 and 8.5. Table 8.4 shows that the fastest-growing markets between 1924 and 1935 were Africa and South-East Asia, followed by British India, Ceylon and South America. Table 8.5, provides a broader perspective. It reveals that by 1935 Japanese exports were available in every continent and were substantial in the Middle East, South America and Australia. Furthermore, in countries as diverse as the Philippines, Java, the United Kingdom, Egypt and the United States, Japan was the largest single foreign supplier.

This breadth of geographical penetration, achieved over such a short period, suggests complex and highly effective commercial strengths and strategies. One such element was the Japanese transportation and commercial services infrastructure. This was particularly evident in the Chinese market, for which one analysis of Japanese and British costs showed that savings in shipping, insurance, and Chinese wholesale margins gave Japanese firms a 10% price advantage over British ones — quite apart from any initial differences in production costs. However, in contrast to the Chinese case, where geographical proximity and cultural

Table 8.5. JAPANESE IMPORT SHARES IN VARIOUS MARKETS, 1935

	Japanese market share (%)	*Next largest supplier (market share, %)*
Egypt	73 (market leader)	Britain (16)
U.S.A.	57 (market leader)	Britain (11)
India	51 (market leader)	Britain (47)
Java	83 (market leader)	Britain (2)
China	72 (market leader)	Britain (25)
Philippines	64 (market leader)	U.S.A. (31)
Turkey	21 (second supplier)	Italy (24)
Australia	32 (second supplier)	Britain (66)
Colombia	26 (second supplier)	Britain (45)
Sweden	14 (second supplier)	Britain (53)
French West Africa	10 (third supplier)	France (51)
Argentina	9.9 (third supplier)	Britain (48)

Source: Derived from data in ILO, *The World Textile Industry*, p. 83.
Note: market shares for China are calculated from import *value* in £ sterling; all other data from import quantities.

factors clearly favoured Japan, the Japanese also set about systematic data collection, analysis and cultivation of the textile markets of Africa — a region in which they were at almost every disadvantage — but where nonetheless their competitors spoke freely of their superior approach.

The underlying explanation of Japan's advance in world textile markets was comparative advantage based on low labour costs. Yet, other Asian economies had comparable costs and access to western technology, so it is important here also to explain the success of Japan in particular in competition with other low-cost producers. The critical factors seem to have been technical versatility; the use of technical strengths to achieve specific marketing objectives; the effectiveness of large trading companies in researching and communicating precise market needs and developing efficient marketing systems; and the capacity of the state and the private sectors to negotiate adequate outlets, despite a rising tide of anti-Japanese protectionism and the emergence of a world where market linkages were increasingly being replaced by 'managed trade'.

If we take the first two points, the analysis of Japan's cloth exports by major type (unbleached, bleached, dyed, patterned etc.) suggests that with unbleached fabrics Japan's export penetration was not evenly

Table 8.6. JAPAN AND BRITAIN: SHARES OF TOTAL JOINT
EXPORTS OF COTTON PIECE-GOODS, BY TYPE, 1924–36
(*% shares*)

		1928	*1930*	*1933*	*1936*
Grey/unbleached	Japan	36	54	62	75
	Britain	64	46	38	25
White/bleached	Japan	8	16	42	45
	Britain	92	84	58	55
Coloured	Japan	33	44	50	56
	Britain	67	56	50	44

Source: ILO, *The World Textile Industry*, p. 131.

spread across markets with varying levels of income but was greatest
at the lower and higher ends. In other words, Japan was a major
exporter of these fabrics both to poor countries in South-East Asia
and Africa, and to rich ones such as Canada, Australia, Sweden and
the United States, to which Japan also sold bleached and higher-quality
finished goods. Thus while Japan's main strength lay in the continued
exploitation of its early competitive advantage in cheaper wares, it was
also achieving success in more sophisticated products and making
strategic use of this in the struggle to oust the British from markets
as far apart as India and South America.[30] This progressive ability to
operate at all levels of quality is illustrated in Table 8.6, which shows
that while Japan started in 1928 from a point of inferiority to Britain
in all three products (unbleached, bleached and coloured fabric), by
1936 it had achieved dominance in two and come close to equality in
the third.

How were this progress and versatility achieved? Technical
capabilities were crucial at the lower as well as the higher end of the
market because sales in Asia and Africa, where consumers had low
incomes and literacy, depended significantly on a firm's ability to
establish brand names and in many cases visual brand-images that the
market would associate with value, quality and efficiency of delivery.
Here, company integration and technical progress made important
contributions, since they ensured consistency of quality in all the
downstream operations (dyeing, finishing, packaging and transportation) to match the rising standards made possible by integrated
spinning and weaving. Thus integration and technical progress not

30. ILO, *The World Textile Industry*, p. 76; Seki, *The Cotton Industry*, pp. 144–5.

only lowered unit costs but contributed to the establishment of brand loyalties in low-income economies while, at the same time, enabling Japan to make strategic moves upmarket against the British in economies as diverse as India and Argentina.

The marketing and commercial skill of the Japanese cotton industry was much commented on by foreign analysts in the late 1920s. In Europe and America, Japan produced for the fashionable requirements of smart but depression-affected consumers, while in South Asia it excelled in indigenous clothing, including sarongs, slendangs and saris, and sharply undercut the prices of domestic handicraft producers. Once established in the key high-volume products areas, the Japanese companies specialised in distribution with the same efficiency as they did in production. Thus a British report published in 1928 noted that in the key area of grey unbleached cloth, the Japanese actually had higher manufacturing costs than some competitors, but that by concentrating on limited lines Japanese companies achieved profitable sales with margins of 5% to 10%, compared to the 15% normal for British companies.[31]

The role of trade diplomacy in expanding Japanese world wide sales has already been touched on, but the most important example related to the complex problems of British and Japanese interaction in the Indian market, and it is to this that we now turn.

Japan, India and the evolution of managed trade in textiles

The importance of India to the textile industry of Japan emerged from the triangular relationship between those two countries and Britain. In the eighteenth century, Indian textiles — sophisticated, high-quality products such as muslins — were imported into Britain by the East India Company, but by late in that century trade was beginning to flow the other way as British manufactured goods found markets in India, where they displaced traditional handicraft production. A substantial share of these exports consisted of unbleached wares that were dyed in India to Indian tastes. By 1850 India had become Lancashire's most important market, absorbing 25% of British cloth exports.[32]

31. *Report on Trade and Industry*, Part 3, *The Textile Industry*, London: HMSO, 1928, pp. 104–7.

32. Overall surveys of this subject are included in Sung, *Stages of Industrial Development in Asia*, ch. 4; Kulkarni, *History*; Sandberg, *Lancashire in Decline*; Farnie, *The English Cotton Industry*; and Basudev Chaterji, *Trade, Tariffs, and Empire. Lancashire and*

There were several early attempts to take British manufacturing technology to India, but only in the 1850s did major concerns like the Bombay Spinning and Weaving Company become established. These pioneer enterprises were largely financed with the profits made in handling the cotton import trade by Parsee businessmen who, in addition to financing machine production, also initiated the export of raw cotton.

The industry prospered strongly during the American civil war and although this boom passed, it later benefited from heavy investment first in irrigation (necessary for cotton cultivation)[33] and then in railways. The latter not only enlarged the geographical span of raw cotton purchasing but also expanded markets for finished goods and enabled the manufacturing sector to move inland where labour costs were lower and domestic inland markets were closer at hand.[34]

By 1882, India had become a net exporter of yarn, and in the following year its industry sold more to China than Lancashire. By 1913–14 further expansion had made India the world's seventh-largest foreign trader and the fourth-largest producer of cotton goods. With easy access to British technology, ample domestic raw cotton supplies, cheap labour and a large internal market based both on population size and the perfect suitability of cotton clothing to its climate, India appeared at this stage to be on the way to achieving a major place in the international textile trade. The main reason why this position was not consolidated and expanded was Japan. Japanese competition was effective in three successive arenas: the Japanese domestic market, the Chinese market and the Indian domestic market. We have already seen how Japan displaced India from its domestic thread market in the 1890s by switching from Chinese to Indian raw cotton, by technical and blending improvements and by benefiting from Indian exchange rate policy. However, the task of displacing India from the Chinese market, where Indian goods were firmly entrenched, took longer. The process, however, was helped by the Japanese consolidation of its presence in Manchuria after the Russo-Japanese war. This

British Policy in India, 1919–1939, Delhi: Oxford University Press, 1992. The latter is an outstandingly interesting and comprehensive study.

33. The irrigation of Sind Province (involving 7 million hectares) was the largest contemporary irrigation project in the world.

34. The textile centres of Ahmedabad, Cawnpore and Madras were notably successful in displacing British imports.

strengthened its access to China and enabled Japan to exceed the
Indian market share by 1914 and achieve market dominance by the
mid-1920s.[35]

India's loss of its major yarn markets produced a serious imbalance
between the scale of spinning and weaving capacity; in response,
Indian firms expanded cloth and piece-goods manufacture. During the
First World War the Indian industry prospered while at the same time
the Japanese took advantage of Lancashire's temporary problems to
increase their penetration of the Indian market. In 1912–13 Japanese
cloth exports were less than 1 million yards; by 1918–19 they had
risen to 207 million yards, representing 35% of the grey cloth market.
This expansion gave the impetus for the further post-war growth.[36]

India's growing yarn output and the role of imports in the domestic
market in the 1920s are illustrated in Table 8.7, where it can be seen
that its domestic output grew steadily but unspectacularly. Imports
as a share of the home market peaked in 1921–22 but Japan's role
as a supplier rose markedly, with growing competitive strength
against Britain in the higher yarn counts. An overview of the cloth
industry is given in Table 8.8, which in one way reinforces the yarn
data by showing that the expansion of the Indian textile industry was
steadily increasing India's capacity for textile self-sufficiency (this trend
was supported by powerful domestic political pressures generated by
the Swadeshi movement).[37] Yet at the same time as Indian output
tripled, exports fell absolutely. When we turn to imports, we find
the British share falling from 97% before the First World War to less
than half of the market by 1935, when the British share of imports
was overtaken by Japan's. For Lancashire the loss of India was
catastrophic. Before the war India had taken 36% of British piece-
goods output, but by 1938 this share had fallen to 3%. Thus the loss
of India to Indian import substitution and Japanese competition alone
accounted for a contraction of the British piece-goods industry by
one-third.[38]

35. Nishikawa, *Japanese imperialism*, p. 283; Sung, *Stages of Industrial Development*,
pp. 142ff.

36. Kulkarni, *History*, p. 162.

37. The Swadeshi movement encouraged the boycotting of foreign goods and the
purchase of Indian goods, especially those made in the handicraft sector. The movement gained great authority after its adoption by the Congress Party in September
1920. Kulkarni, *History*, p. 74.

38. Robson, *The Cotton Industry in Great Britain*, p. 10.

Table 8.7. THE INDIAN YARN MARKET, 1913/14–1926/27
(*million lb.*)

	Domestic output	Index of output	% exported	% of imports in domestic consumption	Japan/Britain shares of imports	Japan's share of imports yarn counts 31–40	Japan's share of imports yarn counts 41 +
1913–14	683	100	30.3	12.1	2.3/85.7	38	n.a.
1921–22	694	102	12.7	18.1	26.1/70.2	36	10.5
1926–27	807	118	6.1	13.7	53.9/40.7	92	53.8

Source: Nishikawa, *Japanese imperialism*, p. 275.

Table 8.8. OUTPUT, SELF-SUFFICIENCY AND THE SOURCES OF IMPORTS IN THE INDIAN CLOTH MARKET, 1913/14–1935
(million linear yards)

	1913–14	1928–29	1935
Mill output	1,164	1,893	3,555
(Handloom output)	n.a.	(1,080)	(1,460)
Net imports	3,135	1,913	1,033
Exports	89	149	68
Indian self-sufficiency (%)	28	52	79
Indian % of output exported	7.6	7.9	1.9
Sources of imports (%):			
– Britain	97	75.2	47.3
– Japan	.3	18.4	50.9
– Others	2.6	6.1	1.8

Source: ILO, *The World Textile Industry*, p. 124.

The reasons for Japanese success were partly variations on themes already elaborated but there were special Indian elements in the story. In broad terms India's textile problems reflected the lack of any strategic government leadership in industrial policy as well as the unfavourable domestic and exchange-rate policies of the British administration. In particular, domestic deflation to balance the budget and the overvaluation of the rupee were severe handicaps in the 1930s, a time when Japan was redoubling its efforts by expansion and devaluation.[39] The Indian industrialists also complained that the *laissez-faire* policies imposed by the administration since the 1880s had sacrificed the interests of India to those of Lancashire.[40] Critics familiar with the textile sector itself also noted many other weaknesses. These included the failure to invest in and diffuse known technologies, excessive dependence on the English textile machinery industry and weaknesses of the corporate structure associated with the managing agency system.[41]

39. These issues are well explored in A.K. Bagchi, *Private Investment in India, 1900–1939*, Cambridge University Press, 1972.

40. Kulkarni, *History*, ch. 5.

41. The issue of investment and technique is dealt with by Bagchi, *Private Investment, passim*. Some Indian firms did adopt advanced techniques, including the Toyoda loom and the Casablanca high draft spinning system. The main problem was the failure to diffuse and develop a domestic machine-making industry.

Table 8.9. THE RELATIVE PRICES OF JAPANESE AND BRITISH COTTON
GOODS IN THE INDIAN MARKET, 1931/32 AND 1939/40
(Japanese prices with British = 100)

	Grey goods	*White goods*	*Coloured goods*
1931–2	97	81	70
1939–40	55	66	53

Source: Bagchi, *ibid.*, p. 244.

A particularly interesting aspect of the comparative strengths of the
Indian and Japanese industries arose from their labour situations. The
evidence suggests that while Japanese workers were not particularly
highly motivated, they had decisive advantages in health, literacy,
training and factory-level management that enabled Japanese firms to
achieve much more efficient working practices and productivity.[42]

Turning now to the question of Japanese–British competition in
India, the fundamental reality for Britain was Japan's increasing price
competitiveness in all sectors reflecting both productivity trends
and exchange-rate movements.[43] Price trends in three product areas
are shown in Table 8.9. Price competitiveness was reinforced by
intensive Japanese marketing efforts in India. Even critics such as
Kulkarni noted its thoroughness and the attention paid to the 'foibles'
of the ordinary Indian consumer, about which domestic manufacturers
would hardly bother themselves and Lancashire would know nothing
at all. The report by A. S. Pearse also throws light on the marketing
issue: he explored the 'evil smells and filth' of the wholesale bazaars
of Calcutta and Bombay, where he never met another European but
did uncover a tightly organised syndicate of fifteen dealers working

42. Gary Saxonhouse and Yukihiko Kiyokawa, 'The supply and demand for
quality workers in the cotton textile industries in Japan and India', *Papers and
Proceedings of the Conference on Japan's Historical Development Experience and the Contemporary Developing Countries: Issues for Comparative Analysis*, Tokyo: International
Development Center of Japan, 1978. This paper makes sophisticated use of the detailed
official 1897 survey of Japanese mills to analyse the early Japanese position. Among
the authors' findings are the following points: namely, that Indian firms failed to take
advantage of the ring system to substitute cheaper for more expensive types of labour,
and that whereas Indian textile workers in the 1920s were largely illiterate, half the
Japanese textile labour force were literate by 1897. Indeed, by 1924, 94.5% had
received exposure to primary education.

43. Chatterji, *Trade, Tariffs, and Empire*, pp. 184–5.

exclusively on behalf of Japanese importers in Bombay. This was a system he compared unfavourably to the ill-organised, hands-off efforts of European firms. He also illustrated the general point that the scale, coordination and international information networks of Japanese companies, especially their heavy use of the telephone and telegraph, enabled them to take advantage of events with a speed and effectiveness impossible for smaller firms with scanty access to information, and with financial resources that were quite inadequate for major commercial operations.[44] Despite all this, there were types of cotton goods where Lancashire maintained superiority, but Indian consumers, faced with drastically lower Japanese prices for somewhat inferior goods, maximised their welfare by opting to buy them.[45]

Textiles, trade friction and the beginnings of managed international trade

The turmoil in world textile markets during the world depression and the Japanese penetration of British-ruled markets in India and elsewhere led to the demise of free trade as the mechanism by which competitive struggles were fought out. The response of Britain — the biggest loser from shifts in the textile balance of power — led to a new era in which trade was increasingly 'managed' by agreed national restrictions that were the outcome of completely new forms of bargaining. The Indian textile market and the Britain–India–Japan commercial triangle were an important focus of these develoments.[46]

The pressure for textile protectionism in Britain began in the early 1920s, when the collapse of the post-war boom in 1921 and loss of overseas markets led to reductions, first in weaving capacity and then in yarn. The depression after 1930 accentuated the problem and increased sensitivity to the Japanese advance. This advance was well documented not only by intelligence from firms in the market but also by the meticulous commercial reports of British consular officials in

44. Pearse, *The Cotton Industry of India*, pp. 192–3.

45. Chatterji, *Trade, Tariffs, and Empire*, pp. 163–5.

46. This section is based on the works of Robson, Hubbard, the ILO, Nishikawa and Kulkarni, cited earlier. A very useful book, which ranges well beyond its title, is Shimizu, *Anglo-Japanese Trade Rivalry in the Middle East in the Inter-war Period*.

Japan.[47] Excluding Japan from third markets by non-commercial means was difficult. Its access to India was guaranteed by the Indo-Japanese Commercial Convention, and Japan had similar rights in the Dutch East Indies. As a member of the League of Nations till 1933, it was entitled to an 'open door' in British East Africa and similar treatment in League Mandated Territories, which included substantial areas of Africa and the Middle East. British problems in India were compounded not only by the intensity of the political Swadeshi movement but also by the fact that India had been granted fiscal autonomy in 1921, after which Britain could only hope for a minor influence on Indian tariff policies.

By 1931 total British piece-goods exports had declined by more than 70% from their pre-war peaks and by 1932 the fundamental decision to abandon free trade had been made and embodied in the Import Duties Act and Ottawa Agreements. The latter were intended to combine protectionism with the development of a colonial preference system that would stimulate trade within the British Empire. British duties on yarn and cloth were raised to 10% and 20% respectively.

In India, meanwhile, not only had tariffs on textiles been raised to new levels by 1930–32, but pressure was also growing for the abrogation of the Indo-Japanese Commercial Convention. This pressure came both from domestic Indian manufacturers, who really wished to exclude all imports, and from Lancashire exporters who saw their old market disappearing to Japanese competition.[48] Abrogation and the establishment of new agreements were finally achieved in 1933 and 1934, accompanied by a 75% tariff on piece-goods from non-British sources. This prohibitive act was primarily directed against Japan.

For Japan, the Ottawa agreements and the abrogation of its treaty with India represented a severe challenge both worldwide and in India, which in 1929 accounted for 32% of Japan's total piece-goods exports. Further, British political influence was a potential barrier to Japanese trade in Africa and the Middle East, both of which were identified as markets with major growth potential. The attempt to exclude Japan from India, accompanied as it was by hostile measures in markets

---

47. The *Commercial Reports* from the Foreign Office officials in Japan for the 1920s and 1930s were of a particularly high standard. So expert did these officials (especially George Sansom) become that they were called upon to play a key role in the tripartite textile negotiations in 1933–34.

48. Chatterji, *Trade, Tariffs, and Empire*, ch. 8.

such as Egypt, Malaya and Australia, simply could not be allowed to succeed.[49]

Japan's ability to respond to the Indian crisis reflected the benefits of forty years of commercial activity in India. From the very beginning of the shipping arrangements designed to bring raw cotton from India, Japanese merchants had been encouraged to fill the outward sailings of the NYK vessels with any merchandise they could sell. As the years passed, these businesses prospered and were supported by Japanese banking and commercial houses in the subcontinent. Japanese economic strengths in India in the 1930s also reflected the effectiveness of the Indo-Japanese Association, set up in its original form in 1902 and already fully operational before the First World War. The first president was former premier Okuma Shigenobu, and on his death he was succeeded by Shibusawa Eiichi.[50] By the 1930s more than 2,000 Japanese companies were exporting to India not only textiles, but also a wide variety of manufactures including clocks, watches, cameras, chemicals, car components, printing machinery, power plant, turbines, switching gear and capital equipment of all kinds. Japanese companies explored every aspect of India and its economy, and although major activity in cotton, banking, shipping and related activities was concentrated in Bombay and Calcutta, Japanese businessmen were also to be found in remote up-country corners of the subcontinent, always seeking new ways to enlarge business. Thus by the 1930s India had become a larger export market for Japan than China and in 1932 was actually the second largest individual market worldwide after the United States.[51] On the import side, in addition to raw cotton, the Japanese imported a variety of goods including pig-iron, iron and steel, and tobacco.

Japanese imports were the crucial strength that Japan had in negotiations with India, for while British mills lacked the technology to use Indian raw cotton, Japanese blending technology had enabled Japan

49. ILO, *The World Textile Industry*, p. 131; Nishikawa, *Japanese imperialism*, pp. 7ff. Data on Indian tariff changes are also detailed in *ibid.*, p. 291.

50. The Association had as its foreign adviser no less a person than Sir Claude Macdonald, the former British Ambassador to both Peking and Tokyo. Its area of responsibility included not only British India but also the whole of South and South-East Asia including the Dutch and French colonies. Indo-Japanese Association, *A Glimpse of Japan's Business and her Trade with India*, Tokyo, 1939.

51. See work cited above and, for details of the companies involved, Indo-Japanese Association, *The Indo-Japanese Business Directory, 1939–40*, Tokyo, 1939.

to become India's biggest raw cotton purchaser. The largest of the Japanese cotton-trading companies, Toyo Menkwa, operated on a scale sufficient to employ 400 Indian staff and controlled a purchasing network that penetrated the remotest cotton-growing districts.[52]

In response to the Indian tariff onslaught, the Bokyo used its plenary powers in 1933 to order the total suspension of cotton purchasing by Japanese companies in India. This precipitated a multi-faceted crisis, and negotiations between London, Delhi and Tokyo, partly on Indian and partly on global problems, began in Simla in the summer of 1933 and continued into the next year. In the Indian case, the resolution eventually reached stipulated quotas for Japanese imports to be matched by guaranteed purchases of minimum amounts of raw cotton.[53]

Agreement on the global issues proved much more elusive. In essence, what the British negotiators were seeking in the spring of 1934 was a partition of global markets that would essentially preserve current levels of Japanese exports but prevent their future growth. This was not acceptable to Japan, whose diplomatic and industry spokesmen pressed for the retention of a liberal trading system, insisting that Japanese prosperity required continuous expansion of exports.[54]

In May 1934 Britain ordered the imposition of a quota system for textile imports into all its colonies except Hong Kong and those in East Africa, and encouraged further elaboration of the imperial preference tariff system elsewhere. While in principle these measures affected all third parties, they were in practice directed at Japan.

The worldwide disputes. Similar disputes between Japan and other colonial territories broke out in the same period. By 1935, 122 countries had imposed restrictions on Japanese textile imports, and those on textiles and other products in the Philippines and the Dutch East Indies were particularly serious.[55] In the East Indies, Japan had

52. Sung, *Stages of Industrial Development*, pp. 144ff; Nishikawa, *Japanese imperialism*, ch. 1.

53. The Indians consistently complained that the Japanese broke the export quota agreements by exporting through Hong Kong.

54. These negotiations are described in the standard sources but of particular interest are comments by key Japanese participants reported in Ando's oral history, *Testimony on Showa economic history*, vol. 1, pp. 283–307.

55. See papers of the conference on International Commercial Rivalry in Southeast Asia in the Inter-War Period, held at Shimoda, Japan, 1988.

Table 8.10. COLONIAL AND WORLD MARKETS FOR
BRITISH TEXTILE EXPORTS, 1909/13–1938

	1909/13	1927/31	1938
Index of total exports	100	27	21
Exports to India (% share)	39	23	21
Exports to India, Dominions and Quota Colonies (% share)	50	46	60
Exports to all other markets (% share)	50	54	40

Source: Cotton Board, *Report of the Committee to Enquire into Post War Problems*, London, 1944, quoted in Robson, *The Cotton Industry in Britain*, p. 11.

built a wide-ranging export trade, not only by competitive pricing but also by careful study of local markets, shipping rebates and the establishment of retail systems that completely circumvented the indigenous one, enabling them to control shop prices.[56] As a result, the Japanese share of all imports had risen from 11.6% in 1929 to 31% in 1933, with the Japanese not only threatening to dominate textiles but also holding between 50% and 90% of market shares in commodities as diverse as bicycle components, glass, toys, beer, cement and electric lamps. The Dutch responded in 1934 by instituting quotas, but Japan once again used its bargaining power as a major purchaser of oil, rubber and sugar to produce a final package of restrictions in 1937–38 that was not too unfavourable to its interests.

The result of all this restrictive activity is not easy to summarise. With textiles, protection succeeded in the sense that it raised the share of Britain's production sold to Empire markets (see Table 8.10). However, as the first line of this table shows, this larger share was only part of a diminishing total. Japan's exports, on the other hand, continued to perform surprisingly well. This ability to find new outlets and do well even in restricted ones reflected the skills of the trade associations and commercial diplomats as well as two other factors. The first of these arose because the world economy was basically colonialised. Thus, most important commercial negotiations were with powers responsible for geographical groupings that included

56. Hiroshi Shimizu, 'A study of Japan's commercial expansion into the Netherlands Indies from 1914 to 1941', *Bulletin of the Faculty of Nagoya University of Commerce and Business Administration*, vol. 34, no. 2, March 1990, pp. 43–76.

raw material producers who needed Japanese purchases; these were particularly important because, apart from the largely self-sufficient Soviet Union, Japan was the one industrial economy in the world that was actually growing. Secondly, the consumers in the low-income colonial markets which the metropolitan authorities were trying to protect were highly sensitive to the declines in their living standards caused by the exclusion of cheap Japanese goods. Because of this, the local colonial governments were equally sensitive. In Ceylon, for example, the anti-Japanese import quotas had to be imposed by Orders-in-Council from London because the colonial administration would not implement them voluntarily and thereby deprive the poorest sections of the population of affordable clothing. Similarly in Indonesia, the bargaining over restrictions in the 1930s reflected Japanese raw material purchasing power and Dutch fears that the loss of Japanese imports might be politically destabilising.

While Japan was learning the arts necessary to live with trade restrictions, many Japanese continued to question whether their country should not itself rationalise and expand its own imperial system, creating an economic bloc that would lessen Japanese vulnerability to economic fluctuations and to political factors beyond the control of Japanese policy-makers.

Part III
THE ROLE OF TECHNOLOGY

9

BUILDING THE TECHNOLOGICAL
INFRASTRUCTURE

'If an oriental had any idea how enormous the world of knowledge is, they would simply sit down and fold their hands, stupified by the prospect, and convinced that it was hopeless to begin what no one could finish.' — *North China Herald*, January 13, 1893

'Achieving "a rich country and a strong military" is the most urgent duty ahead of us; and the essence of this is the development of people.' — Fukuzawa Yukichi[1]

The framework for analysis

In the 1990s the Japanese economy is instinctively associated with a high level of technological achievement. Most analysts have argued that technological performance has been an important element in Japan's international economic success, and see Japan, Europe and the United States engaged in a triangular technological competition, the outcome of which will shape the economic structures of the twenty-first century.

Technology issues were equally important to Japan before 1937, and although earlier issues were somewhat different to contemporary ones, an analysis of them is indispensable to understanding the long-term evolution of Japan's international economic relations. Before attempting to unravel the Japanese experience, however, it is important to define the boundaries of the discussion and enumerate the questions to which we seek answers.

The fundamental point on which the arguments here are based is that a society's technological capacity should be defined so as to take a comprehensive view of the productive process, a view that takes account of the following elements: core physical processes requiring

---

1. Quoted in Morikawa, *The sources of the Japanese style of management*, pp. 42–3. In both Japan and China, the concept of education used in contexts such as this (*yosei* in Japanese, *peixun* or *peiyang* in Chinese) goes far beyond utilitarian training to embrace a strong Confucian component of moral formation.

capital goods; ancillary physical processes; human skills required for the direct operation of core and ancillary processes; and research, design, managerial and commercial skills necessary to establish and coordinate the physical processes, dispose of output to the best commercial advantage and develop cheaper processes and new or variant products. For example, steel production involves core facilities such as blast-furnaces, converters and strip mills; ancillary facilities such as those used to transport raw materials around the plant; the literacy, numeracy and specialised skills required for direct operation of the plant; and the overall skills needed for management of the entire physical and commercial operation.

By this definition, *technological progress* is defined as changes in any of the elements that produce either new products or new processes for producing old ones. Change of this kind is a central dynamic of long-run development. *Product* innovation stimulates demand, expands the economy through linkages between new and old productive structures, and provides competitive advantages for innovative firms in domestic and international markets. *Process* innovation reduces the costs of existing goods and plays a central role in the struggle for domestic and international competitiveness. Although significant, the distinction between product and process innovation must not be exaggerated since the research and development that produce them often overlap. In practice, the overall pattern of innovation is of major product innovation leading to a continuous stream of process innovations as competitors catch up (technically and commercially) with the pioneer.[2]

Any useful discussion of an economy's technological progress must include measurements that enable us to analyse its movements over time, to identify its progress in different parts of the economy, and to see the whole in international perspective. Unfortunately nearly all such measurements have difficulties and ambiguities attached to them. One approach is simply to identify and list new products and processes as growth takes place. Another is to measure progress as reflected in the trend of physical output per worker. For the economy as a whole or for sub-sectors of it, it is also possible first to estimate the con-

---

2. In the petrochemical industry, for example, nine major modern products stimulated 180 new processes at a rate of one every two years for each product. Robert Stobaugh, *Innovation and Competition: The Global Management of Petrochemical Products*, Boston, MA: Harvard Business School Press, 1988, pp. 22–7.

tributions to growth by labour and capital, and then to attribute the 'unexplained' growth to technological improvement. This last approach embodies the broad definition of change suggested at the outset of the discussion, where account has to be taken not only of changing physical facilities, but also of improving human skills and organisational abilities. For developing economies in which technological progress is initially a process of 'catching up', foreign trade measures of self-sufficiency in important technologically intensive activities may also be useful. However, care must be taken with these, because the most dynamic economies combine rapid progress in import substitution with a voracious appetite for learning from the moving technical frontier; thus they have large two-way flows of trade influenced by technological factors.

Let us now move on to the policy issues which technology raises for economic management at all levels of an advanced market economy. During the past seventy years 'technology-consciousness' has grown enormously. At the level of the firm, successful enterprises must foster working methods and cultures of behaviour that enable them to seek information, choose from new or improved technologies currently available, and participate in the processes of technology diffusion. At the same time, larger firms engage in efforts to shift the frontiers of fundamental knowledge and develop new products and processes by the application of theoretical knowledge. In this world, far from being short-term profit maximisers who are competitive by virtue of the correct use of known technologies, firms are sophisticated mechanisms faced with complex time-horizons and business choices, and each engaged on a unique path of search, experience and learning.

At the national level, rising technology-consciousness means that governments are aware that domestic progress and international competitiveness depend on trends in technology which they can influence. This awareness has grown rapidly since the Second World War, and it is scarcely an exaggeration to say that the collapse of the European Communist economies reflected their inability to create and diffuse new technology.

National technology policy operates directly in at least three spheres: first, education, research and development (especially fundamental research, which is beyond the interests and time-horizons of all but the largest private companies); secondly, defence and national security; and thirdly, commercial sectors where government involvement is widely accepted as normal because, for special reasons, private efforts are likely to be too small or otherwise inadequate to the public interest. The pharmaceutical and agricultural industries are good examples of this. Government influences technology indirectly in a variety of ways, of which the most important are financial support and tax incentives to encourage firms to invest in research and development, the establishment of patent systems, and policies on competition and international trade that affect willingness and ability to innovate. The fundamental realities underlying these decisions are that innovation is expensive and risky and that it is neither feasible nor in the public interest for the financial benefits of innovation to be captured only by the firm or individual making it.

This situation gives rise to two paradoxes. The first is that if firms compete intensively through the normal mechanism of price-cutting, then low profits and market uncertainty will tend to discourage innovation, whereas a climate of competition will encourage diffusion of the innovations that do appear. The second paradox is that if patenting is *highly* restrictive and firms succeed in maintaining commercial secrecy, this may encourage innovation but the public benefit will be correspondingly limited. This is because diffusion throughout the economy will be discouraged by the legal and cost barriers to the adoption of new techniques. Thus in a market economy the fundamental problems of technology policy are: how far should government act directly to support private innovation? And how should it devise incentives that combine the encouragement of innovation on the one hand with maximum diffusion on the other?[3]

For developing economies the main technology policy issues are how to select industries to expand by acquiring known techniques from advanced economies; how to determine what adaptation of such technologies is feasible and to their competitive advantage; how to identify traditional technologies that can be preserved and developed in hybrid form; and how to decide the extent, time-scale and mechanisms for subsidising both the acquisition of intrinsically complex technologies and the development of an overall infrastructure of knowledge and skill. Generally such choices should reflect the comparative advantages of poorer countries (especially relatively low

3. The clearest statement of these dilemmas is Kenneth J. Arrow, 'Economic welfare and the allocation of Resources for Invention' in National Bureau of Economic Research, *The Rate and Direction of Inventive Activity, Economic and Social Factors*, Princeton University Press, 1962, pp. 609–26.

labour costs) and the dynamic benefits of key technologies, especially where these are at an early stage of their life. These economic choices may to some extent be subordinated to strategic, military considerations that override them.

A key to these policy conundrums is the fact that over at least the past 250 years technology appears to have advanced in surges of linked innovations — each one defining a 'technological epoch'. Thus while minor and even quite major innovations may disturb the structure of the economy and influence its international competitiveness, epochal advances, by definition, have ramifications not only for all sectors of the economy but also for economic organisation and probably for the social and political order as well. Between the mid-eighteenth century and our own time there have been four or five such epochs.[4]

For the follower nation, the feasibility of entry and catching up in the mainstream of a particular technological epoch depends on finding solutions to the problems of how to mobilise capital to invest in the physical equipment necessary to participate in the epoch; how to catch up on the learning experience of pioneer firms and nations; how to acquire the contextual scientific knowledge that surrounds each epoch and is essential to participate in its development; and, finally, how to remove any special, circumstantial cost disadvantages that may affect a particular follower economy. In general, it is most beneficial to join an epoch just after it has passed beyond the earliest phase of a major innovation. This is because at the outset the risks and costs of acquiring new contextual knowledge are both high, whereas later in its cycle, the epoch still has a long life ahead of it in which followers have a good chance of making their own product and process innovations, while pioneers will not have established too much of a lead in secret or proprietary experience, which they can then either deny to followers or sell only at a high price.[5]

---

4. This view is elaborated by Christopher Freeman and Carlota Perez, 'Structural crises of adjustment: business cycles and investment behaviour' in Giovanni Dosi *et al.* (eds), *Technical Change and Economic Theory*, London: Pinter, 1988, pp. 38–66 and by Carlota Perez and Luc Soete, 'Catching up in technology: entry barriers and windows of opportunity', *ibid.*, pp. 458–79.

5. Stobaugh shows that for his nine petrochemical products the probability of a major process innovation declines continuously throughout the life of a major product innovation, while the highest probability of minor process innovation actually occurs in the first third of a five-decade life. Stobaugh, *Innovation and Competition*, pp. 26–7.

The Japanese technology problem

Before 1937 the Japanese technology problem was consistent with that of the classic follower-nation, hence the the main problem for government and the private sector was not how to advance the technological frontier with major inventions, but how to get anywhere near to it at all; how to emulate known technologies, not create new ones. Japan's achievements in emulation were striking and in some phases extraordinarily so; thus to explain them we must discuss their nineteenth-century origins and Japan's place in the history of the technological epochs discussed above and sketched in Fig. 9.1. The last epoch shown continued till after the Second World War, being finally superseded only by the electronic epoch in which we are now living.

The onset of each epoch was marked by a group of watershed innovations, leading to the transformation of old industries and the creation of new ones. One thread ran consistently through the story, namely the inter-related progress in metallurgy, the materials sciences and tool-making. Starting with Cort's puddling process in Britain in 1783, progress in iron- and steel-making made possible a stream of innovations in toolmaking (by Maudslay, Clements and Bramah), which in turn improved the early manufacture of engines and textile and mill machinery. Further metallurgical advances in the first half of the nineteenth century led to tools for planing metal surfaces and generating accurate screws, gear-wheels and other components to the new standards required by users (Whitworth, Nasmyth, Howe and Whitney). Finally, by the turn of the century, when the leadership of the industry had passed to the United States and, increasingly, Germany, firms such as Brown & Sharpe and Pratt & Whitney had created the universal milling and grinding machines that paved the way for metal components of the accuracy required by mass-production processes and by the aero engine and automobile.

Japan benefited in its efforts to catch up from the fact that it had already acquired many of the relevant social capabilities and, in traditional form, manufacturing disciplines which were needed. These are reflected in a long history of learning and empirical innovation in the traditional economy. In agriculture, long-term improvements in productivity and product variety had been achieved by advances in biological, mechanical and water engineering techniques, and there is evidence that these improvements were supported by some under-standing of the need and potential for such changes. The urban economy, too, developed the capacity to produce a vast and changing range of commodities. Many of these required specialisation of tasks; sophisticated manual skills in wood, metals and other materials; institutionalised systems of training and apprenticeship; large scales of production, and the organisation of complex chains of activity linking product design to final sale.[6] However, the traditional economy lacked modern sources of power, an advanced knowledge of metallurgy and machine tool-making, and the underpinning of both by a modern financial system and a much deeper theoretical understanding of the contextual knowledge surrounding modern technology.

We can see from Fig. 9.1 that Japan's first efforts at catching up began at the favourable early stage of the West's second major technological epoch. Thus although at mid-century both Japanese and westerners perceived an enormous technological gap between Japan and the world at large, this was not entirely the case. Many of the innovations that so alarmed the Japanese in both the civil and military spheres were relatively new; and they (and the achievements of the first epoch) were often the products of men who were brilliantly imaginative but grounded in practice rather than theoretical science — in contrast to the formally educated, laboratory-based innovators who rose to prominence later in the century.[7] Thus while the Japanese at first almost wholly lacked the contextual theoretical knowledge

6. Many of these points are discussed in *EHOJ*, vols 1–2, and in Nakane and Oishi, *Tokugawa Japan*, esp. chs 3 and 6. The extent and character of manual skills and metal-working are emphasised by Odaka Konosuke in Minami Ryoshin and Kiyokawa Yukihiko (eds), *Nihon no kogyoka to gijutsu hatten* (Japanese industrialisation and technological development), Tokyo: Toyo Keizai Shimposha, 1987, pp. 217–20 where it is pointed out that in some areas 9% of households were *shokunin*, i.e. engaged in production of guns, swords, coins and other metal-working pursuits, sometimes in large-scale establishments. A fuller interpretation of the role of the *shokunin* is pro-vided in Odaka Konosuke, *Shokunin no sekai kojo no sekai* (The world of the craftsman and the world of the factory), Tokyo: Libro Porto, 1993.

7. James Nasmyth summed up his handicraft approach to engineering as follows: 'The truth is that the eyes and the fingers — *the bare fingers* — are the two principal inlets to sound practical instruction . . . No *book* knowledge can avail for that purpose [Nasmyth's italics].' Samuel Smiles (ed.), *James Nasmyth Engineer: An Autobiography*, London: John Murray, 1883, p. 97.

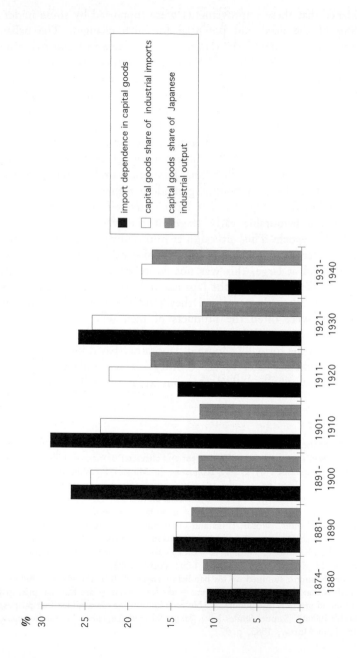

Fig. 9.1. IMPORT SUBSTITUTION AND DEVELOPMENT IN CAPITAL GOODS, 1874–1940

surrounding new processes and products, their craftsmen can be said to have possessed a stock of experience that stood proxy for that accumulated by western innovators and which therefore served to lower the cost for Japan of catching up. Further, the relevance of this experience and its commercial implications were reinforced by the initial entangling of the new technological processes, even in the West, with the contemporary demands for older, traditional types of artifact.

Nothing conveys the full flavour of the western technological world in the decade of the *kaikoku* better than a careful analysis of products on show at the Great Exhibition of 1851. Here we find the newer machines and technologies side by side, and in some cases merging with the crafts and the 'industrial arts'. Indeed, in the 1850s innovations in steam-power and machine-tools were *process* innovations which seemed as important in making traditional products to new standards as they were in making possible the creation of *product* innovations such as the modern railway and ocean steamer. In these traditional industrial arts — especially metal-working and ceramics — the Japanese craftsmen, with their long traditions, deep skills, receptive attitudes, discipline and low wages, were well equipped to compete immediately.[8]

All this is elaborated later, but we can turn immediately to one example of the early 'gap'. In 1842 James Nasmyth patented his steam-hammer: an enormous block of metal that could be lifted by means of a steam-driven piston and then either dropped or forced downwards by steam pressure. The hammer could not only be adapted for the driving of massive piles of the kind needed for bridges and public works, but it also became the essential tool for forging large pieces of metal for shipbuilding and the manufacture of construction steel, steam-engines, ships and guns — all products which we think of as the very essence of the nineteenth-century technological

---

8. In the best guide to this exhibition, within a few pages of illustrations of the latest machine-tools, we find work in lace, papier-mâché, ornamental glass, bronze and enamelled silverware. See *The Illustrated Exhibitor, passim*. The application of steam machinery to traditional industrial arts is also discussed in Asa Briggs, *The Age of Improvement*, London: Longman, 1975, pp. 470–1.

revolution.[9] As early as 1860, however, the British representative in Japan observed an operating Nasmyth hammer in a forging shop in Nagasaki, together with a complete working steam-engine, all entirely made by the Japanese who had never seen such a machine themselves and had constructed it with the help of plans in a book and a Dutch engineering instructor. Deeply moved, Alcock described the scene as 'one of the most extraordinary and crowning testimonies of Japanese enterprise and ingenuity, which leaves all the Chinese have ever attempted far behind'.[10]

Finally, although in many ways the timing of the Japanese technological revolution was favourable, the problem was that the pace of western progress in this epoch was accelerating. In the first, late eighteenth-century epoch progress had been rather slow because neither metallurgy nor machine-tool-making had reached the standards necessary to convert the ideas of the early engineers and engine-makers into safe, workable products.[11] But as the watershed innovations of the second epoch were concentrated in the period from the 1820s to the 1840s, they facilitated a torrent of new and transformed products in mid-century, including steam-engines, locomotives and screw-driven iron ships.[12] And in the late nineteenth century the process of acceleration repeated itself, producing diesel, petrol and electric motors and entire new industries based on advances in the electrical and chemical sciences. Quantification is obviously difficult,

9. Nasmyth and his hammer are discussed in Aubrey F. Burstall, *A History of Mechanical Engineering*, London: Faber and Faber, 1963, esp. pp. 207–8; and by L. T. C. Rolt, *Victorian Engineering*, London: Penguin, 1970, *passim*. A contemporary appreciation of its significance is provided in William Fairbairn, *Iron: Its History, Properties and Processes of Manufacture*, Edinburgh: A. & C. Black, 1869, pp. 132–5. By the 1870s the largest steam-hammers in the world were at the Woolwich Arsenal and the Creusot works in France, where they were used mainly for the manufacture of cannon. Benjamin Vincent (ed.), *Haydn's Dictionary of Dates and Universal Information relating to all Ages and Nations* (16th edn), London: Moxon, 1878, p. 709.

10. Alcock, *The Capital of the Tycoon* vol. 1, pp. 82–4.

11. A nineteenth-century account of these innovators is Samuel Smiles, *Industrial Biography: Iron Workers and Tool Makers*, London: John Murray, 1876.

12. A striking measure of the overall pace of world technology acceleration during the *kaikoku* is the trend of registered patents in the United State. The annual rate of registrations in the thirty years after 1860 was no less than twenty-nine times higher than that during the seventy years preceding it. See Armytage, *A Social History of Engineering*, p. 179; Thomas C. Cochran and William Miller, *The Age of Enterprise: A Social History of Industrial America*, New York: Harper, 1961, pp. 14–15.

but according to one estimate, 1876–1900 was the peak period for new innovations between the mid-eighteenth and twentieth centuries, with an innovation rate almost seven times that of 1750–75.[13] Nonetheless, by the time that European and American innovation was preparing the ground for the third epoch, Japanese capabilities were sufficiently advanced to enter this epoch too at a favourable point, and to begin the process of manipulating their limited technological capabilities in ways that maximised their international commercial effectiveness.

One sector where technology was bounding ahead with particular vigour was military equipment. As we shall see, it was here that between the 1860s and 1914 Japan and other countries found their national security dependent on the availability of techniques that were changing literally from year to year. This compelled follower nations to combine domestic technological development with imports from the technical leaders: e.g. large warships from Britain; guns, ammunition and special steels from Germany; and torpedo-boats from France.

The technological challenge, 1853–1918

In Japan's history of technological improvement, the First World War was a major watershed. Before it, Japan was making the initial transition from traditional to modern technology, which involved catching up on both the first and early stages of the second western epoch. By the end of the war, however, Japan had demonstrated modern engineering and management capabilities in a range of industries including textiles, mining, railways, shipbuilding, civil construction, armaments and metallurgy. Progress thereafter took the form of continuing to raise standards in existing industries while acquiring the techniques to enter other industries of the third epoch

---

13. The best systematic history of technology for this period is Charles Singer *et al.*, *A History of Technology* vol. 4: *The Industrial Revolution. c. 1750–c. 1850*, and vol. 5, *The Late Nineteenth Century*, Oxford University Press, 1958. Even more interesting are contemporary accounts including Robert Routledge, *Discoveries and Inventions of the 19th Century*, repr. London: Bracken Books, 1989, while for the very important French perspective see Louis Figuier, *Les Grandes Inventions Modernes dans les Sciences, l'industrie et les Arts*, Paris: Hachette, 1910. For surveys of individual subjects, *EB* (esp. the 11th edn) remains incomparably useful. The data on innovation rates in 1750–1950 are quoted in Dosi, *The Economics of Technical Change and International Trade*, p. 41.

such as vehicles and aeroplanes — industries almost as new in the West as they were in Japan.

Almost invariably, the acquisition of new industrial technology reflected a deliberate, planned programme of import substitution — a policy described in the Japanese literature as *kokusanka* (lit. 'converting to domestic production') — and in most cases was followed by the planned achievement of export competitiveness.

To clarify the nature of technology policy in this period it is helpful to distinguish between the 'strategic' and 'commercial' realms. In the former, Japan acquired new technologies to meet the urgent national imperatives of military and economic security.[14] In the latter, choices were governed largely by economic considerations. Thus because motivation in the strategic realm transcended narrow economic calculation, success in technology transfer here usually depended on direct government activity or on subsidisation of the private sector. In the commercial realm, by contrast, the government's role was to provide the infrastructure and assist firms to survive the lengthy learning processes needed to make new technologies competitive.[15] While it is true that for a country as poor as Japan in the nineteenth century the economic consequences of choices in the strategic sphere could not ultimately be ignored, the distinction between the two spheres provides a key to Japanese technology policy.

Within the strategic sphere, priority was given to the basic technology of military repellence. The *kaikoku* could not have occurred if Japan had possessed naval and gunnery resources equal to those of the western powers. Achievement of this technology to such a qualitative standard was therefore essential.[16] This process was

14. The military influence on technology is fully discussed in Nakaoka Tetsuro *et al.* (eds), *Kindai Nihon no gijutsu to gijutsu seisaku* (Technology and technology policy in modern Japan), Tokyo: Tokyo Daigaku Shuppankai 1986, esp. chs 1 and 3, and is also a major theme of Hayashi Katsuya, *Nihon gunji gijutsushi* (A history of Japan's military technology), Tokyo: Haruki Shoten, 1957 and Koyama Koken, *Nihon gunji kogyo no shiteki bunseki* (An historical analysis of Japan's military industries), Tokyo: Ochanomizu Shobo, 1972. A pioneering English-language article on the subject is K. Yamamura, 'Success Ill-gotten? The role of Meiji militarism in Japan's technological progress', *Journal of Economic History*, vol. xxxvii, no. 1, March 1977, pp. 113–35.

15. A specific statement that costs could be ignored in planning strategic industries is made in 'The policy of nurturing [*ikusei*] bureaucratically-controlled military industry', MITI, *A history of policy*, vol. 18, *Kikai kogyo* (Machinery), pp. 6–7.

16. See the letter on naval issues by Ii Naosuke to the Bakufu (1853), translated in Beasley, *Select Documents*, pp. 117–19.

substantially complete by the late 1900s, in the sense that Japan had by then acquired both the broad scientific knowledge and the key production experience that were relevant, although at the design level Japan was still basically derivative and production often depended on imports of key materials or components. In the course of this progress, Japan inevitably acquired offensive as well as defensive military capabilities. Moreover, the metallurgical, mechanical and electrical engineering skills required in the strategic sphere spilled over into the commercial one with important benefits for trade. Some of these benefits were not revealed till the 1920s and 1930s and others were not fully exploited till after the Second World War, by which time the government had been supporting the strategic industries by one means or another for more than sixty years.

In addition to these militarily inspired developments, part of the technology acquired for rapid import substitution and export expansion in consumer goods in the early Meiji period must also be counted as 'strategic' in the sense that its underlying purpose was national economic survival. For under the 'free trade' conditions imposed by the Ansei treaties, Japan's economic and financial stability in the 1870s stood to be destroyed by the trade flows reflecting western technological superiority, especially in factory-made textiles. To compete with such imports Japan had to reach productivity and quality levels in spinning and weaving within 'tolerable' range of western imports ('tolerable' in the sense that lower than western levels of productivity and quality were offset by lower wage costs and prices which compensated consumers for any inferiority of quality).[17] In textiles the achievement of competitiveness and the transfer of the industry from the strategic to the commercial sphere were rapid, mainly because policy in this industry was working with the grain of Japan's underlying comparative advantage.

In the purely commercial sphere, the government's main tasks were to build a basic infrastructure of human skills, research and efficient private economic institutions, to seek out and disseminate new knowledge, encourage the newly-created private sector to adapt western techniques in ways that would drive commercial competitiveness

17. This issue is explored by Kiyokawa in Minami and Kiyokawa, *Japanese Industrialisation*, ch. 5, and in his article 'Technological gaps and the stabilisation of transferred technology: the case of cotton textiles' in Ohkawa Kazushi and Minami Ryoshin (eds), *Kindai Nihon no keizai hatten* (Economic development of modern Japan), Tokyo: Toyo Keizai Shimposha, 1975, pp. 249–82.

Table 9.1. THE RATE OF GROWTH OF PRIVATE INDUSTRY AND
THE CONTRIBUTION OF TECHNICAL PROGRESS TO INCREASES
IN LABOUR PRODUCTIVITY, 1908–1938 (% per annum)

	Growth-rate of industry	Growth-rate of labour productivity	Contribution of technical progress to labour productivity	Share of technical progress
1908–10	5.41	3.85	.44	12%
1911–20	7.85	4.65	1.55	32%
1921–30	5.03	4.1	2.96	62%
1931–38	7.86	4.69	3.42	85%
Average	6.71	4.4	2.38	54%

Source: Estimates by Minami based on the LTES series. R. Minami, *The Economic Development of Japan. A Quantitative Study*, London: Macmillan, 1986, pp. 104–7.
Note: Industry is defined here to include mining, manufacturing, construction and infrastructure. Labour productivity increases may be attributed either to an increase in the amount of capital equipment per worker or to some form of technical progress. The right-hand column estimates the contribution of the latter to the increase in labour productivity, *not* to the overall rate of growth of industry.

forward, and in many cases provide transitional protection where time was needed for Japan to achieve the skills and shift in comparative advantage necessary to make a technology competitive.

An overview of Japan's technology performance. Before we look at technology policy and the experience of individual industries, we need some feel for the extent and changing pace of technological progress in Japan before 1937. In Table 9.1 we can see estimates of the contribution of technical progress in the broad sense to the growth of the manufacturing and mining sectors. This is not a perfect indicator of technological capabilities, but does clearly relate to it. Although the data relate only to 1908–38 and to the private sector of industry, this does not seriously distort the message. The average rate of growth of the sector over the four periods is 6.71%. Labour productivity in the same period grew by 4.4%, and more than half of this was accounted for by technical progress. Moreover, the share of technical progress rose markedly through the four periods, reaching 85% in the 1930s.

A second measure of technical progress is the time-lag between original western innovations and their introduction into Japan. In Table 9.2 this point is illustrated by data for the metallurgical sector.

Table 9.2. JAPANESE-EUROPEAN TECHNOLOGY GAPS
IN METALLURGY, 1858–1909

Technique	European innovation	Japanese adoption	Place	Gap (years)
Charcoal-fired furnace	*ca.* 1700	1858	Kamaishi	160 +
Coke-fired furnace (Darby)	1717	1894	Tanaka works	177
Crucible steel (Huntsman)	1740	1882	Tsukuji arsenal	142
Reverberatory furnace (Smeaton)	1766	1850–2	Saga ironworks	86
Puddling method (Cort)	1784	1875	Kamaishi	91
Hot power bellows (Neilson)	1828	1875	Kamaishi	47
Air-blown steel converter (Bessemer)	1856	1901	Yawata steelworks	45
Open hearth process (Siemens-Martin)	1863	1890	Osaka arsenal	27
Stassano electric arc furnace	1899	1909	Dobashi electric steelworks	10

Sources: This Table was suggested by a diagram in Nakaoka, *Technology and technology policy*, p. 14. I have supplemented and adjusted Nakaoka's data with other materials. A useful account of early Japanese iron-making and the transition to modern methods in the latter half of the nineteenth century is K. Okada *et al.*, *Tatara kara kindai seitetsu e* (From Tatara to modern iron making), Tokyo: Heibonsha, 1990. A complete referenced chronology of the industry is in H. Iida, *Nihon tekko gijutsushi* (A history of Japanese iron and steel technology), Tokyo: Toyo Keizai Shimposha.

Note: The precise dating of some of the western innovations is often difficult. Thus the gap illustrated here is only approximate and may in some cases be exaggerated since western dates are for inventions and patents rather than commercial use, while the Japanese data are for early use.

The innovations here fall into three groups. In the first we have blast-furnaces fired by wood and charcoal and a very early small-scale steel-making process. For this group the technology gap between Japan and Europe is about 150 years. The second is a group of three intermediary techniques, including the reverberatory furnace developed in Britain in the latter part of the eighteenth century, for which the gap is less than 100 years. In the final group we have the major nineteenth-century steel-making innovations, for which the gap is on average twenty-

Table 9.3. OUTPUT AND SELF-SUFFICIENCY IN SELECTED
INDUSTRIES, 1880–1938

Turning-point	Domestic output = imports	Exports begin	Exports > imports	Gap between first and last turning-points (years)
Cotton cloth	1880	1883	1909	29
Cotton thread	1889	1890	1897	8
Textile machinery	1922	1907	1929	7
Sheet steel	1923	1900	1934	11

	Year	Home output	Imports	Exports	Total sales	Home output as share of total sales
Cars (units)	1925	376	5,202	0	5,578	7%
	1938	16,479	20,500	0	36,979	45%

Sources: Yamazawa, *Japanese economic development*, pp. 248–51; MITI, vol. 18, *Machinery*, p. 337.

seven years. For the last innovation in this group, the electric arc furnace, the gap has narrowed to ten years. Moreover, as we see in the next chapter, in some technologies the gap between western and Japanese adoption fell to only one or two years, and by the early twentieth century, when significant adaptation of foreign techniques occurred, Japan was actually moving ahead of world standards.[18]

A final group of indicators in Fig. 9.2 and Table 9.3 display technological progress in the form of growing Japanese self-sufficiency in important sectors and industries. In Fig. 9.2 we can see the changing weight of capital goods as a proportion of total imports of manufactured goods and the rise and fall of the foreign contribution to the total supply of capital goods available to the economy. Thus the peak

18. It is important to note that Japan's adoption of these processes was not uniform because the Japanese combined foreign implant technology with modernisation of traditional iron-making. For the latter, some older western techniques were appropriate forms of intermediate or hybrid technology.

foreign contribution to capital goods supply was in 1900–10, when it reached 30%, but by the 1930s Japan was more than 90% self-sufficient in this crucial sector. The top part of Table 9.3 shows changing self-sufficiency in cotton yarn, cotton cloth, textile machinery and steel, as indicated by three watersheds. These are: the point at which domestic production accounts for more than half of consumption, the beginning of exports, and the point where exports exceed imports. To put this picture in perspective, in the bottom panel of the table are data for the motor-car industry, in which none of the turning-points was reached before 1937 although technological capabilities were improving and the level of self-sufficiency was rising.

We shall now examine the Japanese technology policies that lay behind these data, starting with the government as a provider of skills, information networks, special legislation and the policies of standardisation and 'rationalisation'.

Government and the technology infrastructure

Late Tokugawa society responded to the challenge of western intrusion with a series of technology initiatives. Basic metallurgical and mechanical skills were developed, information on western technologies was actively sought, educational and training centres were established and important advances were made in navigation, shipbuilding and armament manufacture. However, these efforts were sporadic, geographically fragmented and hampered by the misunderstanding and anti-foreign mania that were the product of 200 years of Seclusion.

After 1867, the power to make and implement technology policy was concentrated in a new centralised government structure, to which were entrusted most of the arsenals, dockyards and other assets in which the late Tokugawa technological efforts had been concentrated.[19] During the Meiji period authority over technology policy was distributed in the following way. The implementation of policies with direct military significance was the responsibility of the Army and Navy Ministries (Rikugunsho and Kaigunsho), established in 1872, both of which had specialised sections whose duty it was to choose,

19. Nakaoka, *Technology and technology policy*, pp. 173ff. and chs. 4, 5. A great deal of material on this is in MITI, *A history of policy*, vols: 1–2, Sosetsu (Summary). Translations of many key documents are included in McLaren, *Japanese Government Documents*, parts 1 and 2.

acquire and test western weapons, and then organise their importation and domestic production (*kokusanka*) plans as appropriate. These ministries, moreover, were directly concerned not only with importing and import substitution in weaponry but also with the communications, machinery, vehicle, engineering and other industries of military significance.

The second key institution was the Ministry of Public Works (Kobusho). This operated from 1870 to 1885 and its technological mission was spelled out in the terms of reference published in 1872 in which it was charged with developing Japan's engineering capabilities and with technology transfer in the advanced and heavy industries not covered by the military bureaucracy. In particular, it was responsible for mining, railways, iron-making, telegraphs, electricity, machinery and lighthouses.[20] Of these, the electrical and communications industries were in the course of accelerated development in the West, and responsibility for them was taken over by the new Ministry of Communications (Teishinsho) in 1885. As their military significance became increasingly obvious, much of this work was transferred to the military sphere.

The duties of the Army, Navy and Public Works ministries left the technology policy of the traditional and light industry sectors unaccounted for and these became the responsibility of the Ministry of Home Affairs (Naimusho), established in 1873. This extremely important ministry had bureaux for agriculture and engineering, and its responsibilities included the technical modernisation and establishment of quality standards in silk and textiles, industries that remained at the heart of Japan's export expansion till 1937. It was responsible for the Meiji version of the policy of *shokusan kogyo*, which it implemented partly by the direct acquisition of foreign knowledge

20. The expansion of Japan's maritime relations and its dangerous coastline made lighthouse construction extremely important in Meiji Japan. Lighthouse construction techniques were advancing rapidly at this time, not only in the ability to erect safe structures but also in the development of new optical techniques and illuminants for increasing the brilliance of light. Of the 221 foreigners working for the central government in 1872, 48 were lighthouse experts, exceeded in number only by the 49 railwaymen. See 'Lighthouses' in Routledge, *Discoveries and Inventions*, pp. 490–503; 'Lighthouse', *EB* (11th edn); and Emi, *Government Fiscal Activity*, p. 116. Of the lighthouse specialists, the most famous was R. H. Brunton who alone built 26 lighthouses and whose diary has recently been published: Richard Henry Brunton, *Building Japan, 1868–1876*, Folkestone: Japan Library, 1991.

and partly by the establishment of factories embodying such technologies in 'model' form appropriate for Japanese copying.[21]

This early system evolved significantly during the Meiji period. One landmark was the reorganisation in 1880–81 that produced the Ministry of Agriculture and Commerce (Noshomusho), which was split in 1925 into the separate Ministries for Agriculture and Forestry and for Commerce and Industry (Shokosho). Another, wider change was the establishment of the Cabinet system in 1885 and of a Parliament in 1890. After the latter year the budget, through which government technology policies were financed, became a central topic of public and political controversy.

By the late Meiji, as the public bureaucracy proliferated and specialised and as the role of the private sector expanded, responsibility for technology policies became fragmented and lost the high degree of centralisation and direction that marked the early arrangements. During the mid-1920s, however, the government resurrected its role in major policy initiatives for standardisation and rationalisation which, after 1925, became the main domestic task of the Ministry of Trade and Industry.

Education, training and communication networks

The success of policies to transfer and diffuse technology depended heavily on the performance of the educational system, on private company efforts in training and on the efficiency of all forms of communication. The formal educational system was the most tangible of these, although to quantify its impact precisely is impossible. The system consisted of elementary, lower and higher secondary and post-secondary elements. Within these, at both higher and post-secondary levels, specialised and vocational forms of education became available.[22]

Educational efforts, however, were not a Meiji innovation, since much had already been achieved in the Tokugawa period. By the early nineteenth century the Japanese schooling system comprised temple

21. Ishii emphasises the military basis of the whole *shokusan kogyo* programme. Ishii, *Economic history*, pp. 67ff.

22. Basic sources for this section are R. P. Dore, *Education in Tokugawa Japan*, London: Routledge and Kegan Paul, 1965, and Herbert Passin, *Society and Education in Japan*, Tokyo: Kodansha, 1982.

(*terakoya*), shogunal, *han* and various private (*shijuku*) schools, which between them offered not only basic educational facilities to almost all classes of society but in some cases also undertook the teaching of foreign languages and the military, geographical, medical, commercial and other useful sciences. One factor responsible for the widespread penetration of Tokugawa education may have been the class structure. This was restrictive in many ways but nonetheless did not (as in China) restrict literacy and learning to a narrow élite; rather it encouraged a wide spectrum of the population to acquire a degree of education. Whatever the cause, at least one respectable estimate is that before 1867 40% to 50% of the Japanese male population had meaningful literacy, which was reflected in vigorous networks of publishing, bookselling, and itinerant libraries. From as early as 1692 we have a bookseller's catalogue containing 7,300 items, and in the early nineteenth century the three great cities of Osaka, Kyoto and Edo had between them nearly 2,000 publishers, supported by hundreds of booksellers and libraries.[23]

The transformation of the traditional system of education was gradual. Although centralised administrative arrangements were put in place in the 1870s the national attendance rate at elementary school as late as 1892 was only 55%; while in 1895 there were still only 1,600 university students in a population of 45 million. Not till the mid-1900s did even primary-level enrolment rates begin to approach 90%. By 1940, however, data on educational attainments show accelerating progress (see Table 9.4).[24] Financially, this growth reflected the fact that government expenditure on education never dropped below 10% of all central government expenditures; by 1935 it accounted for 2.7% of the Gross National Product.[25] Qualitatively, what particularly impressed contemporary observers was the highly vocational and targeted character of the education offered by the system. For example, third-year Meiji secondary pupils spent a quarter of all lesson time studying foreign languages. In the post-secondary sector most institutions specialised in technology or commercial studies, while emphasis on foreign languages continued. British observers were particulary

23. Nakane and Oishi, *Tokugawa Japan*, ch. 4.
24. Ohkawa and Kohama, *Lectures on Developing Economies*, 1989, pp. 219–27.
25. UNCTAD, *Case Studies in the Transfer of Technology: Policies for Transfer and Development of Technology in Pre-War Japan*, New York, 1978, p. 31.

Table 9.4. EDUCATIONAL INDICATORS, 1900–40
(school attainment levels of the population of working age [15–64])

	1900	1920	1940
% Completed primary education	14.3	44.8	62.9
% Completed post-primary education	.2	2.9	4.5
% Undertaken supplementary continuation of education	0	4.5	10.9
Absolute numbers of students in secondary and higher education specialising in science and education	3,021	48,089	148,515

Sources: Ohkawa and Kohama, *Lectures on Developing Economies*, p. 224; UNCTAD, *Case Studies*, p. 32.

Japanese emphasis on commercial skills, and a Foreign Office special report for 1899 concluded: 'There is certainly no school in the U.K. which can compare with the higher commercial school in comprehensiveness and minuteness of programme.'[26]

In the three imperial universities in Tokyo, Kyushu and Tohoku engineering was a core subject from the outset. Of these institutions Tokyo was the most important, having established its College of Engineering on the advice of a Japanese delegation that toured England in 1872. Among the early foreign teachers it recruited was W. E. Ayrton, who succeeded in establishing the first laboratory in the world for teaching applied electrical engineering. In 1877 it was already possible for a leading British engineer to observe that the Tokyo College of Engineering was becoming the largest institution of its kind in the world and by the early twentieth century it had twenty-nine chairs covering eight branches of engineering, chemistry and mining.[27] Over the longer term, the stock of university-trained engineers in Japan rose from 1,500 in 1900 to 55,000 in 1934. The

26. Foreign Office, 'Report on Commercial Education in Japan by Mr A. H. Lay', *BPPJ*, vol. 10, pp. 465–75.
27. Armytage, *A Social History of Engineering*, pp. 233–4; Stead, *Japan by the Japanese*, p. 637. The engineer was Sir Norman Lockyer, strong advocate of improved technical education in Britain and deeply aware that Britain was falling behind Germany. He later became well known for his address to the British Association, 'The Influence of Brain Power on History'.

evolution of the post-secondary sector as a whole ensured that each type of institution served a particular segment of the economy (e.g. government, large companies, small companies etc.) thereby ensuring that no single favoured sector of the economy monopolised the supply of skills.[28] In other words, although the Japanese embarked on a path of accelerated technology advancement a few decades later than the western countries, in the public sector they quickly achieved levels of professionalism and systemisation in some aspects of the task that were clearly ahead of Britain and rivalled those of contemporary Germany.[29]

Beyond formal education, Meiji pioneers also developed both training within firms and the information networks necessary for the efficient diffusion of newly-arrived technologies. Again the Tokugawa base for this process was sound. It included systems of 'in-house' training in merchant establishments and the traditional crafts, and there is much evidence of continuity between the Tokugawa skill-base and its Meiji and later successors, of which metallurgical skills were particulary important.[30] The Tokugawa period also provided a base for publication, while physical communication networks were also efficient and improving all the time. Osaka, Kyoto and Edo were all connected by fast official courier runs and by even faster private ones; these land-based connections were complemented by three great shipping networks — the eastern, western and Kamigata 'circuits' — which effectively encircled the Japanese coastline, linking every part of it to Osaka and Edo.

These traditional channels of communication were strengthened after 1867, first by political unification and then by new technologies of communication and rising standards of education and literacy. The latter were reflected in an upsurge of new publications. As early as

---

28. Minami and Kiyokawa, *Japanese industrialisation*, p. 16.

29. See the argument of Nakaoka Tetsuro in his review of Tetsu Hiroshige's *Kagaku no shakaishi* (A social history of science in modern Japan), 1973, in *Japanese Studies in the History of Science*, no. 15, 1976, pp. 163–8.

30. See especially the article by Odaka Konosuke, 'The contribution of craft workers [*shokunin*] to the metallurgical industry', *Keizai kenkyu* (Economic research), vol. 37, no. 3, July 1986, pp. 221–33. Odaka describes in a number of case-studies the links between traditional metal-working and the development in Japan of western bicycle, armaments and engineering industries. Odaka has described other aspects of early modern systems of in-house training in his study *Kigyo uchi kyoiku no jidai* (The age of in-house education), Tokyo: Iwanami Shoten, 1993, ch. 3.

the 1880s, Japan published 550 newspapers and periodicals, of which seventeen dailies and 116 periodicals were produced in Tokyo alone. Between 1897 and 1911 the number of Japanese newpapers tripled. Circulation of the large dailies had reached 100,000 by 1911, and by the 1920s the *Osaka Asahi* and the *Osaka Mainichi* were both selling close to a million copies daily. Improvements in the dissemination of information through the press were paralleled in book publishing, and this overall development was encouraged not only by government but also by business leaders such as Shibusawa Eiichi, who actually regarded the collection and diffusion of information as the central function of locally based business associations.[31] On these foundations, Japan was to become the most information-intensive society in the world.

Foreign skills and training

In the early Meiji technology transfer, foreigners were recruited to remedy deficiencies in Japan's stock of expertise and skill and to initiate the acquisition of the theoretical and contextual knowledge necessary for applying and adapting the new technologies. A summary of the foreigners hired between 1870 and 1900 is given in Table 9.5, with the data broken down to show the role of the public and private sectors and the main fields of specialisation for which Japan had to look to outsiders. Here we see that at first the public sector was the main employer of foreigners, among whom science teachers and engineers predominated, but by the 1880s and 1890s the private sector had taken the lead, with business skills being particularly sought after. The costs of these direct purchases of human skills were high. Between 1873 and 1882 expenditure on foreign salaries equalled 11% of the entire national educational budget, and in the Ministry of Public Works the salaries of foreign experts accounted for 67% of the

---

31. Data on the press in the 1880s are quoted by the English journalist Henry Norman, *The Real Japan*, p. 42, and in Gluck, *Japan's Modern Myths*, pp. 171, 232–3. Shibusawa's concept of an information-intensive economy and the role of private sector trade associations in this are discussed in Kimura, *Shibusawa Eiichi*. pp. 22–5. In the 1950s Japan was publishing more books than any other country in the world and more than twice as many as the United States. Fritz Machlup, *The Production and Distribution of Knowledge in the United States*, Princeton University Press, 1962, pp. 208–9.

Table 9.5. FOREIGN EXPERTS HIRED IN JAPAN, 1870–1900

	1870s	1880s	1890s	1870–90
Science teaching	1,300	1,698	3,566	6,564
	(72.8)	(40.8)	(17.6)	(34.5)
Engineering	2,210	2,613	2,070	6,893
	(58.6)	(19.6)	(6.8)	(28.2)
Business	593	897	566	2,056
	(76.4)	(53.6)	(44.7)	(57.7)
Other	1,698	1,244	277	3,219
	(39.2)	(8.)	(6.5)	(24.7)
Total	5,801	6,453	6,479	6,193
	(57.9)	(27.8)	(16)	(33.1)

Note: Data in brackets are % hired by public sector.
Source: UNCTAD, *Case Studies*, p. 21.

Ministry's budget in 1877 and 42% of it over the fifteen-year period 1870–85.[32] But while such 'consultancy' proved expensive and was dispensed with as soon as possible, the contribution these foreigners made was enormous.[33] Many were unusual and gifted men — nearly half of them were British, the next largest groups were German and American — and between them they were largely responsible for the establishment of the shipping, shipbuilding, mining, chemical, electrical, textile, vehicle, aeronautics and other engineering and science-based branches of industry.

At the same time as foreigners were being hired and brought to Japan, knowledge was also being obtained by Japanese students who were sent abroad in accordance with the systematic plans of government ministries, most of which had this responsibility included in their formal remit of duties.[34] Table 9.6. summarises data on the destinations and subjects of study of students and government officials sent abroad up to 1895.

Industry-wide policies

Incentives and Patents. The most fundamental incentive for technical advance provided by the Meiji government was the establishment of

32. Emi, *Government Fiscal Activity*, pp. 114–24.
33. Typically ten times as expensive. *Ibid.*, p. 120.
34. Nakaoka, *Technology and technology policy*, pp. 171–87.

Table 9.6. DESTINATIONS OF STUDENTS AND OFFICIALS SENT
ABROAD AND SUBJECTS STUDIED, 1868–95

	% of total students	% of officials	Subjects studied	1881	1890
U.S.A.	24	7	Military	52	67
Britain	21	20	Language	15	0
Russia	4	4	Machinery/ships	7	8
France	17	16	Law	5	2
Germany	18	2	Medicine	7	5
Total	601	3,783	*Total*	101	61

Source: Emi, *Government Fiscal Activity*, pp. 122–3.
Note: The 'military' category includes men sent either by ministries or by the army or navy.

markets, companies and the systems of law which these required. Two
other devices specifically designed to encourage personal innovation
were the offering of prizes and awards in addition to the patent system.
Prizes were often won at exhibitions designed to speed the diffusion
of new technology, and they conferred great personal honour. Notable
innovations whose creators were honoured in this way included the
garabo (the hybrid technology cotton throstle spindle), the Japanese
automatic loom and the Ikegai G-type lathe, which won the premier
award at the First National Machine Tool Exhibition in Osaka in 1921.

Patents posed a more complex challenge since, as argued earlier,
a balance has to be struck between the financial advantages offered
to innovators and the barriers such rewards create to the diffusion
of information that is in the interests of the economy as a whole.
Nonetheless, the background to the active Japanese patent policy was
the widely-held view that protection of intellectual property rights
in Britain and America had been one of the keys to the explosion
of innovative activity in those countries in the first half of the nineteenth century.[35]

Embryonic concepts of patent law and intellectual property were

35. Compared to the security provided to intellectual property on the Continent,
in Britain protection was such that a contemporary could remark: 'Almost every inven-
tion seeks, as it were, refuge in England, and is there brought to perfection.' Paul
Johnson, *The Birth of the Modern. World Society, 1815–1830*, London: Weidenfeld and
Nicolson, 1991, p. 572. For data on America see Cochran and Miller, *The Age of
Enterprise*, pp. 14–15.

embodied in early Meiji legislation but these were fairly weak.[36] In the 1890s foreign complaints about Japanese pirating of western patents and trademarks made the subject an important element in the treaty revision negotiations. As a result, Japan agreed to join the Paris Union for the Protection of Industrial Property and then sought to make the changes required to harmonise domestic law and international obligations. In spite of this, complaints continued and fundamental differences between western and Japanese systems remained. Whereas in American legislation, for example, the fundamental purpose of patent law was the defence of private rights, in Japan much greater weight was given to the public interest.[37] For example, patent rights in Japan had to be exercised within three years, otherwise, if the public interest was held to be at risk, they could be taken over. Further, no patents were permitted in the pharmaceutical industry and any patent could be expropriated or revoked in the public interest. One other feature of the Japanese system was the 'utility patent', a device copied from Germany enabling a degree of protection to be offered for relatively minor innovations to existing technology. In the Japanese context, where copying and adaptation were the main tasks of technology transfer, this proved very useful.

Despite its unusually restrictive character, the Japanese patent system was actively used and a clear distinction emerged between the role of patent and utility models. Patents tended to be used in the new, heavy and 'transplanted' industries, while utility registrations were common in light and traditional industries where piecemeal technical change was the main mode of advance. Further, although the state reserved its rights so clearly, patenting was important even in the defence industries. For example, the Miyabara boiler system was patented in 1897 and became almost the exclusive system of the Japanese Navy between 1905 and 1912.[38]

---

36. Patent legislation was promulgated in 1871, 1885, 1888 and 1890. Bilateral patent provision between Japan and Britain was agreed in the 1894 Treaty of Commerce and Navigation. See 'The protection of industrial property', Stead, *Japan by the Japanese*, pp. 644–5; R. Ishii, *Japanese Legislation in the Meiji Era*, Tokyo: Pan-Pacific Press, 1958, pp. 602–3.

37. See 'Patents', in *EB* (11th edn); UNCTAD, *Case Studies*, pp. 25–8.

38. MITI, vol. 18, *Machinery*, p. 143.

Special legislation

Industries judged to be technologically strategic and in need of early government guidance and support were treated by the government as special cases. Major industries which had special supportive legislation included electricity, shipbuilding, steel, pharmaceuticals, machine-tools, vehicles and aeronautics.[39] In each case, planned import substitution was the central objective and the legislation ensured the provision of whatever technical, financial and protective support was necessary to guarantee the industry's survival and eventual viability. In the long run, however, direct legislation was bound to have a diminishing role and to be supplanted by more general policies to encourage industrial modernisation and technology transfer. Two such policies were standardisation and rationalisation.

Standardisation

The development and diffusion of industrial standardisation is a normal feature of mature industrial systems and an important factor in the technological progress of developing ones. Its advantages include the definition and stabilisation of quality levels, the promotion of interchangeability and mass-production methods, and a lowering of both design and repair costs. For economies engaged in learning new technologies, specification of standards is essential in order to speed diffusion and to ensure that necessary and desirable adaptations of advanced technologies do not result in chaotic inefficiencies. Although standardisation has its costs, estimates suggest that these are recovered quickly in both advanced and learning economies.[40]

Standardisation can be either a 'top-down' (government-led) or 'bottom-up' (industry-led) process. The former is typical of developing and the latter of more advanced economies. In this framework Japan may be thought of as a developing economy in which the government

39. The legislation and discussion of these cases are all documented in MITI, esp. the volume on *Machinery*.
40. This section is based mainly on articles in *EB* (14th and 1951 edn); MITI, vol. 18, *Machinery*, esp. pp. 283ff.; MITI, *A history of policy*, vol. 9, *Sangyo gorika* (Industrial rationalisation) *passim* and the very important article by Yukihiko Kiyokawa and Shigeru Ishikawa, 'The significance of standardization in the development of the machine tool industry: The cases of Japan and China', parts 1 and 2, *Hitotsubashi Journal of Economics*, vol. 28, no. 2, 1987, pp. 123–54; vol. 29, no. 1, 1988, pp. 73–88.

played the leading role in standardisation. However, the reality is less simple, since government played a lead role in most of Japan's industrial policies. In fact, the time-lag between Japan's standardisation programmes and those of western economies was not very significant.

Standardisation came relatively late to American and European industry, and a prerequisite for it was the progress made in the analysis of the properties of steel between the 1830s and the end of the century. The potential uses of modern iron and steel were so numerous, and the potential dangers so correspondingly great (exploding steam-engines, collapsing bridges and buildings), that fully defined specifications were essential if metals were to be fully exploited. Proper specifications depended not only on advances in the theoretical analysis of materials stress (fatigue, yields points, elasticity etc.) but also on the availability of instruments capable of recording the measurements suggested by theory. These prerequisites were increasingly met between the 1830s and 1860s, although there was at first little specialisation in these fields and its pioneers tended to be men who combined practical and theoretical skills.[41] A key event in materials testing was the construction of Wöhler's fatigue-testing machine in the 1850s, and several testing centres using such equipment opened in the 1870s.[42]

Work on metals continued in the early twentieth century as alloy, special and pre-hardened steels were developed, and as the principles of standardisation were extended to the machinery, electrical and chemical industries. Construction-steel and machine-tool manufacture were particulary crucial sectors. In America, standardisation of structural steel revolutionised bridge and skyscraper building, and for machine-tool manufacture new measurable concepts of speed, accuracy, rigidity and durability were developed that made standardisation

41. William Fairbairn was an outstanding example of a pioneer in mill, engine, ship and bridge construction, who found himself compelled to become a leader in materials analysis. In 1835, for example, Fairbairn and Hodgkinson were commissioned by the British Academy to investigate the properties of iron obtained by the hot and cold blast methods and to do this they developed 38 tests of transverse strength. William Pole (ed.), *The Life of Sir William Fairbairn partly written by himself* (1877), repr. Newton Abbot: David and Charles, 1970, pp. 159–60.

42. These issues are discussed in Burstall, *A History of Mechanical Engineering*, pp. 288–94, 369–76 and Rolt, *Victorian Engineering*, ch. 5.

central to the feasibility of systems of mass-production.[43] But in spite of all these advances, Schlesinger's authoritative standards for the machine-tool industry were not finally published till as late as 1938.

In relation to this gradual development, Japan's progress towards standardisation cannot be considered to have been slow. It is true that typical Japanese standards, particularly in machine-tools, were well behind western standards for most of this period but the concept of standardisation and its value as a device for promoting technical advance and productivity were grasped early. For example, preliminary electrical standards were set in 1896 and 1908, the Army set screw-thread standards in 1902, the Navy set a variety of shipbuilding standards in 1903, and the Ministry of Agriculture and Commerce set building standards in 1905.[44]

Standardisation in military technology, though pursued, was more difficult because the normal Japanese practice of importing several examples of any machine meant that these were almost certain to embody both metric and imperial measurement systems. Further, inter-departmental variations in some standards did develop.

A major decision in favour of metrification was taken in 1920, and in 1921 the First National Machine-Tool Exhibition led directly to the establishment of the Japanese Engineering Standards (JES). Under JES a modest 530 standards had been set by 1941, mainly in shipbuilding, steel and electrical engineering. The JES were generally lower than the Schlesinger standards and were available in two versions: one for large-scale modern establishments and another for small workshops. Nonetheless, standardisation during the inter-war years had a measurable impact on the technology level of Japanese industry, and it was on this foundation that, under the extreme pressure of war production, standardisation and mass production accelerated after 1941.[45]

---

43. One contemporary observer who fully grasped the significance of standardisation in economic development was Alfred Marshall, esp. in his *Industry and Trade*, ch. 3. The link between metallurgy, standardisation and mass-production is discussed in James P. Womack *et al.*, *The Machine that Changed the World*, New York: Rawson Associates, 1990, ch. 2.

44. MITI, vol. 18, *Machinery*, pp. 284ff.

45. Kiyokawa and Ishikawa analyse uniquely detailed data on the level of Japanese machine tool technology in the inter-war years in 'The significance of standardization' part 1, pp. 136–42. As early as the 1920s Japanese appreciation of the crucial nature of the machine-tool industry was attracting American attention. See Arthur Jackson, 'Automatic machine tools in Japan', *Far Eastern Review (FER)*, Nov. 1922, pp. 691–2.

Rationalisation

Government technology leadership in the inter-war period took two main forms: direct leadership in new and military technologies and indirect leadership using the framework of rationalisation policy. Rationalisation was directed at entire sectors or industries, and in implementing it the government sought again to resolve the Meiji dilemma of how to combine its own leadership with encouragement of a vigorous and independent private sector. It did this in the 1920s by legislation encouraging the formation of 'bottom-up' industrial associations whose policies it strongly influenced.

The Japanese regarded rationalisation as a package of policies that would enable them to respond to the unfavourable world economic situation of the 1920s.[46] Although their plans are now seen in the West as a precursor of the post-war Japanese 'industrial policy', at the time the Japanese saw nothing essentially original in them, since both the Germans and the Americans had developed similar concepts of industrial guidance.[47] The Japanese did, however, choose and adapt the contents of their policy package in ways that seemed appropriate to their circumstances.

Japan's perception of the world economic situation in the early 1920s was of one in which long-standing patterns of specialisation and exchange had been disrupted by war, in which new nationalistic and imperialistic trends towards industrial self-sufficiency were strong and the country's newer and more modern industries were threatened by competitive pressures from the West, especially America.[48] As we saw in Chapter 6, these pressures were partly a question of exchange-rate misalignment but the Japanese also believed that structural trends were improving the competitive power of the advanced economies.

46. This section is based largely on MITI, vol. 9, *Industrial rationalisation*. This volume includes not only documentation and comment but also an extensive survey of the subject by N. Yoshino. The basic definition of rationalisation is in pp. 3–11.

47. In 1927 the League of Nations World Economic Conference had an entire committee working on the meaning of rationalisation for industrial economies. Rationalisation in this sense was often the implementation of 'scientific management' in large-scale enterprises. In Germany the definition of the *Reichskuratorium für Wirtschaftlichkeit* (Board of National Efficiency) was much broader. Insight on these issues is contained in L. Urwick, *The Meaning of Rationalisation*, London: Nisbet, 1929, *passim*.

48. The Japanese noted in particular the nationalism of the central European economies emerging from the collapse of the Austro-Hungarian empire.

The latter were doing this by raising investment per worker, greatly enlarging scales of production, introducing 'scientific' systems of enterprise management, and, on the basis of standardisation and engineering advances, moving rapidly towards methods of mass-production that generated productivity standards far beyond those achieved in Japan. In other words, the Japanese saw the world economic challenge of the 1920s as a 'technology' challenge in the broad sense. They were seeing the acceleration of the fourth technology epoch and sought to respond to it with both technical advance and institutional changes.

In thinking about their new strategy, Japanese analysts argued that the industrial revolution should be divided into two phases. In the first, inter-firm differences in technology, productivity and costs would be the normal state of affairs and could be expected to rise and fall as a result of the competitive process. In this phase, *laissez-faire* and low levels of direct government involvement in private industry were appropriate (the first phase in the Japanese economy was judged to extend from about 1890 to the 1920s). In the second phase, however, industrial survival required that old regimes be radically reformed. There were several reasons for this. One was the growth of political barriers to foreign raw materials and to markets, which meant that firms could not function properly without state assistance to overcome them. Meanwhile, in the factory, the rising scale and technological and capital-intensiveness of production called for new techniques of planning and inter-firm cooperation which led ultimately to enormous concentrations of economic power. These changes could not be expected to materialise efficiently from competitive processes, nor could they be maintained in ways acceptable to the public interest if government were not involved. In some ways, the call for co-operative rather than competitive relations between firms echoed the early Meiji period when pioneer Japanese capitalists had great difficulty with the concept of competition and never embraced it in its western form.[49] Throughout the 1920s the urgency of these issues was continuously reinforced by trade crises.

---

49. When translating Chambers' *Economics*, Fukuzawa had been unable to find a Japanese equivalent of 'competition'. See Kiyooka, *The Autobiography of Fukuzawa Yukichi*, p. 201. Shibusawa's concept of information sharing and cooperation through chambers of commerce is also difficult to reconcile with textbook concepts of competition.

The administrative and legislative framework to implement ratio-nalisation was constructed in the 1920s, first by the old Ministry of Agriculture and Commerce and then, after 1925, by its successor. Between 1930 and 1937 responsibility for rationalisation belonged to the Temporary Production Rationalisation Bureau (*Rinji Sangyo Gorikakyoku*) within the Ministry of Trade and Industry, and the main legislative act was the Important Industries Control Law.[50] Under this, government industrial associations were encouraged to engage in all forms of rationalisation, standardisation and elimination of excess and technologically obsolescent capacity, and to form export cartels. The government encouraged firms to make organisational and technical improvements with equal energy, especially in the newer industries. One firm that did this was Mitsubishi Electric, which contracted with Westinghouse Corporation for the transfer of new technology and help in managing what the company described as a 'shift from so-called Japanese to scientific management methods'.[51]

Technology was central to Japanese national policies from *kaikoku* to the late 1930s. The overriding objective of this policy was import substitution for strategic and commercially important goods. Military hardware fell into the first category throughout this period, while ships, steel and cotton were examples of goods that were initially strategic but later became partly or wholly commercial.

The sources and implementation of technology policy evolved significantly during this period. In the early phase, government impor-ting of model plants and the direct hiring of foreign expertise were the main approaches followed. Later, as domestic skills expanded, the private sector's role in technology transfer grew and increasing importance came to be given to the foreign training of Japanese employees and purchases of foreign technology by licence.

The vitality of technology in Japanese business was partly a reflec-tion of the seemingly instinctive, enthusiastic grasp of the issues by Japanese businessmen (a significant number of whom were engineers) and their capacity, even in Japan's 'competitive' phase, to collaborate in the task of diffusion. Equally impressive were the university spe-

50. MITI, vol. 9, *Industrial rationalisation*, pp. 12–16, 158–66.
51. MITI, vol. 18, *Machinery*, pp. 258–88.

cialists, many of whom at first were foreign, who advised the government on new industries and acted as bridges to the private sector in the making of plans for import substitution. Throughout the period the governmental infrastructures in education, training and patent laws all played identifiable roles in encouraging not only technology transfer, but also, increasingly, adaptation and innovation.

In the inter-war years the world economic crisis and accelerated technical advance in the West reinforced the urgency of technology issues. In response, the government developed a whole new approach to industrial development and created a programme of measures to ensure that Japanese industry would survive and grow. In the 1920s industrial policies were initiated against the background of an adverse exchange rate; in the 1930s fiscal, exchange-rate and industrial policies were all working in the same direction with remarkable results, despite the intensely unfavourable world economic environment.

10

TECHNOLOGY AND TRADE IN THE STRATEGIC INDUSTRIES

'It was a farewell to wooden ships, to sails and yards, to the old Navy of Nelson's time. Henceforth came the era of steam and iron, of torpedos and electricity; of what is called Science . . .' — comment on the last Royal Navy circumnavigation by sail, 1870

'The enemy has been sighted; the Combined Fleet is moving to annihilation. The waves are high but the day is clear.' — Admiral Togo, before destroying the Russian fleet with Western technology at Tsushima, 1905

Shipbuilding

The Japanese shipping industry had reached two important milestones by the end of the First World War. Japan could construct naval and merchant vessels comparable in technology to those made in European or American yards, and although this was accomplished in the early 1900s by extensive use of foreign steel and components (especially engines) in Japanese-made hulls and superstructures, by 1918 there was no aspect of shipbuilding technology where Japanese capabilities fell significantly below world standards. Secondly, vessels from Japanese yards had a record of sales to both Japanese and foreign customers that made shipbuilding a commercial as well as technological success. Although supported by subsidies, Japan had become the fifth-largest owner of steam-vessels in the world by 1911, and by 1918 was recognised as one of the great maritime powers of the world.[1] For a country where the construction of oceangoing ships was forbidden between 1636 and 1853, and which as late as the 1840s was almost wholly deficient in the techniques for making and sailing them, these achieve-

---

1. Data on world shares of shipping are from *EB* (11th edn), vol. 24, p. 872. In the NYK, foreign employees (mainly captains and engineers) fell as a percentage of the workforce from 28% in 1886, to 5% in 1910 and to a tiny fraction (one man) in 1918. Data in Appendix to *Golden Jubilee History of the Nippon Yusen Kaisha 1885–1935*, Tokyo: Nippon Yusen Kaisha, 1935.

ments can only be described as amazing. This section attempts to explain how they were accomplished.[2]

The objectives of naval and shipping policy. Naval strength was a major policy objective in Japan from the late Tokugawa period to the end of the Pacific war. In its early stages the policy was implemented by a combination of foreign purchases and the acquisition of skills for naval construction, but during the 1890s the drive for import substitution and self-sufficiency became dominant, as was made explicit by Rear-Admiral Sasao, Director of the Naval Construction Corps, in a speech in 1904: 'It is, perhaps, hardly necessary to point out how important it becomes to promote our industries connected with shipbuilding, in order that we may drive out foreign made goods altogether from ships built in this country.'[3]

Parallel to strategic considerations was the broader argument that shipbuilding and the creation of a Japanese merchant marine were essential to the free development of Japanese trade. Foreign monopolies of shipping, shipbuilding and maritime insurance were all devices that had enabled foreigners to constrict Japanese trade policies in the early Meiji period, and the central importance of shipping was strongly supported by representatives of the private sector such as Shibusawa, who as a banker did much himself to support both shipping and shipbuilding industries.[4] Moreover, the development of these industries was clearly understood to require the acquisition not only of engineering capabilities but also the skills of navigation, naval design and organisation, and the management capabilities necessary to organise successful shipping companies.

2. The development of Japanese shipping had already impressed foreign observers in the late 1890s. For example a correspondent of the *North China Herald* commented: 'What other nations are doing [in ship construction] may be described as progress; but what Japan is doing must be described as a phenomenon', *NCH*, Dec. 17, 1897. A post-First World War article in similar vein is 'Remarkable development of Japanese shipping: The past and present of the Osaka Shosen Kaisha illustrates the extraordinary progress made in ship owning and operation in Japan', *FER*, April 1919, pp. 350–5.

3. Quoted in a comprehensive and expert foreign evaluation of Japanese shipbuilding in 1906. Charles Albertson, 'Equipment and capacity of the dockyards and shipbuilding plants of Japan', parts 1 and 2, *FER*, Feb. 1906, pp. 237–40, and *FER*, March 1906, pp. 288 94.

4. On national shipping policies and Shibusawa see MITI, vol. 18, *Machinery*, pp. 86–7; Kimura, *Shibusawa Eiichi*, p. 32.

Initial conditions and structural difficulties. In the sixteenth century, the construction of three-masted ships influenced by western designs had made the Japanese the fastest and most successful pirates in the Far Eastern seas. The restrictions on shipbuilding imposed in 1636 stunted but did not destroy domestic shipbuilding skills, since coastal and river-borne transport were important in the traditional economy. None-theless, late Tokugawa vessels had very limited capacities, even as sailing ships. They could not sail close to the wind and lacked the design and structural strength that enabled contemporary western vessels to make trans-oceanic voyages.

The serious study of western shipbuilding began in the 1840s and intensified after the forcible opening of Japan by Perry, itself essen-tially a naval event.[5] In 1855 the shogunal naval training school was established at Nagasaki, and by 1860 the Japanese grasp of celestial navigation was sufficient to pilot a foreign-built ship from Japan to San Francisco. Thus in only five years Japan had acquired a working knowledge of one entire branch of the skills necessary to establish a navy and shipping industry.[6] During the last Tokugawa years the French helped to establish an important naval arsenal at Yokosuka, and Japanese enthusiasm for steamships bounded forward with an enthu-siasm that on occasions was as naive as it was impressive.[7]

By 1867 Japan had assembled a navy of nine foreign-built warships with a combined engine power of 2,000 h.p. Seven of these vessels were screw-driven, and one, obtained from America, was part ironclad. Between them, the shogun and the *han* authorities had a further 125 vessels, all sail-driven and with wooden hulls.[8] The scale of the Meiji

5. Discussion of Tokugawa naval policies is in Hayashi, *A history*, pp. 82ff.

6. One of the passengers on this remarkable voyage was Fukuzawa Yukichi, who commented that 'as long as I was on a ship navigated by western methods, I had no fear', Kiyooka, *The Autobiography of Fukuzawa Yukichi*, p. 117. Subsequent research has raised the point that the contribution of the American officer travelling with this ship may have been more than nominal.

7. A first-hand account of Yokosuka written in 1867, a few months before the Meiji Restoration, is included in De Beauvoir, *Pékin, Yeddo, San Francisco Voyage Autour du Monde*, pp. 224–43. De Beauvoir also describes a revealing incident in which the Japanese ordered a fine modern steamship from Dents (the British merchants). They immediately expelled the foreign engineers and sailors and steamed off in high spirits. Unfortunately no one knew how to stop the craft, and they had to steam round in circles until rescued by a French engineer (p. 188).

8. Stead, *Japan by the Japanese*, pp. 121–5, and U. Kobayashi, *Military Industries of Japan*, Oxford University Press, 1922, pp. 15–23.

Table 10.1. TOTAL H.P. OF ENGINES OF
JAPANESE NAVAL SHIPS, 1867–1907

1867	2,040
1872	3,078
1893	96,263
1903	518,040
1907	1,045,383

Source: Stead, *Japan by the Japanese*, pp. 121–5.

naval expansion that followed is shown by Table 10.1, in which
change is indicated by the combined horsepower of the engines of the
Japanese navy.

The problems facing Japanese maritime development in this period
were technological, economic and commercial. Technologically, the
fundamental difficulty was that the quality and technical standards of
contemporary shipbuilding were set by Britain and other advanced
economies, and little compromise on these standards was possible if
Japan was to become an international naval or shipping power.[9] The
chasm between the traditional Japanese and western shipping worlds
was even reflected in language, with English being used for technical
commands on western-style Japanese ships and English and Dutch providing the vocabulary of the early western-style shipyards.

The gap between traditional Japanese and nineteenth-century western
shipbuilding is well illustrated by the width of the *range* of skills,
technologies and materials involved.[10] Early nineteenth-century shipbuilding began with the attachment of simple steam-engines to wooden
boats, but it quickly advanced to the construction of iron hulls. The

9. In the early 1880s the government established standards for insurable ships were
largely based on Lloyd's and German rules. At first many Japanese ships did not reach
these, which was why the government had to establish the Tokyo Marine Insurance
Company. See, *Commercial Report* 1881, part 1, *BPPJ*, vol. 7, p. 26. Later, when warships were constructed in private yards, standards were maintained by naval inspectors
who were described by a foreign specialist as 'the most critical of any of the world's
great naval powers'. See 'Yokohama Engine and Ironworks Ltd.', *FER*, April 1911,
p. 397.

10. The main sources on marine technology used here are E. C. Smith, *A Short
History of Marine Engineering*, Cambridge: Babcock & Wilcox at the Cambridge
University Press, 1937, and articles on relevant topics in the *EB* (11th to 1951 edns).
Among nineteenth-century sources two are of particular interest: William Fairbairn,
Iron Shipbuilding, London: Longmans, Green, 1865, and J. W. King, *The Warships of*

dramatic expansion in ship size that followed reflected the fact that, while larger ships required additional motive power to the square to drive them, the same expansion of size provided them with additional coal-carrying capacity to the cube. In principle, then, the larger the ship, the greater was its range and power, and the major problem was to improve hull construction to take advantage of this theorem in the construction of enormous ships. This problem was largely solved by mid-century, by which time shipbuilding already involved a combination of metallurgy, engineering, mathematics and metal-forging and fabricating skills. In the 1860s the development of new gun technologies led directly to iron cladding and fully armoured warships.[11]

Late nineteenth-century advances in shipbuilding included further improvements in hulls, engines, boilers and superstructures. Emulating and improving on these required advanced knowledge of the material, mechanical and electrical sciences, as well as sophisticated capabilities in metal manufacture and fabrication. In the naval case, large warships were increasingly armed not only with heavy, hydraulically-mounted guns but also with torpedoes and mines. They were navigated by specialised instruments and controlled by centrally-located electrical communications systems. From the 1880s onwards the vulnerability of large ships to torpedoes spurred the development of torpedo-boats and increased the importance of anti-torpedo destroyers. To be effective these smaller craft had to be powered by super-heated steam boilers and intricate compound and triple-expansion engines, both requiring designers and constructors at the leading edge of several technologies.[12] A summary of the major events and achievements of western shipbuilding and their timing is set out in Tables 10.2 and 10.3.

Europe: A Description of the Construction, Armour, and Fighting Power of the Ironclads of England and other European Powers of the Present Day, Portsmouth: Griffen, 1878. The former contains analysis of the construction of the Great Eastern and is a landmark in the literature of naval architecture; the latter is a report by the Chief Engineer of the US Navy that describes the entire European warship situation at the apogee of British supremacy in 1875–76. The report includes detailed specifications of individual British warships and discussion of issues relating to engines, boilers, torpedoes and naval yard organisation.

11. This factor was the main reason for the conversion of the British Admiralty to iron shipbuilding. See Pole, The Life of Sir William Fairbairn, ch. 20.

12. MITI, vol. 18, Machinery, pp. 140–4, emphasises this point and argues that naval shipbuilding became the driving force in the advancement of Japanese heavy industry technology.

Table 10.2. WESTERN SHIPBUILDING PROGRESS: KEY EVENTS, 1836–95

1836	Screw propeller patented by Ericsson
1840	British Admiralty rejects iron ships
1853	Compound steam engine patented by Elder
1858	Publication of General Douglas's *On Naval Warfare with Steam*
1859	*La Gloire* — first seagoing ironclad, constructed in France
1861–4	British Admiralty Iron Armour Committee sits
1862	Triple expansion engine patented by Elder
1864	First torpedo constructed by Whitehead
1865	Publication of William Fairbairn's *Iron Shipbuilding*
1870	HMS *Captain* founders at sea leading to new inquiry into ship design
1872	Report of the British Committee on the Design of Ships of War
1875	Steam registrations exceed sail registrations at Lloyd's
1883	Nordenfeldt constructs first submarine
1895	Turbine engine patented by Parsons

This scenario of western progress had serious economic consequences for Japan since it required that modern shipbuilding should be, from the outset, large in scale and intensive in use of capital and special skills. Hence there were few opportunities in the core processes for developing transplanted technologies by lowering quality standards or for labour-intensive adaptation. Modern shipbuilding was an industry in which Japan's underlying comparative disadvantages were maximised.

Although in naval construction economic considerations were in principle subordinate to strategic ones, high construction costs did matter, and expenditure on shipbuilding became the most politically controversial aspect of the national budget in the early years of Japan's parliamentary democracy.[13] Over the longer term, Japanese shipbuilding had to be competitive in every way if it was to supply the needs of Japan's new private-sector shipping companies: this was because these companies had to break into international shipping cartels in which technical and commercial standards, largely set in London, were among the means used to exclude newcomers such as the

13. In the second session of the Imperial Diet the naval expenditure budget for two battleships and a despatch boat was rejected. Building, however, went ahead and the budget was accepted after the Emperor personally guaranteed to pay ¥1.8 million over six years towards the costs of these vessels. Major political disputes over the naval estimates were also commonplace in Europe, especially Germany, where the Kaiser repeatedly intervened to overrule parliamentarians. See material in Robert K. Massie, *Dreadnought: Britain, Germany and the Coming of the Great War*, London: Cape, 1992.

Table 10.3. WESTERN SHIPBUILDING PROGRESS: SPECIFICATION IMPROVEMENT IN KEY SHIPS, 1823–1906

	Ship	Hull	Weight (tons) defined as gross displacement	Boiler pressure (lbs per sq. inch)	Indicated horse-power (IHP)	Max. speed (knots)	Notes
1823	HMS Lightning	Wood	1,800 (est.)	2–3	100 (nom.)		First steam vessel to see naval action
1833	HMS Medea	Wood			220	10	One of first group of steam fighting vessels
1838	Great Western	Wood	2,300	15	700	8.5	Paddle-driven — first successful Atlantic liner
1840	Nemesis	Iron			120		First iron warship (built for East India Company)
1843	Great Britain	Iron	5,780	25	1,500	11	First single screw driven liner
1858	Great Eastern	Iron	32,160	30	11,000	13	Paddle and screw; double-hulled
1859	HMS Victoria	Wood	7,000		4,200		Sail power with auxilliary steam
1871	HMS Devastation	Iron	9,330	30	7,000	14.2	First steam-driven warship
1876	HMS Inflexible	Iron & steel	11,880	60	8,000	14	24-in. armour
1877	HMS Lightning	Iron	28.7	120	400	18.6	First British torpedo-boat
1884	Umbria	Steel	13,300	110	14,500	19	Cunard liner; Atlantic crossing reduced to 6 days
1894	Torpedo-boat Forban (French)	Steel	126		3,975	31	World speed record-holder
1898	HMS Diadem	Steel	11,000	300	16,500	20.5	Vertical triple expansion engine
1902	Kaiser Wilhelm II (German)	Steel	26,000	213	42,000	23.71	State of the art liner
1906	HMS Dreadnought	Steel	17,900		23,000 (turbine)	21.6	New class battleship; turbine-powered; used Krupp steels
1907	Mauretania	Steel	42,000	195	70,000	26.06	First major advance in scale on the Great Eastern

Sources: Main sources, articles in EB (11th edn); Smith, A Short History; Basset-Lowke, Ships and Men; King, The Warships of Europe.

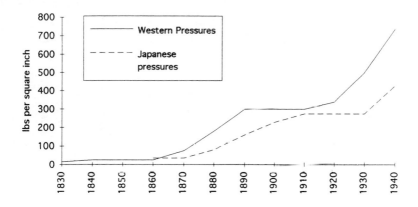

Fig. 10.1. WESTERN AND JAPANESE BOILER PRESSURES, 1830-1940

Sources: As Tables 10.3 and 10.4
Note: The very high pressures achieved in the West in the late 1930s are those of the German battle-cruisers *Scharnhorst* and *Gneisenau*. These used sophisticated steam turbines operating at 735 lb. per sq. inch and achieved speeds of 32 knots. See also Smith, *A Short History*, ch. 20, for data on similar progress in passenger-ship engines.

Japanese. While the purely technical problems of shipbuilding were serious, it was their combination with economic and commercial disadvantages that was so formidable.

Technical achievements in naval shipbuilding. Table 10.4 summarises the technological achievements of Japanese naval shipbuilding, and focuses mainly on change in eight technical characteristics as exemplified in selected ships built between 1863 and 1941. Since the ships included vary significantly in size and purpose, simple progression of these indicators cannot always be interpreted as progress. Nonetheless, improvements in hull materials and in engine and boiler types are fairly unambiguous. Perhaps most useful of all is the record of the rising pressure capacity of boilers. Pressure capacity depended on increasing

Table 10.4. TECHNOLOGICAL PROGRESS IN JAPANESE NAVAL SHIPBUILDING EXEMPLIFIED IN KEY SHIPS

	Name	Type	Displacement (tons)	Hull	Engine type	Boiler pressure (lbs per sq. inch)	Propellers	IHP	Maximum speed	Notes
1863	Chiyoda	Gunboat	138	Wood	Simple 2-cylinder	36	1	60	5	First gunboat and engine MIJ
1880	Torpedo-boats nos 1–4	Torpedo-boats	40	Steel	Compound			430	14.4	Kit from Yarrow assembled at Yokosuka
1884	Kaimon	Gunboat	1,358	Wood	Compound	60	1	1,267	12	Three-masted barque
1888	Musashi	Gunboat	1,502	Composite	Compound	70	1	1,622	13	Fitted Krupp guns
1888	Chokai	Gunboat	614	Iron	Compound	80	2	606	10.25	First iron gunboat
1892	Oshima	Gunboat	640	Steel	VTE	160	2	1,217	16	First VTE fitted and MIJ
1892	Torpedo-boat no. 10	Torpedo-boat	53	Steel	Compound		1	525	20	First torpedo-boat MIJ
1903	Harusume	Torpedo destroyer	375	Steel	VTE	190	2	5,600	29	First destroyer fitted with VTE MIJ; Thorneycroft plans with adaptations
1904	Otowa	3rd-class cruiser	3,000	Steel	VTE	230	2	10,000	21	Completed in 20 months by radical redesign of construction sequence
1907	Tsukuba	Armoured cruiser	13,750	Steel	VTE		2	23,260	21	First MIJ engine of more than 20,000HP; Miyabara boilers

Year	Name	Type	Displacement	Material	Engine			Power	Speed	Notes
1907	*Ituki*	Armoured cruiser	15,600	Steel	Curtis turbine	235	2	22,500	21	First Curtis turbines fitted in Japan
1908	*Mogami*	Despatch boat	1,350	Steel	Parsons turbine			8,000	23	First Parsons turbines fitted to Japanese warship; built by Mitsubishi
1909	*Satsuma*	Battleship	19,150	Steel	VTE		2	17,500	18.25	Largest ship in the world by displacement
1910	*Kawachi*	Dreadnought class battleship	22,000	Steel	Curtis turbine		2	25,000	20	First Japanese *Dreadnought*; first Curtis turbines MIJ (by Kawasaki)
1915	*Haruna*	Battle-cruiser	27,500	Steel	Curtis turbine	250/275	4	64,000		Built by Kawasaki
1915	*Fuso*	Battleship	36,000	Steel	Brown/Curtis turbine	275	4	40,000	22.5	First battleship complete with armament MIJ
1941	*Yamato*	Battleship	72,000	Steel	Kampon turbine	375		150,000 (SHP)	27	Largest and most heavily-armed battleship in history
1941	*Shokaku*	Aircraft-carrier	26,675	Steel	Kampon turbine	428	4	160,000 (SHP)	34	Most powerfully-engined vessel in the Navy

Sources: MITI, vol. 18, *Machinery*, esp. pp. 142–5 and Table 39; Kobayashi, *The Military Industries of Japan, passim*.; A. J. Watts and B. G. Gordon, *The Imperial Japanese Navy*, London: Macdonald, 1971; H. Jettschura, D. Jung and P. Mickel, *Warships of the Imperial Japanese Navy, 1869–1945*, London: Arms and Armour Press, 1977. The last two volumes are very comprehensive but lack some key technological detail available in MITI and Kobayashi. Some datings in this table are hard to verify because from plan to final armament and fitting out could take up to eight years.

Notes: VTE: Vertical Triple Expansion Engine; MIJ: Made in Japan; IHP: Indicated Horsepower.

metallurgical and engineering sophistication and was consistently sought in order to maximise speed, irrespective of vessel size. High pressures were also crucial to the development of turbines which were essential for the economy and vibration-free power needed on both battleships and long-distance liners. In Fig. 10.1, an attempt is made to show the shipbuilding technology gap in terms of boiler pressures. This is inevitably a crude but useful exercise. The western data illustrate the slow take-off between the 1830s and 1860s, acceleration during the 1880s and 1890s, and a final acceleration in the 1930s. Against this we see Japan beginning boiler-making at the end of the first western phase and effectively narrowing the technological gap by the First World War. Thereafter Japan made one more advance (in the battleship *Yamato*), while western constructors moved ahead again in the 1930s.

When we synchronise the overall western and Japanese chronologies, some important facts emerge. The first is that although western ironclads were growing in armament and protective strength during the 1860s, naval architects did not solve the fundamental engineering problem of stabilising gun-laden ships till 1870–71. Thereafter progress in hull construction, engine-power, armour and armament was rapid. The speed of change in the period crucial for Japan's early learning — the 1860s to the 1880s — was prodigious, whether measured by size, engine-power, protective armament or firepower; and the adoption by the Admiralty of compound steam-engines in the 1870s gave subsequent British ships the power and economy for global operation.[14]

Western demonstrations in Asia of these new shipbuilding and gun technologies were highly influential in Japan. One early sign of their power, reported in detail to the Japanese, was the Anglo-Chinese Opium war of 1839–42. To prosecute this, the East India Company built in great secrecy the first iron steamship ever to engage in naval warfare. Armed with 32-pound guns, the *Nemesis* was especially designed for offensive action in Chinese river and coastal locations, and proved her worth by her capacity to travel great distances and then fight with many fewer repair problems than wooden boats.[15] The

14. By the late nineteenth century the development of engine technology had reduced the engine weight needed to produce one unit of horsepower from about 600 lb. in the 1840s to 50 lb. in the 1890s. Smith, *A Short History*, p. 255.

15. The *Nemesis* was owned by the East India Company but manned by Royal Navy officers. She left Britain giving a false destination and on her outward voyage

Nemesis thus demonstrated an entirely new potential for trans-oceanic warfare, and in combination with the British fleet her fire-power was so great that 'in *nine minutes* Chusan's docks, forts and buildings were a heap of smoking ruins' (original emphasis).[16]

In 1860, China was again a victim of improved western technology, this time when it provided the first ever field experience for the Armstrong breech-loading guns. By a remarkable chance, 1860 was the year in which Japanese visitors to New York inspected the West's most advanced shipbuilding technology, embodied in *The Great Eastern*.[17] But the demonstration that most deeply affected Japanese opinion was the shelling of Kagoshima in 1863, a ferocious bombardment in which the British navy, again employing the new Armstrong guns, destroyed three Japanese steamships, five giant Taiwanese trading junks, and left Kagoshima 'a mass of ruins and flames'.[18]

This pattern of western intimidation continued right into the Meiji period, by which time Asian countries were responding to the West with sufficient naval modernisation to make irrelevant the old Opium War rule that 'a single frigate is worth a thousand junks'. Thus while new naval technologies and fleet expansion were key factors in the French decision to build a colonial empire in Indo-China, this expansion accelerated the Asian response and brought western naval power deep within the Japanese sphere of interest.[19] In 1883–84 the French not only attacked the coasts of Southern China and Vietnam but

---

was the first iron ship to cross into the Southern Hemisphere. After the Opium War she returned to service in India where her iron hull was examined and found to be in excellent condition, despite several beachings. The story of this ship is given in great detail in W. D. Bernard (ed.), *Narrative of the Voyages and Services of the Nemesis from 1840 to 1843, and of the Combined Naval and Military Operations in China* (2 vols), London: Henry Colburn, 1844. See esp. ch. 1.

16. This quotation, together with an account of the event and a print showing two steam vessels supporting British warships firing on Chusan, is in *China Illustrated*, London: Fisher and Sons, n. d., vols 1–2, pp. 91–3.

17. James Dugan, *The Great Iron Ship*, London: Hamish Hamilton, 1954, p. 65.

18. The bombardment of Kagoshima is analysed in J. M. Spaight, *Air Power and the Cities*, London: Longmans, Green, 1930, pp. 52–8. The performance of the Armstrong guns at Kagoshima was the subject of a Parliamentary White Paper, *Kagoshima — Admiral Kuper's Official Report of the Performance of the Armstrong Guns in the Action at Kagoshima*, April 4 1864.

19. E. H. Jenkins, *Histoire de la Marine Française des origines à nos jours*, Paris: Albin Michel, 1977, ch. 14.

also proceeded to blockade Formosa. In these engagements they used advanced guns and small torpedoes to attack the Chinese ships, some of which were designed by Americans, manned by German officers and armed with Krupp and Nordenfeldt guns.[20]

So successful were Japan's efforts to catch up that by the late Meiji era its naval performance was increasingly monitored by the West and played an ever more influential role in western naval planning. Indeed, because of the relative tranquility of the western seas, the Sino-Japanese and Russo-Japanese naval battles represented the only serious conflicts in which western constructors could observe their own most recent technology in action.[21]

Although in the early stages of catching up the 'hardware' of Japanese naval warfare was almost entirely foreign, the Japanese were active from the outset in mastering and improving the 'software' of naval design, strategy and tactics. The significance of this requires some understanding of the gap that had opened up in the late 1880s between the technical choices available and the limited understanding in western navies of how they could be used. In design, the new technologies posed crucial choices in which designers had to trade off unprecedented potential speed, steel protection and firepower against each other. In tactics, officers had to work out how to take advantage of the new designs adopted — a problem which the British navy, still easily the world's greatest, found quite difficult since it was still run by men who preferred sailing to steaming, gave higher marks to shiny decks than to knowledge of gunnery techniques,

20. The significance of this event is mentioned in Figuier, *Les Grandes Inventions*, p. 51. The person responsible for these attacks was Admiral Courbet, a former Director of the French Torpedo School and pioneer of torpedo warfare; he was also a national hero. Courbet's attack on Foochow in 1884 was particularly devastating: 'In less than half an hour the [Chinese] fleet had been utterly destroyed and several thousand were dead and wounded.' Quoted in Chère, *The Diplomacy of the Sino-French War*, p. 47. A vivid account of the modernising Chinese navy and the use of French torpedoes against it in the Formosan blockade is Louis Boussenard, 'Les Torpilleurs de L'Amiral Courbet', *Journal des Voyages*, 2nd series, nos 41 and 42, 1897, pp. 226–8, 247–50.

21. For the years between 1800 and 1816, Haydn lists fifty-two major naval battles. Between 1816 and 1905 only four are listed: the Battle of Navarino in 1827 (fought in the Nelson tradition) and one-sided engagements off Egypt, Lagos and China. *Haydn's Dictionary of Dates Containing the History of the World to the Summer of 1906* (24th edn), London: Ward Lock, 1906, pp. 913–14.

A late Meiji porcelain factory. A contemporary photograph, revealing the role of child labour. This was the cause of much trade friction down to the 1920s. A large proportion of the output was exported, and millions of these objects are still to be found around the world today.

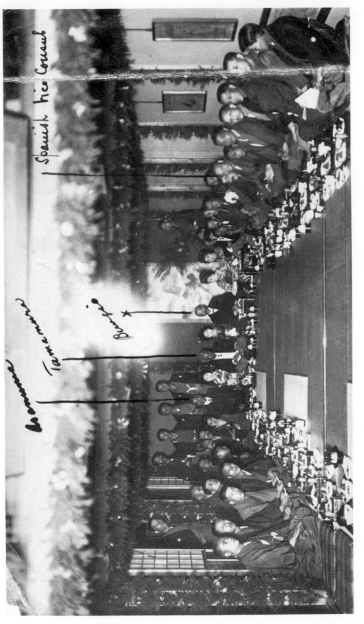

A technology transfer business dinner, 1913. The European guest of honour was the author's great-uncle, Mr B. Wesson, who represented Kodak Eastman in Japan before the First World War. On his right is a member of the Asanuma family, the founders of Japan's first photographic retail shop and famous as makers of wooden-plate cameras in the Meiji period.

Emperor Hirohito inspects the Nikon field telescope in the late 1920s. From Kogaku Kogyoshi Henshukai, *Nihon no kogaku kogyoshi*.

Fifty years of technological development. The camera is the Nikon S2 rangefinder of the early 1950s, the first of Nikon's big successes in the post-war camera market. The kettle is of cast-iron, made in traditional style probably around 1900.

The battleship *Yamato*. One of the few photographs available, showing the warship on trials.

The Nakajima *Kotobuki* aero-engine, regarded as the first to be entirely designed and manufactured in Japan. It was made in substantial numbers and used to power several important aircraft.

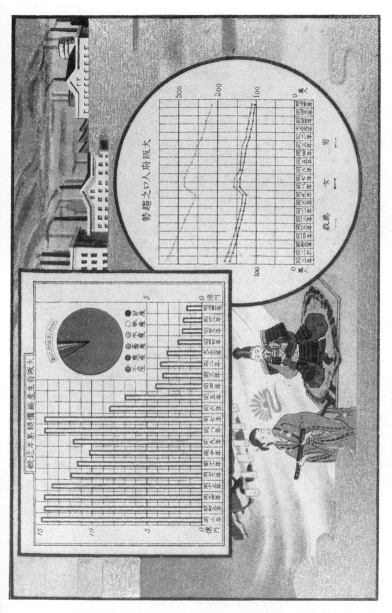

The population revolution as seen in the 1920s (data read from right to left). This contemporary coloured postcard shows the growth of population and industrial output in Osaka, 1909–28. The population increased by 2.3% annually, but industrial output by over 13%.

Migrants dedicate themselves at the Meiji shrine in Tokyo before leaving for Manchuria. They were probably destined for armed rural settlements.

The world's largest opencast mine developed by the SMR at Fushun. This mine, together with the Anshan ironworks, was the largest of the SMR's industrial activities outside the railway itself.

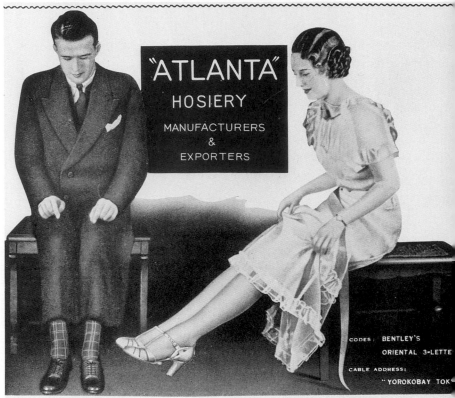

NAIGAI AMIMONO CO., LTD.,
NO. 3, 5-CHOME, NISHIGINZA, KYOBASHI, TOKYO.

Advertisement for Japanese hosiery, late 1930s. The deadly effectiveness of Japanese competition in the hosiery trade was commented upon by British consular reports in the late 1920s and 1930s. Parallel to Japanese efforts to match the needs of low-income consumers in Asia and Africa was a determined effort to appeal to fashion-conscious, depression-affected Western consumers.

and who as late as 1896 were training crews in the techniques of swordsmanship used by Nelson in the Napoleonic wars for ship-to-ship grappling.[22]

The Japanese, by contrast, plunged immediately into these problems as their naval development programme got under way in the 1880s, and as they faced the Chinese navy that had been equipped with what were, by contemporary standards, two enormous German warships of 7,000 tons displacement. Acting on the advice of their French naval counsellor, Emile Bertin, the Japanese decided not to go down the route of seeking the biggest of everything with imported ships, but instead built up their domestic construction facilities and, by use of these and selective foreign purchases, implemented a policy of using smaller ships with exceptionally powerful armament. They also embraced the revolutionary new technologies embodied in torpedoes, torpedo-boats and mines, of which the French at that time were probably the world's best exponents.[23]

These policies and Japanese 'software' skills were fully exhibited in the war with China (1894–95), where the technically larger Chinese fleet was annihilated in a single day. In the Russo-Japanese conflict, Japan again made particularly effective use of mines and torpedoes and, by use of sampans mounted on modern ships, succeeded to a limited extent in combining traditional and modern technologies.[24] Indeed, since both the Russian and Japanese navies had basically equal access to western naval technologies, Japan's success in the Russo-Japanese naval conflicts suggests that Japanese utilisation and adaptation of these

22. The Germans were no better, believing that their new warships would be used to ram the enemy at a time when guns could sink ships at several thousand yards. Massie, *Dreadnought*, pp. 168ff.

23. Louis Emile Bertin was seconded under contract to the Japanese government from 1885 to 1890. He continued the tradition of Leonce Verny, the founder of Yokosuka, but with responsibility not only for arsenal development and administration but also for ship design, foreign orders and long-term naval budgets. Bertin encouraged the Japanese to develop new, unprecedentedly powerful torpedoes and envisaged the day when they would be launched from submarines. Christian Dedet, *Les fleurs d'acier du Mikado*, Paris: Flammarion, 1993.

24. The use of sampans for rapid and silent landings of troops was observed by a British reporter whose book has unique insights into the day-to-day functioning of the Japanese navy at that time. H. C. Seppings Wright, *With Togo: The Story of Seven Months Active Service under his Command*, London: Hurst and Blackett, 1905, p. 76.

technologies must have been a key factor in their success.[25] The war also marked the Japanese breakthrough into the high-speed indigenous construction of large ships, notably the *Ikoma* and *Tsukuba*, the most heavily-armed cruisers ever built up to that time.

So seriously was the Russo-Japanese naval conflict taken in the West that it gave rise to an urgent British study. In the autumn of 1905, influenced both by the Russo-Japanese naval war and by German naval expansion, a committee of the British Admiralty recommended the immediate construction of the *Dreadnought* class battleship and of heavy cruisers on Japanese lines. Although HMS *Dreadnought* (1906) set new world standards in speed and firepower, significant refinements to the *Dreadnought* systems were incorporated in HMS *Bellerophon* (1907) in the light of still further study of Japanese naval techniques.[26]

The process of learning

The overall framework of the advance in Japanese shipbuilding is found in plans that were initially focused on fairly limited objectives set by the Department of the Navy. But between 1882 and 1907 Japan drew up a series of increasingly ambitious naval programmes which were continually expanded. The 1882 plan was for forty-two vessels, of which 20 had been completed by 1889. The third plan (1896) was for 676 vessels and this was rolled over into even larger plans in 1904 and 1907. The financial consequence of these plans

25. An exhaustive first-hand study of the naval aspects of the war is Captain Nicolas Klado, *The Battle of the Sea of Japan*, London: Hodder and Stoughton, 1906. Klado, a Russian naval officer, analysed the technical, organisational and personal factors in Russia's defeat. The technical appraisal is in ch. 3, where the author particularly emphasises the Japanese use of torpedo-boats and skills in the matching and placing of guns and vessels. A modern analysis of the Battle of Tsushima and its naval and technological consequences is Alberto Santoni, *La Battaglia di Tsushima*, Rome: Ateneo, 1985, esp. chs. 4, 6.

26. The crucial lessons learned from the Russo-Japanese naval conflict, especially from the battle of Tsushima, were the need for speed and the danger presented by torpedoes. This fact strengthened the case for vessels armed exclusively with very large guns capable of accurate firing at 6,000 to 7,000 metres. Modern work on this subject includes Arthur J. Marder, *From the Dreadnought to Scapa Flow* (vol. 1); *The Road to War, 1904–1914*, Oxford University Press, 1961, *passim*; Massie, *Dreadnought*, esp. part 3, and Robert Jones, *The Battleship Dreadnought*, London: Conway Maritime, 1992, esp, p. 9, for comment on Japanese factors in British armament decisions. A detailed, near-contemporary account of these developments from the British view is contained in 'Ship', *EB* (11th edn).

was a growth of naval expenditures from ¥3.1 million in 1881 to ¥81 million in 1908.[27]

The basic sequence for all military technology transfer was, first, to buy several foreign examples of a specific weapon; secondly, to organise exhaustive testing procedures and selection conferences; thirdly, to encourage the adaptation and improvement of foreign designs where feasible; and fourthly, when specifications were finally agreed, to establish production arrangements in either the public or the private sectors or some combination of the two. Where domestic production was initially impossible or inadequate, as was usually the case, imports were arranged.

Japan's determination not merely to emulate but also to exceed western naval technologies as soon as possible is reflected in the fact that even while still at the importing and early learning stage, the Japanese navy hired the most prestigious naval architect in Britain to oversee the building of its first warship.[28] Later the Japanese insisted on British shipyards building to specifications *higher* than those being supplied to the British Admiralty. This process started in the torpedo-boat class and ultimately led to the point where, by their expansion of the capabilities and performance of these vessels, the British shipbuilder Yarrow considered Japan to have effectively invented the destroyer.[29]

27. Kobayashi, *Military Industries of Japan*, pp. 52–8 and 121–2; Hayashi, *A history*, pp. 108–10, 126ff.; Koyama, *An historical analysis*, esp. pp. 120–7; Okuma, *Fifty Years of New Japan*, vol. 1, ch. 8.

28. The architect was Sir Edward Reed, former Chief Constructor to the British Admiralty.

29. For example, in 1885 the British Royal Navy ordered 54 first-class torpedo-boats, of which the largest was 127 feet long with 700 h.p. engines. In the same year the Yarrow yard constructed for the Japanese a kit of parts for the *Kotaka* which, when made up at Yokosuka in 1888, was 166 feet long and powered by 1,400 h.p. engines. See Smith, *A Short History*, p. 259, and Kobayashi, *Military Industries of Japan*, p. 59. Discussion of Yarrow's Japanese business may be found in various sources and especially in ch. 10 of Lady Yarrow's *Alfred Yarrow: Life and Work*, London: Chapman and Hall, 1924. This practice was repeated with both the *Mikasa* and *Kongo* class battleships in 1899 and 1910. The former was built in British yards to Japanese specification, again by a combination of specification and ultimately self-construction. In terms of armament, the Japanese were the first to mount 15-, 16- and 18-inch guns. See J. D. Scott, *Vickers: A History*, London: Weidenfeld and Nicolson, 1962, ch. 4, and articles on the *Kongo* and the *Yamato* in J. N. Westwood, *Fighting Ships of World War Two*, London: Sidgwick and Jackson, 1975.

In the 1898 naval programme Japan ordered the *Mikasa* battleship from Vickers in Britain. The vessel achieved an unprecedented combination of firepower and protective strength, which caused doubts in Britain over the wisdom of allowing even a friendly foreign power access to vessels more powerful than those of the British navy.[30] This process of adaptation and improvement continued throughout the 1900s, notably in the deployment of unprecedentedly heavy armour. This led ultimately to the modern concept of the heavy cruiser, a vessel smaller than a battleship but equivalent to it in offensive power by virtue of its speed and armour.[31] Japan sought at this early stage to minimise risks and implemented its policy of 'copy, improve, innovate' by purchasing ships from a range of foreign shipbuilders and by buying at least two models for domestic trial and adoption of crucial techniques.[32]

To acquire domestic construction skills, foreigners were allowed to build ships in Japan with specialised manpower hired from abroad. At the top level, several outstanding naval constructors were brought to Japan, including Charles Dickenson West, who for twenty-five years held the chair of Mechanical and Marine Construction at Tokyo University. Use was also made of the shipyards of western firms and managers who built up Japanese skills, first by repair and refitting work and then by building vessels with rising levels of specification.[33] Comprehensive repair capability for modern ships was claimed as early as 1876.

For the building of large, sophisticated vessels the process of learning consisted of Japanese hulls and superstructures being initially fitted with foreign engines, boilers and specialised components; then, by

30. The significance of the *Mikasa* was that its main guns were concentrated in a strongly fortified central position, allowing the rest of the ship to be evenly protected with heavy Krupp steel. As Admiral Togo's flagship, the *Mikasa* withstood enormous bombardment in the Russo-Japanese war. Details of its novel construction are analysed in Alex Richardson, *Vickers and Sons and Maxim Ltd: Their Works and Manufactures*, Engineering, 1902, pp. 109–10.

31. See sources cited in notes 29 and 30.

32. In marine engines, Parsons and Curtis turbines were adopted and assigned to the Mitsubishi and Kawasaki shipyards respectively. The story of the transfer of turbine technology is in MITI, vol. 18, *Machinery*, pp. 140–56.

33. For example, Kirby and Co., who had previously made wooden, steam-powered vessels, began construction of Japan's first significant iron ships in 1881. At one time the Osaka Tekko yard was also under British management. See 'shipbuilding' in Foreign Office, *Commercial Report, 1881, BPPJ*, vol. 7, p. 26.

stages, imported materials and parts were manufactured domestically. For smaller ships, examples were initially assembled from imported kits, but domestic capabilities were rapidly developed. For example, kit assembly of torpedo-boats was used from 1880 to 1890 (boats 1–5). For boats 6–9, hulls were bought in but engines were made in Japan. Total domestic capability was achieved with torpedo-boat 10, completed in 1892. However, no sooner had Japan acquired this capability than the first-generation torpedo-boats were surpassed by superior rivals, especially those built by Normand in France. Normand's torpedo-boat, *Forban*, powered by superlative triple-expansion engines and innovatory 'Normand'-type boilers, broke the world sea-speed record in 1895. To maintain naval parity with Russia, Japan had again to supplement domestic construction with imports from Yarrow and Normand; thus in 1904–5 boats from both firms were ranged against each other in the service of the Japanese and Russian navies.[34] This pattern was repeated for the last time after the British battleship *Dreadnought* again made contemporary Japanese skills obsolete. Japan responded in 1910 by ordering four new battleships: the *Kongo*, to be built by Vickers in Britain, and three sister-ships, to be built in Japan with assistance from Vickers.

The most striking feature of the technology acquisition process revealed by Tables 10.2, 10.3 and 10.4 is that in every significant aspect of marine construction, Japanese learning went — albeit rapidly — through almost all the stages traversed by western innovators. They started in the 1860s with small, wholly wooden craft, powered by simple steam-engines with auxiliary sail. At this stage, lack of appropriate materials rather than lack of construction skills posed a greater problem to pioneer yards such as Ishikawajima.[35] Gradually, the sophistication of hull materials increased until hulls entirely fabricated from steel became standard. Engine technology moved from simple to compound and triple steam expansion types, to turbines in the early 1900s, then

34. The Normand yard began ship construction in the eighteenth century and reached its apogee under the great engineer J. A. Normand, when its specialisation in engine and boiler technology bore fruit in exceptionally fast torpedo-boats and destroyers. A full account of the yard, including the specifications and details of ships supplied to Japan, are in Jean de la Varende, *Les Augustin-Normand. Sept Générations de Constructeurs de Navires*, Mayenne (France), 1960.

35. See the acount of Ishikawajima's construction of the *Asahi Maru* in 1854. *Ishikawajima jukogyuo kabushiki kaisha 108 nenshi* (The 108-year history of Ishikawajima Heavy Industries), Tokyo, 1961, pp. 187–8.

to diesel. There was even one major experiment in electrically powered craft in the early 1920s.[36] Similar progression can be observed in the screw and boiler systems. Although a latecomer, Japan did not by-pass major stages of vessel development, and impressive as were some of its technological leaps, none actually exceeded that represented by the British *The Great Eastern* in 1858 (Table 10.3). This is not to imply that progression was smooth, for it was not. But under the driving imperatives of the navy, and equipped with detailed intelligence of the state of the art elsewhere, Japanese shipbuilders pursued advanced models until they were mastered.

By the 1900s Japanese hull, engine and boiler construction were beginning to embody significant improvements on transferred technologies. Particularly notable were the success of the Miyabara boiler system, improvements in condenser technology, the revolutionary re-design of hull and bow shapes to facilitate high-speed manoeuvring, and the ability to load more guns and armour on each class of ship than any other navy had done before. Between the World Wars, Japanese strengths in naval shipbuilding were finally brought to a peak with the building of aircraft-carriers equalled only in scale by those of the United States,[37] the largest long-distance submarines ever built,[38] highly innovative torpedoes[39] and, finally, battleships of unprecedented

36. 'Japan's first electric steamer', *FER*, Jan. 1921, p. 12.

37. The first purpose-built aircraft-carrier in the world was the *Hosho*. Constructed in 1922, it was equipped with a copy of the Sperry Gyro Stabiliser. It survived the battle of Midway and was finally scrapped in 1947. For details of the Sperry equipment, see F. P. Purvis, 'Japan's contribution to naval architecture', *FER*, August 1925, pp. 577–8.

38. The STo-type submarine ordered in 1942 was in effect a submersible aircraft-carrier. It could carry three seaplane bombers accompanied by 18,000 kg. of bombs and its unique four sets of diesel engines gave it a radius of action of 37,000 miles. Watts and Gordon, *The Imperial Japanese Navy*, pp. 351–3.

39. Westwood has argued: 'Of all the submarine fleets, that of the Imperial Japanese Navy was provided with the best torpedos,' Westwood, *Fighting Ships*, p. 131. By the early 1930s Japanese engineers had solved the problems of oxygen-enriched and oxygen-powered torpedo engines, and the attack on Pearl Harbor was made feasible by new solutions to the problems of shallow launching from aeroplanes. A naval attaché in Tokyo in the 1930s, George Ross (who was fluent in Japanese and exceptionally able), actually discovered details of Japanese advances in torpedo propulsion but the British Admiralty rejected his reports as incredible. See S. E. Morison, *History of United States Naval Operations in World War Two* (13 vols), Boston: Little, Brown, 1947–64, vol. 3, p. 23; 'Return to Pearl Harbor', *National Geographic*, vol. 80 no. 6, Dec. 1991. Details of Ross's career are from his obituary, 'Rear-Admiral George Ross', *Daily Telegraph*, Aug. 9, 1993.

sophistication and firepower, each nearly twice as large as any other battleship in the world.[40]

The full engineering details of the battleship *Yamato* will never be known because its plans were destroyed during the American bombing of the Kure naval shipyard. However, it clearly marked an extraordinary achievement. Its scale was enlarged to the point where no American capital ship of equal size could enter the Panama Canal, and its hull design was only finalised after more than fifty models had been tank-tested. Each of its gun-turrets weighed 2,774 tons — more than the weight of a large destroyer — and its 18.2-inch guns were the largest ever built, transmitting more than twice the blast of contemporary 16-inch guns. To be useful at their full range of 40 kilometres, these guns were guided by rangefinders 15 metres in length, themselves a separate development which most specialists agree were the most remarkable optical achievement of the pre-war Nikon company.[41] The ship contained yet another innovation: a neon strip-lighting system developed by Toshiba. The 150,000 h.p. turbine engines that drove the vessel were exceeded in size only by those of the Japanese *Zuikaku*-class aircraft-carriers.

Apart from actual warship production and the success of import substitution, two other aspects of naval progress were important at this time. First, the techniques required by shipbuilding became a force for the expansion of related industries — notably steel-making, mechanical and electrical engineering and, for ballistics development, chemicals. Many of these ancillary activities were developed 'in house', and many too had important spillover effects in the commercial sector. Metallurgy was one such activity: the navy had begun to press for

40. Summaries and evaluations of these achievements are in Watts and Gordon, *The Imperial Japanese Navy*; M. Ito, *The End of the Imperial Japanese Navy*, London: Weidenfeld and Nicolson, 1956, esp. pp. 68–73 (on the *Yamato*, *Shinano* and *Musashi*); Ronald H. Spector, *Eagle Against the Sun. The American War with Japan*, New York: Viking, 1985, pp. 43–7. Further details of the *Yamato*, together with reconstructed drawings are in Janusz Skulski, *The Battleship Yamato*, London: Conway Maritime Press, 1988.

41. Details of Nikon's naval work, together with close-up photographs of the *Yamato's* equipment, are included in Kogaku Kogyoshi Henshukai, *Nihon no kogaku kogyoshi* (History of the Japanese optical industry), Tokyo: Optical Industry History Editorial Committee, 1955. The *Musashi* and its optical equipment are illustated in *Nippon kogaku kogyo kabushiki kaisha yonjunenshi* (The forty-year history of the Nikon Company), Tokyo, 1957, pp. 126–7.

Japanese steel as early as 1878, and in the late 1880s the French adviser Bertin insisted on implementing steel-making standards in Osaka comparable to those of Krupp and the French.[42] By the 1890s the Japanese had concluded that even their reduced dependence on imported steels for guns and ships was an unacceptable strategic weakness. This led directly to the foundation of the Yawata and Muroran steel companies.[43] Related to metallurgy was machine-making, and an important example of such spillover was the early provision by the Yokosuka shipyard of technical support and a steam-engine for the Aichi Cotton Mill.[44]

A second spillover from naval construction was the development of private-sector shipbuilding capability. Japan was of course not alone in experiencing this close interplay between the public and private sectors and between advances in civilian and military uses of new technology: the development of the Vickers company and the career of individual engineers such as Marc Birkigt are outstanding cases in point.[45] In shipbuilding especially, the wartime role of the merchant marines made these distinctions academic.[46]

In Japan the first generation of Japanese-made naval vessels had been built in public naval shipyards, but as early as 1898 the private Kawasaki yard claimed the capability to build a complete cruiser, with

42. He required the Osaka steelmakers to supply in three major grades of quality, together with many other steel types needed for specialised functions in ship construction. Dedet, *Les Fleurs*, p. 293.

43. H. Iida, *A history of Japanese iron and steel technology*, pp. 244ff.; Nakaoka, *Technology and technology policy*, pp. 210–11.

44. MITI, *Textiles*, vol. 15, p. 18.

45. Birkigt graduated from the University of Geneva in engineering and physics in 1878 and quickly found himself working on artillery problems in an ordnance factory. At that time, ordnance work was considered professionally equivalent to the most sophisticated postgraduate research. In the 1900s Birkigt switched to car-building and in 1911 invented the twin overhead camshaft engine. During the First World War he made aero-engines embodying water cooling, forced lubrication, monobloc aluminium construction methods, and overhead camshaft systems. These engines were exceptionally efficient and one of Birkigt's twenty-one international licensees was Mitsubishi. After the war, he made what many regard as the world's most beautiful high-powered car — the Hispano-Suiza. In 1941 he returned to military work with designs for what became the standard 20 mm. cannon used in British Royal Air Force fighters.

46. The great German transatlantic passenger liners that sailed from Hamburg in the Edwardian era were designed from the outset for easy conversion to armament carrying and rapid wartime deployment.

Table 10.5. IMPORT SUBSTITUTION IN WARSHIPS, 1883–1924
(*% shares by tonnage*)

Origin of naval vessels	1883–1906	1907–23
Naval shipyards	24.3	47.9
Imports	74.3	7.2
Private shipyards	1.4	44.9

Source: MITI, vol. 18, *Machinery*, p. 153.

steel plate as the only essential import. By the 1890s, in engine-building and other branches of marine construction, large private yards such as Mitsubishi and Kawasaki had become important centres of technology transfer and innovation, with new technologies being applied in naval and civilian ships.[47] As a result, the joint expansion between the Russo-Japanese war and 1924 of state facilities and the private sector enabled the completion of the import substitution process in warships.

Shipbuilding in the private sector

Between *kaikoku* and the First World War the private shipbuilding sector consisted of three types of yards: those specialising in traditional Japanese-style (*wa*) ships, those established to build western-style ships, and those in the process of transition from Japanese to western techniques, a type which became numerous towards the end of the period.[48] The technical frontier in shipbuilding was clearly in the western yards, and the basic problem faced by private yards was how to survive a long period of learning without the consistent financial support of the order provided to naval yards by government procurement. As argued earlier, the intrinsic difficulties and scale of modern techniques impeded the adaptation of western techniques or progress through the gradual modernisation of traditional yards. If we date the

47. The Kawasaki claim is reported in 'The Kawasaki shipyard', reprinted from the *Kobe Chronicle* in *NCH*, Sept. 5, 1898.

48. This section is based on several sources of which the following are particularly important: Minami and Kiyokawa, *Japanese industrialisation*, ch. 8; Nakaoka, 'On technological leaps of Japan as a developing country 1900–1940', *Osaka City University Economic Review*, no. 22, 1987, pp. 1–25, and articles in the *Far Eastern Review*. The latter specialised in shipping and shipbuilding and is a unique source of expert western views on Japanese progress in shipbuilding and technology generally.

'western' private sector from 1884 (the purchase of the Nagasaki Iron Works by Mitsubishi), we may define the private sector's economic task as being to maintain financial viability for the twenty to thirty years needed for catching up not only in the technologies of ship-building but also in the management skills needed for commercial com-petitiveness in the industry.[49]

Learning and technical achievements in the private sector. The learning process in private yards is best illustrated by the experience of impor-tant yards. Ishikawajima, Mitsubishi and Kawasaki were all late Tokugawa yards built for the direct transfer of western technology. Initially taken into the public sector in 1867, they were then privatised in the 1880s.

Ishikawajima was established by the Mito clan in 1853 to learn western shipbuilding technology. It built the *Asahi Maru* in 1854 and Japan's first steam warship, the *Chiyodagata*, in 1862. In its early days it mixed Japanese with western skills, and as late as 1893 was one of only four Japanese private shipyards capable of making metal hulls. Ishikawajima was an outstanding example of the ability of shipyards to diversify into cognate engineering technologies from which they could earn the profits to sustain progress in difficult shipbuilding. Together with Kawasaki, Nakajima and Mitsubishi, Ishikawajima became a pioneer in aircraft and jet engine construction during the Second World War. The progress of the Mitsubishi yard is sum-marised in Table 10.6, where we can see how the yard proceeded directly to the building of western ships in the 1880s and then followed a phased approach, culminating in three trans-Pacific passenger liners. The key vessel in this sequence, which clearly represented a leap more than an incremental step, was the *Hitachi Maru*, built in 1898, which was four times larger and nearly five times more powerful than its predecessor built two years earlier. After this success the company went on in 1908 to build the *Tenyo Maru*, a vessel that outstripped all western standards and broke the world record for the San Francisco run on its maiden voyage. It is true that its engines and many of its components were imported, but in building its third great Pacific liner

---

49. Of the Mitsubishi yard it was said, 'Immediate returns were looked upon as a very secondary consideration, the whole aim of the firm being to equip an establish-ment of which Japan might be proud in respect to both workmanship and business integrity.' 'The Mitsubishi Dockyard and Engine Works at Nagasaki', *FER*, April 1911, p. 376.

Table 10.6. THE GROWTH OF THE MITSUBISHI SHIPYARD

	No. of ships built	Total gross tonnage	Total IHP	Workforce
1898	4	7,703	4,225	3,340
1903	8	13,078	11,463	5,658
1908	4	23,332	36,417	9,011
1909	4	29,596	33,379	5,903
Total 1898–1909	93	155,056	192,833	

Table 10.7. KEY VESSELS PRODUCED BY THE MITSUBISHI SHIPYARD

	Name	Gross tonnage	Other specifications
1883	Kosuge Maru	1,500	Wood, simple engine
1887	Yugao Maru	206	Iron, compound engine
1890	Chikugawa Maru	610	Steel, triple expansion 483 h.p.
1896	Suma Maru	1,593	Steel, triple expansion 853 h.p.
1898	Hitachi Maru	6,172	Steel, triple expansion 3,847 h.p.
1908	Sakura Maru (armed Volunteer Fleet steamer)	3,200	Steel, Parsons turbines, 8,500 h.p. Miyabara boilers
1908	Tenyo Maru	13,454	Steel, Parsons turbines 20,608 h.p. triple propeller system

Source: Nakaoka, 'Technological leaps'; 'The Mitsubishi dockyard and engine works at Nagasaki', *FER*, April 1911, pp. 375–87.
Notes: 1. The *Kosuge Maru* was built in the the old Nagasaki shipyard during its last year in public ownership. Although not strictly a Mitsubishi ship, it was in the direct line of development.
2. The *Tenyo Maru* was one of a trio of ships that included the *Chiyo Maru* and the *Shinyo Maru*.

the *Shinyo Maru* in 1911, Mitsubishi did not merely use its license to construct Parsons turbines but actually advanced Parsons technology with an improved condenser system.[50]

50. From *EB* (11th edn), vol. 24, p. 887. The *Tenyo Maru* was fitted with advanced heating and air cooling systems, telephones, a nursery, darkroom, barber's shop, hospital and luxurious smoking and staterooms. The turbine engines and triple propeller system of this class provided the unprecedented stability sought in a luxury liner. 'The *Tenyo Maru*, Japan's new palatial greyhound', *FER*, August 1908, and 'The *Shinyo Maru*, the Toyo Kisen Kaisha's new Pacific greyhound', *FER*, October 1911. The latter has photographs and a discussion of the Mitsubishi condenser system. Descriptions of the luxury NYK liners are also to be found in *Golden Jubilee History of the Nippon Yusen Kaisha*, 1885–1935.

Kawasaki was another yard which, though small, was technologically distinguished. By the early twentieth century it was making extensive use of electrical machinery. It was responsible for a number of important naval as well as merchant vessels, was a pioneer in advanced engine building, and was the first shipyard to export its output.[51]

The learning process in both the Mitsubishi and Kawasaki yards included a long preliminary phase of repair, renovation and modification of foreign-built ships. It included intensive study of foreign techniques, the use of especially commissioned foreign designs and blueprints, and the employment of supervisors and engineers from overseas. Mitsubishi judged itself able to dispense with on-site western engineers by 1896 but it retained a nominal western presence to reassure customers for its large liners. By the 1900s private yards were at the forefront in both the adoption and improvement of western technologies. Kawasaki developed the Miyabara boiler system and combined it with improved versions of the Curtis turbine, for which it held the Far Eastern license; Mitsubishi upgraded Parsons engines and fitted the *Shinyo Maru* with the best sonic depth-sounding devices on any ship sailing the Pacific, as well as with a wireless system with the unparalleled range of 3,000 miles. It was the application of this type of progress to warships that enabled the navy to dispense with western-built warships so quickly.

However, progress was not as smooth as may appear from retrospective description. Difficulties and disappointments were encountered, and major financial risks were taken in moving from one phase of technology to the next. However, the yards were consciously operating a long-term financial strategy and it was the general understanding among the private customers of the yards that overcoming short-term problems was critical to Japan's overall economic wellbeing. Nonetheless, the financial survival of the yards depended on various special forms of government financial support and guidance, imaginative management and the exploitation of varied profit-making opportunities.

Government support came by four different routes. First, after an early period of *laissez-faire* trade, low profitability and shipbuilding bankruptcies, the government developed a competition policy in shipping that ensured that one company (NYK) was guaranteed viability

51. 'The Kawasaki Dockyard Company Ltd.', *FER*, April 1911, pp. 391–5.

as Japan's flagship carrier, and as the market expanded, it allowed the emergence of other lines.

Secondly, government payment for shipping services during the Formosan expedition (1874) and the Satsuma rebellion (1877) and then the Sino-Japanese war provided financial windfalls of enormous proportions to the private shipyards and shipping companies.[52] For example, windfall profits from the Sino-Japanese war financed the private sector's most dramatic and risky technological enterprises — the successive construction of the *Suma Maru* and the *Hitachi Maru* during 1896–98.

Thirdly, there was the impact of the Shipping Subsidy Law. This initially encouraged shipping companies to buy large ships of any origin, but in amended form it provided incentives in the form of subsidies to ensure that as many of these as possible would be built in Japan. These subsidies, while not large, were sufficient to encourage the immediate building of the *Hitachi Maru* and the establishment of a new trans-Pacific line (the Toyo Kisen Kaisha). They were also crucial to companies on the margin of viability or for establishing scheduled services on new routes. In a poor year such a subsidy could make the difference between profitability and loss.[53] Foreign com-

52. Foreign observers noted that every time shipping was expanded in national emergencies, the same vessels subsequently appeared to open new commercial routes. 'The development of navigation in Japan', *NCH*, Aug. 14, 1896. During the Sino-Japanese war, shipping companies' profits were inflated by special government fees (*goyosen*) earned for transporting 631,000 men, 56,000 horses and their feed, and over 250,000 tons of goods. In shipbuilding, Mitsubishi earned 95% of its profits in 1895 from special government work. Details in MITI, vol. 18, *Machinery*, pp. 80ff. For an overview of these issues see 'State and war in Japanese shipping history' in Y. Tominaga, *Kotsu ni okeru shihonshugi no hatten* (The development of capitalism in transportation), Tokyo: Iwanami Shoten, 1957, pp. 96–163.

53. Useful articles on shipping policy are those by Miwa, Nakagawa and Wray in T. Yui and K. Nakagawa (eds), *Business History of Shipping. Strategy and Structure*, University of Tokyo Press, 1985. Shipbuilding subsidies were a key component of the wider policy of 'import substitution in the machinery industry' (*kikai kogyo kokusanka*). Details of this and of the laws and the ships which were subsidised are given in MITI, vol. 18, *Machinery*, pp. 96ff., 152ff. An example of the significance of the subsidies for shipping companies in a weak market is illustrated in the accounts of the Osaka Shosen for 1914, a year in which subsidies were larger than total profits. The stabilising effect of subsidies will have been a factor in the willingness of this and other companies to maintain high rates of investment through the major commercial downturns such as those that followed the Russo-Japanese war and the First World War, a policy which surprised and impressed western observers. See 'Remarkable development of Japanese shipping', *FER*, April 1919, pp. 350–5.

petitors were certain that these subsidies were effective. One American line claimed to have been closed by their effect, and the British shipowner John Swire reported that with their aid the NYK was 'sweeping the board both down and up [to Australia]'.[54] However, apart from Britain and the United States, nearly all contemporary shipping nations provided large open subsidies of some sort.[55] What was distinctive about Japan was the strong bias towards a combination of technical modernisation and commercial expansion. Thus while Japan's subsidy law was encouraging shipbuilders and shipping lines to go for advanced hull designs and new engine technologies, the French were operating an expensive programme of subsidies designed to encourage the development of advanced *sailing* ships.[56]

Finally, government support for private shipbuilding was not confined to policy and special financial arrangements, for when all else failed the government acted by direct legislation. The most important example of this was the law of 1885 which specifically forbad the building of Japanese-style ships of more than 500 *koku* capacity. This decision was taken because this was still a profitable activity at a time when the government wished to concentrate all available resources into the struggle to acquire western techniques.[57]

Given the scale of other commitments, special government support could only supplement the efforts made by the private sector to build up its own profitability. One way in which a yard could acquire funds for innovation was by developing successful businesses in the repair and refitting trades and by taking increasing volumes of work from the naval yards. Mitsubishi, having the advantage of the enormous Tategami dry dock, was particularly successful in this. The yards also

54. The American problem was highlighted after the failure of the Shipping Subsidy Bill in the American Congress and is described in 'Blow to American shipping', *FER*, April 1907, p. 340. For the Swire comment see Sheila Marriner and Francis E. Hyde, *The Senior John Samuel Swire: Management in Far Eastern Shipping Trades*, Liverpool University Press, 1967, p. 94.

55. The British gave modest subsidies in the form of postal contracts. See Sidney Pollard and Paul Robertson, *The British Shipbuilding Industry, 1870–1914*, Cambridge, MA: Harvard University Press, 1979, pp. 222–6; H. J. Dyos and D. H. Aldcroft, *British Transport: An Economic Survey from the Seventeenth Century to the Twentieth*, London: Penguin, 1974, chs. 8, 9, 11.

56. 'Japanese shipping subsidies', *FER*, June 1908, pp. 26ff. French subsidy policy is discussed in Theodore Zeldin, *France, 1848–1945: Anxiety and Hypocrisy*, Oxford University Press, 1981, ch. 8, 'Technology', esp. pp. 284–5.

57. MITI, *Machinery*, vol. 1, pp. 86–7.

used metal-fabricating and engineering skills developed in shipbuilding to diversify into other businesses. The Kawasaki shipyard, for example, also made iron and bronze castings, all-purpose boilers, machine tools, locomotives and rolling-stock, bridge girders, armaments, power machinery, mining equipment and the carriage sets for the Hiogo city electric tramway system, as well as manufacturing every conceivable kind of ship for sale at home and abroad. A third source of profit was foreign technology licences. To cite the case of the Kawasaki yard again, the company controlled licences for cantilever-framed hulls, Curtis turbines, Miyabara boilers, Schmidt engine superheaters and GEC electric locomotives. These licences usually conferred rights of construction and also of profitable resale in East and South-East Asia.[58]

Valuable and important as all these activities were, the fundamental factor underpinning private-sector shipyard development was the health of Japanese shipping companies. This in turn depended on the success of the companies in local services, long-distance coastal runs, East Asian regional lines (incorporating routes to China, Taiwan, Manchuria, Hong Kong and South-East Asia) and trans-oceanic lines to India, Australia, North and South America and Europe. Each of these four markets required ships of appropriate size and type, ranging from small, Japanese-style ships for local services to the very large modern ships needed for trans-oceanic crossings.

In all except the most localised of these markets, there was serious competition in the 1870s and 1880s, but as the Meiji economy grew, Japanese shippers eventually established themselves in both the long-distance coastal and local lines, thereby underpinning the expansion of the Osaka Tekko and Kawasaki yards. In addition, regional lines flourished after Japanese expansion in Formosa, Korea, Manchuria and the Yangtze valley, thereby generating profits for the Kawasaki, Mitsubishi and Osaka yards. At the top end, growing business on the trans-oceanic lines supported Mitsubishi and other large yards.[59]

The link between market expansion and technical progress was not

58. 'The Kawasaki Dockyard Company Ltd.', *FER*, April 1911, pp. 391–5.

59. The general expansion of the companies is concisely explained in William D. Wray, 'Shipping from Sail to Steam' in Marius B. Jansen and Gilbert Rozman (eds), *Japan in Transition: From Tokugawa to Meiji*, Princeton University Press, 1986, pp. 248–70. The intense competitiveness on Asian routes is a theme of the early part of Marriner and Hyde, *The Senior John Samuel Swire*. The relationship between markets and shipbuilding is explained in Nakaoka, 'Technological leaps'.

simply a matter of the former paying for the latter. The relationship was much more dynamic, since Japanese shipowners and shipbuilders competed not only by emulating western techniques, but also by going beyond them in ways that sharpened their competitive strengths, especially in East Asia and the Pacific where they saw their most promising markets. For example, in 1911 Mitsui ordered British ships for the coal trade embodying a novel cantilever construction that gave larger loading space and greater seaborne stability. For the Chinese coastal and Yangtze valley lines, Japanese yards built vessels that had the unusual combination of strength, power and shallow drafts necessary for the peculiar conditions met in these waters.[60] For the great trans-oceanic routes, vessels were designed to optimise speed and luxury, with care being taken to meet the tastes and requirements of the various passenger groups being competed for. Thus while Edwardian gentlemen travelling first class enjoyed 'exquisite cuisine', panelled lounges decorated in white and gold, open fires in winter, air-conditioning in summer and the 'general air of comfort so beloved of the English', the Toyo Kisen Line added to their second and steerage classes a special 'Chinese' class to improve competitiveness in this commercially significant segment of the market.[61]

Skill in segmenting the market and competing by qualitative attractions was very important in shipping because prices (i.e. shipping tariffs) were generally fixed by shipping conferences, of which Japanese lines became active members.[62] Japan's shipping lines, moreover, were part of a wider strategy to compete in the provision of international travel services that included the linking of shipping routes to the South Manchurian Railway to provide direct services to Europe and connecting both railways and shipping to Japanese hotels which,

60. 'Navigating the upper Yangtze', *FER*, Jan. 1921, p. 11.
61. The *Tenyo Maru* accommodated 78 first-class, 238 second-class, 791 steerage and 1,260 'Chinese' steerage passengers. See the articles cited above on the three Mitsubishi liners. An earlier example of a trans-Pacific liner built in Britain to Japanese specification and embodying similar features is discussed in 'The Toyo Kisen Kaisha's new steamer *Nippon Maru*', *NCH*, Dec. 24 1898. Japanese skills in 'non-price competition' in passenger ships were specifically noted by analysts. It may well have been the case that the cheaper classes subsidised the more expensive one. This was later to be the case on the South Manchurian Railway, where travellers in the luxurious first class were subsidised by those travelling in the 'hard'.
62. The Far Eastern conferences were very much the creation of Swire. The NYK, after some early price cutting, joined in 1896.

like the Pacific liners, matched any that could be found in the region.[63]

By 1914, though still small by British standards, Japanese shipping and shipbuilding had achieved parity in many ways with any country in the world. It was the country's dominant and most advanced heavy industry, directly responsible for growth in steel and other related industries. In the naval sphere, Japanese vessels built before the war not only reached world standards but illustrated in several ways the Japanese capacity to innovate as well as emulate. On the foundations laid by Meiji shipbuilders and shipping companies, Japan took advantage of the special circumstances of the First World War to bring about a spectacular expansion in its activities. In 1914 the volume of imported ships had been equal to 55% of domestic output, but by 1919 output had increased elevenfold, while imports had fallen to nothing. In the same period shipping earnings transformed Japan's invisible balance of payments from a deficit of ¥6.5 million to a surplus of over ¥500 million.[64]

After the war, the profits generated in shipping were used to engender diversification into new technologies and new forms of import substitution. The achievement of Japanese shipbuilders was recognised in requests from the American government and others to assist the rebuilding of their merchant marines.

State-led import substitution in other strategic industries: guns, aircraft, communications, electrics and optics

The experience of import substitution in shipbuilding has been dealt with in some detail because it is so important and because it illustrates

63. It was said of the new Yokohama Grand Hotel that its 'magnificent salle de fête and wine café adjacent constitute quite the finest set of entertaining and banqueting rooms in the Far East,' 'The new Grand Hotel at Yokohama', *FER*, Nov. 1908, pp. 196–7.

64. Oishi Kaichiro (ed.), *Nihon teikokushugishi: dai ichiji dai senki* (The history of Japanese imperialism. The First World War), Tokyo: Tokyo Daigaku Shuppankai, 1985, gives a detailed analysis of the development of industry in the war. Shipping and shipbuilding are discussed on p. 54 and pp. 199–204. Wartime shipping profits were so notorious that they gave rise to the phrase *fune narikin* (to become a millionaire through ships), Arisawa Hiromi (ed.), *Showa keizaishi* (The economic history of the Showa period), Tokyo: Nihon Keizai Shimbunsha, 1976, pp. 5–6.

graphically the key features of technology transfer in the strategic sector. However, planned import substitution was taking place in many other industries and by 1937 was either well advanced or had at least laid the foundations for rapid development after the Second World War.

Here we examine two strategic industries, guns and aeroplanes, and three others, communications, electric light bulbs and optics which, while strategic at the beginning, were the foundations of what later became great commercial developments. In turning to the military industries we must remember that the Franco-Prussian war of 1870–71 (Meiji 3–4) was the first war in which armaments on both sides were the products of factory mass-production and in which troop transport was by train. The significance of this new integration of civilian and military industry was not lost in Japan, where the impact of military activities on the trade cycle was to be large and where the railways were nationalised in the strategic interest in 1906.[65] The Satsuma rebellion and the wars with China and Russia were each important factors in the expansion of civilian industry and in improvements in its technological capabilities. This was because military requirements for manufactured goods extended far beyond the capacities of the army and navy arsenals and created a demand for goods for which domestic capacity was either slight or non-existent.[66]

Gun-making. Gun manufacture is one of the best examples of the impact of army and naval procurement on technical progress in Japanese industry. Japan had a solid foundation for gun-making. There was a three-hundred-year-old tradition of copying western firearms (Chapter 1) and it was estimated that the total stock of imported rifles during the late Tokugawa period amounted to nearly half a million pieces. But these advantages were soon lost, since the opening of Japan and the Meiji Restoration coincided almost exactly with a gun-making revolution in the West. Whereas improvements in gun-making between the Napoleonic and Crimean wars (1853–56) had been only marginal, by the early twentieth century the power, range and accuracy of all kinds of western guns had been transformed by

65. See E. A. Pratt, *The Rise of Rail Power in War and Conquest, 1833–1914*, Westminster: P. S. King, 1915, esp. the chapter on the Franco-Prussian war.

66. As late as 1913 the army's requirements for civilian goods included 436,000 sets of horseshoes. Kobayashi, *Military Industries of Japan*, p. 99.

Table 10.8. PHASES OF TECHNICAL PROGRESS
IN GUN-MAKING, 1841–1908

1841	Prussia adopts the needle gun (bolt-action, breech-loading rifle).
1862	Invention of the Gatling (machine) gun.
1857–67	Development of rifled steel gun-barrels by Armstrong and Whitworth in Britain.
1866–71	Britain, France, Sweden, Russia and Italy adopt breech-loading military rifles.
1870–71	German bombardment of Paris and Strasbourg with Krupp guns demonstrates the power of contemporary ordnance.
1882	Maxim gun patented (advanced machine-gun).
1886	French adopt smokeless gunpowder.
1907–08	Japanese stabilise army gun models with the Rifle of the 38th Year, the Japanese Hotchkiss machine-gun and the Field-Gun of the 38th Year.

major improvements in steel casting and machine-tool accuracy as well as by the development of mechanisms for automatic weapons and machine-guns.[67] In the later nineteenth century, the pacemaker in big gun-making was Krupp, with its secret techniques for the production of ever larger and finer steel barrels.[68] The main phases of this revolution are set out in Table 10.8.[69]

67. Machine-tool accuracy was particularly crucial for the improvement in small arms. During the 1870s, small arms specifications required a reduction in tolerances from hundredths to thousandths of an inch. In 1874–76, the American firm of Brown Sharpe provided the key to this with their Universal Cyclindrical Grinding machine. This breakthrough thus coincided almost exactly with both the early years of Meiji military development and, in Europe, with the unification of Germany, whose machine-tool and weapons makers rapidly moved to the forefront of this technology.

68. The scale and technological intensity of the Krupp enterprises were extraordinary. The gun-making facility employed 100 furnaces working 24 hours a day as well as 310 steam-engines for metal fabrication. In a workforce of 50,000, Krupp employed 5,000 engineers and in the early 1900s the Krupp factories consumed half a million tonnes of coke and 700,000 tonnes of oil a year in Essen alone. Even in 1910, self-preservation still forced half of the world's modern armies, including the Japanese, to buy Krupp guns. *EB* (11th edn), vol. 20, pp. 210–12; Routledge, *Discoveries and Inventions*, pp. 127–60. For a vivid account of the Krupp enterprises based on a personal visit see Jules Huret, *En Allemagne. Rhin et Westphalie*, Paris: Charpentier, 1907, pp. 322–61.

69. This section is based on articles on 'rifles', 'guns', 'machine-guns' and 'ordnance' in *EB* (11th edn), articles in the general technology works referred to in ch. 9 and, of particular value, W. W. Greener, *The Gun and its Development*, (9th edn) London: Cassell, 1910. Greener was himself an innovatory gun-maker, responsible for the first

Keeping abreast of these developments was critical for national security. The Prussian victories between 1864 and 1871 over Denmark, Austria and France, and the Turkish resistance against Russia in 1877–78, were each attributed to superior gun technology. And as we have seen both China and Japan were attacked in the 1860s by forces employing advanced guns.[70] Japan was aware of these unfolding technologies. As early as the war over Schleswig-Holstein in 1864, two Tokugawa students undergoing naval training in the Netherlands succeeded in obtaining the passports and introductions necessary to inspect the war from both sides of the fighting front. Particulary impressed by the Schreider rifle and Krupp breech-loading field-gun, they even attempted — unsuccessfully — to inspect the Krupp factories at Essen.[71]

The rapid Japanese response to new gun technologies was reflected in the development of metallurgy. The qualities and strengths of the metals needed for guns were initially high and rose rapidly as ever higher standards of accuracy and distance were called for and as the explosive power of ordnance increased. Thus the demand for modern steel in Japan was closely related to gun-making requirements. Developments specifically related to gun-making and ordnance included the installation of an innovatory reverberatory furnace at the Osaka arsenal in 1882, the use of a giant steam-hammer for metal forging in the Tokyo arsenal in 1895 and the first production of nickel-chrome steel (for 24 mm. cannon shells) at Osaka in 1901.[72]

In addition to steel for barrel-making, Japan had to keep pace with the mechanisms needed for breech-loading techniques, automatic rifles,

---

expansionary bullets, and although his interests were more in sporting guns, his book has full descriptions of contemporary military rifles and detailed accounts of the trials in which newer, more sophisticated weapons were tested against earlier models.

70. In the Russo–Turkish wars, the Turkish advantage included breech-loading Krupp artillery, and Winchester repeating and Peabody-Martini rifles.

71. These students were Miyanaga Takaaki and Akamatsu Noriyoshi, both of whom were to have important careers in the defence and government establishments. Although unable to gain access to Krupp's factories, they did manage to get an invitation to dinner with the great industrialist himself. Details based on materials in Takahashi Miyanaga, *Bakufu Oranda ryugakusei* (Japanese students in the Netherlands in the Bakufu period), Tokyo, 1982.

72. The connection between steel and naval gun-making as well as shipbuilding is emphasised by Nakaoka, *Technology and technology policy*, p. 211. Other data from Kobayashi and Yamamura.

quick-firing field guns, machine-guns, and all forms of naval ordnance. The army and navy monitored international data on these, hired French, Belgian and Italian specialists to help them keep pace and, during the Meiji period, successfully arranged for Japanese to learn from the Krupp and Creusot works. But although rapid progress was made and mass production of rifles was well established by the 1870s, keeping up with advances in automatic weapons and Krupp metallurgical specifications was an endless problem. After both the Chinese and Russian wars, emergency imports and a major upgrading of domestic skills were essential to maintain required capabilities.[73] The Russians in particular imported very advanced gun technologies and hence were a constant threat to neighbours less well equipped than they.[74] Comparative data for field guns and naval ordnance around 1907–10 suggest that by a combination of imports and import substitution Japan had achieved parity with international standards in these categories of weapons.[75]

The spillover effects from gun-making, in conjunction with those from shipbuilding, were considerable. The arsenals and later the Yawata and Muroran steel plants were pioneers in the production of Japanese textile and other machinery. They also made steel for railways and engaged in bridge-building and a variety of civil engineering projects. In the 1900s Japanese steel plants actually had labour productivity levels about one-third of those found in similar plants in the west. This reflected low skill levels in operating new plant and a deliberate, and quite rational policy of substituting labour for capital in ancillary operations.[76] In the 1920s wage inflation and inappropriate exchange-rate policies destroyed this early competitiveness, but as always government policies found a way (through concentration, rationalisation and development of the private financial market) to allow the industry to prolong its learning and maintain its trajectory of labour productivity

73. Hayashi discusses the particularly serious re-evaluation that took place after the Sino-Japanese war in *A history*, pp. 120–6. See also Nakaoka on the continuing problems with guns and munitions, pp. 203–9.

74. A great deal of information on Armstrong and Krupp guns and competition is in Scott, *Vickers: A History*, ch. 1.

75. Detail on Japanese gun-making is in Nakaoka, *Technology and technology policy*, and in Kobayashi, *Military Industries of Japan*. The international comparative data are in *EB* (11th edn), vol. 20, pp. 210–19.

76. Tetsuji Okazaki, 'Import substitution and competitiveness in the pre-war Japanese iron and steel industry' in Etsuo Abe and Yoshitaka Sukuzi (eds), *Changing Patterns of International Rivalry: Some Lessons from the Steel Industry*, University of Tokyo Press, 1991, pp. 166–90.

improvement until it finally emerged as the world leader in the late 1960s.[77]

Communications and electrical industries. These industries were barely in existence at the time of the Meiji Restoration, and it was the military bureaucracy that led research in telegraph, telephone and wireless communications. As a result, the Japanese navy was the first of the world's navies to have a wireless communication system, and both the Sino-Japanese and Russo-Japanese wars were followed by major programmes of communication expansion.[78] Although the overall rate of diffusion of telephones for civilian purposes was still low early in the century, the direct line installed between Tokyo and the naval base at Sasebo in 1904 was the second-longest direct inter-city line in the world, exceeded only by the connection between Boston and Galveston, Texas. Expansion programmes were particularly developed to improve communications within the Japanese empire; in Korea, for example, 71% of all telephone capacity in 1905 was controlled by the army.

In the electrical sector, the government's role was important but less direct. It set standards and agreed explicit programmes of import substitution, but this was an industry where collaboration with private business was essential. Within this sector, the electric bulb industry is a good illustration of how collaboration to reduce import penetration worked.[79]

Electric lighting was important in Japan for both street lighting and household use and for facilitating night-work in textile factories. In 1884–85 the government agreed its first import substitution plan and in 1885 specialists were sent to the Philadelphia Electrical Exhibition and to bulb manufacturing plants in Europe and the United States. Between 1886 and 1891 a number of private-sector Japanese bulb manufacturers were set up, and in one of them, Tokyo Denkyu, a government-supported experimental manufacturing facility was established. By 1890 domestic production was established in several companies, but inadequate skills, especially in glass-making and the small scale of production kept costs higher and quality lower than competing imports.

77. Okazaki, in Abe and Suzuki, *Changing Patterns*, pp. 166–90.

78. Nakaoka, *Technology and technology policy*, p. 210. General information for this section is from MITI, *Machinery*, vol. 18, p. 119 and pp. 225–33.

79. Based on the account in MITI, *op. cit.*, pp. 243ff., and Nakaoka, *op. cit.*, pp. 200–2.

The Sino-Japanese war gave the industry a temporary boost but the struggle against imports resumed in the late 1890s. In 1901 imports of bulbs reached their highest level ever. Thereafter, however, the industry was transformed by three developments. First, in 1904 the government used its newly-won tariff autonomy to put a 10% tariff on bulb imports. Secondly, in the same year General Electric and Tokyo Denki established a technical cooperation agreement, which within a short time gave the Japanese company the right to use the newly-developed tungsten filament. Finally, imports were seriously disrupted during the Russo-Japanese war and shipping costs rose, giving domestic production a chance to expand and, at last, obtain the necessary economies of scale. By 1914 the industry was fully established at home and by the 1920s had become a successful exporter in East and South-East Asia.

Lenses and optical equipment. The transfer of western optical knowledge to Japan started as early as the seventeenth century with the first Japanese copies of western-made spectacles. However, although some basic skills were transferred, Japanese inability to make optical glass made imported lenses (or Japanese lenses made with 'blue plate' glass from the Netherlands) the superior choice throughout the Tokugawa period.[80] The situation changed radically in the early Meiji period. There were renewed Japanese efforts to improve lens-making and the development of an active import trade in western photographic goods enabled Asanuma Tokichi, formerly a merchant dealing in traditional drugs and pharmaceuticals, to establish Japan's first photographic store, the Asanuma Shokai, in 1871. Asanuma and others moved quickly from selling to manufacture, with sufficient progress in the latter for Asanuma to win second prize for camera design and construction with a wooden camera displayed at the Paris Exposition of 1900.[81]

Japanese military awareness of optics intensified in the Russo-Japanese war, when reconnaissance and rangefinders for field-guns became serious issues. Lense-making was an advanced western technology

80. Tatsuzo Ueda, *The Development of the Eyeglass Industry in Japan*, Tokyo: United Nations University Press, 1979. The Jesuits brought spectacles as gifts in the sixteenth century, and the oldest spectacles in Japan are two European pairs that belonged to Tokugawa Ieyasu.

81. See John R. Baird, *The History of the Japanese Camera*, Yakima, WA.: Historical Camera Publications, 1990, ch. 1.

constantly driven forward by Zeiss. By the 1900s this firm had established clear supremacy in research, development and manufacturing techniques, yet was happy to license foreign manufacturers. In this way it was able to limit to some extent the incentives for American and other European competitors to catch up. Although Japan's first lens factory opened in 1876, it was not till the suspension of European supplies of optical glass in the First World War that the urgency of the need to establish an independent, world-class Japanese lens-making capability was fully understood. During the war, the navy established a facility for optical goods which, with difficulty, began producing lenses of reasonable quality. By the end of the war it was clear that the optical requirements of land, sea and air conflict were going to be large, and a number of companies appeared. Of these, Nikon was to be by far the most important. Founded in 1917 through an amalgamation of three existing companies, it enjoyed the support of the navy and Mitsubishi. Its first successful products were binoculars for the Japanese navy and as early as 1919 the company seized the opportunity to supply the Russians with a consignment of 2,000 instruments.[82]

In the early post-war years, Nikon cooperated with military and academic specialists in an intensive programme of learning and technology transfer. As soon as post-war diplomatic conditions allowed, the company sent students and technological scouts to four European countries and, with the help of eight German lens-making specialists and mathematicians who settled in Japan, began the transfer of the best European techniques. In 1923 the great Kanto earthquake destroyed the Navy's experimental glass–making plant, and the responsibility for this work was transferred to Nikon, for which the navy bought a second 500 kg. glass furnace in 1925. The Washington Conference naval agreements of 1922 led to a sharp decline in Japanese defence and naval expenditure, and Nikon spent the rest of the 1920s in conditions close to insolvency — a period described in the company history as the 'era of bitter struggle' (*kuto jidai*). But because the company was crucial to Japan's military import substitution, some contract

82. This section is based mainly on the encyclopaedic Kogaku Kogyoshi Henshukai *History of the Japanese optical industry* and the four Nikon company histories. The introduction to the former emphasises that it was written to preserve a record of the secret achievements of the pre-war Japanese optical designers and producers. Of the Nikon histories, the most important are the first (1942) and last (1993).

work did continue in conjunction with a new optical research centre established by the navy in 1924. By 1928 the last of Nikon's foreign employees returned to Europe and in the same year Sunayama Kakuya, the company's chief lens designer, visited a series of European lens-makers before returning to design Nikon's first commercial photographic lens.[83]

Orders from the army following the Manchurian invasion of 1931 transformed the industry's prospects. Between 1925 and 1936 Nikon increased output threefold and research and development expenditures eighteenfold.[84] The resumption of naval construction and the establishment of a new naval optical testing unit at the Yokosuka base in the 1930s provided still more work for Nikon and other private sector optical manufacturers.

Because their work was for the military, it is hard to document the activities of the Japanese optical companies in these years, or to estimate precisely the technological level they had reached. However, our sources do throw light on the activities of the larger companies. They reveal that the range of instruments produced was huge and included many varieties of telescopes, binoculars, gun-sights, range-finders, navigational instruments, periscopes, and the photographic equipment needed for reconnaissance. Among these instruments were the legendary fifteen and twenty eight metre Nikon 'mast' telescopes, which were used to look over forests (see pp. 280–1), a five-metre long, lorry-mounted reconnaissance camera for the army, and a battery of ten fifteen-metre rangefinders for the *Yamato*, the construction of which involved an accuracy of prism construction sixty times greater than that conventionally applied.[85]

By the 1940s Japanese quality standards were equal or superior to those of any other country, including Germany. Captured Japanese optics were described by the US War Department as 'outstanding' and Japanese binoculars, with their superior lens coating and night viewing abilities, were among the most sought-after trophies of

83. Sunayama's report is in *Nippon kogaku* (1957), pp. 151–7.

84. *Nippon kogaku nijugonenshi* (The twenty-five year history of the Nikon Company), Tokyo, 1942, pp. 197–8 and *Nikon nanajugonenshi* (The seventy-five year history of Nikon), Tokyo, 1993, chs. 1–2. The latter reports an explosion in the number of patents filed in the early 1930s.

85. Details of these instruments are in *Nippon kogaku* (1957), p. 479; *Nikon nanajugonshi* (1993), pp. 77–8.

American naval officers.[86] At the end of the war, Nikon alone was employing 23,000 workers in nineteen factories.

The speed of Nikon's re-orientation to civilian markets may be judged from the following. Japan surrendered to the Allies on 14 August 1945. On 1 September the company established fifteen working groups to assess the potential for civilian production of seventy Nikon products and, by the 20th of that month, thirty-eight had been selected. Nine days later, production plans for these were ready for submission to the Occupation authorities.

The speed of this process was undoubtedly influenced by Nikon's pre-war experience in the production of civilian binoculars, scientific instruments, camera lenses and the magnificent eight inch reflector telescope for the Imperial observatory, which is still in use today. At this stage, cameras were given top priority in terms of further research only, but within a year trial production of miniature cameras had begun.

Four Nikon innovations proved critically important to Japanese competitiveness in the post-war period, namely: lens-coating (for submarine periscopes);[87] prism-making (for submarine periscopes and the vital component of the reflex camera); mass production techniques (to meet demand for binoculars in the latter part of the war when skilled labour was unobtainable); and early experimentation with the integration of optical, mechanical and electrical techniques. By the early 1950s the superior quality of Japanese optics was recognised worldwide. In the following decades, the Japanese industry went on to dominate the world market, first through the reflex camera revolution and later by the application of electronics to cameras and optical instruments.[88]

What is so striking in the four Nikon company histories is the long-term consistency of the company's belief that, whatever the circum-

86. US War Department, *Handbook on Japan's Military Forces*, Washington, D.C.: Government Printing Office, 1944, p. 29; and S.E. Morison, *History of United States Naval Operations in World War Two*, vol. 3, p. 24.

87. The thirty-two optical elements of the standard Nikon ten-metre naval periscope were responsible for large light losses. Japanese submarine commanders wished to use these periscopes in the low light of dawn and early evening, and put severe pressure on Nikon to improve them. This was done by developing new coating techniques to minimise light loss. These advances were later found greatly to enhance the performance of camera lenses with as few as four elements; thus coating was probably the single most important reason why post-war Nikon lenses became superior to German ones.

88. The conversion to civilian markets and camera development are described in *Nikon nanajugonenshi* (1993), ch. 3 and Robert Rotolin, *The Nikon Rangefinder Camera*, Brighton: Hove Foto Books, 1983.

Table 10.9. TECHNICAL PROGRESS IN AEROPLANES, 1908–18

		Weight (lb.)	Lifting surface	h.p.	h.p. per 1,000 lb.	Speed (m.p.h.)
Wright	1908	1,000	540	25	25	40
Martinsyde F4	1918–19	2,290	330	300	130	145
Handley-Page V/1500	1918–19	24,100	2,900	1,440	60	90

Source: 'Aeronautics', *EB* (12th edn), p. 22.

stances, the key to success is absolute technological leadership. This philosophy was reflected in the high level of resources devoted to education, training and research, regardless of the company's current financial position. From the First World War to 1945 the drive to emulate and surpass western technical levels was dominated by Japanese defence and imperial goals. Yet even when the industry was forced to make a revolutionary adaptation to market forces in the post-war period, the underlying philosophy of action remained precisely the same.

Aircraft. In looking finally at aircraft, we are turning to the study of a latecomer industry, unknown at the time of the Meiji Restoration, and an industry which might reasonably be considered the last industrial revolution before the arrival of the microchip. Thus by the time Japanese learning in this field began, the governmental and corporate capabilities necessary for sophisticated technology transfer had already been acquired. In the West the first significant aeroplane flights only took place between 1908–9, and at the outbreak of war in 1914 aeroplanes were still largely the preoccupation of brilliant, individualistic engineers. All this was transformed by the war, in which aircraft were used first for reconnaissance and later for combat and bombing. The acceleration of technical development under war conditions is illustrated by comparing the Wright plane with two planes built in 1918–19 (see Table 10.9).

The industrial consequences of aircraft development may be judged from the facts that in France alone 51,000 planes and 92,000 aero-engines were built during the four years of the war. These were machines of rising performance in speed, attainable altitudes and manoeuvrability.[89]

---

89. Maurice Percheron, *L'Aviation Française*, Paris: Fernand Nathan, 1948, p. 106. The Spad was the outstanding French plane, several of which were bought by the Japanese army.

In the inter-war years technical progress in the industry continued, taking three main forms: the substitution of metals for wood, improved
fuselage and wing designs and ever more powerful engines. For all of
these improvements the development of new methods for fabricating
and welding duralumin and nickel alloy steels was critical.

Aeronautical development was studied closely in Japan, where it was
immediately taken with the greatest official seriousness and a firm
grasp of its military potential.[90] It was never in any important sense
a civilian industry. Balloon reconnaissance had been practised by the
army since the 1870s, and in 1909 a major military investigation into
aircraft was mounted in the wake of the flights by the Wright
brothers, Blériot and Farman.[91] In 1910 two army officers became
the pioneers of Japanese flying by demonstrating their abilities on
imported planes. In 1911 one of these pioneers, with the auspicious
name of Captain Tokugawa, designed an improved Farman model
which, when constructed by the army balloon unit, became the first
plane made in Japan. Japanese-flown planes were used briefly in China
in 1914, and by the end of the war both the navy and the army had
established separate research units and flying corps. Even before the
war, the exceptional importance and dangers of the industry were
recognised in an Imperial rescript that provided pensions for killed and
wounded aviators as well as prizes for long-distance flights.[92]

During the 1920s the industry remained basically dependent on
public-sector interest.[93] The navy and army brought in teams of

---

90. Eiichiro Sekigawa, *Pictorial History of Japanese Military Aviation*, London: Ian
Allen, 1974, ch. 1. Other basic sources used for the history of Japanese aviation are
Masatake Okumiya and Jiro Horikoshi, *The Zero Fighter*, London: Cassell, 1958;
Nihon Hankyu Kyokai (ed.), *Nihon hankyushi* (A history of Japanese aviation), Tokyo,
1956; Shibusawa Ton, *Hikoki rokujunen* (Sixty years of aeroplanes), Tokyo: Toshokan
Shuppansha, 1973; and materials in MITI, vol. 18, *Machinery*, esp. pp. 188ff. and
308–19. The most important English sources, which include comprehensive photo-
graphs, drawings and technical details from 1910 down to the 1940s, are René J.
Francillon, *Japanese Aircraft of the Pacific War*, London: Putnam, 1979, and Robert
C. Mikesh and Shorzoe Abe, *Japanese Aircraft, 1910–1941*, London: Putnam, 1990.

91. This was the Rinji Kikyu Kenkyukai (Provisional Committee for Balloon
Research), a joint navy and army organisation.

92. 'Japan in 1913', *NCH*, Jan. 24, 1914.

93. While Britain and France had 108 and 57 private airfields respectively in 1922,
Japan had *none*. 'Aviation in Japan: A new opening for American machines', *FER*,
July, 1922, pp. 453–4.

foreigners to advise them on technology and organisation and, between them, imported examples of all the important monoplanes, biplanes and seaplanes currently in use and under development in the West. They also bought licences for the manufacture of all important aero-engines.[94]

As early as 1929 and with renewed determination after 1932, Japan launched programmes to achieve total import substitution and self-sufficiency in aircraft technology. As a result, data on aircraft production and performance in the 1930s were largely kept secret; most western observers of Japan's achievement in capturing the Tokyo to London speed record failed to appreciate the true significance of the event, regarding the flight as a prank, which was in fact nearly the case for many of the early western pioneer flights.

The nature of the *kokusanka* programme for production in the aircraft industry differed from that in the older strategic industries. One reason for this was that both the army and the navy were seeking to attach the new technology to their forces, and rivalry between them was so intense that they would not share either research or basic performance data. Another factor was that by the 1920s the private sector had the capacity to handle contracts for production and for research and development. Thus the public sector was not called upon to bear all of the financial and organisational costs of pioneering the new technologies in aircraft manufacture. These private-sector strengths were found in two distinct types of company. One group consisted of the old shipyards, with their broad and diversified engineering skills, their long experience and their huge accumulated profits from the First World War. Mitsubishi, Kawasaki and Ishikawajima were the main examples of this type. The other group were companies founded by brilliant aeronautical engineers or companies converted from very different initial technologies. The outstanding examples of this group

94. The army hired Colonel Faure, who came with sixty-nine staff and Spad fighters from France. The navy hired Sir Francis Sempill, who brought with him a team of twenty-nine instructors and a collection of Blackburn Swifts, Gloster Sparrowhawks and two seaplanes. Sempill reported that his Japanese pilots were 'fearless' and superior to his English ones. The Renault, Gnome and Mercedes-Benz were initially judged the best engines for the Japanese to copy and use. Key foreign designers active in Japan were Dr Baumann from Germany and Herbert Smith of Sopwith in Britain. See MITI, vol. 18, *Machinery*, pp. 188ff.; Sekigawa, *Pictorial History*, pp. 19–22; 'The Japanese as airmen', *NCH*, April 7, 1923.

were Nakajima and Aichi.[95] In all types of company, one common strength was that, because of the totally new character of the technology, not only the most brilliant but generally the youngest engineers had to be used, irrespective of all normal conventions of craftsmanship and seniority.

During the 1920s the companies studied western machines, sent staff abroad and developed relationships with key foreign partners. Because of inter-service rivalry, most companies belonged either to the 'navy group' or to the 'army group', with Mitsubishi, the most powerful of all, working in both.[96] Both the army and the navy developed the practice of inviting the private sector to compete for contracts to develop their major aircraft, and although the practices of secrecy were damaging, the evidence suggests that the competitiveness generated by the triple rivalry of individual entrepreneurs, services and companies provided stimuli and mechanisms for technical progress as powerful as anything found in market economies.[97] The overall system was certainly effective enough to ensure that as early as 1936, the industry believed that by a combination of engine power, innovative aerodynamic design and development of extra super duralumin, all embodied in the A5M ('Claude') fighter and G3M ('Nell') long-distance bomber, Japan had reached, and in some ways surpassed, world standards in warplane design and production.[98]

95. Important materials on Nakajima and his circle are in Nakagawa Ryoichi *et al.* (eds), *Nakajima enjinshi wakai gijutsusha shudan katsuyaku* (The history of Nakajima aero-engines: The activities of a group of young engineers), Tokyo: Kantosha, n.d.

96. In 1925 Nakajima, Kawasaki and Mitsubishi were invited to compete for a light bomber contract and the navy later invited Mitsubishi and Nakajima to tender for their key fighter contract. Sekigawa, *Pictorial History*, pp. 22, 53. Membership of the army and navy 'groups' is listed in MITI, vol. 18, *Machinery*, p. 316.

97. When Admiral Yamamoto observed the progress of Mitsubishi army bombers in the early 1930s, he overruled his subordinates and insisted on transferring the design and development of the the G3M bomber to Mitsubishi and the private sector. See discussion in Richard M. Bueschal, *Mitsubishi: Nakajima G3M 1/2/3 in Japanese Naval Service*, London: Osprey, 1972.

98. The key state-of-the-art machines purchased by the Japanese for study in the 1930s were the Clark GA43 sold by General Aviation to Mitsui in 1934 and the proto-type DC4 acquired as late as 1939. The GA43 was a low-winged, all-metal, duralumin aircraft. The DC4 certainly influenced the Mitsubishi G3M. J. P. Gardiner, 'Design trajectories for airplanes and automobiles during the past fifty years' in Christopher Freeman (ed.), *Design, Innovation and Long Cycles in Economic Development*, London: Design Research Publications, 1984, pp. 185–213. The overall judgement of Japan's

The key information for judging the progress and technological level attained by the industry are analyses of the comparative performance of Japanese and Allied aircraft manufactured between 1937 and 1945. First, let us take three examples from the fighter class. In 1937 the navy commissioned Mitsubishi to build a fighter with a combination of performance specifications that in all important respects surpassed those of any contemporary western aircraft.[99] This was the Zero ('Zeke') series, which saw early active duty in the war against China. The Zero's dominance in China was so great that during a raid on Chengtu four Zeros actually landed on the Chengtu airfield, enabling Japanese aircrews to attack Chinese planes on the ground.[100] The significance of this early performance was not grasped by foreign observers at the time, but as soon as the Pacific war began in earnest, Allied analysts agreed that the plane had fulfilled all its design intentions. The Zero retained fighter supremacy in the Pacific until overtaken by new American planes, in particular the F6F Grumman Wildcat in 1942–43. Indeed, as one American authority has noted, 'It [the Zero] was the first carrier-based aircraft to equal or surpass the performance of the best contemporary land based fighters; it was superior to *any* fighter in the United States Army or Navy at the outbreak of war.'[101] The same year saw the appearance of the Hien Type 5, which was clearly superior not only to the contemporary Curtis P40E but also to the Messerschmidt P404, an example of which had been tested in Japan.[102] Finally, the Nakajima Ki 84, with a 2,000

technical level is that of Horikoshi Jiro, the head of the Zero fighter design team at Mitsubishi, quoted in Okumiya and Horikoshi, *The Zero Fighter*, pp. 73–5. 'Claude' and 'Nell' were American codenames for these aircraft, whose correct designations were often unknown at the time.

99. The key stimuli to development of this class of carrier-borne fighter were the performances of an imported Northrop Gamma in 1933 and a Fairchild A942 in 1936.

100. Wanda Cornelius and Thayne Short, *Ding Hao: The American Air War in China 1937–1945*, Gretna, LA: Pelican, 1980, pp. 97–8.

101. The quotation is from Spector, *Eagle against the Sun*, p. 46. Okumiya and Horikoshi, *The Zero Fighter*, is the most authoritative and technical source on this aircraft. Details of the Zero models are also in Francillon, *Japanese Aircraft*, and H. P. Willmott, *Zero A6M*, London: Arms and Armour Press, 1980. The Zero can be seen on video and, for real enthusiasts, a specialised dealer in California could still supply a complete working aircraft as recently as 1990.

102. Francillon, *Japanese Aircraft*, pp. 112–19, and William Green, *Famous Fighters of the Second World War*, London: Macdonald, 1960, pp. 107–10.

h.p. engine, entered the war in 1945. A captured version of this plane was later taken to California for exhaustive analysis, from which it emerged that its engine was equal to its contemporary Pratt and Whitney counterpart and that its overall performance (measured by a combination of speed, rate of climb and manoeuvrability) was superior to all contemporary western competitors including the Super-marine Spitfire and Hawker Hurricane.[103]

Among larger planes was the Mitsubishi G3M ('Nell'), for which the navy let its first development contracts in 1932.[104] The early versions of this plane were fitted with Rolls Royce engines, but these were replaced by Mitsubishi engines based on Rolls Royce and Benz designs. In 1938 a group of G3Ms accomplished bombing missions in China which were the first trans-oceanic missions in aviation history, and the ones covering the longest distance ever. In 1941 the same planes took western experts by surprise in the role they played in the sinking of the battleships *Repulse* and *Prince of Wales*, an action which ended British naval supremacy in the Far East.[105]

Some western analysts have emphasised that Japanese aircraft were derivative in design, implying that at best the Japanese industry was still in the phase of technological catching-up. There is truth in this viewpoint, yet the extent of catching-up can be illustrated by the fact that when a planned post-war transfer of aerospace technology from America to Japan was undertaken, it was found that of the hundreds of processes involved in aircraft construction, Japan lacked only three.[106]

However, catching-up was not the whole story. In 1937 the Air Ministry could realistically ask Nakajima to prepare designs for a plane capable of attacking the world speed record. By assiduous study of

103. *Nakajima K1-84*, Fulbrook, CA: Aero Publishers, 1965.

104. See Bueschal, *Mitsubishi: Nakajima G3M 1/2/3.*; Francillon, *Japanese Aircraft*, pp. 350–7; and for an excellent recent analysis of this plane, Bernard Millot, 'Le Mitsubishi G3M "Nell" ', *Le Fanatique de l'Aviation*, Oct. 1991, pp. 18–27.

105. The British underestimation of Japanese airpower in this episode is documented in Correlli Barnett, *Engage the Enemy More Closely: The Royal Navy in the Second World War*, London: Hodder and Stoughton, 1991, ch. 13.

106. These were chemical milling techniques, spray mat processes for icing control and high temperature treatments for steel. Among the 181 'hardcore' components in the transfer programme for the F-104J, lack of the relevant technical capability was a factor in only ten items and in no case was it the sole factor. G. R. Hall and R. E. Johnson, *Transfers of United States Aerospace Technology to Japan*, Santa Monica, CA: Rand Corporation, 1968, pp. 32–3.

foreign advances Mitsubishi was by the late 1930s arguably among the world's leading constructors of air-cooled engine systems as well as a pioneer in aerodynamic design and the use of duralumin and other specialised metals in airframe and wing construction. Japanese manu-facturers also made innovations in instrumentation, specialised glass cockpits, auto-pilot systems, self-sealing and disposable auxiliary fuel tanks, split wing-flap devices and torpedo and radio communications systems. Towards the end of the war, Japanese development resources were stretched to intense limits, but despite overwhelming difficulties major innovations in rocket- and jet-powered planes reached an advanced stage of development. The problem of skill shortages and production bottlenecks prevented these prototypes from reaching the stage of production.[107]

Having achieved such success in military technology transfer and import substitution, it might seem puzzling that Japan came to lose the war. Clearly this question involves issues far beyond the scope of this study, but the answer does relate to the weaknesses and pecu-liarities of Japan's achievements in international technology transfer.

The first and overwhelming problem for the Japanese was simply that by the peak of the war (1943–44) they were outproduced by the United States in key sectors such as aircraft by a factor of 10–1. This reflected the massive resources which the United States had avail-able for production and the efficiency with which these resources were used. By the late 1930s American industry had been widely permeated by advanced systems of mass production, many pioneered by the automobile industry. By contrast, Japan, while advanced in design development and prototype manufacture, did not have a com-parable grasp or dissemination of mass production. Aircraft manufac-ture illustrated this clearly. For most of the war Japanese planes were still works of art — built individually or in small batches, with pro-duction depending 'heavily on the skill of workers able to do fine

---

107. Mitsubishi made a rocket-powered interceptor. This was inspired by the Messerschmitt Me 163B, of which a specimen was sunk en route to Japan in a German submarine. In the final months of the war, rocket-powered suicide planes reached 576 m.p.h. and Nakajima, always in the van, produced his *Kikka* engine for a prototype twin-engined fighter which flew only twice. Details in Francillon, *Japanese Aircraft* and *Famous Airplanes of the World: Army Experimental Fighters* (title in English, text in Japanese), Tokyo: Burin-Do, 1990. Further details of Japanese experimental planes of all kinds are in Mikesh and Abe, *Japanese Aircraft, 1910–1941*.

machining with comparatively simple universal machine tools . . . [and on] workers . . . strongly influenced by traditional craftsmanship, relying more on experience and manual skill than on scientific calculations and technical instructions'.[108] Towards the end of the war manufacturers were working hard to change this, especially in the aircraft industry, but by then it was far too late.[109]

Secondly, although Japan was at the forefront in many technologies and ahead in some, in certain critical areas it remained behind, if only marginally so. The outstanding example of this was the lack of fully developed and fitted naval radar systems. Radar was a technology still only at the developmental stage at the start of the war; failure to match western progress in this field proved fatal to Japan in the battles of Midway and Guadalcanal, where the ability to find and identify the enemy in poor visibility proved decisive. Even so, the narrowness of the technological gap may be judged from one estimate that in radar technology it was a matter of a mere six months.[110]

Finally, there was a wider problem, discussed in the next chapter. While the late nineteenth-century use of patriotism to drive technology transfers in civilian industry had notable successes, by the 1930s the Japanese were allowing their confidence in a combination of religious patriotism, the gigantic and the technically remarkable to outweigh all broader, common-sense considerations: 'We believed that our strength lay, not in massed physical power, but in the perfection of expertness. Pyramidding through each succeeding generation, this philosophy was apparently the unrealized inheritance of the modern Japanese Army and Navy.'[111] At a practical level, plane-makers were

108. The quotation is from Tetsuro Nakaoka, 'Production management in Japan before the period of high speed economic growth', *Osaka City University Economic Review*, no. 17, 1981, pp. 7–24.

109. Y. Hashiguchi, *Hankyuki kogyo no noritsu zoshin* (Increasing the efficiency of the aeroplane industry), Tokyo, 1944.

110. This problem and related issues are discussed in 'Analysis of the Defeat' in Mitsuo Fuchida and Masatake Okumiya, *Midway*, Annapolis: Naval Institute Press, 1955 (repr. 1988), pp. 232–48. See also John Deane Potter, *Yamamoto*, New York: Paperback Library, 1971, pp. 284, 320–1; and the judgement of another Japanese participant, Lt. Commander M. Hashimoto, *Sunk! The Story of the Japanese Submarine Fleet, 1942–1945*, London: Cassell, 1954, pp. 118–19.

111. Quotation from Okumiya and Horikoshi, *The Zero Fighter*, p. 163. Further evidence of the linking of patriotism and technology is the Foreword to the 1942 history of Nikon, which elaborates the point that, driven by patriotism, 'mass production and superlative technology will be the decisive keys determining victory or defeat

accused of developing gimmicks while ignoring more serious weaknesses in their aircraft; more fundamentally, the leadership failed to
appreciate either the quantitative shortcomings of Japanese industry or
the significance of contemporary developments in airpower for the
effectiveness of the large battleship. In a sense, therefore, the very
brilliance of the Japanese achievement in military technology transfer
and the misplaced self-confidence this generated became liabilities
which contributed to the eventual defeat.[112]

---

in the war'. *Nippon kogaku* (1942), p. 4. Something similar is also present in Part 2:
'Industrial Expansion due to Racial Traits', esp. ch. 6, 'Technical achievement and
the Japanese spirit' of Ginjiro Fujihara's *The Spirit of Japanese Industry*, Tokyo:
Hokuseido Press, 1940.

112. Some individuals did indeed understand the issues, but interservice rivalry
and communication failures made rational behaviour impossible. The fantastic
character of their thinking and the failure of Japanese leaders to communicate with
each other are themes of Masao Maruyama, 'Thought and behaviour patterns of Japan's
wartime leaders' in his *Thought and Behaviour in Modern Japanese Politics*, Oxford
University Press, 1963. The fatal gap between the rationality needed to create Japan's
war technology and the irrational psychology of those using it was perceptively
analysed by a contemporary Chinese intellectual, Chiang Monlin, a university vice-
chancellor who later had a distinguished career as an economic planner in Taiwan.
Chiang's observations on this issue were prompted by the sight of dead Japanese
airmen surrounded by both the scientific apparatus of aerial warfare and fragments
of Buddhist and Shinto charms. Chiang Monlin, *Tides from the West: A Chinese
Autobiography*, New Haven: Yale University Press, 1947, pp. 235–6.

11

TECHNOLOGY AND TRADE IN THE COMMERCIAL SECTOR

The three industries with which we are concerned here are cotton textiles, tea and silk. All three had long histories of traditional technology and all, initially at least, depended on domestic agriculture for their raw materials. Technology provided the keys to export expansion in tea and silk, and to both import substitution and exporting in cotton textiles, which eventually became the most successful commercial export of all. The urgency of cotton import substitution for national economic survival required that the industry be initially regarded as 'strategic', and therefore to be subsidised at almost any cost.

Cotton textiles

The main trend of technology development in textiles has already been outlined in Chapters 7 and 8. Here we briefly recapitulate the technological elements of that story, summarise its rationale and attempt to explain the unfolding progress in terms of government and company technology policies.

The key technology phases already discussed may be summarised as follows:

Phase

I	1867–	The importation of British spinning machinery.
II	Early 1880s	The choice by the private sector of large scale, steam-driven spinning plants using imported raw cotton.
III	Late 1880s	The decision to substitute ring for mule spinning.
IV	1890s–1920s	Further development of ring technology; the adoption of High Draft (Casablancas) systems and the diffusion of automatic looms.
V	1920s–1930s	The gradual achievement of world technological levels in spinning and weaving, making increasing use of domestic capital equipment and the close integration of technology and marketing strategies.

The rationale behind this sequence of decisions was that, compared to factory-made output, Japan's traditional textiles were unsuitable in kind and far too high in cost to stem the flow of imports, or to form a base for export expansion at a later date. It was therefore essential for Japan to shift to modern factory methods, although these were to be adapted as much as possible to allow hybrid technologies in the early Meiji period and substitution of labour for capital, especially low-cost female labour, throughout the entire period.

The introduction of western technology required capital, knowledge of contemporary foreign textile technologies and the acquisition by the Japanese of the skills to construct and operate new factories. Since capital markets in early Meiji were lacking and private-sector capacities for investigation of foreign conditions were minimal, government involvement in the initial establishment of the industry was indispensable. Even when it was established, time would be required for basic operating and managerial skills to be learned; hence some form of continuing subsidisation or protection would be necessary. In fact, this phase of direct assistance lasted till the mid-1880s, but even then shortfalls in Japanese skill levels required plant to be worked intensively by shift-work to achieve the further cost reduction needed for the industry to become competitive.

Once minimal competitiveness had been realised in the lower counts of the yarn market, the industry's progress took the form of further imports of plant, further adaptation and innovation of foreign technologies and rising blue- and white-collar skill levels. At first development was mainly concentrated in spinning but it later extended to the weaving sector. By the late 1930s Japan was broadly equalling or exceeding world standards of quality and of labour and machine productivity. Let us now consider the national and company policies responsible for this progress.

The first phase of technological development started with the establishment of the Kagoshima Cotton Spinning Works in 1867 and ended in 1889, when there was a clear turning-point in the industry's growth-rate and other aspects of its development. Even at the end of this period, the competitive capacity of the industry was weak, although a bridgehead had been established and national bankruptcy from excessive textile imports averted. This was accomplished through a strategy that facilitated the co-existence of traditional, modern and intermediate technology.[1] Traditional technology was important in

1. The key sources on cotton textile technology used here are Nakaoka, *Technology and technology policy*, ch. 1, part 2, and ch. 3; 'The role of domestic

weaving, which survived by exploiting the benefits of cheap imported yarns, low-cost household labour and close proximity to the domestic market. In spinning, however, factory production quickly made the traditional technology unviable.

At the other end of the spectrum, modern technology was introduced into the state-owned 'model' factories and into the private factories equipped with machinery procured by the government. Since state-owned enterprises made losses, and the equipment supplied to the private sector was subsidised, the government bore the direct cost of this protection. After 1879 the private sector was encouraged to take the lead in technology transfer and by the mid-1880s it had the knowledge, organisation and access to capital to do so.

During this difficult transitional period, an important role in maintaining domestic yarn production was played by the output of the *garabo* workshops.[2] The *garabo* spinning machine was an intermediate form of technology, in essence a semi-mechanised version of hand-spinning, and its emergence was no accident, in the sense that the traditional textile industry had developed complex, largely wooden, semi-mechanised machines well before the arrival of imported cottons. Government encouragement and market incentives drew on this achievement to produce a machine that was economically appropriate to the circumstances, for although only six to eight times as productive as hand-spinning, low labour costs enabled *garabo* output to compete against imported yarn produced on machinery at least twenty times as productive as hand-spinning. *Garabo* output peaked as early as 1887, and thereafter enjoyed a short further life spinning waste from

technical innovation in foreign technology transfer: The case of the Japanese cotton textile industry', *Osaka City University Economic Review*, no. 18, 1982, pp. 45–62; Y. Kiyokawa, 'The choice of technology in textiles: from the mule to the ring' in Minami and Kiyokawa (eds), *Japanese industrialisation*, pp. 83–107; 'Technological gaps and the process of stabilising imported technology, with special reference to the experience of the textile industry' in Ohkawa and Minami, *Economic development*, pp. 249–82; MITI, *Textiles*, vol. 1, *passim*, and articles by G. Ranis and G. Saxonhouse in K. Ohkawa *et al.* (eds), *Japan and the Developing Countries: A Comparative Analysis*, Oxford: Basil Blackwell, 1985.

2. The *garabo* is well treated in Nakaoka's work and in Y. Kiyokawa, 'Entrepreneurship and innovation in Japan: An implication of the experience of technological development in the textile industry', *The Developing Economies*, vol. XXII, no. 3, September 1984, pp. 211–36. An account of the inventor with photographs of the machine is in *Nihon keizaishi jiten*, vol. 2, pp. 1757–60. Data on *garabo* output from MITI, *Textiles*, vol. 15, p. 133.

Japanese spinning factories before its extinction in the face of the modern industry.

The leadership in this early technology strategy had to come from the government — or, to be more precise, the Trade Encouragement Bureau of the Ministry of Home Affairs (Naimusho Kanshokyoku). Apart from financing model mills, the government relied heavily on National Industrial Exhibitions (*naikoku kangyo hakurankai*), 'Competitive' Exhibitions (*kyoshinkai*) and International Exhibitions. The last of these was used to introduce Japanese products to the world and obtain intelligence on foreign techniques and markets, while the former two served to encourage domestic diffusion of knowledge.[3] These devices were obviously relevant to western technology acquisition, but were also important in the brief but successful diffusion of the *garabo*.[4]

The second phase of technology development, from 1890 to 1919, witnessed a major transfer of initiative to the private sector. We saw earlier how the successful establishment of the Osaka Boseki had depended on correct technical choices. These choices reflected Shibusawa's method of handling technology problems rather than any inspired guesses made by him. From the outset, this method was to ensure that while the best western techniques and technicians were used where needed, the key management role in the company was played by a Japanese with personal expertise in the theory and practice of cotton technology. Yamanobe Takeo was personally recruited for this role by Shibusawa in 1879 while the latter was visiting London to establish the Mitsui branch office.[5] Shibusawa persuaded Yamanobe to drop his study of economics in favour of courses in mechanical engineering in London, which were followed by shopfloor experience and study in Manchester and Blackburn, Lancashire. After returning to Japan, Yamanobe played a decisive role in all the initial technological decisions of the Osaka Boseki, and in 1887 he travelled to England again to arrange the purchase of the firm's first ring-spinning machines. His key role in the company continued in the early 1900s, and he ended his career as the first chairman of the Toyo Boseki, the merged company formed with the explicit objective of enhancing technology capabilities.[6]

3. MITI, *Textiles*, vol. 15, pp. 3–9, 92–3, 115ff.

4. *Ibid.*, pp. 145–6.

5. This account of the technological policies of the Osaka Boseki and the Toyo Boseki are mainly based on Takamura, *An introduction; Toyo boseki nanajunenshi* and MITI, *Textiles*, vol. 15.

6. *Toyo boseki nanajunenshi*, pp. 148–9.

An important development in the 1900s came with the early experiments with automatic looms. However, these were not very successful, either with foreign or with Japanese models. Nonetheless, the emergence of large firms embracing both spinning and weaving began to focus attention on the problems of weaving technology and on the potential for technical progress in integrated companies. Although domestic competitiveness may have abated somewhat by comparison with the boom years of the 1890s, the problems of international competitiveness provided powerful incentives for cost reduction and quality improvement throughout this period.

In the inter-war phase from 1920 to 1937 the industry responded to adversities with renewed drives for technical improvement. In the 1920s these adversities included the post-war slump, an over-valued yen, the Kanto earthquake and uncertainties in the China market. After the Ottawa Agreements of 1932 circumvention of Britain's Imperial Preference became the explicit goal of technology policy, for which the national framework was supplied by government policies for private-sector concentration and 'rationalisation' and by its encouragement of technology-sharing in many forms. But in spite of this revival of government interest, the private sector was the main engine of progress. An important indicator of the importance attached to these problems at the Toyo Boseki was the establishment of special organisations to handle them. The first of these was the Technology Research Society (*Gijutsu Kenkyukai*), established in 1923 for work on spinning. In 1925 the company set up the Spinning and Cloth Joint Research Society (*Boseki-Menpu Rengo Kenkyukai*) to promote integrated research.[7]

The main objectives of company research in the 1920s were lower fault rates, increased quality range and raised output per machine and per person. These problems were approached from many angles. The introduction and improvement of new equipment had a high priority, but much effort was also put into simplified factory layouts, quality control procedures, factory environmental improvements (especially air-conditioning) and the introduction of Taylorian and standardisation principles wherever appropriate. Technical standardisation was found particularly important since it enabled different factories, united in new merged companies, to work effectively together. In advancing all these programmes, the Toyo Boseki found that the attitudes and

7. *Ibid.*, pp. 21, 179–201.

approaches of the young graduates (*gakko shusshinsha*) and the older workshop-based technicians (*jitchi agari no nenkosha*) were often at odds.[8] As far as possible, management insisted that the conflicting groups should work out their differences on the shop-floor. The company also encouraged technical progress through inter-plant competitions for cost reduction and quality improvement.

In spinning, much effort was put into the pre-factory stages of cotton handling and preparation, while on the shop-floor high draft systems and quality improvement to British and American standards were pursued.[9] In weaving, the search for successful automatic loom technologies was intensified, and in the Toyo Boseki, at least, this was done in an entirely objective way. For example, in one round of factory testing, ten automatic loom models from four Japanese and six Western manufacturers were analysed.

Closely related to technical research and diffusion programmes was a systematic effort to measure their results, particularly in terms of cost reduction. This was intrinsically difficult since what was required was that a huge variety of factory outputs be reduced to a common physical denominator so that it could be compared with common raw material and labour costs. In the Toyo Boseki the company's accountants borrowed techniques developed by the former Mie Company which enabled them to reduce all counts of yarn to a single (twenty-count) measure. This system was known as 'cotton spinning standard cost accounting', and its principles were later extended to weaving. Once adequate measures of efficiency were in place, factories that lagged behind in cost reduction were descended on by specialists from company headquarters and their problems solved.

The long-term results of these strategies cannot easily be summed up. One indicator of what was achieved is the improvement of labour productivity in spinning, illustrated in Fig. 11.1, which shows two distinct phases of productivity growth: a steady annual growth of 3% to 4% in 1891–1926 followed by nearly 9% in 1927–35. In the first period we are looking at the results of continuous learning in the basic ring technology, and in the second at the impact of high draft techniques, electrification and a variety of welfare and incentive measures.

Productivity improvement in the 1920s made possible the smooth abolition of night work. In the early stages of planning for this, the

8. *Ibid.*, pp. 179ff.
9. *Ibid.*, p. 197.

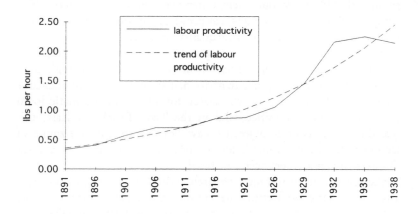

Fig. 11.1. LABOUR PRODUCTIVITY IN SPINNING, 1891–1938

Source: Data from materials in Shindo, *op. cit.*, n. 10.

25% cost increase that the loss of seven working hours represented was seen as bound to lead to wage-rate reductions. However, so successful were companies in advancing mechanisation, in substituting female for male labour (through layout and mechanical simplification) and in raising worker motivation through welfare and environmental improvement that no wage-rate reductions were necessary.[10]

10. Shindo, *Labour in the Japanese Cotton Industry*, is particularly interesting on the implementation of the factory law and on the productivity enhancement achieved by improved welfare and by environmental and educational provision in the 1920s. See esp. pp. 65–78. In the case of air-conditioning, experiments showed that humidity caused workers to suffer serious short-term fatigue and loss of body weight when temperatures reached 28 degrees C. Substantial productivity gains were therefore available from implementing measures to control these factors. In the Toyo Boseki, automation of weaving was accomplished using a mixture of Northrop and Toyoda looms. Data on capital intensity, labour productivity and output in the Toyo Boseki company for the crucial years 1928 to 1931 are in *Hyakunenshi Toyobo* (The hundred-year history of Toyobo) (2 vols), Osaka: Toyobo, 1986, vol. 1, ch. 4.

A measure of qualitative progress in textiles is illustrated in the performance of one of the Toyo Boseki's key plants, the Tomita factory. Here continuous spinning improvements took counts from the very low level of 8 before the First World War to the phenomenal range of 100–160 by 1940–41, with counts as high as 200 being achieved in trial production. In weaving, by the late 1930s the Tomita factory was using its range of yarns to produce no less than 380 varieties of cloth. Between them, these varieties could mount competitive attacks in almost any segment and in any geographical location in the world market.[11]

Tea and silk

Tea and silk were the main export industries in the *kaikoku* period. Between 1867 and the early 1900s their function was to earn foreign exchange during the learning period in cotton. This led to significant import substitution and eventual export expansion. Part of the success of export expansion in tea and silk depended on improved procurement, quality control, promotion and international marketing, but our concern in this chapter is rather the way in which technical progress influenced cost reduction and quality enhancement. The crucial difference between these two industries and cotton textiles was the gap between the traditional techniques and the best foreign ones. In tea and silk the gap was smaller than in cotton, and competition from factory-processed imports was not an issue. In other words the industries were viable in their traditional forms but could be made more competitive and thus able to supply larger volumes by improved techniques.

The production of tea is a combination of cultivation of tea plants and the processing of the harvested leaves. The agricultural improvement of the industry mainly took the form of the development of specialised 'tea gardens' and the application of increasing quantities of fertiliser and of various mechanical improvements. The progress in processing, which is our focus here, took the form of mechanisation.

---

11. See, 'Product up-grading and market expansion' and 'Towards diversified management' in *Toyo boseki nanajunenshi*, pp. 284ff. The Tomita plant used the leading technology available — English spinning and Swiss weaving machines — in their drive for up-market quality.

There were substantial economic parameters bearing on mechanisation. Between 1880 and 1935 the price of tea relative to other agricultural commodities fell by 66% while real wages in the industry rose by 194%. Export markets were highly competitive, with tastes shifting from East to South Asian teas, although domestic demand grew strongly with rising incomes. Under these pressures, productivity improvements were essential to the industry's survival.[12]

The technological options open to processors included various degrees of mechanisation. This meant that for a given price of tea, different technological options were appropriate, depending on the levels of wage costs. As these costs rose, the degree of mechanisation could be increased. As tea was a rather localised rural industry, wage variations between localities could be a significant factor in this decision. The evidence shows that under these circumstances a gradual process of mechanisation took place with a pattern of technological shifts through time reflecting the pattern of economic pressures transmitted through trends in wages and tea prices.

The story of technological progress in silk is more complex and can only be outlined here.[13] The agricultural elements of the industry are climate and soil appropriate to the mulberry bush, which provides the food for the silkworms. The silkworms eject their thread in the form of cocoons, which are heated to kill the live chrysalides and then sorted for use and quality. The selected cocoons are then briefly heated in water and the primary reeling process begins. Reeled silk is then further wound and 'thrown' until the final product, categorised by count and quality, is ready for sale or processing.

Systems of raw silk manufacture may be very primitive. In Japan traditional silk manufacture was largely a part-time activity in rural households, employing simple wooden implements. This silk was hand-spun and known as *zakuri*. The Tokugawa authorities rightly identified silk as their major export activity, and in the early Meiji period a similar view led to the importation of the most famous of

12. The principal source of data for this section is Niitani Masahiko, 'The choice of technique in the tea industry' in Minami and Kiyokawa, *Japanese industrialisation*, pp. 24–42. See also materials on tea in Ohara and Okata, *Trade and Industry*.

13. R. Minami, 'The choice of technology in the silk industry' in Minami and Kiyokawa, *Japanese industrialisation*, pp. 43–63. Ishii, *An analysis of the history of Japan's silk industry*, esp. chs 2–3; Akira Ono, 'Technical progress in silk industry in pre-war Japan — types of borrowed technology', *Hitotsubashi Journal of Economics*, vol. 27, no. 1, 1986, pp. 1–10; 'Silk', *EB* (11th edn).

all government 'model' factories, the Tomioka Silk Filature.[14] This firm, which was completed in 1872, was a major technological and social innovation since it involved not only substituting steam-power and iron reeling basins for hand-powered wooden equipment, but also replacing household activity with a French factory system, complete with limited working hours, formal discipline and Sunday observance.

The Tomioka Filature was not financially successful in its original form, the fundamental reason being that it represented an unnecessarily advanced model of innovation, adapted neither to Japanese resource endowments nor to the social conditions. In spite of this, the transfer of technology it represented was significant, since with study and experience the Japanese could use and adapt elements of it in ways that immediately improved productivity and led over time to the establishment of hundreds of economically efficient, Japanese-style filatures. This process of advance was facilitated by the full range of government support discussed in the cotton section and was reinforced by the highly competitive nature of the industry. Thus if we take cross-sectional snapshots of Japanese silk technology between the 1890s and the 1930s, we observe the co-existence of different technological levels, indicated by variations in types of capital equipment and sources of motive power, and an accumulation of learning and minor innovations that may be classified as adaptations of western techniques to suit Japanese conditions or as improvements in the traditional *zakuri* silk-making methods.

The net effect of this was a history of steady progress in the industry's labour productivity. Between 1890 and 1935 this grew by 3.6% per year, with rates in the modern and *zakuri* sectors being respectively *ca.* 4.6% and 2.2%. There was little variation in the rate of improvement other than a flattening of the upward curve between 1926 and 1931. This performance, while not spectacular, was sufficient to take Japan to world leadership in the international silk trade, in spite of China, which had previously been dominant, having distinctly more favourable natural conditions.

14. MITI, vol. 15, *Textiles*, pp. 25ff. and Y. Kiyokawa, 'Transplantation of the European factory system and adaptations in Japan: the experience of the Tomioka Filature', *Hitotsubashi Journal of Economics*, vol. 28, no. 1, June 1987, pp. 27–39.

The success of Japanese technology transfer before 1937

Technology was central to Japanese trade performance before 1937, and progress in trade was impressive whether measured by new fields successfully entered or by continuous progress in techniques already acquired. Six factors seem to have played particulary important roles in this success.

First, although the gap between Japanese and western technology seemed large in the 1850s, it was smaller than was often supposed. Japan missed the first epoch of innovation and industrial revolution in the West, from the 1770s to the 1820s, but faced the challenge of technology transfer within the first decade or so of the long second epoch from the 1830s to the 1870s. Japan's ability to seize and enjoy the unfolding advantages of this critical epoch reflected the benefits of the country's reservoir of traditional skills in metallurgy, machinery and textiles and the successful mobilisation of the national effort under the direction of imported western specialists. Its traditional industrial skills were capable of rapid diffusion and of initiating forms of minor product and process innovation almost immediately.

Secondly, leaders in both public and private sectors grasped the comprehensive nature of the technology acquisition process and thereby ensured that the acquisition of equipment was accompanied by development of the full range of skills and knowledge and by business systems needed to adapt and exploit such equipment to the maximum effect. The western specialists brought with them not only working experience of the new technologies but, increasingly, the wider scientific and contextual knowledge needed for further Japanese discrimination, adaptation and innovation. Public and private investment in the domestic skill and intellectual infra-structure accelerated after the Meiji Restoration. By the turn of the century, therefore, Japan was largely able to dispense with the direct involvement of western specialists in the established technologies, although learning in the fourth epoch, from the 1900s to the 1930s, made use of foreign direct investment, and further imports of western specialists and technological alliances with western companies were needed in the inter-war years, especially in new industries such as aviation and optics.

Thirdly, the government played a crucial role in technology transfer by providing institutional, legal and knowledge infrastructures and supporting individual industries. The character of such assistance varied according to the nature of the gap between traditional and western technology and on the capacity of market forces to support it. In the military and most heavy industries, the technical gap was large and inflexible, domestic market support was necessarily weak, and the forces of comparative advantage worked against an economy where labour was plentiful but capital and skill remained relatively scarce. In these circumstances government subsidisation through procurement, tariffs or other forms of protection was essential and often of very long duration. Shipbuilding, metallurgy and engineering eventually secured a degree of viability and even of export success up till 1937, but the main achievement of these industries before the Second World War was successful import substitution. The optics industry, on the other hand, never achieved more than minimal civilian market support and therefore depended on government demand right down to 1945.

Though costly, the ultimate results of government support for the strategic industries were remarkable. By the early 1950s these industries had restructured and adapted to both domestic and world markets to such a degree that by 1971 metallurgical and machinery producers alone accounted for 68% of all exports and Japan had achieved world export leadership in steel, shipbuilding and optical products — the key objectives of the pre-war *kokusanka* programme.

In the commercial and light industries the problems were different. In cotton textiles, the technical gap was less formidable and Japan's underlying comparative advantage was favourable. Thus government support, while crucial at first, quickly gave way to private activity. In tea and silk, moreover, where the technological gap could be very small and export prospects immediate, an infrastructure of advice, encouragement and quality control was all that was needed to encourage the successful development of adapted and hybrid technologies that formed the basis of the industries' competitive success.

Fourthly, emphasis on the government's role should not obscure the importance of the private sector. In strategic and high-technology industries, although government support was indispensable, the technological initiative passed quite rapidly to the private sector, first in shipbuilding and electrics and later in aircraft — an industry where demand came almost entirely from public sources. And even Nikon, though closely supported and influenced by the public sector, was always a commercial company, watching its balance-sheets as well as its technological research budgets.

Apart from direct aid of various kinds, tolerance and even encouragement of controlled markets and monopoly profits were important in ensuring that private firms had the resources to support innovation over long periods of initiation and development.

In textiles, the private sector was completely in control by the 1880s. The striking feature in this case is the ability of the industry's leadership to choose and develop technologies that led to continuous productivity improvements. Indeed, although important technical innovations were introduced, their impact is often hard to detect in the long upward curves of productivity, which were based on a combination of improvements and adaptations of imported capital equipment, rising skill levels and improved managerial practice (see Fig. 11.1).

Fifthly, Japan's technological receptivity was matched by the eagerness of the West to supply what Japan was seeking. Thus in the 1900s, as Japan's objectives and capabilities began to rise significantly, its businessmen could live *à la carte* on menus selected from the world's technological leaders. One extraordinary embodiment of this eclecticism was the late Meiji headquarters of the Yokohama Specie Bank, which was built using marble and granite from six different Japanese quarries, electrical systems from Germany, glass from Pilkington Bros. in England, steel from Carnegie, elevators from Otis and windows from Henry Hope of Birmingham.[15] The textile industry was another that benefited from the openness of the world economy and the willingness of British machinery manufacturers in particular to market their products worldwide.

In heavy industry it is the transfers in the military area that are especially remarkable, since these could have been restrained by strategic considerations. However, various influences worked in Japan's favour. One was that the great powers had been largely at peace since the treaty of Vienna (1815), and this encouraged trade in weapons and related technologies. Thus in the 1860s the British could seriously contemplate relying for their long-term provision of guns on Krupp and in the 1870s willingly supplied the design capacity for Germany's finest warship. While international rivalry in this period did not generally threaten the great powers, there was intense competition among second-class ones. For such countries localised wars could be won or lost on the basis of narrow technological advantage, and the prestige of buying from the technological leaders was considerable. By the turn of the century, however, technological

15. *FER*, June 1905, pp. 12–14.

competitiveness was becoming universal. For example, Anglo-German naval rivalry became so keen in the first decade of the twentieth century that Sir Alfred Yarrow persuaded the British Admiralty to replace an entire class of destroyers in order to close the 3-knot speed gap that had opened up between British and German designs.

In the face of these pressures military development moved swiftly. Of crucial importance for countries such as Japan, this military development was located largely in the private sector in the West where the pressure to export was intense given that domestic demand was insufficient to maintain large-scale, fully utilised production facilities. Hence national governments encouraged export sales to lower their own budgetary burdens and keep firms in business when domestic demand was slack. So intense were these pressures in Britain that W. H. White of Armstrong's exploited the mutual naval anxieties of the Japanese and Chinese governments by promising to deliver to both parties the latest technology and total design confidentiality.[16]

Serious doubts about the provision of offensive military technology to foreign governments were raised in the late 1890s and grew in intensity in the run-up to the First World War. By that time, however, Japan's armaments industry was well advanced and whatever doubts western governments may have felt, foreign orders remained critical to financial viability in the western private sector in the 1900s. Later, between the World Wars, drastic reductions in defence spending and a depression in western engineering and military industries again facilitated the transfer of western technology, most notably in aviation. In the 1920s western air forces and companies supplied large-scale technical support to Japan and their willingness to do so was linked closely to restrictions on domestic armament programmes and fierce competition in home markets.[17] Similarly, the Japanese availed them-

16. Pollard and Robertson, *The British Shipbuilding Industry*, pp. 219–20. Chapter 10 of this work discusses the whole issue of state support for shipbuilding in this period. White was a former Admiralty man who moved into the private sector as Director of Naval Construction for Armstrong's. In British shipbuilding in the nineteenth century, this kind of *amakudari* ('descent from heaven') was common, and proved important in maintaining the public–private sector relationship.

17. For example, after the Sparrowhawk's early success with the Japanese Navy, the Gloster Aircraft Company offered Nakajima licences for the Gloster Gambet, which enabled Nakajima to win an inter-Japanese procurement competition for a new naval plane in 1926. Gloster's keenness for this contract reflected lack of success in Britain and employment anxieties in Gloucestershire. The Gambet was eventually modified and fitted with the first completely original Japanese engine, the Nakajima *Kotobuki*. See Derek N. James, *Gloster Aircraft since 1917*, London: Putnam, 1987, pp. 157–60.

selves of important innovations and aviation patents in the 1930s largely through the apathy of western governments.[18]

Finally, although careful examination of disparate sources throws some light on Japan's crossing of the frontier from traditional to modern technology, there remains something extraordinary about the speed of Japanese learning and diffusion of skills. As we have already seen, this aptitude was as obvious to foreigners in the sixteenth and seventeenth centuries as it became in the nineteenth and twentieth. A further part of the answer can perhaps be found in two phenomena. The first is that dedication to techniques for the perfect crafting of physical objects has deep roots in the Japanese psyche, going back to the eighth century:

The correct (religious) way to build a house, forge a sword, or brew liquor had been, from earliest times . . . imbued with a peculiar guarantee of success through its dependence on a divine patron who established rules and divided labor and in whose honor the chanties were sung . . . The carpenter's try square and plumb bob, as well as his simple yet sufficient rule of thumb formulas of angles and proportions, have all been embedded in Shinto rhymes and patters and aids to memory that were were liturgy, litany and sound sense[19]

As if to reinforce the significance of this seemingly abstruse point, carpenters even today engage in Shinto rituals at the key moments of ground-breaking, ridge-raising and the ceremonial completion of building projects.[20] A second, related point is that the watershed between traditional and modern technology is less clear-cut than is often assumed. The accumulation of skills in design and tool-making and the adaptation of technologies to meet the complex market demands of a traditional economy in some way constitute a vast

18. Access to technologies in the special metals on which new standards in engine and airframe construction depended was freely available to Japan. Nakajima in particular imported special steels and the Clark GA 43 that incorporated them. This is discussed in James A. Rabbitt, 'Nickel alloys and steels in the aeronautical industry', *FER*, June 1934, pp. 274–6. Japanese manufacturers were the first in the world to make use of western patent rights to fit bombers with Sperry automatic pilot systems and radio direction finders, both important for Pacific navigation. See Bueschal, *Mitsubishi: Nakajima G3M.* Even in this field, however, the flow was two-way as western manufacturers used Japanese techniques for developing radar antennae.

19. Langdon Warner, *Japanese Sculpture of the Tempyo Period: Masterpieces of the Eighth Century*, Cambridge, MA: Harvard University Press, 1964, pp. 25–6.

20. William H. Coaldrake. *The Way of the Carpenter: Tools and Japanese Architecture*, New York: Weatherhill, 1990, pp. 3–5.

storehouse of 'blueprints' from which society can summon knowledge long after the human bearers of skills have passed away and the technological environment has changed beyond recognition. We have already seen how the technical and commercial sophistication of the traditional textile industry enabled it to modernise speedily and with selectivity in the Meiji era, and that Japan's traditional metal-working skills were ultimately channelled into the arms, bicycle and modern machinery industries. Similar stories can be told of the trans-formation of a small group of late Tokugawa watchmakers into Seiko, the twentieth century's most successful and innovative watch manu-facturer; of the carpenters who adapted their pattern and technology handbooks (*hiinagatabon* and *gijutsusho*) to illustrate western bricklaying in the early Meiji; and of the glassmakers, many originally specialised in making Buddhist icons, who progressed from copying Dutch telescopes and spectacles in the Tokugawa to work on contemporary German optics in the late nineteenth and twentieth centuries.

This continuity of skills certainly impressed nineteenth-century western observers. British toolmakers, for example, estimated that there were in use in Japan at least 1,300–1,400 varieties of traditional woodworking tools, and they believed that it was the store of skills implicit in these that enabled the Japanese to copy their own machine-made wares with such extraordinary speed and accuracy. Moreover when Belgian and Scottish iron pipes were imported to build the Tokyo water system, the Japanese contractors explained why they demanded of the pipes an accuracy associated by Europeans with watchmaking:

We have been accustomed for 300 years past to absolute flawlessness in artistic works, and our young tyros, fresh from theoretical training in the University, with little or no practical experience, cannot be made to under-stand that the perfection naturally looked for in a work of art is impossible in mere utilitarian work.[21]

Japan's modern technological achievement reflected, therefore, not only the favourable timing of its entry into the technological

---

21. 'Japan Report for the Year 1895', *BPPJ*, vol. 10, p. 57. The end to this story is the problem of the Japanese firm that was instructed by an IBM subsidiary to supply to an acceptable quality level of three defects per 10,000 parts. The firm replied (perhaps with tongue in cheek): 'We Japanese have hard time understanding North American business practices. But the three defective parts per 10,000 have been included and are wrapped separately. Hope this pleases.' Quoted in John Bank, *The Essence of Total Quality Management*, Englewood Cliffs, NJ: Prentice-Hall, 1992, p. 26.

revolution in the West, imaginative organisation and a consistency of leadership that provided long-term support to uncompetitive activities, but also the vast and, by its nature, immeasurable stock of human capital available to it in the nineteenth century. This capital comprised the skills of the men and women who lived and worked through the transition and the accumulated 'blueprints' and 'implicit knowledge' inherited from former generations. While this human capital had deep historical roots, its scale and power were undoubtedly nurtured during the long Tokugawa peace during which demand expanded and practical craftsmen responded with innovation, and for the first time began to circulate manuals and pattern-books containing what had once been secret, family-based skills.[22]

22. The concept of 'implicit knowledge' is from the lectures of Michael Polanyi, published as *The Tacit Dimension*, London: Routledge and Kegan Paul, 1967. The economic significance of this concept is elaborated by Richard R. Nelson and Sidney G. Winter in *An Evolutionary Theory of Economic Change*, Cambridge, MA: Belknap Press, 1982, pp. 76–85, 118–21. Here the authors cite the phenomenon of identical machines working perfectly in one country but not in another, quoting Polanyi's explanation: 'Even in modern industries the indefinable knowledge is still an essential part of technology.' I link this concept to that of 'blueprints' or 'designs,' as discussed by Paul Romer in his article 'Endogenous technical change', *Journal of Political Economy*, vol. 98, no. 5, part 2, Oct. 1990, pp. 71–102. The seventeenth- and eighteenth-century dating for the vast expansion of Japanese design books is clear from the literature on both textiles and carpentry.

Part IV
WAR, EMPIRE, TRADE AND INVESTMENT

12

THE IMPERIAL BACKGROUND AND
THE CASE OF TAIWAN

'We rejoice therefore to report that, thanks to the Great Guardian Spirit, who through unbroken ages has continually guided His Majesty the Emporer and each of His Imperial Ancestors, and thanks also to the generous way in which the Formosan Administration has been upheld by the State, our plans for the colonization of the island have been crowned with a great measure of success.' — Goto Shimpei, chief of civil administration, Formosa, 1905[1]

At several points in earlier chapters we have seen the close relationship between trade and the economy on the one hand and policies for the enhancement of Japanese power on the other. The Tokugawa Seclusion, the early Meiji transplantation of new industries, the Matsukata nurturing of the private sector, and import substitution in the defence industries are all examples of economic programmes implemented to achieve strategic and political as well as economic objectives. In these last chapters these threads are gathered together to illustrate ways in which Japan's external economic relations have been shaped by war and imperial expansion. The subject is complex and controversial. Much post-war Japanese economic literature ignores the issues, and authors often explain Japanese trade patterns by changing comparative advantage and other purely economic factors. And although Marxist economic historians have done much research on the issues, their work is often highly specialised and rarely reaches audiences beyond Japan.

Two groups of questions have particulary engaged those tackling the subject. First, was Japan's an accidental imperialism, responding to irresistible external pressures? Or was there an underlying genius of expansion within Japan, contained during the Tokugawa but released by Japan's re-entry into the world economy after 1868? And secondly, what was the balance between strategic and economic factors at the various stages of Japan's imperial expansion? Was Japan's economic strategy so dependent on international trade that it was

1. Quoted in Yosaburo Takekoshi, *Japanese Rule in Formosa*, London: Longmans, Green, 1907, p. v.

335

bound to founder? Or indeed was there a logical thread of thought and coordinated action at all?[2]

Resolving these issues is far beyond our scope here. However, what is certain is that between 1895 and 1937 Japan, through force of arms, successfully extended its control throughout Korea, Taiwan, the Liaotung Peninsula and the South Manchurian Railway Zone, and eventually into Manchuria itself. At the same time, Japan was advancing its interests by direct foreign investment and loans in China generally and in Shanghai especially. These moves all had important economic implications, for they influenced the regional and commodity composition of Japanese foreign trade and stimulated Japanese flows of investment, technology and human resources. The character and inter-relationship of all these elements is therefore a key to understanding the pattern of Japan's pre-war international economic relations and their post-war legacy. Central to this pattern was Japan's attempt after 1937 to incorporate China and South-East Asia into a planned, self-sufficient economic bloc. The details of this expansion were ill thought-out and the experiment itself lasted a relatively short time, but in some ways it represented a logical conclusion to much that preceded it and was the culmination of one particular pattern of Japan's external economic relations.

In the space of three chapters only the essentials and highlights of this story can be told; the argument is therefore organised by distinguishing three kinds of 'colonial' economic linkage. These are economic penetration supported by direct political control, exemplified by the colonisation of Taiwan; economic penetration with indirect control, as in Manchuria; and commercial strength created by successful direct foreign investment, exemplified by Japanese investment in the Chinese cotton textile industry. Before looking at these cases, however, we need to consider the context in which they all developed.

2. An excellent political overview of the issues is W. G. Beasley, *Japanese Imperialism, 1894–1945*, Oxford University Press, 1987. Two collections of papers with valuable contributions on economic problems are Ramon H. Myers and Mark Peattie (eds), *The Japanese Colonial Empire, 1895–1945*, Princeton University Press, 1984; and Peter Duus *et al.* (eds), *The Japanese Informal Colonial Empire, 1895–1937*, Princeton University Press, 1989. A recent Japanese survey of the economic issues of the inter-war empire is K. Ono, *Senkanki no Nihon teikokushugi* (Japanese imperialism in the inter-war period), Tokyo: Sekai Shisosha, 1985.

The context of Japanese imperialism

Japan's imperial expansion took place in an environment containing distinct political and economic ingredients, which we should briefly recapitulate.

Competing imperialisms in the Far East. First, the Far East has had a history of continuous rivalries between nations each believing in its own divine, supranational mission in the region. It was within this competitive framework that Japan had to find its own place.[3]

Both China and Japan had long-standing claims to forms of universal sovereignty that relegated the rest of the world to tributary status; both vied with each other to enforce these claims on third parties, especially Korea. Let us take Japan first. Japan had intermittently accepted Chinese supremacy, but it made its last tribute mission to China in 1549.[4] The Koreans, who had recognised Japanese claims for centuries, switched to Chinese protection in 1460 only to suffer the horrendous punishment of Hideyoshi's invasions from Japan in 1592–98. Although this invasion failed, the Koreans subsequently placated Japanese claims to the extent of agreeing to nominal tribute missions, with expenses paid by the Japanese. These missions continued from 1623 till 1832. After 1867 the Meiji government attempted to re-assert its special status in Korea and was rebuffed. Japan subsequently removed Korea from the Chinese tributary system through its victory in the Sino-Japanese war, and in 1911 proceeded to annex it formally.

Disputes over Asian suzerainty were by no means matters of purely intra-Asian interest. We have already seen how the forms of western trading relations in Asia were determined by the etiquette of oriental imperialisms in the seventeenth and eighteenth centuries. As late as 1873 European ambassadors were publicly humiliated by the Chinese Emperor T'ung Chih, who insisted on summoning them to his presence in a remote and draughty hall, customarily used to receive the ambassadors of barbaric, tributary nations.[5]

3. An authoritative work on early intra-East Asian relations that emphasises the Japan-centric as distinct from Sino-centric view of the world is Ronald P. Toby, *State and Diplomacy in Early Modern Japan: Asia in the Development of the Tokugawa Bakufu*, Stanford University Press, 1991.

4. From archaeological evidence we know that Japan had some form of vassal status as early as the Han dynasty (202 BC to 220 AD). Huang, *China: A Macro History*, p. 52.

5. This incident is described by Curzon, whose book is a fascinating first-hand glimpse of the Far East, especially Korea, on the eve of the Sino-Japanese war. George N. Curzon, *The Problems of the Far East: Japan, Korea, China*, London: Longmans, Green, 1894, pp. 291–2.

The Europeans also had their own notions of providential destiny. The sixteenth-century Portuguese pioneers believed firmly in the high purposes they served, and so great was the shock of the Dutch decline in Asia in the late eighteenth century that it was described by one contemporary as the divine finger, pointing out to man 'the utter instability of everything in this sublunary world'.[6]

By the nineteenth century the Russians and British had become the most active Asian expansionaries. In the spirit of their predecessors, the Russian Tsars, inheritors of the Byzantine imperial tradition, established an empire that at its fullest extent stretched from Siberia in the north to Persia in the south, and from the Caspian sea in the west to the Pacific in the east. While in 1894, George Nathaniel Curzon, the future Viceroy of India, dedicated his study of the Far East 'to those who believe that the British Empire is, under providence, the greatest instrument for good that the world has seen and who hold, with the writer, that its work in the Far East is not yet accomplished'.[7]

Only four years after Curzon's dedication, America's war with Spain inflamed its sense of Asian destiny. Armed with the iron-clad battleship, 'the leviathan, arbiter of human destinies alike on land and sea', the Americans reached for the leadership of a new, ultimately world-dominating Pacific community, a community in which 'the late acquisitions of the United States in the West Indies and the Pacific [Hawaii and the Philippines] are simply on a line with the world's policy of territorial acquisition.'[8] This view of the Asia-Pacific region and its economic future was widely shared and not simply a vision. Indeed, early in the century it was already supported by rail, telegraph and shipping networks, linking everywhere from New England and Vancouver to Nagasaki, Vladivostok, the Ladrones and Australia. Belief in the region was enthusiastically shared by American industrialists at the end of the nineteenth century: American textile exporters still made half their worldwide sales to China, and the burgeoning steel and engineering industries saw Asia as the key market for heavy industry exports.[9]

6. Stavorinus, *Voyages*, vol. 3, p. 422.
7. Curzon, *Problems of the Far East*, preface.
8. Hubert Howe Bancroft, *The New Pacific*, New York: Bancroft, 1900, pp. 2–7.
9. See two articles by J. R. Jernigan, 'China trade possibilities. Opportunities which Americans should not overlook', *NCH*, Nov. 28, 1898; 'The Pacific Ocean — The commercial arena', *NCH*, Jan. 23, 1899.

The scramble for colonies. A second element in the background to Japanese imperialism was the late-nineteenth-century western scramble for uncolonised territory. So successful was this that between 1878 and 1914 the proportion of the world's surface controlled by western powers increased from 67% to 85%.[10] Africa was the most spectacular theatre for this expansion, and this left China, with its failing dynasty, its vast fragmented polity and its deep structural obstacles to economic modernisation, as the last potential victim of international partition. Japan, just across the water and bound to it by economic, cultural and historic ties, saw a Chinese partition from which it was excluded as a great danger.[11]

The aftermath of the First World War. A third and later ingredient of Japanese imperialism was the experience and aftermath of the First World War. The war had caused unparalleled destruction of life and capital so that in many ways reconstruction of previous conditions was impossible. On the positive side it stimulated the rapid dissemination of new techniques of mass-production and the creation of virtually new industries. It also led to the rise of huge firms whose market power raised fundamental questions about the future of the competitive economy, and whose performance was to depend on the new science of industrial management. Outside the narrow circle of the old industrial powers, the war had also provided the opportunity for industrialists in Latin America, southern Europe and Asia to supply their own domestic markets and to export to markets where in normal times they could not have been competitive.

After the war the new industrial revolution was followed by an agricultural one. In Latin America and the white colonies of Australasia and Canada a new class of modern farmers, supported by inflows of foreign capital, began to combine vast land resources with capital-intensive forms of production that resulted in unprecedented advances

10. Data quoted in Edward W. Said, *Culture and Imperialism*, London: Chatto and Windus, 1993, p. 6.

11. In 1897 these fears were abundantly realised by the Germans, who had suddenly decided in the mid-1880s that they needed colonies. Tirpitz sailed up the eastern coast of China and selected Tsingtao as a naval base and Shantung as a sphere of influence, forcing the Chinese to submit. The Germans behaved with such cruelty and stupidity in their new sphere of influence that they were largely responsible for provoking the Boxer Rebellion, which nearly led to the massacre of the entire foreign community in Peking.

in agricultural productivity. In the long run these improvements in industrial and agricultural performance were beneficial, but in the inter-war period they placed intense pressures of adjustment on the rest of the world.[12] Post-war economic problems were compounded by the decline of London as a stabilising financial centre and the corresponding rise of the United States, which although it was now the world's largest creditor was unwilling to perform the pre-war role of the London market.

All these developments were relevant to Japan. We have already seen how the new industrial economics and the ending of wartime conditions created problems for Japanese trade and industry in the early 1920s. The collapse of world agricultural prices in the 1930s led to the protection of Japanese agriculture and a major economic restructuring in the Japanese colonies. Changes in the world financial system were also important to Japan. Between 1905 and 1914 the London market had been critically helpful to Japan in its maintenance of the gold standard and national solvency. In the 1920s the management of its chronic balance of payments problems was made that much more difficult by the changing balance of western financial power.

The end of migration and trade protectionism. The problems of inter-war economic adjustment were compounded by two new rigidities in the world system. The first was the closing of most of the world to further Asian immigration and the second was the rise of protectionism, typified by the American Smoot-Hawley tariff of 1930 and the Ottawa system of Imperial Preference of 1931. The migration problem has to be seen in the context of increasing anxiety over the relatively rapid growth of population in poor countries and the worsening economic disparities that resulted. Such disparities had been alleviated in the nineteenth century by mass migration from Europe to North America and to some extent also by migration from Asia to both North and South America. With the closing of the migration door, the problems of countries such as Japan deepened.

As is argued in more detail in the next chapter, the 1920s were a decade in which the processes of Japanese development and structural change were intrinsically difficult. Agriculture had grown as a result of an initial once-for-all burst of efficiency in the early Meiji period and the subsequent spread of superior practices from Japan's advanced areas to its more backward ones. Further growth required significant

12. Ono, *Japanese imperialism*, ch. 1.

investment in new technologies and adaptation to changing tastes as consumers' incomes rose. In industry, the Japanese problem was to make the transition from the relatively simple technologies of textiles and consumer goods to the more complex ones of the skill- and capital-intensive industries. Finally, in foreign trade Japan had to extend its localised successes in textile exporting to become competitive in new categories of goods and in parts of the world far removed from the local Asian markets of its early export achievements. Under any circumstances these transitions would have been demanding; under inter-war conditions, without some basic changes in the rules of the game, they were perhaps impossible.

The colonisation of Taiwan, 1895–1945

Taiwan (once known as Formosa) is an island 90 miles off the east coast of China, approximately 240 miles long and 60 to 80 miles wide. It is almost tropical, although there are significant climatic variations between north and south. About two thirds of its terrain is mountainous, and in the late nineteenth century a similar proportion was covered by forest. Taiwan is rich in economic resources, and the climate is suitable for cultivating rice, sugar, tea, vegetables and fruit, as well as forestry. Fish are abundant and the configuration of natural water resources is favourable to hydro-electric generation, which eventually formed the basis of the island's early industrialisation.

Despite its proximity to China, Taiwan has had a somewhat loose political connection to the mainland for much of its history, with a tendency to break free at times of dynastic upheaval. Its core population consisted of eight aboriginal tribes, although today the Chinese dominate the racial structure. This dominance reflects waves of economic immigration from the Chinese coastal regions over several centuries and a final flood of political immigration from all parts of China in 1949. The island's location and its impenetrable inland areas have made it a natural centre of piracy and illegal trading, much of it stimulated by the Chinese and Japanese Seclusion laws. The Dutch controlled the island from 1623 to 1642, and its full incorporation into the Ching empire did not take place till the late seventeenth century.[13]

---

13. The early classics dealing with the history of Formosa are James W. Davidson, *The Island of Formosa Past and Present*, New York: Macmillan, 1903, and Campbell, *Formosa under the Dutch*.

In the decades before the Japanese arrival in 1895, Taiwan was a problematic, generally lawless place, in which headhunters and cannibals wandered freely. But in spite of sporadic murders, poor administration and Chinese hostility, western businessmen based in the Chinese treaty ports had begun by the 1850s to develop an interest in the island's resources and, in 1858, it was visited by a British hydrographical expedition.[14] Tea, rice, camphor and opium became the most popular trades.[15] Four treaty ports were opened and ships flying thirteen different flags called at one of them, Takow, during 1864.[16] In the decades that followed various western powers were reported to be considering annexation but it never came about.

The Japanese had a long history of legal and illegal ties with the island. In 1609 Tokugawa Ieyasu unsuccessfully invited the islanders to recognise Japanese suzerainty, and a few years later a governor of Nagasaki — a city with which Taiwan did much trade — attempted to take the island by force. This history and the island's proximity inevitably made its affairs a matter of concern to the Meiji government. Japan undertook a punitive mission there in 1874 and thereafter kept a careful watch on the island.[17] Then in 1895 China was forced to

14. This expedition to survey 'the coast of Tartary' was launched in 1856 after an incident in which the Russians, using superior charts, had escaped a naval confrontation by making a passage from the Gulf of Castries to the Sea of Okhotsk. The British survey ships finally left Nagasaki for England in 1861. The account of this work includes unique material on Hong Kong, Korea and Japan and its frontispiece is a photo of Ito Hirobumi, 'four times Premier of Japan and a friend of England', to whom the book is dedicated by the leader of the expedition and author of its history, William Blakeney, *On the Coasts of Cathay and Cipango Forty Years Ago*, London: Elliot Stock, 1902. Ch. 4 deals with Taiwan and the Pratas Reef.

15. A vivid, personal account of these years is W. A. Pickering, *Pioneering in Formosa: Recollections of Adventures among Mandarins, Wreckers, and Head Hunting Savages*, London: Hurst and Blackett, 1898. See also Robert Fortune, *A Residence Among the Chinese*, London: John Murray, 1857, ch. 11. Fortune reported that although violence in the coastal areas was declining in the 1850s, it was still believed that the Taiwanese aboriginals lived in trees.

16. Dennys, *The Treaty Ports*, has a full account of Formosa and its treaty ports, pp. 291–325.

17. The kid-gloved nature of these early relations was illustrated in 1892 when the Japanese consul from Foochow, Uyeno Senichi, visited the island. Uyeno invited a local chief to an alcoholic picnic lunch with the words, 'I humbly ask you to allow me to meet you by the river side, where we may sit on the soft sands close by the pellucid water.' 'A Japanese Explorer in Taiwan', *NCH*, March 18, 1892. Post-colonial treatment of the chiefs was much harsher.

cede the island to Japan[18] as part of a settlement following the Sino-Japanese war that included a variety of important economic concessions to Japan.

Although Taiwan was to become Japan's most successful colony and an important part of the Japanese trade and foreign investment network, purely economic motives can hardly have been dominant in the initial decision to colonise,[19] for apart from its sugar, the Japanese could not at that time have been aware of the island's full economic potential. This did not become clear until new and much more complete information about the island's resources could be combined with a broad understanding of the new rice-growing technologies that were being developed early in the 1900s.

The Japanese regarded their governing of Taiwan as a crucial experiment by which they would not only join the ranks of the western imperial powers, but would then surpass them through the development of a superior form of colonial relationship. For whereas white man's colonialism was judged to be exploitative, inimical to indigenous development and the cause of net economic loss to the home-country; Japanese colonialism was to be developmental, racially unbiased and fiscally self-sufficient, leading ultimately to political and economic integration with Japan.[20] Many observers, contemporary and retrospective, agreed that the Taiwanese colonisation achieved its main aims; indeed it is remarkable that as early as 1907 the economic historian, Takekoshi Yosaburo, could entitle the first chapter of his book on Taiwan 'A brief survey of our successes'.[21]

18. The treaty of Shimonoseki was followed by three supplementary treaties and protocols, largely dealing with Japanese economic rights in China. These rights included arrangements governing direct investment, mining, taxes, navigation and long-distance fishing. Texts of these treaties are located in John V. A. MacMurray, *Treaties and Agreements with and concerning China, 1894–1919* (2 vols), New York: Oxford University Press, 1921.

19. On this issue generally, see Peter Duus, 'The economic dimensions of Meiji Imperialism', in Myers and Peattie, *The Japanese Colonial Empire*, pp. 80–127.

20. Yanaihara Tadao, *Teikokushugi ka no Taiwan* (Taiwan under imperialism), Tokyo: Iwanami Shoten, 1988 (first published in 1928), pp. 12–13; Takekoshi, *Japanese Rule in Formosa*, ch. 2.

21. In 1910 Taiwan was visited by the British Ambassador, Sir Claude Macdonald. Sir Claude was highly impressed with the Japanese administration, which consulted him on his experiences in the African colonies. 'The Japanese in Formosa', *The Times*, March 23, 1910. The Japanese benefited from violent anti-German feelings in the First World War and this is reflected in 'Japan in Formosa', *NCH*, April 22, 1916. A later,

The colonial development of Taiwan has been periodised in many ways. For our purposes the fundamental phases are 1895–1920, 1921–31 and 1932–45. In the first phase the foundation strategy for the island's development as an agricultural colony was established and it flourished in the special circumstances of the First World War. In the second this strategy reached maturity with strong progress in agriculture and foreign trade. In the third phase, internal and external developments made new strategies for Taiwan's economic development essential. We will now look at each in more detail before attempting to summarise the significance of the whole Taiwanese colonial experience.[22]

Foundation strategies, 1895–1920. In the early years of colonialism, military control was a major problem. The turbulent Taiwanese had a long history of insurrections and clan warfare, and in the case of the hardiest aboriginal groups complete subjugation was not complete till the early 1920s. This issue had significant economic implications because the costs of pacification constituted a high proportion of government spending.[23]

The basic financial problem faced by the colonial government was that Japan's domestic fiscal situation in the decade after 1895 was extremely tight and pressure for the island to achieve its own fiscal

---

still very positive view is George Barclay, *Colonial Development and Population in Taiwan*, Princeton University Press, 1954.

22. Key sources used for this section are Samuel P. Ho, *Economic Development of Taiwan, 1860–1970*, New Haven: Yale University Press, 1978; Taiwan Yinhang Jingji Yanjiushi (ed.), *Riju shidai Taiwan jingjishi* (An economic history of Taiwan under Japanese occupation) (2 vols), Taipei: Taiwan Yinhang, 1958; Tu Zhao-yan, *Nihon teikokushugi ka no Taiwan* (Taiwan under Japanese imperialism), Tokyo: Tokyo Daigaku Shuppankai, 1975 (also available in a Chinese language edition in Taiwan). Pre-war books still rich in data and ideas include Yanaihara, *Taiwan*, and Takahashi Kamekichi, *Gendai Taiwan keizairon* (The economy of modern Taiwan), Tokyo: Okura Shobo, 1937. Yanaihara was a Christian Marxist and the 1988 edition of his book contains an interesting sketch of his life and work.

23. Between 1895 and 1901 military expenditure fell by 75% in absolute terms, and administrative expenses, including pacification, fell from 32.6% of total spending in 1902 to 13.2% in 1912. Data from Okura Zaibatsu Kenkyukai, *Okura zaibatsu no kenkyu. Okura to tairiku* (Research into the Okura zaibatsu. Okura and the [Chinese] mainland), Tokyo: Kondo Shuppansha, 1982, p. 69; Huang Tong *et al.* (eds), *Riju shidai zhi Taiwan caijing* (Taiwan finance under the Japanese occupation), Taipei: Lianjing Chubanshe, 1988, p. 14.

balance was therefore intense. Fiscal balance and independence from Japanese budgetary support were rapidly achieved. This was done in the short run by the creation of state monopolies in key commodities including tobacco, opium, salt and camphor. At the same time, in the early 1900s the government also prepared the basis for its longer-term tax-base with a series of exhaustive surveys of the island's resources. These included the establishment of what became a highly sophisticated population census system and full trigonometric and cadastral surveys of land and land-ownership.[24]

Given the physical conditions of Taiwan and the complex, largely unwritten legacy of land-ownership systems, surveying and the establishment of an accurate cadastral record were such immense tasks that they were said to dwarf even the great Meiji surveys of Japan in the 1870s. The surveys took seven years to complete and involved teams of up to 800 surveyors and officials; their results included a set of maps showing the island in extreme detail on a scale of 600:1. However, difficult as this work was, its completion marked a turning-point, since it established a basis for agricultural taxation and reform and provided information for potential investors in Japan. Most important of all, at the end of the process the government of Taiwan had basically removed the phenomenon of absentee landlordism and itself emerged as the island's predominant landowner. It used this position not only to provide the economic foundations for a select group of Japanese companies involved in exploiting the primary product sector, but also to shape its own strategies for agricultural development and control. Overall, the quality of the Japanese population, land, resource and ethnographic surveys was so high that they have made Taiwan the most minutely documented colonial development in history.

Other infrastructural tasks included the unification of weights and measures and the establishment of systems of currency and banking. A key institution was the Bank of Taiwan,[25] the establishment of which Matsukata Masayoshi regarded as an urgent priority and as central to the creation of an environment attractive to private investors. As Japanese Minister of Finance, he was personally listed as

---

24. Taiwan Yinhang, *An economic history*, vol. 1, pp. 2–5, and Takekoshi, *Japanese Rule in Formosa*, ch. 5.

25. *Taiwan ginkoshi* (A history of the Bank of Taiwan), Tokyo: Taiwan Ginkoshi, 1964, pp. 7–8.

the bank's largest single shareholder.[26] Taiwan joined Japan on the gold standard in 1904 no doubt also under Matsukata's influence, and links with Japan and East Asia were further strengthened by harbour construction and the opening of a network of subsidised shipping services.[27] Internal road and rail transport was another early priority, and between 1897 and 1904 nearly 2,000 miles of telegraph cable were laid.

As the elements of civil order and other prerequisites for a market economy moved into place, Governor-General Kodama turned to the problem of Taiwan's long-term economic development.[28] This required careful structuring of the roles of public and private sectors and had to take into account the profound pessimism over Taiwan's economic future common in both government and private business circles.[29] The approach developed was based on close and conscious parallels to early Meiji practice, and in the scenario that unfolded the role of the state was inevitably important. State investment took the lead in the provision of physical infrastructure, especially communications and transport, and this accounted for most of the activity in the island's first twenty-year plan. The state was also called upon to open foreign trade, develop human resources, improve agriculture, create an attractive environment for private foreign capital, and provide the framework necessary for Taiwan's colonial economic future.

The role of the private sector and Okura. Despite the dominance of the government, the tasks left to the private sector were important The activities of the Okura Company and the development of the sugar industry give a clear indication of their nature.

Okura's business origins were in gun-running for the winning side in the Meiji Restoration. From this experience the company's

---

26. Matsukata held 10,000 out of 50,000 shares and Okura Kihachiro (see below) held 2,652. Okura Zaibatsu Kenkyukai, *Okura zaibatsu*, p. 77.

27. Yanaihara, *Taiwan*, p. 65.

28. The key figures in the early administration of Taiwan were the Governor-General, Kodama Gentaro, and his Chief of Civil Administration, Goto Shimpei. The latter was responsible for the highly researched approach to colonial administration and had a famous library of Taiwanese materials. As we shall see, both re-appear in Japanese colonial history, with Goto as the President of the South Manchurian Railway.

29. This section is based on Okura Zaibatsu Kenkyukai, *Okura zaibatsu*, ch. 1–2.

founder, Okura Kihachiro, drew the important conclusion that while military matters could be left to soldiers, many opportunities for private enterprise existed in logistics, provisioning and transportation. Okura provided support for Japan's first military intervention in Taiwan in 1874 and moved quickly to take advantage of the island's full colonisation after 1895.[30] At first Okura's activities in Taiwan were essentially in trading, but as opportunities arose, the company extended itself into construction and production. As it enlarged its activities, so its corporate philosophy expanded. Okura later claimed that the Taiwan experience was the basis for his business empire; from it he had developed strong views about Japan's long term strategy for overseas economic expansion. According to Okura, the key to this expansion was the combination of trade and direct foreign investment. The primary role of foreign investment would be to extract and transport raw materials, followed by the establishment of a wide variety of productive and service industries. Okura envisaged a central role in this expansion for trading companies such as his own, since they alone had the organisation, human resources, capital and ability to reap economies of scale and scope. Close cooperation with government was an essential part of the Okura philosophy. He believed that only government could establish the political and diplomatic conditions for successful direct investment, and afford the risks inherent in large projects in economies still at an early stage of economic development. Put another way, the Okura philosophy was an extension of the domestic Meiji *shokusan kogyo* policies to the world of overseas economic relations.

Following this philosophy, Okura was active in the early formation of Taiwanese economic policy. He encouraged Kodama and his Chief Administrator, Goto Shimpei, to take an optimistic view of Taiwan's export potential; Okura's company itself became actively involved in construction, railway-building, forestry, sugar and other forms of agricultural production. Okura was also instrumental in encouraging Tokyo-based businessmen to examine the investment opportunities afforded by Taiwan, and he established a tripartite Taiwan development council, bringing together bureaucrats, politicians and businessmen in a characteristically Japanese framework of public–private sector cooperation. Later, Okura men trained in Taiwan played an important

---

30. A key source for these comments is 'The Okura strategy for overseas advance', *op. cit.*, pp. 106–32.

role in the expansion of the company's activities in China, Manchuria and elsewhere. So intertwined were the Okura business interests and Japanese colonial expansion that when the empire collapsed, so did nearly all the company's business. Like the South Manchurian Railway, Okura was a company that was born and died in war.

The growth of the sugar industry. Sugar became the central focus of the first phase of Taiwan's colonial development.[31] We have already seen how the Tokugawa government had sought to transfer sugar technology from Asian trading partners, and although Japanese *per capita* sugar consumption in the early Meiji period was only one seventh of that found in Britain, the foreign exchange costs of sugar imports were so serious that the government identified sugar and textiles as the two most important commodities for an active programme of import substitution. These early plans made some progress, but Japanese cane production costs in the south were high, while the new technique of sugar-beet cultivation in the north, though energetically developed, was still too expensive to compete with imports.[32] The problems of the domestic sugar industry were partly climatic and ecological and partly a reflection of the inefficiency of Japan's small-scale farming, for while the Japanese sugar-processing factories were increasingly using modern techniques by the late 1890s, the industry as a whole was held back by problems in Japanese agriculture.

Taiwan was clearly a promising location for sugar production and imperial import substitution. Cane cultivation had been introduced by the Dutch in the seventeenth century, and as early as 1900 Kodama went to Tokyo to persuade Masuda Takashi and the Mitsui Company to invest in the Taiwanese sugar industry. He also ordered an expert inquiry into the industry, the report of which was published the

31. Based on materials in Okura Zaibatsu Kenkyukai, *Okura zaibatsu*; Ito Shigeru (ed.), *Taiwan seito kabushiki kaishashi* (The history of the Taiwan Sugar Company), Tokyo: Taiwan Seito Kabushiki Kaisha, 1939; Yanaihara, 'Taiwan's sugar imperialism', *Taiwan*, part 2, pp. 203–84.

32. Cane sugar was cultivated in Okinawa and the Ryukyus and in Shikoku and Chugoku (the Ryukyus, after their long history of dual allegiance, were annexed by Japan in 1879). Matsukata learned of sugar-beet cultivation at the Paris Exposition of 1878. On his return to Japan, he encouraged its cultivation in the Hokkaido countryside and organised the establishment of a sugar-beet processing plant in Sapporo. Yanaihara, *Taiwan*, pp. 215–16.

following year.[33] As a result of this it was agreed that Taiwanese sugar be protected in domestic markets, that large-scale plantations for cane-growing be established, that fertilisation and irrigation be increased, and that improved varieties of cane and advanced techniques of sugar processing be imported. Thus not only was Taiwan to be a better location for sugar cultivation than the metropolis, but the colonial context also made it possible to ensure that a modern factory-processing sector would be matched by the efficiency of plantation cane cultivation.

Kodama decided that sugar was an ideal industry for the private sector and the Taiwan Sugar Manufacturing Joint Stock Company, founded with the support of the Bank of Taiwan and the Mitsui Bank, was the instrument chosen to implement this policy.[34] The standard *shokusan kogyo* formula of private ownership and a guaranteed minimum rate of return was applied. Land for the plantations came partly from reclamation, partly from stocks of untitled arable land identified during the cadastral survey, and partly by means of confiscation from large landowners. The industry was supported with tariffs and a sugar consumption tax and by marketing systems agreed with the Mitsui Trading Company.

Under these arrangements, the model company was so profitable that by 1914 it had attracted several large Japanese companies to join it. During the First World War a worldwide sugar shortage made this industry exceptionally profitable, and both the companies and the Taiwan government benefited. Indeed, this success had a highly favourable impact on the island's whole economy because government revenues from sugar were used for major projects that formed the basis for development in other parts of the agricultural and trading sectors.

By 1920 the Kodama–Okura strategies for Taiwan's economic development seemed well established. They had laid the foundations for Taiwanese growth and, more broadly, had enabled Japan to penetrate the economy of the Chinese eastern seaboard provinces

---

33. This was the *Togyo kairyo ikensho* (Proposals for improvement of the sugar industry) by Dr Nitobe, head of the Industrial Bureau. See Okura Zaibatsu Kenkyukai, *Okura zaibatsu*, pp. 92–7, and Ito, *The history of the Taiwan Sugar Company*, chs 1–2.

34. Not only was Mitsui the largest individual shareholder with 1,500 shares, but Masuda himself also appears to have held a further 500 in his own name. Ito, *The history of the Taiwan Sugar Company*, pp. 83–7.

through the banking system.[35] There had only been one divergence from the original, publicised policies. It had been stated that Taiwan would seek foreign investment from western as well as Japanese sources, but in the event only Japanese links were developed. Even in trades such as tea, where western merchants had been active and dominant before 1895, the strength of the Japanese banks and trading houses, combined with government discrimination through differential shipping tariffs and other devices, eventually reduced the foreigners to an insignificant role.[36] In spite of this, the overall strategy of state capital preparing the way for the private sector worked. The data in Fig. 12.1 illustrate the pattern precisely.

Agriculture and development in the 1920s

Let us now look in more detail at Japan's agricultural strategy in Taiwan. Although the supply of staple grains was not a major element in Japan's early plans for Taiwan, it definitely became one. During the quinquennium 1893–97 Japanese imports of rice exceeded exports for the first time, and in a bad year such as 1898 imports accounted for 14% of the total rice supply.[37] By the 1910s the problem was becoming serious. While the demand for food rose rapidly with industrialisation and urbanisation, the supply side was becoming more strained — partly because the early and relatively easy gains from the Meiji policies had been accomplished and partly because the disincentive effects of the Meiji landlord system were increasing.[38] Although

35. Financial penetration into the Chinese eastern seaboard was an explicit part of the Bank of Taiwan's foundation remit. By 1912 it was issuing currency and notes to circulate in Canton, Foochow and other South China ports. 'Japanese capital in China', *NCH*, April 6, 1912. Between 1916 and 1919 its overseas loans (excluding those to Japan) were larger than loans to Taiwan borrowers; between 1917 and 1924 foreign accounts were growing more rapidly than Taiwanese ones. Tu, *Taiwan under Japanese imperialism*, pp. 307–15.

36. By 1910 Lawton could report, 'If anything, it is more difficult for [foreign] capital to gain a foothold in Taiwan than it is in Japan itself'. Lancelot Lawton, *Empires of the Far East* (2 vols), London: Grant Richards, 1912, vol. 2, p. 1102. The role and fate of foreign capital is fully analysed by Yanaihara, *Taiwan*, pp. 33–49.

37. Data on trade and production is from Ajia Keizai Kenkyujo (ed.), *Nihon nogyo hyakunen norinsui sangyo ruinen tokeihyo* (A hundred years of Japanese agricultural annual statistics), Tokyo: Norin Tokei Kyokai, 1969, table 60, pp. 240–1.

38. Y. Hayami. *A Century of Agricultural Growth in Japan. Its Relevance to Asian Development*, University of Tokyo Press, 1975, pp. 60–1.

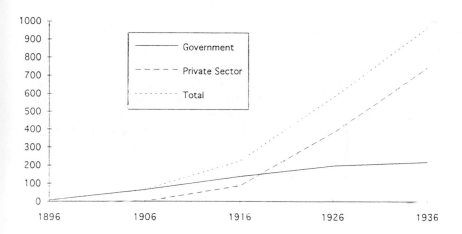

Fig. 12.1. GOVERNMENT AND PRIVATE INVESTMENT
IN TAIWAN, 1896–1936 (*millions of yen*)

Source: *Taiwan ginkoshi*, p. 71.

Japanese policy-makers were prepared to accept total import dependence in raw cotton, there was a deep reluctance to depart from some
form of basic self-sufficiency in food.[39] During the inter-war years,
the problems persisted and were reflected in stagnant rice yields.[40]

39. Kawano Shigeto, *Taiwan beikoku keizairon* (The rice economy of Taiwan),
Tokyo: Yuhikaku, 1941, pp. 10–11. This book is the most important single study
of the subject. It integrates technical and institutional issues and was written under
the guidance of Japan's most important modern agricultural economist, Tobata Seiichi.

40. Between 1920 and 1935 rice yields grew at less than one-third of the rate
achieved between 1885 and 1920. Data in Hayami, *A Century of Agricultural Growth
in Japan*, p. 120. The best technical account of the pre-war problems in Japanese
agriculture is still Ohkawa Kazushi *et al*. (eds), *Nihon keizai to nogyo. Seicho bunseki*
(The Japanese economy and agriculture: A growth analysis) (2 vols), Tokyo: Iwanami
Shoten, 1956, esp. chs 1–2.

These issues first erupted as matters of public concern at the end of the First World War. Between January 1917 and December 1919, rice prices more than tripled and popular dissatisfaction was expressed in the rice riots of July–September 1918, which to the older politicians must have been uncomfortably reminiscent of the rice and inflation riots of the 1860s, which had helped to destroy the old political order of Japan.[41] To appreciate the unfolding nature of this crisis we need to see it in its international and regional contexts. It then becomes clear that although the development of colonial food imports and the protection of domestic farming were eventually to solve the Japanese food problem, this outcome was far from predictable in the 1920s and early 1930s, when the overall situation still appeared precarious. One reason for this was the paradox that, while developments in the 'white' colonies were ensuring the adequacy of world *grain* supplies, the problem for Japan was the supply of *rice*. For many consumers the two were reasonable substitutes, but not for the Japanese. The rice issue thus requires careful attention.

The world rice economy. Rice is a highly specialised product that needs the climatic and soil conditions that are found mainly in monsoon Asia. It may be produced by systems of widely varying sophistication and productivity and it is characteristic of the monsoon economies that rice itself accounts for a disproportionate share of all food consumption. In the 1930s it was estimated that 630 million people derived more than 40% of their calorie intake from rice, and that for 375 million the proportion was more than 60%.[42] Rice cultivation is also deeply associated, particularly in Japan, with traditional social arrangements and even religious practices. This is one reason why rice issues have an importance that goes far beyond questions of nutrition, taste or food security.

In 1930–35, the twelve countries of monsoon Asia accounted for more than 95% of the world's rice output,[43] and within the region

---

41. Rice price data are for Tokyo. See Takekazu Ogura, *Agricultural Development in Modern Japan*, Tokyo: Fuji Publishing, 1968, p. 188. The rice riots were extremely frightening and widespread. In Kyoto, rioters cut telephones, overturned streetcars and looted shops. In all, several hundred people were killed. See 'The rice riots in Japan', *NCH*, Aug. 17, 24 and 31, 1918.

42. V. D. Wickizer and M. K. Bennett, *The Rice Economy of Monsoon Asia*, Stanford, CA: Food Research Institute, 1941, p. 116.

43. *Ibid.*, p. 23.

Table 12.1. MAJOR NET IMPORTERS OF RICE IN ASIA, 1931–35
(% shares of total Asian imports)

India	Japan	Dutch East Indies	China	British Malaya	Ceylon
26	30	7	20	9	9

MAJOR NET EXPORTERS OF RICE IN ASIA, 1931–35
(% shares of total Asian exports)

Burma	French Indo-China	Thailand	Sub-total	Korea	Taiwan	Sub-total
42	16	20	(78)	15	7	(22)

SOURCES OF SUPPLY OF JAPANESE RICE IMPORTS (GROSS), 1931–35
(% shares)

Korea	Taiwan	Other
65	30	5

Source: Wickizer and Bennett, *op cit.*, Appendix Tables, pp. 320–5.

China and India accounted for nearly two-thirds of the total output. Most Asian rice was consumed close to the point of production, and less than 10% of it entered international trade.[44] Only five of the monsoon economies were major rice exporters: Burma, French Indo-China, Thailand, Korea and Taiwan. Japan, India and China were the largest importers, and Table 12.1 summarises the rice trade of monsoon Asia in 1931–35. The importance of Taiwan in Japan's imported food supply is clear from these figures and their strength reflects the effort put into colonial rice cultivation, especially up to the end of the 1920s. However, outside of the Japan-Taiwan-Korea triangle, regional food security in the inter-war years remained unsatisfactory, which is of great relevance in judging the total situation. Data for China are uncertain, but estimates for the other eleven monsoon economies show that between 1921 and 1935 population was growing more rapidly than rice output. They also show that in the three key 'non-Japanese' export economies — Burma, Thailand

44. *Ibid.*, p. 28.

and French Indo-China — output per head actually declined between the 1920s and 1930s.[45]

The problem of the Asian rice supply was not insoluble, since it was clear at the time that the transfer of best current practice could substantially raise Asian yields, as the Japanese were demonstrating in Taiwan. But outside the colonial framework, the mechanisms to achieve such technology transfers were weak; hence the problems of supply remained very real.[46]

Rice policy in Taiwan. The first stage of Japanese colonial rice policy lasted from 1897 till 1907. During these years the land surveys were completed and standards for grading and exports were established. No major agronomic changes were made at this time, although as early as 1901 Kodama had forecast the long-term possibility of tripling Taiwanese rice output. By 1907 the government was ready to embark on comprehensive agrarian development. This programme included selection of improved seed varieties, encouragement for increased fertiliser application and, critically, long-term investment in major water projects for which the public finance was just becoming available. In combination, these measures could be expected to enable Taiwanese farmers to extend double cropping and to increase yields along the lines already established in Japan.[47]

---

45. *Ibid.*, pp. 188–94.

46. For example, yields in Laos in the 1930s were less than one-fifth of contemporary Japanese yields. Data on differential Asian yields and their changes over 1931–80 are tabulated in Randolph Barker and Robert W. Herdt, *The Rice Economy of Asia*, Washington, DC: Resources for the Future, 1985, p. 47. This issue is also at the heart of Ishikawa Shigeru's study, *Economic Development in Asian Perspective*, Tokyo: Kinokuniya, 1967, ch. 2.

47. This section is based on Kawano, *The rice economy*; Taiwan Yinhang, *An economic history*, ch. 2; Tu, *Taiwan under Japanese imperialism*, pp. 159–271. It is important to bear in mind that while Japanese policies in Taiwan bore a strong initial resemblance to the Meiji policies of achieving growth by the spread of old, best practices and by selection from traditional seed varieties (known as the *rono* policy), Taiwanese development also reflected the lessons learned in Japan between the 1870s and early 1900s and Japan's participation in the rapid, worldwide development of scientific plant-breeding thereafter. By the early 1900s the Japanese had not only clarified the importance for yields of increased fertiliser and public investment in water control but were also achieving sophistication in producing new rice varieties. Between 1900 and the 1920s, Japanese plant technologists advanced from the selection of best traditional varieties to the development of 'pure line' and finally hybrid varieties. This progression is described in detail for the case of cold-climate varieties for use

The introduction of new seed varieties was central to the rice strategy.[48] At first the policy was to select and improve existing varieties (*zairai kairyo*). Later, the *horai* group of varieties was introduced to improve yields and to satisfy the tastes of Japanese consumers. Experiments with *horai* lasted from 1911 till 1922, and from 1926 onwards it was actively distributed to the peasants in what Kawano called 'the age of *horai*'.[49] Starting in the north, where climatic conditions were closest to Japan, *horai* was gradually extended south, where the varieties had to adapt to the fully tropical conditions. By the 1940s *horai* was sown on 60% of the total rice area.[50]

The success of the new varieties depended not only on fertiliser application (for which special incentives were provided) but above all on new systems of irrigation. Total expenditure on irrigation in the 1920s was equal to half the entire amount spent from 1900 till 1944. Half of this expenditure came directly from the government, representing more than 25% of all funds raised through public bond offerings. Particularly remarkable was the huge Chianan project, which eventually irrigated 20% of the island's cultivated area and affected the production of 10% of all peasant households.[51] This project facilitated new, complex systems of multiple cropping and rotation and enabled higher yields of the new rice varities to be obtained.[52]

---

in the 'internal colony' of Hokkaido by M. Takahashi, *The History and Future of Rice Cultivation in Hokkaido*, Tokyo: United Nations University, 1980.

48. The scale of Japanese efforts may be judged from the fact that between 1931 and 1940, more than 5,000 crossbred rice varieties were developed for trial. Barker, 'Varietal improvement', *The Rice Economy of Asia*, pp. 54–9.

49. Kawano, *The rice economy*, chs. 1–2. See also Carole Carr and Ramon H. Myers, 'The agricultural transformation of Taiwan: the case of Ponlai rice, 1922–42' in R. T. Shand (ed.), *Technical Change in Asian Agriculture*, Canberra: Australian National University Press, 1973, pp. 28–50.

50. The difference between the northern and the southern climates may be judged from the fact that whereas in the north the ratio between the lowest and highest monthly rainfalls was approximately 5:1, the contrast in the tropical south between the drier winter and the monsoon peak raised this ratio to 28:1. The southern climate created serious mildew problems for *horai* varieties, which had originally been developed for the more northerly climate of Japan.

51. Ho, *Economic Development of Taiwan*, p. 37; Ono, *Japanese imperialism*, p. 119, 145; Yanaihara, *Taiwan*, pp. 60–1.

52. The full Chianan system had eleven cropping patterns, each operating over a three-year period. These rotated sugar, rice, green fertiliser and other crops in different combinations. A chart of the system is shown in Taiwan Yinhang, *An economic history*, vol. 1, p. 35.

The basic institutional element in the rice strategy was the decision to create and transform a small-scale farm sector worked by the indigenous population. In a situation where Japanese political control of the island was complete but separate from economic control, this scheme was in contrast to that found in Korea, where land was confiscated for large-scale agricultural projects, owned by Japanese and worked partly by immigrants. It was also in contrast to the sugar plantation system that eventually gave the sugar processors direct control of 80% of the cane they required. Thus whereas the implementation of sugar policy was largely a matter of installing select Japanese companies and providing them with appropriate privileges, financial signals and power over land, the Taiwan rice policy called for a difficult combination of market development and special incentives, supplemented by education, novel cooperative institutions such as the Irrigation and Farmers Associations, and even direct controls such as water allocation.[53]

The need for market development was well illustrated by the *horai* revolution. To be successful, this required a major change in what had largely been a subsistence system. Since *horai* rice was developed to suit Japanese tastes, and the Taiwanese peasants preferred not to consume these varieties, they had to exchange their output, through the market, for foods that were acceptable to them. Thus in place of the gradual development of commercialisation that is normal as market systems expand, the conversion of Taiwan into a source of food for the Japanese consumer required, for many Taiwanese peasants, an almost instant conversion to a market-dominated farming life. Levels of commercialisation varied by region, but by 1936–38 more than 75% of the rice harvest passed through the market.[54]

The complexities and drawbacks of the market were quite apparent in the 1920s and were illustrated by the Chianan project. This project took the high-yielding *horai* varieties into southern Taiwan where they came into direct competition with sugar at a time when the trend in the relative price of sugar was already encouraging peasants to increase

---

53. Control was also exercised through the market structure, which consisted of 400,000 rice-growing households, 700 private hulling operations and the four Japanese trading companies who handled exports. Tu, *Taiwan under Japanese imperialism*, pp. 204–5. In Taiwan (as in Japan in the 1920s) even the police played an active role in the administrative control of agriculture when necessary.

54. For purposes of comparison, the comparable rate in mainland China (i.e. state purchase and tax as a proportion of output) was still below 20% in the late 1970s. Kenneth R. Walker, *Food Grain Procurement and Consumption in China*, Cambridge University Press, 1984, p. 182.

the planting of rice. Since Taiwanese sugar was far more important to Japan than rice, this had to be stopped. To achieve this, the authorities had to use their power over water allocations to enforce their planting priorities on the farmers.[55]

Achievement of agricultural goals. The 1920s was the decade in which Japan obtained the fullest benefits from the development of Taiwan as an agricultural colony. At the heart of this achievement was the further expansion of sugar and rice and the large-scale investment in irrigation systems that they required.[56] With sugar, the strategy of the companies was to improve the productivity of both plantations and processing mills. Greater mill productivity was sought through the adoption of the most advanced known techniques of mechanisation for the conveyance, rolling and crushing of cane. So advanced were these techniques that contemporary photographs of the facilities rarely have more than one or two people visible in them.

On the plantations the intensification of cultivation was achieved by the adoption of imported, high-yielding, large-stemmed varieties of cane as well as by improvements in land formation, irrigation and pest control. At the same time, mechanisation of planting, harrowing and transporting cane was advanced with steam-driven machinery. The impact of these programmes was remarkable. In the ten seasons 1920/21 to 1929/30, sugar yields rose by 11% compound per year. In the season 1928–29, the Japanese empire at last achieved the self-sufficiency in sugar sought by the Tokugawa shoguns, with even a surplus for export.[57] By 1935 Taiwanese sugar accounted for 82% of the combined production of Japan and Taiwan.[58]

Progress in rice was equally impressive. Improved irrigation and the use of quick-ripening varieties enabled double cropping of rice to be extended from 29% of the arable area in 1905 to 56% in 1941.[59] Yields rose correspondingly (see Table 12.2). Taiwanese rice supple-

55. Compared to a rice price of 100, the relative sugar price between 1915 and 1930 fell from 235 to 70. These data and a full discussion of the use of water to control peasant planting are in Tu, *Taiwan under Japanese imperialism*, pp. 79–87.

56. Ono, *Japanese imperialism*, pp. 117–21.

57. Ito, *The history of the Taiwan Sugar Company*, ch. 7; 'The problems of the Formosan sugar industry. How Japan is meeting competition by the application of intensive cultivation and seed selection', *FER*, Nov. 1930, pp. 611–14.

58. The role of Taiwanese sugar in the Japanese market is discussed in Takahashi, *The economy of modern Taiwan*, ch. 5.

59. Taiwan Yinhang, *An economic history*, p. 31.

Table 12.2. INDICATORS OF AGRICULTURAL DEVELOPMENT
IN TAIWAN, 1900–40

LAND EXPANSION AND IMPROVEMENT

	Index of arable area	Arable land as % of total land	% of arable land irrigated
1898–1900	100	10.2	n.a.
1918–20	201	20.6	39.9
1938–40	244	23.9	61.7

YIELDS OF RICE AND SUGAR

	Rice	Sugar
1900	100	100
1918–20	147	104
1938	215	248

Source: Basic data from Taiwan Yinhang, *An economic history*, vol. 1, pp. 30–1, 37–43.

mented the domestic rice supply in Japan — at lower prices. This competitiveness reflected the lower incomes of Taiwanese cultivators, the advantages of their larger plots and a climate that enabled a higher proportion of the land to be doubled cropped. The price advantage of Taiwanese rice led to rapid penetration of the Japanese market, and although the overall contribution of Taiwan to the total Japanese rice supply in the 1930s was only 6%–7%, its share of the *marketed* rice needed to feed urban areas was as high as 17%.[60] Taiwanese harvests were also more consistent than domestic ones, hence Taiwan played the additional role of stabilising the Japanese market.[61]

Taiwan's colonial role after 1931

The role of Taiwan as a colonial economy changed fundamentally during the 1930s. One reason for this was the move towards agricultural protectionism in Japan. Contemporary analysts noted that

60. More than 70% of Taiwanese rice went to the markets of Tokyo, Osaka, Kobe and Nagoya. Kawano, *The rice economy*, pp. 295–6.
61. Instability indexes for the Japanese and colonial harvests for 1918–37 are calculated by Kawano, *ibid.*, pp. 108–9.

1931 was the first year in which total supplies of rice available in Japan exceeded their estimated requirements. This turning-point coincided with the onset of a severe worldwide agricultural depression. The combination of the low-cost food supplies available on world markets and the distress of Japanese domestic agriculture created a new agenda for colonial policy-makers. With rice, pressures for protection became intense and ultimately had to be acceded to.[62]

For commodities other than rice, the role of colonial supplies had to be questioned where these could only be produced at prices in excess of world prices. Sugar was a central issue here. Remarkable as Taiwanese development had been, climatic and ecological reasons caused cane sugar costs to remain well above those in Java and Cuba. In addition, world markets generally had also been invaded by low-cost supplies of beet sugar.[63] The problem was manifested in 1930 when Cuban exporters appeared on the Chinese mainland market quoting prices that the Taiwan-based companies could only match with difficulty. An additional problem for the Taiwan government was the fact that the development of irrigation — intended to benefit both rice and sugar — was more effective in raising rice than sugar yields. During the 1930s this led to higher land costs and hence to still higher sugar costs.[64]

By 1937 other, new elements were entering the calculations. Japanese economic strategists were beginning to think of a much wider geographical sphere of planned economic cooperation, including

---

62. A series of control measures were introduced between 1921 and 1933 but these were largely ineffective. In 1934–39, virtually no foreign rice was allowed into Japan and colonial supplies were strongly discouraged at source. Bruce F. Johnston, *Japanese Food Management in World War II*, Stanford, CA: Food Research Institute, 1953, ch. 4.

63. The relationship between Java, Japan and the Taiwanese sugar problem may be deduced from an important article by Peter Boomgaard, 'Treacherous cane. The Java sugar industry between 1914 and 1940' in Bill Albert and Adrian Graves (eds), *The World Sugar Economy in War and Depression, 1914–1940*, London: Routledge, 1988. This explains that up to 1870 all Javanese sugar went to Holland, but that after 1872 Javanese sugar had to find Asian outlets. In the 1930s the introduction of new varieties in Java was driving up yields at a time when protectionism and the slump were reducing demand.

64. Higher land costs were a general indicator of Taiwan's rising level of development and its declining comparative advantage in agriculture. Colonial government surveys in 1923 and 1929 had already indicated the small and declining potential for both land reclamation and agricultural development. Takahashi, *The economy of modern Taiwan*, p. 94.

the Dutch East Indies and other South-East Asian economies capable of producing sugar and tropical commodities. These Asian economies were seen not only as low-cost sources of imports but also as major export markets for Japanese manufactures, which they would only be able to acquire through new systems of managed trade and barter. Thus space had to be made for these new sources of agricultural imports, which greatly weakened the case for continued preservation of existing Japanese sugar arrangements.[65]

These broad considerations led ultimately to a far more positive re-evaluation of Taiwan's economic future. Within the division of labour envisaged by what was to become the Greater East Asian Co-Prosperity Sphere, Taiwan was to move well beyond the stage of intensive agricultural specialisation. According to this scenario, Taiwan was to shed its rice and tropical product exports in favour of South China and South-East Asia, so that it could then industrialise on the basis of the heavy investments already made in hydro-electricity. It was recognised that to support this there would have to be an inflow of Japanese migrants with appropriate high-level skills.[66] It was also anticipated that, with the disappearance of the British from Singapore and Hong Kong, the well-established triangular trading system of Taiwan, Kobe and Osaka would become the commercial hub of the Asia Pacific region, with Taiwan as the 'base [*kyoten*] of our country's southward development'.[67] Thus waves of secondary

65. Takahashi's fundamental argument was that Taiwan's economy would be transformed by a combination of the new world agricultural situation and the emergence of an international trading system made up of bloc economies. Takahashi referred to the former as the product of 'a new industrial revolution', i.e. a revolution that reinforced agriculture's supply side with use of tractors and chemical fertilisers, and was at the same time profoundly changing demand by the development of man-made fibres. He also argued that oversupply in agriculture was itself one of the factors accelerating barter and bloc based systems, since only such systems could provide a secure foundation for rational trade in agricultural products. See Takahashi, *The economy of modern Taiwan*, especially chs 1–2.

66. Immigration policy is the underlying agenda of 'The situation with regard to Taiwan's population', *Takushoku shoreikan kiho* (The quarterly journal of the Department for Encouraging Colonisation), no. 1, Jan. 1939, pp. 111–76. See also Takahashi, *The economy of modern Taiwan*, p. 44.

67. Takahashi, *The economy of modern Taiwan*, p. 345. See also the later unfolding of these ideas outlined in 'Taiwan and the southerly [economic] sphere' in Taiwan Keizai Nenpo Kankosha, *Taiwan keizai nenpo* (Taiwan economic yearbook), Tokyo: Kokusai Nihon Kyokai, 1942, part 3.

Table 12.3. ECONOMIC AND TRADE INDICATORS
FOR TAIWAN, 1910–35,
(% per annum, trend growth rates)

Population	Net Domestic Product	Industrial production	Agricultural production	Railway freight · movement	Export volume
1.88	4.03	5.81	2.94	9.76	6.6

Source: Basic series from Ho, *Economic Development of Taiwan*, p. 27.

Table 12.4. THE CHANGING EXPORT STRUCTURE OF
TAIWANESE FOREIGN TRADE, 1911–38

	% of exports sent to Japan	Commodity structure of exports		
		Foodstuffs	Raw materials	Capital and consumer goods
1911–15	66	75	10	13
1916–20	75	73	13	9
1921–25	73	77	8	9
1926–29	77	78	7	9
1930–35	87	87	7	6
1936–38	90	90	5	6

Source: Ho, in Myers and Peattie, *The Japanese Colonial Empire*, pp. 396–7.

and tertiary development, together with the specialisation of agriculture away from sugar and rice, constituted the formula for the development of Taiwan in the 1940s.

Conclusions

The economic growth of Taiwan under Japanese rule was impressive and is summarised by the indicators shown in Table 12.3, and the impact of this development on the Taiwanese export structure and the increasing Japanese orientation of the economy is shown in Table 12.4. In the perspective of Japan's objectives at the time, the colonisation of Taiwan has to be judged a success. Growth was achieved and output and export structures were shifted in the desired direction by a combination of government activity and Japanese corporate control. The contribution of Taiwan to the Japanese food supply has been discussed above. To some extent also, Taiwan was developed as a market for

Table 12.5. THE RATES OF GROWTH OF REAL WAGES AND PER CAPITA INCOME IN TAIWAN, KOREA AND JAPAN, 1915–38
(% per annum)

	Gross Domestic Expenditure (1920/24–1935/38)	Wages in manufacturing (male) (1915/17–1931/33)	Wages in agriculture (female) (1915/17–1931/33)
Taiwan	1.93	5.6	2.8
Korea	.27	1.9	.8
Japan	2.04	5.1	1.2

Sources: As Chart 12.2 and Toshiyuki Mizoguchi, 'Consumer prices and real wages in Taiwan and Korea under Japanese rule', *Hitotsubashi Journal of Economics*, vol. 13 no. 1, June 1972, pp. 40–56.

Japanese manufactured exports. However, although it served as a destination for skilled Japanese in government, management and professional work, the attempt to develop small-scale farming and make Taiwan an outlet for surplus Japanese rural migrants failed.

The experience of colonial development was less harsh and socially divisive for Taiwan than for Korea. This was mainly because the Japanese reorganised basic production in Taiwan particularly from within existing structures, controlling and evolving, rather than destroying and replacing them with foreign implants. Apart from organisation, the Japanese contribution to Taiwan in human terms was the large number of professionals who became indispensable to the island's technological revolution, especially in agriculture, and to whose skill the increase in agricultural yields is the most remarkable single testimony. In terms of human welfare, while food consumption showed little improvement, it did not at any point markedly decline as it did in Korea. A summary of the progress and relative levels of per head income in Taiwan, Korea and Japan is shown in Fig. 12.2. Table 12.5 lists wage data which reveal a considerable improvement in real incomes, in stark contrast to the Korean experience. In addition to the gains shown here, the Taiwanese population also made what are to some extent unquantifiable gains from government expenditures on health and education. In the case of health, the environment was improved to the point where even the Japanese lived more healthily in Taiwan than in Japan. Fig. 12.3 shows the improvements

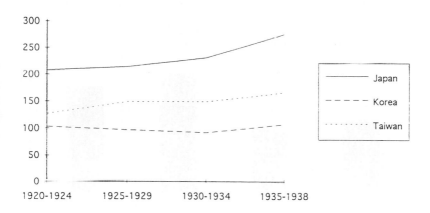

Fig. 12.2. GROSS DOMESTIC EXPENDITURE PER CAPITA,
JAPAN, KOREA AND TAIWAN, 1920–38
(*yen at 1934–36 prices*)

Source: Data from Ono, *Japanese imperialism*, p. 155.

in Taiwanese fertility and mortality and compares them with those
for Japan.[68]

In education, the drive for literacy in the Japanese language was
especially important. This was actively supported by the government
in normal schooling and part-time programmes for adults and for
workers from every sector of the economy. Indeed, the education
programme of colonial Taiwan even extended to supporting Japanese-
language schools in three major cities on the east coast of China.[69] In

68. Barclay, *Colonial Development and Population in Taiwan*, p. 238.
69. An excellent contemporary account of these educational programmes is to be
found in the offical publication from Taiwan Sotokufu, *Taiwan jijo* (Conditions in
Taiwan), Taipei: Taiwan Jiho Hakkosho, 1933, ch. 9. (The accuracy and value of this
compilation is attested by a note from the British Consular Office in Tamsui, appended
to the Foreign Office copy of the book.)

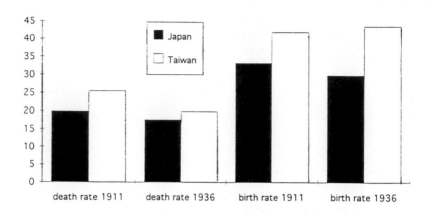

Fig. 12.3. BIRTH AND DEATH RATES IN TAIWAN AND JAPAN, 1911–36
(rates per 1,000 of population)

Source: 'The situation with regard to Taiwan's population', *The Monthly Journal of the Department for Encouraging Colonisation*, pp. 134–7. Full details of the programme of disease eradication and other health measures are in Barclay, *Colonial Development and Population in Taiwan*, ch. 6.

addition to the importance of formal education, the Taiwanese also benefited from the training given to Taiwanese employees in the government and private sectors. This was a significant gain, for by 1944 there were nearly a quarter of a million Taiwanese in industrial occupations of some kind.[70]

Japan's colonial activities contributed in various ways to Taiwan's post-war economic success. Colonial development established a rapid trajectory of growth, a market culture and an economy with the highest exports per head of any country in Asia, including Japan. In agriculture — the focus of Japan's most intensive colonial efforts —

70. By 1944 there were nearly a quarter of a million Taiwanese in the industrial sector — Tu, *Taiwan under Japanese imperialism*, p. 146.

Japanese-led development not only ensured Taiwan's post-war food self-sufficiency but also enabled the sector to remain the largest source of Taiwanese export earnings till the late 1960s. This post-war growth reflected the pre-war investments in infrastructure and in research and development. It also reflected the survival of the cooperative and agricultural extension structures initiated by the Japanese, which then flourished in the post-war era, complemented by a successful land reform.

The other institutional legacy of the colonial period was the scale and tradition of the public sector. The public sector remained at the core of Taiwanese industrial development down to the early 1980s, both in the sense that enterprises inherited from the Japanese were retained and developed and that creative use was made of new public sector initiatives. Even today, elements of the old Japanese structures persist, especially in relation to landholding. In 1939 the ten largest Japanese agricultural corporations accounted for nearly one-fifth of Taiwan arable land; all of this was inherited by the Taiwanese public sector. Among these holdings, those of the Taiwan Sugar Company have remained so substantial that privatisation of the corporation in this century was still not deemed feasible in the early 1990s.

However, there were some negative aspects to the Japanese period. The colonial government distorted development by creating an over-specialised agricultural economy. The Japanese also left a legacy of high population growth and failed to train the Taiwanese in the higher-level professional and managerial skills. However, these problems proved not to be too serious. Migration from the mainland solved the problem of high-level manpower, population growth proved a spur rather than a barrier to development, and the market orientation of the system enabled it to respond quickly with the restructuring required for a more balanced development. Thus the ending of the colonial era arguably posed more problems for the Japanese economy than for Taiwan, for the very success in developing colonial agriculture had enabled Japan to postpone the difficult issues of a domestic land reform. Hence agriculture was one of the first Japanese economic problems that had to be addressed in 1945.

13

THE ECONOMIC EXPANSION OF JAPAN
IN MANCHURIA

'With an annual increase of 1,300,000 in the population of the Empire, Japan is facing the gravest problem that has ever disturbed the equilibrium of a modern state ... Japan stands at the crossroads and, placing her problems before the world, asks in no uncertain tone: *"What are you going to do about it?"*' — George Bronson Rea, *Far Eastern Review*, November 1930

'During a world upheaval with bombs dropping from the sky and bursting all around, one is apt to wonder what caused these terrible things to happen.' — Chiang Monlin, Kunming, 1942

The exploratory phase in Manchuria, 1860–1918

Japan started to involve itself in Manchuria in the late nineteenth century as a drive to acquire political influence and to exploit opportunities for trade and direct investment. In 1931 it proceeded to full-scale occupation and proxy rule through a puppet regime, and this was followed by the invasion of China between 1937 and 1945. Throughout the whole of this period, economic, political and strategic objectives were closely related, although the interests of businessmen, politicians and the military were often in open conflict.[1]

---

1. General sources for this section include T. Hoshino, *Economic History of Manchuria* Seoul: Bank of Chosen, 1921; Sun Kungtu and Ralph Huenemann, *The Economic Development of Manchuria in the First Half of the Twentieth Century*, Cambridge, MA: Harvard East Asian Monographs, no. 28, 1969; Kang Chao, *The Economic Development of Manchuria: The Rise of a Frontier Economy*, Ann Arbor: Michigan Papers in Chinese History, no. 43, 1983; Manshushi Kenkyukai (eds), *Nihon teikokushugi ka no Manshu* (Manchuria under Japanese imperialism), Tokyo: Ochanomizu Shobo, 1972; Zhang Cheng-da, *Dong-Bei jingji* (The north-eastern economy) (2 vols) Taipei: Chunghwa Chubanshe, 1955; the files of the *North China Herald* and *Contemporary Manchuria*. I have also drawn upon earlier work on the subject, including Christopher Howe, 'Japan's economic experience in China before the establishment of the People's Republic of China: A retrospective balance sheet', in Ronald Dore and Radha Sinha (eds), *Japan and World Depression Then and Now: Essays in Memory of E. F. Penrose*, London: Macmillan, 1987, pp. 155–77.

For our purposes, the Manchurian story started with the Russo-Chinese and Tientsin treaties of 1858–60, and was subsequently punctuated by three war settlements: those for the Sino-Japanese war in 1895, for the Russo-Japanese war in 1906 and for the First World War in 1919–22. Each of these settlements provided the framework for the next stage of foreign and Japanese economic involvement in Manchuria and China proper.[2] The Russo-Chinese treaties of 1858 and 1860 ceded to the Russians vast territories north of the Heilong (Amur) river and between the Ussuri river and the Pacific, thereby transforming Russia into a Pacific power with access to the sea at Vladivostok. By the Treaty of Tientsin (1840), the British were allowed to open a consulate in Newchang, a port at the mouth of the Liao river in the south of Manchuria. From these beginnings a vast and largely empty region, traditionally preserved as the homeland and hunting ground of the Manchu aristocracy, began a process of development which by 1931 had given it a pivotal position in the economy of East Asia and thrust it to the forefront of world politics.

The economic growth of the region was at first tentative and conducted at a modest pace. British consular officials in Newchang encouraged the export of soya beans and other agricultural products that could be floated downriver on junks from the interior. But although soya bean exports grew at a steady 4%–5% *per annum* between the 1860s and the 1890s, and although the port accounted for about half of all Manchurian trade by the turn of the century, Newchang was iced up for four to five months of the year and the consular reports suggest little in the way of frenetic commercial activity.[3] On the contrary, they describe a leisured life of skating in winter and cricket against visiting British sailors in summer. There were tea-parties, concerts, treaty-port gossip and genteel dances often

2. A helpful introduction to the early treaties and the complex history of relations in the region is 'Prologue to the Crisis' in B. L. Putnam Weale, *Manchu and Muscovite*, New York: Macmillan, 1904, pp. 1–65.

3. Data on the growth of the soya bean trade from Sun, *The Economic Development of Manchuria*, p. 15. Further details on the soya bean and its uses and processing may be found in Alexander Hosie, *Manchuria: Its Peoples, Resources and Recent History*, London: Methuen, 1904 and China Imperial Maritime Customs, *The Soya Bean of Manchuria*, Shanghai, 1911.

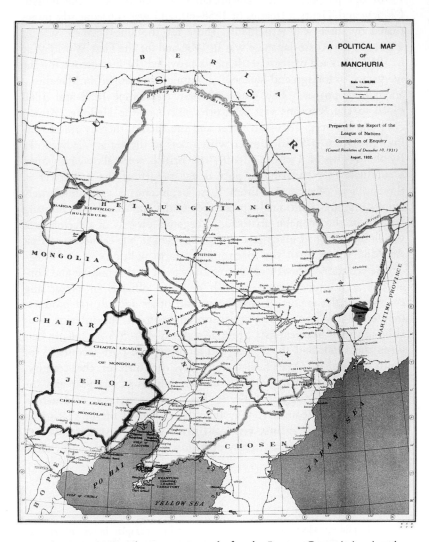

Manchuria in 1932. The map was made for the Lytton Commission inquiry into the Japanese invasion of that country.

timed to mark the changing seasons.[4] From the north, however, the Russians used their strength to begin an energetic penetration of Manchuria, spurred by the economic potential of railway and waterway development. For by using the spring and summer tides of the Sungari and Heilong rivers, one could travel over 3,000 miles by boat, linking Nicolaievsk on the Sea of Ohkotsk, Vladivostok and central Manchuria with the commercial heartland of China on the upper Yangtze and in Shanghai.

At the same time as the Russians advanced from the north, Newchang became the southern port of entry for migrant Chinese peasants seeking a better life in Manchuria than they could find in the overpopulated, marginal agricultural lands of the North China Plain. The Japanese also began to develop interests in a region rich with agriculture and raw materials, which by the 1890s was also thought of as an important potential market for Japanese manufactured exports. Further, because of its border with Korea it also fell within the sphere of strategic national interest. But in spite of all these initiatives, Manchuria in the 1890s was still largely an empty country of mountain and forest and vast uncultivated plains that were the roaming-grounds of Mongol pastoralists, bandits and a motley assortment of commercial adventurers. Hunters could still shoot antelope, wild boar, bears, cats, foxes, sables, tigers and leopards, and although prospectors had reported the presence of gold, iron, coal and other mineral resources, these had not been seriously developed.[5]

The Sino-Japanese war quickened international competitiveness and the pace of Manchurian economic development. By the Treaty of Shimonoseki (1895) Japan at first gained — and was then forced to cede back — the Liaotung peninsula. However, the crucial point of the settlement was that it gave Japan 'great power' status in China, and with it the right to make direct industrial investments and enjoy

---

4. Life and events in Newchang were reported to the weekly *North China Herald* as part of that paper's round-up of treaty-port news. This description is based on issues in the first half of 1890. The Consular Reports of T. T. Meadows, who moved to Newchang in 1861, were regarded as classics of their kind, even in the nineteenth century. See the account of Newchang in Dennys, *The Treaty Ports*, pp. 538–45.

5. Hosie, *Manchuria, passim.*; 'Manchuria' in Lawton, *Empires of the Far East*, vol. 2, pp. 1109–1358; the files of the *North China Herald*.

other commercial privileges.[6] As a result, Japanese activity in Manchuria accelerated between 1895 and 1904; textile exporters made significant inroads into Chinese and Manchurian markets, and industrial investments were supported by vigorous expansion of commerce, banking and transport. Among the trading companies Mitsui, Mitsubishi and Okura were particularly active.

The most visible point of conflict at this time was the striving by foreigners for railway concessions — a form of economic expansion widely seen as giving effective political control.[7] Initially the Russians were the most successful in this, securing between 1896 and 1898 the right to occupy the Liaotung peninsula and to build the Chinese Eastern Railway (CER). The latter was an immense potential economic gain. The original Russian plan had been to connect the Pacific with Europe via Russian Siberia but this was proving immensely difficult and expensive. Thus the CER was in effect a 900-mile short-cut that took the railway from the Khingan mountains across the rich Sungari plain and on to Vladivostok.[8] Later, the Russian system was extended south from the junction at Harbin to link with a branch line

<hr />

6. Full details of the major treaties and other instruments relevant to Japanese expansion in China and Manchuria are in vol. 1 of MacMurray, *Treaties and Agreements*. The scale of unequal treaty-making in China during the period after 1840 was considerable. A recent Chinese study fills 52 pages with a listing of the titles, including 100 treaties and supplementary instruments made by the Japanese, compared to 73 items listed for Britain. Li Bo-lu *et al.* (eds), *Jiu Zhongguo bu pingdeng tiaoyue shihua* (An historical account of the unequal treaties of old China), Xian: Shanxi Renmin Chubanshe, 1992, pp. 246–97.

7. P. H. B. Kent, *Railway Enterprise in China: An Account of its Origin and Development*, London: Arnold, 1907. This source has a valuable appendix of the legal instruments governing railway concessions. S. H. Chou, 'Railway development and economic growth in Manchuria', *China Quarterly*, no. 45, Jan.–March 1971, pp. 57–84. On the political significance of railways, a contemporary observer commented: '. . . Communications have acquired such vast significance that it may be truly said that they constitute today the most tangible evidence of sovereignty . . . left in the hands of aliens, surrounded by their own troops, what you have is *de facto* military occupation . . .' B. L. Putnam Weale, *The Truth about China and Japan*, New York: Dodd, Mead, 1919, p. 88. Much the same could be said of the control of telegraph wires.

8. In this period the Russians also obtained rights to acquire lands and administrative powers in the railway 'zone', police the zone with troops, undertake forestry development, navigate on the Sungari river and various other communications and extra-territorial priviliges. These all constituted disastrous precedents when the balance of power changed and the Japanese inherited these rights along with the CER.

from Newchang. The completion of this network was a significant engineering achievement, undertaken by a company charged with broad developmental tasks that went far beyond conventional railway management. In this important sense the CER was both a symbol of Russia's ambitions to colonise the region and, a forerunner of the Japanese South Manchurian Railway Company (SMR).

The defeat of Russia in the Russo-Japanese war led to a major shift in the Manchurian balance of power and was the starting-point for a further vigorous phase of Japanese prospecting, espionage, market research and economic expansion throughout the region.[9] By the Treaty of Portsmouth (1905) the Japanese finally obtained not only the Liaotung peninsula (known as the Kwantung Leased Territory) but also the southern part of the CER and the strip of land along which it was built, known as the SMR zone. Although the zone was only 62 metres wide and had an area of 298 square kilometres in total, it proved a significant concession because the Japanese then interpreted their rights as allowing them to develop economic activities in parts of Manchuria to which they had no other legitimate claims.[10]

The railway and its properties were entrusted to the South Manchurian Railway Company. Founded in 1906 by imperial ordinance, the SMR was financed by international and Japanese capital and run by a board and a series of presidents whose background and functions reveal the mixture of economic, governmental and military functions

9. A strong tradition of state espionage had been handed down from Tokugawa times, and some commentators noted that Japan's success in the Russo-Japanese war could be regarded as the culmination of ten years of successful intelligence work in Manchuria. Spies were often disguised as pedlars, photographers and barbers. Military and economic intelligence were substantially interchangeable and teams of Chinese-speaking Japanese students were notably active in the latter. See Lawton, *Empires of the Far East*, vol. 1, pp. 282–4, 330–1; 'Japanese espionage in China', *NCH*, May 17, 1913; and, Dana G. Munro, 'Prospects in Manchuria', *FER*, July 1913, pp. 61–5.

10. The Leased Territory was 2,462 sq. km. The legal case against Japan's administration of this land is expounded in, Herbert Hantao Wu, *Japan's Acts of Treaty Violation and Encroachment upon the Sovereign Rights of China in the North-Eastern Provinces (Manchuria)*, Peking: North-Eastern Affairs Research Institute, 1932 (repr. Taipei, 1972). Ch. 3 deals with the controversy over the SMR zone land. The Japanese view of the zone is explained in 'A review of the thirty-year Japanese administration of the Kwantung Leased Territory and the SMR Zone', *Contemporary Manchuria*, vol. 3, no. 1, Jan. 1939, pp. 57–79.

that the railway was to perform.[11] Against strong Chinese opposition, the Manchurian line was soon joined to the Japanese-built Korean railway, a system which traversed a wild and mountainous terrain, and whose construction, with 205 bridges, 24 tunnels and 213 culverts, was described by a contemporary western expert as 'an engineering feat' and 'a triumph'.[12] When fully developed, the SMR and its associate systems circled half the globe with luxurious air-conditioned trains which reduced the time needed to travel to East Asia from Europe by two-thirds and the cost, compared with that of the sea voyage, by more than half. In addition, the company was encouraged to expand into virtually any business enterprise, often in conjunction with Okura and other large trading firms. Notable SMR businesses included the world's largest opencast coal mine at Fushun and what became China's most important iron and steel works at Anshan.[13]

Between 1905 and the First World War Japanese economic expansion in Manchuria intensified. Direct investment in railways and mines was the leading edge of this penetration but there were other economic prizes to be had. After a visit to the area in the same period, Yamanobe Takeo of the Osaka Boseki reported: 'In our eyes the purchasing power of the Manchurians is almost boundless.' Manchuria itself was 'one of the best markets in the world for cotton textiles . . . I have come back loaded with hope'.[14]

Industrial advance was supported by both banking penetration and

11. The origins of the SMR and a detailed analysis of its Board are in Ando Hikataro (ed.), *Mantetsu* (The South Manchurian Railway), Tokyo: Ochanomizu Shobo, 1965, ch. 1–2. A contemporary survey of the SMR is in a series of articles in the *FER*, Feb., April and Nov. 1909. An excellent recent analysis of the subject is R. H. Myers, 'Japanese imperialism in Manchuria: The South Manchuria Railway Company, 1906–1933' in Duus, *The Japanese Informal Colonial Empire*, pp. 101–32. A positive, propagandist account of the SMR, emphasising its developmental, non-colonising role, is Henry W. Kinney, *Modern Manchuria and the South Manchuria Railway*, Dairen, 1928. Kinney was later kidnapped on an SMR train by anti-Japanese patriots and suffered various humiliations. See Edgar Snow, *The Far Eastern Front*, London: Jarrold, 1934, pp. 238–9.

12. 'The railways of Manchuria and Korea. Probable instruments of war do valuable work in times of peace', *FER*, no. 5, April 1918, pp. 143–53.

13. The government order establishing the SMR lists six major business sectors which it may enter, adding that it may enter any other business as well with permission. The order also requires that within the zone area, the SMR is responsible for education, health and physical infrastructure. MacMurray, *Treaties and Agreements*, vol. 1, pp. 557–8.

14. Quoted in Lawton, *Empires of the Far East*, vol. 2, pp. 1180–1.

the expansion of trading companies.[15] Banking made inroads by virtue of the acceptability of Japanese banknotes based first upon silver (still the preferred metal of the Chinese after 400 years) and later gold.[16] Okura quickly laid the foundations of an empire in trade, mining, metallurgy, forestry, warehousing and agriculture and Mitsui Bussan was equally active. Mitsui had arrived in Manchuria as early as 1890 when Yamamoto Jotaro, a young man in the company's Shanghai office, was sent to reconnoitre business prospects. At that time he was probably the only domestically recognised Japanese businessman in Manchuria. From the outset the company maintained close relations with the SMR: it received most of the SMR orders in the post-1905 boom, and in turn provided the SMR with soya bean freight, its most profitable business. By 1927 Yamamoto had changed careers, cementing the relationship by becoming President of the SMR.[17] The soya bean was the heart of the Mitsui business in Manchuria, for which the company laid the early foundations by establishing a monopoly of the trade. It did this through the efforts of its indefatigable agents, who tramped the remote Manchurian countryside, buying directly 'in every out-of-the-way bean-growing district' and by the imaginative use of the Japanese army telegraph system, through which it maintained unrivalled control of market information.[18]

To establish their power in the Manchurian cities, the Japanese did not hesitate to seize economic assets by force or fraud. One writer

15. Banking aggression was facilitated by the ease with which gold-based Japanese banknotes drove out Chinese and Russian rivals. 'Manchurian currency', *NCH*, April 12, 1907.

16. The Russians had tried to use the CER to establish acceptability of their paper currencies but had failed. See 'The defeat of the travelling rouble', ch. 15 in Putnam Weale, *Manchu and Muscovite*. In this book Putnam Weale described the Russo-Chinese Bank as 'the Jesuit of politico-finance'.

17. Valuable material on this subject is included in *Mitsui tokuhon* (The Mitsui reader), Tokyo: Ajia Shobo, 1943, esp. 'Mitsui Bussan and the development of Manchuria', pp. 262–91. Just how hard direct buying must have been is suggested by the pioneer medical missionary Dugald Christie. 'Made up roads are non existent. Rough tracks lead across the country from village to village, usually below the level of the surrounding land, and deep ruts are worn by heavy carts conveying the produce of the district to the nearest mart . . . in times of rain these roads become streams or a succession of ponds or quagmires, and the weary mules have to struggle on at a snail's pace'. *Thirty Years in Moukden, 1883–1913*, London: Constable, 1914, p. 65.

18. The quotation is from 'Stray notes from Manchuria', *NCH*, Feb. 24, 1912. The telegraph point is from *Mitsui tokuhon*, pp. 262–91.

commented: 'To the victor belong the spoils, and the average Japanese adventurer acted on the old adage. If a house looked good to him he occupied it, if the natives did not show due respect to the victor, he was pummelled and put through a course of jiujitsu.'[19] Once in charge, Japanese nationals pushed forward their commercial advantage not only by skilful strategy and hard work but also by stolen trademarks and preferential post, telegraph and freight rates, customs manipulation and other tricks.[20]

Economic imperialism was supplemented by cultural expansion. Desperate for modern learning, the younger generation of Chinese were eager to study under any auspices. They learned from the growing numbers of Japanese teachers at home, while thousands also went to Japan for university education, many on Chinese government scholarships. Japan's impact on the Chinese intellectual liberation was so great that it was to influence Sino-Japanese relations for more than three generations, even at the time when it was reported that 'almost any book on any subject in various branches of human knowledge may be procured in China and it is a noteworthy fact that there are many Chinese who are perfectly able to read books and papers in the Japanese language.'[21]

Through all this conflict and expansion, the Japanese often retained the warm and influential support of foreign observers. After the Sino-

19. 'Japanese in Manchuria', *FER*, Feb. 1909, pp. 297ff. See also Lawton, *Empires of the Far East*, vol. 2, p. 1163. 'The Japanese acted as though they were conquerors in a conquered land . . . [they] inaugurated a period of tyranny far worse than any which might have preceded it.' The Japanese seizure of Korean economic assets was equally ruthless but largely unreported. The English writer E. T. Bethell, who did provide graphic reports and established an independent Korean newspaper to publicise what was happening, was forcibly silenced by the Japanese with the shameful connivance of British Foreign Office officials. See 'E. T. Bethell and the Taehan Shinbo', *Korea Journal*, April 1984, pp. 39–44. In 1960 Bethell was retrospectively made a Hero of the Korean Revolution.

20. 'Trade in Manchuria', *NCH*, May 24, 1907; Lawton, *Empires of the Far East*, vol. 2, pp. 1155–86; 'Prospects in Manchuria. A brief survey of American commercial interests', *FER*, July 1913, pp. 61–5.

21. 'Japanese educational influence in China' , *NCH*, March 1, 1907. Zhou Enlai was just one of the future rulers of China who studied in Japan and who, after the break with the Soviets in 1960, instinctively turned to Tokyo for economic support. Zhou was personally involved in the 1962 negotiations with the Japanese leader Takasaki, even to the extent of setting the long-term trade targets. See Christopher Howe, 'China, Japan and Economic Interdependence in the Asia Pacific Region', *The China Quarterly*, no. 124, Dec. 1990, pp. 674–5.

Japanese war the poet and traveller Sir Edwin Arnold argued that Japan was the 'champion of progress, justice and international development' and that its people had done (in the war) 'what any Englishman would have done in his place'.[22] And while the British community in Newchang might come to regret that 'the sleepy, happy-go-lucky days of the last century ... were lost forever', British policy after the Russo-Japanese war was determined by the Anglo-Japanese alliance and the Anglo-Japanese naval co-operation which this entailed.[23] It was also influenced by the views of businessmen such as the chairman of Shell, Marcus Samuel, who went on record at a meeting of his company in 1904 with this significant statement:

I am thoroughly convinced that, had Russia not been justly tackled by Japan, Manchuria would have been lost to European trade, and particulary to our company ... Besides this, I am convinced that, with the progressive and able administration of the Japanese, trade both in Corea and Manchuria will advance far more rapidly than it would have done under the reactionary policy of the Russian Government. I have had practical proof of how able the Japanese are in their civil administration, by seeing what giant strides Formosa has made since it has been under their guidance.[24]

It is true that post-war conflicts with American business in Manchuria were serious but only when Japan issued its 'Twenty-One Demands'

---

22. 'Sir Edwin Arnold's defence of Japan', *NCH*, Oct. 12, 1894. The *North China Herald* itself took a much more guarded view of these events.

23. 'Newchang', *NCH*, March 4, 1910. The naval relationship was important because it enabled Britain to withdraw its fleet to face Germany, and gave Japan completely new status in the east. However, the absurd heights of the Anglo-Japanese relationship are well exemplified by the last verse of A. C. Benson's *Ode to Japan* (1902).

> *But best, if knit with love,*
> *As fairer days increase, We twain shall learn to prove*
> *The world-wide dream of peace;*
> *And, smiling at our ancient fears,*
> *Float hand in hand across the golden years.*

The 'twain' are Britain and Japan. (Quoted in Blakeney, *On the Coasts of Cathay and Cipango Forty Years Ago*, p. 347.)

24. 'The oil trade in the east', *NCH*, Nov. 4, 1904. Ironically, it was the exclusion of the foreign firms from Manchuria by the Oil Monopoly Law of 1935 that finally opened the eyes of western powers to the exclusive nature of Japanese ambitions in Manchuria. T. A. Bisson, *American Policy in the Far East, 1931–1940*, New York: Institute of Pacific Relations, 1940, p. 32.

in 1915 did international anxieties over the reality of the Japanese 'open door' policy in Manchuria become widespread.[25]

The First World War provided the crucial point of transition between the peaceful trade-oriented Japanese expansion in Asia during the Meiji era and the emergence in the 1920s of a much more aggressive approach, in which territorial acquisition and military factors were fundamental.[26] With active British support, Japan took control of German possessions in China and the south Pacific. Japanese newspapers reflected the country's growing confidence in China with open demands that the rising tide of anti-Japanese economic boycotts be confronted by direct Japanese political intervention.[27] At the same time Japanese businessmen in Manchuria were reported by competitors to be expanding their activities through their customary minute attention to market detail.[28] By 1918, when the British remained largely dismissive of the Japanese commercial threat in China, the Americans were becoming concerned.[29] During the war, while Britain's share of China's foreign trade fell from 20% to 12%, Japan's rose from 21% to 38%. Even more striking was the development of the foreign communities in China and Manchuria. We see from Fig. 13.1 that even before the war there had been nearly ten times as many Japanese in China as British. While the British community declined during the war, the number of Japanese nearly doubled, and the number of Japanese firms in China rose from 955 to 4,483.[30]

Looking at this data, it might be asked why the discrepancy between

25. The concept of the 'open door' was not restricted to Manchuria. In 1905 the Germans advanced this principle in an effort to stop the growth of French influence in Morocco. Massie, *Dreadnought*, p. 355.

26. Hajime Shimizu, '*Nanshin-ron*: its turning point in World War I', *The Developing Economies*, Dec. 1987, pp. 386–402.

27. In 1915 the *Osaka Mainichi* demanded the replacement of President Yuan Shih-kai in retaliation for anti-Japanese economic boycotts. 'Chinese boycotts of Japan', *NCH*, June 10, 1915.

28. 'Japanese in Manchuria. Efforts to capture German trade', *NCH*, Jan. 2, 1915. The writer refers to the 'minute attention [of the Japanese] as to what is actually required', and complains of the 'distinct lack of energy and foresight' on the part of the British.

29. The Americans had a series of hard-working and perceptive consuls in Newchang, Darien, Mukden and Yokohama and their reports provided accurate analyses of both the potential of Manchuria and the dangers of Japanese domination.

30. A comprehensive analysis of the issues which is very critical of the British is W. S. Ridge, 'Is Anglo-American trade with China threatened by Japan', *FER*, Sept. 1919, pp. 613–17.

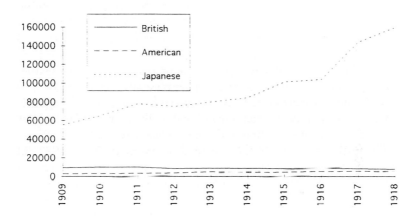

Fig. 13.1. NUMBERS OF BRITISH, AMERICAN AND JAPANESE
BUSINESSMEN IN CHINA, 1909–18

Source: As note 28.

Britain and Japan was quite so large and what was the economic
significance of the Japanese numbers. First, of course, the proximity
of China and Manchuria to Japan meant that Japanese seeking an
improvement in their quality of life could easily migrate. In addition
to such migrants, there were also men left in Manchuria at the end
of the Russo-Japanese war who found careers in small-scale trade and
other ways. But the greatest difference was that the Japanese expansion
into these regions was on all economic fronts: industrial, financial and,
above all, commercial, a point which western analysts of the competition in Manchuria never tired of emphasising. American goods were
usually supplied via stocks held in Shanghai or Japanese ports and sold
through complex networks of Chinese traders, and had to carry the
costs of expensive expatriate staff. In contrast, Japanese goods were
marketed through commercial networks staffed by Japanese living as
cheaply as the Chinese; these were financed by Japanese banks at rates

far below those effectively applying to their competitors (Chinese or foreign) and supplied the market through Japanese-controlled post office and communications systems.[31] It was not only the expatriate workers themselves who raised costs for the western companies. According to the Mitsui merchant Masuda Takashi, who had a lifetime's experience to draw on, the British and Americans were also much disadvantaged by their wives, who lacked the qualities of their hardworking and adaptable Japanese counterparts.[32] Thus in textiles and other labour intensive exports, the Japanese advantages of low production and transport costs were reinforced by cultural and linguistic affinities, by intensive market research and by the power of inexpensive but highly effective banking and commercial networks.[33]

The final settlements of the war made between 1919 and 1922 did not fulfil the whole of Japan's wartime demands, which at times had amounted to the establishment of an 'Asiatic Monroe Doctrine' that would largely have excluded the West from China. Nonetheless, the settlements did meet many of its objectives. Important new economic concessions were obtained and the leases on the Liaotung peninsula and the SMR zone, which were due to expire in 1923 and 1938, were extended respectively to 1997 and 2002. Moreover, as the evidence above indicates, by the early 1920s the Japanese corporate invasion of China and Manchuria was reaching formidable proportions, irrespective of legal arrangements and diplomacy.

31. The pro-Japanese administration of the Manchurian postal and customs system was a sore topic with western businessmen. For example, see the official Japanese admission, 'Without a knowledge of the Japanese postal regulations, a foreigner is liable to misunderstand [how to get letters and goods delivered promptly] . . .' in 'Japanese post office in Manchuria: A reply to criticisms', *NCH*, Sept. 9, 1922.

32. Nagai Minoru (ed.), *Jijo Masuda Takashi o-den* (The autobiography of Masuda Takashi in later life), Tokyo: private press, 1939 (copy in University of Tokyo Economics Department Library). See especially the chapters on 'The strengths of the Japanese', pp. 469–74 and 'Japanese wives', pp. 503–7. The latter begins with the statement: 'The development of Japanese foreign trade has put many burdens on the wives.'

33. For an American view of Japanese competitiveness see the report of the American Consul in Mukden, Fred Fisher, 'Commercial activities in Manchuria', *FER*, March 1913, pp. 433–4. The Japanese view of the issue is described in 'Competition with American and European traders', *Mitsui tokuhon*, pp. 283–6. This emphasised direct buying and the advantages of the Japanese in their financial and communications systems.

Japan's economic problems in the 1920s

To grasp the economic background to the Japanese expansion in Manchuria after 1918 one must understand the nature of the external and domestic difficulties confronting the Japanese economy in the 1920s. The first of these was the problem of trade.

Trade balance and structure. The three main trade problems facing Japan in the 1920s were a persistent trade deficit and continuing anxieties about the ability to pay for raw materials and food imports; a structural failure to achieve export competitiveness in the new skill- and capital-intensive industries; and a growing geographical imbalance in trade relations. Of these, the second was the central issue, while the other two were essentially reflections of it, aggravated by the problem of the uncompetitive exchange rate, discussed in Chapter 6.

This structural problem may be summarised in the following way. Between the 1880s and early 1900s Japan succeeded in completing a large measure of import substitution in cotton textiles and began an almost simultaneous transition to exporting. From 1900 onwards there was a process of diversification into the heavier and more skill-intensive industries, reflecting the beginnings of tariff protection and, more important, subsidisation in the form of preferential government and military orders. Steel, ships, machinery and equipment for railway systems gained notably in this process. This diversification was soon reflected in exporting, notably to Asian markets where Japanese companies could compete by using labour-intensive techniques and by offering low prices for goods with quality levels appropriate to these markets. During the First World War the virtual disappearance of many western suppliers to Asia encouraged a rapid acceleration of import substitution, notably in steel, machinery, shipbuilding and chemicals. This advance was not reflected in comparable gains in exports. After the war, western competition resumed in Japan's home and export markets alike, and the impact of this was reinforced by the restrictions placed on Japanese naval spending by the Washington Conference. The result was a sharp depression in Japanese heavy industry, rising machinery and metal imports, and a deepening imbalance between internal and external industrial development. This problem is illustrated by data for the machinery industry shown in Fig. 13.2, where we see the beginnings of machinery output for the home market, followed within five years by machinery exports. At first the pace of

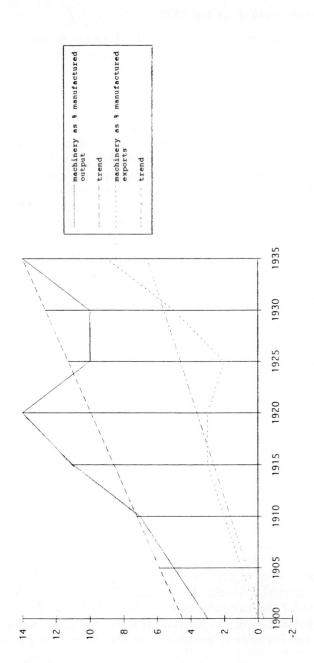

Fig. 13.2. MACHINERY AS % OF DOMESTIC MANUFACTURING OUTPUT AND OF MANUFACTURED EXPORTS

Source: Data from Appendix tables in Ohkawa, *Patterns of Japanese Economic Development.*

change in the industry's share of domestic and external sales remained approximately the same, but while the internal share accelerated in the war years, the external share failed to gain commensurately. The post-war slump and the problems of the early 1920s are clearly visible.[34]

The problems of the heavy sector were not simply a failure to achieve price competitiveness. A structural mismatch of capacity and demand was also important, particularly in steel, where between 1910 and 1918 the share of steel output absorbed by the military had risen from a range of 10% to 15% to one of 30% to 32%. This military demand tended to be highly specific, being focused on speciality and high-quality steels. Thus the post-war collapse of military spending left this specialised capacity idle at a time when rising demand necessitated growing imports of more ordinary types of steel, notably from India. This depressive effect was particularly strong in firms such as Yawata and Sumitomo, whose expansion had been closely tied to army and navy procurement.[35]

Thus at a time when Japan's import requirements for capital goods and raw materials were expanding, export earnings were still pre-dominantly drawn from a narrow range of products. Indeed, coal and tea had all but disappeared as significant exports, and by the 1920s the four Meiji export staples (coal, tea, silk products and cotton tex-tiles) had effectively been reduced to the two textiles, both of which faced problems. Textiles were highly dependent on sales to China, where domestic import substitution and a rising tide of anti-Japanese boycotts in the 1920s made the future of the market uncertain.[36] In the 1930s silk was to prove vulnerable to competition from man-made

34. Excellent discussions of the post-war problems of the Japanese economy, their world context and their relevance to imperialist policies in the 1930s are in Ono, *Japanese imperialism*, ch. 1; Sumiya, *The Showa depression*, part 1; and, Oishi, *Japan's inter-war external economic relations*, ch. 1.

35. This point is emphasised by Nagura Bunji in his extensive study of the origins of the Japanese steel industry, *Nihon tekkogyoshi no kenkyu* (Research into the history of the Japanese steel industry), Tokyo: Kondo Shuppansha, 1984. For data on military use and individual companies see pp. 300–1, 354–9.

36. Major anti-Japanese boycotts took place in 1905, 1908–9, 1915, 1919, 1921, 1923, 1925, 1927, 1928–29 and 1931–32. A comprehensive primary source for the details of these campaigns is the *North China Herald*. A summary of their history is included in Study no. 8, *Memorandum on Boycotts and Japanese Interests in China* in League of Nations, *Appeal by the Chinese Government and Supplementary Documents to the Report of the Commission of Enquiry* (the Lytton Commision) (2 vols), Geneva: League of Nations, 1932, pp. 208–32. The Chinese also threatened Japanese interests by spreading the boycott movement throughout the Dutch East Indies and other places with large Chinese populations.

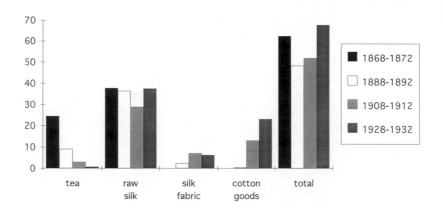

Fig. 13.3. THE ROLE OF FOUR MAJOR COMMODITIES
IN THE EXPORT STRUCTURE, 1868–1932
(% shares)

Source: Summarised from Miyohei Shinohara, *Growth and Cycles in the Japanese Economy*, Tokyo:
Kinokuniya, 1962, p. 49.

fibres and the changing nature of the American market.[37] The
dimensions of this problem are illustrated in Fig. 13.3.

The commodity composition of trade had important implications
for geographical imbalance. The broad structure of Meiji trade had
allowed Japanese exports of tea and silk to pay for imports of manufactured goods from Europe and America. However, while demand both
for American capital goods and raw materials (especially raw cotton
and oil) remained strong in the inter-war years, export diversification
and the penetration of western markets at the rate needed to compen-
sate for the decline of such exports as silk, failed to materialise. This

37. The problem of silk and the silk markets of New York and Yokohama are
extensively analysed in Sumiyami, *The Showa depression*, part 2.

problem was noted in Chapter 5 where it was shown that in the American case, while America's share of Japanese imports fell only marginally from 31% to 28% between 1919 and 1940, America's share of Japanese exports rose to a peak of 36% in 1929 and then fell dramatically to only 11% by 1940.

The broad political dimension of trade, as perceived in Japan in the 1930s, is summed up in Table 13.1, which shows the direct and colonial control structure of Japanese markets for the whole of the Asia Pacific region (including the United States), a region that consistently accounted for 70% to 80% of Japanese foreign trade between 1914 and 1936.

In the 1920s the government responded to these problems first by encouraging rationalisation of the textile sector, and subsequently by strengthening the small-scale export sector, where the combination of low wages, labour-intensive techniques and low-cost electrification made Japanese competitiveness strong. This was the origin of the Export Industries Association Law of 1925. For the longer term, however, an alternative strategy was to supplement rationalisation with the development of political ties that would assist market penetration and develop the Asian markets for Japanese heavy industry exports in particular. Such initiatives had begun well before the First World War. Japan's first exports of ships had gone to China and the construction of the Korean and Manchurian railways had provided opportunities for the metals and engineering industries. During the war further efforts had been made to expand heavy industry exports, sometimes with great success. Between 1914 and 1919 the volume of shipbuilding exports increased more than tenfold, China and India were identified as key potential markets for heavy industry goods, and the war even provided opportunities in China for Japan to make its first foreign sales of sophisticated electrical goods.[38] By 1929 the Asian share of Japanese exports of metallurgical, machinery and chemical products was 86%, 89% and 62% respectively.[39]

Asian markets of particular interest to Japan were those with the

38. For example, Mitsui installed the first telephone system in the Chinese city of Hankow, 'Japan's trade with China', *NCH*, June 10, 1916. Shipbuilding data quoted in Sumiyami, *The Showa depression*, p. 16.

39. These data come from a report that fully articulated Japanese inter-war anxieties. The article compared these export shares with the fact that 73% of the land and 50% of the population of Asia were controlled by western powers or Russia. Mitsubishi Keizai Kenkyujo, *International economic relations in the Pacific*, part 3.

Table 13.1. POLITICAL STRUCTURE OF JAPANESE EXPORT
MARKETS AND SOURCES OF IMPORTS WITHIN THE
ASIA PACIFIC REGION, 1914–36

% of Japanese export markets controlled by:	1914	1929	1936	Index of export growth to 1936 (1914 = 100)	Factors explaining relative performance
Britain	17	19	24.2	587	Textile exports to British Empire
U.S.A.	42.1	49.9	32	315	Silk export/price collapse
Netherlands	1.1	4.6	6.3	2,364	Textiles and light industry sales to Dutch East Indies
Manchuria and the Kwantung Leased Territory	7.9	9.9	24.3	1,273	See text
China	29.4	14.8	7.8	110	Boycott and other problems
All areas	100	100	100	**414**	
% of Japanese import sources controlled by:				Index of import growth to 1936 (1914 = 100)	
Britain	43.1	30.8	33.8	416	Diversification from Indian raw cotton
U.S.A.	24.8	39.3	39.7	849	Demand for raw materials and capital goods
Netherlands	5.2	4.5	5.1	516	Oil from Dutch East Indies
Manchuria and the Kwantung Leased Territory	10.9	12.6	10.7	523	See text
China	1.9	9.2	6.9	353	
All areas	100	100	100	**531**	

Source: Basic data from Mitsubishi Keizai Kenkyujo, *op. cit.*, p. 488.

potential to supply raw materials, as they had the potential to engage in balanced, friction-free trade. This brings us to the wider issue of raw materials and their place in the problem of the Japanese trade balance.

The raw material problem. In the early Meiji period, Japan had appeared relatively well endowed with raw materials. The trade sector reflected a comparative advantage in agriculturally-based products, coal and metals. When the modern textile industry developed, domestic raw cotton was available to supply it. However, as we have seen, there was a decisive shift to imported cotton when the textile industry expanded and raw material requirements became more demanding. Thereafter export production required an increasing quantity of raw materials to be imported, and later, as the heavy industries expanded, there was a consequential demand for capital goods and imports of coke, iron ore, fuel, wood and other materials. In the 1920s the metallurgical problem was becoming increasingly a cause for concern. In the United States *per capita* consumption of iron and steel had increased from 5 lb. in 1820 to 597 lb. in 1920, and to 809 lb. in 1923. Contemporary requirements for the raw materials to match these levels of consumption in industrial economies outdated all earlier judgements about self-sufficiency and the significance of raw material control.[40] In addition to the metals issue there was the question of the food supply, which intensified after the rice riots of 1918. The combined effects of the rising demand for heavy industry goods and raw materials during the 1920s are shown in Table 13.2, where we see that while silk was enjoying its final period of success as Japan's staple export, there were huge increases in the net foreign exchange costs of wheat, sugar, machinery and oil. Copper and wood were actually transformed from trade surplus to trade deficit industries, and coal was making the same transition.

The supply of iron ore, coal and coke had always been a problem for the Japanese iron and steel industry, and this was a factor in Japan's pre-war interest in Manchuria and China, as shown in Table 13.3. The iron ore supplies of the Yawata Company provide an insight into the evolution of Japan's dependence on imported ore. We see in this table that domestic supplies were soon exhausted, and that thereafter China

40. H. Foster Bain, *Ores and Industry in the Far East*, New York: Council on Foreign Relations, 1933, ch 1.

Table 13.2. THE BALANCE OF PAYMENTS COSTS OF RAW MATERIAL
AND HEAVY INDUSTRY. NET IMPORTS, 1910–19 AND 1920–29
(millions of yen)

	1910s: deficit or surplus by commodity	*1920s: deficit or surplus by commodity*	*% increase in cost of deficit per commodity*
Rice	− 324.4	− 493.5	+ 52
Wheat and flour	− 72.1	− 518.5	+ 619
Sugar	− 75.5	− 332.7	+ 340
Raw cotton	− 1,108.7	− 1,413.7	+ 28
Wool	− 376.8	− 1,647.6	+ 337
Silk	+ 3,340.7	+ 8,053.9	Growing surplus
Steel	− 1,134	− 1,699.4	+ 50
Copper	+ 376.8	− 252.8	Surplus to deficit
Wood	+ 79.5	− 677.5	Surplus to deficit
Machinery	− 156.6	− 1,333.4	+ 751
Fertiliser	− 667.5	− 1,550.2	+ 132
Oil	− 131	− 576.3	+ 340
Coal	+ 162.5	+ 11.9	Declining surplus

Source: Ono, *Japanese imperialism*, p. 38.

Table 13.3. SOURCES OF ORE FOR THE YAWATA STEEL COMPANY
(% shares)

	1901–11	*1912–21*	*1922–30*	*1931–40*
Korea	28.2	32.6	13.1	6.9
China	61	63.5	47.6	29.8
India/Malaysia		3.1	37.6	52
Other	10.8	.8	1.7	11.3

Source: Yawata seitetsujo yonjunenshi (The fifty-year history of the Yawata Steel Company), 1950, p. 78.

and later South-East Asia (mainly Malaya) became the main sources
of ore. The expansion of Chinese supplies was not the result of conventional trading but a consequence of Japanese direct investment in the
Hanyebing complex in the Yangtze valley.[41] This investment had

41. This section is based on Nagura, *Research into the history of the Japanese steel
industry*, ch. 1, parts 2–3; Sheng Chuan-han, *Hanyebing gongsi shilue* (Outline history
of the Hanyebing Company), Zhongwen Daxne Chubanshe, 1972. This source has
the Chinese texts of the documents relating to Yawata and the Yokohama Specie
Bank.

been made legally possible by the provisions of the Sino-Japanese war settlement and was initiated in 1902 by Okura specifically to guarantee ore supplies to the Imperial Yawata Steel Company (founded in 1901). Japanese investments sometimes took the form of loans provided by Okura and Mitsui but were more often loans by the Ministry of Finance via the Yokohama Specie Bank. Repayment with interest was taken from the proceeds of the sales of ore made by the company.[42]

The relative decline of Chinese supplies in the 1920s reflected growing difficulties with these arrangements. Nationalist and anti-Japanese sentiment in the Yangtze valley became a powerful force in the 1920s and the Hanyebing role declined accordingly. This key episode illustrated the essential point that, even with effective co-operation between the Japanese public and private sectors, control of foreign raw materials through financial mechanisms was not enough to ensure the stability of supply needed for Japan's strategic industries. As Hanye-bing output fell back, the metallurgical role of Malaya, where costs were low, and of Manchuria, where Japan carried much more direct political weight, rose.[43] The total picture of the control of iron ore supplies in China and Manchuria in 1927 is seen in Table 13.4.

The food supply. The issue of food has been discussed extensively in Chapter 12. Manchuria offered no major solutions to the rice problem as such, but it did hold possibilities for developing cold-climate rice production. The significance of this had been demonstrated for the first time in Hokkaido, a region with climatic features similar to those of Manchuria, where settlement between the 1870s and 1920 served as a model for inter-war colonisation.[44] In addition to modest rice potential, Manchuria had massive agricultural resources of other kinds, including unique strengths in soya bean production and extensive forestry resources. Above all, its underpopulated land appeared, in all its forms, as a potential solution to the problem of the 'surplus' Japanese rural population. Opinion differed over the potential size of

42. A listing of the loans made between 1902 and 1930 is in *Zhongguo jindai gongyeshi tzuliao 1895–1914* (Materials on China's modern industrial history 1895–1914), Beijing: Kexue Chubanshe, 1957, part 1, pp. 119–26.

43. Bunji Nagura, *The Prewar Japanese Steel Industry and Iron Ore Resources in South East Asia: The Development of Malaysian Iron Ore by the Ishihara Sangyo Company*, Tokyo: United Nations University, 1981.

44. The Hokkaido theme and its Manchurian relevance is in *Manshu kaitaku nenkan* (The Manchurian colonisation yearbook), Tokyo: Manshukoku Tsushinsha, 1941.

Table 13.4. CONTROL OF IRON ORE SOURCES, IN CHINA, 1927

		Ore under 'Sino-Japanese' control		
Hanyebing	*Anhui province mines*	*Manchuria (Okura-controlled)*	*Manchuria (SMR-controlled)*	*Total Japanese-controlled*
111,073	233,250	70,000	371,000	785,323

Ore under exclusive Chinese control	*Total ore output from all sources*	*Sino-Japanese-controlled ore as % of total*
76,623	861,946	91.1%

Source: John E. Orchard, *Japan's Economic Position. The Progress of Industrialization*, New York: MacGraw-Hill, 1930, p. 330.
Note: There were significant variations in scale and shares of output during the 1920s.

the cultivated area, but even with the pessimistic estimate of 25 million hectares, the proportion of uncultivated land was large. This is clearly shown in Table 13.5.

Population and migration. The population growth of Japan during the early phases of Meiji industrialization had been modest. The growth-rate rose from below 1% in the 1870s to a peak of 1.7% in 1930. By comparison with the growth rates of 2% to 4% common among developing countries after 1945, these figures do not suggest that population was a major obstacle to development. But this is not how the matter was seen at the time. One reason for this perception was that although it was low by contemporary standards, population growth after 1868, was rapid by comparison with the population stagnation of the two previous centuries. Secondly, the scope for further labour absorption in agriculture was extremely limited since, even in the 1870s, Japanese agriculture was labour-intensive and except in Hokkaido almost all the potentially cultivable land had been occupied. Thus new increases in population had to be absorbed in industry and the tertiary sector. The most authoritative recent estimates of the labour absorption process in the 1920s are shown in Table 13.6, which presents striking data. They show population growing at an unprecedented rate, the working-age population growing faster than the total

Table 13.5. UNCULTIVATED LAND AS A % OF POTENTIAL
CULTIVATED AREA IN MANCHURIA

	Uncultivated % based on a 33 million ha. potential	Uncultivated % based on a 25 million ha. potential
1887	92	89
1908	77	70
1914	71	62
1930	62	50
1940	54	40

Sources: Chao, *The Economic Development of Manchuria*, p. 9; Sun and Huenemann, *The Economic Development of Manchuria* pp. 21–7; Manchoukuo Yearbook Company, *The Manchoukuo Yearbook 1942*, Hsinking, 1942, p. 419.

Table 13.6. POPULATION AND EMPLOYMENT IN JAPAN:
THE BALANCE SHEET FOR 1920–30

	Absolute change	Growth rate p.a.
Population	+ 13,927,000	+ 1.42
Population aged 15–60*	+ 9,006,000	+ 1.88
Total employment, of which	+ 2,332,000	+ 0.69
services	+ 2,097,000	+ 2.78
agriculture	− 77,000	− 0.05
manufacturing industry	+ 164,000	+ 0.35

Source: Umemura Mataji (ed.), *Rodo ryoku* (Manpower), Tokyo: Toyo Keizai Shimposha, 1988 (Ohkawa, *LTES*, vol. 2), Tables 2 and 9.
Note: These data are given as an *indicator* of shifts in the population of normal working age. They are only an indicator, because large numbers of people outside this age-group also worked.

population, agricultural employment in decline, and manufacturing employment growing at *less than one-fifth* of the rate of increase of the working-age population. Umemura's data show that most of the increase in employment in the 1920s consisted of work in commerce, hotels and restaurants, sectors where labour can easily be absorbed at the expense of the incomes of existing workers. Although these data are far more accurate than anything available at the time, contemporary analysts had enough information to grasp the broad issues. Their first source of anxiety was an increase in the birth-rate from 32.2 per 1000 in 1918 to 36.2 per 1000 in 1928. By the mid-1920s, the annual population increase was around one million, a figure far in excess of the expansion of employment in modern manufacturing industries. Secondly, analysts were concerned that the raw material and food

requirements for each additional member of the population was growing.[45] And thirdly, extrapolation of contemporary trends suggested a
future population of 70–100 million, figures which were believed to
make a major demographic crisis unavoidable. Projections of this order
led directly to demands for Japan to find reliable outlets for its 'excess
population' abroad.[46]

It should be remembered that reliable population data only became
available after the 1920 census, and that in the 1920s both demographic
and international trade theory were still at an early stage of development. Demographic analysis of the long-term issues called for estimates
of the underlying or 'intrinsic' trends in fertility and mortality, not
estimates of the crude rates. On the basis of appropriate information
it would have been possible to judge whether the demographic revolution, clearly under way in Europe and the United States, was beginning in Japan — or alternatively whether Japan shared with the rest of
Asia the exceptional and persistent levels of fertility believed by many
to be typical of 'oriental' races.[47]

Against this background several views of the problem emerged. The
mainstream thought, which certainly dated from as early as the 1890s,
emphasised the intractable nature of the problem and the urgent need
for population outlets to relieve the internal pressure on resources.[48]
During the 1920s the problem of population and the need for emigration outlets came to the top of the domestic and international political
agenda. Efforts at settlement were intensified on the domestic and colonial front, with the government taking compulsory purchase powers
over all uncultivated land and providing increasing subsidies to private
emigration companies. At the international level, Foreign Minister
Shidehara described US immigration restrictions as 'irreconcilable with
the rules of international comity and justice', and claimed that Japan's

45. In his analysis of the balance of payments problem, Junnosuke Inouye (see ch. 6)
commented: 'It is the food problem which is of such desperate importance.' Inouye,
Problems, p. 209.

46. A brilliant contemporary survey of the issues and the protagonists is E. F.
Penrose, *Population Theories and their Application, with Special Reference to Japan*, Stanford, CA: Food Research Institute, 1934.

47. The question of 'oriental fertility' and other myths about the Japanese population were dealt with by Penrose in *Population Theories*, ch. 4.

48. For example, Okura had argued in the 1890s that 'surplus labour' was central
to the case for colonisation, since it was the enemy of the capital accumulation and
development needed for the deepening of Japanese economic development. Okura
Zaibatsu Kenkyukai, *Okura zaibatsu*, pp. 110–12.

role was to supply developing countries with capital *and labour*.[49] Alarmist views were reinforced by many foreign commentators and demographers, several of whom saw global political stability threatened by the polarisation of the world into rich countries where population was tending to decline and poor ones where population growth was still high and opportunities for migration small.[50] In the 1930s and 1940s the official Japanese view changed. Faced with the challenge of managing an empire and with the prospect that Japanese modernisation of Chinese health conditions would lead to unprecedented increases in the Chinese population,[51] population policy led to deliberate attempts to increase the size and quality of the Japanese population.[52]

The unfairness of Japan's predicament was seen to lie in the fact that a great era of international population migration had been brought to a close by a wave of racist anti-Japanese migration restrictions. Between the 1820s and the late 1920s, 60 million people are estimated to have migrated from one continent to another. In the early phase of this migration it was possible, for example, for a Briton to migrate to America for a £10 fare with no formalities. The peak years of European migration under this liberal regime were the decade before the First World War.[53] In the late nineteenth century the Japanese and the Chinese became active participants in this process, with migrant

49. 'Baron Shidehara's graphic survey', *NCH*, Jan. 23, 1924.

50. Examples of this view are included in the publications of the International Labour Office and the Institute of Pacific Relations; W. R. Crocker, *The Japanese Population Problem*, London: Geo. Allen and Unwin, 1931; Warren S. Thompson, *Population and Peace in the Pacific*, University of Chicago Press, 1946. A. M. Carr-Saunders, *World Population: Past Growth and Present Trends*, Oxford University Press, 1936 (esp. ch. 18), was particularly influential.

51. Odabashi Josu, 'China's population and vital rates' in Toa Keizai Kenkyujo, *Toa keizai kenkyu nenpo* (East Asia economic research yearbook), Tokyo: Nihon Hyoronsha, 1942, pp. 231–67.

52. This problem is analysed retrospectively in Irene B. Taeuber, *The Population of Japan*, pp. 336–9. The demographic requirements of the Greater East Asian Co-Prosperity Sphere were explained by a sophisticated contemporary demographer, Okazaki Ayanori, in *Shintoa kakuritsu to jinko seisaku* (The establishment of the New East Asia and population policy), Tokyo: Okura Shobo, 1941. Okazaki forecast a population of 120 million by the year 2020. This figure was actually reached in 1984 and current estimates of the peak Japanese population are 135 million, expected to be attained in the year 2013. See Okazaki, p. 25 and Okurasho Insatsukyoku, *Showa 63 nenkan tokei handbuku* (1988 statistical handbook), Tokyo, 1988.

53. Carr-Saunders, *World Population*, ch. 4.

communities springing up in Hawaii, California, Siam, Guatemala, North Borneo, Fiji, Brazil, Australia and Canada. Migrants were often highly successful economically, acquiring land and almost monopolising certain trades such as the Californian suburban fruit and vegetable markets.[54] However, opposition to 'orientals' became virulent. In California 'rich and poor, educated and uneducated, all express abhorrence of the 'little brown monkeys' and determination to expel them.'[55] This opposition was formalised in anti-Japanese legislation in the state of California, which was later supported by a US Supreme Court decision of 1922 and by the US Immigration Act of 1924.[56]

In contrast to the simple but politically powerful views of the Japanese population pessimists, a subtler scenario was developed by the Japanese economic demographer, Uyeda Teijiro. This had important implications for trade policy. Uyeda's first contribution to the subject was a major piece of research that correctly showed, by careful analysis of the post-1920 statistics, that age-specific fertility in Japan was on the decline and that a demographic revolution was indeed coming to Japan.[57] As an economist, Uyeda also used Bertil Ohlin's new theory of comparative advantage to make the fundamental point that a country's 'optimum' population size need not be determined by the supply of land. A country where land and raw materials were scarce, he argued, must use its comparative advantage to specialise in manufacturing. While these points emphasised that the Japanese population

54. By 1912 80% of the Los Angeles vegetable market was in the hands of Japanese and in Honolulu only the Japanese immigrants were rich enough to drive cars. 'Japanese in Hawaii and California', *NCH*, Aug. 24, 1912.

55. Lawton, *Empires of the Far East*, vol. 1, ch. 15; the quotation is on p. 404.

56. Morse and MacNair, *Far Eastern International Relations*, pp. 980–2 and Donald R. Nugent, *The Pacific Area and Its Problems. A Study Guide*, New York: Institute of Pacific Relations, 1936, ch. 11.

57. According to Irene Taeuber, Professor Takeo Soda was the first Japanese to use age-specific vital rates to estimate future population size. However, Uyeda's estimates became better known and his integration of demography and economics was a crucial contribution to the debates. A key work is Uyeda Teijiro, *Nihon jinko seisaku* (Japan's population policy), Tokyo: Okura Shobo, 1937. Uyeda's analysis influenced Penrose, who made it known in the West. A valuable contemporary account of his life and thought is Odabashi Josu, 'Uyeda Sensei and research into Japanese population problems' in Dr Uyeda Teijiro Memorial Collected Works, vol. 4, *Jinko oyo toa keizai no kenkyu* (Research into the theory of population and the East Asian economy), Tokyo: Kagakushugi Kogyosha, 1943, pp. 3–28. This volume also contains interesting papers on the population problems of the Pacific war period, including one by Tobata Seiichi on reverse migration.

problem was not intrinsically insoluble, Uyeda recognised and analysed the population-related issues facing Japan, especially unemployment, the social stresses of excessive urbanisation and the need for food and raw material imports. Uyeda's solutions to this complex of problems looked partly to the development of post-capitalist planning institutions in Japan and even more to the establishment of an international framework that would allow Japan to develop its full comparative advantage in the export of manufactures. By the mid-1930s, Uyeda had concluded that such a framework would have to be one of managed trade between economic blocs, rather than free trade in a liberal environment.

Advance in Manchuria without political control, 1919–1930

During the 1920s the Japanese continued their economic advance into Manchuria impelled both by the economic and demographic factors just discussed and, increasingly, by strategic considerations. The possibility of war and the need for the resources and technology to fight the West had been factors in Japanese policy from the moment Japan was forced to hand back the Liaotung peninsula in 1895 — it was also an open influence on the development of Taiwan — and thus the emergence of the strategic factor in Manchurian policy was the revival of an old theme.[58] By the 1920s Russia and then America were both seen as potential enemies in an Armageddon for which some analysts could even predict a date. To counter this challenge, Japanese military theorists came to the view that Japan would need to control and mobilise a large economically-integrated territorial bloc.[59]

58. Evidence for these matters is often not easy to find but the comments by Matsukata on the 'Triple Intervention' of 1895 and the 'post [Sino-Japanese] war financial plan' are revealing, as is Kodama's remark on the strategic significance of Taiwan. For Matsukata, see *Koshaku Matsukata Masayoshi den* (The biography of Count Matsukata Masayoshi) (2 vols), Tokyo: Koshaku Matsukata Masayoshi Denki Henshukai, 1935, repr. 1992, pp. 543–54, 609–41. Kodama's speech of 1901 is quoted in Ramon H. Myers, 'Taiwan as an Imperial Japanese colony 1895–1945', *Journal of the Institute of Chinese Studies*, vol. 6, no. 2, 1973, p. 434.

59. The key source for this discussion is Mark R. Peattie, *Ishiwara Kanji and Japan's Confrontation with the West*, Princeton University Press, 1975. Also of value is Narusawa Yomezo, *Ishiwara Kanji* (in Japanese), Tokyo: Keizai Oraisha, 1969. Narusawa emphasises the highly supportive attitude of young Japanese such as Ishiwara to the 1911 Chinese revolution. Revealing quotations emphasising Ishiwara's concerns about the Japanese population and food problem and Manchuria's part in their solution are in Takemori Kazuo, *Mantetsu koboshi* (The rise and fall of the South Manchurian Railway), Tokyo: Akita Shoten, 1970, pp. 86–8.

Financial diplomacy and direct investment. In the immediate post-war years Japan's most visible form of expansion in Manchuria was a programme of financial diplomacy. By 1920 Japanese banks were totally dominant and as the domestic Manchurian currency, the *fengpiao*, collapsed, a yen-based economy emerged although the yen was then still off the gold standard.[60]

Banking and currency aggression was paralleled by the 'Nishihara' loans (1917–18), so named after the entrepreneur who organised them. These were government loans ostensibly for productive investment projects in mining and infrastructural development, but their actual purpose was to increase Japanese influence in a fragmenting Chinese political situation. Most of the money was used for bribery and payment of warlord armies, and when the loans went into default the Japanese Finance Ministry had to assume responsibility to limit the otherwise disastrous consequences for the Japanese banking system.[61]

Direct investment by Japanese firms also gathered pace in the 1920s so that by the end of the decade, the overall and relative scale of Japanese investment in Manchuria had reached the levels shown in Table 13.7. Here we see that by 1926 investment in Manchuria surpassed that in China proper and Korea and was substantially larger than that in Taiwan. Within this total, the SMR accounted for more than half of all investment up to 1935. Among private firms, Okura's activities continued on a huge scale. In mining and metals, for example, the company was producing by 1930, 582,000 tonnes of coal, 131,000 tonnes of coke, 141,000 tonnes of iron ore and 85,000 tonnes

60. The dominant role of Japanese banks by the 1920s is described in Hoshino, *Economic History of Manchuria*, p. 276, and Zhang, *The north-eastern economy*, pp. 51–4. The collapse of the Manchurian *fengpiao* and its replacement by the yen for wage settlements and contracts among Chinese is described in 'Japanese currency in Manchuria', *NCH*, March 13, 1926; 'Manchurian money madness', *NCH*, Feb. 4, 1928; 'Mukden's currency troubles', *NCH*, March 17, 1928.

61. Between Jan. 1917 and July 1918, Japanese interests made 36 major loans to China. Some were openly for 'general purposes' but others were to finance industrial and Japanese projects. Security for these loans took the forms of property, gold mines, forests, local tax revenues and, in some cases, Japanese rights to operate industrial enterprises. 'The loan craze in China', *FER*, Aug. 1918, pp. 335–8; 'How Japan finances China', *FER*, Sept. 1918, pp. 362–4; Beasley, *Japanese Imperialism*, pp. 117–18. The Japanese financial crisis created by the non-payment of the Nishihara loans is described in 'Tangles over Japanese loans to China', *NCH*, Aug. 5, 1922; 'The Nishihara loans', *NCH*, Feb. 6, 1926.

Table 13.7. JAPANESE INVESTMENTS IN MANCHURIA,
KOREA AND TAIWAN, 1926–36
(millions of yen, %)

	1926	1930	1936
Manchuria	1,402 (33.3)	1,757 (32.6)	2,919 (36.4)
China proper	1,166 (27.7)	1,446 (26.8)	1,994 (24.8)
Korea	1,127 (26.7)	1,507 (27.9)	2,409 (30)
Taiwan	519 (12.3)	685 (12.7)	707 (8.8)

Source: Estimates by Yamamoto, *EHOJ*, vol. 6, p. 261.

of iron and steel. Okura also had investments in railways, forestry, logging, chemicals, paper, construction and fisheries.[62]

Economic performance. The economic development of Manchuria from the late 1880s up to 1930 is summarised in Table 13.8. In absolute terms, the population had grown from 13 million in 1900 to more than 31 million in 1931. Industrial development in the Liaotung peninsula accelerated after Japan took control in 1905, as did soya bean output and exports, which actually doubled in the decade 1917–27. The role of the SMR in transporting soya and other exports made the 1920s its golden age and this prosperity and expansion were reflected in the performance of the company's Japanese suppliers of rolling stock and other equipment. SMR revenues almost doubled in the 1920s, reaching their historic peak in the financial year 1929/30.[63]

In spite of this growth, the Japanese economic situation in China and Manchuria during the 1920s was in several important ways deteriorating. The Japanese advance stimulated violent opposition from politicians, consumers and labour unions. Further, one of the underlying economic attractions of Manchuria had been its emptiness, but this

62. Extensive details of the Okura and other Japanese investments in Manchuria are to be found in Okura Zaibatsu Kenkyukai, *Okura zaibatsu*, pp. 326–68. Regular reports appear in issues of *The Manchoukuo Yearbook*. A short contemporary western survey of Japanese and other investments on the eve of the Japanese takeover is Study no. 7: *Chinese, Japanese and other Foreign Investments in Manchuria* in League of Nations, *Appeal*, vol. 2, pp. 199–207.

63. 1929 was the SMR.'s peak year in terms of total revenue, freight revenue and profits. Details in Myers in Duus, *The Japanese Informal Colonial Empire*, pp. 112–15; East Asia Economic Investigation Bureau, *The Manchoukuo Year Book, 1934*, Tokyo, 1934, pp. 646–7.

Table 13.8. KEY INDICATORS OF ECONOMIC
DEVELOPMENT IN MANCHURIA, 1900–30
(% per annum)

Indicator		Growth rate
Population	1887–1930	5.6
Area of cultivated land	1887–1930	4.8
Industrial output in the Kwantung Leased Territory	1910–29	12
Freight carried by Chinese Eastern Railway	1903–24	11
Total foreign trade	1899–1929	6.6
Exports of soya beans	1909–29	4.5

Sources: Population, cultivated area and foreign trade data are from Chao, *The Economic Development of Manchuria*, pp. 9–10; industrial output data are from Sun, *The Economic Development of Manchuria in the First Half of the Twentieth Century*, p. 94; CER freight from Chou; and soya export totals are in Xu Dao-fu, *Zhonngguo jindai maoyi tongji tzuliao* (Trade statistics of modern China), Shanghai: Renmin Chubanshe, 1983, p. 190.

was disappearing under the pressure of Chinese immigration. As is shown in Table 13.5, while 92% of the potential cultivated area was unused in 1887, by 1930 that proportion had fallen to 50% — still large but much diminished, especially in the light of the rising influx of Chinese migrants.[64]

Developments in the outside world were also alarming. By 1931 the impact of the Wall Street crash and other depressive factors on worldwide economic stability were becoming apparent, and in Russia, Japan's old Manchurian rival, Stalin was industrialising with programmes that threatened to strengthen Russian military capability at a time when technology had just made Tokyo vulnerable to air attack from Vladivostok. Of particular concern to Japan was the establishment of Soviet steel plants of unprecedented scale and technical modernity in eastern locations such as Magnitogorsk. Finally, Japan remained under intense competitive trade pressures, although Manchurian markets were beginning to help its heavy goods exporters. Above Japan in the economic hierarchy was America, whose advantages in the heavy and skill-intensive industries were increasing, while below it were China and India, where economic development manifested itself in import substitution and also in successful exporting to other parts of Asia.

64. Between 1927 and 1930 just under 4 million Chinese migrants arrived in Manchuria by train or boat and although nearly 2 million returned in the same years, the scale of this influx was clearly a portent. Study no. 3, *Chinese Migrations to Manchuria* in League of Nations, *Appeal*, vol. 2, pp. 108–21.

Although the economic and strategic case for Japan's seizure of Manchuria in 1931 may appear persuasive in retrospect, two further points about this period remind one of the complex and contradictory forces at work. First, although early international enthusiasm for Japan's new Asian role was diminishing, foreign attitudes to Japanese policies in Manchuria and China in the 1920s often remained supportive. All foreign businessmen sought a secure climate for trade and direct investment, and to many the Japanese seemed the most likely and best motivated to deliver this. The American publisher George Bronson Rea was a striking example of this view. Not only did Rea fully support Japanese demands for open markets and parity of treatment in such issues as international migration and investment, but he even proposed that the United States should support Japanese expansion in China and Manchuria, subject to an agreed division of labour that would allow unfettered access to these markets for Japanese light industry, while reserving for the Americans the markets for heavy and engineering goods.[65]

The second point is that most Japanese businessmen appear to have opposed military violence. In 1911 Japan had generally supported the Chinese republican revolution and believed that its role was to support Chinese nationalism in an Asia-wide movement to rid the continent of westerners. This view was wholly consistent with the Okura philosophy of business imperialism, since the latter sought to tread carefully between the extension of Japanese influence and outright war. Patrolling Chinese rivers with Japanese gunboats and maintaining a powerful presence was one thing; total war was quite another. Okura's strategy was to rid China and Manchuria of foreigners and then develop the country with Japanese direct foreign investment. He was well aware that his investment strategy depended on the willing cooperation of the Chinese business and working classes. Elements of all these attitudes persisted into the 1920s, as the case of the textile investors in Shanghai makes clear in the next chapter.

---

65. A classic Rea article is 'The New Open Door Doctrine. Japan's Plea for Equal Opportunity', *FER*, Nov. 1930, pp. 594–6. This article manages to endorse both the moderate Foreign Minister Shidehara and the contemporary Japanese protagonists of expansion. It criticises the anti-Japanese policies of the British, the Indians, the Russians, the Californians, the Egyptians and the Greeks, and describes American efforts to open the Manchurian door before the First World War as a 'sordid intrigue'. The market sharing proposal is in 'Shall America fight for China or cooperate with Japan?', *FER*, March 1920, pp. 151–3.

Development and trade in Manchukuo, 1931–1937

By 1931 the Japanese army had concluded that Japan could not achieve its objectives in Manchuria by indirect control, and that the construction of a new state was therefore necessary. Thus after the seizure of power in 1931, the political framework in Manchuria became that of the puppet state of Manchukuo, an entity legally separate from the rest of China.

Goals and planning. The economic objectives of Manchukuo were ambitious. They included the comprehensive growth of the economy in ways calculated to supplement Japanese development, and looked forward to the eventual creation of a China-Manchuria-Japan economic bloc. This programme was to be accomplished through Japanese army leadership and through the creation of 'a new unparalleled system' of planning and administration, a system that would, in General Araki's words, 'make Manchuria a paradise on earth'.[66]

The emergence of the Manchurian system reflected development within and outside of Japan. Within it, economic concentration in the old *zaibatsu* groupings such as Mitsui or Mitsubishi had become intensely unpopular, and this unpopularity had been heightened by the belief that the *zaibatsu* had benefited from Japan's removal from the gold standard in 1931. The interest in economic reform was reinforced by a widespread belief that new economic systems were developing throughout the world which gave the state a much more direct and powerful role. Both the New Deal in America and the emergence of state ownership and central planning in the Soviet Union were quoted as examples of this trend.[67] Because changing the Japanese domestic system presented many difficulties, Manchuria came to be seen not only by the army but also by economists and intellectuals as a place

66. 'General Araki's speech', *NCH*, May 3, 1932. The theme of Manchukuo as a middle way between capitalism and Soviet Communism becomes very strong after 1936 and is illustrated in Takayoshi Matsuo (ed.), *Manshukoku no konpon rinen to Kyowakai no honshitsu* (The fundamental concept of Manchukuo and the nature of the Concordia Association), *Gendaishi shiryo* (Materials on modern history), vol. 9 part 2, Tokyo: Misuzu Shobo, 1964, pp. 737–40; Matsuo, *The Manchoukuo Yearbook 1942*, Hsinking: The Manchoukuo Yearbook Company, 1942, ch. 6.

67. For an American view see Staley, *World Economy in Transition*, and for British opinions see Arthur Salter (ed.), *The World's Economic Crisis and the Way of Escape*, London: Geo. Allen and Unwin, 1932, and J. M. Keynes, *The End of Laissez Faire*, London: Hogarth Press, 1926.

where Japan could create a planning system capable of remedying domestic weaknesses and enabling it to play a central role in the new world of superpower economic blocs.[68]

At the centre of the Manchurian system were the state, banking and economic organs, all dominated or monopolised by Japanese personnel. Below these was an industrial hierarchy ranging from the big Japanese companies down to small indigenous enterprises. From the moment of Japan's takeover, the quasi-governmental role of the SMR, which had played a crucial role in providing the army with economic intelligence, was removed. Even so, the railway and its associated activities remained a crucial part of the Manchurian economic system.[69]

The government outlined its objectives for the economy in a series of statements leading to the establishment in 1934 of a new tripartite system of planning. This divided the industrial economy into large companies specialising in defence-related activities that were to be directly planned; engineering, chemical and mining companies whose development was to be kept under review but not subject to rigorous, direct planning; and other companies, mostly smaller or Chinese-owned, that were allowed to develop in accordance with market requirements. After 1935 the role of the army in planning and control increased, as was apparent in the Ishiwara plan of 1936 and then in the Five-Year Plans of 1936 and 1942.[70]

The state's assumption of the leading role in planning and finance was not meant to preclude the inflow of private investment either from Japan or from the rest of the world. There were precedents for a private role in Japanese overseas expansion. The SMR had received considerable funds through the London market, and in the 1920s the New York market had supported the colonisation of Korea by marketing bonds for the Oriental Development Company. However,

68. Takahashi Kamekichi was an excellent example of an economist who saw Manchukuo as an opportunity to create a more rational economic system. See his *Manshu keizai to Nihon keizai* (The Manchurian economy and the Japanese economy), Tokyo: Chiyogura Shobo, 1934, and comments by Howe in Dore and Sinha, *Japan and World Depression*, pp. 167–8.

69. This is mentioned in the memoirs of Yamaguchi Yuji, leader of the Manchurian Youth League, *Kieta teikoku Manshu* (Vanished Imperial Manchuria), Tokyo: Mainichi, 1967, p. 104. A brilliant Western report of the Manchurian takeover and the early 1930s was that by Edgar Snow, whose contemporary insights into the psychology of the army leadership of Araki, Honjo and Minami are still interesting. See *The Far Eastern Front*, ch. 6.

70. Manshushi Kenkyukai, *Manchuria under Japanese imperialism*, ch. 1.

Table 13.9. PRIVATE INVESTMENT FLOWS FROM
JAPAN TO MANCHUKUO TO 1941
(millions of yen)

	Mitsui	*Mitsubishi*	*Sumitomo*	*Okura*	*Total all sources*
To 1925	10.143	3.362	5.237	84.98	112.264
1932	2.15	2.15	2.15	–	6.45
1933	.25	–	1.95	–	20.225
1934	23.09	6.587	31.05	.54	84.842
1935	10.35	20	–	11	61.332
1936	35.478	15.915	3.8	3	107.973
1937	24.98	14.234	3.25	1	111.364
1938	13.6	3.95	3.15	12.25	105.6
1939	35.6			70	215.950
1940	.108	5.55			28.108
1941	.195			6.019	66.214
% of total	17	8	5	21	100

Source: Manshushi Kenkyukai, *op. cit.*, p. 55.

since the old *zaibatsu* were unwelcome in Manchuria and state planning and an anti-capitalist ideology did not encourage other private investors, the private capital inflow from this sector was disappointing. An exception among the 'new *zaibatsu*' that did invest was Nissan, a company that played an important role in Manchurian industrial development. Looking further afield, the Manchurian government's search for American investment went on right up to the eve of the Pacific War; it was still talking of financing future plans through the world capital market as late as 1942.[71]

Policies for industry and agriculture. The main thrust of industrial policy was to develop the extractive, metallurgical and heavy industries, and investment policy supported this. Manchuria was also seen as the location for Japan's most technologically-advanced industries. Among the products produced in Manchuria were chemicals, cars, aeroplanes and

71. Cho Yukio, 'An enquiry into the problem of importing American capital into Manchuria' in Dorothy Borg and Shumpei Okamoto (eds), *Pearl Harbor as History: Japanese-American Relations, 1931–1941*, New York: Columbia University Press, 1973, pp. 377–410.

optical goods, all of which were seen as essential industries if Manchuria was to perform its strategic function as a bulwark against Russia and a reserve base against America.[72]

Economic policies for agriculture were also important. Modern Manchuria and the revenues of the SMR had been built on the country's success in becoming the world's largest exporter of soya beans, and the further growth and diversification of agriculture were crucial to the realisation of its potential for absorbing 'surplus' Japanese population. To achieve all this, Manchurian administrators devised an endless series of plans. There was a thirty-year plan for wool, a twenty-five-year plan for wheat and ten-year plans for cotton and livestock. The government also developed cold climate rice growing and pioneered the introduction of sugar beet into Manchuria. The SMR was active in this sector, supporting a range of agricultural research projects that used plots of land along the railway, often farmed by retired railway guards. But the main problem for agriculture in the 1930s was that Manchuria's role as an exporter was deeply affected by the world agricultural depression, and this undermined the short-run impact of agricultural plans and policies.

Labour and immigration. The Japanese population of Manchuria and the Kwantung Leased Territory grew from a few thousands in the early 1900s to nearly a half a million in 1934. To put these data into perspective, Table 13.10 shows the whole of the 1934 overseas Japanese population in the Asia Pacific and Manchuria and their occupational structure. This table reveals that whereas the numbers of Japanese in agricultural employment were significant in the Americas and other parts of the Pacific Basin, most Japanese in Manchuria were employed in industry, communications, public service and, above all, commerce.

The serious organisation of emigration from Japan began in 1927 with two events: the establishment of a Department of Overseas Affairs, charged with responsibilities for emigration and colonisation, and the formation of a Commission for the Study of Population and

---

72. Important roles in Manchukuo's build-up of the advanced industries were played by Ayukawa Gisuke of the industrial conglomerate, Nissan, and by Goko Kiyoshi of Mitsubishi Heavy Industries. For a life of the latter and an account of his role in developing aeronautics and high technology in Manchukuo, see Nihon Keizaishi Kenkyukai, *Kindai Nihon jinbutsu keizaishi* (A biographical economic history of modern Japan), vol. 2, pp. 232–59.

Table 13.10. THE JAPANESE OVERSEAS POPULATION AND
ITS OCCUPATIONAL STRUCTURE, 1935

	Manchuria and the Liaotung Leased Territory	*The Pacific (Hawaii etc.)*	*The Americas*	*Total (incl. other areas)*
Population	480,229	205,074	160,789	1,146,462
Population in classified occupations (of which % shares)	287,033	73,053	58,907	509,966
Agriculture	2	40	37	20
Fishing	1	5	4	2
Mining	2	1	1	1
Industry	20	13	9	15
Commerce	28	14	26	26
Communications	19	4	3	12
Public service	22	3	4	14
Other	6	20	16	10

Source: Data from Mitsubishi Keizai Kenkyukai, *International economic relations in the Pacific*, p. 481

Food Supply.[73] The latter lasted only three years but the former was active in different manifestations till the 1940s. The history of migration in Manchuria had three stages. In the early stage, which lasted till the takeover of 1931, small numbers were settled along the railway zone without any significant economic success. This was followed by the 'experimental' stage, which included the settlement of groups of armed immigrants and the establishment in 1933 of a full migration administration (the Yiminbu) to work with the Tokyo ministry. Finally, there began from 1936 the stage of large-scale migration and planning with yet another new organisation — the Manchuria Colonisation Company — to provide resources.[74]

73. The Commission and its background are described in Ryoichi Ishii, *Population Pressure and Economic Life in Japan*, London: P. S. King, 1937, ch. 3. Ishii was himself a member of the Commission.
74. This history is fully documented in Kita Itsuo, *Manshu kaitakuron* (The colonisation of Manchuria), Tokyo: Meibundo, 1944. Migration and labour issues are also surveyed in Manshushi Kenkyukai, *Manchuria under Japanese imperialism*, ch. 3.

According to the most ambitious of the Manchurian immigration plans, 5 million migrants were to go to Manchuria over a twenty-year period, thereby raising the Japanese share of the population to 10%. This plan was supported by state finance and by vigorous propaganda campaigns in which happy migrant farmers were shown working in the broad, abundant Manchurian landscape.[75] As war approached and the First Five-Year Plan got under way, the Manchurian authorities became increasingly concerned with the shortage of the skilled immigrants from Japan needed to ensure the success of their heavy and high technology industries. Again, various plans were made, including a scheme for the direct allocation of graduates students from Japan.

A summary of the Manchurian experience

Economic performance. Between 1929 and 1941, the Gross Domestic Product of Manchuria grew at nearly 4% per year and at 1.8% per head. The success of Manchuria's industrialisation programme is indicated by the rise of industry's share of output from 12.9% to 20.3% in the same period and by the fact that the Liaotung peninsula achieved the distinction of being the first part of China in which the non-agricultural population exceeded the agricultural one. Against the background of world depression, especially in agriculture, this development was impressive. It left Manchuria with a *per capita* income 50% higher than the rest of China and with substantial heavy industries and significant advances in agriculture. In human terms, however, the cost was high and the Japanese failed to leave any significant legacy of industrial and managerial skills in the Chinese workforce.[76]

However, when the specific Japanese objectives for raw materials imports, export markets, population outlets and the creation of a self-sufficient economic bloc are considered, the results were generally

75. Sino-Japanese labour problems are discussed in Christopher Howe, *Wage Patterns and Wage Policies in Modern China, 1919 1972*, Cambridge University Press, 1973. The bibliography includes a listing of key Japanese-language works on the subject to be found in the old SMR research library, now held by the Library of Congress, Washington, DC.

76. After 1945 the Chinese were unable to operate what was left of the Anshan iron and steel works. M. Gardner Clark, *The Development of China's Steel Industry and Soviet Technical Aid*, Ithaca, NY: School of Industrial and Labor Relations, 1957, p. 3.

disappointing. Exhaustive surveys and substantial investment for raw materials and metallurgical development continued throughout the 1930s. Fushun and Anshan grew rapidly and the Japanese succeeded in finding several valuable raw materials, including magnesite, fluorspar, graphite and molybdenum. Nevertheless, they failed to locate Manchuria's vast oil reserves and in the 1940s still lacked rubber, tin and tungsten. The supply of raw cotton, wool and timber also remained major problems.[77] Variable iron ore quality and the lack of coking coal hindered development in metallurgy, and when war came the Manchurian bases proved vulnerable to air power. The fundamental problem was that the raw-material requirements of industry — especially the new highly sophisticated industries — were so far-ranging and complex that only free access in a multilateral trading world could supply what was needed.[78] The relative weakness of the Japanese materials position, even including the resources of the entire Japan-Manchuria-China bloc, is summarised in Table 13.11.

Manchuria's output was not vital for the metropolitan food supply because the combined produce of domestic farmers in Taiwan, Korea and Japan proved adequate. Even the Manchurian soya bean cake declined steeply in importance as domestic ammonium sulphate and other chemical fertilisers became abundant and cheap in the 1930s. As war approached and fighting began in China in 1937, the overall net effect of Japan's search for raw material security was to draw it first

77. This judgement, based on scattered data, is confirmed by the summary in Takemura Kazuo, *Taitoa keizai shigen taikan* (A survey of the economic resources of the Greater East Asian Co-Prosperity Sphere), Tokyo: Nichi-Su Tsushinsha, 1942, pp. 33–5.

78. A detailed account of the problems of the iron and steel industry in China and their pre-war origins is Clark, *The Development of China's Steel Industry and Soviet Technical Aid*, esp. chs 1, 5 and 6. The success of US air attacks is described in United States Strategic Bombing Survey, *The Effects of Strategic Bombing on the Japanese War Economy*, quoted in Alan S. Milward, *War, Economy and Society, 1939–1945*, London: Geo. Allen and Unwin, 1977, pp. 166–77, 318–19. The wider problem is illustrated by the fact that to make a motor car required 795 different raw materials, starting with acetic acid, acetylene and alcohol, and ending with zinc sulphate, zinc sulphide and zirconium. To make a telephone required thirty-five major materials, many uniquely sourced as far apart as South America, the Arctic Circle, South Africa, Sweden, Australia and China. From *The World Buys a Motor Car* (1938), quoted in Staley, *World Economy in Transition*, pp. 24–8.

Table 13.11. JAPANESE SUPPLIES OF INDUSTRIAL MATERIALS
RELATIVE TO THE U.S.A. AND THE SOVIET UNION, 1938
(% of world totals)

	Japan	Japan-Manchuria-China bloc	U.S.A.	Soviet Union
Coal	0	.009	35.9	9.9
Oil	0	0	60.4	11.1
Iron ore	0	2.3	31.9	17.8
Aluminium	0	0	30.0	10.4
Raw cotton	0	12.4	39.1	11.3

Source: Takemura, *A survey of the economic resources of the Greater East Asian Co-Prosperity Sphere,* pp. 9–10.
Notes: 1. Zero figures indicate supplies are not statistically meaningful. 2. Takemura's study is premised on the view that raw material control is essential for military success and the author compares annual consumption rates of key materials for the two World Wars, showing increases of two- and threefold in the Second, pp. 8–9.

into North China and later into South-East Asia, but even these desperate moves did not solve the problems.[79]

Manchuria also proved disappointing as an outlet for 'surplus' population. In 1930 there were about 1,000 Japanese rural migrants there, mainly settled under the SMR schemes. By the late 1930s, after years of planning and propaganda, there were 800,000 Japanese in Manchuria altogether but still only about 80,000 peasants – a minuscule number in relation to any estimate of 'surplus population'. The problem was that Japanese peasants, however poor, preferred not to migrate to a country where incomes were very low, where the indigenous population was violently hostile and where conditions, especially in winter, were so harsh. The migration plans for skilled labour were not much more successful. For example, the plan for skilled migration achieved only one-sixth of its target numbers in 1939, and skill shortages remained a serious constraint on Manchurian industry throughout the whole of the war.

79. The early stages of the drive into North China are described in Takafusa Nakamura, 'Japan's economic thrust into North China, 1933–1938: Formation of the North China Development Corporation' in Akira Iriye (ed.), *The Chinese and the Japanese: Essays in Political and Cultural Interactions,* Princeton University Press, 1980, pp. 220–51.

Foreign trade. Foreign trade played the central role in stimulating the development of the modern Manchurian economy, and the soya bean had been by far the most important commodity in the trade sector. This was still the case in 1936, in spite of all the intensive industrialisation efforts of the Manchukuo government. In that year, agricultural products accounted for 85% of the major export items, and soya beans and related products alone still accounted for 65% of exports. Metallurgical and coal products accounted for 11%.[80] In other words, development did not go beyond import substitution.

In the earlier part of this chapter it was argued that part of the problem of Japanese foreign trade in the 1920s was the failure to sustain the export shift to heavy industry goods that began during the First World War. Colonial expansion helped this problem, at least superficially; both Manchuria and the Kwantung Leased Territory offered protected markets for Japanese heavy industry goods. The effect of this outlet is illustrated in Fig. 13.4, which compares the structure of Japanese exports to those two markets with the structure of Japanese exports worldwide. This shows clearly that while Japan's exports to the world reflected Japan's advantage in textiles and light industry, Manchuria became a market for heavy industry exports and thereby did contribute to the process of learning that eventually led to Japanese heavy industry competitiveness in the 1950s and 1960s.[81] Manchurian heavy industry planning also provided a school for bureaucrats and economic planners who later returned to play an important role in the Japanese industrial bureaucracy of the post-war era.

The overall role of Manchuria in the Japanese trade system in 1935 is illustrated in Table 13.12. We see here that the Japanese empire is defined as including Manchukuo, which accounted for only one-third of Japan's exports in 1936 and exactly the same proportion of imports. The small trade surplus that Japan ran in the same year was divided in a similar way. Manchuria was the one economy with which Japan

80. 'The foreign trade of Manchoukuo', *Contemporary Manchuria*, vol. 3, no. 2, April 1939, pp. 1–20.

81. See esp. Minoru Sawai, 'The rolling stock industry and the "Manchurian" market with special reference to the 1930s' in Oishi, *Japan's inter-war external economic relations*, pp. 131–70. This deals with the growing importance of Manchuria for Japanese exports of rolling stock and illustrates at the micro level the contribution of the Manchurian market to the correction of the internal–external imbalance problem. The article also shows that Mitsui was the most important of the trading houses in this business.

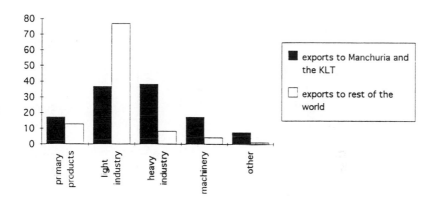

Fig. 13.4. DIFFERENTIAL EXPORT STRUCTURE TO MANCHURIA AND
THE K.L.T COMPARED TO THE REST OF THE WORLD, 1935
(% shares)

Source: EHOJ, vol. 6, pp. 248–9.

had a large surplus — without it there would have been a large deficit
with the empire as a whole. However, much of this surplus represented purchases of Japanese goods tied to Japanese investment, so that
cumulatively the scale of the deficits and investment outflows were
approximately the same in the 1930s.

Although this analysis is based on a post-war reconstruction of the
statistics, these trends were understood at the time. One important
analysis published in 1942, in which the definition of 'empire' was
enlarged to take account of Japan's wartime expansion into South-East
Asia, showed exactly the same problem with little sign that the trend
could be made more favourable. Indeed, the trends could be interpreted
as meaning that the Greater East Asian Co-Prosperity Sphere was
increasingly inclined to internal deficits that had to be offset by
surpluses with the outside world.[82] Another influential viewpoint

82. Takemura, 'Japan's trade relations with the Greater East Asia Co-prosperity
Sphere', *A survey of the economic resources of the East Asian Co-Prosperity Sphere*, ch. 3,
pp. 76–80.

Table 13.12. THE OVERALL STRUCTURE OF JAPANESE TRADE WITH MANCHURIA, THE EMPIRE AND THE REST OF THE WORLD, 1936 (millions of yen)

	Manchuria and the Kwantung Leased Territory	Korea	Taiwan	All parts of the Japanese empire	Third countries	Total
Japanese exports, 1936, to:	468.946	544.252	210.055	1,275.000	2,279.998	3,555.843
% shares	13.2	15.3	5.9	35.9	64.1	100
Japanese imports, 1936, from:	216.522	522.880	333.246	1,200.724	2,146.581	3,347.305
% shares	7.5	15.6	10	35.9	64.1	100
Trade balance	+252.424	+21.372	−123.191	+74.276	+133.417	+208.538

Source: Derived from *EHOJ*, vol. 6, p. 244.

was that of the great trade theorist Akamatsu and this was much more positive. It acknowledged the immediate trade problem but suggested that the full development of the East Asia regional economy, with Japan as its advanced core, would enable the 'flying geese' pattern of development to spread Japanese industrialisation to China and the rest of the region. This of course could be accomplished only by the expulsion of the western powers, who naturally wished to avoid the painful readjustments that Asian economic success would entail and therefore sought to impede the development of a Japan-centred Asia and impose the trade and industrialisation patterns that suited them.[83]

In the light of subsequent history, this last argument is fascinating, even prophetic. For the phase of western adjustment to East Asian industrialisation that Akamatsu wanted to accelerate in the 1940s, with all the dilemmas it entailed, actually started in earnest in the 1980s. In 1942, however, all this was premature. Japan's inter-war quest for raw material security, population outlets and a predictable framework for its international trade were all rational objectives in their time. Nonetheless, the degree of specialisation that Japan had developed by the 1920s meant that a multilateral pattern of trade, in which there was an important place for exports to both the rich western economies and to their spheres of influence in the developing world, was essential. Any immediate attempt to balance trade bilaterally within the Asian region or achieve self-sufficiency in technologically advanced goods was bound to fail. Even partial success involved the Japanese economy in exorbitant costs.

However, there was one element in Japan's inter-war economic expansion for which the economic rationale was much stronger and which pointed the way to a much more satisfactory role for Japan in the Asian economy. This was the expansion of textile investment into China, to which we must now finally turn.

---

83. Akamatsu, K., 'The historical pattern of East Asian trade' in Toa Keizai Kenkyujo, *East Asia economic research yearbook*, pp. 73–131. The argument that the western powers used unfair methods to stop Japan's structural transformation by impeding its industrial exports to China fits in with contemporary claims that America and Britain would not allow Japanese goods into Manchuria although their prices were lower.

14

JAPAN'S TRADE AND DIRECT INVESTMENT IN THE CHINESE TEXTILE INDUSTRY

THE ELEMENTS OF AN ALTERNATIVE MODEL

'The swift capture of the Chinese textile market by Japan is indeed a miracle of modern commercial history.' — Kang Chao, 1977

On July 16, 1923, the daughter of the Japanese Consul General in Shanghai, Miss T. Funatsu, cut the launching cords of the *Katata* with a silver axe. The *Katata* was the second Japanese gunboat to be built jointly by Japanese and Chinese workmen in a Japanese shipyard in Shanghai. Because it was designed for river patrols, its triple expansion engines gave it a speed of 16 knots with a normal draft of only 40 inches. As the cords parted and the boat slid down the slipway towards the water, a large red and white ball secured under the boom burst open, releasing a shower of confetti on to the water below and a flock of pigeons (symbolising peace) into the sky above. More than one thousand Japanese, Chinese and European visitors enjoyed the spectacle. They were supplied with tea and refreshments and, before leaving, each was presented with a small paperweight in memory of the occasion. During the afternoon a message of congratulation from the Minister of the Navy in Tokyo, Admiral Takarabe, was read to the assembly. After this, Consul General Funatsu addressed his guests in the following words: 'We Japanese people are not anxious to build and place these gunboats on the Yangtze, but in view of the present situation in China the Japanese government deems it absolutely necessary to construct gunboats which can sail up the Yangtze, for the protection of the lives and property and other interests of Japanese residents.'

After a brief spell of duty in Manchuria, Mr Funatsu was subsequently released from the diplomatic service to enter the world of business. In 1926 he was back in Shanghai, this time as Director-General of the Japan Cotton Millowners' Association. In December of that year, the Association gave a dinner for leading members of the foreign community at the Majestic Hotel, and Mr Funatsu was called on to address his fellow-businessmen, British, French, and American, who were attending the dinner, together with the newly-appointed British Minister in China, Miles Lampson. He told them:

It was naturally not easy for one who had been trained in the diplomatic service of his country to leave that service late in life and to enter upon a career in business . . . [but] the more I realise the possibilities of my position and the more I realise what the shareholders, directors and managers of the Japanese cotton mills in China are trying to do, the happier I am that I have undertaken my present work.

For we Japanese have a huge investment and a great responsibility in this city. We employ about 70,000 labourers, whose welfare is our special care and in whose interests much of our Association's work is done. The mere business of managing a cotton mill and making a profit has nothing to do with our Association. We exist for something more than that. We exist to improve the industry, to develop the finest friendship between our competitors of other nationalities and ourselves, to maintain the most cordial relations between the management and the labourer, and to provide for the labourer as favourable conditions as the production of the industry will permit.

The story of Mr Funatsu and his career, his aspirations and the receptions he attended encapsulate almost perfectly the last important thread in Japan's pre-war international economic relations and the ambiguities which these involved. This is the thread that combines trade with private foreign direct investment, and both of these with the transfer of technology and competitiveness to the mutual benefit of Japan and the recipient economy. The ambiguities in this line of development arose from two problems: that contemporary imperialisms did not provide a suitable environment for such activities and that other elements in Japan had other purposes in China.[1]

1. This chapter relies heavily on two major secondary sources and the files of the *North China Herald*. The former are Takamura Naosuke, *Kindai Nihon mengyo to Chugoku* (The modern Japanese textile industry and China), Tokyo Daigaku Shuppankai, 1982, and Kang Chao, *The Development of Cotton Textile Production in China*, Cambridge, MA: Harvard University Press, 1977. Details and the story of Mr Funatsu and the Yangtze patrols are from 'A new Japanese Gunboat built in Shanghai', *NCH*, July 7, 1923; 'A second Japanese Yangtze gunboat', *NCH*, July 21, 1923; 'Japanese cotton industry: Aims of the Millowners' Association in China. contribution to happier conditions', *NCH*, Dec. 4, 1926. There was nothing intrinsically surprising about the Japanese patrols, since in 1923 the chambers of commerce of Hong Kong and Canton were both demanding similar patrols in the Pearl River delta, based on fears that they could be cut off from essential food supplies and other resources by free-shooting bandits and warlords preying on river shipping. See 'River patrols in China', *NCH*, July 21, 1923.

This final chapter outlines the Japanese experience of direct investment in Chinese textiles and points to its longer-term significance.

The cotton industry in China

China had a vast traditional cotton industry, with a history only exceeded by that of India, whence the Chinese learned many textile skills. Using handicraft methods and mainly part-time rural labour, the Chinese traditional weaving sector was producing 1.9 billion square yards of handloom cloth annually in the early 1900s, with its output rising to a peak of 2.6 billion yards in 1928–31.[2]

In the second half of the nineteenth century this traditional supply was supplemented by imports of western machine-made yarn and cloth. Because of the size of the Chinese population, even quite small volumes of imports *per capita* made an impressive impact on exporters' output and an even greater one on their dreams for the future. The value of cotton imports more than doubled between 1870 and the early 1890s and then quadrupled again by the 1920s. For Britain, the world's leading exporter, the combined imports of India, China and Japan rose from approximately one-tenth to a half of total exports between 1830 and 1880, with access to China being greatly eased by control of the entrepot port of Hong Kong. For the Americans, as was shown in Chapter 12, China was even more important, accounting by itself in the 1890s for half their total textile exports.[3]

The growth of imports led in China, as it had done in Japan, to the potential for import substitution, and by the 1890s this process was actively under way. So successfully was this implemented that by 1917 domestic yarn production was greater than imports, as by 1927 were exports.[4] Import substitution in cloth was harder to achieve, as it had been in Japan, but by the late 1930s considerable progress was being made. In these processes of modernisation, import substitution and export development, the role played by the Japanese cotton textile industry was crucial.

Japan's textile interest in China. We have seen the importance of China to the early development of the modern Japanese textile industry. In

2. Chao, *The Development*, pp. 232–3.
3. *Ibid.*, p. 89; Takamura, *China*, ch. 1.
4. Chao, *The Development*, p. 92.

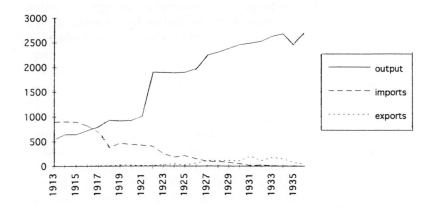

Fig. 14.1. OUTPUT, IMPORTS AND EXPORTS OF
COTTON YARN IN CHINA, 1913–36

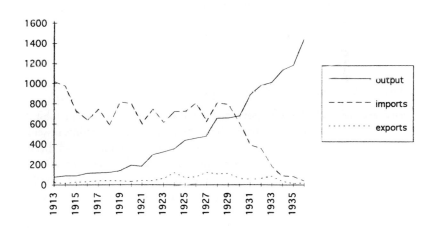

Fig. 14.2. OUTPUT, IMPORTS AND EXPORTS OF
COTTON CLOTH IN CHINA, 1913–36

Source of both Figures: Takamura, *China*, p. 98.

the late 1880s it became Japan's first source of the foreign raw cotton that made its machine-made yarn internationally competitive. To exploit this, Japanese companies (notably Mitsui) opened offices in Shanghai to purchase raw cotton and lay the foundations for a long-term business relationship with China. China was also Japan's first major market for textile exports. In the early stages access to the China market was difficult, despite underlying cost competitiveness and the specialised ability of Japanese companies to satisfy the Asian demand for textiles that were rough, hard-wearing and cheap. The Sino-Japanese war transformed this situation. Not only did it give great impetus to domestic industrial development, but it gave Japan new status in Korea. In China it finally enabled Mitsui and others to dispense with the entire traditional distribution network. This was something in which the western powers were never successful, partly because too few of their staff could speak Chinese and partly because of the inability of most westerners to understand the extraordinarily complex local Chinese monetary systems.[5]

As a result, the China market (including Hong Kong) was absorbing 94% of Japanese yarn exports by 1897, and total yarn exports of 140,000 bales accounted for 25% of all yarn output. In 1899 exports reached 340,000 bales, absorbing an astonishing 43% of output. From this time onwards, the textile development of Japan was inextricably related to exports, which in turn were inextricably related to the evolution of the China market.[6]

Direct investment in the Chinese textile industry

Phase one: 1890–1922. The potential for import substitution in China had interested westerners from the outset. Before the Shimonoseki treaty ending the Sino-Japanese war in 1895, foreigners had been forbidden by law to invest directly in China. Within months of the agreements, the Bokyo had made a long-term Japanese plan for textile investment. This first initiative made little progress, but several

---

5. Takamura, *China*, chs. 2 and 3; *Mitsui tokuhon*, pp. 219ff. Takahashi, *Development*, vol. 1, ch. 4. Takamura and Takahashi emphasise at many points in their work the advantage that the Japanese enjoyed in their relatively easy access to the Chinese language.

6. Takamura, *China*, p. 50. As an entrepot, Hong Kong absorbed a large amount of imports with unknown final destinations.

Japanese investments came on stream in Shanghai, building on twenty years of commercial development in China.[7]

The interest of Japanese business in direct investment in textiles was based on two factors: the need to establish secure outlets for Japanese yarn exports in foreign cloth mills and the stagnation of the domestic rate of textile growth. Where the first of these factors was concerned, the Japanese feared that other direct investors would use their Chinese weaving mills as outlets for their own yarn and thus cut out Japanese yarns. The slowing of domestic growth reflected partly the fact that import substitution was past its peak, and partly the difficulties in exporting which arose from Japan's new status as a gold standard economy. With lower wage costs and the benefits of a silver standard currency that was tending to depreciate against gold, Chinese mills were thus a rational prospect.

The First World War dramatically accelerated this development. Pre-war development had not been profitable for all, but by 1917 the cotton trade in Shanghai was awash with money, being described as 'exhilarating as well as phenomenal'. Throughout China, output and exports grew rapidly, drawing the Chinese-owned mills in particular on to a rapid learning curve in technology, management and commercial relations.[8] By 1919–22, Japanese wage-rises and the failure to readjust the post-war exchange rate destroyed Japanese competitiveness in the lower-count yarns and lower-graded cloths. By transferring output to China the Japanese could combine their commercial networks and their sophisticated knowledge of textile management and technology with Chinese labour costs. This would enable them both to produce output that would protect their position in the Chinese market and to compete in the new Asian export markets. Japanese businessmen also had to devise strategies later for coping with Chinese boycotts and with the impact on exports of the anticipated raising of protective tariffs after the recovery of Chinese tariff autonomy, which in fact

7. These early initiatives were in association with Mitsui and the Naigai Wata Company, both of which had long experience in Shanghai business as raw cotton dealers.

8. 'Shanghai Cotton Manufacturing Co. Ltd.', *NCH*, Sept. 22, 1917. Before the war some investors found money so hard to make that a distant, unlikely prospect ('a blue moon') was described as happening 'when the cotton mills pay a dividend'.

occurred in 1931.[9] Thus the total post-war strategy for the Japanese textile industry did not consist only of domestic rationalisation and technological and product upgrading (as discussed in Chapter 8); it also involved the transfer to China of a large share of textile productive capacity. This entire programme was essentially financed with the reserves accumulated during the war boom.

The outflow of textile capital to China was so vigorous that between 1920 and 1924 the three largest companies were installing spindles in China at the same rate as in Japan. By 1924 there were over 1 million spindles in China, and of these, four-fifths were in Shanghai, although Japanese investors were moving increasingly to other cities where land costs were lower and labour was cheaper and less politically explosive.[10]

The total flow of investment in terms of spindles is shown in Table 14.1, where we see that by 1925, despite the slow pace of the early Japanese investment, the Japanese accounted for 38% of the capital installed in the spinning sector. Furthermore, they had established themselves as the overwhelmingly dominant foreign investor whose performance would therefore be a major factor in the performance of the entire Chinese industry. Table 14.2, summarising the full post-war story for both spinning and weaving, shows the strength of Japanese direct investment in China, the decline and fall of other foreigners and the stubborn development of the Chinese-owned sector in spite of all difficulties.

The efficiency of the Japanese mills

The success of the Japanese mills in China was demonstrated by their ability to compete with Chinese mills, by their ability to overtake and dominate other foreign (notably British and American) textile investors, and by their important role in exporting. The explanation of how all this was accomplished falls into two parts, the first relating to the experience of the pre-war pioneer investors and the second, more

9. The Chinese tariff issue dragged on for much of the 1920s. Having fought to regain their own tariff autonomy just a few years previously, the Japanese defended China's right to autonomy in principle while in practice attempting to ensure that Japan's economic interests would not be harmed by new protection.
10. Takamura, *China*, pp. 116–32.

Table 14.1. THE CHINESE SPINNING INDUSTRY AND ITS
FOREIGN COMPONENTS, 1890–1925

	Chinese spindles	Japanese spindles	English spindles	Total
1890	35,000			35,000
1895	174,564			174,564
1900	336,722		80,548	497,270
1905	355,588	23,912	80,548	540,048
1910	497,448	55,296	80,548	713,292
1919	658,748	332,922	244,088	1,235,758
1925	1,866,232	1,268,176	205,320	3,339,728

Source: Ishii, *Economic history*, p. 231.

Table 14.2. CHINESE, JAPANESE AND OTHER
FOREIGN TEXTILE CAPACITY IN CHINA, 1913–36

	Chinese spindles	Japanese spindles	Other	Chinese looms	Japanese looms	Other
1913	521,000	112,000	233,000	2,707	886	1,210
1927	2,099,000	1,370,000	205,000	13,459	13,981	2,348
1936	2,920,000	2,485,000	230,000	25,503	28,915	4,021

Source: Takamura, *China*, p. 98.
Note: 1927 was selected for the 1920s as a peak-year for exports.

comprehensive explanation to the situation as it developed in the inter-war years.[11]

In the pre-war period, Japanese performance was reflected in superior levels of productivity and in high and rising profit and dividend performance. The superior productivity of Japanese mills was mainly explained by three factors. First, Japanese mills were staffed in their upper technical echelons by Japanese expatriates whose numbers, levels of training and experience were all high in relation to competitors. This meant that factory layouts and work organisation

11. This subject is dealt with in Takamura, *China*, ch. 6; Chao, *The Development*, ch. 6.; Pearse, *Japan and China*, part 2.

were good and — most important — that high standards of maintenance and continuous smooth running of machinery were achieved.
Secondly, the Japanese factories transferred and adapted their skills in
the technology of mixing raw cottons to Chinese conditions to achieve
results superior to those of their rivals. Thirdly, training programmes
were instituted for Chinese workers. These were of great significance,
for while the mills in Japan could rely on the state to provide the
'infrastructure' of basic workforce literacy and numeracy, this was not
so in China. Most Shanghai cotton workers came from rural Kiangsu
and in consequence were at first remote from factory culture and
burdened with rates of illiteracy of as much as 30% or even 50%.
Of all these factors success in training and maintaining an adequate
labour supply seem to have been the most important, and Japanese successes were in sharp contrast to the failure of the British textile
investments in particular.[12]

In the inter-war years, three groups of factors were important in
determining Japanese performance: technology, human resource
management and financial and commercial skills. The elements of
technological superiority included the tendency for Japanese mills to
be larger in scale and to have much higher rates of electrification and
newer and technically superior machinery. This was especially so after
the 1920s investment boom when the Japanese mills in China, most
of all the new ones outside Shanghai, benefited from the rapid transfer
of improvements in technology being made at the same time in Japan.
The Japanese gained major benefits from economies of scale and the
introduction into these plants of the latest Toyoda automatic looms
and high draft spinning systems.

Machine supremacy was reinforced by skilled human resource
management. Training and shift-working systems were both important, and the Japanese appear also to have operated with higher proportions of technical staff and lower proportions of administrative staff
than their Chinese rivals. The latter were in fact plagued by a combination of overmanning and poor staff selection, reflecting the intensely

---

12. 'Why it [textile investment] does not pay in Shanghai', *NCH* Dec. 18, 1901.
This article emphasises that the failure of British investments was due to the problems
of language, lack of skills and commitment by the local labour force and the overall
error of 'dumping down' an industry in China that was naturally only appropriate
to certain geographical locations in the world.

nepotistic tendencies of Chinese management (as powerful today as they were before 1937).[13]

Finally, the financial, commercial and top management skills of the Japanese companies are also clearly evident. At every stage from investment through to production and distribution, competitors claimed that Japanese companies had access to capital at lower cost than either foreign or Chinese competitors. The margin against the Europeans and Americans was probably not large but against the Chinese, whose financial system remained underdeveloped, the gain was large and a significant factor in total costs.

In raw cotton buying and in sales and distribution, the Japanese companies naturally continued to rely heavily on Mitsui and the other trading companies, especially Naigai Wata. It was reported that 70% of their output was handled by these companies, which by the 1920s had over forty years' experience in buying raw cotton and selling exports throughout Asia and, increasingly, throughout the world. Japan's commercial advantages, which have already been discussed, were probably decisive in explaining the rapid decline of other foreigners in both direct foreign investment and textile importing.

The question of Japanese textile production efficiency was not only much debated in the Shanghai trade but was also the subject of highly expert analysis. The commentators agreed on the generally excellent performance of the Japanese mills and noted two particular factors in addition to the points already mentioned. The first was the originality of Japanese methods and their ability to adapt their transferred expertise to Chinese conditions with minute precision and efficiency. The British in particular seemed never to grasp that Lancashire methods could be improved upon and simply tried to transfer techniques *en bloc*.[14] Thus, as one writer put it, 'In cotton mill management at

13. 'Advice to Chinese Cotton Millowners. Retiring expert addresses native industrialists on future expansion', *FER*, July 1919, pp. 504–5. In this speech, Mr James Kerfoot of Jardine Matheson told the Chinese Millowners' Association that every key to competitiveness was available to them, provided they could overcome the inefficiencies caused by nepotism.

14. This section and quotations are taken from a very detailed analysis by 'Sub Rosa' and comments by 'Progress', writing in the *North China Herald*. Many articles and letters in this paper were pseudonymous. 'Sub Rosa' was almost certainly a British specialist wishing to protect his employability in the western sector, who wrote his articles and letters to explain why the Japanese mills had a 20% productivity advantage over competitors. See 'Cotton spinning for success', *NCH*, Feb. 9, 1918; and a letter from 'Progress', Feb. 16.

least we cannot accuse the Japanese of being imitators only — they have gone one better and *studied conditions and met them* [emphasis added].' The particular issue seized upon by this analyst was the problem of the tendency of threads to break in the great heat and high humidity found in the summer months in eastern China. The Japanese experience in the Osaka region must have been helpful here and the solution was to invest much more heavily than normal in the machinery used for the preparatory stages of blowing, carding, drawing and slubbing before the final process of spinning.

The second factor was the technical literacy of senior managers and the long-term strategic outlook of Japanese shareholders, whose qualities were implicitly compared with their British equivalents by an exasperated contemporary analyst: 'The [British] mill directors probably devoid of technical knowledge, the mill advisors satisfied to keep their jobs ... [and] the shareholders indifferent and looking more towards "jumping in and jumping out" at the right moment than caring what the spindle point rendering is.'

In summing up this issue, we must remember that the precise nature of Japanese cost advantages in China has to be considered by comparing them not only with competitors in China itself, but also with costs in Japan. Estimating these advantages is obviously difficult and must have changed significantly over time. Takamura has summarised the data for spinning as shown in Table 14.3. Even allowing for the considerable problems of estimation, these data show clearly why Japan transferred output of lower-count yarn to China and why, as direct

Table 14.3. COMPARATIVE COSTS OF SPINNIING 20-COUNT YARN
(per bale)

	Japanese mills in Japan (1928)	Japanese mills in China (1928)	Japanese mills in China (1935)	Chinese mills in China (1928)
Energy	5.5	5.0	4.8	5.5
Wages	20.0	9.2	5.8	10.5
Taxes (for 1935: tax and interest payments)	4.0	.5	2.7	15.0
Total costs	42.0	22.0	20.4	43.7

Source: Takamura, *China*, p. 183.
Note: 1928 data are in Japanese yen; 1935 data are in Chinese yuan.

investors, the Japanese China mills were so successful in both the Chinese and export markets.

The Japanese in China

The history of the Japanese commercial community in China began well before Japan embarked on the path of advancing its economic interests by force. Its consulate in Shanghai opened in 1872, and in the 1870s and 1880s Japanese ships were seen in the harbour there ever more frequently. Japanese firms began to arrive in earnest during the 1880s and in the years that followed, as business increased, the Japanese settled down and began the creation of a lively expatriate community in what became one of the world's most vibrant and cosmopolitan colonial cities.[15]

In 1907 the community was honoured with a one-day visit from H.I.H. Prince Fushimi, who toured the native city in the morning and took tiffin at the NYK offices in the afternoon.[16] The next year a substantial Japanese Club was opened, and by the outbreak of war the Japanese were a respected group in the international business community. The international Shanghai Cotton Millowners' Association distributed seats on its committee in proportion to the shares of spindles owned. In 1914 this gave three seats to the westerners and two each to the Chinese and Japanese. Of the Japanese, Mr Kawamura offered at one time to withdraw because of his inability to attend every meeting, but this suggestion was decisively rejected by the chairman (from Jardine's) on the grounds that his knowledge of the trade was indispensable.[17] By the 1920s Japanese goods were common in the department stores, some fine schools for Japanese children had been opened,[18] and a Japanese contingent even won the cup for the best contribution to the International Volunteer Corps, a prize which the Japanese community itself had public-spiritedly donated.[19] In 1923

15. See especially the contributions of Lucian Pye and Marie Claire Bergère in Christopher Howe (ed.), *Shanghai: Revolution and Development in an Asian Metropolis*, Cambridge University Press, 1981.

16. 'Prince Fushimi in Shanghai', *NCH*, Feb. 22, 1907.

17. 'Cotton Millowners Association', *NCH*, April 25, 1914.

18. In 1926 there were 2,700 children at the Japanese schools. Of the latter the most distinguished was the Japanese High School for Girls. The girls at this school could certainly get a better education than was possible in Japan, for in addition to learning the arts of Japanese housekeeping in a small, Japanese-style room, they studied physics, chemistry, history and music. 'Japanese school in Shanghai', *NCH*, June 27, 1926.

19. 'The Japanese cup presented', *NCH*, July 1926.

they added cultural to economic and political expansion through the Association of the Culture of the Great East, which had as part of its mission the dissemination of Japanese ideology in Asia. By the same year Japanese shipping dominance on the Upper Yangtze foreshadowed an extending regional commercial influence.[20]

The major shift of textile capital in the early 1920s that consolidated all these elements was almost entirely an economic phenomenon. As Japanese labour costs rose, the pressure for specialisation increased. For Japan this meant not only moving towards the more capital-intensive industries, but also towards increased intra-industry specialisation. As the domestic Japanese textiles moved up-market, it was logical to combine Japanese industrial and commercial skills with cheaper Chinese labour in a complex pattern of geographical specialisation, driven by foreign direct investment. This process was accelerated by a mistaken Japanese exchange-rate policy, but that too represented an error of economic rather than political policy.

As we saw in Table 14.2, Japan's success in textile manufacturing was at the expense of foreign rivals. The Chinese industry, in spite of difficulties, expanded impressively, and one factor in this was the technical and managerial spillover from the Japanese mills. The benefits of this spillover were apparent in the short run and were later taken to Hong Kong by the Shanghaiese industrialists who in the 1950s initiated the fastest, textile-based industrialisation the world has ever seen.[21]

As foreign direct investment increased and the Japanese wartime empire spread, the extent and complexity of Japanese company interests grew correspondingly. This is clear from the development of financial and trading companies, but the industrial cases are more remarkable, and of these an outstanding example was the Toyo Boseki. The extent of this company during wartime is illustrated in Table 14.4, from which we see that by the 1940s the old Osaka Boseki, founded as a spinning company in a single city in the 1880s, had not only become a world leader in its original activity but had also extended this to cover all aspects of the textile sector. It had then integrated backwards to ensure its raw material supply and had finally

20. 'Japan's Association of Culture', *NCH*, April 23, 1923. The shipping information refers to the river from Ichang to Chunking and is reported in *NCH*, July 21, 1923; 'Japanese in the Upper Yangtze trade', *NCH*, April 7, 1923.

21. Judith Mary Nishida, 'The Japanese Influence on the Shanghaiese Textile Industry and Implications for Hong Kong', unpubl. M. Phil. thesis, University of Hong Kong, 1990.

Table 14.4. THE MAIN LOCATIONS AND ACTIVITIES OF THE TOYO
BOSEKI COMPANY AND ITS ASSOCIATED COMPANIES, 1940–44

	No. of main locations	Activities
Japan	91	Factories and offices engaged mainly in all branches of the textile trade
Malaysia, Indonesia, Philippines, Hong Kong and South Seas	29	Factories, offices, farms and plantations, engaged mainly in the cotton, textile, sesame oil and tobacco industries
China and Manchuria	55	Factories, mines and offices engaged in: *Textiles* cotton spinning and weaving, dyeing, printing, woollens, clothing manufacture *Light industry* paper, flax processing, sesame oil, soya bean processing, tobaccco *Heavy industry* shipbuilding, steel, mining, coal processing, man-made fibres, chemicals, machine tools, oil, aircraft, engineering, rubber tyres, electricity supply *Service sector* property development companies

Source: Based on data in *Toyo boseki nanajunenshi*, appendix map, pp. 715–30.

spread horizontally into cognate activities such as chemicals and man-made fibres as well as into the heavy industries.

From the onset, the Japanese government was involved in this overseas expansion. In the early Meiji years the government was involved in almost everything, but this was explicable in the circumstances of the time and even today no fundamental shift of private-sector international business policy would be possible without official approval. At first Japan's official role in China consisted largely of general encouragement, of establishing the 'Maeda tripod' of trading house/ banking/industrial collaboration and of providing subsidised shipping services linking Shanghai and the Chinese ports to Japan and other parts of Asia. By 1917 the Japanese Foreign Ministry was encouraging the textile companies to invest in China, since it foresaw the inevitability of Chinese tariff autonomy and its possible effects on Japanese trade.[22]

By the late 1920s the growing militarisation of Japanese policy led to sharp divisions. In the mid-1920s the Japanese businessmen in Shanghai called for sharp diplomatic and other sanctions against the Chinese boycott movement,[23] but as the Japanese military rose to power in China, westerners observed a widening split between the Japanese army, which wanted China as a population outlet, and the private business sector, which sought only reasonable political stability and the opportunity for further commercial expansion and direct investment — in other words, the continued implementation of the original Okura philosophy.[24] In the end, however, all were drawn into the violence and disaster of the Manchurian takeover and the Sino-Japanese war.

The fact that Japan's pre-war international economic entanglements ended so badly has overshadowed the entire pattern of economic development in Asia since the Second World War. But this should not obscure the significance of the earlier, purely economic elements of the kinds discussed in these last three chapters. Not only did Japanese involvement in Asia profoundly influence the economies it touched, but through the processes of trade and investment expansion the Japanese themselves also learned a huge range of skills. They learned how to research foreign economies and their resources, institutions, technologies and monetary systems. They learned how to nurture foreign markets from small beginnings over long periods of time. They learned how to adapt their technologies to local conditions, how to manage multinational companies and compete as traders and direct investors, and how to develop diplomacy in the service of economic policy. Finally, and perhaps most important of all, there is the

22. 'Japanese spinners' anxiety', *NCH*, March 24, 1917.

23. See the demands of the Shanghai Japanese Chamber of Commerce in 'Japanese Merchants and the Boycott', *NCH*, June 23, 1923.

24. 'Japanese cotton mills in China. Expression of opinion by men in the trade', *NCH*, May 14, 1927.

paradigmatic image of the pre-war Japanese businessman — the Mitsui soya bean buyer on the rutted Manchurian roads — progressing slowly but never giving up.[25]

If all this had been studied with more care, there would have been less surprise at the post-war success of Japan in the world economy and perhaps a greater ability to cope with its consequences.

---

25. The verb for exactly this concept of persistence is *ganbaru*. As you walk up a mountain in Japan, descending climbers encourage you with the cry '*Ganbatte kudasai*' ('Stick with it, please!').

15

CONCLUSIONS

'For the economic state of a people does not emerge simply from the preceding economic conditions, but only from the preceding total situation.' — Joseph A. Schumpeter, *The Theory of Economic Development*

Japan's emergence as a power in world trade has been neither sudden nor a wholly economic event. On the contrary, it is the end-product of a lengthy process in which Japanese understanding of the outside world, trade and other relationships has expanded in stages, interacting as it did so with the changing world environment.

The earliest Japanese trading exchanges were with Asian neighbours. Then in the sixteenth century there began the first cycle of contact with Europeans and later with partners from the Americas. Stimulating and economically useful as these contacts were, they were also profoundly destabilising for a society already suffering the consequences of its medieval institutions having collapsed in the late fifteenth century. Thus, from the early seventeenth to the mid-nineteenth century, Japan's leaders restricted foreign contacts mainly, though not exclusively, to Asian partners. During this long period, the domestic economy grew in size, diversity, and technical and institutional sophistication. Thus although the price of Seclusion was a loss of contact with key elements of the scientific and economic revolutions of post-Newtonian Europe, the prolonged years of isolation seem to have deepened in every way the Japanese capacity for learning and problem-solving.

In the mid-nineteenth century the rampant expansion of western industrialisation led to a re-opening of Japan, although the motivation for this was more closely related to western interest in China than to the economic promise of Japan itself. But once the Tokugawa spell had been broken, Japan proved to be by far the most able student of western economic modernisation. Without entirely destroying traditional structures and values, its people learned how to devise new economc institutions and to mobilise resources for the acquisition of new skills and technologies. The driving force in all this was not national (let alone individual) enrichment as such, but the need for an economic and technological base capable of maintaining Japanese

426

nationhood and independence. Thus, although the Japanese borrowed many of the institutions and mechanisms of capitalism (private property, joint stock companies, financial markets etc.), and although strategic factors had necessarily to be linked to economic ones, the motive power of the system always included elements from outside the economic realm.

In the 1890s, to the stupefaction of contemporary western observers, Japan emerged not only as an exporter of primary products and oriental exotica, but as a serious competitor in the markets for manufactured goods. This entry on to the world economic stage coincided with the last phase of western imperial expansion, in which traditional players such as Britain and France were joined by newcomers such as Germany and the United States, both of which were backed by formidable and growing domestic economic power bases. Japan asserted its own Asian claims through the medium of its war with China in 1894. Thereafter its pattern of economic development began to be influenced by its own expansion of overseas political power, but within this framework progress was very much a reflection of successful industrial development and the achievement of a rational international division of labour.

An underlying factor in Japan's economic development was its success in mastering a widening range of technological transfer and adaptation. Timing was helpful here, because Japan's pursuit of modernisation began within a few decades of the Western era of steam and iron; thus, by the late nineteenth century, Japan had joined the new industrial revolution based on the sciences of chemistry and electricity and the invention of the internal combustion engine.

We saw in Part III that transfer and innovation in technology rests on three types of knowledge. The first is the open, formal knowledge of production processes of the kind that can be codified, transmitted and ultimately embodied in commercially valuable patent formulations. The second is the tacit, informal knowledge that is the product of practice and experience. In the traditional world such knowledge is often jealously guarded by the craftsman and may be transmitted through family lines and apprenticeship arrangements; but in the modern world it is often preserved by the practice of commercial secrecy. The third, and more abstract form, is the theoretical or contextual knowledge essential for the stage when innovation becomes a conscious objective, pursued with the aid of specialists working *outside* the workshop or factory.

Traditional Japan had an impressive record of increasingly market-driven transfers and innovation based on tacit and even open varieties of knowledge, but it lacked contextual knowledge of the kind that the West had derived from the intellectual revolutions of the seventeenth to nineteenth centuries. (Even today, the chemical processes of fine steel manufacture are imperfectly understood, yet traditional Japanese swordsmiths learned, by trial and error, to forge the finest blades east of Damascus.)

This framework governed the patterns of Japan's modern technological progress. Thus in traditional industries, such as tea and silk, there was substantial continuity with the past. This was reinforced by government-led, selective modernisation, urged from above and supported by the new incentives of the emerging market economy from below.

The case of cotton textiles, on the other hand, was a transitional one. For while the traditional technological trajectory had some life in it (e.g. the *garabo* spinning system), within a generation the demands of modern, large-scale production called for a decisive break with the past and the establishment of large private companies to carry the burden of technology transfers and innovation.

Finally, in the heavy and new technology industries (shipbuilding, electricals, optics etc.) the benefits of the traditional legacy were much weaker and the new institutional framework had to transfer open, tacit and contextual forms of knowledge and support companies over the long periods of learning during which new technologies, left solely to market forces, would have failed.

The strategic and military requirements of Japan were an important factor in this last sector. From the outset, however, economic and commercial considerations also had a large role to play, and the vital early leadership of the state was soon reinforced by the technological vision of the private sector and of the outstanding Japanese engineer-businessmen who provided its leadership.

The unfolding progress of technological transfer and learning was the basis of long-term achievements in productivity and innovation and hence eventually of Japanese success in foreign markets. Moreover, these were integrated with growing abilities in marketing, transport, finance and other service activities and reinforced by them. Thus even in the 1930s, when industrial progress was so impressive, the rate of company formation was actually higher in the service than in the manufacturing sector. Particularly important was the pioneering success of the Japanese in researching the needs of consumers in very poor countries and then in developing the most suitable quality, cost and technology choices to satisfy these demands.

Development and export expansion were also supported by the willingness of Japanese companies to exchange information and cooperate in the furtherance of their joint interests. In addition, their capacity to work with government on long-term strategies and the coordination of everything from education and language learning to finance, marketing and transportation proved advantageous. The combined effect of consistent strategic thinking and of a 'package' of competitiveness was remarked upon by the French in Africa, the British in India and China, the Dutch in South-East Asia and the Americans in Manchuria and the Philippines. As the economy matured in the 1920s, simple trade gave way to Japanese-led regionalisation of trade and production exemplified in a China trade and investment boom that prefigured similar 'China booms' in the 1970s and 1990s.

One final factor in this long-term configuration of progress and competition was language. The Japanese recognised as early as the seventeenth century that foreign language learning was a key to the control of trade and to intellectual development generally. However, there is little evidence of foreigners being willing to invest in a comparable learning of Japanese. This had two effects. First and most obvious was the competitive asymmetry that arose as the Japanese progressively mastered foreign markets, while foreigners found their penetration of Japan impeded by the language barrier. Secondly, while the Japanese could benefit from the growth of every form of public knowledge in the West, foreigners were largely excluded from Japanese knowledge, whether circulating in the public domain or through the consciously developed corporate networks of the private sector. Thus, insofar as knowledge and its diffusion is the engine of economic growth, the Japanese created a vital advantage for themselves, which they largely retain to this day.

The problem of geographical balance was central to the development of Japanese foreign trade. Japan's dilemma during the inter-war years was that its resource endowment and relatively low technological level made it dependent for imports on Western and especially American trade, while its export competitiveness was greatest in the markets of developing low-income economies, mainly in Asia. Access to these latter markets was impeded by well-established colonial structures and in the 1930s by the erosion of the world system of multilateral trade caused by the depression. Thus the achievement of a satisfactory regional balance of economic activity through free flows of trade and investment was impossible.

These urgent issues were intensified for Japan by persistent trade deficits and a perceived problem of population growth. But efforts to achieve a regionally balanced economic system within Asia by political and military dominance ultimately acquired a momentum that was totally destructive of Japan's own interests. This engulfing tragedy derived partly from the incomplete character of the Meiji revolution and its consequences, and partly from the structural economic factors outlined above. Even today, when circumstances are so different, the working out of Japan's regional economic relationships remains a long way short of a satisfactory resolution.

Although the thesis of this book is that an understanding of the present world economy calls for a more detailed knowledge of the Japanese past, it is not argued that the defining characteristics of Japanese economic development were all in place by the 1940s. The progress of Japan in the world economy after 1945 involves issues hardly touched upon here. They still need far more research.

SELECT BIBLIOGRAPHY

WESTERN LANGUAGE MATERIALS (BOOKS)

Abe, Etsuo, and Suzuki Yoshitaka (eds), *Changing Patterns of International Rivalry: Some Lessons from the Steel Industry*, University of Tokyo Press, 1991.

Albert, Bill, and Adrian Graves (eds), *The World Sugar Economy in War and Depression, 1914–1940*, London: Routledge, 1988.

Alcock, Sir Rutherford, *The Capital of the Tycoon: A Narrative of Three Years' Residence in Japan* (2 vols), London: Longmans, Green, 1863.

Aldcroft, Derek H., *From Versailles to Wall Street, 1919–1929*, London: Penguin Books, 1987.

Allen, G. C., and Audrey Donnithorne, *Western Enterprise in Far Eastern Economic Development: China and Japan*, London: Geo. Allen and Unwin, 1954.

American-Japanese Trade and Treaty Abrogation Special Report, San Francisco: Japanese Chamber of Commerce, 1939.

Anesaki, Masaharu, *History of Japanese Religion, with Special Reference to the Social and Moral Life of the Nation*, London: Kegan Paul, 1930.

Armytage, W. H. G., *A Social History of Engineering*, London: Faber and Faber, 1961.

Avril, Philip, *Voyages en divers États d'Europe et d'Asie. Entreprise pour découvrir un nouveau chemin à la Chine*, Paris: Claude Barbin, 1692.

Bagchi, A. K., *Private Investment in India, 1900–1939*, Cambridge University Press, 1972.

Bain, H. Foster, *Ores and Industry in the Far East*, New York: Council on Foreign Relations, 1933.

Baird, John R., *The History of the Japanese Camera*, Yakima, Washington: Historical Camera Publications, 1990.

Bancroft, Hubert Howe, *The New Pacific*, New York: Bancroft, 1900.

Bank, John, *The Essence of Total Quality Management*, Englewood Cliffs, NJ: Prentice-Hall, 1992.

Barclay, George, *Colonial Development and Population in Taiwan*, Princeton University Press, 1954.

Barker, Randolph, and Robert W. Herdt, *The Rice Economy of Asia*, Washington, DC: Resources for the Future, 1985.

Barnett, Correlli, *Engage the Enemy More Closely: The Royal Navy in the Second World War*, London: Hodder and Stoughton, 1991.

Barreto, Mascarenhas, *The Portuguese Columbus. Secret Agent of John II*, London: Macmillan, 1992.

Bartholomew, J. G., *A Literary and Historical Atlas of Asia*, London: J. M. Dent (n.d.).

Bassett-Lowke, W. J., and George Holland, *Ships and Men*, London: George G. Harrap, 1946.

Beasley, W. G., *Select Documents on Japanese Foreign Policy, 1853–1868*, Oxford University Press, 1955.

——, *A Modern History of Japan*, London: Weidenfeld and Nicolson, 1963.

——, *The Meiji Restoration*, Stanford University Press, 1973.

——, *Japanese Imperialism, 1894–1945*, Oxford University Press, 1987.

Beazley, C. R., *Prince Henry the Navigator*, New York: G. P. Putnam, 1903.

Becker, William H., and Samuel F. Wells, Jr., *Economics and World Power: An Assessment of American Diplomacy since 1789*, New York: Columbia University Press, 1984.

Bellah, Robert N., *Tokugawa Religion*, Glencoe, IL: Free Press, 1957.

Bernard, Henri, *Matteo Ricci's Scientific Contribution to China*, Peking: Henri Vetch, 1935.

——, (ed.), *Lettres et Mémoires d'Adam Schall, SJ. Relation Historique*, Tientsin: Hautes Études, 1942.

Bernard, W. D. (ed.), *Narrative of the Voyages and Services of the Nemesis from 1840 to 1843, and of the Combined Naval and Military Operations in China*, (2 vols), London: Henry Colburn, 1844.

Bernstein, Michael A., *The Great Depression: Delayed Recovery and Economic Change in America, 1929–1939*, Cambridge University Press, 1988.

Bisson, T. A., *American Policy in the Far East, 1931–1940*, New York: Institute of Pacific Relations, 1940.

Black, John R., *Young Japan, Yokohama and Yedo: A narrative of the settlement and the city from the signing of the treaties in 1856 to the close of the year 1879* (2 vols), Yokohama: Kelly and Walsh, 1880, 1881.

Blakeney, William, *On the Coasts of Cathay and Cipango Forty Years Ago*, London: Elliot Stock, 1902.

Borg, Dorothy, and Shumpei Okamoto (eds), *Pearl Harbor as History: Japanese-American Relations, 1931–1941*, New York: Columbia University Press, 1973.

Boxer, C. R., *A Portuguese Embassy to Japan, 1644–1647*, London: Kegan Paul, 1928.

——, *Jan Compagnie in Japan, 1600–1817*, The Hague: Martinus Nijhoff, 1936.

——, *The Great Ship from Amacon: Annals of Macao and the Old Japan Trade 1555–1640*, Lisbon: Centro de Estudios Historicos Ultramarinos, 1959.

——, *Fidalgos of the Far East, 1550–1770* (2nd edn), Oxford University Press, 1968.

——, *The Portuguese Seaborne Empire, 1415–1825*, London: Hutchinson, 1969, repr. Manchester: Carcanet Press, 1991.

——, *The Christian Century in Japan, 1549–1650*, Berkeley: University of California Press, 1974.

——, *The Dutch Seaborne Empire*, London: Penguin Books, 1990.

Braudel, Fernand, *Capitalism and Material Life, 1400–1800*, New York: Harper and Row, 1967.

——, *The Mediterranean and the Mediterranean World in the Age of Philip II* (2 vols), London: Collins, 1972.

——, *Civilisation and Capitalism 15th–18th Century*, vol. 1: *The Structures of Everyday Life*; vol. 3: *The Perspective of the World*, London: Collins, 1984.

——, *L'identité de la France, les hommes et les choses*, Paris: Arthaud-Flammarion, 1986.

Briggs, Asa, *Victorian People*, London: Penguin Books, 1967.

——, *The Age of Improvement*, London: Longman, 1975.

——, *Victorian Things*, London: Batsford, 1988.

British Parliamentary Papers, Japan (10 vols), Shannon: Irish University Press, 1971.

Brooke, Lord, *An Eyewitness in Manchuria*, London: Eveleigh Nash, 1905.

Brunton, Richard Henry, *Building Japan, 1868–1876*, Folkestone: Japan Library, 1991.

Bueschal, Richard M., *Mitsubishi Nakajima G3M 1/2/3 in Japanese Naval Service*, London: Osprey, 1972.

Burstall, Aubrey F., *A History of Mechanical Engineering*, London: Faber and Faber, 1963.

Byram, Leo, *Petit Jap Deviendra Grand! L'Expansion japonaise en Extrême-Orient*, Paris: Berger-Levrault, 1908.

Campbell, William, *Formosa under the Dutch, described from Contemporary Records*, London: Kegan Paul, 1903 (repr. Taiwan, 1987).

Carr-Saunders, A. M., *World Population: Past Growth and Present Trends*, Oxford University Press, 1936.

Carter, George R., *The Tendency towards Industrial Concentration*, London: Constable, 1913.

Chao, Kang, *The Development of Cotton Textile Production in China*, Cambridge, MA: Harvard University Press, 1977.

——, *The Economic Development of Manchuria: The Rise of a Frontier Economy*, Ann Arbor: Michigan Papers in Chinese History, no. 43, 1983.

Chapman, S. J., *The Lancashire Cotton Industry*, Manchester University Press, 1904.

Chatterji, Basudev, *Trade, Tariffs and Empire. Lancashire and British Policy in India, 1919–1939*, New Delhi: Oxford University Press, 1992.

Chaudhuri, K. N., *Trade and Civilisation in the Indian Ocean: An Economic History from the Rise of Islam to 1750*, Cambridge University Press, 1985.

Chère, Lewis M., *The Diplomacy of the Sino-French War (1883–1885): Global Implications of an Undeclared War*, Bloomington, IN.: Cross Road Books, 1988.

Chesters, J. H., *Iron and Steel*, London: Nelson, 1951.

Chiang, Monlin, *Tides from the West: A Chinese Autobiography*, New Haven: Yale University Press, 1947.

China Illustrated (2 vols), London: Fisher and Son (n.d.).

China Imperial Maritime Customs, *The Soya Bean of Manchuria*, Shanghai, 1911.

Christie, Dugald, *Thirty Years in Moukden, 1883–1913*, London: Constable, 1914.

Cipolla, Carlo M. (ed.), *The Fontana Economic History of Europe*, vol. 1: *The Middle Ages*; vol. 3: *The Industrial Revolution*, London: Collins, 1972/3.

——, *Before the Industrial Revolution: European Society and Economy, 1000–1700*, 2nd edn, London: Methuen, 1980.

Clark, M. Gardner, *The Development of China's Steel Industry and Soviet Technical Aid*, Ithaca, NY: School of Industrial and Labor Relations, 1957.

Coaldrake, William H., *The Way of the Carpenter: Tools and Japanese Architecture*, New York: Weatherhill, 1990.

Cochran, Thomas C., and William Miller, *The Age of Enterprise: A Social History of Industrial America*, New York: Harper, 1961.

Cooper, Michael (trans. and ed.), *This Island of Japan: João Rodrigues's account of 16th Century Japan*, Tokyo: Kodansha, 1973.

Cooper, Michael, *Rodrigues the Interpreter: An Early Jesuit in Japan and China*, New York: Weatherhill, 1974.

'[A] Copy of the Japan Diary Received per a Danish Ship, July 18, 1674', Appendix to Kaempfer, *The History of Japan*.

Cordier, Henri, *Histoire Générale de la Chine, et de ses Relations avec les Pays Étrangères* (4 vols), Paris: Paul Geuthner, 1920.

Cornelius, Wanda, and Thayne Short, *Ding Hao. The American Air War in China, 1937–1945*, Gretna, LA: Pelican, 1980.

Cosenza, M. E. (ed.), *The Complete Journal of Townshend Harris*, New York: Doubleday, 1959.

Craig, Albert M., *Choshu in the Meiji Restoration*, Cambridge, MA: Harvard University Press, 1961.

Crocker, W. R., *The Japanese Population Problem*, London: Geo. Allen and Unwin, 1931.

Crouzet, François, *The Victorian Economy*, London: Methuen, 1982.

Curzon, George N., *The Problems of the Far East: Japan, Korea, China*, London: Longmans, Green, 1894.

Dames, Mansel Longworth (ed.), *The Book of Duarte Barbosa*, vol. 1, London: Hakluyt Society, 1918.

D'Elia, M. Pasquale, *Fonti Ricciane. Storia dell'Introduzione del Cristianesimo in Cina, scritta da Matteo Ricci* (3 vols), Rome: Libreria dello Stato, 1942–49.

D'Herbelot, *Bibliothèque Orientale ou Dictionnaire Universel*, Maastricht: Dufour et Roux, 1776.

Davidson, James W., *The Island of Formosa Past and Present*, New York: Macmillan, 1903.

De Beauvoir, Le Comte, *Pékin, Yeddo, San Francisco. Voyage autour du Monde*, vol. 3, Paris: Plon, 1872.

de Backer, A., A. Carayon and C. Sommervogel, *Bibliothèque de la Compagnie de Jésus* (9 vols) Brussels, 1890–1900.

de Barros, João, and Diego de Couto, *Da Asia, Dos Feitos, que os Portuguezes fizeram no descubrimento, e conquista dos mares, e terras do Oriente* (24 vols), Lisbon: Na Regia Officina Typografia, 1778–88.

Dedet, Christian, *Les fleurs d'acier du Mikado*, Paris: Flammarion, 1993.

Dennys, N. B. (edited by Frederick L. Mayers), *The Treaty Ports of China and Japan Guide Book and Vade Mecum*, Hong Kong, 1860 (repr. San Francisco, 1977).

Department of Agriculture and Commerce (Japan), *Japan in the Beginning of the Twentieth Century*, London: John Murray, 1904.

Department of Overseas Trade, *Economic Conditions in Japan*, London: HMSO, 1930–32.

Dermigny, Louis, *La Chine et L'Occident. Le Commerce à Canton au XVIIIème Siècle, 1719–1833* (4 vols), Paris: SEVPEN, 1964.

Dore, R. P., *Education in Tokugawa Japan*, London: Routledge and Kegan Paul, 1965.

Dore, Ronald, and Radha Sinha (eds), *Japan and World Depression Then and Now: Essays in Memory of E. F. Penrose*, London: Macmillan, 1987.

Dosi, Giovanni, *et al.* (eds), *Technical Change and Economic Theory*, London: Pinter, 1988.

Dosi, Giovanni, Keith Pavitt, Luc Soete, *The Economics of Technical Change and International Trade*, New York: Harvester, 1990.

Dugan, James, *The Great Iron Ship*, London: Hamish Hamilton, 1954.

Duus, Peter, Ramon H. Myers and Mark Peattie (eds), *The Japanese Informal Colonial Empire, 1895–1937*, Princeton University Press, 1989.

Dyos, H. J., and D. H. Aldcroft, *British Transport. An Economic Survey from the Seventeenth Century to the Twentieth*, London: Penguin Books, 1974.

East Asia Economic Investigation Bureau, *The Manchoukuo Year Book, 1934*, Tokyo, 1934.

Eichengreen, Barry (ed.), *The Gold Standard in Theory and History*, New York: Methuen, 1985.

Emi, Koichi, *Government Fiscal Activity and Economic Growth in Japan, 1868–1960*, Tokyo: Kinokuniya, 1963.

Encyclopaedia Britannica, 11th (1910), 12th (1922) and 13th (1930) edns, New York. 14th edn (1951), Chicago.

'[An] Enquiry, whether it be conducive for the good of the Japanese Empire, to keep it shut, as it now is, and not to suffer its inhabitants to have any Commerce with foreign nations, either at home or abroad', Appendix to Kaempfer, *The History of Japan*.

Fairbairn, William, *Iron Shipbuilding*, London: Longmans, Green, 1865.

——, *Iron: Its History, Properties and Processes of Manufacture*, Edinburgh: Adam and Charles Black, 1869.

Fairbank, John K. (ed.), *The Chinese World Order: Traditional China's Foreign Relations*, Cambridge, MA: Harvard University Press, 1968.

——, *Trade and Diplomacy on the China Coast: The Opening of the Treaty Ports, 1842–1854*, Cambridge, MA: Harvard University Press, 1953.

Famous Airplanes of the World: Army Experimental Fighters (title in English, text in Japanese), Tokyo: Burin-Do, 1990.

Farnie, D. A., *The English Cotton Industry and the World Market, 1815–1896*, Oxford: Clarendon Press, 1979.

Febvre, Lucien, and Henri-Jean Martin, *The Coming of the Book: The Impact of Printing, 1450–1800*, London: Verso, 1984.

Figuier, Louis, *Les Grandes Inventions Modernes dans les Sciences, L'Industrie and les Arts*, Paris: Hachette, 1910.

Foreman-Peck, James, *A History of the World Economy: International Economic Relations since 1850*, Brighton: Wheatsheaf Books, 1983.

Fortune, Robert, *A Residence Among the Chinese*, London: John Murray, 1857.

——, *Yedo and Peking: A Narrative of a Journey to the Capitals of Japan and China*, London: John Murray, 1863.

Fox, Grace, *Britain and Japan, 1858–1883*, Oxford University Press, 1969.

Francillon, René J., *Japanese Aircraft of the Pacific War*, London: Putnam, 1979.

Freeman, Christopher (ed.), *Design, Innovation and Long Cycles in Economic Development*, London: Design Research Publications, 1984.

Frost, Peter, *The Bakumatsu Currency Crisis*, Cambridge, MA: Harvard East Asian Monographs, 1970.

Fuchida, Mitsuo and Okumiya Masatake, *Midway*, Annapolis, MD: Naval Institute Press, 1955.

Fujihara, Ginjiro, *The Spirit of Japanese Industry*, Tokyo: Hokuseido Press, 1940.

Geyl, Pieter, *The Netherlands in the 17th Century, part 2: 1649–1715*, London: Ernest Benn, 1964.

Glaman, Kristoff, *Dutch–Asiatic Trade, 1620–1740*, The Hague: Martinus Nijhoff, 1981.

Gluck, Carol, *Japan's Modern Myths: Ideology in the Late Meiji Period*, Princeton University Press, 1985.

Golden Jubilee History of the Nippon Yusen Kaisha, 1885–1935, Tokyo: Nippon Yusen Kaisha, 1935.

Goodman, Grant K., *Japan: The Dutch Experience*, London: Athlone Press, 1986.

Grande Encyclopédie, La, Paris: Société Anonyme de la Grande Encylopédie (n.d.)

Gray, Albert (ed.), *The Voyage of François Pyrard of Laval to the East Indies, the Maldives, the Moluccas and Brazil* (2 vols), London: The Hakluyt Society, 1887–88.

Green, William, *Famous Fighters of the Second World War*, London: Macdonald, 1960.

Greener, W. W., *The Gun and its Development* (9th edn), London: Cassell, 1910.

Guth, Christine M. E., *Art, Tea, and Industry: Masuda Takashi and the Mitsui Circle*, Princeton University Press, 1993.

Gutzlaff, Charles, *China Opened* (2 vols), London: Smith, Elder, 1838.

Hall, G. R., and R. E. Johnson, *Transfers of United States Aerospace Technology to Japan*, Santa Monica: Rand Corporation, 1968.

Hanley, Susan B., and Kozo Yamamura, *Economic and Demographic Change in Pre-Industrial Japan, 1600–1818*, Princeton University Press, 1977.

Hao, Yen-p'ing, *The Commercial Revolution in Nineteenth-Century China: The Rise of Sino-Western Capitalism*, Berkeley: University of California Press, 1986.

Harootunian, H. D., *Toward Restoration: The Growth of Political Consciousness in Tokugawa Japan*, Berkeley: University of California Press, 1970.

Hashimoto, Lieut.-Cmdr. M., *Sunk! The Story of the Japanese Submarine Fleet, 1942–1945*, London: Cassell, 1954.

Hayami, Y., *A Century of Agricultural Growth in Japan: Its Relevance to Asian Development*, University of Tokyo Press, 1975.

Hazard, Paul, *The European Mind, 1680–1715*, Harmondsworth: Penguin Books, 1964.

Hishida, Seiji G., *The International Position of Japan as a Great Power*, New York: Columbia University Press, 1905.

Ho, Samuel P., *Economic Development of Taiwan, 1860–1970*, New Haven: Yale University Press, 1978.

Hoshino, T., *Economic History of Manchuria*, Seoul: Bank of Chosen, 1921.

Hosie, Alexander, *Manchuria: its Peoples, Resources and Recent History*, London: Methuen, 1904.

Hosono, Masanobu, *Nagasaki Prints and Early Copperplates*, Tokyo: Kodansha, 1978.

Howe, Christopher, *Wage Patterns and Wage Policies in Modern China, 1919–1972*, Cambridge University Press, 1973.

—— (ed.), *Shanghai: Revolution and Development in an Asian Metropolis*, Cambridge University Press, 1981.

Huang, Ray, *China. A Macro History*: Armonk, NY: M. E. Sharpe, 1990.

Hubbard, G. E., *Eastern Industrialization and its Effects on the West, with Special Reference to Great Britain and Japan*, Oxford University Press, 1935.

Huret, Jules, *En Allemagne. Rhin et Westphalie*, Paris: Bibliothèque Charpentier, 1907.

Illustrated Exhibitor, The, nos 1–30, June–Dec., 1851.

Indo-Japanese Association, *A Glimpse of Japan's Business and her Trade with India*, Tokyo, 1939.

———, *The Indo-Japanese Business Directory, 1939–40*, Tokyo, 1939.

Inouye, Junnosuke, *Problems of the Japanese Exchange, 1914–1926*, Glasgow: Robert Maclehose, 1931.

International Commercial Rivalry in Southeast Asia in the Inter-War Period, papers from a conference held at Shimoda, Japan, 1988.

International Labour Office, *The World Textile Industry Economic and Social Problems*, London: P. S. King, 1937.

Iriye, Akira (ed.), *The Chinese and the Japanese: Essays in Political and Cultural Interactions*, Princeton University Press, 1980.

Ishii, Kanji, *International Factors in the Formation of Banking Systems: Japan, 1810–1914* (mimeo).

Ishii, Ryoichi, *Population Pressure and Economic Life in Japan*, London: P. S. King, 1937.

Ishii, Ryosuke, *Japanese Legislation in the Meiji Era*, Tokyo: Pan-Pacific Press, 1958.

Ishikawa, Shigeru, *Economic Development in Asian Perspective*, Tokyo: Kinokuniya, 1967.

Israel, Jonathan I., *Dutch Primacy in World Trade, 1585–1740*, Oxford University Press, 1989.

Ito, M., *The End of the Imperial Japanese Navy*, London: Weidenfeld and Nicolson, 1956.

James, Derek N., *Gloster Aircraft since 1917*, London, Putnam, 1987.

Jansen, Marius B., and Gilbert Rozman (eds), *Japan in Transition: From Tokugawa to Meiji*, Princeton University Press, 1986.

Jansen, Marius B. (ed.), *The Cambridge History of Japan*, vol. 5: *The Nineteenth Century*, Cambridge University Press, 1989.

Jansen, Marius B., *China in the Tokugawa World*, Cambridge, MA: Harvard University Press, 1992.

Jayne, K. G., *Vasco de Gama and his Successors* (repr.), London: Methuen, 1970.

Jenkins, E. H., *Histoire de la Marine Française des Origines à Nos Jours*, Paris: Albin Michel, 1977.

Jentschura, H., D. Jung and P. Mickel, *Warships of the Imperial Japanese Navy, 1869–1945*, London: Arms and Armour Press, 1977.

Jenyns, Soame, *Ming Pottery and Porcelain*, London: Faber and Faber, 1953.

Johnson, Chalmers, *MITI and the Japanese Miracle: The Growth of Industrial Policy, 1925–1975*, Stanford University Press, 1982.

Johnson, Paul, *The Birth of the Modern: World Society 1815–1830*, Weidenfeld and Nicolson, 1991.

Johnston, Bruce F., *Japanese Food Management in World War II*, Stanford, CA: Food Research Institute, 1953.

Jones, E. L., *The European Miracle: Environments, economies and geopolitics in the history of Europe and Asia* (2nd edn), Cambridge University Press, 1990.

Jones, Robert, *The Battleship Dreadnought*, London: Conway Maritime, 1992.

Kaempfer, Engelbertus, *The History of Japan* (trans. J. G. Scheuchzer, 2 vols), London, 1727–28.

Keene, Donald, *The Japanese Discovery of Europe, 1720–1830*, Stanford University Press, 1969.

Kent, P. H. B., *Railway Enterprise in China: An Account of its Origin and Development*, London: Edward Arnold, 1907.

Keynes, J. M., *The End of Laissez Faire*, London: Hogarth Press, 1926.

Kindleberger, Charles P., *The World in Depression, 1929–1939*, The Pelican History of the World Economy in the Twentieth Century, London: Penguin Books, 1987.

King, Frank H. H., *The History of the Hong Kong Banking Corporation: The Hong Kong Bank in the Period of Imperialism and War, 1895–1918*, Cambridge University Press, 1988.

King, J. W., *The Warships of Europe: A Description of the Construction, Armour, and Fighting Power of the Ironclads of England and other European Powers of the Present Day*, Portsmouth (England): Griffen, 1878.

Kinney, Henry W., *Modern Manchuria and the South Manchuria Railway*, Dairen, 1928.

Kircher, Athanasius, *China Monumentis qua Sacris qua Profanis, nec non variis Naturae & Artis Spectaculis*, Amsterdam: Waesberge en Weyerstraat, 1667.

Kiyooka, Eiichi (ed.), *The Autobiography of Fukuzawa Yukichi*, Tokyo: Hokuseido Press, 1948.

Klado, Captain Nicolas, *The Battle of the Sea of Japan*, London: Hodder and Stoughton, 1906.

Kobayashi, U., *Military industries of Japan*, Oxford University Press, 1922.

Koizumi, Kazuko, *Traditional Japanese Furniture*, Tokyo: Kodansha, 1986.

Kulkarni, V. B., *History of the Indian Textile Industry*, Bombay: Bombay Millowners' Association, 1979.

Kuznets, Simon, *Modern Economic Growth. Rate, Structure and Spread*, New Haven: Yale University Press, 1967.

Lach, Donald F., *Asia in the Making of Europe* (3 vols in 9 books), University of Chicago Press, 1965–93.

Ladurie, E. LeRoy, *Histoire du Languedoc*, Paris: Presses Universitaires de France, 1974.

Landes, David S., *The Unbound Prometheus: Technological Change and Industrial*

Development in Western Europe from 1750 to the present, Cambridge University Press, 1969.

Latourette, K. S., *The History of Early Relations between the United States and China, 1784–1844*, Transactions of the Connecticut Academy of Arts and Sciences, vol. 22, New Haven: Yale University Press, 1917.

Lau, D. C., *Confucius the Analects (Lun yü)*, Hong Kong: Chinese University Press, 1983.

Lawton, Lancelot, *Empires of the Far East* (2 vols), London: Grant Richards, 1912.

Le Japon à l'Exposition Universelle de 1878, Paris: Commission Impériale du Japon, 1878.

League of Nations, *Appeal by the Chinese Government and Supplementary Documents to the Report of the Commission of Enquiry* (2 vols), Geneva: League of Nations, 1932.

Lee, O-Young, *The Compact Culture: The Japanese Tradition of 'Smaller is Better'*, Tokyo: Kodansha, 1991.

Linnemann, Hans (ed.), *Export-Oriented Industrialization in Developing Countries*, Singapore University Press, 1987.

Linschoten, John Huighen van, *His Discours of Voyages into ye East and West Indies*, London: John Wolfe, 1598.

Ljungstedt, Anders, *An Historical Sketch of the Portuguese Settlements in China and of the Roman Catholic Church and Mission*, Boston: Munroe, 1836 (repr. Hong Kong, 1992).

Lockwood, William W., *Trade and Trade Rivalry between the United States and Japan*, New York: American Council of Pacific Relations, 1936.

—— (ed.), *The State and Economic Enterprise in Japan*, Princeton University Press, 1965.

Machlup, Fritz, *The Production and Distribution of Knowledge in the United States*, Princeton University Press, 1962.

Martelli-Chautard, M., *L'Expansion Japonaise en Afrique*, Paris: Comité de l'Afrique Française, 1934.

MacMurray, John V. A., *Treaties and Agreements with and concerning China, 1894–1919* (2 vols), New York: Oxford University Press, 1921.

MacNair, H. F., *Modern Chinese History Selected Readings*, Shanghai: Commercial Press, 1923.

Maddison, Angus, *Phases of Capitalist Development*, Oxford University Press, 1986.

Maffei, R. P. Giovan Pietro, *Le Historie delle Indie Orientali tradotte di Latino in Lingua Toscana da M. Francesco Serdonati Fiorentino, con una scelte di lettere scritte delle Indie*, Venice: Damian Zenaro, 1589.

Maine, Henry Sumner, *Ancient Law: Its Connections with the Early History of Society, and its Relation to Modern Ideas*, London: John Murray, 1861.

Major, R. H., *The Life of Prince Henry of Portugal surnamed the Navigator and its results*, London: A. Asher, 1868.

Manchoukuo Yearbook Co., *The Manchoukuo Yearbook, 1942*, Hsinking, 1942.

Marder, Arthur J., *From the Dreadnought to Scapa Flow. The Road to War, 1904–1914*, Oxford University Press, 1961.

Maritiem Museum 'Prins Hendrick', *350 jaar Nederland-Japan*, Rotterdam, 1959.

Marriner, Sheila, and Francis E. Hyde, *The Senior John Samuel Swire. Management in Far Eastern Shipping Trades*, Liverpool University Press, 1967.

Marshall, Alfred, *Industry and Trade. A study of industrial technique and business organization: and of their influences on the conditions of various classes and nations*, London: Macmillan, 1919.

——, *Money, Credit and Commerce*, London: Macmillan, 1923.

——, *Principles of Economics*, vol. 1, London: Macmillan (2nd edn 1891 and 8th edn 1936).

Martini, M., and J. Blaeu, *Novus Atlas Sinensis*, Amsterdam: Blaeu, 1655.

Maruyama, Masao, *Thought and Behaviour in Modern Japanese Politics*, Oxford University Press, 1963.

——, *Studies in the Intellectual History of Tokugawa Japan*, University of Tokyo Press, 1974.

Massie, Robert K., *Dreadnought. Britain, Germany and the Coming of the Great War*, London: Jonathan Cape, 1992.

Mathieu, Caroline, *Guide to the Musée d'Orsay*, Paris: Editions de la Réunion des Musées Nationaux, 1987.

Matsukata, Masayoshi, *Report on the Adoption of the Gold Standard in Japan*, Tokyo: Government Press, 1899.

——, *Report on the Post Bellum Financial Administration in Japan, 1896–1900*, Tokyo: 1901.

McClain, James L., *Kanazawa. A Seventeenth Century Japanese Castle Town*, New Haven: Yale University Press, 1982.

McClaren, W. W., *Japanese Government Documents*, Transactions of the Asiatic Society of Japan, Yokohama: Kelly and Walsh, 1914.

Mémoires concernant l'histoire, les sciences, les moeurs & les usages des Chinois, par les missionnaires de Pékin (14 vols), Paris: Nyon l'Ainé, 1776–81.

Mendoza, Gonzalez de, *Histoire du Grand Royaume de la Chine, situé aux Indes Orientales*, Lyon: François Arnouilet, 1609.

Mikesh, Robert C., and Shorze Abe, *Japanese Aircraft, 1910–1941*, London: Putnam, 1990.

Milburn, William, *Oriental Commerce*, London: Black Parry, 1813.

Milward, Alan S., *War, Economy and Society, 1939–1945*, London: Geo. Allen and Unwin, 1977.

Minami, Ryoshin, *The Economic Development of Japan: A Quantitative Study*, London: Macmillan, 1986.

Ministry of Finance (Japan), *Financial and Economic Annual of Japan*, Tokyo, 1905.

Mitsubishi Economic Research Bureau, *Japanese Trade and Industry Present and Future*, London: Macmillan, 1936.

Mokyr, Joel (ed.), *The British Industrial Revolution: An Economic Perspective*, Boulder, CO: Westview Press, 1993.

Montanus, A., *Ambassades Mémorables de la Compagnie des Indies Orientales des Provinces Unies vers les Empereurs du Japon contenant plusieurs choses remarquables arrivées pendant le voyage des Ambassadeurs*, Amsterdam: Jacob de Meurs, 1680.

Morison, S. E., *History of United States Naval Operations in World War Two* (13 vols) Boston: Little, Brown, 1947–64.

Morley, James W. (ed.), *Dilemmas of Growth in Pre-War Japan*, Princeton University Press, 1971.

Morse, H. B., *The Trade and Administration of China*, London: Longmans, Green, 1921.

——, and H. F. MacNair, *Far Eastern International Relations*, Shanghai: Commercial Press, 1928.

Murdoch, James, *A History of Japan* (3 vols), London: Kegan Paul, 1925–26.

Myers, Ramon H., and Mark Peattie (eds), *The Japanese Colonial Empire, 1895–1945*, Princeton University Press, 1984.

Nagura, Bunji, *The Prewar Japanese Steel Industry and Iron Ore Resources in South East Asia: The Development of Malaysian Iron Ore by the Ishihara Sangyo Company*, Tokyo: United Nations University Press, 1981.

Nakajima K1-84, Fulbrook, CA: Aero Publishers, 1965.

Nakane, Chie, and Shinzaburo Oishi (eds), *Tokugawa Japan: The Social and Economic Antecedents of Modern Japan*, University of Tokyo Press, 1990.

National Bureau of Economic Research, *The Rate and Direction of Inventive Activity, Economic and Social Factors*, Princeton University Press, 1962.

[A] *Narrative of the success of an Ambassage sent by John Maatzukyer de Badem, General of Batavia, unto the Emperour of China and Tartary*, London: John Maycock for John Nieuhoff, 1669.

Nelson, Richard R., and Sidney G. Winter, *An Evolutionary Theory of Economic Change*, Cambridge, MA: Belknap Press, 1982.

[A] *New History of China, containing a Description of the Most Considerable Particulars of that Vast Empire, written by Gabriel Magaillans of the Society of Jesus, Missionary Apostolic*, London: Thomas Newborough, 1688.

Nishida, Judith Mary, 'The Japanese Influence on the Shanghaiese Textile Industry and Implications for Hong Kong', unpubl. M. Phil. thesis, University of Hong Kong, 1990.

Noma, Seiroku, *Japanese Costume and Textile Arts*, Tokyo: Heibonsha, 1974.

Norman, E. H., *Japan's Emergence as a Modern State: Political and Economic Problems of the Meiji Period*, New York: Institute of Pacific Relations, 1940.

Norman, Henry, *The Real Japan*, London: T. Fisher Unwin, 1892.

North, Douglass C., and Robert Paul Thomas (eds), *The Growth of the American Economy to 1860*, New York: Harper and Row, 1968.

Nugent, Donald R., *The Pacific Area and its Problems: A Study Guide*, New York: Institute of Pacific Relations, 1936.

Obata, Kyugoro, *An Interpretation of the Life of Viscount Shibusawa*, Tokyo: Daiyamondo Jigyo Co., 1937.

Ogura, Takekazu, *Agricultural Development in Modern Japan*, Tokyo: Fuji Publishing, 1968.

Ohara, Keishi and Tamotsu Okata (eds), *Japanese Trade and Industry in the Meiji-Taisho Era*, Tokyo: Obunsha, 1957.

Ohkawa, Kazushi and Hirohisa Kohama, *Lectures on Developing Economies*, University of Tokyo Press, 1989.

——, G. Ranis and L. Meissner (eds), *Japan and the Developing Countries: A Comparative Analysis*, Oxford: Basil Blackwell, 1985.

——, and Miyohei Shinohara (eds), *Patterns of Japanese Economic Development: A Quantitative Appraisal*, New Haven: Yale University Press, 1979.

Okuma, Count (ed.), *Fifty Years of New Japan*, London: Smith, Elder, 1909.

Orchard, John E., *Japan's Economic Position: The Progress to Industrialization*, New York: McGraw-Hill, 1930.

Papers and Proceedings of the Conference on Japan's Historical Development Experience and the Contemporary Developing Countries: Issues for Comparative Analysis, Tokyo: International Development Centre of Japan, 1978.

Parliamentary White Paper, *Kagoshima — Admiral Kuper's Official Report of the Performance of the Armstrong Guns in the Action at Kagoshima*, April 4, 1864.

Parry, J. H., *Europe and the Wider World, 1415–1715*, London: Hutchinson, 1969.

——, *The Age of Reconnaissance, Discovery, Exploration and Settlement, 1450–1650*, Berkeley: University of California Press, 1981.

——, *The Discovery of the Sea*, Berkeley: University of California Press, 1981.

Paske-Smith, M., *Western Barbarians in Japan and Formosa in Tokugawa Days, 1603–1868*, New York: Paragon, 1968.

Passin, Herbert, *Society and Education in Japan*, Tokyo: Kodansha, 1982.

Pearse, Arno S., *Japan and China: Cotton Industry Report*, Manchester: International Federation of Master Cotton Spinners and Manufacturers, 1929.

——, *The Cotton Industry of India*, Manchester: International Federation of Master Cotton Spinners and Manufacturers, 1930.

Peattie, Mark R., *Ishiwara Kanji and Japan's Confrontation with the West*, Princeton University Press, 1975.

Pegolotti, Francesco Balducci (ed. Allan Evans), *La Practica della Mercatura*, Cambridge, MA: Mediaeval Academy of America, 1936.

Penrose, Boise, *Travel and Discovery in the Renaissance, 1420-1620*, Cambridge, MA: Harvard University Press, 1952.

Penrose, E. F., *Population Theories and their Application, with Special Reference to Japan*, Stanford: Food Research Institute, 1934.

Percheron, Maurice, *L'Aviation Française*, Paris: Fernand Nathan, 1948.

Pickering, W. A., *Pioneering in Formosa: Recollections of Adventures among Mandarins, Wreckers, and Head Hunting Savages*, London: Hurst and Blackett, 1898.

Polanyi, Karl, *The Great Transformation: The Political and Economic Origins of Our Time*, Boston: Beacon Press, 1957.

Polanyi, Michael, *The Tacit Dimension*, London: Routledge and Kegan Paul, 1967.

Pole, William (ed.), *The Life of Sir William Fairbairn partly written by himself*, 1877 (repr. Newton Abbot: David and Charles, 1970).

Pollard, Sidney and Paul Robertson, *The British Shipbuilding Industry, 1870–1914*, Cambridge, MA: Harvard University Press, 1979.

Potter, John Deane, *Yamamoto*, New York: Paperback Library, 1971.

Pratt, E. A., *The Rise of Rail Power in War and Conquest, 1833–1914*, Westminster: P. S. King, 1915.

Prestage, Edgar, *The Portuguese Pioneers*, London: A. & C. Black, 1966.

Putnam Weale, B. L., *Manchu and Muscovite*, New York: Macmillan, 1904.

——, *The Truth about China and Japan*, New York: Dodd, Mead, 1919.

Redesdale, Lord, *Memories* (2 vols), London: Hutchinson (n.d.).

Rein, J. J., *The Industries of Japan*, London: Hodder and Stoughton, 1894.

Reischauer, Haru Matsukata, *Samurai and Silk: A Japanese and American Heritage*, Cambridge, MA: Belknap Press, 1986.

Report of the Committee on Finance and Industry (The Macmillan Report), London: HMSO, 1930 (repr. 1961).

Report on Trade and Industry, part 3: *The Textile Industry*, London: HMSO, 1928.

Requien, Marcel, *Le Problème de la Population au Japon*, Paris: Paul Geuthner, 1934.

Richardson, Alex, *Vickers and Sons and Maxim Ltd: Their Works and Manufactures*, London: Engineering, 1902.

Richesse de la Hollande, La, [Elie Luzac] (2 vols), London, 1788.

Robson, R., *The Cotton Industry in Britain*, London: Macmillan, 1957.

Rolt, L. T. C., *Victorian Engineering*, London: Penguin Books, 1970.

Rotolin, Robert, *The Nikon Rangefinder Camera*, Brighton: Hove Foto Books, 1983.

Routledge, Robert, *Discoveries and Inventions of the 19th Century*, repr. London: Bracken Books, 1989.

Rozman, Gilbert, *Urban Networks in China and Tokugawa Japan*, Princeton University Press, 1973.

Said, Edward W., *Culture and Imperialism*, London: Chatto and Windus, 1993.

Sakai, Naoki, *Voices of the Past: The Status of Language in Eighteenth-Century Japanese Discourse*, Ithaca, NY: Cornell University Press, 1992.

Salter, Arthur *et al.*, *The World's Economic Crisis and the Way of Escape*, London: Geo. Allen & Unwin, 1932.

Sandberg, Lars, *Lancashire in Decline: A Study in Entrepreneurship, Technology, and International Trade*, Columbus: Ohio State University Press, 1974.

Santoni, Alberto, *La Battaglia di Tsushima*, Rome: Edizioni dell'Ateneo, 1985.

Satow, Sir Ernest M., *The Voyage of Captain John Saris to Japan, 1613*, London: The Hakluyt Society, 1900.

Schafer, Edward H., *The Golden Peaches of Samarkand*, Berkeley: University of California Press, 1963.

Schama, Simon, *The Embarrassment of Riches: An Interpretation of Dutch Culture in the Golden Age*, London: Collins, 1987.

——, *Patriots and Liberators: Revolution in the Netherlands, 1780–1813*, London: Fontana Press, 1992.

Schumpeter, E. B. (ed.), *The Industrialization of Japan and Manchukuo, 1930–1940: Population, Raw Materials and Industry*, New York: Macmillan, 1940.

Schurhammer, Georg, *Francis Xavier: His Life, His Times* (4 vols), Rome: Jesuit Historical Institute, 1977.

Scott, J. D., *Vickers: A History*, London: Weidenfeld and Nicolson, 1962.

Seki, Keizo, *The Cotton Industry of Japan*, Tokyo: Japan Society for the Promotion of Science, 1956.

Sekigawa, Eiichiro, *Pictorial History of Japanese Military Aviation*, London: Ian Allen, 1974.

Seppings Wright, H. C., *With Togo: The Story of Seven Months Active Service under his Command*, London: Hurst and Blackett, 1905.

Shand, R. T. (ed.), *Technical Change in Asian Agriculture*, Canberra: Australian National University Press, 1973.

Shibusawa, Keizo (ed.), *Japanese Society in the Meiji Era*, Tokyo: Obunsha, 1958.

Shimizu, Hiroshi, *Anglo-Japanese Rivalry in the Middle East in the Inter-war Period*, London: Ithaca Press, 1986.

Shindo, T., *Labour in the Japanese Cotton Industry*, Tokyo: Japan Society for the Promotion of Science, 1961.

Shinjo, Hiroshi, *History of the Yen*, Tokyo: Kinokuniya, 1962.

Shinohara, Miyohei, *Growth and Cycles in the Japanese Economy*, Tokyo: Kinokuniya, 1962.

Sims, Richard, 'French Policy towards Japan, 1854–1894', unpubl. Ph.D. thesis, University of London, 1968.

Singer, Charles, E. J. Holmyard, A. R. Hall and Trevor I. Williams, *A History of Technology*, vol. 4, *The Industrial Revolution, c. 1750–c. 1850*; vol. 5, *The Late Nineteenth Century*, Oxford University Press, 1958.

Skulski, Janusz, *The Battleship Yamato*, London: Conway Maritime Press, 1988.

Smiles, Samuel, *Industrial Biography: Iron Workers and Tool Makers*, London: John Murray, 1876.

—— (ed.), *James Nasmyth Engineer: An Autobiography*, London: John Murray, 1883.

Smith, Adam, *Wealth of Nations* (ed. James E. Thorold Rogers), Oxford University Press, 1869.

Smith, E. C., *A Short History of Marine Engineering*, Cambridge: Babcock and Wilcox/Cambridge University Press, 1937.

Smith, Thomas. C., *The Agrarian Origins of Modern Japan*, Stanford University Press, 1959.

——, *Native Sources of Japanese Industrialization, 1750–1920*, Berkeley: University of California Press, 1988.

Snow, Edgar, *The Far Eastern Front*, London: Jarrold, 1934.

Solomou, Solomos, *Phases of Growth, 1850–1973: Kondratieff Waves and Kuznets Cycles*, Cambridge University Press, 1990.

Sotheby's, *Atlases, Travel, Natural History and Topographical Prints*, London: Sotheby's, 1989.

Souza, George Bryan, *The Survival of Empire, Portuguese Trade and Society in China and the South China Sea, 1630–1754*, Cambridge University Press, 1986.

Spaight, J. M., *Air Power and the Cities*, London: Longmans, Green, 1930.

Spalding, W. F., *Eastern Exchange: Currency and Finance*, London: Pitman, 1918.

Spector, Ronald H., *Eagle Against the Sun: The American War with Japan*, New York: Viking, 1985.

Staley, Eugene, *The World Economy in Transition: Technology vs. Politics, Laissez Faire vs. Planning, Power vs. Welfare*, New York: Council on Foreign Relations, 1939.

Stavorinus, Rear Admiral John Splinter, *Voyages to the East Indies* (3 vols) (trans. Samuel Hull Wilcocke), London: G. G. and J. Robinson, 1788.

Stead, Alfred (ed.), *Japan by the Japanese: A Survey by the Highest Authorities*, London: Heinemann, 1904.

Stinchecum, Amanda Mayer, *Kosode: 16th–19th Century Textiles from the Nomura Collection*, New York: Kodansha, 1984.

Stobaugh, Robert, *Innovation and Competition: The Global Management of Petrochemical Products*, Boston, MA: Harvard Business School Press, 1988.

Sugiyama, Shinya, *Japan's Industrialization in the World Economy, 1859–1899: Export Trade and Overseas Competition*, London: Athlone Press, 1988.

Sun, Kungtu and Ralph Huenemann, *The Economic Development of Manchuria in the First Half of the Twentieth Century*, Cambridge, MA: Harvard East Asian Monographs no. 28, 1969.

Sung, Jae Koh, *Stages of Industrial Development in Asia: A Comparative History of the Cotton Industry in Japan, India, China and Korea*, University of Philadelphia Press, 1966.

Swaen, Paulus, *Zipangu: The Mapping of Japan*, Geldrop, 1993.

Swain, David L., *Science and Culture in Traditional Japan*, Cambridge, MA: MIT Press, 1978.

Taeuber, Irene B., *The Population of Japan*, Princeton University Press, 1958.

Takahashi, Kamekichi, *The Rise and Development of Japan's Modern Economy: The Basis for Miraculous Growth*, Tokyo: Jiji Press, 1969.

Takahashi, M., *The History and Future of Rice Cultivation in Hokkaido*, Tokyo: United Nations University Press, 1980.

Takekoshi, Yosaburo, *Japanese Rule in Formosa*, London: Longmans, Green, 1907.

——, *Economic Aspects of the Civilisation of Japan* (3 vols), London: Geo. Allen and Unwin, 1930.

Tarn, William W., *The Greeks in Bactria and India* (2nd edn), Cambridge University Press, 1951.

Thistlethwaite, Frank, *The Great Experiment: An Introduction to the History of the American People*, Cambridge University Press, 1955.

Thompson, Warren S., *Population and Peace in the Pacific*, University of Chicago Press, 1946.

Tippett, L. C., *A Portrait of the Lancashire Textile Industry*, Oxford University Press, 1969.

Toby, Ronald P., *State and Diplomacy in Early Modern Japan: Asia in the Development of the Tokugawa Bakufu*, Stanford University Press, 1991.

Toson, Shimazaki, *Before the Dawn* (trans. William Naff), Honolulu: University of Hawaii Press, 1987.

Trebilcock, Clive, *The Industrialization of the Continental Powers, 1880–1914*, London: Longman, 1981.

Tsuchiya, Takao, 'An Economic History of Japan', *Transactions of the Asiatic Society of Japan*, 2nd series, vol. 15, 1937.

Tsunoda, Ryusaku, Wm. Theodore de Bary and Donald Keene (eds), *Sources of Japanese Tradition*, New York: Columbia University Press, 1958.

Ueda, Tatsuzo, *The Development of the Eyeglass Industry in Japan*, Tokyo: United Nations University Press, 1979.

UNCTAD, *Case Studies in the Transfer of Technology: Policies for Transfer and Development of Technology in Pre-War Japan*, New York, 1978.

Urwick, L., *The Meaning of Rationalisation*, London: Nisbet, 1929.

US War Department, *Handbook on Japan's Military Forces*, Washington, DC: Government Printing Office, 1944.

Utley, Freda, *Lancashire and the Far East*, London: Geo. Allen and Unwin, 1931.

——, *Japan's Feet of Clay*, London: Faber and Faber, 1937.

Uyeda, Teijiro, *Small-scale Industries of Japan: The Electric Light Industry*, Tokyo: Institute of Pacific Relations, 1936.

Valignano, Alessandro, *Historia del Principia y Progresso de la Compania de Jesus en las Indias Orientales (1542–64)* (ed. Josef Wicki), Rome: Institutum Historicum SJ, 1944.

van der Post, Laurens, *Yet Being Someone Other*, London: Penguin Books, 1984.

Varende, Jean de la, *Les Augustin-Normand. Sept Générations de Constructeurs de Navires*, Mayenne, France, 1960.

Vincent, Benjamin (ed.), *Haydn's Dictionary of Dates and Universal Information relating to all Ages and Nations*, 16th edn, London: Moxon, 1878; 24th edn, London: Ward Lock, 1906.

Voyages de Mr. de Thevenot, Paris: La Veuve Biestkins, 1694.

Wakeman, Frederic, Jr., *The Great Enterprise: The Manchu Reconstruction of Imperial order in Seventeenth Century China* (2 vols), Berkeley: University of California Press, 1985.

Walker, Kenneth R., *Food Grain Procurement and Consumption in China*, Cambridge University Press, 1984.

Wallace, Alfred Russell, *The Wonderful Century: The Age of New Ideas in Science and Invention*, London: Swan Sonnenschein, 1908.

Wallach, Sidney (ed.), *Narrative of the Expedition of an American Squadron to the China Seas and Japan*, London: Macdonald, 1954.

Warner, Langdon, *Japanese Sculpture of the Tempyo Period: Masterpieces of the Eighth Century*, Cambridge, MA: Harvard University Press, 1964.

Watson, Ernest, *The Principle Articles of Chinese Commerce (Imports and Exports)* Shanghai: Maritime Customs, 1930.

Watts, A.J., and B.G. Gordon, *The Imperial Japanese Navy*, London: Macdonald, 1971.

Westney, D. Eleanor, *Imitation and Innovation: The Transfer of Western Organizational Patterns to Meiji Japan*, Cambridge, MA: Harvard University Press, 1987.

Westwood, J.N., *Fighting Ships of World War Two*, London: Sidgwick and Jackson, 1975.

White, Fifi, *Japanese Folk Textiles*, Kyoto: Shikosha, 1988.

Wickizer, V.D., and M.K. Bennett, *The Rice Economy of Monsoon Asia*, Stanford: Food Research Institute, 1941.

Williams, Harold S., *Tales of the Foreign Settlements in Japan*, Tokyo: Charles Tuttle, 1958.

Williams, S. Wells, *The Middle Kingdom* (2 vols), New York: Wiley and Halstead, 1857.

Willmott, H. P., *Zero A6M*, London: Arms and Armour Press, 1980.

Wills, John E., Jr., *Pepper, Guns and Parleys: The Dutch East India Company and China 1622–1681*, Cambridge, MA: Harvard University Press, 1974.

Womack, James P., *et al.*, *The Machine that Changed the World*, New York: Rawson Associates, 1990.

Wu, Herbert Hantao, *Japan's Acts of Treaty Violation and Encroachment upon the Sovereign Rights of China in the North-Eastern Provinces (Manchuria)*, Peking: North-Eastern Affairs Research Institute, 1932 (repr. Taipei, 1972).

Yamazawa, Ippei, *Economic Development and International Trade: The Japanese Model*, Hawaii: East–West Center, 1990.

Yarrow, Lady, *Alfred Yarrow: Life and Work*, London: Chapman and Hall, 1924.

Yui, T., and K. Nakagawa (eds), *Business History of Shipping. Strategy and Structure*, University of Tokyo Press, 1985.

Yule, Sir Henry, and Henri Cordier (eds), *The Book of Ser Marco Polo* (3rd edn, 3 vols), London: John Murray, 1903, 1920.

——, *Cathay and the Way Thither, being a collection of Medieval Notices of China* (2nd edn, 2 vols), London: The Hakluyt Society, 1913–16 (repr. Taipei, 1966).

Zeldin, Theodore, *France 1848–1945: Anxiety and Hypocrisy*, Oxford University Press, 1981.

ASIAN LANGUAGE MATERIALS

Ajia Keizai Kenkyujo (ed.), *Nihon nogyo hyakunen norinsui sangyo ruinen tokeihyo* (A hundred years of Japanese agricultural annual statistics), Tokyo: Norin Tokei Kyokai, 1969.

Ando Hikataro (ed.), *Mantetsu* (The South Manchurian Railway), Tokyo: Ochanomizu Shobo, 1965.

Ando Yoshio (ed.), *Showa keizaishi e no shogen* (Testimony on Showa economic history) (3 vols), Tokyo: Mainichi Press, 1965.

Arisawa Hiromi (ed.), *Showa keizaishi* (The economic history of the Showa period), Tokyo: Nihon Keizai Shimbunsha, 1976.

Ayuzawa Shintaro and Okubo Toshiaki, *Sakoku jidai Nihonjin no kaigai chishiki* (The Japanese understanding of the outside world in the era of the Seclusion), Tokyo: Kengensha, 1953.

Bokyo hyakunenshi (The hundred-year history of the Japan Cotton Spinners' Association), Osaka: Nihon Boseki Kyokai, 1982.

Fujii Mitsuo, *Senkanki Nihon seni sangyo kaigai shinshutsu no kenkyu* (Researches into the history of the overseas advance of the inter-war Japanese textile industry), Tokyo: Minerva Shobo, 1987.

Fujita Teiichiro *et al.* (eds), *Nihon shogyoshi* (A history of Japanese commerce) Tokyo: Yuhikaku, 1978.

Gaimusho Joyakukyoku, *Kyu joyaku isan* (Compendium of old treaties. 3 parts in 4 books) Tokyo: Gaimusho, 1930–36.

——, *The Washington Conference, 1921–1922: Treaties and Resolutions*, Tokyo: Gaimusho, 1922.

Hamashita Takeshi and Kawakatsu Heita (eds), *Ajia koiken to Nihon kogyoka, 1500–1900* (The Asian trade sphere and Japanese industrialisation, 1500–1900), Tokyo: Libro Porto, 1991.

Hashiguchi Y., *Hankyuki kogyo no noritsu zoshin (Increasing the efficiency of the aeroplane industry)*, Tokyo, 1944.

Hayashi Katsuya, *Nihon gunji gijutsushi* (A history of Japan's military technology), Tokyo: Haruki Shoten, 1957.

Honjo Eijiro (ed.), *Meiji Ishin keizaishi kenkyu* (Research into the economic history of the Meiji Restoration), Tokyo: Yamamoto Sansei, 1931.

Hori Tsuneo, *Meiji keizai shisoshi* (A history of Meiji economic thought), Tokyo: Meiji Bunken, 1975.

Huang Tong *et al.* (eds), *Riju shidai zhi Taiwan caijing* (Taiwan finance under the Japanese occupation), Taipei: Lianjing Chubanshe, 1988.

Hyakunenshi Toyobo (The hundred year history of Toyobo) (2 vols), Osaka: Toyobo, 1986.

Iida H., *Nihon tekko gijutsushi* (A history of Japanese iron and steel technology), Tokyo: Toyo Keizai Shimposha, 1979.

Ishii Kanji, *Nihon sanshigyoshi bunseki* (An analysis of the history of Japan's silk industry), Tokyo: Tokyo Daigaku Shuppankai, 1972.

——, *Nihon keizaishi* (Economic history of Japan), Tokyo: Tokyo Daigaku Shuppankai, 1976.

——, *Kaikoku to Ishin* (The opening of the ports and Restoration) Tokyo: Shogakukan, 1989.

——, and Sekiguchi Hisashi (eds), *Sekai shijo to Bakumatsu kaiko*, (The world market and the opening of the ports at the end of the Tokugawa period), Tokyo: Tokyo Daigaku Shuppankai, 1982.

Ishikawajima jukogyo kabushiki kaisha 108 nenshi (The 108-year history of lshikawajima Heavy Industries), Tokyo, 1961.

Isobe Kiichi, *Dento sangyoron* (The theory of traditional craft production), Tokyo: Yuhikaku, 1985.

Ito Shigeru (ed.), *Taiwan seito kabushiki kaishashi* (The history of the Taiwan Sugar Company), Tokyo: Taiwan Seito Kabushiki Kaisha, 1939.

Kanemori Hisao, *Nihon no boeki* (Japanese foreign trade), Tokyo: Shiseido, 1965.

Kawano Shigeto, *Taiwan beikoku keizairon* (The rice economy of Taiwan), Tokyo: Yuhikaku, 1941.

Kimura Masato, *Shibusawa Eiichi*, Tokyo: Chuo Shinsho, 1991.

Kita Itsuo, *Manshu kaitakuron* (The colonisation of Manchuria), Tokyo: Meibundo, 1944.

Kogaku Kogyoshi Henshukai, *Nihon no kogaku kogyoshi*, (History of the Japanese optical industry), Tokyo: Optical Industry History Editorial Committee, 1955.

Kojima Kiyoshi, *Ronso keizai seicho to Nihon boeki* (The debate on economic growth and Japanese foreign trade), Tokyo: Kobundo, 1960.

—— (ed.), *Gakumon henro* (A pilgrimage of learning), Tokyo: Seikai Keizai Kenkyukai, 1975.

Koshaku Matsukata Masayoshi den (The biography of Count Matsukata Masayoshi) (2 vols), Tokyo: Koshaku Matsukata Masayoshi Denki Henshukai, 1935, repr. 1992.

Koyama Koken, *Nihon gunji kogyo no shiteki bunseki* (An historical analysis of Japan's military industries), Tokyo: Ochanomizu Shobo, 1972.

Li Bo-lu et al. (eds), *Jiu Zhongguo bu pingdeng tiaoyue shihua* (An historical account of the unequal treaties of old China), Xian: Shanxi Renmin Chubanshe, 1992.

Manshu kaitaku nenkan (The Manchurian colonisation yearbook), Tokyo: Manshukoku Tsushinsha, 1941.

Manshushi Kenkyukai (ed.), *Nihon teikokushugi ka no Manshu* (Manchuria under Japanese imperialism), Tokyo: Ochanomizu Shobo, 1972.

Maruyama Masao, *Bunmeiron no gairyaku o yomu* (On reading [Fukuzawa's] '*An outline theory of civilization*'), Tokyo: Iwanami Shoten, 1986.

Minami Ryoshin and Kiyokawa Yukihiko (eds), *Nihon no kogyoka to gijutsu hatten* (Japanese industrialisation and technological development) , Tokyo: Toyo Keizai Shimposha, 1987.

MITI, *Shoko seisakushi* (A history of policy towards commerce and industry), vol. 9: *Sangyo gorika* (Industrial rationalisation), Tokyo: MITI, 1961.

——, vol. 3: *Gyosei kiko* (Administrative structures), 1962.

——, vols 5–6: *Boeki* (Foreign trade), 1965, 1971.

——, vols 15–16: *Seni kogyo*, (Textiles), 1968, 1972.

——, vol. 18: *Kikai kogyo* (The machinery industry), 1976.

——, vols 1–2: *Sosetsu* (Summary), 1985.

——, *Tsusho hakusho* (Trade white paper), various years.

Mitsubishi Keizai Kenkyujo, *Taiheiyo ni okeru kokusai keizai kankei* (International economic relations in the Pacific), Tokyo: Nihon Hyoronsha, 1937.

Mitsui tokuhon, (The Mitsui Reader), Tokyo: Ajia Shobo, 1943.

Miyamoto Mataji (ed.), *Shohin ryutsu no shiteki kenkyu* (Historical research into the circulation of commodities), Kyoto: Minerva Shobo, 1967.

Miyamoto Mataji, *Kamigata konjyaku* (The Kyoto-Osaka district today and yesterday), Tokyo: Isseido, 1972.

—— et al. (eds), *Nihon boekijin no keifu* (The lineage of Japanese merchants), Tokyo: Yuhikaku, 1980.

Miyamoto Matao, *Kinsei Nihon no shijo keizai: Osaka kome shijo no bunseki* (The market economy of early modern Japan: A study of the Osaka rice market), Tokyo: Yuhikaku, 1988.

Morikawa Hidemasa (ed.), *Nihongata keiei no genryu* (The sources of the Japanese style of management), Tokyo: Toyo Keizai Shimposha, 1973.

Morikawa Hidemasa *et al.* (eds), *Kindai Nihon no keieishi no kiso chishiki* (Basic knowledge of the history of modern Japanese management) Tokyo: Yuhikaku, 1974.

Nagai Minoru (ed.), *Jijo Masuda Takashi o-den* (The autobiography of Masuda Takashi in later life), Tokyo, 1939.

Nagura Bunji, *Nihon tekkogyoshi no kenkyu* (Research into the history of the Japanese steel industry), Tokyo: Kondo Shuppansha, 1984.

Nakagawa Ryoichi *et al.* (eds), *Nakajima enjinshi wakai gijutsusha shudan katsuyaku* (The history of Nakajima aero-engines: The activities of a group of young engineers), Tokyo: Kantosha, n.d.

Nakamura Takafusa, *Meiji-Taishoki no keizai* (The economy of the Meiji-Taisho period), Tokyo: Tokyo Daigaku Shuppankai, 1985.

Nakaoka Tetsuro, *et al.* (eds), *Kindai Nihon no gijutsu to gijutsu seisaku* (Technology and technology policy in modern Japan) Tokyo: Tokyo Daigaku Shuppankai, 1986.

Narusawa Yomezo, *Ishiwara Kanji*, Tokyo: Keizai Oraisha, 1969.

Nawa Toichi, *Nihon bosekigyo no shiteki bunseki* (An historical analysis of the Japanese textile industry), Tokyo: Choryusha, 1949.

Nihon boeki seiran (Foreign trade of Japan: a statistical outline), Tokyo: Toyo Keizai Shimposha, 1975.

Nihon Ginko Hyakunenshi Iinkai (ed.), *Nihon ginko hyakunenshi* (The hundred-year history of the Bank of Japan) (7 vols), Tokyo: Nihon Ginko, 1982–86.

Nihon Hankyu Kyokai (ed.), *Nihon hankyushi* (A history of Japanese aviation), Tokyo, 1956.

Nihon keizai no kahi teki bunseki, 1868–1970 (An analysis of currency in the Japanese economy, 1868–1970), Tokyo: Sobunsha, 1984.

Nihon Keizaishi Kenkyukai, *Kindai Nihon jinbutsu keizaishi* (A biographical economic history of modern Japan) (2 vols), Tokyo: Toyo Keizai Shimposha, 1955.

Nihon keizaishi jiten (A dictionary of Japanese economic history) (3 vols), Tokyo: Nihon Hyoronsha, 1940.

Nihon yusen kabushiki kaisha nanajunenshi (The seventy-year history of the NYK), Tokyo, 1956.

Nikon nanajugonenshi (The seventy-five year history of Nikon), Tokyo, 1993.

Nippon kogaku kogyo kabushiki kaisha gojunen no susumi (Fifty years of progress of the Nikon Company), Tokyo, 1967.

Nippon kogaku kogyo kabushiki kaisha nijugonenshi (The twenty-five-year history of the Nikon Company), Tokyo, 1942.

Nippon kogaku kogyo kabushiki kaisha yonjunenshi (The forty-year history of the Nikon Company), Tokyo, 1957.

Nishikawa Hiroshi, *Nihon teikokushugi to mengyo* (Japanese imperialism and the cotton industry) Kyoto: Minerva Shobo, 1987.

Nishikawa Joken, *Yonjunikoku jinbutsu zusetsu* (illustrations of the people of forty-two countries), Edo, 1720.

Odaka Konosuke, *Shokunin no sekai kojo no sekai* (The world of the craftsman and the world of the factory), Tokyo: Libro Porto, 1993.

——, *Kigyo uchi kyoiku no jidai* (The age of intra-enterprise education), Tokyo: Iwanami Shoten, 1993.

——, and Yamamoto Yuzo (eds), *Bakumatsu Meiji no Nihon keizai* (The Japanese economy in the late Tokugawa and Meiji periods), Tokyo: Nihon Keizai Shimbunsha, 1988.

Ohkawa Kazushi *et al.* (eds), *Choki keizai tokei* (Long-term economic statistics) (14 vols), Tokyo: Toyo Keizai Shimposha, 1965–.

Ohkawa Kazushi *et al. Nihon keizai to nogyo. Seicho bunseki* (The Japanese economy and agriculture. A growth analysis) (2 vols), Tokyo: Iwanami Shoten, 1956.

Ohkawa Kazushi and Minami Ryoshin (eds), *Kindai Nihon no keizai hatten* (Economic development of modern Japan), Tokyo: Toyo Keizai Shimposha, 1975.

Oishi Kaichiro (ed.), *Nihon teikokushugishi: dai ichiji dai senki* (The history of Japanese imperialism: The First World War), Tokyo: Tokyo Daigaku Shuppankai, 1985.

——, *Senkanki Nihon taigai keizai kankei* (Japan's inter-war external economic relations), Tokyo: Nihon Hyoronsha, 1992.

Okada K., *et al.*, *Tatara kara kindai seitetsu e* (From Tatara to modern iron making), Tokyo: Heibonsha, 1990.

Okazaki Ayanori, *Shintoa kakuritsu to jinko seisaku* (The establishment of the new East Asia and population policy), Tokyo: Okura Shobo, 1941.

Okura Zaibatsu Kenkyukai, *Okura zaibatsu no kenkyu Okura to tairiku* (Research into the Okura zaibatsu. Okura and the [Chinese] mainland), Tokyo: Kondo Shuppansha, 1982.

Okurasho Insatsukyoku, *Showa 63 nenpan tokei handbuku* (The 1988 statistical handbook), Tokyo, 1988.

Ono K., *Senkanki no Nihon teikokushugi* (Japanese imperialism in the inter-war period), Tokyo: Sekai Shisosha, 1985.

Saito Osamu, *Puroto kogyoka no jidai* (The age of proto-industrialisation), Tokyo: Nihon Hyoronsha, 1984.

Sampei Takako, *Nihon mengyo hattatsushi* (A history of the development of the Japanese cotton industry), Tokyo: Keio Shobo, 1941.

Sheng Chuan-han, *Hanyebing kongsi shilue* (*Outline history of the Hanyebing Company*), Hong Kong: Zhongwen Daxue Chubanshe, 1972.

Shibusawa Ton, *Hikoki rokujunen* (Sixty years of aeroplanes), Tokyo: Toshokan Shuppansha, 1973.

Showa sangyoshi (A history of industry in the Showa period) (3 vols) Tokyo: Toyo Keizai Shimposha, 1952.

Sugiyama Shinya and Ian G. Brown (eds), *Senkanki Tonan Ajia keizai habatsu* (Inter-war economic frictions in South-East Asia), Tokyo: Dobunkan, 1990.

Sumiyami Kiyo, *Showa kyoko* (The Showa depression), Tokyo: Yuhikaku, 1974.

Taiwan ginkoshi (A history of the Bank of Taiwan), Tokyo: Taiwan Ginkoshi, 1964.

Taiwan Keizai Nenpo Kankosha, *Taiwan keizai nenpo* (Taiwan economic yearbook), Tokyo: Kokusai Nihon Kyokai, 1942.

Taiwan Sotokufu, *Taiwan jijo* (Conditions in Taiwan), Taipei: Taiwan Jiho Hakkosho, 1933.

Taiwan Yinhang Jingji Yanjiushi (ed.), *Riju shidai Taiwan jingjishi* (An economic history of Taiwan under Japanese occupation) (2 vols), Taipei: Taiwan Yinhang, 1958.

Takahashi Kamekichi, *Manshu keizai to Nihon keizai* (The Manchurian economy and the Japanese economy), Tokyo: Chiyogura Shobo, 1934.

——, *Gendai Taiwan keizairon* (The economy of modern Taiwan), Tokyo: Okura Shobo, 1937.

——, *Tokugawa hoken keizai no kenkyu* (Research into the Tokugawa feudal economy), Tokyo: Toyo Shokan, 1941.

——, *Nihon kindai keizai keiseishi* (The history of the formation of the modern Japanese economy) (3 vols), Tokyo: Toyo Keizai Shimposha, 1968.

——, *Nihon kindai keizai hattatsushi* (The development of the modern Japanese economy) (3 vols), Tokyo: Toyo Keizai Shimposha, 1983.

——, *Watashi no jissen keizaigaku* (My practical economics), Tokyo: Toyo Keizai Shimposha, 1976.

Takahashi Miyanaga, *Bakufu Oranda Ryugakusei* (Japanese students in Holland in the Bakufu period), Tokyo, 1982.

Takamura Naosuke, *Nihon bosekigyoshi no josetsu* (An introduction to the Japanese cotton textile industry), Tokyo: Tokyo Daigaku Shuppankai, 1971.

——, *Kindai Nihon mengyo to Chugoku* (The modern Japanese textile industry and China), Tokyo: Tokyo Daigaku Shuppankai, 1982.

Takayoshi Matsuo (ed.), *Gendaishi shiryo* (Materials on modern history), vol. 9, part 2, Tokyo: Misuzu Shobo, 1964.

Takemori Kazuo, *Mantetsu koboshi* (A history of the rise and fall of the South Manchurian Railway), Tokyo: Akita Shoten, 1970.

——, *Taitoa keizai shigen taikan* (A survey of the economic resources of the Greater East Asian Co-Prosperity Sphere), Tokyo: Nichi-Su Tsushinsha, 1942.

Takushoku Shoreikan, *Takushoku shoreikan kio* (Quarterly journal of the Department for Encouraging Colonisation), 1939.

Toa Keizai Kenkyujo, *Toa keizai kenkyu nenpo* (East Asia economic research yearbook), Tokyo: Nihon Hyoronsha, 1942.

Tokyo Daigaku gakujutsu zasshi sogo mokuroku (University of Tokyo Catalogue of Scientific Periodicals in Japanese Language), Tokyo,1986.

Tominaga Y., *Kotsu ni okeru shihonshugi no hatten* (The development of capitalism in transportation), Tokyo: Iwanami Shoten, 1957.

Toyama Shigeki, *Meiji Ishin* (The Meiji Restoration), Tokyo: Iwanami Shoten, 1951.

——, *Meiji ishin to jindai* (The Meiji Restoration and today), Tokyo: Iwanami Shoten, 1968.

Toyo boseki nanajunenshi (The seventy-year history of the Toyo Spinning Company) Tokyo, 1953.

Tu Zhao-yan, *Nihon teikokushugi ka no Taiwan* (Taiwan under Japanese imperialism), Tokyo: Tokyo Daigaku Shuppankai, 1975.

Umemura Mataji, *Rodo ryoku* (Manpower), Tokyo: Toyo Keizai Shimposha, 1988 (Ohkawa, *LTES*, vol. 2).

—— *et al.* (eds), *Nihon keizaishi* (Economic history of Japan), Tokyo: Iwanami Shoten, 1988–.

Umezu Kazuro, *Nihon no boeki shiso* (Japanese foreign trade thinking), Kyoto: Minerva Shobo, 1963.

Uyeda Teijiro, *Nihon jinko seisaku* (Japan's population policy), Tokyo: Okura Shobo, 1937.

——, Memorial Collected Works, vol. 4, *Jinko oyo toa keizai no kenkyu* (Research into the theory of population and the East Asian economy), Tokyo: Kagakushugi Kogyosha, 1943.

Uehara Kenzen, *Sakoku to han boeki* (Seclusion and *han* trade), Tokyo: Yaegaku Shobo, 1981.

Xu Dao-fu, *Zhongguo jindai maoyi tongji tzuliao* (Trade statistics of modern China), Shanghai: Renmin Chubanshe, 1983.

Yamaguchi Kazuo, *Bakumatsu boekishi* (A history of foreign trade in the late Tokugawa period), Tokyo: Chuo Koronsha, 1943.

Yamaguchi Yuji, *Kieta teikoku Manshu* (Vanished imperial Manchuria), Tokyo: Mainichi, 1967.

Yamazawa Ippei, *Nihon no keizai hatten to kokusai bungyo* (Japanese economic development and the international division of labour), Tokyo: Toyo Keizai Shimposha, 1985.

—— and Yamamoto Yuzo, *Boeki to kokusai shushi* (Foreign trade and international payments), Tokyo: Toyo Keizai Shimposha, 1979. (Ohkawa, *LTES*, vol. 14).

Yanaihara Tadao, *Teikokushugi ka no Taiwan* (Taiwan under imperialism), Tokyo: Iwanami Shoten, 1988 (first published in 1928).

Yawata seitetsujo yonjunenshi (The fifty-year record of the Yawata Steel Company), 1950.

Zhang Cheng-da, *Dong-Bei jingji* (The north-eastern economy) (2 vols), Taipei: Zhonghua Chubanshe, 1955.

Zhongguo jindai gongyeshi tzuliao 1895–1914, (Materials on China's modern industrial history, 1895–1914), Beijing: Kexue Chubanshe, 1957.

ARTICLES AND BOOK CHAPTERS

Akamatsu Kaname, 'The historical pattern of East Asian trade' in Toa Keizai Kenkyujo, *Toa kizai kenkyu nenpo*, pp. 73–131.

Albertson, Chas., 'Equipment and capacity of the dockyards and shipbuilding plants of Japan', parts 1 and 2, *FER*, Feb. 1906, pp. 237–40, and March 1906, pp. 288–94.

Allen, G. C., 'The cotton industry' in Schumpeter, *The Industrialization of Japan and Manchukuo, 1930–1940: Population, Raw Materials and Industry*, pp. 568–95.

Arrow, Kenneth J., 'Economic welfare and the allocation of resources for invention' in National Bureau of Economic Research, *The Rate and Direction of Inventive Activity: Economic and Social Factors*, pp. 609–26.

Bernard, Jacques, 'Trade and finance in the middle ages, 900–1500' in Cipolla, *The Fontana Economic History of Europe*, vol. 1: *The Middle Ages*, pp. 274–80.

Boussenard, Louis, 'Les Torpilleurs de L'Amiral Courbet', *Journal des Voyages*, 2nd series, nos. 41, 42, 1897.

Brauer, Kinley J., '1821–1860: Economics and the diplomacy of American expansion' in Becker and Wells, *Economics and World Power: An Assessment of American Diplomacy since 1789*, pp. 55–118.

Cho Yukio, 'An enquiry into the problem of importing American capital into Manchuria' in Borg and Okamoto, *Pearl Harbor as History: Japanese–American Relations 1931–1941*, pp. 377–410.

Chou, S. H., 'Railway development and economic growth in Manchuria', *The China Quarterly*, no. 45, March–June 1971, pp. 57–84.

Crawcour, E. Sydney, 'The Tokugawa heritage' in Lockwood, *The State and Economic Enterprise in Japan*, pp. 36–42.

Duus, Peter, 'The economic dimensions of Meiji Imperialism' in Myers and Peattie, *The Japanese Colonial Empire, 1895–1945*, pp. 80–127.

Freeman, Christopher, and Carlota Perez, 'Structural crises of adjustment: business cycles and investment behaviour' in Dosi, *Technical Change and Economic Theory*, pp. 38–66.

Gardiner, J. P., 'Design trajectories for airplanes and automobiles during the past fifty years' in Freeman, *Design, Innovation and Long Cycles in Economic Development*, pp. 185–213.

Hayami Akira and Kito Hiroshi, 'The historical demography of the common people' in Umemura, *Nihon keizaishi*, vol. 2, pp. 267–310.

Howe, Christopher, 'China, Japan and Economic Interdependence in the Asia Pacific', *The China Quarterly*, no. 124 (Dec. 1990), pp. 674–5.

———, 'Japan's economic experience in China before the establishment of the People's Republic of China: A retrospective balance sheet' in Dore and Sinha, *Japan and World Depression Then and Now: Essays in Memory of E. F. Penrose*, pp. 155–77.

Jackson, Arthur, 'Automatic machine tools in Japan', *FER*, Nov. 1922, pp. 691–92.

Jansen, Marius B., 'The Meiji Restoration' in Jansen, *Cambridge History of Japan*, vol. 5: *The Nineteenth Century*, pp. 308–66.

Kiyokawa Yukihiko, 'Entrepreneurship and innovation in Japan: an implication of the experience of technological development in the textile industry', *The Developing Economies*, vol. XXII, no. 3 (Sept. 1984), pp. 211–36.

———, and Ishikawa Shigeru, 'The significance of standardization in the development of the machine tool industry: the cases of Japan and China', parts 1 and 2, *Hitotsubashi Journal of Economics*, vol. 28, no. 2 (1987), pp. 123–54, and vol. 29, no. 1 (1988), pp. 73–88.

———, 'Technological gaps and the stabilisation of transferred technology: the case of cotton textiles' in Ohkawa and Minami, *Kindai Nihon no keizai hatten*, pp. 249–82.

———, 'The choice of technology in textiles: from the mule to the ring' in Minami and Kiyokawa, *Nihon no kogyoka to gijutsu hatten*, pp. 83–107.

———, 'Transplantation of the European factory system and adaptations in Japan: the experience of the Tomioka Filature', *Hitotsubashi Journal of Economics*, vol. 28, no. 1 (June 1987), pp. 27–39.

Maruyama Masao, 'Kaikoku', *Koza gendai rinri*, 1959, pp. 282–312.

Miwa Ryoichi, 'Maritime policy in Japan: 1868–1937' in Yui and Nakagawa, *Business History of Shipping: Strategy and Structure*, pp. 123–52.

Millot, Bernard, 'Le Mitsubishi G3M "Nell"', *Le Fanatique de L'Aviation*, October 1991, pp. 18–27.

Minami Ryoshin, 'The choice of technology in the silk industry' in Minami and Kiyokawa, *Nihon no kogyoka to gijutsu hatten*, pp. 43–63.

Minoru Sawai, 'The rolling stock industry and the "Manchurian" market with special reference to the 1930s' in Oishi, *Senkanki Nihon no taigai keizai kankei*, pp. 131–70.

Mizoguchi Toshiyuki, 'Consumer prices and real wages in Taiwan and Korea under Japanese rule', *Hitotsubashi Journal of Economics*, vol. 13, no. 1 (June 1972), pp. 40–56.

Moriya Katsuhisa, 'Urban networks and information networks' in Nakane and Oishi, *Tokugawa Japan*, pp. 97–123.

Myers, Ramon H., 'Japanese imperialism in Manchuria: The South Manchuria Railway Company, 1906–1933' in Duus and Myers, *The Japanese Informal Colonial Empire, 1895–1937*, pp. 101–32.

———, 'Taiwan as an Imperial Japanese colony, 1895–1945', *Journal of the Institute of Chinese Studies*, vol. 6, no. 2, 1973, p. 434.

Nakagawa Keiichiro, 'Japanese shipping in the nineteenth and twentieth centuries: strategy and organization' in Yui and Nakagawa, *Business History of Shipping: Strategy and Structure*, pp. 1–33.

Nakamura Takafusa, 'Japan's economic thrust into North China, 1933–1938: Formation of the North China Development Corporation' in Iriye, *The Chinese and the Japanese. Essays in Political and Cultural Interactions*, pp. 220–51.

Nakaoka Tetsuro, review of Tetsu Hiroshige's *Kagaku no shakaishi, Japanese Studies in the History of Science*, no. 15 (1976), pp. 163–68.

——, 'Production management in Japan before the period of high speed economic growth', *Osaka City University Economic Review*, no. 17 (1981), pp. 7–24.

——, 'The role of domestic technical innovation in foreign technology transfer: The case of the Japanese cotton textile industry', *Osaka City University Economic Review*, no. 18 (1982), pp. 45–62.

——, 'On technological leaps of Japan as a developing country, 1900–1940', *Osaka City University Economic Review*, no. 22 (1987), pp. 1–25.

——, 'The textile history of Nishijin (Kyoto): East meets West', *Textile History* 19(2) (1988), pp. 117–41.

Niitani Masahiko, 'The choice of technique in the tea industry' in Minami and Kiyokawa, *Nihon no kogyoka to gijutsu hatten*, pp. 24–42.

Nishikawa Shunsaku and Amano Masatoshi, 'Han industrial and economic policies' in Umemura, *Nihon keizaishi*, vol. 2, pp. 173–218.

Odabashi Josu, 'China's population and vital rates' in Toa Keizai Kenkyujo, *Toa keizai kenkyu nenpo*, pp. 231–67.

——, 'Uyeda Sensei and research into Japanese population problems' in Dr Uyeda Teijiro Memorial Collected Works, vol. 4: *Jinko oyo toa keizai no kenkyu*, pp. 3–28.

Odaka Konosuke, 'The contribution of craft workers [*shokunin*] to the metallurgical industry', *Keizai kenkyu*, vol. 37, no. 3 (July 1986), pp. 221–33.

Oguchi Yujiro, 'Bakufu finances' in Umemura, *Nihon keizaishi*, vol. 2, pp. 128–71.

Ono Akira, 'Technical progress in silk industry in pre-war Japan — types of borrowed technology', *Hitotsubashi Journal of Economics*, vol. 27, no. 1 (1986), pp. 1–10.

Patrick, Hugh T., 'The economic muddle of the 1920s' in Morley, *Dilemmas of Growth in Pre-War Japan*, pp. 217–66.

Perez, Carlota, and Luc Soete, 'Catching up in technology: entry barriers and windows of opportunity' in Dosi, *Technical Change and Economic Theory*, pp. 458–79.

Purvis, F. P., 'Japan's contribution to naval architecture', *FER*, August 1925, pp. 577–78.

Rabbitt, James A., 'Nickel alloys and steels in the aeronautical industry', *FER*, June 1934, pp. 274–76.

Romer, Paul, 'Endogenous technical change', *Journal of Political Economy* vol. 98, no. 5, part 2 (Oct. 1990), pp. 71–102.

Saito Osamu, 'Population fluctuation, east and west' in Odaka and Yamamoto, *Bakumatsu Meiji no Nihon keizai*, pp. 29–47.

Sakudo Yotaro 'The management practices of family businesses' in Nakane and Oishi, *Tokugawa Japan*, pp. 147–66.

Saxonhouse, Gary and Yukihiko Kiyokawa, 'The supply and demand for quality workers in the cotton textile industries in Japan and India' in *Papers and Proceedings of the Conference on Japan's Historical Development Experience and the Contemporary Developing Countries: Issues for Comparative Analysis*, Tokyo: International Development Center of Japan, 1978.

Shimizu Hajime, '*Nanshin-ron*: its turning point in World War I', *The Developing Economies* (Dec. 1987), pp. 386–402.

Shimizu Hiroshi, 'A study of Japan's commercial expansion into the Netherlands Indies from 1914 to 1941', *Bulletin of the Faculty of Nagoya University of Commerce and Business Administration*, vol. 34, no. 2 (March 1990), pp. 43–76.

Shinbo Hiroshi and Hasegawa Akira, 'The dynamics of production and circulation', Umemura, *Nihon keizaishi*, vol. 1, pp. 217–70.

Sugiyama Shinya, 'Japanese textile exports and trade frictions' in Sugiyama and Brown, *Senkanki Tonan Ajia keizai habatsu*, pp. 77–108.

——, 'The international environment and foreign trade' in Umemura, *Nihon keizaishi*, vol. 3, pp. 185–7.

Takeno Yoshi, 'Seclusion and the Hosokawa *han*' in Miyamoto, *Shohin ryutsu no shiteki kenkyu*, pp. 213–30.

Vos, F., 'Iets over Nederlandse woorden in het Japans' in Maritiem Museum 'Prins Hendrick', *350 jaar Nederland-Japan*, pp. 40–2.

Yamamoto Yuzo, 'Management of the colonial territories' in Umemura, *Nihon keizaishi*, vol. 6, pp. 231–74.

Wray, William D., 'Shipping from Sail to Steam', in Jansen and Rozman, *Japan in Transition. From Tokugawa to Meiji*, pp. 24–70.

Wray, William D., 'NYK and the commercial diplomacy of the Far Eastern Freight Conference, 1896–1956' in Yui and Nakagawa, *Business History of Shipping. Strategy and Structure*, pp. 279–305.

Yamamura Kozo, 'Success Illgotten? The role of Meiji Militarism in Japan's technological progress', *Journal of Economic History*, vol. XXXVII, no. 1 (March 1977), pp. 113–35.

INDEX

Abyssinia, 4
Adams, Will, 20
Aden, 10, 19
Adler, Solomon, xv
Africa, 171–5
agriculture: development in Tokugawa
   Japan, 52–4; European views on
   Tokugawa, 31, 31 *n. 99*;
   development in white colonies,
   339–40; Japanese crisis, 340–1;
   labour absorption, 391; world
   depression in, 340; *see also* Taiwan,
   Manchuria, rice, sugar
Aichi Tokei Denki KK/Hikoki KK
   (Aichi Watch and Electric/Aircraft
   Company), 310
aircraft engines: Gnome, 309 *n. 94*;
   Mercedes-Benz, 309 *n. 94*;
   Mitsubishi Hiro, 91, 312; Nakajima
   Homare, 45, 312; Nakajima Kikka,
   313 *n. 107*; Nakajima Kotobuki,
   329, *n. 17*; Pratt and Whitney R
   2800, 312; Renault, 309 *n. 94*;
aircraft types: Blackburn Swift, 309
   n. 94; Clark GA 43, 310 *n. 98*, 330;
   Curtis P40E, 311; Douglas DC4,
   310 *n. 98*; Fairchild A942, 311
   n. 99; Farman, 308; Gloster Gambit,
   329 *n. 17*; Gloster Sparrowhawk,
   309 *n. 94*, 329 *n. 17*; Grumman F6F
   Wildcat, 311; Hawker Hurricane,
   312; Hien Type 5, 311;
   Messerschmidt P404, 311;
   Messerschmidt Me 163B, 313
   n. 107; Mitsubishi A5M ('Claude'),
   310–11; Mitsubishi A6M ('Zero'),
   311; Mitsubishi G3M ('Nell'), 310,
   312; Nakajima Ki 84, 311;
   Northrop Gamma, 311 *n. 99*;
   SPAD, 307 *n. 89*; Spitfire, 312;
   Wright Brothers, 307
aircraft industry: 307–15; groups of

companies, 310; import
   substitution, 309; inferiority of
   production methods, 313;
   innovations, 312–13
aircraft carriers, 286
Akamatsu Kaname, 410
Albuquerque, Alfonso, 10
Alcock, Sir Rutherford: 44, 77, 78;
   strategy for Far East, 46–7; on
   Japanese living standards, 54; on
   corrupting effect of trade, 85; on
   gold speculation, 140; on Japanese
   technical skills, 244
Alexandria, 4, 6
Allen, G.C., xvi
Amsterdam, 13, 30 *n. 97*, 35
Ansei Treaties, *see* Treaty
Anshan Iron and Steel Works, 372,
   403 *n. 76*, 404
Arabia, 5
Arai Rioichiro, 98
Araki, Gen. , 398
Arnold, Sir Edwin, 375
Arrow War, 46
Asahi Maru (steamship), 291
Asanuma Tokichi (Shokai), 303
Asia: trade with Europe in middle
   Ages, 3–5; spice trade, 12–13;
   textile industry development, 204–5
Ayrton, W. E. (engineering professor),
   255
Azov, Sea of, 4

Baghdad, 5
Bakuhan (Bakufu rule of *han*), 70
balance of payments, long run trends
   116–22; *see also* capital flows
Bank of Japan, 148
Bank of Taiwan, 345
Baumann, Dr (German aircraft
   engineer), 309 *n. 94*